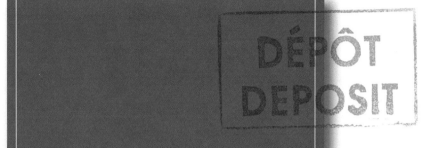

Who Is Responsible?
Fact Finding Report

Cat. No: CP32-86/2-2005E
ISBN: 0-660-19533-X

Available through your local bookseller or through
Publishing and Depository Services
Public Works and Government Services Canada
Ottawa, Ontario
KIA OS5

Telephone: (613) 941-5995
Orders only: 1 800 635-7943
Fax: (613) 954-5779 or 1 800 565-7757

Internet: http://publications.gc.ca

(1A1
CP32
2005 W 33
v. 1

Commission d'enquête sur
programme de commandites et
les activités publicitaires

Juge John H. Gomery
Commissaire

Commission of Inquiry into the
Sponsorship Program and
Advertising Activities

Justice John H. Gomery
Commissioner

November 1, 2005

To Her Excellency
The Governor General in Council

May it please Your Excellency:

As Commissioner appointed by Order in Council P.C. 2004-110 which was
promulgated on February 19, 2004 pursuant to Part I of the *Inquiries Act*, in
accordance with the Terms of Reference assigned therein, I have inquired into and
respectfully submit this Fact Finding report on the sponsorship program and
advertising activities of the Government of Canada, entitled "Who Is
Responsible?"

John H. Gomery
Commissioner

Complexe Guy-Favreau
200, boul. René-Lévesque ouest
C.P. 608, Montréal (Québec)
H2Z 1X4

Guy-Favreau Complex
200 René-Lévesque Blvd. West
P.O. Box 608, Montreal, Quebec
H2Z 1X4

(514) 283-8093 télécopieur / fax (514) 283-8138

CONTENTS

FREQUENTLY USED ACRONYMS

Acronym	Definition
ADM	Assistant Deputy Minister
AEB	Audit and Ethics Branch
AG	Attorney General
AMG	Advertising Management Group
AOR	Agency of Record
APORD	Advertising and Public Opinion Research Directorate
APORS	Advertising and Public Opinion Research Sector
BDC	Business Development Bank of Canada
CCSB	Communication Coordination Services Branch
CIO	Canada Information Office
DM	Deputy Minister
EA	Executive Assistant
EX	Executive Group
FAA	Financial Administration Act
FIP	Federal Identity Program

ICA	Institute of Canadian Advertising
LPCQ	Liberal Party of Canada (Quebec)
PCO	Privy Council Office
PMO	Prime Minister's Office
PRPCSS	Public Relations and Print Contract Services Sector
PWGSC	Public Works and Government Services Canada
QRT	Quick Response Team
TB	Treasury Board
TBS	Treasury Board Secretariat

ACKNOWLEDGEMENTS

The work involved in conducting an inquiry of this kind is enormous and far beyond the capacity of any one individual. There is an unfortunate tendency to attribute all of the success of a public inquiry to the person who conducts it, and to overlook the contributions of the team of workers who assemble and organize the evidence before it is presented in public. I want to thank the administrative organization, ably directed by Executive Director Sheila-Marie Cook, and to acknowledge the remarkable support that has been given to the Commission by all the people who assisted her, and to apologize for not naming them individually.

Special thanks are due to the legal team that toiled ceaselessly for months on end to prepare the evidence and to present it before me. The four leaders of the team, Bernard Roy, Q.C., Neil Finkelstein, Guy Cournoyer and Marie Cossette, are outstanding lawyers who deserve to be recognized for their efforts in making the inquiry as successful as it has been. My personal legal counsel, Laura Snowball, has been and continues to be of invaluable assistance, both at the hearings and in the preparation of the present Report. Her keen and critical mind has enabled me to avoid all kinds of mistakes.

Finally, as she has done for more than twenty years, my executive assistant Maxine Hoffer has typed, retyped, and retyped again every word of what turned out to be a massive manuscript, never complaining, and working with efficiency and speed that left me no respite. I could not manage without her.

PREFACE

On February 10, 2004, I was asked to preside over the Commission of Inquiry into the Sponsorship Program and Advertising Activities of the Government of Canada. I really did not know what I was getting into. All I knew about the problems that were the subject of the Report of the Auditor General was what I had read in the newspapers and seen on television. Like other Canadians I had been shocked to read and to hear of such mismanagement of a government program and waste of public funds. One of the reasons I accepted the appointment was that I was curious "to get to the bottom" of the situation, and I believed that a Commission of Inquiry was an excellent method of learning the truth of what had happened.

The Report that follows chronicles a depressing story of multiple failures to plan a government program appropriately and to control waste—a story of greed, venality and misconduct both in government and advertising and communications agencies, all of which contributed to the loss and misuse of huge amounts of money at the expense of Canadian taxpayers. They are outraged and have valid reasons for their anger.

With the vital assistance of a talented and hard-working team of lawyers and forensic accountants, my role as Commissioner has been to investigate and report on the facts, and to attribute blame where the facts lead to that conclusion. It is not within my jurisdiction to make findings of civil or criminal responsibility, for the very good reason that the Commission's Inquiry was not a trial, even though it had many of the characteristics of a judicial process, using lawyers and rules of legal procedure. None of the persons and organizations which are criticized in the Report, directly or by implication, had the advantages that our legal system gives to a defendant in a civil or criminal trial, so no one should jump to the conclusion that someone has been found guilty of an infraction, or was civilly responsible for what was done.

One of the disadvantages of a public inquiry is that it may seem that justice has been done. This perception is misleading for the reason I have just given, and also for another reason: the dramatic revelations at public inquiries and the media attention given to them tend to distort reality and to make the misconduct that the inquiry uncovers appear to be more widespread than it really was. I fear that that has occurred in this case.

Because of the sensational nature of some of the evidence presented at the Commission's hearings, the publicity given to it, and the political context in which the Inquiry took place, the impression may have been created that in Canada the administration of public affairs by the federal government is generally careless, incompetent, and motivated by improper considerations. People may also be persuaded that the persons involved in Canadian political life are inspired by improper motives, and unscrupulous.

Let me suggest that the Inquiry proves the contrary. Without diminishing the importance of the findings of impropriety and wrongdoing in the Report, the evidence presented reveals that, in general, the administration of government programs by the federal bureaucracy is competent and praiseworthy, a conclusion that has been emphasized by the Auditor General herself.

Let me also suggest that a system of government that would impose upon itself a searching inquiry by an independent commissioner, armed with the authority to compel the production of incriminating documentation from the public administration and able to subpoena witnesses from every level of society, with a far-reaching mandate to investigate and report on matters that could prove to be embarrassing to the Government itself, is proof that our democratic institutions are functioning well and objectively. There are very few countries in the world where an inquiry commissioner has the power to summon the sitting Prime Minister and his predecessor, to be examined under oath concerning their administration of public affairs and their involvement in what is publicly referred to as a scandalous affair. The fact that the Inquiry has been held demonstrates that in this country persons at even the highest levels of government are accountable for their actions, not only to Parliament but also to the citizenry.

There is no reason for the public's confidence in the integrity of our democratic institutions to be shaken. In the administration of the Sponsorship Program, certain government officials failed to meet the high standards of ethical behaviour that our laws and traditions expect, and political interference in the Program and in the advertising activities of the government resulted in deviations from acceptable standards. The persons responsible for these irregularities have been identified and reproached for their errors and misconduct. The procedure for uncovering wrongdoing is ponderous and expensive, but in the long run it works fairly well. Canadians should not forget that the vast majority of our public officials and politicians do their work honestly, diligently and effectively, and emerge from this Inquiry free of any blame.

On a personal note, I have attempted in the Report to use plain language, accessible to Canadians in all walks of life, and free from legalese and bureaucratic jargon. My intent has been to write using terms that anyone can understand, in the belief that the citizens whose interests were betrayed by the persons responsible for the "sponsorship scandal" are entitled to know and understand what occurred. Any attempt to summarize all the evidence that was presented would have resulted in a Report so long and detailed that it would be read by no one, so I have opted to report on what I consider to be the most important facts, and to leave the rest to scholars and the like, who are able, if they wish, to read all of the transcriptions and to examine the volumes of exhibits.

Since the use of acronyms in the government is very prevalent, I have had a table prepared of those acronyms and abbreviations that appear frequently in the Report. As well, there are two annexes. One is a table listing the names of each individual of importance who is mentioned in the Report, with a brief description of his or her position and role in the matters which are described in the Report. The other Annex is a chronology of events during the period under review. The Appendices include the most important documents that readers may wish to consult.

CHAPTER I

INTRODUCTION

1.1

Appointment of the Commissioner/Terms of Reference

On February 10, 2004, a Report prepared by the Auditor General of Canada was deposited in the House of Commons, thereby becoming public.[1] The Prime Minister of Canada immediately announced that the Government of Canada intended to appoint me, in accordance with the *Inquiries Act*,[2] to act as a commissioner to conduct an inquiry into the questions raised by Chapters 3 and 4 of the Report.[3]

Section 2 of the *Inquiries Act* authorizes the Governor in Council, that is to say the Privy Council or Cabinet, whenever it deems it expedient, to "cause an inquiry to be made into and concerning any matter connected with the good government of Canada or the conduct of any part of the public business thereof." In accordance with that provision, a Privy Council decision[4] was approved on February 19, 2004, confirming my appointment as Commissioner, defining my duties and authorizing me to adopt procedures, engage personnel and generally to conduct an independent but fair public inquiry, respecting the rights of interested and affected parties. This decision, a copy of which is attached to this Report as Appendix A, is usually referred to as the Terms of Reference of the Commission.

Specifically, the Terms of Reference direct me

> ...to investigate and report on questions raised, directly or indirectly, by Chapters 3 and 4 of the November 2003 Report of the Auditor General of Canada to the House of Commons with regard to the sponsorship program and advertising activities of the Government of Canada, including
>
> (i) the creation of the sponsorship program,
>
> (ii) the selection of communications and advertising agencies,
>
> (iii) the management of the sponsorship program and advertising activities by government officials at all levels,
>
> (iv) the receipt and use of any funds or commissions disbursed in connection with the sponsorship program and advertising activities by any person or organization, and
>
> (v) any other circumstance directly related to the sponsorship program and advertising activities that the Commissioner considers relevant to fulfilling his mandate...

The Terms of Reference then go on to instruct me to make recommendations, based on the factual findings made according to the preceding paragraphs, to prevent mismanagement of sponsorship programs or advertising activities in the future, taking into account certain initiatives which were adopted by Cabinet and announced concurrently with the announcement concerning the appointment of the present Commission. Those initiatives and my recommendations will be the subject of a second report; the present Report will restrict itself to reporting on my factual findings made with reference to what is cited above in my Terms of Reference.

It should be noted immediately that the Terms of Reference do *not* instruct me to make any inquiry into the Government policies or political decisions which led to the creation of the Sponsorship Program, or which might have motivated the advertising activities of the Government of Canada. Accordingly, I am not entitled and do not intend to express opinions with respect to the wisdom or appropriateness of those political decisions. Although I was invited to offer my opinions on such subjects by the submissions of certain parties, I decline to do so since I do not consider that they fall within the scope of my mandate. My mandate, like the mandate of the Auditor General, is restricted to examining the implementation of the political decisions that led to the creation of the Sponsorship Program and the implementation of political decisions concerning its advertising activities, not the political decisions themselves.

However, it may be necessary for me on occasion to make reference to the political decisions and policies which led to the creation and which guided the management of the Sponsorship Program, to enable a fuller understanding of the reasons for any errors or mismanagement that might have occurred. Such references should not be interpreted by the reader as an indication that the Commission is questioning the wisdom of those decisions and policies, an area which is not within its jurisdiction.

Although this Report is limited to the making of factual findings, it will be necessary on occasion to clarify certain legal issues, such as the definition of the word "program" as it is used in federal legislation, or the concept of ministerial responsibility. These legal issues are dealt with only to assist the reader to understand what is being said, and to explain some of the factual conclusions. I am not rendering a legal judgment or opinion in these matters.

I.2
The Report of the Auditor General (November 2003)

The Report of the Auditor General of Canada was completed in November 2003 and delivered to the Speaker of the House of Commons; but, since Parliament was not at that time in session, and since the Auditor General of Canada reports directly to the House of Commons and not to the government of the day, the Report became public only when the next session of Parliament commenced, on February 10, 2004. Chapter 3 of the Report deals with the Sponsorship Program during the period from 1997 until August 31, 2001, and Chapter 4 deals with advertising activities of the Government of Canada during that same period. These two chapters are attached to this Report as Appendix B.

The Auditor General's Report, which constitutes a severe criticism of the way that the federal government ran the Sponsorship Program, and which comments disapprovingly on certain government management practices in the field of advertising, will be the subject of Chapter II of this Report.

1.3
The Public Hearings

The initial organization of the Commission required the engagement of counsel, securing of premises, the hiring of personnel and experts, and the initial organization and examination of masses of documentation. On May 7, 2004, I made a public opening statement, and in it I announced the procedure that would be followed in the Commission's inquiry and the principles that would guide its public hearings and the administration of the evidence to be presented. A copy of the opening statement is attached to this Report as Appendix C. I will not repeat here what was said at that time, but I report with some pride that the intentions which were then announced have been, in my view, substantially realized. The hearings have been conducted respecting those principles which the Commission undertook to follow, namely, independence, fairness, thoroughness, expedition and efficiency.

Public hearings took place commencing in Ottawa on September 7, 2004, for approximately six months and continuing in Montreal until June 17, 2005. One hundred seventy-two witnesses were heard, some of them for several days and some on more than one occasion, over a total of 136 hearing days. A lits of witnesses who testified is attached as Appendix D.

Ordinarily the deliberations of Cabinet are secret and privileged, but the Government of Canada agreed to waive this privilege by two Orders in Council[5] which permitted a full inquiry to be made of the question of how certain decisions were reached when the Sponsorship Program was first conceived.

Twenty-five participants were granted standing and attorneys representing them were in attendance at the hearings at various stages, some throughout the hearings and some only occasionally. A list of the participants who were granted standing and the attorneys who represented them is attached as Appendix E.

A vast quantity of documentary evidence was put into evidence and forms part of the record of the Commission. A list of the exhibits, many of which are books of documents, is attached as Appendix F. As Commissioner, I have systematically avoided taking cognizance of any document or evidence which has not been produced into the record at the public hearings, although I am conscious that Commission counsel have had access to many documents that I have not seen and have had meetings and discussions with witnesses and other persons on matters that are not part of the evidence that I have heard. Commission counsel have respected my expressed wishes that any information acquired in this fashion should not be communicated to me. This Report has been written solely on the basis of the evidence in the public record.

Notices in accordance with section 13 of the *Inquiries Act*[6] were duly sent to the persons who might be the subject of findings of misconduct or unfavourable comments in this Report, to give them an opportunity to be heard. During the last week of the public hearings, closing submissions were made by counsel representing interested parties and intervenors. Most of them filed detailed written submissions, which have been useful in the preparation of the present Report. Other persons filed written submissions but chose not to make oral submissions. Whether oral or written, all submissions have been taken into consideration in preparing the present Report.

I.4
Incidental Proceedings and Rulings

Prior to and in the course of the public hearings, ten incidental rulings were made, orally or in writing, copies of which are attached as Appendix G. They may be briefly described as follows:

1. On July 5, 2004, I decided which parties would be granted full standing before the Commission, and which would be granted intervenor status only, giving reasons for my decision in each case.

2. On July 19, 2004, a ruling decided which parties would be recommended for government funding of their counsels' fees. Supplementary rulings on funding were subsequently made on October 26, 2004, April 4, 2005 and April 6, 2005.

3. On October 28, 2004, giving reasons, I dismissed an application presented on behalf of Mr. Joseph Charles Guité, who sought an order that his testimony be heard *in camera*,[7] be the subject of a publication ban, or be postponed to a later date – until after his pending criminal trial.

4. On November 22, 2004, after hearing lengthy representations on the subject, I maintained an objection made on behalf of Mr. Guité, giving detailed reasons for any decision, and ruled that he could not be cross-examined with respect to allegedly contradictory declarations he had made in his testimony before the Public Accounts Committee of the House of Commons.[8] This decision was the subject of an application for judicial review presented before the Federal Court of Canada on behalf of Mr. Alfonso Gagliano, which was dismissed by Madam Justice Danielle Tremblay-Lamer on April 27, 2005.[9]

5. On February 1, 2005, I dismissed an application seeking my recusal presented on behalf of the Right Honourable Jean Chrétien. This decision was the object of an application by Mr. Chrétien for judicial review, which was contested by the Attorney General of Canada.[10] The Commission was allowed to intervene to a limited extent. The application was scheduled to be heard by the Federal Court on June 7, 2005, but on May 30, Mr. Chrétien discontinued his proceeding. The Commission requested the Court to set aside the discontinuance and to reschedule the hearing, but its motion was dismissed.[11]

6. On March 29, 2005, giving reasons, I maintained in part three applications presented by Messrs. Jean S. Brault, Paul Coffin and Joseph Charles Guité for a publication ban with respect to their forthcoming testimony on the grounds that publication of some parts of their depositions might prejudice their right to a fair trial on pending criminal charges against them. After completion of the testimony of each witness, I varied my initial ruling and partially lifted the publication ban.

7. On April 13, 2005, I dismissed a request presented by counsel for Malcolm Media Inc. and Mr. Luc Lemay seeking an order to keep confidential certain documents containing financial information about them.

8. On May 20, 2005, I dismissed an application made on behalf of Mr. Alfonso Gagliano which sought to produce into the record of the Commission a transcript of the evidence of Mr. Guité before the Public Accounts Committee.

9. On June 2, 2005, I heard a motion presented on behalf of the Right Honourable Jean Chrétien seeking two orders: that Commission counsel be required to make public submissions with respect to the factual findings which could be supported on the evidentiary record at the end of Phase I of the hearings; and that Commission counsel be required not to provide advice to the Commissioner other than in public, in respect of the present Report. Counsel for Jean Pelletier, Alfonso Gagliano and Ranald Quail all supported the conclusions of the motion. Counsel for the Attorney General of Canada made submissions, but neither supported nor opposed the motion. Counsel for the Commission opposed the motion. For brief reasons given orally, the motion was dismissed.

10. During the hearings, I heard motions presented by two participants who, having received notices in accordance with section 13 of the *Inquiries Act*, requested particulars with respect to the notices. These motions, which were heard and decided *in camera* to protect the confidentiality of the notices and the identity of the persons concerned, were dismissed.

1.5
Scope of the Present Report

It should be emphasized that in accordance with the Terms of Reference of February 19, 2004, the primary purpose of the present Report is to make factual findings concerning the Sponsorship Program and advertising activities of the Government of Canada. However, paragraph (k) of the Terms of Reference specifically directs me to perform my duties "without expressing any conclusion or recommendation regarding the civil or criminal liability of any person or organization," and I am further instructed by that paragraph "to ensure that the conduct of the Inquiry does not jeopardize any ongoing criminal investigation or criminal proceedings." To satisfy these restrictions, the Commission avoided presenting or referring to evidence which is or has been the subject of three criminal prosecutions initiated by the Attorney General of Quebec against Messrs. Jean S. Brault, Joseph Charles Guité and Paul Coffin, who are alleged to have committed certain criminal acts in relation to the Sponsorship Program. In my opinion these restrictions have not unduly limited the thoroughness and efficiency of the work of the Commission.

With respect to the injunction not to express any conclusion or recommendation regarding the civil or criminal liability of any person or organization, I am taking particular care in this Report to avoid such expressions. The reader should not interpret anything said in the Report as an indication that I have come to any conclusions or opinions on the subject of the possible civil or criminal liability of anyone.

One has to be conscious that the rules of evidence and the procedure followed at a commission of inquiry are very different from those of a court. The findings of fact that I have reached may not necessarily be the same as those which would be reached in a court. There are no legal consequences attached to my determinations as a commissioner. My Report is not a judgment, and my findings are not enforceable and would not bind courts called upon to consider the same subject matter. My findings are simply findings of fact and statements of opinion that I have reached at the end of this Inquiry and which are supported by evidence in the record of the Inquiry.

My first duty is, therefore, to describe what happened. This obliges me to resolve conflicts in the evidence. There are many such conflicts, and I intend to express my conclusions as to which evidence I accept and which I do not. Indeed, the Report would be incomplete if I did not do so. More importantly, coming to conclusions on the evidence is necessary to fulfill my mandate. The Report would be of little value to the citizens of Canada or its government if it did not include findings as to the causes of any mismanagement or misconduct that might have occurred. The recommendations that I am called upon to make in the second Report will be based upon what I consider to be the reasons for the mismanagement revealed by the present Report; coming to conclusions as to what those reasons were, and identifying any persons who failed to fulfill their responsibilities, are essential parts of this Report. The legal consequences of any mismanagement or misconduct will, however, be left to another forum.

Just as it is important to identify persons who failed to fulfill their responsibilities or who might have been guilty of misconduct, it is equally important in this Report to identify persons who, on the basis of the evidence, are innocent of any misconduct or mismanagement. Such persons who, in the publicity surrounding the Commission or elsewhere, might have been accused or suspected of improprieties, are entitled to have any blemishes to their reputations explained or removed.

As an initial finding, which will be expanded upon in the pages that follow, it became apparent to me throughout the hearings that, with virtually no exceptions, the conclusions of the Auditor General of Canada, expressed in Chapters 3 and 4 of her 2003 Report to Parliament, have been confirmed. With only one exception of a purely technical nature, relating to the purchase of horses by the RCMP, no one has seriously suggested to me that any of her conclusions were unfounded.

What the Commission has been able to do, which the Auditor General could not do since her jurisdiction is limited to an audit of the institutions of the Government itself, was to compel the giving of evidence under oath and the production of documents, as well as to push its inquiry beyond the boundaries of government administration and investigate the receipt and use of funds and commissions disbursed in connection with the Sponsorship Program. This has led us to investigate the actions and conduct of communication agencies, which were purportedly acting on behalf of the Government of Canada to administer sponsorship projects and to supervise the promoters of events and activities sponsored by the Government of Canada. The Commission also looked into the commissions and fees charged by the agencies for their services. The use or misuse by certain communication agencies of funds derived from the Sponsorship Program, and the improper involvement of those agencies in the financing of the Liberal Party of Canada where that occurred, have also been investigated.

To recapitulate, the present Report intends to describe the actions of the persons and organizations at every level within the administration of the Government that might be blamed for mismanagement of public funds, or other misconduct. It will also report on the actions of persons and organizations outside the Government who might have unfairly or improperly taken advantage of such mismanagement and misconduct.

The Report will also examine the question of ministerial responsibility in an attempt to determine to what extent, if any, Ministers of the Crown might be held to be responsible for administrative improprieties, for their actions, for the absence of oversight, or for other omissions or inaction.

One of the main purposes of a public inquiry is to enable concerned citizens to learn firsthand what occurred when allegations of the improper use of public funds have been made. By following the public hearings they are able to arrive at informed opinions as to who might be held responsible for any errors or mismanagement that might have occurred affecting what the *Inquiries Act* calls "the good government of Canada." The first role of the Commissioner is to conduct hearings that serve to facilitate the understanding of the public, while ensuring at the same time that the presentation of the evidence is done fairly and dispassionately, to avoid premature or unfounded conclusions from being reached which risk damaging the reputations of persons innocent of any wrongdoing, impropriety or negligence.

I now embark upon my second role, which is to summarize the evidence and to attempt to make sense of what often appears to be a confused and confusing jumble of facts and documentation. Without forgetting the advertising activities of the Government, which will be dealt with later, let me start by providing an overview of the Sponsorship Program, which was the subject of the greatest proportion of the evidence presented to the Commission. Much of what is said in this preliminary section will be repeated in greater detail in the chapters that follow.

1.6
A Short History of the Sponsorship Program

What later became known as the Sponsorship Program had its beginnings in the fiscal year 1994-95, when the advertising section of the Department of Public Works and Government Services Canada (PWGSC), managed by Mr. Joseph Charles Guité, disbursed about $2 million from its normal operating budget for what were described as "special programs," such as the subsidization of heavily publicized automobile races, in exchange for the prominent display of advertisements for various federal government departments and agencies. This kind of activity was repeated in 1995-96, when nearly $22 million was disbursed by PWGSC for advertising rights at similar events and for expenses related to the promotion of national unity. At this time, the objective was to give publicity to certain government programs such as the campaign against the use of tobacco, in addition to an intention to advertise the federal programs and presence in general.[12]

Following the very close result of the referendum in Quebec on October 30, 1995, the Government of Canada, at a special meeting of Cabinet held on February 1 and 2, 1996, decided that it should, among other measures taken to counteract the sovereignty movement in Quebec, take steps to make the federal presence more visible, in Canada generally but particularly in Quebec. This would take the form of advertising and displays at community, cultural and sporting events. The advertising service of PWGSC was assigned this task.[13] Because Mr. Guité was accustomed to using the services of advertising agencies to assist the Government in its advertising activities, and because his section did not have sufficient personnel possessing the necessary training and experience to look after what proved to be an extensive program, he chose to contract with advertising and communication agencies that were asked to manage and administer the sponsorships to which the Government of Canada had agreed.[14] In effect, the advertising and communication agencies were engaged to act on behalf of the Government of Canada to organize and manage these sponsorships and to see to it that the Government received the publicity and visibility for which it was paying. In exchange for their services, these agencies would receive remuneration in the form of commissions and fees paid for what were referred to as production costs.[15]

At the time the decision was made to embark upon this program, the Minister of PWGSC was the Honourable Diane Marleau. She was only marginally involved in the creation of the Sponsorship Program, which was directed in its initial stages, at the request of the Prime Minister, by Mr. Jean Pelletier, his Chief of Staff,[16] with the assistance of the Privy Council Office. All of this was done in collaboration with Mr. Guité. When the Honourable Alfonso Gagliano replaced Ms. Marleau as Minister of PWGSC in June 1997, he took a much more active role in the direction of the Sponsorship Program, gradually replacing Mr. Pelletier's supervision of the work of Mr. Guité.[17]

In August 1999, Mr. Guité retired from the public service. He was replaced as head of the Communication Coordination Services Branch (CCSB), which was the name of the section within PWGSC that handled sponsorships and advertising, by Mr. Pierre Tremblay. Until his transfer to the public service a few months earlier, Mr. Tremblay had been the Executive Assistant of Mr. Gagliano, that is to say the political and administrative head of the Minister's office.[18]

At or about this time, Daniel Leblanc of the Globe and Mail was making his first requests for information about the Sponsorship Program in accordance with the *Access to Information Act*.[19] The first request was made in September 1999,[20] and further requests were being processed during the early months of 2000,[21] eventually leading to a series of newspaper articles which made the problems affecting the Program a matter of public discussion.[22]

In the meantime, in or about February 2000, because of a scandal that had erupted concerning major administrative problems that arose in the Department of Human Resources Development, it was decided by Mr. Gagliano or by Deputy Minister Ranald Quail (the question of who made the decision is a matter of controversy) to order an internal audit of the Sponsorship Program.[23] The audit report was presented to Mr. Gagliano in September 2000 and disclosed a number of irregularities in the administration of the Program. He says that he ordered a temporary suspension of the Program until a plan could be implemented to mitigate the risks identified in the audit, at which time the Program would be reinstated.[24] Given that contracts were issued as early as November 2000, the moratorium, if in fact it occurred, was of a very short duration.[25]

On September 1, 2001, after CCSB had been merged with the Canada Information Office, the new organization, named Communication Canada, assumed responsibility for the administration of the Sponsorship Program. Communication Canada, under the leadership of Mr. Guy McKenzie, created for the first time an administrative structure to handle sponsorship contracts, using known and published criteria and standard procedures.[26]

In January 2002, Mr. Gagliano was replaced as Minister of PWGSC by the Honourable Don Boudria, who was advised in May 2002 by the Auditor General that, on the basis of certain findings with respect to three sponsorship contracts she had been investigating, she was referring the files in question to the RCMP and was undertaking a complete audit of the Sponsorship Program from 1997 to 2001. By now the problems associated with the Program had become the subject of daily questions in the House of Commons and extensive critical media coverage.[27] On May 23, 2002, Prime Minister Chrétien made a major speech in the House of Commons in which he announced a number of new initiatives designed to restore public confidence in the integrity of the Government.[28]

On May 26, 2002, Mr. Boudria was replaced as Minister of PWGSC by the Honourable Ralph Goodale, who was instructed by Prime Minister Chrétien to "go in there, find out what is the problem and fix it." Within

24 hours Mr. Goodale was able to determine that the problems with the
past administration of the Program were of such gravity and importance
that it would be best to suspend it again. The moratorium was partially lifted
on July 22, 2002, and when the Program was resumed in September of that
year, Communication Canada had the responsibility of administering it
under new rules and without using the services of communication or
advertising agencies as intermediaries.[29]

In December 2003, when the Right Honourable Paul Martin took office
as Prime Minister, the first action taken by the new Cabinet was to cancel
the Sponsorship Program. A few months later, Communication Canada was
dismantled.[30]

From 1994 to 2003, the amount expended by the Government of Canada
for special programs and sponsorships totalled $332 million, of which
44.4%, or $147 million, was spent on fees and commissions paid to
communication and advertising agencies. These amounts do not include sums
of money expended on the salaries of the public servants who worked on
the administration of the Sponsorship Program, or the costs of their offices;
nor do they include the costs of the numerous audits and investigations which
have been conducted over the years as a result of the mismanagement of the
Program and the abuses to which it gave rise. And of course the figure of
$332 million does not include the costs incurred by the Government of Canada
as a result of the appointment of the present Commission of Inquiry.

1.7
Brief Overview of Federal Government Advertising

The federal government is one of the largest advertisers in the country. From
April 1994 to March 2003, it issued advertising contracts totalling $1.1 billion,
out of which 53% was for media placement. In that period, almost 50% of
these contracts went to three agencies, Vickers & Benson, BCP and
Groupaction.[31]

Endnotes for Chapter I

1 Office of the Auditor General of Canada, *Report of the Auditor General to the House of Commons: Government-Wide Audit of Sponsorship, Advertising, and Public Opinion Research* (Minister of Public Works and Government Services Canada 2003).

2 RSC 1985, c. I-11.

3 Chapter 3 – The Sponsorship Program; Chapter 4 – Advertising Activities.

4 PC 2004-110.

5 PC 2004-119, February 20, 2004; and PC 2004-986, September 14, 2004.

6 Section 13 reads: "No report shall be made against any person until reasonable notice has been given to the person of the charge of misconduct alleged against him and the person has been allowed full opportunity to be heard in person or by counsel."

7 A Latin phrase commonly used by the legal profession, meaning the hearing would be conducted in private.

8 On April 22 and 23, 2004.

9 *Gagliano v. Canada (Attorney General)*, 2005 FC 576.

10 *Chrétien v. Canada (Attorney General)*, F C file T-404-05.

11 *Chrétien v. Canada (Attorney General)*, 2005 FC 925 (Madam Prothonotary Aronovitch).

12 Exhibit P-106(A), tab3.

13 Testimony of Mr. Gagliano, Transcripts vol. 67, pp. 11565-11566, 11582-11583 (OF), pp. 11562-11563, 11578-11579 (E).

14 Testimony of Mr. Guité, Transcripts vol. 33, p.5667(OE), pp.5674-5675(F); Testimony of Mr. Lefrançois, Transcripts vol.53, p. 9135(OF), pp.9131-9132(E).

15 Testimony of Mr. Guité, Transcripts vol. 33, p.5667(OE), pp.5674-5675(F).

16 Testimony of Mr. Pelletier, Transcripts vol. 71, pp. 12402-12403 (OF), pp. 12393-12394 (E); Testimony of Mr. Chrétien, Transcripts vol. 72, p. 12568 (OF), p. 12557 (E).

17 Testimony of Mr. Guité, Transcripts vol. 33, pp. 5676-5677 (OE), pp. 5685-5687 (F); Testimony of Mr. Guité, Transcripts vol. 37, p. 6409 (OE), p. 6427 (F).

18 Exhibit P-20, paras. 84, 88.

19 RSC 1985, c. A-1.

20 Testimony of Ms. Lloyd, Transcripts vol. 38, p. 6560 (OE), p. 6567 (F).

21 Testimony of Ms. Francoeur, Transcripts vol. 38, p. 6645 (OF), 6644-6645 (E); Exhibit P-115, p. 12; Exhibit P-116, p. 6; Exhibit P-117, p. 13.

22 Exhibit GC-15; Exhibit P-115, p. 46; Exhibit P-200, p. 46; Exhibit P-214, p. 142.

23 Testimony of Mr. Turner, Transcripts vol. 16, p. 2550 (OE), p. 2561 (F); Testimony of Mr. Gagliano, Transcripts vol. 67, pp. 11550-11551 (OF), pp. 11549-11550 (E); Exhibit P-45, paras. 116-117.

24 Testimony of Mr. Gagliano, Transcripts vol. 69, p. 11983 (OF), pp. 11974-11975 (E).

25 Exhibit P-428(D), p. 747.

26   Exhibit P-127(A), tab A, pp. 8-10.

27   Testimony of Mr. Boudria, Transcripts vol. 128, pp. 24216-24218, 24224-24225 (OF), pp. 24214-24217, 24222-24223 (E); Testimony of Mr. Goodale, Transcripts vol. 128, p. 24083 (OE), pp. 24083-24084 (F).

28   Testimony of Mr. Boudria, Transcripts vol. 128, p. 24190 (OE), p. 24196 (F).

29   Testimony of Mr. Goodale, Transcripts vol. 128, pp. 24083-24096 (OE), pp. 24083-24097 (F).

30   Testimony of Mr. Goodale, Transcripts vol. 128, p. 24098 (OE), p. 24099 (F).

31   Exhibit P-428(A), pp. 16, 20, 69.

CHAPTER II

THE AUDITOR GENERAL'S REPORT OF NOVEMBER 2003

2.1
Genesis in March 2002

In March 2002 the Honourable Don Boudria, who was then the Minister of Public Works and Government Services Canada (PWGSC), asked the Auditor General of Canada to investigate three contracts, totalling $1.6 million, that had been awarded by PWGSC through its Communication Coordination Services Branch (CCSB) to Groupaction Marketing Inc. in 1996, 1998 and 1999.[1] These contracts had been the subject of many questions in the House of Commons and had attracted considerable media commentary.

On May 6, 2002, the Auditor General reported to the Minister that her audit of these contracts had revealed significant shortcomings at all stages of the contract management process. She advised him that her findings had led her to refer the matter to the RCMP. She also announced that, on the basis of the facts which she had learned during her investigation of these files, she had decided to undertake a government-wide audit of all of the advertising and sponsorship activities of the Government of Canada since 1997.[2]

On the basis of this initial Report of the Auditor General, Prime Minister Chrétien, on May 23, 2002, spoke to the House of Commons and announced an eight-point action plan which included changes to the legislation governing the financing of political parties and candidates for office.[3] In his speech the Prime Minister acknowledged that "it appears that some mistakes were made." He did not go into the details of the problems with the House of Commons, because he did not know precisely what they were and because there were ongoing investigations by the police and by the Auditor General.[4] His intent was to reassure the public that the Government was doing what was necessary to correct the situation and that the matter could be dealt with effectively by the Auditor General and the police.[5]

At the time that the Auditor General announced her intention to conduct a full-scale audit of the Sponsorship Program, she was under the impression that it had been initiated in 1997 at about the time CCSB was created as a branch of PWGSC.[6] We now know that certain sponsorship initiatives had been undertaken by the Government through the predecessor of CCSB, known as the Advertising and Public Opinion Research Service (APORS), as early as 1995, and that what is now referred to as the Sponsorship Program was commenced in the spring of 1996.[7]

Since the Government's advertising activities were also being administered by CCSB, the same service that was in charge of the Sponsorship Program, the Auditor General undertook at the same time an audit of the advertising activities of the federal government.[8] In each case her audit dealt only with the period from November 1997, when CCSB was created, until 2001.

The Auditor General learned in the course of her audit that the Sponsorship Program had been the subject of an internal audit conducted by PWGSC in 2000. That internal audit had revealed serious administrative shortcomings which PWGSC had made attempts to remedy.[9] Similar problems had been uncovered in an earlier audit of the Government's advertising activities conducted by outside auditors, Ernst & Young, in 1996.[10] These audits will be discussed in Chapter VII of this Report.

The Auditor General reported that the Sponsorship Program was created as a result of concerns about the visibility of the federal presence across Canada, but particularly in the Province of Quebec. One of the vehicles for promoting the visibility of the federal government was sponsorships. The Government of Canada would agree to provide organizations with financial assistance to support cultural and community events. In exchange, an organization would agree to provide visibility for the federal government by, for example, displaying the Canada wordmark and other symbols, such as the Canadian flag, at its events and on promotional material. Sponsorships were intended to encourage a positive perception of the federal government through its association with popular events in fields such as sports, entertainment and culture.[11]

2.2
Summary of the Auditor General's Conclusions

The Auditor General's Report of November 2003 is highly critical of the Government's handling of the Sponsorship Program. Under the heading "Overall Main Points," she summarizes her findings in the following paragraphs:[12]

1. We found that the federal government ran the Sponsorship Program in a way that showed little regard for Parliament, the *Financial Administration Act*, contracting rules and regulations, transparency, and value for money. These arrangements—involving multiple transactions with multiple companies, artificial invoices and contracts, or no written contracts at all—appear to have been designed to pay commissions to communications agencies while hiding the source of funding and the true substance of the transactions.

2. We found widespread non-compliance with contracting rules in the management of the federal government's Sponsorship Program, at every stage of the process. Rules for selecting communications agencies, managing contracts, and measuring and reporting results

were broken or ignored. These violations were neither detected, prevented, nor reported for over four years because of the almost total collapse of oversight mechanisms and essential controls. During that period, the program consumed $250 million of taxpayers' money, over $100 million of it going to communications agencies as fees and commissions.

3. Public servants also broke the rules in selecting communications agencies for the government's advertising activities. Most agencies were selected in a manner that did not meet the requirements of the government's contracting policy. In some cases, we could find no evidence that a selection process was conducted at all.

Chapter 4 of the Auditor General's Report deals with the advertising activities of the Government of Canada. In it, critical observations are made concerning deficient management practices by public servants; the Auditor General takes care to specify that her comments and criticisms do not apply to the persons with whom the Government contracted for advertising services.[13]

In her testimony at the hearings of the Commission, the Auditor General and her colleagues on her panel described their audit objectives as follows:[14]

- whether the Government had exercised adequate control over the Sponsorship Program, public opinion research, and advertising activities;

- whether the program and activities were duly reported to Parliament; and

- to what extent the Government had taken corrective action as a result of previous audits and reviews.

The entities audited were CCSB and its successor, Communication Canada, which were believed to be the two main agencies responsible for the management of the Sponsorship Program, as well as the two central agencies with oversight responsibility, the Treasury Board Secretariat and the Privy Council Office. Included in the audit were the Government agencies and Crown

Corporations that had received money from the Government through the Sponsorship Program.[15]

The Auditor General comes to eight principal conclusions, which may be summarized as follows:

1. *Parliament's role was not respected* in that Parliament was not informed of the Sponsorship Program's existence and objectives.[16] There had been no advice or direction from the Government as to how the Program was to be implemented, and no strategic plan. In fact, the Auditor General had been unable to determine how the decision to create the Program had been made, or by whom. None of PWGSC's performance reports to Parliament mentioned the Sponsorship Program prior to 2001. The Auditor General was of the opinion that in such performance reports there should have been specific mention of the Sponsorship Program, given its importance.[17]

2. *There was a breakdown in internal controls*, due in part to the fact that the contracting and payment procedures followed at CCSB violated basic principles of segregation of duties and oversight. Essentially a deputy head is obliged, by reason of section 32 of the *Financial Administration Act* and related Treasury Board policies, to ensure that procurement, requisitions for payment, and certification for payment according to section 34 of the *Financial Administration Act* are kept separate and performed by different persons. This did not occur.[18]

    Personnel at CCSB told the representatives of the Office of the Auditor General that Mr. Guité, the Executive Director of CCSB, decided, without their involvement, on events to be sponsored, amounts to be allocated and the selection of agencies. He held discussions with the Minister's office or representatives of the Prime Minister's Office at various times, and then instructed them to prepare contract requisitions and to forward them to procurement staff for the completion of contracts. The Executive Director then approved payments to the contracted communication agencies. The concentration of all these functions in the hands of one public servant constituted a serious irregularity. The Auditor General also found that the Sponsorship Program operated without written guidelines, and that events and the amounts of money granted to them by way of sponsorships appeared to be decided arbitrarily and on an *ad hoc* basis.[19]

3. *There were problems related to the selection of agencies.* According to the Government Contracting Policy and particularly Appendix Q,[20] which governs the selection of advertising agencies, suppliers should have been selected competitively[21] according to procedures that were frequently not followed.[22]

    Until 2001, for sponsorship contracts, PWGSC used communication agencies from three lists of pre-qualified suppliers that were approved for another purpose. Two of the lists had been created in 1995, and one in 1997. None of the agencies on the three lists of pre-qualified suppliers had been selected in conformity with the required competitive process. In every case there were serious irregularities.[23]

4   *Files were poorly documented.* Section 12.3.1 of the Contracting Policy of the Government provides that:[24]

> Procurement files shall be established and structured to facilitate management oversight with a complete audit trail that contains contracting details related to relevant communications and decisions including the identification of involved officials and contracting approval authorities.

The Auditor General found that there was a general lack of documentation in the files, which usually did not contain any assessment of a project's merits (indeed, there were no criteria in existence for assessing merit) or a documented rationale supporting the level of funding approved. There was a general lack of visibility plans and post-mortem reports that would permit evaluation of value received for money spent.[25]

5. *Amendments were made irregularly.* The Auditor General found that 21% of the audited files had been amended without any explanation of the reasons for the amendments or of how such amendments were in the best interests of the Government.[26]

6. *There were serious problems relating to section 34 certification and payment.* Although sponsorship files invariably included a signature certifying that the requirements of section 34 of the *Financial Administration Act* had been satisfied, in many instances the Auditor General saw insufficient evidence in the file supporting that signature. Some payments were made on the basis of lump-sum invoices, with no supporting documentation; or there was no record of who had performed the work, and no post-mortem report showing that the sponsored event had taken place and that the Government had received the visibility for which it had paid. In many cases, the file contained only a contract and an invoice.[27]

7. *Commissions and production costs were excessive.* The Auditor General found that of about $250 million spent in Sponsorship Program expenditures, over $100 million was paid to communication agencies as production fees and commissions. The latter sum could be roughly broken down into $16.9 million in agency commissions, calculated at 12% of sponsorship values; $4.3 million in Agency of Record commissions, calculated at 3% of sponsorship values; and $85.4 million in production costs. It was the $85.4 million in production costs that was of particular concern to the Auditor General. They included sums expended through subcontracting, and she could not be sure from the documentation in the files if further commissions had been charged in the subcontracts. Although there must have been some value received for the commissions and fees spent, there was little evidence to justify this.[28]

In her testimony, the Auditor General agreed that the problem was not with commissions as such. The Program had been established in such a way that communication agencies would do most of the management of the Program, giving advice on what to sponsor, taking care of administrative details and ensuring that the requested visibility was received. Her quarrel was with the amounts charged as production costs that would normally be covered by the commission of 12%. Her view was that the commission should have been a management fee paid to manage the whole activity, and that additional production costs should have been charged only on an exceptional basis.[29]

8.   *The Government's Transfer Payments Policy was not observed.* The final area of criticism was related to sponsorship of Crown Corporations and agencies, such as Via Rail, Canada Post, the Business Development Bank and the RCMP. In the course of the audit, the Office of the Auditor General learned of arrangements between PWGSC and communication agencies to transfer sponsorship funds to these corporations and agencies. PWGSC did not enter into contracts directly with the Crown Corporations to which it was transferring money; rather it contracted with communication agencies, to which it paid commissions to transfer money to the Crown Corporation or agency concerned.[30] The Auditor General takes the position that these transfers violate the intent of the Transfer Payments Policy, which aims to ensure that grants, contributions and other transfer payments are not used as a substitute for financing a Crown Corporation's operating or capital requirements.[31]

The Auditor General expressed the view that if a Crown Corporation or agency requires additional funds, it must go to Parliament to seek additional funds through supplemental appropriations. To do otherwise amounts to a bypass of parliamentary controls and oversights.[32]

In addition, there was little or no value for the money paid as commissions to transfer these funds from PWGSC to the Crown Corporation or agency concerned.[33]

The Report of the Auditor General includes a number of case studies which serve to illustrate the above findings most eloquently.[34]

With respect to the Auditor General's audit of the advertising activities of the Government of Canada, the audit objective was to determine whether in contracting for advertising services the federal government ensured that it obtained the best value for the Crown in a process that was transparent and gave equitable access to suppliers of advertising services. The objective was also to determine whether departments ensured that their advertising campaigns were designed to achieve the expected results and whether there was a corporate approach to advertising activities and their coordination.[35]

As a general conclusion, the Auditor General found that the Government of Canada failed to meet its obligation to allow suppliers equitable access to government business and obtain best value in selecting advertising agencies. She also found that most of the advertising agencies chosen to supply advertising services to the various departments of government that needed their assistance were selected in a manner that did not comply with the Government Contracting Policy.[36] All of the evidence presented to the Commission relating to advertising contracts, including the report submitted by Kroll Lindquist Avey (the "Kroll Report," which is reproduced as a separate volume of this Report—Forensic Audit), is consistent with the Auditor General's findings.

The Report of the Auditor General disclosed serious shortcomings relating mostly to the Sponsorship Program, but also to the general advertising activities of the Government of Canada. She made her findings on the basis of an audit of the books and records of the Government of Canada supported by interviews with public servants. However, there were limits on how far she could go in her investigation.

2.3
Additional Scope of a Commission of Inquiry

The present Commission of Inquiry has had many advantages which the Auditor General did not have. It has been able to subpoena records from third parties and to compel witnesses from within and outside the Government to testify under oath, whether they were inclined to cooperate with counsel for the Commission or not. In this way, a fuller and more complete examination of the shortcomings described in the Auditor General's Report has been possible. As already indicated, everything that the present Inquiry learned tends to validate the conclusions of the Auditor General's Report on the Sponsorship Program and government advertising activities, except that in many cases the irregularities and mismanagement that she described were clearly worse and more widespread than the Auditor General had learned or imagined, particularly with respect to sponsorship.

It is not necessary for the present Report to repeat what is disclosed in the Report of the Auditor General, especially since Chapters 3 and 4 are available to the interested reader as Appendix B to this Report. However, it should be noted that the objectives of an audit are to verify if the books and records of an organization have been properly maintained and accurately represent its financial results and situation. It also seeks to discover if the management of the organization which is being audited is conforming to established laws, regulations and policies, and whether there has been maladministration. In extreme cases, the audit may reveal the commission of criminal acts. Audits would not be required if the owners of the organization were correct to presume that every one of its employees was perfectly competent and honest and had not committed any errors. In other words, the function of an auditor is necessary because sometimes people are in error, incompetent or dishonest. Good management requires that these possibilities be anticipated, envisaged and discouraged.

But before launching into a description of what went wrong, it is important first to examine the structure, organization and operation of the Canadian government and how "good government" is supposed to function. That will be the subject of the next chapter.

Endnotes to Chapter II

[1]   Testimony of Ms. Fraser, Transcripts vol. I, p. 43 (OE), p. 46 (F); Exhibit P-I(A), pp. IO-II.

[2]   Exhibit P-I(A), p. IO.

[3]   Exhibit P-2IO(D), p. 754.

[4]   Testimony of Mr. Chrétien, Transcripts vol. 72, p. I264I (OF), pp. I2625-I2626 (E), Exhibit P-2IO(D), pp. 754-759.

[5]   Testimony of Mr. Chrétien, Transcripts vol. 72, pp. I264I-I2645 (OF), pp. I2626-I2629 (E).

[6]   Office of the Auditor General of Canada, *Report of the Auditor General to the House of Commons: Government-Wide Audit of Sponsorship, Advertising, and Public Opinion Research* (Minister of Public Works and Government Services Canada 2003), chapter 3, para. 3.6.

[7]   The recent history of sponsorships initiatives is discussed more fully in Chapter IV of this report.

[8]   Exhibit JC-IO, tab 3.

[9]   Office of the Auditor General of Canada, *Report of the Auditor General to the House of Commons: Government-Wide Audit of Sponsorship, Advertising, and Public Opinion Research* (Minister of Public Works and Government Services Canada 2003), chapter 3, para. 3.95.

[10] Exhibit P-3(A), tab 3.

[11] Office of the Auditor General of Canada, *Report of the Auditor General to the House of Commons: Government-Wide Audit of Sponsorship, Advertising, and Public Opinion Research* (Minister of Public Works and Government Services Canada 2003), chapter 3, paras. 3.5-3.7, 3.14.

[12] Office of the Auditor General of Canada, *Report of the Auditor General to the House of Commons: Government-Wide Audit of Sponsorship, Advertising, and Public Opinion Research* (Minister of Public Works and Government Services Canada 2003), chapter 3, para. 3.I.

[13] Office of the Auditor General of Canada, *Report of the Auditor General to the House of Commons: Government-Wide Audit of Sponsorship, Advertising, and Public Opinion Research* (Minister of Public Works and Government Services Canada 2003), chapter 4, paras. 4.I, 4.6.

[14] Testimony of Ms. Fraser, Transcripts vol. I, p. 58 (OE), p. 62 (F); Exhibit P-I(A), p. I4

[15] Testimony of Mr. Campbell, Transcripts vol. I, pp. 6I-62 (OE), pp. 66-67 (F); Exhibit P-I(A), pp. I5-I6.

[16] Office of the Auditor General of Canada, *Report of the Auditor General to the House of Commons: Government-Wide Audit of Sponsorship, Advertising, and Public Opinion Research* (Minister of Public Works and Government Services Canada 2003), chapter 3, para. 3.IOO.

[17] Testimony of Ms. Fraser, Transcripts vol. I, pp. 95-IO2 (OE), pp. IOI-IO8 (F).

[18] Exhibit P-I(A), p. 26.

[19] Office of the Auditor General of Canada, *Report of the Auditor General to the House of Commons: Government-Wide Audit of Sponsorship, Advertising, and Public Opinion Research* (Minister of Public Works and Government Services Canada 2003), chapter 3, paras. 3.20-3.23, 3.I20-3.I22; Exhibit P-I(A), p. 27.

[20] See Chapter V, Section 5.3, for a fuller description of Appendix Q and the circumstances of its adoption.

[21] Testimony of Mr. Minto, Transcripts vol. I, pp. II6-II7 (OE), pp. I23-I24 (F); Exhibit P-I(A), pp. 28-29.

22   *Office of the Auditor General of Canada, Report of the Auditor General to the House of Commons: Government-Wide Audit of Sponsorship, Advertising, and Public Opinion Research* (Minister of Public Works and Government Services Canada 2003), chapter 3, paras. 3.49-3.54; chapter 4, paras. 4.20-4.31.

23   Testimony of Mr. Minto, Transcripts vol. 1, pp. 124-126 (OE), pp. 130-132 (F); Exhibit P-1(A), pp. 29-30.

24   Testimony of Mr. Minto, Transcripts vol. 1, pp. 133-134 (OE), pp. 139-140 (F).

25   Testimony of Mr. Minto, Transcripts vol. 1, pp. 134-136 (OE), pp. 140-142 (F); Exhibit P-1(A), p. 31.

26   Testimony of Mr. Minto, Transcripts vol. 1, pp. 150-151 (OE), pp. 156-157 (F); Exhibit P-1(A), p. 31.

27   Testimony of Mr. Minto, Transcripts vol. 1, pp. 137-138 (OE), pp. 143-144 (F); Exhibit P-1(A), pp. 35-37.

28   Testimony of Mr. Minto, Transcripts vol. 1, pp. 152-157 (OE), pp. 158-164 (F); Testimony of Ms. Fraser, Transcripts vol. 2, p. 294 (OE), p. 313 (F); Exhibit P-1(A), pp. 31-37.

29   Testimony of Ms. Fraser, Transcripts vol. 2, pp. 329-331 (OE), pp. 332-334 (F).

30   Office of the Auditor General of Canada, *Report of the Auditor General to the House of Commons: Government-Wide Audit of Sponsorship, Advertising, and Public Opinion Research* (Minister of Public Works and Government Services Canada 2003), chapter 3, para. 3.43.

31   Testimony of Mr. Minto, Transcripts vol. 1, pp. 163-166 (OE), pp. 170-174 (F); Testimony of Ms. Fraser and Mr. Minto, Transcripts vol. 1, pp. 67-76 (OE), pp. 73-82 (F); Exhibit P-1(A), pp. 37-41; Exhibit P-2(A), tab 17; Office of the Auditor General of Canada, *Report of the Auditor General to the House of Commons: Government-Wide Audit of Sponsorship, Advertising, and Public Opinion Research* (Minister of Public Works and Government Services Canada 2003), chapter 3, para. 3.43.

32   Testimony of Ms. Fraser, Transcripts vol. 1, pp. 108-111 (OE), pp. 115-117 (F).

33   Office of the Auditor General of Canada, *Report of the Auditor General to the House of Commons: Government-Wide Audit of Sponsorship, Advertising, and Public Opinion Research* (Minister of Public Works and Government Services Canada 2003), chapter 3, para. 3.35.

34   *Office of the Auditor General of Canada, Report of the Auditor General to the House of Commons: Government-Wide Audit of Sponsorship, Advertising, and Public Opinion Research* (Minister of Public Works and Government Services Canada 2003), chapter 3, pp. 10-20.

35   Exhibit P-1(A), p. 66.

36   Office of the Auditor General of Canada, *Report of the Auditor General to the House of Commons: Government-Wide Audit of Sponsorship, Advertising, and Public Opinion Research* (Minister of Public Works and Government Services Canada 2003), chapter 4, paras. 4.24-4.31.

CHAPTER III

STRUCTURE, ORGANIZATION AND OPERATION OF THE GOVERNMENT OF CANADA[1]

3.1
General Principles of Responsible Government

Canada is a constitutional monarchy and a democracy with a system of responsible parliamentary and cabinet government based on the British Westminster model. The structures and conduct of executive authority are governed by law and by conventions and customs that have evolved and been developed over the history of responsible government in Canada. Constitutionally and technically, the power of the State flows from the Crown; in reality, the Crown acts only on the advice of its Ministers, who collectively form the Cabinet and are chosen by the Prime Minister. The government may remain in office only so long as it retains the confidence of a majority of the members of the House of Commons.

Responsible government in Canada is based on the individual and collective responsibilities of Ministers to Parliament. Ministers of the Crown are responsible for the conduct of government. They are accountable to Parliament.

Three words are used to designate the duties of Ministers: responsibility, accountability and answerability. The meanings of these words are the subject of learned writings which are not in every respect in agreement, and the application of the concept of ministerial responsibility will vary according to the circumstances of each particular case. Nonetheless, some basic principles can be stated.

A Minister is responsible for the department of which he or she has the overall direction and management. I will come back later to the concept of ministerial responsibility, to attempt to describe it more completely.

A Minister is accountable in that he or she must render an account to Parliament of how his or her ministerial responsibilities have been carried out. The Minister must take corrective action should problems have occurred, must correct any problems that have been identified, and must accept the consequences if the problem is attributable to the Minister's own actions or inactions.

Answerability refers to a duty to inform and explain to Parliament what has occurred in a department of the Government. A Minister is answerable to Parliament for the department under his or her jurisdiction, even if the subject of the questions refers to the administration under a previous Minister.[2] Accordingly, answerability is narrower in scope than accountability in that it entails neither responsibility to take action nor the personal consequences associated with accountability.

3.2
The Prime Minister and the Prime Minister's Office (PMO)

The Prime Minister is the leader of the political party that has been able to form a government that has the confidence of the House of Commons, usually by holding a majority of the seats or through coalition with another party or parties. The Prime Minister is responsible for organizing the Cabinet, providing the direction necessary to maintain its unity and setting the broad course of government policy. The Prime Minister is responsible for allocating Ministers' portfolios, establishing their mandates and standards of conduct, identifying the priorities for their portfolios and clarifying the relationships among Ministers.

As head of government, the Prime Minister has special responsibilities in the areas of national unity, national security, and intergovernmental and international affairs. In his testimony, the Right Honourable Jean Chrétien said that Canadian unity had been his number one priority as Prime Minister.[3] This may have led him to take a special interest in certain areas under the responsibility of individual Ministers. There are no established limits to restrict the involvement of the Prime Minister and his or her senior staff in whatever issue they decide to take over and manage. The Prime Minister's accountability for the Government as a whole is heightened by such direct involvement,[4] but in principle each Minister retains primary responsibility for what is done within his or her portfolio, and is accountable for it.

The Prime Minister is supported politically by the PMO and bureaucratically by the Privy Council Office (PCO). Although these are separate organizations, they are expected to work closely together to ensure that consistent timely advice is provided on the subjects of greatest importance to the Prime Minister.

The PMO includes political staff headed by the Chief of Staff. They provide advice on policy development and appointments, draft speeches and other public statements for the Prime Minister, and generally assist in dealing with matters of a political dimension. The Chief of Staff works more closely than anyone else with the Prime Minister, or at least that was the case when Jean Pelletier was Prime Minister Chrétien's Chief of Staff, which covers the period under review by this Commission. They met on a daily basis. Mr. Pelletier was among a select group of advisors and was the Prime Minister's closest collaborator. The evidence discloses that no one else had that kind of access.[5]

3.3
The Privy Council Office

The Privy Council Office is responsible for providing the Prime Minister with non-partisan and non-political advice on government policy and operations. The head of the PCO is the Clerk of the Privy Council, who also acts as Secretary to the Cabinet and is the head of the public service. In effect, the Clerk of the Privy Council is the Prime Minister's Deputy Minister, and meets with the Prime Minister and his or her Chief of Staff every morning. Jocelyne Bourgon became Clerk of the Privy Council on March 28, 1994, and occupied that post for almost five years. She was succeeded by Mel Cappe on January 18, 1999.

The PCO, as the Prime Minister's department, has a primary mandate to provide support for all of the Prime Minister's areas of responsibility. This mandate includes determining the Government's priorities and agenda, providing support for the Cabinet decision process and providing general assistance for the Prime Minister's chosen priority areas.

3.4
Ministerial Responsibility[6]

"Ministerial responsibility" has to do with the relationship between a Minister and public servants working in the department of which the Minister has charge.

So far as the Minister's department is concerned, law, tradition or convention dictate that the Minister has sole authority for the management and direction of the department to which he or she has been appointed. However, within the Government as a whole, the Minister is only one member of a team, so that the principle of Cabinet solidarity requires that the Minister seek the approval of or inform other members of the Cabinet about policies and decisions that may have relevance to other portfolios and the conduct of government as a whole. In addition, the Minister must be mindful of the obligation to report to Parliament, which represents the citizens of Canada and has a duty to safeguard the public purse. Parliament can discharge this obligation only if it is kept informed of the commitment and disbursement of public monies by individual Ministers and their departments.

The principle of a Minister's accountability to Parliament is well described in the following extract from *Governing Responsibly: A Guide for Ministers and Ministers of State:*

> Clear Ministerial accountability to Parliament is fundamental to responsible government, and to ensuring that Canadians have confidence that their government is acting in an open, honest and transparent manner. A Parliament that makes real decisions requires parliamentarians who have and can use information and tools to promote the interests of the regions they live in, and to hold the government to account for its decisions. The Prime Minister expects Ministers to place a high priority on ensuring that Parliament and its committees are informed of departmental policy priorities, spending plans, and management challenges. Ministers are expected to seek the views of parliamentarians and parliamentary committees on future plans and priorities, and to dedicate time to consulting and engaging their colleagues in Parliament in order to earn their support. These elements are key to bringing the public will and the purpose of a government into productive alignment.

Parliament confers the powers of the state on Ministers on the condition that they, and through them the officials under their management and direction, be accountable to Parliament for their actions. Parliamentary review of spending is a key element of this accountability.[7]

One of the difficulties in the attribution of ministerial responsibility derives from the size of modern government. Most commentators say that it is not fair today to hold a Minister responsible for errors or maladministration attributable to departmental officials if the Minister was not aware of them. The exception occurs if it can be determined that the Minister failed to ensure that appropriate systems were in place to manage the risks that led to those errors or instances of mismanagement. This subject is addressed in paragraphs 70 and 71 of the Attorney General's written submission to this Commission:

[Emphasis added]

70. Ministerial accountability does not require that the Minister be aware of everything that takes place in his or her department. Similarly, accountability does not mean that the Minister must accept blame, for example, by resigning, whenever something goes wrong in his or her department. Accountability and blame are different: *blame applies only if problems are attributable to the action or inaction of the Minister.*

71. To support a Minister's accountability for a department, the Minister and his or her Deputy Minister must work together to understand the level of detail in which the Minister expects to be involved in the department's work. This will vary according to the circumstances and style of individual Ministers. Broad direction rather than transactional engagement is the norm, especially with respect to administrative matters, although Ministers will give more specific direction on key priorities such as Cabinet documents and Treasury Board submissions. *But, whatever the level of detail in which the Minister becomes involved, the Minister and Deputy Minister need to ensure that appropriate systems are in place to manage the risk of problems and to correct them when they occur.*[8]

The foregoing paragraphs reflect similar views found in Chapter 6 of *Responsibility in the Constitution,* under the heading "Ministers and Their Departments":

[Emphasis added]

The legislative bases for the departments of government make explicit the individual responsibility of the ministers who preside over them, and as has been noted, provide one of the legal bases of the minister's responsibility. The way in which ministers fulfil their responsibilities and are called to account for the exercise of their statutory authority is subject to practice and convention. All departmental acts provide for the formal appointment of the minister by the Crown (informally on the advice of the Prime Minister), set out the powers, duties, and functions for which the minister will be responsible, *and give him or her the management and direction (control and supervision) of the financial and public service resources deployed in the department.* These statutory provisions are given life through the conventions of the constitution, which determine at any given time the way in which ministers fulfil their respective roles and the circumstances of their answerability to Parliament for their actions, and offer further safeguards through the conventional responsibility of ministers collectively.

The individual responsibility of the minister requires that he or she be personally responsible for the activities carried out under his or her authority. This concept is fundamental to the long struggle to impose responsibility on the exercise of power. Parliament has insisted that ministers be directly accountable to it by being part of it. Ministers are, therefore, assailable on a daily basis for their actions and those of their officials.

The duties of the minister are set out in the statutes and are usually very general in character, leaving it to the minister to propose specific means of fulfilling them; these are then presented to Parliament in the estimates for its approval. If the minister wishes to seek an appropriation for a program whose provision is not covered in the general duties set out in the departmental Act, it is usually necessary for the minister to seek the necessary authority through legislation. Normally, however, *the duties described in the minister's acts cover a wide variety of functions, ranging from policy formulation and program development to program implementation and departmental administration.* These functions, whether policy, program, or administration, may be devolved upon the minister's senior permanent adviser in the latter's quality as the minister's deputy.[9]

It is therefore incumbent upon a Minister, according to law and the relevant government policies, to work with the public service to ensure that the proper implementation of government policy is delivered through the program or activity under the Minister's charge. Mr. Alex Himelfarb, the present Clerk of the Privy Council, testifies that when policies are to be translated into action, they have to be implemented jointly by the Minister, his or her department and the public service. He expands upon this concept in the following extract from his testimony:

Mr. Himelfarb: Now, it is true—and to be fair to all the parties, it is true that in a large department, a complex department, a minister cannot possibly be expected to know all the details, nor is anyone implying that they would, but they can't expect to know all the details or all the aspects of a program, and the style of ministers and their relationship with deputies varies extraordinarily. There is a lot of flexibility. There are some active ministers that one might describe as micromanagers, positively or negatively, depending on one's view, who are much more actively on top of the details and others who trust much more the public service to do that. In a sense, that is a shared accountability and the public service has to—that, by the way, does not in any way diminish the accountability of the elected official. It is non-delegatable.

The Commissioner: If he chooses not to micromanage, he nevertheless remains responsible?

Mr. Himelfarb: Exactly so. Exactly so, Commissioner.[10]

Some witnesses and the submissions made by certain participants take the position that individual Ministers and Cabinet are limited to formulating policy and that it is the responsibility of their administrative officials, directed by the appropriate Deputy Minister, to implement the policy. Thus, if errors occur in the implementation of policy of which the Minister is unaware, he or she bears no responsibility other than the obligation to take the appropriate corrective measures. According to the proponents of these submissions, the Minister is entitled to assume that the public servants charged with the implementation and administration of the policy decisions made by the Government will act honestly and competently and will, of their own volition, adopt appropriate practices and procedures in so doing.

For example, the Honourable Alfonso Gagliano, when interviewed on September 8, 2003, by a representative of the Office of the Auditor General, stated that the role of politicians is to make policy, but that public servants run the Government.[11] If there are problems in the management of programs, they are often hidden from the Minister, who will only learn of the problems from the media.[12]

Mr. Pelletier testifies that Prime Minister Chrétien, on taking office in 1993, met with all of the Deputy Ministers and expressed the view that they would be entirely responsible for government administration, and that the politicians would be responsible only for policy decisions. Here is how Mr. Pelletier describes what Mr. Chrétien said at that meeting:

> [Unofficial Translation]
>
> He clearly indicated that the deputy ministers were the heads of the bureaucracy and that the bureaucracy's territory was everything administrative and legislative; and that the political elements were the responsibility of the office of each minister, under the direction of an executive assistant, if you will, a chief of staff.
>
> I was at that meeting between the Prime Minister and the deputy ministers and agency heads, and clearly this was extremely enlightening for me, I would say, because it signalled to me what the subsequent policy of the Prime Minister's Office would be, namely, that we handled the political aspects. We had no administrative responsibilities. We had no administrative authority. We did not have to give instructions to public servants, and if such instructions had to be given, they were to come either from the deputy minister of the department concerned or from the Clerk of the Privy Council.

Nonetheless, Mr. Pelletier acknowledges that subordinate officials might obtain advice from the Prime Minister's Office about a program such as the Sponsorship Program, all the while retaining full responsibility for any administrative decisions, even those made following suggestions from persons such as Mr. Pelletier himself. Mr. Pelletier does not consider this to be political interference in administrative matters. Here is an extract from his testimony referring to Mr. Joseph Charles Guité, the public servant in charge of the implementation of the Sponsorship Program:

> [Unofficial translation]
>
> So, he frequently consulted the Prime Minister's Office in order to get our opinion, which was perfectly logical for us, because, as I explained earlier, one of the roles of the Prime Minister's Office is to provide relevant political advice.
>
> Therefore, since the program—and I stress that this advertising program had a political but non-partisan scope—it was perfectly normal that the Prime Minister's Office be consulted, and that it give its opinion. I believe, moreover, that, in his testimony, the current Deputy Minister of Public Works told the Commissioner that if Guité had not consulted the Prime Minister's Office he would have been shirking his responsibilities, and I agree completely.
>
> So, we gave our opinion. Guité showed up with the lists. The only kind of lists I saw were lists with names of events and the amounts requested. I never saw any lists with the names of agencies or intermediaries who had been designated to handle specific files, let alone details about the payment of the intermediaries.[13]

3.4.1 Exempt Staff

Ministerial responsibility for a department is to be distinguished from the Minister's responsibility for the political staff (also known as "exempt staff") in his or her office. The Minister chooses to employ his or her staff members (they are "exempt" from the general authority of the Public Service Commission, including the appointment process governing public servants) and works with them closely. According to *Governing Responsibly: A Guide for Ministers and Ministers of State*,[14] a Minister *is personally* responsible for the actions of his or her political staff. Therefore, if a staff member becomes involved in the department's program administration, the Minister is directly and personally responsible for any consequences, including unfortunate ones, of such involvement. Some activities undertaken in a Minister's office by exempt staff are subject to Treasury Board rules and policies such as travel and hospitality allowances.[15] If political staff were to breach those rules or policies, again the Minister would be personally responsible.

3.4.2 Ministerial Responsibility for Program Administration

As appears from authorities cited earlier, the proposition that Ministers and their political staff have no responsibility whatsoever for seeing to the proper implementation and administration of government programs and policies is an inadequate and incomplete expression of the principle of ministerial responsibility. A Minister must give attention to policy and program implementation and, in concert with the Deputy Minister, be assured that adequate means to deliver government policies are in place. It is the Minister's responsibility to see that the political decision or program has been sufficiently defined so that no misinterpretation of its objectives can occur. The Minister should take steps, in consultation with the Deputy Minister, to see to it that trained personnel are available to administer any new initiatives. The establishment of proper procedures and oversight are particularly important where the discretionary expenditure of public funds is involved. Above all, the Minister should give sufficient directions to the Deputy Minister so that the Deputy will be able to supervise properly the actions of the subordinate personnel who will administer the program and activities foreseen by the policy.

If the Minister fails to take these precautions, he or she cannot subsequently take refuge in the claim of being unaware of problems until they arose and became public. In other words, a Minister can be reproached for inaction as much as for positive actions that lead to unfortunate results. Willful ignorance of administrative inadequacies will not suffice to disengage a Minister from responsibility for failures within the department.

3.5
Role and Responsibilities of the Deputy Minister

For information and guidance on this topic, the Commission relies on a government publication entitled *Guidance for Deputy Ministers*, last modified on June 20, 2003. It states general principles applicable to the period relevant to the Commission's mandate. It begins by defining the responsibilities of Ministers of the Crown as being collective, in support of the Cabinet team; and individual, for their performance in carrying out the responsibilities of the portfolio assigned to them.[16]

The responsibilities of a Deputy Minister are best understood in the context of the support they provide to Ministers. The Deputy Minister is the principal source of support for a Minister in fulfilling his or her collective and individual responsibilities. In particular, the Deputy Minister is responsible for ensuring:

- sound advice on policy development and implementation;

- effective departmental management; and

- fulfillment of authorities that have been assigned to the Deputy Minister or his officials.[17]

With respect to the obligation to provide advice to the Minister, the publication describes this obligation in the following paragraph:

> The Deputy Minister supports both individual and collective ministerial responsibilities with respect to policy development and implementation. The Deputy Minister is counted on to provide the highest quality of advice on all relevant dimensions of a departmental issue, be they economic, social or administrative. Within the priorities, objectives and standards established by the government, the Deputy Minister must provide advice on the possible impact of initiatives on the public, the department, and the government. Advice must be timely and candid, presented fearlessly, and provide the best

> possible policy options based on impartial review of the public
> good and the declared objectives of the Minister and the
> government. Advice must challenge, guide and clarify, and
> generate new possibilities for improving the lives of Canadians.
> It must also demonstrate policy coherence from the perspective
> of departmental and portfolio management.[18]

In the foregoing extract, emphasis is put upon the importance of the advice
to be given to the Minister on policy development and implementation. It
must be assumed that the decisions are to be made by the Minister, probably
on the basis of the advice received, but that the Deputy Minister is not the
person making the decision. This concept corresponds to what has already
been said concerning ministerial responsibility and the obligation of the
Minister to work with the Deputy Minister and to give direction to him or
her concerning the development of policy and its implementation. These
matters are not left to the entire discretion of the Deputy Minister.

The relationship of the Deputy Minister with the political employees
("exempt staff") of the Minister's office is the subject of a short paragraph
in the publication, which reads:

> The Deputy Minister needs to be attentive to maintaining
> good working relations with the Minister's office in providing
> complementary support to the Minister. It is important to
> remember, however, that exempt staff of a Minister do not have
> the authority to give direction to public servants. When they
> ask for information or convey a Minister's instructions, it is
> normally done through the Deputy Minister.[19]

In his testimony Mr. Ronald Bilodeau, a former Associate Secretary of the PCO,
described the relationship between a Deputy Minister and his or her Minister
and stated that the role of the political official is not only to be in charge of
political matters, but also to have an awareness of management and administrative
matters. The role of a Deputy Minister is to be in charge of management and
its administration, and also to be sensitive to the political side. Each must clearly
understand his or her role and work together as a partnership.

Mr. Bilodeau went on to say that decisions made in a department are made by the Minister. Sometimes legislation gives specific responsibility to the Deputy Minister, but the final responsibility is that of the Minister. Ministers may exercise some discretion in what they delegate to their Deputy Ministers and what decision-making authority they retain. If there is a disagreement between a Minister and a Deputy Minister, the Minister may contact the Prime Minister, and the Deputy Minister may contact the Clerk of the Privy Council, and the problem would be worked out between them.[20]

Generally speaking, the Deputy Minister runs his or her department and the Minister should avoid interfering in the day-to-day management of the department, even though the Minister is responsible for it. Nevertheless it is sometimes difficult to prevent the people in the department from communicating directly with their Minister. The Honourable Marcel Massé, who has long experience not only as a politician but also as a senior public servant, says that the appropriate policy to follow is to ensure that the Deputy Minister is immediately informed about any contact between one of his or her subordinates and the Minister, so that the Deputy Minister is always aware of the information that is being conveyed. Without remaining current on such contacts, a Deputy Minister could lose control of his or her department. According to Mr. Massé, Deputy Ministers cannot be held accountable or responsible for decisions in which they had no part.[21]

Ms. Bourgon agreed that a Deputy Minister would have the following obligations in the context of the management of a project or a program:

- to ensure that there was the appropriate structure in place to address the project or program;

- to require that there were appropriate policies in place to administer the program;

- to require and ensure that the program was staffed by apparently competent people; and

- to require and ensure that there was an appropriate risk management scheme in place.

She added that the Deputy Minister must always be assured that the program or project is within the authority of the department, that the managers assigned to it have clear delegated authority and that normal information management systems are in place so that the Deputy Minister can receive feedback on the project.[22]

3.6
Treasury Board

The Treasury Board, supported by its Secretariat, functions as the Government's management board, overseeing the operations of the entire federal government. It is created by section 5 of the *Financial Administration Act*[23] (FAA), which provides that the Board shall consist of the Minister of Finance and four other members of Cabinet, and shall be presided over by the President of the Treasury Board, who is also a member of Cabinet.

Section 7 of the *Financial Administration Act* enumerates the areas of jurisdiction of Treasury Board, which include general administrative policy in the public service of Canada; the organization of the public service of Canada; financial management, including estimates, expenditures and procedures; and personnel management.

The role of Treasury Board has been modified over the years. Prior to legislative changes in 1966 resulting from the recommendations of the Glassco Royal Commission,[24] it presided over a highly centralized system for authorizing expenditures and a standardized accounting system. The Glassco Commissioners concluded that this operated as a disincentive to effective departmental management and argued, in effect, for a reassertion of ministerial authority through a higher degree of ministerial autonomy. In a post-Glassco environment the mantra became "let the managers manage." However, in 1976 the Auditor General of Canada concluded that financial management and control in the federal government continued to be inadequate. A new Royal Commission was appointed, chaired by Allen Lambert, which noted in its Report in 1979:

> After two years of careful study and consideration, we have reached the deeply held conviction that the serious malaise pervading the management of government stems fundamentally from a grave weakening, and in some cases an almost total breakdown, in the chain of accountability, first within government, and second in the accountability of government to Parliament and ultimately to the Canadian people.[25]

It appears that similar problems in financial management continually reoccur in the administration of the federal government.

At present, Treasury Board performs its role through the following general functions:

- setting management policies and guidelines for departments and agencies in areas such as expenditure management, procurement, human resources and information technology;

- holding departments and agencies to account for how they allocate resources, described generally as "oversight"; and

- acting as the principal employer of the public service.

Treasury Board establishes standards through its policies, but of course it cannot oversee the compliance by Deputy Ministers with respect to every transaction. It exercises its oversight role most actively through its review of Treasury Board submissions for spending initiatives.[26] It also endeavours to ensure that expectations of accountability, legality and propriety are clear for departments. I must say, however, after struggling through books of documents, that clarity is not always a characteristic of its written policy manuals.

In spite of massive documentation and policy directives, the principal expenditure controls are legislative, and consist of sections 32, 33 and 34 of the *Financial Administration Act*:

[Appropriation]

32 (1) No contract or other arrangement providing for a payment shall be entered into with respect to any program for which there is an appropriation by Parliament or an item included in estimates then before the House of Commons to which the payment will be charged unless there is a sufficient unencumbered balance available out of the appropriation or item to discharge any debt that, under the contract or other arrangement, will be incurred during the fiscal year in which the contract or other arrangement is entered into.

(2) The deputy head or other person charged with the administration of a program for which there is an appropriation by Parliament or an item included in estimates then before the House of Commons shall, as the Treasury Board may prescribe, establish procedures and maintain records respecting the control of financial commitments chargeable to each appropriation or item.

[Requisition for Payment]

33 (1) No charge shall be made against an appropriation except on the requisition of the appropriate Minister of the department for which the appropriation was made or of a person authorized in writing by that Minister.

(2) Every requisition for a payment out of the Consolidated Revenue Fund shall be in such form, accompanied by such documents and certified in such manner as the Treasury Board may prescribe by regulation.

(3) No requisition shall be made pursuant to subsection (1) for a payment that

(a) would not be a lawful charge against the appropriation;

(b) would result in an expenditure in excess of the appropriation; or

(c) would reduce the balance available in the appropriation so that it would not be sufficient to meet the commitments charged against it.

(4) The appropriate Minister may transmit to the Treasury Board any requisition with respect to which that Minister desires the direction of the Board, and the Board may order that payment be made or refused.

[Payment]

34 (1) No payment shall be made in respect of any part of the public service of Canada unless, in addition to any other voucher or certificate that is required, the deputy of the appropriate Minister, or another person authorized by that Minister, certifies

(a) in the case of a payment for the performance of work, the supply of goods or the rendering of services,

(i) that the work has been performed, the goods supplied or the service rendered, as the case may be, and that the price charged is according to the contract, or if not specified by the contract, is reasonable,

(ii) where, pursuant to the contract, a payment is to be made before the completion of the work, delivery of the goods or rendering of the service, as the case may be, that the payment is according to the contract, or

(iii) where, in accordance with the policies and procedures prescribed under subsection (2), payment is to be made in advance of verification, that the claim for payment is reasonable; or

(b) in the case of any other payment, that the payee is eligible for or entitled to the payment.

(2) The Treasury Board may prescribe policies and procedures to be followed to give effect to the certification and verification required under subsection (1).[27]

To assist in understanding what these provisions mean, at the risk of oversimplifying, section 32 ensures that funds are available to pay for any goods or services contracted; it means that no government expenditure may be made unless a provision for it has been previously approved by Parliament. Section 33 deals with requisitions for payment; it says that expenditures must be preceded by a requisition by the Minister of the department concerned or his or her delegate, in the form prescribed by Treasury Board regulations. Section 34 ensures that the contracting party has delivered the goods and services and that there is value for money; it says that no payment for goods or services requisitioned by the Government shall be made unless there is a certification on record that the goods or services have been supplied, that they were in accordance with the Government contract which authorized the expenditure, and that the claim for payment is reasonable.

These provisions are supplemented by Treasury Board regulations, which are binding, and guidelines and policies, which are not binding legally, but which must be followed by public servants.

We return briefly to the oversight function of the Treasury Board. The former Secretary, Mr. Jim Judd, insisted in his testimony that the primary lines of defence against spending irregularities are the oversight function that is expected of each department and the systems that should be in place to control spending. He states:

> Given the size and complexity of the federal government, bearing in mind that we are talking about hundreds of different institutions, a multitude of different governance regimes, it is only realistic to expect that departments and agencies, individual institutions of government, have an obligation to have in place appropriate management and oversight and control systems over their operations.[28]

The Commission is left with the impression that Treasury Board no longer considers its oversight function to be an important part of its overall responsibilities.

3.7
The Federal Budget and the Minister of Finance

The Minister of Finance is responsible for preparing the federal Budget. This is the Minister's primary responsibility, although he or she is also charged with developing tax and tariff policy and legislation; managing federal borrowing on financial markets; administering major federal funding and transfers to provinces and territories; developing regulatory policy for the country's financial sector; and representing Canada at international financial institutions.[29]

With respect to the Budget, the Minister of Finance is responsible for establishing the fiscal framework within which overall government spending takes place. He or she is, by tradition, the Vice-President of the Treasury Board. However, by custom the Minister of Finance does not attend Treasury Board meetings except when the President of the Treasury Board is unable to attend or when a matter to be discussed by Treasury Board is of special concern to the Department of Finance.

Once the fiscal framework is set, departments are responsible for the management of the expenditures allocated to them, although Treasury Board has its general oversight role. The Department of Finance and its Minister do not play a role in the oversight of expenditures made by other departments.

When the Minister of Finance prepares a Budget, there are two aspects to consider: revenues and expenses. Revenues come mostly from taxation, and the Government estimates its revenues based upon its calculation of how the economy, employment and inflation will affect revenues from taxation.

On the expense side, there are three basic categories of expenses to take into account:

- spending for which the Government is committed by legislation and over which the Finance Minister has virtually no control;

- debt service charges, over which the Finance Minister has little discretion unless Canada chooses to default on its obligations to its creditors; and

- non-statutory spending, or program spending, the area over which the Finance Minister, in consultation with his or her Cabinet colleagues and the Prime Minister, has discretion.

To prepare the Budget, the Finance Minister goes through the process of reviewing expected revenues and existing spending commitments and determines if there is going to be surplus money, and if so, for what it will be used. If it is decided that the surplus will go to spending, the Finance

Minister takes into account government policy as announced in the Speech from the Throne, the Party's platform and the various spending proposals that have been put before Cabinet. The final result is a Budget that makes an allocation to each department. This is the source of funds for departmental programs.

If the Finance Minister does not put something in the Budget for spending proposals of the department concerned, the process of obtaining new funding is basically over for that department, at least until the next federal Budget. Even if the Finance Minister agrees with a spending proposal and puts it in the Budget, the Minister of the department concerned still requires a number of approvals before he or she can go ahead with the proposed program. None of these approvals comes from the Minister of Finance as such, although as a member of Cabinet he or she is part of the overall Cabinet approval process, like any other Minister.

At some point, the Minister making a spending proposal goes to the Minister of Finance to request that funds be included in the Budget, and must make a presentation to a Cabinet committee to obtain approval in principle for the spending proposal from his or her colleagues.

Once there is a source of funds in the Budget and approval in principle of the proposed expenditure, the Minister goes back to the Cabinet committee, where the proposed project or expenditure is again examined, this time in more detail, before being approved.

Once final Cabinet approval has been obtained, a submission is prepared and goes to Treasury Board, where the proposal is again reviewed in detail. If Treasury Board gives its approval, the proposed spending is prepared for Parliament's approval, as part of the main estimates or supplementary estimates. The Minister can spend money only once Parliament has approved the spending.[30]

The Finance Minister's only role in this process is to set the financial context or the fiscal framework. Once a proposed expenditure has been approved through the presentation of the Budget, his or her responsibility for it comes to an end. The Minister plays no role in granting the various approvals, except to the extent that he or she may exceptionally attend the Treasury Board meeting at which the Treasury Board submission is considered. The Minister of Finance has no responsibility to monitor spending once it has been approved.

Once money has been voted to a department by Parliament, it is primarily the role of the department of the Minister concerned to ensure proper management and compliance with legislation. Although Treasury Board has an overall supervisory function to ensure that departments use money allocated to them in the way intended, the main responsibility for the proper administration of the sums allocated to the department is that of the Minister of that department.

3.8
Public Works and Government Services Canada

The Department of Public Works and Government Services Canada (PWGSC) was created in June 1993 by Order in Council through the merger of two departments, the Department of Public Works and the Department of Supply and Services. In 1996, legislation[31] confirming the merger and establishing the new Department was enacted. Section 5 of this legislation provides:

> The Department shall operate as a common service agency for the Government of Canada, and its activities as a common service agency shall be directed mainly toward providing the departments, boards and agencies of the Government of Canada with services in support of their programs.

Accordingly, PWGSC has a general mandate to operate as a common service agency for the Government and to provide all of its other departments, boards and agencies with goods and services "in support of their programs."

Section 7 of the same legislation provides as follows:

> In exercising the powers or performing the duties or functions assigned to the Minister under this or any other Act of Parliament, the Minister shall
>
> (a) investigate and develop services for increasing the efficiency and economy of the public service of Canada and for enhancing integrity and efficiency in the contracting process;
>
> (b) acquire material and services in accordance with any applicable regulations relating to government contracts...

Although the *Interpretation Act* and the common law[32] provide that any power or responsibility assigned by statute to a Minister may be validly exercised by his or her Deputy Minister or any other person in the Department who is suitably qualified, this provision does not relieve the Minister from his or her responsibilities of oversight. The responsibilities specified in section 7 are of such importance to the Department's function as a common service provider to all government departments that the Minister of PWGSC must take an interest in the contracting process to be followed by public servants in his or her Department. Because the Minister bears the primary responsibility for the Department, he or she is not entitled to leave administrative procedures and regulations to the sole supervision of Department personnel.

The table below, which identifies the various Ministers and Deputy Ministers of PWGSC at the times relevant to this Inquiry, will give the reader a better understanding of what follows in this Report.

Position within PWGSC	Incumbent	Time Period
Minister	David Dingwall	November 1993-January 1996
Minister	Diane Marleau	January 1996-June 1997
Minister	Alfonso Gagliano	June 1997-January 2002
Minister	Don Boudria	January 2002-May 2002
Minister	Ralph Goodale	May 2002-September 2003
Deputy Minister	Ranald Quail	June 1993-April 2001
Deputy Minister	Janice Cochrane	April 2001-June 2003
Deputy Minister	David Marshall	June 2003-present

David Marshall was the incumbent Deputy Minister at the time of writing this Report. His testimony before the Commission provides valuable insight into the problems that affected PWGSC during the years when the Sponsorship Program was operating, and he has put into effect measures designed to reduce the likelihood that such problems will reoccur. His testimony will be of value to the Commission when it comes to make recommendations to the Government, in Phase II.

In the Statement of Evidence submitted on behalf of PWGSC is the following paragraph:

[Emphasis added]

7. The Minister of PWGSC is responsible for the Department and, thus *there is a requirement for daily interaction between the Minister, his or her staff, and departmental officials*. The reasons for these interactions vary but may include such matters as briefings on Treasury Board submissions, presentations on major departmental initiatives, preparation for Question Period and discussions on key communications issues. It is generally the case that these interactions are through the Deputy Minister's Office…[33]

The same submission contains the following paragraphs concerning the relationship between PWGSC and the Treasury Board Secretariat:

10. PWGSC interacts with the Treasury Board Secretariat (TBS) in many different contexts. First, because of the number of operational programs for which PWGSC is responsible, it must often seek Treasury Board approvals. PWGSC works with the TBS in preparing Treasury Board submissions. These submissions are necessary to seek access to funds that have already been identified for PWGSC within the fiscal framework and to obtain specific authorities from time to time. For example, Treasury Board approval will be required for contracts whose value exceeds a Minister's authority or for large construction or information technology projects at various stages of their development.

11. Second, there is interaction between the TBS and PWGSC in the preparation of the Main and Supplementary Estimates and the Annual Reference Level Update.

12. Third, PWGSC's financial and contractual activities are driven by Treasury Board policies and guidelines.[34]

3.9
Definition of a "Program"

In his final oral submissions, counsel for the Attorney General of Canada argues that there was no Sponsorship Program in existence until September 1, 2001, when Communication Canada at last established and published formal guidelines, criteria and procedures to govern the administration of sponsorships for the future. The administration of sponsorships without criteria and involving considerable political input may have been risky or even dangerous, but it was not illegal and it did not constitute a program.[35] This submission appears to contradict the Terms of Reference by which this Commission was created, which refer in very specific terms to the creation and management of the Sponsorship Program. It also implicitly contradicts the testimony of many of the witnesses who were directly involved in 1996 in what they themselves describe as the Sponsorship Program, as well as the testimony of the public servants involved in the implementation of the measures decided upon in 1996 by the Government.

The question of whether the administration of sponsorships prior to September 1, 2001, constituted a program is important because the *Financial Administration Act* (FAA) and other legislation create responsibilities and obligations where funds are paid out in the context of a program. For example, section 32 of the FAA imposes upon a person "charged with the administration of a program" the duty to "establish procedures and maintain records respecting the control of financial commitments" made by the Government in relation to the program in question. Other uses of the word "program" appear in sections 7, 11, 29.1 and 32 of the FAA, but nowhere in the Act or other federal legislation is the word defined.

Treasury Board's Statement of Evidence provides a definition of a program as a "formal framework for organizing and undertaking activities so as to achieve a specific and defined set of objectives,"[36] but it does not tell us from where this definition is drawn. Probably it reflects what appears to be the prevailing attitude in the public service, since two witnesses with distinguished records of achievement in the Privy Council Office expressed a similar opinion.[37]

The Commission heard testimony from Ronald Bilodeau, who in 1994, after many years of service as a senior public servant, became Deputy Minister of Intergovernmental Affairs, a ministry that was at that time part of the Privy Council Office. In 1996 he was appointed Associate Secretary of the Privy Council and Deputy Secretary to the Cabinet PCO, which is to say he became the second most senior public servant in the Government, reporting directly to the Clerk of the Privy Council, Jocelyne Bourgon.

In his testimony, Mr. Bilodeau states that, in his opinion, what is described in the Terms of Reference as the Sponsorship Program did not prior to 2001 constitute a program as that word is used in bureaucratic jargon. Rather, it was until then a series of government initiatives, many having elements in common. It was only in 2001 that the Program was publicly announced and given officially approved structure and criteria.

Mr. Bilodeau admits that there is a degree of uncertainty within the public service as to what constitutes a program. In his opinion, in order for a program to exist there would have to have been a detailed proposal submitted to Cabinet and duly approved, which described the objectives sought and which clearly defined who had responsibility for the administration of the program. The following passage from Mr. Bilodeau's testimony expresses his view on the subject:

> [Unofficial Translation]
>
> Mr. Bilodeau: Normally, new programs are created by submitting a detailed proposal to Cabinet, that is, a brief to Cabinet spelling out the program objective, the rationale for the program, the steps, the activities to be funded

	by or carried out under the program, the pros and cons of the program, the person responsible for it, what Treasury Board and the Department of Finance think about it, etc. Consequently, it was a regular process for Cabinet…
Commissioner:	Is it not critical to establish eligibility criteria for programs?
Mr. Bilodeau:	Definitely. In the case of new programs it would be the…
Commissioner:	Definitely, and would there not be a certain amount of interest taken in the way the program is to be administered, the means to be used, and the person who is to be in charge?
Mr. Bilodeau:	Yes, that's true, Commissioner.[38]

Ms. Bourgon testifies that she had come to the same conclusion as Mr. Bilodeau, and that in her opinion there was no program before 2001 for the administration of sponsorship initiatives; they consisted only of lists of projects which were part of the Government's publicity activity. In her view, in order to constitute a program, the publicity activity would have to have been more structured and of greater importance.[39]

Section 12 of the *Interpretation Act* says that every enactment is deemed remedial, and is to be given the "fair, large and liberal construction and interpretation that will best ensure the object of the enactment." In the absence of any definition of what constitutes a government program in the law, the rules of interpretation of statutes require that these words or expressions be given their usual and ordinary meaning. A technical or specialized interpretation of an ordinary word is not to be resorted to unless the context clearly requires it.

In the *Shorter Oxford English Dictionary on Historical Principles*, the word "program" is defined in its general sense as "a definite plan of any intended proceedings." In *Le Petit Robert*, the word "programme" is defined as "suite d'actions que l'on se propose d'accomplir pour arriver à un résultat." In the *Canadian Oxford Dictionary* (Second Edition) the word "program" is defined as "a course of activities or actions undertaken to achieve a certain result."

With respect for the contrary point of view expressed by Ms. Bourgon and Mr. Bilodeau, I have come to the conclusion that the series of projects and initiatives launched by the Government of Canada in 1996, in the circumstances described in the remainder of this Report, constituted a "program" as that term is ordinarily used. Sponsorship initiatives were a series of projects or activities planned and undertaken to accomplish the objective of enhancing the visibility of the federal presence and promoting its programs and services. As such, they fit precisely into the dictionary definitions of the word "program." The fact that the Sponsorship Program was not formally structured and had not been specifically approved by Cabinet, Treasury Board and the Privy Council Office, and that it lacked eligibility criteria and the required bureaucratic oversight, did not make it less of a program, but in fact contributed greatly to the problems and abuses in its implementation that have been described in the Report of the Auditor General.

This completes our description of how the Government of Canada generally functions in the areas relevant to this Commission of Inquiry.

Endnotes to Chapter III

---

[1] This chapter relies on the testimony of Ms. Jocelyne Bourgon, a former Clerk of the Privy Council, and on the testimony of Mr. Alex Himelfarb, the present occupant of that office, the most senior position in the public service.

[2] Testimony of Mr. Himelfarb, Transcripts vol. 12, pp. 1889-1894, 1905 (OE), pp. 2009-2014, 2027-2028 (F).

[3] Testimony of Mr. Chrétien, Transcripts vol. 72, pp. 12506 (OF), p. 12502 (E).

[4] Testimony of Mr. Himelfarb, Transcripts vol. 12, pp. 1891-1892 (OE), p. 2012 (F).

[5] Testimony of Mr. Pelletier, Transcripts vol. 71, pp. 12327-12328 (OF), p. 12326 (E).

[6] The written submissions of the Attorney General of Canada and the testimony of Ms. Bourgon and Mr. Himelfarb rely on two government publications, which appear to be authoritative. They are *Responsibility in the Constitution*, prepared by the Privy Council Office in August 1977 and last modified on June 1, 1993 (Exhibit GC-2), and *Governing Responsibly: A Guide for Ministers and Ministers of State* (Exhibit P-35), dated December 2003 and also published by the Privy Council Office. The principles they contain apply to any era.

[7] Exhibit P-35, p. 15.

[8] Exhibit P-474(GG), paras. 70-71.

[9] Exhibit GC-2, VI, pp. 1-4.

[10] Testimony of Mr. Himelfarb, Transcripts vol. 12, p. 1851 (OE), p. 1965 (F).

[11] Exhibit P-200, p. 14, para. 48.

[12] Testimony of Mr. Gagliano, Transcripts vol. 67, pp. 11547-11550 (OF), pp. 11546-11548 (E).

[13] Testimony of Mr. Pelletier, Transcripts vol. 71, pp. 12313-12314, 12391-12393 (OF), pp. 12313-12314, 12383-12384 (E).

[14] Exhibit P-35, p. 33.

[15] Treasury Board Secretariat, "Guidelines for Ministers' Offices," section 3.3.4.3, Meals; section 6.1.3, Travel Expenses—Ministerial Staff.

[16] Exhibit P-36.

[17] Exhibit P-36, Part II, "Responsibilities of the Deputy Minister."

[18] Exhibit P-36, Part II, "Responsibilities of the Deputy Minister."

[19] Exhibit P-36, Part III, "Accountabilities of the Deputy Minister."

[20] Testimony of Mr. Bilodeau, Transcripts vol. 47, pp. 8082-8088 (OF), pp. 8082-8088 (E).

[21] Testimony of Mr. Massé, Transcripts vol. 64, pp. 11214-11218 (OF), pp. 11211-11215 (E).

[22] Testimony of Ms. Bourgon, Transcripts vol. 48, pp. 8335-8336 (OE), pp. 8338-8339 (F).

[23] RSC, c. F10.

24   The Royal Commission on Government Organization, 1962 ("Glassco"), recommended, at the broadest level, that departmental management be entrusted with the power of decision in many of the areas that were, at the time, being controlled by Treasury Board staff. The Commissioners concluded that "... the defects in government are the consequence of outmoded concepts of public administration and do not reflect on the calibre of Canada's public servants."

25   Exhibit P-10, pp. 4-7, paras. 12, 13-15, 18, 20, 22.

26   Exhibit P-10, pp. 13-18.

27   RSC 1985, c. F-11.

28   Testimony of Mr. Judd, Transcripts vol. 4, p. 593 (OE), pp. 595-596 (F).

29   Exhibit P-51, p. 1.

30   Testimony of Mr. Martin, Transcripts vol. 73, pp. 12690-12693, 12698-12705 (OE), pp. 12691-12694, 12700-12708 (F).

31   *Department of Public Works and Government Services Act*, SC 1996, c. 16.

32   In particular, section 24(2) of the *Interpretation Act*, RSC I-23, and the "Carltona principle" endorsed by the Supreme Court of Canada in *R. v. Harrison*, [1977] 1 SCR 238, and in *Comeau's Sea Foods Ltd. v. Canada*, [1997] 1 SCR 12.

33   Exhibit P-20, p. 2.

34   Exhibit P-20, p. 3.

35   Testimony of Mr. Lussier, Transcripts vol. 136, p. 25709 (OF), p. 25706 (E).

36   Exhibit P-10, p. 54.

37   Testimony of Mr. Bilodeau, Transcripts vol. 46, pp. 7917-7918 (OF), pp. 7882-7884 (E); Testimony of Ms. Bourgon, Transcripts vol. 47, pp. 8163-8164 (OF), pp. 8163-8164 (E).

38   Testimony of Mr. Bilodeau, Transcripts vol. 46, p. 7918 (OF), p. 7883 (E).

39   Testimony of Ms. Bourgon, Transcripts vol. 47, pp. 8163-8164 (OF), pp. 8163-8164 (E).

CHAPTER IV

ORIGINS OF THE
SPONSORSHIP PROGRAM

Let us next examine how the Government functioned in practice in its advertising activities and in the administration of the Sponsorship Program, starting with the election of a new government in November 1993, when the Liberal Party of Canada, headed by the Right Honourable Jean Chrétien, won a majority of the seats in the House of Commons.

4.1
Evolution of the Management of Advertising Services within PWGSC

Prior to the election of the Chrétien government in 1993, government advertising was managed by the Advertising Management Group (AMG), an organization within Public Works and Government Services Canada (PWGSC) directed by Joseph Charles Guité. At some point in time the name of the AMG was changed to the Advertising and Public Opinion Research Directorate (APORD), and a year or two later it again was renamed to become the Advertising and Public Opinion Research Sector (APORS), always under Mr. Guité's direction.[1] These did not involve important structural changes. This Report will, from time to time, use the acronym APORS to describe the various organizations headed by Mr. Guité prior to the formation of the Communication Coordination Services Branch (CCSB) in 1997.

AMG and APORS were never large organizations. In 1994, only about 16 people worked there, of whom only five were involved in advertising; the others worked on public opinion research or other matters. The five who worked mostly in advertising were Mr. Guité as Director; Andrée LaRose as his Deputy and the person in charge of agency-selection procedure; Huguette Tremblay, who worked with Mr. Guité continuously from 1987, fulfilling a variety of functions until the latter left the public service in August 1999; Denyse Paquette, who worked as Mr. Guité's assistant; and Mario Parent, who dealt mainly with the contracting process. Other employees such as Allan Cutler, Marie Maltais, Evelyn Marcoux, Paul Lauzon and David Myer came and went over the years. They sometimes tried to introduce reforms or to effect changes to the very loose way in which the organization was operated by Mr. Guité, but without success.[2]

Until November 1994, the contracting function necessary to the activities of APORS was handled by a separate division of PWGSC, known as the Public Relations and Print Contract Services Sector (PRPCSS). This arrangement led to conflicts between Mr. Guité and the people at PRPCSS. Generally, Mr. Guité was impatient with delays and with the bureaucratic processes governing the issuance of contracts.[3] He was proud of his reputation as someone who was "results oriented" and who would cut through red tape as required.

On November 21, 1994, Mr. Guité wrote a letter to his superior, who at that time was the Assistant Deputy Minister, Richard Neville, to inform him about the continuing dispute he was having with PRPCSS as a result of its slowness in completing contracts. In the letter he proposed various options to rectify the problem. His primary recommendation was that clear instructions be given to PRPCSS that once a requisition had been approved by Mr. Guité's group, PRPCSS was to issue an advertising contract without delay. The second option was to delegate the contracting authority to the client department, subject to prior approval from Mr. Guité's group. The third option was to assign the contracting function to his own organization, APORS.[4]

While Mr. Guité states that he preferred the first option,[5] the third option was chosen by his superiors, and APORS was given responsibility both for agency selection and for the procurement process, including the signing of contracts.[6] The assignment to his section of complete control of the contracting process left Mr. Guité free to give effect to his conviction, which was obvious to the Commission, that the awarding of advertising contracts should not be the subject of a bureaucratic and competitive process. Apparently it was from this moment in time that he felt free to disregard the requirements of Appendix Q to the Government's Contracting Policy and Guidelines, as approved by Treasury Board. Appendix Q, which applied to advertising and public opinion procurement, had only come into effect about six months earlier. The importance of Appendix Q and Mr. Guité's views about the competitive process in advertising contracts will be the subject of Chapter V of this Report.

In his testimony, Mr. Neville agrees that it was not normal that procurement, contracting authority and agency selection would all be performed by the same individuals in the same group. However, he does not recall anyone ever raising this question during the discussions with the Deputy Minister, Ranald Quail, about transferring the contracting function to APORS.

The transfer of the contracting function to APORS required Allan Cutler, who had formerly performed this work within PRPCSS, to move to APORS, where he came under Mr. Guité's authority. This led to problems. Mr. Cutler was of the view that contracting should be done strictly in accordance with Treasury Board policy, including the requirements of Appendix Q, and he was reluctant to perform his functions in the manner that Mr. Guité would have preferred. This resulted in a conflict, which will be more fully described in Chapter VII of this Report; it need only be mentioned here that Mr. Cutler effectively ceased working within APORS[7], leaving Mr. Guité free to manage it as he wished. No other employee dared to challenge his authority from then on.

In July 1995 there was an organizational shuffle within PWGSC. As a result, APORS came under the authority of a different Assistant Deputy Minister, James Stobbe. Mr. Stobbe was uncomfortable with this new assignment since he had no expertise in advertising or communications, or in the procurement of these services.[8] He tended to defer to Mr. Guité's judgment and decisions in such matters, requiring only that such decisions be reported to him and the Deputy Minister. Such decisions were never questioned, since both Mr. Stobbe and Mr. Quail knew that Mr. Guité was in direct communication with the Prime Minister's Office and, after June 1997, with the Minister of PWGSC, the Honourable Alfonso Gagliano.[9] Such direct contact and exceptional access put Mr. Guité beyond their control for all practical purposes. Following the appointment of Mr. Gagliano as Minister of PWGSC, Mr. Guité was promoted and given new responsibilities with the creation of CCSB in November 1997. Mr. Quail explains in his testimony that the objective in creating CCSB was to streamline operations, improve delivery of services and eliminate duplication, all with a view to reducing the budget of PWGSC as part of program review. CCSB brought together PRPCSS, APORS and a number of other functions within PWGSC, all under the direction of Mr. Guité. As a result he suddenly became the executive director of a much larger organization, consisting of about 220 full-time employees.[10]

However, only the same small group of public servants continued to work on advertising and sponsorships. All witnesses agree that in this part of his work Mr. Guité preferred to make most decisions himself and that he was not comfortable in delegating authority to others. Ms. LaRose testifies that the small team in CCSB that was handling sponsorships could be described as a makeshift operation, having few administrative procedures in place and little structure or organization.[11] Everyone who worked for Mr. Guité on sponsorship files was expected to do a little bit of everything. He preferred to keep tight control over everything. Essentially, sponsorship contracts were handled by a small group consisting of Andrée LaRose, Huguette Tremblay, Denyse Paquette, Paul Lauzon and Mario Parent, all of whom did what Mr. Guité told them to do, whether or not it was in conformity with Treasury Board policy, Appendix Q or the *Financial Administration Act*.[12] There was an atmosphere of secrecy; only the inner circle was informed of decisions, which Mr. Guité announced without explaining. Administrative procedures were informal, and there was little information-sharing.[13]

From time to time other employees joined CCSB to work for varying periods in sponsorship matters. Marie Maltais arrived in May 1998 as Director General of Strategic Communications Coordination, determined to impose order on an obviously unstructured organization. She met with Huguette Tremblay and Denyse Paquette, who were supposed to report to her weekly, and told them that files on sponsorship contracts would have to be kept in order, and contracts properly documented. Nothing happened; the weekly meetings simply did not occur, and Ms. Maltais began to realize that this small group saw no reason to change the unorganized way in which they had always managed their files.[14] To respond to needs expressed by the employees concerned, Ms. Maltais tried to organize training sessions and lectures by persons experienced in handling sponsorship projects. But on three separate occasions, Mr. Guité cancelled the presentations that had been arranged, saying that he did not want a group discussion on sponsorship issues.[15] Finally Ms. Maltais gave up, and moved in January 1999 to the Canada Information Office (CIO) and later to Canada Mortgage and Housing Corporation.

A similar fate awaited Evelyn Marcoux, who joined CCSB for about 18 months. Nominally she was supposed to be Mr. Guité's second-in-command, but she received no cooperation from him. Her attempts to arrange meetings with Mr. Guité were unsuccessful. He finally removed all authority from her when she asked too many questions.[16]

David Myer was named Director General of Procurement in CCSB in June 1998, but he quickly realized that sponsorship contracts were not given the same treatment as other procurement functions. His request to Mr. Guité that procurement be treated uniformly was turned down. Effectively, Mr. Myer was excluded from dealing with sponsorship matters except when Mr. Guité was absent and Mr. Myer would sign documents in his place, including certifications for payment in accordance with section 34 of the FAA.[17] He later came to regret that he had done so.[18]

4.2
Financial Context

National unity initiatives and what came to be known as the Sponsorship Program were undertaken at a time of severe fiscal restraint. There was a concerted effort by the Government to reduce its operating deficit by cutting spending at all levels.

When Mr. Chrétien's Government took power in 1993, one of its highest priorities was to reduce the annual deficit and generally to get the Government's finances under control. The situation as described in testimony by the Right Honourable Paul Martin was perilous—34.5% of every dollar in the Budget went to pay debt service charges. In 1993, the Government's debt was about $487 billion, and about 27.5% of that debt was in foreign hands. The proportion of foreign debt has since been reduced to under 13%. The reduction of foreign debt was particularly important because it put Canada under a great deal of pressure from the international financial community. When Mr. Martin became Mr. Chrétien's Finance Minister in 1993 he was very worried that foreign lenders would withdraw their support of the Canadian Government and require it to increase interest rates, making the deficit situation much worse.

The annual deficit, which had become $42 billion by 1993, was eliminated by 1998. Canada had achieved a balanced budget, and was beginning to reduce its overall indebtedness.[19]

The reduction and eventual elimination of the deficit was the result of drastic cuts in spending and an exercise that came to be known as "program review." Program review was government-wide. It was initiated by Finance Minister Martin, who told all departments of the Government that they would have to review all of their programs and their need for personnel, and to cut back their spending. Program review began in 1994 and proceeded in stages. It was resisted, sometimes fiercely, by other ministers and by the public service, and Mr. Martin had to take a very tough line to secure the spending cuts that he needed to succeed. He was able to prevail due to the unqualified support of Prime Minister Chrétien.[20]

Within PWGSC, program review was something of a nightmare to Mr. Quail. He had worked diligently to meet the savings targets that resulted from the amalgamation of the two departments which preceded PWGSC. Program review then imposed further reductions on the department; for example, between 1995 and 1999 its personnel was cut by 25%, or about 5,800 people. The department's operations budget was reduced by $350 million out of a total of about $2.2 billion. Mr. Quail was very preoccupied by the adjustments necessitated by these cuts, and says that he had little time available to deal with other problems, such as the internal management of APORS.

During the years from 1994 to 1998, program review influenced almost every decision made by the Government of Canada that involved money. Mr. Quail testifies that sponsorship funding was something of an anomaly as there was absolutely no new money for other things.[21] This is confirmed by Jocelyne Bourgon, former Clerk of the Privy Council Office, who advises the Commission that program review resulted in the elimination from departmental budgets of reserves of every kind and description, the only exception being the Unity Reserve,[22] which, as we will see later, was the principal source of funding in the early years of the Sponsorship Program.

4.3
Unity Strategy and the Quebec Referendum

In his testimony, Mr. Chrétien states that any serious examination of the Sponsorship Program must take full account of the circumstances in Quebec when the Program was created and of the climate of political uncertainty during the time in which it operated.[23] When he became Prime Minister in 1993, the official Opposition Party was the Bloc Québécois, which was dedicated to the separation of Quebec from the rest of Canada. In September 1994, Mr. Jacques Parizeau, the leader of its provincial counterpart, the Parti Québécois, was elected Premier of the Province of Quebec, heading a majority government. In the course of the election campaign, Mr. Parizeau had pledged to hold a referendum on the question of the sovereignty of Quebec, which the Parti Québécois advocates, within the first year of taking office. On December 6, 1994, draft legislation anticipating the political independence of the Province of Quebec following a successful referendum on the subject was tabled in the Quebec National Assembly. Eventually the referendum was scheduled for October 30, 1995.

During the months preceding the referendum, the Government members of the National Assembly campaigned ceaselessly to promote the sovereignty option. The Quebec Government and its agencies used the advertising facilities at their disposal to influence public opinion in favour of sovereignty.

Although the federal government was not directly involved and was not in charge of the forces opposing the referendum campaign, it actively participated in the work of the "no" committee. The Honourable Lucienne Robillard, Minister of Citizenship and Immigration, was delegated to the committee by the federal government as the official representative of the Liberal Party of Canada. She was supported by the Associate Secretary of the PCO, Ron Bilodeau, and a team composed of members of his staff.[24]

Funding was needed to finance the federal government's contribution to what was referred to as its National Unity Strategy. Substantial sums were disbursed through APORS as well as by the Department of Canadian Heritage and the PCO.[25] For example, on March 20, 1995, Ms. Bourgon recommended to Mr. Chrétien that he approve the disbursement of $100,000 to two advertising agencies with well-known Liberal affiliations, BCP and Groupe Everest, to defray the cost of their advice with respect to the development of advertising concepts to be used in the period leading up to the referendum.[26] No one appears to have given any thought to the need for a call for tenders before awarding these contracts. They were treated as advertising disbursements by PWGSC.

In a Treasury Board submission dated June 15, 1995, authority was requested to spend up to $20 million to support Canadian Unity initiatives, including $10 million to be disbursed by APORS for advertising, media buys and public opinion research, all under the guidance of the PCO.[27] To emphasize the importance of the need for these funds, and because it constituted an encroachment upon the Unity Reserve,[28] which is under the exclusive authority of the Prime Minister, the submission was signed by Mr. Chrétien himself. Not surprisingly, it was approved by Treasury Board promptly and without question.

A recommendation dated July 19, 1995, to the Prime Minister from the Clerk of the Privy Council refers to a number of national unity initiatives for which approval was sought, including the purchase of space on outdoor billboards at a cost of $2.6 million.[29] The initiative was approved and in the following months Mr. Guité was particularly efficient in using these funds to buy up all the available billboard space in Quebec, thereby depriving the "yes" side of this publicity medium. These results were noted with appreciation by the PCO. In general, during the pre-referendum period, Mr. Guité worked closely with the team in the PCO which had been created to coordinate and assist the National Unity Strategy. He was perceived to be energetic, efficient and expert in the field of advertising. This reputation followed him in the years to come.[30]

The referendum file was extremely important to Mr. Chrétien. He states in his testimony that the maintenance of Canadian unity was his duty and his first priority as Prime Minister. He admits that he was dismayed at the closeness of the referendum result—the federalist side won by only a few thousand votes. Although Mr. Parizeau immediately announced his resignation as Premier of Quebec, he was promptly replaced by Lucien Bouchard, an immensely popular politician in Quebec, who pledged to call a new referendum whenever he felt that "winning conditions" were present. The federal government, led by Mr. Chrétien, took Mr. Bouchard's pledge seriously, as well as criticism that the federal government had not been sufficiently active during the referendum campaign. Mr. Chrétien testifies that his Cabinet was united in its determination to do whatever was necessary to ensure that winning conditions for sovereignty never arose in Quebec.

4.4
Post-Referendum Strategy

The federal government's post-referendum strategy was multi-faceted; advertising activities and sponsorships were only one element of a comprehensive game plan to better inform Quebeckers of the advantages of federalism.[31] Its initiatives consisted of:

- a Resolution passed by Parliament before the end of 1995 affirming the distinctiveness of Quebec;

- legislation to provide to each region of Canada a veto on constitutional change;

- the drafting and introduction of the *Clarity Act*, which is legislation to limit and control any future provincial referendum on sovereignty;

- devolution by the federal government to the Province of Quebec of responsibility for manpower training; and

- the appointment of a Cabinet committee chaired by the Honourable Marcel Massé, Minister of Intergovernmental Affairs, to make recommendations on national unity.

It is the work of the Cabinet committee which is of particular interest and relevance to this Commission. After deliberations, the committee prepared a Report (the Massé Report), dated January 26, 1996, and addressed to the Prime Minister, which was the principal subject of discussion at a special Cabinet meeting held on February 1 and 2, 1996, in circumstances described as a "retreat."[32]

In his testimony, Mr. Massé says that the Cabinet committee came to the conclusion that the federal government had made two fundamental mistakes during the referendum campaign. First, it had not systematically refuted the arguments of its sovereignist opponents; in other words, its communications were not effective. Second, federal Ministers from Quebec and Quebec members of the Liberal caucus were not sufficiently present in regions outside their own constituencies.[33]

With respect to communication strategy in the future, the Massé Report recommended that a new secretariat or agency be created "to develop and implement strategy and tactics in terms of communications and policy;"[34] this was implemented by the creation in July 1996 of the Canada Information Office (CIO).[35] The Report further recommended "a coordinated effort to increase the visibility and presence of Canada in Quebec. Existing and new federal programs and initiatives beneficial to Quebeckers should be prominently, systematically and repeatedly advertised..."[36]

The Report made a further recommendation, reading as follows:

> Ministers recommend a substantial strengthening of the organization of the Liberal Party of Canada in Quebec. This means hiring organizers, finding candidates, identifying ridings that are winnable in the next federal election, and using the most modern political techniques of reaching targeted voters.[37]

Most witnesses agreed that a recommendation to strengthen the organization of the Liberal Party of Canada would not ordinarily form part of a Cabinet committee's report, since Cabinet is expected to deal with the interests of the country as a whole, leaving partisan considerations aside.[38] However, Mr. Pelletier expressed the opinion that it is "angélisme"[39] (Angélisme is a word that does not translate easily into English as used in this context, the closest equivalent being "idealism.") to expect that Ministers of the Crown in a Cabinet meeting, all of whom are members of the same political party, would not discuss partisan politics when they get together. Of course, in this instance it is not a question of informal discussions, but rather the contents of a report.

The inclusion of this recommendation in the Massé Report is an indication of the failure of some members of the Government at that time to consider that any political party other than the Liberal Party of Canada could have a role in promoting federalism in Quebec. This attitude was displayed by the former Executive Director of the Quebec wing of the Liberal Party of Canada, Benoît Corbeil, when he testified.[40] This attitude, which may not have been shared by all members of the Party, is difficult to reconcile with basic democratic values.

At the Cabinet retreat, after extensive discussions, the Massé Report and its recommendations were supported and adopted. The minutes of the meeting include the following statement:

> [Unofficial Translation]
>> The ministers indicated their agreement on a four-track strategy on national unity.
>>
>> ……...
>>
>> Promoting an attachment to Canada, and, lastly a plan to communicate with and reach out to people.
>>
>> Additionally, ministers expressed agreement on the importance of establishing national identity and communication programs in order that the federal government message reach citizens as directly as possible.[41]

Nothing in writing more specific than this statement came out of the Cabinet retreat.

Many of the Ministers who attended the Cabinet meeting of February 1-2, 1996, testified concerning the discussions that preceded the adoption of the recommendations of the Massé Report. The list includes Prime Minister Chrétien, Diane Marleau (Minister of Public Works and Government Services), Paul Martin (Minister of Finance), Marcel Massé (President of the Treasury Board and Minister responsible for Infrastructure), Alfonso Gagliano (Minister of Labour and Deputy Leader of the Government in the House of Commons), Lucienne Robillard (Minister of Citizenship and Immigration), Stéphane Dion (Minister of Intergovernmental Affairs and President of the Privy Council), Pierre Pettigrew (Minister of International Cooperation and Minister responsible for the Francophonie), and Martin Cauchon (Minister of Regional Development in Quebec). Jean Pelletier, who attended the meeting, also testified about the discussions.

All witnesses agree that there were no specific references during these discussions to a Sponsorship Program or to sponsorships as such, but most remember discussions about the importance of increasing the visibility and presence of Canada in Quebec.[42] No one recalls a discussion of the cost of increased government advertising in Quebec, except that Ms. Marleau says that she assumed there would be associated costs which would have to be found somewhere.[43] Mr. Massé says that he recommended that more money be spent on communications, but did not specify how or who would administer any new disbursements.[44]

Mr. Chrétien testifies that while the term "sponsorship" was not mentioned, the possibility of promoting events to enhance the visibility of the Government of Canada was mentioned, without identifying the kinds of events that would be promoted.[45]

Mr. Dion is certain that if it had been stated during the discussions that more funds would be spent on communications and advertising in the Province of Quebec than elsewhere in Canada, he would have objected since he has always believed that spending of this kind should be evenly distributed across the country.[46]

It is fair to conclude from the testimony of all the witnesses heard that, at the February Cabinet retreat, a decision was reached in principle to improve federal government advertising and communications to enhance the visibility of the federal presence in Quebec, but that no specific decisions were made by the Ministers present as to how this was to be accomplished, how it would be financed, or who would be in charge of any initiatives undertaken. It was left up to the Prime Minister's Office, which had primary responsibility for national unity concerns, in consultation with the Privy Council Office, to determine the details of how the decision reached in principle was to be put into effect. No other Minister of the Crown or government agency or ministry was at that time charged with the responsibility for these initiatives.

Mr. Bilodeau explains in his testimony that there was nothing unusual or inappropriate in the development of policy by the Privy Council Office, in consultation with representatives of the Prime Minister's Office, once the broad lines of the policy had been decided by Cabinet. This would be particularly true in the case of matters to do with national unity,[47] for which the Prime Minister has a particular responsibility.

Mr. Chrétien testifies that he decided that the person designated to be in charge of the national unity file was his Chief of Staff, Jean Pelletier.[48] Mr. Pelletier does not dispute this affirmation, but testifies that he does not recall precisely what steps were taken by him to implement the Cabinet decisions of February 1-2, 1996, with respect to increased visibility by the federal government.[49] He acknowledges that he had a meeting with Mr. Guité on April 16, 1996, at which there must have been a discussion of the question of funding certain new initiatives, because a Treasury Board submission seeking authorization to spend important sums of money on specific initiatives had been drafted and was shown to him as early as April 22, 1996. The submission refers to expected spending of $17 million, which is the total amount of a list of proposed sponsorships that Mr. Guité was then in the process of drawing up.

If the specifics of the Sponsorship Program were not identified at the Cabinet meeting of February 1-2, it appears from Mr. Chrétien's testimony that at least the objectives were clearly understood, then or later, by Mr. Chrétien himself. In his prepared statement to the Commission he declares that the intention was to match the initiatives of the Parti Québécois Government in billboard, radio or television advertising, or the sponsorship of community events. He repeatedly refers to these initiatives as a "program," as appears from the following extract from his testimony:

> Sponsorship is much more than billboards and flags. It is involvement with organizers of community events, people that are often opinion leaders in their communities, letting them know that there is also a Government of Canada that relates directly to citizens, that the Government of Canada does more than just collect taxes while the Quebec government delivers programs.
>
> This type of federal presence amongst community leaders was part and parcel of our overall strategy. This is why we committed to spending a significant amount of money every year to be part of community events and we did not restrict the program to Quebec and we did not restrict it to Quebec because the Government of Canada should be present in communities across the country.

> I regret any mistakes that were made in the course of this
> program or any other government program. As Prime Minister,
> I take the ultimate responsibility for everything good and
> everything bad that happens in the government.[50]

In his testimony, Mr. Gagliano, who in June 1997 became Minister of PWGSC and responsible for the Sponsorship Program, echoes Mr. Chrétien's declaration that the objective of the Program was to compete with the Quebec Government and its agencies, such as Hydro-Québec, Loto-Québec and La Société des Alcools du Québec, which were heavily involved in the sponsorship of community organizations and cultural and sporting events. In Mr. Gagliano's view, shared by Mr. Chrétien, the Government of Canada had become practically invisible in Quebec and it was necessary to counteract separatism by increasing the federal government's presence.[51]

Mr. Bilodeau testifies that he recalls that following the Cabinet meeting of February 1-2, there were meetings to discuss the implementation of the policy decisions which had been reached by Cabinet at that time. He cannot recall or explain why responsibility for sponsorships was given to APORS instead of to Canadian Heritage, which might appear to be the natural home for a program to promote Canadian unity, except to say that PWGSC was known to have expertise in the field of advertising.[52] He acknowledges that the effect of the decision was to make PWGSC both the procurement agency and the client department, an abnormal situation, as appears from the following exchange in the course of his testimony.

[Unofficial Translation]

Commissioner:	But for the first time, it was tasked with procuring advertising or retaining the services of advertising agencies for its own use.
Mr. Bilodeau:	That's correct.
Commissioner:	Wasn't there any discussion to the effect that that could pose a problem? Did people not see that it was rather unusual in the workings of government?
Mr. Bilodeau:	Sir, as I indicated to Mr. Roy, I do not recall that we had a formal, ongoing discussion about the options at that time. My sense is that given the Department's expertise in the matter, that is, the procurement of advertising, it was decided that it was perhaps the Department best able to manage sponsorships. But, in so doing, we were taking the Department in a new direction, as you so aptly pointed out. It was turning into a program department as opposed to a service department, in my opinion. That was a big change.
Commissioner:	Obviously, when you purchase advertising for a client, say, the Department of Health or Agriculture, the department in question, which is also the client, automatically exercises a certain level of control.
Mr. Bilodeau:	Very true.
Commissioner:	But, when you buy for yourself, there is no control. Did that not occur to anyone at the time?
Mr. Bilodeau:	It should have, sir. In my opinion, the Department of Public Works, like many departments, has to look after its own needs.[53]

4.5
The Canada Information Office

Another result of the Massé Report and the Cabinet decisions of February 1-2, 1996, was the creation of the Canada Information Office (CIO), a new secretariat or agency intended "to develop and implement strategy and tactics in terms of communications and policy." During the referendum campaign, the use of a Quick Response Communications Team within the PCO had been effective, and similar requirements led to the creation of the CIO.[54] It was created by an Order in Council dated early in July 1996.

Mr. Chrétien took it upon himself to interview Roger Collet in May 1996 for the position of head of the new agency.[55] Mr. Collet was a Franco-Manitoban whose long public service career had culminated with an appointment as Assistant Deputy Minister at Canadian Heritage. He was a strong federalist and was believed by Mr. Chrétien to be a good manager on the basis of his activities in the field of communications during the referendum campaign.[56]

Mr. Pelletier testifies that an indication of Mr. Chrétien's wish to personally oversee the whole unity issue was his decision to take time from his busy schedule to interview Mr. Collet.[57] Normally the hiring of personnel, even at a senior level, is done through the Public Service Commission, except at the Deputy Minister level, which goes through the PCO.

It was decided by Mr. Chrétien, in consultation with the PCO, that the CIO would have an annual budget of $20 million, to be financed by draws from the Unity Reserve. The Treasury Board submissions signed by Mr. Chrétien in 1996 and 1997 reflect this decision. In the first year, nearly $5 million of the $20 million was budgeted for "grants and contributions," although the Minister of Canadian Heritage, Sheila Copps, was not in favour of subsidies being granted by the CIO[58] in competition with other programs in her Ministry. However, Ms. Copps had little control over the CIO, in spite of the fact that it was nominally under the supervision of her ministry. For all practical purposes, Mr. Collet was reporting directly to Mr. Pelletier at the

PMO.[59] Funds were available to subsidize events and projects deemed worthy by Mr. Collet, over and above the $5 million referred to earlier,[60] since a substantial portion of his total budget was not needed for other purposes.

The mandate given to the CIO was to coordinate the Government's communications concerning unity questions, and also to enhance the federal government's presence.[61] The mandate was similar to what APORS was asked to accomplish by advertising and through the Sponsorship Program; that is to say, to increase the visibility of the federal presence in Canada generally, and particularly in Quebec. Mr. Collet had little or no expertise available to him in the assessment, financing and administration of sponsorships. His organization at the CIO was, in 1996 and 1997, rudimentary, and his personnel were inexperienced. Mr. Collet had never before in his career been given the task of organizing from scratch an agency of the importance of the CIO.

Nevertheless, public announcements were made in July 1996 concerning the creation of the CIO and its objectives. Persons and organizations seeking federal subsidies for an event or a project became aware that it had funds available. The parallel mandate of APORS had not been given any publicity, nor had an announcement been made by the Government concerning its readiness to sponsor events. As a result, the CIO was requested by the promoters of events, communication agencies representing such promoters, or Members of Parliament on behalf of their constituents to supply funding in the form of sponsorships. Mr. Collet had no personnel in his newly formed organization to assess or deal with these requests, and since he knew that Mr. Guité's group at APORS had capabilities in that area, it was quickly agreed between them that sums of money would be transferred from the CIO budget to APORS to be used for sponsorships.[62]

Documents indicate that a meeting took place on August 27, 1996, among Mr. Collet, Mr. Pelletier and Jean Carle of the PMO, at which they went over a list of projects to be sponsored by the federal government, or which had already occurred, or for which commitments had been made on the assumption that sponsorship funds would become available to the promoters.[63]

The list is very similar to the list that eventually was attached to the Précis in support of the Treasury Board submission jointly signed by Mr. Chrétien and Ms. Marleau later in the year.[64] It is therefore apparent that as early as August 1996, only a month after the creation of the CIO, it was anticipated by Mr. Pelletier that the CIO would be involved in the financing of sponsorship projects, and that Mr. Collet would be expected to work in close collaboration with Mr. Guité.

The pattern was established. In 1996-97 and subsequent years, an important proportion of the budget allocated to the CIO was transferred to APORS and its successor, CCSB, to be managed and administered as part of the Sponsorship Program.[65]

In spite of good intentions, Mr. Collet was not a gifted administrator. In November 1997, an internal audit of the CIO disclosed serious shortcomings in its administrative practices. In due course, Mr. Collet's shortcomings were recognized, and on July 27, 1998, he was relieved of his post as head of the CIO and replaced by Marc Lafrenière. At the same time responsibility for the CIO was transferred to Mr. Gagliano in his capacity as Chairperson of the Committee of Cabinet on Government Communications.[66]

When Communication Canada was created by Order in Council on September 1, 2001, it was the continuation of the CIO, into which CCSB had been merged, under another name. Consequently, it took over responsibility for all functions previously performed by CCSB.

4.6
Funding for Sponsorships

For the fiscal year beginning on April 1, 1996, funds would be needed to finance the Government's new visibility initiatives to be managed by APORS. Their cost had not been foreseen in the Budget or in the departmental appropriations for PWGSC. The method of providing funds for what became known as the Sponsorship Program in its first and subsequent years is the subject of this section of this chapter.

Mr. Guité must have been advised by someone that APORS would be assigned the task of implementing the Government's new visibility program. It is extraordinary that no witness is able or willing to tell the Commission exactly what transpired in the period following the political decision made by Cabinet on February 1-2 and up to the first meeting between Mr. Guité and Mr. Pelletier on April 16, 1996. It is impossible to believe that there were no meetings or discussions involving the Prime Minister and his staff during that period concerning the implementation of the decision, but Mr. Pelletier purports to have no recollection of what happened.

At some point in time after his April 16 meeting with Mr. Pelletier, Mr. Guité started to prepare a proposed list of events to be sponsored in 1996-97. The list went through several transformations before it was definitively settled upon.[67] The total sum required for 43 sponsorships was $16,138,640. Included in the list is an item entitled "miscellaneous" for $989,000, which is explained in greater detail at the end of the list. There seems to have been confusion as to whether the sum of $989,000 should be added to the amount of $16,138,640, to make an approximate total of $17 million, but it is apparent from a perusal of the list that the total needs were not in fact $17 million but $16,138,640.

In due course the list was annexed to a draft Treasury Board Submission, (see Figure IV-1) which resulted in a series of communications between the Clerk of the Privy Council, Ms. Bourgon, and Prime Minister Chrétien. These communications are of importance in determining who was ultimately responsible for the sums disbursed in the Sponsorship Program. Before reviewing them, however, it should be noted that since January 15, 1996, there had been a new Minister at PWGSC, Diane Marleau, who had particular reasons for wanting to have nothing to do with Mr. Guité.

Figure IV-1: Proposed Sponsorships 1996/97.

1057183 : Front

The Treasury Board   La Conseil du Trésor

NOV 21 1996
SA

PRÉCIS

CONFIDENCE OF THE QUEEN'S PRIVY COUNCIL
DOCUMENT CONFIDENTIEL
DU CONSEIL PRIVÉ DE LA REINE

TB No.N° du CT	824628
Dept/Min.	PWGSC
Prog.	Supply and Services
Date	November 21, 1996
Proposed Handling Procedure à suivre	Appendix

𝒜

SUMMARY:

The Department of Public Works and Government Services Canada (PWGSC) is seeking additional funding totalling $34M, over the next two years, to support the communications priorities of the Government of Canada.

The Advertising and Public Opinion Research Sector (A&PORS) at PWGSC is responsible for, amongst other activities, fulfilling a Government of Canada initiative to promote all its programs, policies and services by means of sponsorship through selective events across Canada. The events are determined on the basis of audience, visibility, timing and potential impact on the government's programs used at such events. Appendix A provides a list of venues that have already been used this fiscal year to fulfil this mandate and which account for the $17,000,000 requested for 1996/97. According to A&PORS, similar venues for sponsorship will be selected for 1997/98 in order to fulfil this mandate.

                                                                Approve

PROPOSAL:

To seek Treasury Board approval to include an item in the 1996/97 Supplementary Estimates for $17M and to establish an item in the 1997/98 Reference Levels for funding to support the communications priorities of the Government of Canada.

COST AND SOURCE OF FUNDS:

Earmarked funds for Unity.

	1996/97	1997/98
($000s)	17,000	17,000

RECOMMENDATION:

Approve as requested.

TBC/CTC 300-28 (Rev.1995/09) (WORD)

1057184 : Front

- 2 -   TB No.:/N° du CT:824628

BACKGROUND:

1.   It is the policy of the government to provide accurate and
timely information to the Canadian public about its policies,
programs and services.

2.   Given the ongoing challenges of National Unity coupled with
the result of the Quebec referendum the need for the promotion
of government programs and services across Canada becomes
particularly evident.

3.   In June 1994, Treasury Board (#821823) approved
modifications to the Treasury Board Contracting Policy to
incorporate the Guidelines on Contracting for Communications,
Public Opinion Research and Advertising. The revised policy
states that all departments must use PWGSC to contract for
public opinion research or advertising services.

4.   PWGSC, through the Advertising and Public Opinion Research
Sector (A&PORS), is responsible for this service in addition to
carrying out the analysis of the impact of the political
situation in all regions of Canada and the subsequent coordination of all initiatives that relate to the promotion and
communication of the government's programs and services.

5.   In carrying out its contracting function, A&PORS ensures
that the creative services, media buys, sponsorships, promotions
and any other marketing initiatives initiated within departments
conform with established Treasury Board policy and guidelines
and that any communications services including advertising and
public opinion research, are competitive as required and
subsequently that appropriate contracts are issued.

6.   A&PORS also provides advisory services to departments and
agencies in the areas of advertising and public opinion research
to ensure that Government of Canada programs and services are
promoted to the fullest extent possible in all departmental
initiatives.

7.   Most recently, A&PORS is responsible for fulfilling a
Government-of-Canada initiative to promote all its programs by
means of sponsorship through selective events across Canada.
The events are determined on the basis of audience, visibility,
timing and potential impact on the government's programs used at
such events. Appendix A provides a list of venues that have
already been used this fiscal year to fulfil this mandate and
which account for the $17,000,000 requested for 1996/97.
According to A&PORS, government programs and services will be
promoted through sponsorship at many of the same/similar events
in 1997/98.

- 3 -   TB No./N° du CT:824628

Appendix A

PROJECT	VALUE ($)
Grand Prix Molson Canada	536,000
Molson Indy Toronto	372,000
Molson Indy Vancouver	325,000
Fête Francophonie Nord America	325,000
Rimouski - 300 ans	218,000
Gala de Tennis	22,000
Défi 737	70,000
Hockey News	80,000
Concours International de musique de Montréal	110,000
Sur la route d'Atlanta	252,000
Expos de Montréal - Fête du Canada	334,800
Canadiens de Montréal	352,000
Concours hippiques de Québec, Blainville, Bromont et Ottawa	419,000
Internationaux de tennis junior du Canada	149,200
Expo Fest '96	300,000
Autobus Sherbrooke Magazine - 1 page	25,000

1057186 : Front

- 4 -   TB No./N° du CT:824628

Les nuits Black - Festival de jazz et de blues Québec	80,000
Journal de Montréal (couverture Grand Prix)	85,000
Guide les loisirs du Québec	40,000
Maximum Blues	75,000
Baseball Club of St. Catherines	40,000
Promotion Kodak	364,000
Skins Game, Classique Du Maurier, Omnium Canadien Bell	94,000
Via Rail - Promotion étudiants	493,000
Expos de Montréal	900,000
Outils promotionnels	900,000
Canada sur deux roues (being amended)	2,400,000
Journal de Montréal "20 ans déjà"	10,840
Montréal '76 - Atlanta '96	22,800
Vélo-culture en ville	10,000
Grand-Prix Players de Trois-Rivières	60,000
Canada Sud	240,000
Imavision	375,000
Ottawa Senators	200,000
Montreal Alouettes	150,000
Canadiens de Montréal	850,000

	- 5 -	TB No./N° du CT:824628
Rafales de Québec		500,000
Rough Riders		275,000
Promotional Items		500,000
Canada Coast to Coast		1,435,000
Miscellaneous (see below)		989,000
Bluenose		975,000
Saumons de l'Atlantique		185,000
TOTAL		16,138,640

Miscellaneous

INFRAS - syndicated study on quebecers values and attitudes (PCO-Intergovernmental Affairs)	60,000
CROP - omnibus questions on quebecers views on Saguenay disaster (PCO-Intergovernmental Affairs)	9,000
ENVIRONICS - survey of Canadians outside Quebec (PCO-Intergovernmental Affairs)	50,000
ENVIRONICS - focus group testing of logos (Canadian Information Office)	20,000
BCP - logo development and consulting fees (Canadian Information Office)	150,000
VICKERS & BENSON - logo development (Canadian Information Office)	50,000
PALMER JARVIS - logo development (Canadian Information Office)	50,000

- -6 -   TB No./N° du CT:824628

COMPASS - logo development   50,000
(Canadian Information Office)

GROUPE EVEREST - logo   200,000
development and consulting fees
(Canadian Information Office)

ENVIRONICS - focus group   50,000
testing of logos (Canadian
Information Office)

TRANSFER BFDRQ - Montréal,   250,000
C'est toi ma ville! Project
coordinated by BFDRQ (PCO-
Intergovernmental Affairs)

CRÉATEC - testing of taglines   50,000
(Canadian Information Office)

TOTAL   989,000

Until January 15, 1996, David Dingwall was the Minister of PWGSC, but in a Cabinet shuffle just a few days before the Cabinet retreat, he was replaced by Ms. Marleau. Previously she had been Minister of Health.

As Minister of Health, Ms. Marleau had had an experience with Mr. Guité which left her uneasy and suspicious concerning his manner of performing his responsibilities. She had requested a change in the advertising agency which looked after the advertising needs of the Health ministry, but a competition conducted by personnel in Mr. Guité's organization had resulted in the selection of the same agency as before. Ms. Marleau would have greatly preferred a new agency and was disturbed and disappointed by the results of the competition.[68]

Her perception of Mr. Guité was again adversely affected when, shortly after her appointment as Minister of PWGSC, he came unexpectedly and without an appointment to her office, saying that he intended to discuss an issue directly with her. He explained to her Executive Assistant that this had been his manner of communicating with her predecessor, Mr. Dingwall. Ms. Marleau preferred that communications with subordinate personnel in her department be made through proper channels, following the usual procedure, and in the presence of her Deputy Minister. She refused to meet directly with Mr. Guité.[69]

She was subsequently informed by her staff that Mr. Guité was having a series of meetings with Mr. Pelletier and Mr. Carle in the Prime Minister's Office. She thought this was irregular, especially when she was not kept informed of the conversations. But, when she raised the subject with her Deputy Minister, Mr. Quail, he seemed taken aback and asked her if she had proof that such meetings were occurring. When she replied "no, I don't have any proof, but I am very worried about this," Mr. Quail told her in a somewhat enigmatic manner to be very careful, which she took as a warning that her future career as a Minister could be in jeopardy. Ms. Marleau says she was shocked by this.[70]

On the basis of these incidents Ms. Marleau adopted, as her policy, that she would have no contact with Mr. Guité except through proper channels. As a matter of fact, she had no direct contact with him at all for the duration of her tenure as Minister of PWGSC, which ended when she was replaced on June 10, 1997, by Mr. Gagliano.[71]

We now know, on the basis of admissions of the parties themselves, that Mr. Guité met in 1996 and 1997 with Mr. Pelletier on several occasions.[72] On a few of these occasions, Mr. Carle, who was employed in the PMO as Director of Operations, was also present.[73] The Director of Operations in the PMO is in charge of the Prime Minister's travel schedule and making arrangements for his public appearances; Mr. Carle needed to know when and where public events would occur in case Mr. Chrétien decided to attend.[74] He fulfilled other, less clearly defined functions in the PMO as well.

For instance, on April 11, 1995, Mr. Pelletier wrote a letter to all Ministers, calling their attention to the new Treasury Board guidelines on communications, advertising and public opinion research (Appendix Q), in which he states:

> [Unofficial Translation]
>
>> At the same time, I would also like to inform you that Jean Carle, Director of Operations, is the individual in the Office of the Prime Minister responsible for ensuring that the policy has been respected.[75]

In his testimony Mr. Pelletier says the wording of the letter is erroneous and that he did not intend to attribute to Mr. Carle responsibilities that more properly belonged to Treasury Board. He only wanted Mr. Carle to supply information to those who needed answers to questions about the new policy.[76] This is not at all what the letter says, and there is no indication in the record that Mr. Pelletier wrote again to the members of Cabinet to explain the true role to be played in the communications policy by Mr. Carle, and to correct the impression given by the letter of April 11, 1995, that Mr. Carle was effectively in charge of the implementation of the Government's new communications policy. It is clear from Mr. Guité's testimony that he believed that Mr. Carle was a much more important person in the PMO than the designation of Director of Operations would suggest.[77]

The purpose of the meetings with Mr. Guité was to discuss lists of sponsorship projects and the amounts to be granted in each case. There are divergences between the testimony of Mr. Guité and the testimony of Messrs. Pelletier and Carle as to how the lists were prepared, the frequency of the meetings, and whether or not the identity of the communication agencies chosen to handle sponsorship projects was part of the discussions; but there is no doubt that meetings occurred, during which Mr. Pelletier and to a lesser extent Mr. Carle would give Mr. Guité advice with respect to the events that should be sponsored and the amounts to be allowed in at least some cases.

In the written submissions made on behalf of Mr. Pelletier, his counsel says that between April 15, 1996, and November 20, 2000, according to his agendas, Mr. Pelletier met Mr. Guité 23 times: twelve times alone, six times with Mr. Carle, one time with Mr. Collet, five times with Mr. Gagliano and twice with Jean-Marc Bard, Mr. Gagliano's Executive Assistant. Considering the volume of work that he had to get through every day and the constraints on the availability of time in his busy schedule, the frequency of Mr. Pelletier's meetings with a mid-level public servant underlines the importance he gave to the Sponsorship Program and the Government's advertising initiatives under Mr. Guité's direction.

Mr. Quail knew that such meetings were taking place, and his advice to Ms. Marleau "to be very careful" about suggesting that such meetings were occurring is surprising.

Accordingly, although Ms. Marleau co-signed a Treasury Board submission in 1996, which was the subject of exchanges between Ms. Bourgon and the Prime Minister, she really knew very little about the reasons why funds were needed or about the subject of sponsorships in general. The list of proposed sponsorships which supported the submission had been discussed with Mr. Pelletier and representatives of PCO, but it was not discussed with her, and she had nothing to do with the administration of the sponsorship contracts that resulted.[78]

By April 22, 1996, it had already been determined that about $17 million would be needed by PWGSC in the current fiscal year in connection with national unity initiatives. It was considered that authorization for the use of these funds would be obtained by way of supplementary estimates, and a draft Treasury Board submission along these lines was prepared and signed by Ms. Marleau, with a space provided for the countersignature of Mr. Chrétien.[79] However, this plan was temporarily abandoned while the subject of a draw on the Unity Reserve was examined. It was finally submitted to Treasury Board in October, and approved in November 1996. In the meantime, there was a degree of urgency to settle the question of funding since many of the proposed disbursements on the list had already been made or were to be made almost immediately. For example, the sponsorship of the Grand Prix Molson Canada ($536,000) was disbursed in the early part of the summer of 1996, as was the amount to be paid to the Montreal Expos ($334,800) for a Canada Day event.[80]

4.7
The Unity Reserve

It is time to provide some details about the Unity Reserve, sometimes referred to as the National Unity Reserve. It constituted a unique source of funds available only to the Prime Minister of Canada, which had existed in previous governments, at least as far back as Prime Minister Trudeau. Under the Mulroney administration, it had been decided in 1991 that $50 million per year would be set aside in the Budgets for the next five years to provide a source of funds to be used as needed by the Prime Minister for expenditures related to national unity. Accordingly, in the annual Budgets for the years up to 1996, a reserve of $50 million was set aside automatically and was included in the fiscal framework without the necessity of a decision each time by the Minister of Finance.[81]

Mr. Martin testifies that starting in 1996 or 1997, it was necessary to specifically include an item of $50 million in the annual Budget for the Unity Reserve. He gave no particular attention to what seemed an apparently minor allocation, which simply continued what had existed previously.[82]

It has always been the prerogative of the Prime Minister to determine the priorities to which the Unity Reserve will be allocated. For example, Prime Minister Mulroney had used it to finance the cost of the ill-fated Charlottetown Constitutional Accord, and in 1995-96 funds were drawn from the Unity Reserve at the request of Prime Minister Chrétien to pay for the federal government's expenditures in connection with the referendum campaign.[83]

In 1996-97, Mr. Chrétien agreed that in addition to the $17 million needed for sponsorships, he would authorize a further draw of $20 million to fund the creation of the Canada Information Office, which came into being as a result of the Cabinet decision of February 1-2, 1996. The Unity Reserve was also used to finance certain other initiatives, costing $11 million, undertaken by the Department of Canadian Heritage, and expenses totalling $5 million incurred by the PCO in strengthening federal-provincial relations.

Access to these funds had to be justified by a Treasury Board submission, which would ordinarily be signed only by the Minister of the department charged with the responsibility for the proper management and administration of the amounts allocated to it. In the case of the $17 million, exceptionally, Mr. Chrétien chose to sign the submission himself.[84] He explains this decision in his testimony as follows:

> Mr. Commissioner, I signed a number of Treasury Board submissions when I was Prime Minister normally for expenditures relating to the Privy Council Office, another organization for which I was directly responsible. I also signed

the Treasury Board submission creating the Sponsorship Program. I wanted to give a clear signal to ministers on the Treasury Board that this settlement of the National Unity Strategy, like all of the strategies, was a priority that needed to be funded despite the fact that very few new spending initiatives were being approved in 1996 as a result of our determination as a government to get the finances of the country in order after years of deficit spending.[85]

Before he signed the submission, Mr. Chrétien received a memorandum from Ms. Bourgon in which she states:

[Emphasis in the original]

It will be critical to ensure that the unity funds are spent efficiently and that the different initiatives currently being developed support a coherent unity communications strategy.

I would therefore recommend that you do not take a decision on any unity initiatives requiring new funding until a formal process for evaluating the merits of such initiatives is put in place.

. . . .

PCO is currently developing options for such a process and I will be reviewing these with you shortly.[86]

On June 17, 1996, Ms. Bourgon wrote a further memorandum to the Prime Minister, reading as follows:

Following our June 6 memo to you regarding accessing funds set aside for national unity, a meeting was held with PCO, affected departments, and your office to review the outstanding pressures on the reserve ($50 million per year in 1996-97 and 1997-98). It is recommended that you approve the allocation of $28 million in 1996-97 and $14 million in 1997-98, to be apportioned as follows:

• to Canadian Heritage, $11 million in 1996-97 and $14 million in 1997-98 for initiatives to strengthen attachment and identity, and to support the Council for Canadian Unity;

- to Public Works and Government Services Canada (PWGSC), $17 million in 1996-97 for communications-related activities to increase federal visibility across the country including enhancement of planned media campaigns and promotion of special events. Of this amount, $10 million will be allocated to short term commitments with the balance of $7 million to be frozen by Treasury Board for use at a later date.

Approval of funding for Heritage and PWGSC will allow planning and programming to begin now for the summer and fall, while retaining sufficient flexibility to fund the agency (estimated to cost about $20 million per year) and to respond to new requirements in 1997-98. If you concur, Canadian Heritage and PWGSC will seek Treasury Board approval next week.[87]

It is apparent from this memo and from Ms. Bourgon's testimony that she was concerned about the lack of "planning and programming" surrounding the communications-related activities to increase federal visibility.

Mr. Chrétien says that he agreed to follow this advice.[88] On June 19, 1996, he authorized a provisional draw on the Unity Reserve for the communications-related activities of PWGSC to the extent of $17 million, of which $10 million was allocated to short-term commitments and the balance of $7 million was frozen by Treasury Board for use at a later date, after a proper Treasury Board submission had been completed and approved.[89] This document was never submitted to Treasury Board.

On October 9, 1996, an amended version of the June 19, 1996, Treasury Board submission was signed jointly by Diane Marleau as Minister of PWGSC and by Prime Minister Chrétien, seeking approval of $17 million for each of two fiscal years, 1996-97 and 1997-98, for funding to support the communications priorities of the Government of Canada.[90] The signatures are on the first page (reproduced in Figure IV-2) of the two-page Treasury Board submission. The submission contains the following admonition, which was repeated in all subsequent Treasury Board submissions seeking funds for the Sponsorship Program:

Figure IV-2: Joint signatures on Treasury Board submission.

1057172 : Front

The Treasury Board of Canada   Le Conseil du Trésor du Canada

PROPOSED
PROTÉGÉ   824628

Public Works & Government Services Canada
Travaux publics et Services gouvernementaux Canada   Ministère

NOV 21 1996

October 09, 1996
le 09 octobre 1996

File — Dossier

T.B. Number — C.T. Nº
Date

SUBJECT

Request to include an item in the 1996-97 Supplementary Estimates and in the 1997-98 Reference Levels.

PROPOSAL

That Treasury Board approve inclusion of an item in the 1996-97 Supplementary Estimates and establishment of an item in the 1997-98 Reference Levels for funding to support the communications priorities of the Government of Canada.

COST

Cost in 1996-97 and 1997-98 will amount to $17,000,000 each fiscal year and will be chargeable to the operating vote of the department of Public Works and Government Services Canada. Refer to Annex A for detailed information.

OBJET

Demande d'inclure un poste au Budget des dépenses supplémentaires 1996-97 et des niveaux de référence de 1997-98.

PROPOSITION

Que le Conseil du Trésor approuve l'inscription d'un poste au Budget des dépenses supplémentaires 1996-97 et d'établir des niveaux de référence pour 1997-98 pour le financement supplémentaire en vue de soutenir les priorités du gouvernement canadien en matière de communication.

COÛTS

En 1996-97 et en 1997-98, les coûts seront de 17,000,000 $ par année financière et seront imputables aux Dépenses de fonctionnement du ministère des Travaux publics et Services gouvernementaux Canada. Consulter l'annexe A pour plus de détails.

APPROVED
NOV 21 1996

APPROUVÉ

Minister of Public Works & Government Services Canada

Prime Minister

Public Works and Government Services Canada through the Advertising and Public Opinion Research Sector will ensure that the creative services, media buys, sponsorships, promotions and any other marketing initiatives conform with established Treasury Board policy and guidelines and that they provide added value to the Crown. In addition, they will continue to ensure that all communications services, including advertising and public opinion research, are competitive as required and subsequently that appropriate contracts are issued.[91]

The submission was later supported by a Treasury Board Précis, dated October 31, 1996, describing in greater detail the uses to which the funds being sought for release would be put. It included the following paragraph:

7. Most recently, A&PORS is responsible for fulfilling a Government of Canada initiative to promote all its programs by means of sponsorship through selective events across Canada. The events are determined on the basis of audience, visibility, timing and potential impact on the government's programs used at such events. Appendix A provides a list of venues that have already been used this fiscal year to fulfil this mandate and which account for the $17,000,000 requested for 1996/97. According to A&PORS, government programs and services will be promoted through sponsorship at many of the same/similar events in 1997/98.[92]

Attached to the Précis is the detailed list of sponsorship events, totalling $16,138,640.

The submission was approved by Treasury Board on November 21, 1996. By that time virtually the entire amount of $17 million authorized for 1996-97 had already been spent.[93]

Ms. Bourgon testifies that it was not really necessary for the Prime Minister to sign the Treasury Board submission in order to obtain the release of the funds. She is of the view that he agreed to co-sign the submission because, unlike other aspects of the unity strategy, which had been well documented and defined, there was no written instrument, other than the Cabinet decision to have a unity strategy, which defined or described the "visibility initiatives."[94]

All witnesses who have testified on this subject agree that it was without precedent for the Prime Minister to sign a Treasury Board submission. Mr. Bilodeau is of the view that the Prime Minister's signature sent a signal to the bureaucracy that he would support the submission with all of the weight of his authority.[95] Ms. Bourgon agrees that the Prime Minister's signature sent a message to everyone about the seriousness of the initiative.[96] As already indicated, Mr. Chrétien himself knew that his signature on a Treasury Board submission would send "a clear signal"[97] to all concerned of the importance he attached to these visibility initiatives that were to be financed with the funds to be released from the Unity Reserve,[98] over which he had complete control. Under such circumstances, it was unlikely that anyone in the machinery of government, whether partisan or bureaucrat, would question a visibility initiative which had the backing of the Prime Minister himself.

Ms. Bourgon testifies that she was concerned about the question of ministerial responsibility for funds allocated from the Unity Reserve on the basis of the Prime Minister's signature.[99] In a memorandum to the Prime Minister dated December 18, 1996, she requested him to make decisions concerning the use of such funds by the CIO and PWGSC, in the latter case referring specifically to the $17 million drawn for each of the current year and year to come. This is what she wrote; the underlining appears in the original text of the memorandum:

>   C. Public Works and Government Services Canada
>
>   • PWGSC accessed the Unity Reserve, <u>on your behalf</u>, on October 21, for $17 million in each of 1996-97 and 1997-98 for sponsoring special events, advertising, enhancement of planned media campaigns to increase federal presence, and the promotion of special events (details at Table 4).
>
>   <u>The funds for 1996-97 had already been spent by the time the submission was approved by Treasury Board</u>

- While, like for any other advertising programs, Mme Marleau is the Minister responsible for the proper administrative and financial procedures in the actual disbursement of the funds, the <u>accountability rests with you for how the funds were spent in 1996-97 as the Unity Reserve was accessed on your behalf by PWGSC</u>.

  Therefore, if questions were to be raised about the actual initiatives supported by these funds, you would need to be ready to respond to them.

- <u>At issue is what support you need to fulfill your accountability</u>. Support could be provided to you by the Intergovernmental Affairs Secretariat or, alternatively by the Ministers having a primary interest in Unity.

<u>Decisions Sought</u>

(5) Do you want to retain the responsibility for these unity monies or do you wish to transfer this responsibility to a Minister?

(6) If you retain the responsibility, do you want PCO or a group of Ministers to review, for your approval, projects which could be funded by the unity monies provided to PWGSC for 1997-98?[100]

The memorandum is self-explanatory. Ms. Bourgon says she was concerned that the Prime Minister had taken on a very large burden of responsibility, and she wanted to be sure that the PCO was serving him well.[101] She obviously thought that a review of future projects by the PCO or a group of Ministers would provide better management of the $17 million allocated to PWGSC for 1997-98 than was the case in 1996-97, when the list of projects had been prepared by APORS and the PMO, with little or no input by the PCO.

Mr. Chrétien did not reply in any way to Ms. Bourgon's memorandum of December 18, 1996. Ms. Bourgon returned to the same subject of concern in a second memorandum, dated September 30, 1997, on the subject of access to the Unity Reserve, which was under pressure due to the number of requests for funding which were pending, including requests by PWGSC for an additional $18.8 million for 1997-98, mainly for the Sponsorship Program, and $50 million for each of the following three years.

This is what she wrote on that subject:

III Upcoming Pressures

This note focuses on the most pressing issues requiring decisions at this time.

Public Works and Government Services Canada Request

- The largest current pressure originates from PWGSC, which is seeking through the Supplementary Estimates multi-year funding from the Unity Reserve: $18.8 million for 1997-98 for a variety of advertising and promotional activities and $50 million for each of the subsequent three years for public opinion research and communications activities.

- A Treasury Board Submission to that effect has been signed by the Minister. As occurred on the last occasion, you will be expected to co-sign this submission (Tab 2).

- While listing the initiatives for 1997-98, this Submission does not provide a breakdown, nor detailed justification for the $150 million proposed to be spent in the following three years. The Unity Reserve, as currently profiled, does not contain sufficient funds in 1998-99 and 1999-2000 to support both the anticipated requests and the current proposal from PWGSC.

- At issue is how the $18.8 million proposal relates to the national unity strategy. PWGSC was already granted $17 million for 1997-98 from the Unity Reserve for advertising.

- An option would be to limit your approval at this time to the request for supplementary funding of $18.8 million for 1997-98, leaving for later the request for $50 million per year for 1998-99 and 1999-00.

- Beyond this lies the question of accountability. While the Minister of Public Works and Government Services Canada is responsible for the proper administrative and financial procedures in the actual disbursement of funds, the accountability rests with you for how the funds are spent when access to the Unity Reserve is approved by you for the PWGSC. The funds themselves reside within and are voted to PWGSC. <u>That said, it is your office which determines to which projects the monies are directed.</u> Should questions arise in the House of Commons, for example, on the initiatives supported by these funds, you might have to respond.

- Hence, at issue as well is the level of support you require to fulfil your accountability. This support could be provided to you by the PCO or, alternatively, by a Minister or group of Ministers.

<u>Decisions Sought</u>

(1) Do you agree to proceed with the PWGSC request for $18.8 M for the current year and to review the funding for future years in the context of budget spending pressures?

(2) Do you want to remain accountable for the unity monies to be administered by PWGSC, or do you wish to transfer this responsibility to a Minister?

(3) If you wish to retain accountability, do you want PCO or a Minister (or group of Ministers) to review, for your approval, projects which could be funded by the unity monies provided to PWGSC?[102]

This memorandum establishes:

- that the PCO was aware that the PMO was determining those projects to which sponsorship monies were being directed;
- that the Prime Minister was accountable for the use of funds drawn from the Unity Reserve on the basis of his signature on a Treasury Board submission;

- that this accountability could be transferred to a Minister, an option that Ms. Bourgon, by repeating the suggestion, apparently favoured; and
- that if the Prime Minister preferred to retain accountability, he could obtain advice or assistance from the PCO or a Minister or group of Ministers, who would review projects to be funded by unity monies.

The memorandum makes it obvious that Ms. Bourgon was uncomfortable with the existing management of the funds being accessed by the Prime Minister's signature. During her testimony she was asked what she meant by the sentence, "It is your office which determines to which projects the monies are directed." She attempted to make a distinction between responsibility (or accountability; she seems to use the words interchangeably) for the nature of the projects envisaged, and responsibility for the particular projects themselves.[103] I was not convinced that such a distinction could be deduced from the text of the memorandum, which is admirably clear.

In any event, Mr. Chrétien declined to respond positively in writing or otherwise to the requests for decisions sought by Ms. Bourgon. As stated by Mr. Pelletier, Mr. Chrétien fully understood his responsibilities and accountabilities, chose to retain them, and became accountable for how the funds, accessed on his behalf by PWGSC, were spent or misspent.[104]

In 1998-99, a further amount of $35 million from the Unity Reserve was allocated to PWGSC for the Sponsorship Program. The evidence shows that the Prime Minister authorized two draws, of $18 million and $17 million.[105] In 1999-2000, the amount dropped to $9 million. By then, the operating budget of PWGSC included, for the first time, an amount of $40 million for "special programs."[106] This was the first time that Members of Parliament were made aware, in the appropriations procedure, that there was a program being administered by PWGSC which involved the discretionary expenditure of funds.[107]

The budgeting of $40 million annually for special programs to be administered by PWGSC continued in the three following years, until the discontinuance of the Sponsorship Program in December 2003.[108]

Details of the source of funds used for the Sponsorship Program will be found in the Kroll Report.

What conclusions can be drawn from the foregoing?

The funds made available to PWGSC for the Sponsorship Program in its first three years were accessed from the Unity Reserve, which was under the exclusive jurisdiction of the Prime Minister. These funds were spent at a time when the Program had not been formalized, adequately defined or publicized. They were allocated according to discretion given to Mr. Guité, working under the direction of the PMO and with its approval. There had been no directions or guidelines given by the PMO or the PCO to anyone as to how the Program was to be administered, what criteria would guide decisions made regarding the use of the funds and who would supervise implementation of the Program.

Although Ms. Marleau may have been, in law, the Minister responsible for the Program until she was replaced by Mr. Gagliano in June 1997, in fact she and her Deputy Minister had nothing at all to do with the management of the Sponsorship Program other than to seek approval for its financing. The Program was run out of the PMO under the direct supervision of Mr. Pelletier, specifically delegated to carry out this responsibility by the Prime Minister. Mr. Pelletier, for all practical purposes, assumed the role, the functions and the responsibilities of a Minister of a department charged with the implementation of a program. Mr. Pelletier failed to fulfill that responsibility in that he did not give adequate direction to the subordinates in PWGSC to whom he was delegating the task of administering a new program.

Mr. Pelletier had been put in charge of the Sponsorship Program[109] by the Prime Minister himself, whose number one priority was the issue of national unity. Mr. Chrétien was personally responsible for the actions or the inaction of Mr. Pelletier and other exempt staff in his office. He resisted or ignored all suggestions from Ms. Bourgon that sponsorship initiatives and related events would be better directed and controlled by a Minister accustomed to program implementation and familiar with its requirements. She was obviously conscious of the irregularity and the danger of allowing exempt political staff to direct discretionary spending, especially during a period of fiscal restraint, when there was no evidence that criteria existed for spending decisions, and procedures for the administration and oversight of the program had not been established.

Mr. Chrétien chose to disregard the warnings of Ms. Bourgon, and on his behalf his Chief of Staff assumed ministerial responsibility for the Sponsorship Program. They cannot take comfort in the wording in the Treasury Board submissions jointly signed by the Prime Minister and the Minister of PWGSC that require PWGSC personnel to observe all the requirements of the Government's Contracting Policy, when those controls and oversight had been deliberately bypassed. By his conduct and involvement, Mr. Pelletier made it impossible for Ms. Marleau and Mr. Quail to fulfill their responsibilities, since they were excluded from any participation in the decision-making process and had no effective control over the actions of Mr. Guité.

Endnotes to Chapter IV

[1] Testimony of Mr. Myer, Transcripts vol. 31 (E) p. 5267 (OE), pp. 5267-5268 (F); Testimony of Ms. Tremblay, Transcripts vol. 20, pp. 3144-3145 (OF), pp. 3143-3145 (F).

[2] Testimony of Ms. Maltais, Transcripts vol. 30, pp. 5183-5190 (OF), pp. 5177-5183 (E); Testimony of Ms. Marcoux, Transcripts vol. 26, pp. 4425-4433 (OF), pp. 4420-4428 (E); Testimony of Mr. Myer, Transcripts vol. 31, pp. 5269-5274, 5290-5298 (OE), pp. 5269-5276, 5294-5303 (F); Exhibit P-100, tabs 9, 10.

[3] Testimony of Mr. Guité, Transcripts vol. 33, p. 5728 (OE), p. 5743 (F); Exhibit P-103(A), tab 21.

[4] Exhibit P-103(A), tab 22.

[5] Exhibit P-103(A), tab 22.

[6] Testimony of Mr. Guité, Transcripts vol. 33, pp. 5748-5749 (OE), pp. 5766-5766 (F).

[7] Testimony of Mr. Cutler, Transcripts vol. 13, pp. 2108-2110, 2146-2147 (OE), pp. 2110-2112, 2151-2152 (F).

[8] Testimony of Mr. Stobbe, Transcripts vol. 40, pp. 6935-6936 (OE), pp. 6942-6944 (F).

[9] Testimony of Mr. Stobbe, Transcripts vol. 40, pp. 6891-6892, 6895, 6932-6933 (OE), pp. 6892-6894, 6897, 6938-6941 (F); Testimony of Mr. Quail, Transcripts vol. 39, pp. 6734, 6792, 6800 (OE), pp. 6739-6740, 6805, 6813-6814 (F).

[10] Testimony of Mr. Quail, Transcripts vol. 39, pp. 6759-6761 (OE), pp. 6767-6770 (F); Testimony of Mr. Guité, Transcripts vol. 33, pp. 5612-5613 (OE), pp. 5613-5615 (F).

[11] Testimony of Ms. LaRose, Transcripts vol. 27, pp. 4674-4675, 4681-4684 (OF), pp. 4726, 4732-4734 (E).

[12] RSC 1985, c. F-11.

[13] Testimony of Mr. Lauzon, Transcripts vol. 26, p. 4399 (OF), p. 4394 (E); Testimony of Ms. LaRose, Transcripts vol. 27, pp. 4683-4684 (OF), p. 4734 (E).

[14] Testimony of Ms. Maltais, Transcripts vol. 30, pp. 5184-5191 (OF), pp. 5178-5183 (E).

[15] Testimony of Ms. Marcoux, Transcripts vol. 26, pp. 4453-4459 (OF), pp. 4445-4450 (E); Testimony of Ms. LaRose, Transcripts vol. 27, pp. 4675-4681 (OF), pp. 4727-4732 (E); Exhibit P-87(A), pp. 107-111; Exhibit P-94.

[16] Testimony of Ms. Marcoux, Transcripts vol. 26, pp. 4430-4432 (OF), pp. 4424-4426 (E), and pp. 4425-4428 (OF), pp. 4420-4423 (E); vol. 25, p. 4257 (OF), p. 4246 (E); Exhibit P-87(A), pp. 153, 156.

[17] Testimony of Mr. Myer, Transcripts vol. 31, pp. 5268-5274, 5288-5289 (OE), pp. 5269-5275, 5291-5292 (F).

[18] This is discussed in the context of the Demers Administrative Review in Chapter VII.

[19] Testimony of Mr. Martin, Transcripts vol. 73, pp. 12690, 12695-12698 (OE), p. 12691, 12696-12700 (F); Exhibit P-213, tab 3.

[20] Testimony of Mr. Martin, Transcripts vol. 73, pp. 12718-12721 (OE), pp. 12722-12726 (F).

[21] Testimony of Mr. Quail, Transcripts vol. 39, pp. 6703-6705 (OE), pp. 6705-6707 (F).

[22] Testimony of Ms. Bourgon, Transcripts vol. 47, pp. 8189-8191 (OF), pp. 8188-8191 (E).

[23] Testimony of Mr. Chrétien, Transcripts vol. 72, p. 12504 (OF), pp. 12500-12501 (E).

[24] Testimony of Ms. Robillard, Transcripts vol. 65, pp. 11231-11232 (OF), pp. 11231-11232 (E).

[25] Exhibit P-88(C), pp. 558-569.

[26] Exhibit P-148 (B), pp. 308-309.

27 Exhibit P-186 (B), tab-12, p. 123.

28 The Unity Reserve will be described in greater detail in Chapter IV, section 4.7.

29 Exhibit P-148 (A), p. 74.

30 Testimony of Mr. Dingwall, Transcripts vol. 60, p. 10553 (OE), p. 10555 (F); Testimony of Mr. Gagliano, Transcripts vol. 69, p. 12046 (OF), p. 12049 (F); Testimony of Mr. Pelletier, Transcripts vol. 72, pp. 12490-12491 (OF), p. 12474 (E).

31 Testimony of Mr. Chrétien, Transcripts vol. 72, pp. 12507-12508 (OF), pp. 12503-12504 (E).

32 Exhibit P-189(A), p. 31 (F), p. 41 (E); Testimony of Mr. Chrétien, Transcripts vol. 72, pp. 12546-12547 (OF), pp. 12538-12539 (E).

33 Testimony of Mr. Massé, Transcripts vol. 64, pp. 11194-11195 (OF), pp. 11193-11194 (E).

34 Exhibit P-189(A), p. 46 (E), p. 37 (F).

35 Testimony of Mr. Massé, Transcripts vol. 64, pp. 11196-11197 (OF), pp. 11195-11196 (E).

36 Exhibit P-189(A), p. 47 (E), p. 38 (F).

37 Exhibit P-189(A), p. 48 (E), p. 38 (F).

38 Testimony of Mr. Dion, Transcripts vol. 62, pp. 10882-10883 (OF), p. 10882 (E); Testimony of Mr. Massé, Transcripts vol. 64, pp. 11198-11200 (OF), pp. 11197-11199 (E); Testimony of Ms. Robillard, Transcripts vol. 65, pp. 11241-11242 (OF), pp. 11239-11240 (E); Testimony of Mr. Pettigrew, Transcripts vol. 66, pp. 11334-11335 (OF), pp. 11333-11334 (E).

39 Testimony of Mr. Pelletier, Transcripts vol. 71, pp. 12354-12355 (OF), pp. 12348-12350 (E).

40 Testimony of Mr. Corbeil, Transcripts vol. 115, p. 21379 (OF), pp. 21356-21357 (E).

41 Exhibit P-189(A), pp. 57-65 at p. 64.

42 Testimony of Ms. Marleau, Transcripts vol. 61 (revised), pp. 10858-10861 (OE), pp. 10860-10864 (F); Testimony of Mr. Chrétien, Transcripts vol. 72 (revised), 12561-12564 (OF), pp. 12551-12552 (E); Testimony of Ms. Robillard, Transcripts vol. 65, pp. 11239-11240, 11242-11243 (OF), pp. 11238-11239, 11242 (E); Testimony of Mr. Cauchon, Transcripts vol. 65, pp. 11296-11297 (OF), pp. 11290-11291 (E); Testimony of Mr. Martin, Transcripts vol. 73, pp. 12742-12743 (OE), pp. 12749-12750 (F); Testimony of Mr. Dion, Transcripts vol. 62, pp. 10879-10881 (OF), pp. 10879-10881 (E); Testimony of Mr. Pettigrew, Transcripts vol. 66 (revised), pp. 11332-11333 (OF), pp. 11332-11333 (E); Testimony of Mr. Pelletier, Transcripts vol. 71, pp. 12356-12357 (OF), p. 12352 (E).

43 Testimony of Ms. Marleau, Transcripts vol. 61 (revised), p. 10864 (OE), pp. 10866-10867 (F).

44 Testimony of Mr. Massé, Transcripts vol. 64, pp. 11201-11202 (OF), pp. 11200-11201 (E).

45 Testimony of Mr. Chrétien, Transcripts vol. 72 (revised), pp. 12561-12562 (OF), pp. 12551-12552 (E).

46 Testimony of Mr. Dion, Transcripts vol. 62, pp. 10931-10934 (OF), pp. 10927-10929 (E).

47 Testimony of Mr. Bilodeau Transcripts vol. 47, pp. 9067-9068 (OF), pp. 8068-8069 (E).

48 Testimony of Mr. Chrétien, Transcripts vol. 72, p. 12568 (OF), p. 12557 (E).

49 Testimony of Mr. Pelletier, Transcripts vol. 71, pp. 12356-12360 (OF), pp.12352-12355 (E).

50 Testimony of Mr. Chrétien, Transcripts vol. 72, pp. 12511-12512 (OF), p. 12507 (E).

51 Testimony of Mr. Gagliano, Transcripts vol. 67, pp. 11603-11606 (OF), pp. 11597-11600 (E).

52 Testimony of Mr. Bilodeau, Transcripts vol. 46, pp. 7897-7899 (OF), pp. 7863-7865 (E).

53 Testimony of Mr. Bilodeau, Transcripts vol. 46, pp. 7898-7900 (OF), pp. 7864-7865 (E).

54 Testimony of Mr. Bilodeau, Transcripts vol. 46, pp. 7897-7899 (OF), pp. 7863-7866 (E).

[55] Testimony of Mr. Chrétien, Transcripts vol. 72, pp. 12563-12564 (OF), pp. 12552-12553 (E); Testimony of Mr. Collet, Transcripts vol. 43, pp. 7286-7289 (OF), pp. 7285-7294 (E).

[56] Testimony of Mr. Collet, Transcripts vol. 43, pp. 7297-7301 (OF), pp. 7302-7306 (E).

[57] Testimony of Mr. Pelletier, Transcripts vol. 71, p. 12492 (OF), pp. 12475-12476 (E).

[58] Testimony of Mr. Collet, Transcripts vol. 43 (revised), pp. 7382-7384 (OF), pp. 7379-7381 (E).

[59] Testimony of Mr. Collet, Transcripts vol. 43 (revised), pp. 7352-7353 (OF), pp. 7352-7353 (E).

[60] Testimony of Mr. Collet, Transcripts vol. 43 (revised), pp. 7385-7386 (OF), pp. 7382-7384 (E).

[61] Exhibit P-131(A), p. 61.

[62] Testimony of Mr. Guité, Transcripts vo. 34, pp. 5830-5831 (OE), pp. 5833-5834 (F).

[63] Testimony of Mr. Collet, Transcripts vol. 43, pp. 7455-7458 (OF), pp. 7452-7455 (E); Testimony of Mr. Pelletier, Transcripts vol. 71, pp. 12372-12373 (OF), pp. 12366-12377 (E); Exhibit P-208(D), pp. 118-119, 197; Exhibit P-106(A), tab 17, pp. 120-130.

[64] Exhibit P-12(A), tab-C, tab-F.

[65] Testimony of Mr. Guité, Transcripts vol. 35, p. 6055 (OE), pp. 6063-6064 (F); Exhibit P-106(A), pp. 166, 173.

[66] Testimony of Mr. Collet, Transcripts vol. 43, pp. 7438-7441 (OF), pp. 7435-7438 (E); Testimony of Mr. Lafrenière, Transcripts vol. 45, pp. 7741-7742 (OF), pp. 7735-7736 (E).

[67] Exhibit P-106(A), tabs 13, 16, 17, tab 19, pp. 162-164; Exhibit P-12(A), tab F.

[68] Testimony of Ms. Marleau, Transcripts vol. 61, pp. 10864-10868 (OE), pp. 10867-10871 (F).

[69] Testimony of Ms. Marleau, Transcripts vol. 62, pp. 10945-10947 (OE), pp. 10945-10948 (F).

[70] Testimony of Ms. Marleau, Transcripts vol. 62, pp. 10947-10950 (OE), pp. 10948-10951 (F).

[71] Testimony of Ms. Marleau, Transcripts vol. 62, pp. 10944-10945 (OE), p. 10945 (F).

[72] Testimony of Mr. Pelletier, Transcripts vol. 71, pp. 12360-12363, 12389-12391 (OF), pp. 12356-12358, pp. 12381-12383 (E); Exhibit P-208(D), p. 115.

[73] Testimony of Mr. Pelletier, Transcripts vol. 71, pp. 12389-12391 (OF), pp. 12381-12383 (E); Exhibit P-208(D), p 115.

[74] Testimony of Mr. Pelletier, Transcripts vol. 71, pp. 12332, 12375-12376, 12394-12395 (OF), pp. 12330, 12369-12370, 12386-12387 (E).

[75] Exhibit P-208(D), p. 27.

[76] Testimony of Mr. Pelletier, Transcripts vol. 71, pp. 12339-12341 (OF), pp. 12336-12339 (E).

[77] Exhibit P-206, pp. 22, 31, 38, 67, 76; Testimony of Mr. Guité, Transcripts vol. 33, pp. 5652-5655 (OE), pp. 5657-5660 (F); Exhibit P-208(D), pp. 118-119, 197; Exhibit P-106(A), tab 17, pp. 120-130; Testimony of Mr. Collet, Transcripts vol. 43, pp. 7455-7458 (OF), pp. 7452-7455 (E); Testimony of Mr. Pelletier, Transcripts vol. 71, pp. 12372-12373 (OF), pp. 12366-12377 (E).

[78] Testimony of Ms. Marleau, Transcripts vol. 62, pp. 10940-10944 (OE), pp. 10949-10944 (F).

[79] Exhibit P-106(A), p. 86.

[80] Exhibit P-106(A), tab 13, Exhibit P-219(A), pp. 115, 118; Exhibit P-225(A), pp. 66-67l; Exhibit P-216, pp. 55, 60.

[81] Testimony of Mr. Chrétien, Transcripts vol. 72, pp. 12515-12516 (OE), pp. 12517-12518 (F); Testimony of Mr. Martin, Transcripts vol. 73, pp. 12743-12745 (OE), pp. 12750-12751 (F).

[82] Testimony of Mr. Martin, Transcripts vol. 73, p. 12753 (OE), pp. 12760-12761 (F).

[83] Testimony of Mr. Chrétien, Transcripts vol. 72, pp. 12541-12543 (OF), pp. 12534-12536 (E).

84 Exhibit P-12(A), tab-1C.

85 Testimony of Mr. Chrétien, Transcripts vol. 72, p. 12513 (OE), pp. 12514-12515 (F).

86 Exhibit P-210(C), pp. 553-554.

87 Exhibit P-210(C), pp. 560-563.

88 Testimony of Mr. Chrétien, Transcripts vol. 72, p. 12605 (OF), p. 12591 (E).

89 Exhibit P-12(A), tab 1A (E), tab 1C (E).

90 Exhibit P-12(A), tab 1C (E).

91 Exhibit P148(A), p. 115.

92 Exhibit P-148(A), p. 123 (E).

93 Testimony of Ms. Bourgon, Transcripts vol. 47, p. 8235 (OF), p. 8235 (E).

94 Testimony of Ms. Bourgon, Transcripts vol. 47, p. 8218 (OF), p. 8218 (E).

95 Testimony of Mr. Bilodeau, Transcripts vol. 46, p. 7878 (OF), p. 7844 (E).

96 Testimony of Ms. Bourgon, Transcripts vol. 47, p. 8220 (OF), p. 8220 (E).

97 Testimony of Mr. Chrétien, Transcripts vol. 72, p. 12513 (OE), p. 12514 (F).

98 Testimony of Ms. Bourgon, Transcripts vol. 47, pp. 8229-8230 (OF), pp. 8229-8230 (E).

99 Testimony of Ms. Bourgon, Transcripts vol. 47, pp. 8227-8230 (OF), pp. 8227-8230 (E).

100 Exhibit P-148(A), pp. 148-149.

101 Testimony of Ms. Bourgon, Transcripts vol. 47, pp. 8227-8230 (OF), pp. 8227-8230 (E).

102 Exhibit P-148(A), pp. 172-173.

103 Testimony of Ms. Bourgon, Transcripts vol. 48, pp. 8262-8264 (OF), pp. 8260-8263 (E).

104 Testimony of Mr. Pelletier, Transcripts vol. 71, pp. 12387-12388 (OF), 12380 (E).

105 Exhibit P-12(A), tabs 3D and 3I.

106 Exhibit P-12(A), table preceding tab 1; Exhibit P-12(B), tab 5A.

107 Testimony of Ms. Fraser, Transcripts vol. 1, pp. 94-102 (OE), pp. 100-108 (F); vol. 2, pp. 291-293 (OE), pp. 310-313 (F).

108 Exhibit P-12(A), table preceding tab 1.

109 Testimony of Mr. Chrétien, Transcripts vol. 72, pp. 12567-12568 (OF), pp. 12556-12557 (E).

Chapter V

SELECTION of ADVERTISING and COMMUNICATION AGENCIES

5.1
Under the Previous Progressive Conservative Government

Prior to November 1993, government advertising was handled by the Advertising Management Group (AMG), consisting of a small group of public servants in the Department of Supply and Services headed by Mr. Joseph Charles Guité, to which were added two political appointees named by the Prime Minister's Office, designated "consultants." The selection and engagement of advertising agencies to assist the Government in its advertising activities were openly done on a political basis. For direction as to how to proceed, Mr. Guité received instructions from the Cabinet committee on Communications. Although at that time Mr. Guité was a relatively minor public servant four or five levels down in the hierarchy from the Deputy Minister within his department, he reported directly to Senator Lowell Murray, who presided over the Committee.[1] The normal chain of command whereby a public servant is expected to take orders from his or her immediate superior was accordingly bypassed. Usually a public servant will deal with politicians only in the presence of the Deputy Minister or his or her representative.

In the preceding Progressive Conservative administration, government departments requiring the services of an advertising agency would inform the AMG, which would then hold a competition to choose the agency to be awarded a contract. However, the list of agencies invited to compete was prepared by the political appointees within the AMG.[2] Advertising and communication agencies having Liberal Party sympathies or connections had little or no chance of getting government business. Mr. Guité believes that once the list of candidates had been prepared, the competition was fair, but of course only agencies acceptable to the party in power had been put on the list.

5.2
Mandate for Change

In the 1993 election campaign, the Liberal Party made it a part of its platform that less money would be spent by the Government on advertising and polling, and that the rules for selecting advertising agencies would be changed to allow fair, open and transparent bidding.[3] As soon as Mr. Chrétien became Prime Minister, he took steps to fulfill these promises, instructing the Treasury Board Secretariat to design and develop a new policy, which became known as Appendix U to the Treasury Board Contracting Policy. It was later designated Appendix Q, by which name it is described throughout this Report. The new appendix, entitled *Policy and Guidelines with respect to Contracting Procedures for Communications, Public Opinion Research and Advertising Services*, came into effect on July 6, 1994.

It is discouraging to see how what appears to have been a sincere attempt to depoliticize an openly biased procurement policy was subverted almost from the very beginning. In his testimony Mr. Guité expressed the opinion that politicians, who rely on advertising agencies to help them get elected, will always contrive to reward their friends in the advertising business once they are in office. Naturally, the advertising agencies are pleased to benefit from such rewards and are tempted to render services to candidates for office at bargain rates during election campaigns, in the hope and expectation that they will eventually get lucrative government business in exchange.[4] What occurred in the development and drafting of Appendix Q lends credence to Mr. Guité's cynicism, at least with respect to some, but not all, politicians.

5.3
Formulation of Appendix Q

The Treasury Board Secretariat had the main responsibility for the conception and development of the new policy guidelines, but had assistance from personnel from the Privy Council Office. The political direction in the development of the guidelines came from the PMO and from the Honourable David Dingwall as Minister of Public Works and Government Services Canada (PWGSC). Mr. Guité, as the acknowledged expert in advertising matters, was delegated to assist in the process, as was his immediate superior in PWGSC, Mr. James Stobbe, and Mr. Richard Neville, who was then Assistant Deputy Minister, Corporate Services, of PWGSC. Mr. Ranald Quail as Deputy Minister also contributed and was kept informed.

The subject of the new government policy concerning advertising was discussed at a Cabinet meeting on January 27, 1994, at which the Prime Minister is recorded as saying that the "process of advertising and polling would have to be much better managed and more transparent than in the past."[5] Nevertheless, there was already reluctance expressed by certain Ministers to do away completely with ministerial discretion in the appointment of advertising agencies to assist them in the advertising needs of their various departments. After discussion, a compromise was reached at the Cabinet level: if as a result of the competitive process two agencies submitted approximately equivalent bids, the Minister concerned would have the right to choose between the two bidders. Eventually this was to become the "10% rule" by which, if two competitive bids were evaluated as being within a range of 10% of each other, either one of them could be accepted at the discretion of the relevant Minister.[6] This was the first undermining of a completely competitive process.

On April 14, 1994, Cabinet gave general approval to the new policy, including the 10% rule.[7] At that time the guidelines had yet to be drafted in final form, but the adoption by Cabinet of the new policy apparently permitted Mr. Chrétien to believe that, for the future, the selection of advertising agencies would be as he had promised the electorate, that is to say open, transparent and competitive. That was what he communicated to his colleagues in the letter written on May 9, 1994,[8] to each Minister of his Cabinet (reproduced in Figure V-1).

Figure V-1: May 9, 1994, letter from Prime Minister Chrétien

PRIME MINISTER · PREMIER MINISTRE

RECEIVED · REÇU May 9, 1994

MAI 10 1994

House of Commons
Chambre des Communes

Dear Colleague,

This letter is further to the recent Cabinet decision on polling, advertising and communications. You will recall that we agreed at that time to ensure integrity in the contracting process and to contain overall expenditures in these areas.

I believe that, by demonstrating restraint, we can save about 25 percent of the average annual cost of advertising and polling. I am setting a ceiling for spending in these areas for 1994-95 of $65 million. If ministers show firm resolve, we will free up millions of dollars that can be reallocated to the government's priorities.

Your department in consultation with Public Works and Government Services Canada and the Privy Council Office is revising government policies to reflect Cabinet's decision. These proposed changes will then be considered by Treasury Board ministers. I would also like you to convene Treasury Board ministers 2-3 times per year to review the advertising and polling expenditures of departments, to ensure that our target is met. The Honourable David Dingwall will assist ministers in this task, by ensuring that expenditures in these areas are closely monitored.

The Honourable Arthur C. Eggleton
President of the Treasury Board and
Minister responsible for Infrastructure
Room 207, Confederation Building
House of Commons
Ottawa, Ontario
K1A 0A6

- 2 -

At Cabinet, we also agreed that contracting procedures for polling, advertising and communications must follow a competitive process, similar to the procurement of other services purchased by the government. Polling and advertising contracts should be open to all qualified suppliers, based on clear criteria, and be subject to a fair and competitive process. Normally, ministers will not be involved in the selection process unless two or more bids are judged to be of equivalent value. In these cases, it will be left to ministerial discretion to choose among these equivalent bids.

You should also ensure that your department supports the government's efforts to become more transparent and accessible. I am therefore encouraging you to release the results of any public opinion research conducted by your department within 90 days of receiving a final report. It may be necessary to withhold some findings using exemptions permitted under the Access to Information Act, but complete disclosure should be the norm.

As you know, your department is now leading the process of ensuring these changes are reflected in the appropriate government policies and procedures. Until such time as they are revised, I expect you and your officials to operate in the spirit of the attached guidelines.

Yours sincerely,

Jean Chrétien

A major debate then ensued concerning the inclusion of price as a criterion in the process of selection of an advertising agency. Early drafts of the proposed guidelines all included price as a relevant factor, and at the Cabinet meeting of April 14, 1994, at which the subject of the new policy was discussed, approval was given to the following statement:

> The competitive process is to be open, possibly incorporating a two-step process when a significant number of suppliers wish to bid. Under this process a convenient number of those deemed best qualified to provide the required service would be requested to submit detailed, priced offers.[9]

In spite of this clear direction, Mr. Guité and the advertising industry, with which he was obviously on very friendly terms, together mounted a concerted campaign to exclude price as a criterion in the selection of advertising agencies.

Mr. Guité acknowledges that he worked very hard to convince the persons at Treasury Board responsible for drafting the guidelines to exclude price as a factor. It was his opinion that the essence of successful advertising is creativity, and that it is impossible to put a price on the creative process. He made representations to that effect to the persons in the Privy Council Office involved in the development of the policy. He also encouraged executives he knew in the advertising industry to lobby to exclude price from the competitive process.[10] Typical of these efforts was a letter sent to him on June 7, 1994, by the President of the Institute of Canadian Advertising,[11] which represented a substantial proportion of the industry. The letter is reproduced in Figure V-2.

*Figure V-2: June 7, 1994, letter from President of the
Institute of Canadian Advertising*

JUN 8 '94 15:37   FROM INSTITUTE OF CDN ADV   PAGE.002

Institute of Canadian Advertising

30 Soudan Avenue, Toronto, Ontario M4S 1V6
Tel. (416) 482-1396 • Fax (416) 482-1856

June 7, 1994

Mr. J.C. Guité   **Via Facsimile**
Advertising Management Group
151 Slater Street
Suite 215
Ottawa, Ontario
K1P 5H3

Dear Mr. Guité: .

                    <u>Advertising Agency Selection - Remuneration</u>

This letter is further to our recent discussions regarding the selection process for advertising
agencies.

It is my understanding of the proposed Federal Government guidelines that, in most respects,
they represent an efficient and fair procedure for interviewing and appointing advertising
agencies. One aspect, however, remains a concern to ICA and that relates to the matter of
agency remuneration and how this important subject is handled in the Government's proposed
guidelines.

The basic service of any advertising agency is to generate ideas. These would include regular
creative and publicity materials, but also cover media and distribution ideas, research ideas,
positioning and philosophy ideas and strategic ideas. It is a well-accepted industry position that
<u>ideas cannot be, and should not be, purchased on the basis of price or remuneration</u>. Ideas are
generated by creators and artists and agency services should be likened to musicians or sculptors,
not to the acquisition of hard-goods or services such as insurance, computer software or banking.

Experience has shown our industry that an advertiser who selects an advertising agency largely
on the criterion of price is buying a very short-term or non-existent benefit. It would be
counter-productive for the Federal Government (or any other reputable advertiser) to determine
agency selections on a low price or lowest price basis.

It is important, however, to recognize that agencies should be compensated on an astute,
competitive basis. A thorough procedure of searching for the proper agency should be based
on other criteria; then compensation can be negotiated with the chosen finalist.
                                                                       2

7160549

PW - 008996
JUN 8 '94 15:38   FROM INSTITUTE OF CDN ADV   PAGE.003

Mr. J.C. Guité
<u>Advertising Management Group</u>   <u>Page 2</u>

The following quotation on this subject is from a well-respected publication, "Managing Agency
Relations" of the Association of National Advertisers, Inc.:

> "Advertisers often focused on cost reduction, as such, ignoring the question of
> how best to maintain the quality or value of the agency service they received. In
> many instances the desire to reduce costs was so strong that advertisers lost sight
> of the fact that there would inevitably be some kind of reaction to reduced
> compensation on the part of the agencies."

The ANA has long recognized the peril of being guided by price and recommends that it not
play an important part of the selection process.

It is hoped that the proposed guidelines will correctly position the matter of agency remuneration. It's a critically important consideration and will have a significant effect on the future
efficacy of government programmes.

Our organization would be pleased to provide further information or dialogue on this subject if
you wish.

Sincerely,

John G. Sinclair
President
JGS:hc

A letter along the same lines, dated June 7, 1994, was written to Mr. Guité by Claude Boulay in his capacity as President of the Association des agences de publicité du Québec.[12] Mr. Boulay was also the president of Groupe Everest and a part owner of the agency which would later be designated as Agency of Record for the Government; in those capacities he was enabled to profit enormously from the fees and commissions generated from the Sponsorship Program, which, of course, at the time he wrote the letter was no more than a future possibility.

Mr. Guité had frequent and easy access to Mr. Dingwall. He showed the Minister these and other letters he had obtained from representatives of the advertising industry, and he gradually was able to persuade Mr. Dingwall that price should be dropped from the guidelines.[13]

On this subject, Mr. Guité's testimony is contradictory. When he first testified at the Ottawa hearings of the Inquiry, he indicated that he had, over time, persuaded Mr. Dingwall to exclude price from the criteria. When he reappeared at the Montreal hearings, he stated that Mr. Dingwall, together with his Executive Assistant Warren Kinsella, had at no time wanted price to be a factor; otherwise, politicians would not be able to hire the agencies they favoured, which had been involved in their election campaigns.[14] On this subject as on others, Mr. Guité was not entirely a reliable witness.

Mr. Dingwall in his testimony acknowledges that there was a debate over whether to include price as a criterion. His Deputy Minister, Mr. Quail, appropriately supplied information and arguments on both sides of the question. The Assistant Deputy Minister, Mr. Neville, was in favour of retaining price as a factor,[15] whereas Mr. Guité, whom he described as their "advertising guru," wanted it out, and supplied him with evidence of representations from the private sector to the effect that price should not be part of the selection criteria. He allowed himself to be persuaded by Mr. Guité,[16] and Mr. Neville admits that he lost the argument.[17]

Probably Mr. Dingwall's version is to be preferred to that given by Mr. Guité in Montreal. In any event, no matter how the change in position was arrived at, price ceased to be a criterion for what was supposed to be a competitive process when Appendix Q reached the final form in which it was approved by Treasury Board. All references to price in Appendix Q had by then disappeared, although there were references to "value." The final decision to exclude price must have been made at the last minute: a draft of the guidelines, dated June 10, 1994, would have made price a factor worth 30% of the evaluation of a candidate, as appears from the following extract from the document:

2A The contracting authority will determine "best value" by using the following criteria and criterion weighting (whose sum is a possible total value of 1000 points) in evaluating the bids from prospective suppliers of "advertising services":

i   PRICE 300 points   30%

All forms of remuneration and payment schedules and structures, including administrative and management fee schedules; premiums; commissions; interest; taxes and duties

ii   EXPERIENCE 250 points   25%

Professional qualifications; track record; previous experience with government accounts; availability of senior personnel, talent, professionals; strength of support services.

iii   CREATIVITY 250 points   25%

Innovation; imagination; inventiveness; originality in proposal; understanding and development of program and media planning requirements, including cost effectiveness.

iv   KNOWLEDGE   100 points   10%

Awareness of institutional goals and government objectives; sensitivity to affected publics.

v   SUITABILITY 100 points   10%

Adaptability, motivation, commitment of the prospective supplier and its staff through interview and project proposal[18]

On this draft, opposite the paragraph headed "PRICE," is the handwritten notation "out." In his testimony, Mr. Dingwall said that he does not know whose handwriting this is.[19]

In its final form, Appendix Q[20] foresees either open bidding for an advertising contract or the creation of a pre-qualified suppliers list by a selection process, followed by competitive bidding for each contract by the agencies which had succeeded in having their names retained on the list. Open bidding would be used only in connection with advertising contracts.

5.4
Contracting Rules for Sponsorships

For sponsorship contracts, the process leading to inclusion of agencies on a pre-qualified suppliers list was invariably used. It was supposed to be a two-step process.

The first step for selecting a contractor consists of what is called pre-qualification. The contracting authority, which would always be PWGSC, issues a public call for agencies wishing to supply the stated advertising and communication needs of a particular department. Agencies are asked to communicate their interest and complete a questionnaire, prepared by PWGSC, intended to establish their capabilities, relevant experience and expertise. The completed questionnaires are then evaluated by a selection committee, usually consisting of six persons, representing the department involved, the public and representatives of PWGSC. These examiners individually evaluate the questionnaires on the basis of the criteria established in the guidelines; the results are combined, and in this way each application is rated. In some instances, some of the best applicants are invited to make oral presentations before the selection committee. The desired number of applicants having the best ratings are then placed on a pre-qualified suppliers list, subject to approval by the Minister of the department concerned. This pre-qualified suppliers list remains in effect for a year or more.

The second step in the process occurs when the department has a specific advertising need. At that time, all the agencies on the pre-qualified suppliers list are invited to bid competitively. The best bid results in the awarding of a contract.

On February 2, 1995,[21] the Government made an important policy decision. The interpretation of the requirement in Appendix Q that "only Canadian owned and controlled companies will be considered for advertising contracts"[22] was changed from 51% to 100% ownership.[23] According to a briefing book prepared on October 12, 1995, the change was announced by Mr. Guité to the advertising industry on directions given by Mr. Dingwall's office,[24] and was supported by the PMO at the highest level.[25]

The policy change generated a flurry of memos within the Government. The first one was sent by Jocelyne Bourgon, the Clerk of the Privy Council, to Jean Pelletier, the Prime Minister's Chief of Staff, on May 16, 1995. Another unsigned memo prepared around August 31, 1995, from Ms. Bourgon to the Prime Minister, deals with the same issue. While this memo may not have been seen by Mr. Chrétien, it would appear from notations on the document that it was discussed with Mr. Pelletier.

While both memos attribute the policy change to Mr. Dingwall, months later PCO was not able to confirm whether Mr. Dingwall's office had "consulted within government before making this change." PCO also believed that Mr. Dingwall made the change "after receiving representations from various Canadian firms." Other memos, prepared for Mr. Quail or by Mr. Quail for Ms. Bourgon, do not include any official notice of the change in the interpretation of the policy, which is strange given its importance.

That the announcement of the policy change took place on February 2, 1995, is confirmed by industry magazine articles.

Two advertising agencies that applauded the change, BCP and Vickers & Benson,[26] which are close to the Liberal Party, benefited from the new interpretation and became the biggest recipients of advertising contracts reviewed by this Commission.[27] More important, the change took effect on

February 2, 1995, the first day of the Heritage Canada selection process, which will be reviewed later, by which both BCP and Vickers & Benson, along with three other agencies, were selected. This cannot be mere coincidence. Mr. Guité expresses the opinion that this requirement favoured agencies friendly to the Liberal Party, all of which at that time were 100% Canadian owned.[28] The documentary evidence supports his testimony. Once again, it would appear that political considerations affected the formulation of an administrative policy.

5.5
Irregularities in the Application of the New Contracting Policy for Advertising

In practice, the requirements of Appendix Q for a second step, the competitive bidding process, were totally disregarded. In many instances there were also irregularities in the preparation of the pre-qualified suppliers list, but in all cases the second step was simply ignored. Sometimes only one supplier would pass the pre-qualification and would therefore automatically qualify for all of the advertising contracts from the department. Where there was more than one agency on the pre-qualified suppliers list, Mr. Guité would simply choose which of them would get the contract, with or without input from the department seeking advertising assistance.

No one in the Government admits to having been aware that the careful procedure prescribed in Appendix Q was being systematically disregarded by the Executive Director of the service involved.[29] It is difficult for an outsider to understand how such a total disregard for a carefully crafted and important government policy could have been unknown by everyone, but according to all of the witnesses who testified on this question, that appears to have been the case.

Mr. Guité was required by Treasury Board to report periodically upon the implementation of Appendix Q. He dutifully forwarded reports through Mr. Quail to Treasury Board, in which he stated that the requirements of Appendix Q were being strictly observed and that all advertising contracts were being let competitively. This was simply untrue. On May 25, 1995, the Honourable

Art Eggleton, who was then President of the Treasury Board, wrote to Mr. Chrétien to advise him that a reduction of expenditures on advertising was in accordance with expectations, and that "I have every expectation that the information which will be provided…on the level of competitive contracting which has been achieved will be another source of satisfaction."[30] On June 2, 1995, an aide-memoire to the Ministers of the Treasury Board reports that for the period between July 1 and December 31, 1994, advertising contracts exceeding $30,000 were 100% competitive.[31] This report, we may presume, was based upon the information being provided by Mr. Guité.

On August 4, 1995, Mr. Chrétien responded to Mr. Eggleton:

> [Emphasis added]
>
>> I am impressed with the high percentage of contracts awarded on a competitive basis. It appears that we have been able to deliver on our commitment to make the process more open and competitive. I trust we will not allow this early success to in any way diminish our resolve to improve the contracting process. *I would ask you and your officials to remain vigilant over the awarding of polling and advertising contracts.*[32]

The Commission has not been informed by anyone of any vigilance brought to bear on the administration of Mr. Guité's organization. He proceeded for the next five years, until he retired in 1999, to award advertising contracts, and sponsorship contracts which he considered to be a form of advertising, to agencies essentially as he pleased and without the slightest pretense of respecting a competitive process. No one appears to have questioned the procedures which he was following, and no one, from his immediate superiors on up to the highest levels, ever bothered to verify whether or not Mr. Guité and the employees under him were awarding advertising contracts in accordance with Appendix Q. Indeed, from 1995 on, he was explicitly exempted from making any further reports to Treasury Board with respect to the success achieved in implementing the new *open, transparent and competitive* policy.[33]

5.6
Tourism Canada Contract

An example of how advertising contracts were awarded without respecting the competitive process is cited by the Auditor General in Chapter 4 of her November 2003 Report at page 6.[34] Because this particular contract was the subject of testimony lasting for several days, and because it furnishes a good example of how Appendix Q was circumvented, it deserves to be described in some detail.

In July 1994, almost immediately after the formal adoption of Appendix Q as a Treasury Board policy, Mr. Guité, as Director General of the Advertising and Public Opinion Research Sector (APORS), published a notice of a competition to be held to select an advertising agency to provide a full range of marketing support services to Tourism Canada, an agency of Industry Canada, whose mission was to promote tourism in Canada. The notice listed the requirements of the agency to be selected, the last of which was "substantial knowledge of Tourism Canada's prime prospect – residents of the United States."[35]

A large number of advertising agencies indicated an interest in the competition and completed questionnaires.[36] After the agencies had been evaluated, several of them, including Vickers & Benson and BCP, were invited to make presentations to the selection committee on September 14 and 15, 1994. Following these presentations, the selection committee prepared its report, dated September 19, 1994, addressed to Tourism Canada, in which it indicated that Vickers & Benson had been given the highest score of 529 points and had been rated by all the members of the committee as the best agency for this contract. BCP had the second highest score of 509 points and was rated in second place by five out of six members.[37] The report concludes as follows:

Committee Recommendation

> On the basis of the review described, the Committee wishes to make the following recommendation:
>
>> That Vickers & Benson of Toronto be awarded the advertising/communications contracts for Tourism Canada.
>
>> Should Tourism Canada wish or have a need for more than one agency, the Committee recommends that the additional agency(ies) be selected based on the ranking established by the Committee.[38]

The report was submitted to the Honourable John Manley, Minister of Industry Canada, who approved it.[39] The letter from the DM seeking his approval contains the following paragraphs:

> The department agrees with the Committee's findings and recommends that you approve the selection of Vickers and Benson of Toronto as the agency responsible for the United States component of our tourism marketing program. If any additional funding is provided for that market, it would be added to their contract.
>
> Given the possibility of additional funding being allocated to tourism marketing for a domestic program, we recommend that if such funding is provided, you approve the selection of BCP Advertising as the agency responsible for that program.[40]

A letter dated October 6, 1994, addressed to BCP,[41] advises it that another agency had been chosen to act as Tourism Canada's advertising agency, but Yves Gougoux, the president of BCP, testifies that his agency has no record of having received the letter.

On October 25, 1994, Prime Minister Chrétien made a speech to a tourism industry conference in which he announced a significant increase in government funding for tourism advertising.[42] In the weeks following, PWGSC awarded contracts to Vickers & Benson for Tourism Canada's advertising programs in the United States and the Pacific Rim, while BCP was awarded the contract for advertising in Canada.[43]

Although Mr. Guité expressed the opinion in his testimony that BCP was awarded this contract, which brought it over $65 million in government business over the next decade,[44] as a result of Mr. Gougoux's direct intervention with the Prime Minister or the PMO, this allegation is totally unsubstantiated and flatly denied by Mr. Gougoux. The notes made by personnel of the Office of the Auditor General of a telephone interview they had with Tom Penney of Tourism Canada were introduced into evidence.[45] Mr. Penney is reported as saying that there had been an intervention with the PMO by Mr. Gougoux, but this affirmation does not appear to be based upon personal knowledge of the alleged intervention and is probably the result of what Mr. Penney had been told by Mr. Guité. His statements, not made under oath, represent hearsay evidence which is not reliable. The Commission is not persuaded that any such intervention took place, and has no reason to disbelieve Mr. Gougoux's testimony.

Nevertheless, the procedure leading up to the awarding of a contract to BCP was flawed. If the intention of APORS was to award contracts to more than one agency, the notice of the competition should have so stated, and the reference to "required substantial knowledge of the U.S. market" may have discouraged some prospective applicants, possessing Canadian experience only, from participating in the competition.

Although there is no evidence of any impropriety committed by BCP, the way in which it obtained the Tourism Canada contract led to suspicions, unfounded in fact but nonetheless damaging to its reputation, that it obtained the contract because of its well-known connections to the Liberal Party of Canada, for which it has repeatedly worked during election campaigns. Such suspicions also tend to undermine the confidence of the public that advertising contracts are to be awarded on the basis of the capacity and experience of the agency concerned, and not on the basis of its political connections. The Commission agrees with the Auditor General that the availability of substantial new funding for Tourism Canada advertising activities in Canada as well as in the United States made it necessary to hold a new competition, open to all interested parties, in which the new objectives of Tourism Canada were clearly stated.[46]

The Auditor General's review of advertising contracts also included irregularities with respect to Justice Canada's firearms advertising campaign, Industry Canada's advertising campaign for the Year 2000 ("SOS 2000") and the advertising campaign related to the *Clarity Act* ("Project lumière"). These irregularities will be more fully discussed later in this Report in relation to Jean Brault, Gilles-André Gosselin and Paul Coffin.[47]

5·7
Use of Communication Agencies for Sponsorships

Since the personnel within PWGSC handling advertising were insufficient in number to administer by themselves the events and projects that were to be sponsored, they had always used communication agencies for this purpose. The agency was paid a commission as compensation for managing the sponsorship. Mr. Guité believed that 15% of the amount of the sponsorship was the industry-standard commission rate payable for the placement of advertising in the media, and gave no thought to the possibility of negotiating, or attempting to negotiate, a lower commission rate, even for sponsorships of great value.[48] As will be seen, employing a standard commission rate of 15% sometimes resulted in ludicrously exaggerated commissions being paid to agencies that often had little to do in exchange for this compensation.

When the sponsorship contract required the agency to do creative work such as designing posters or writing promotional material, the agency was allowed to charge additional sums for such work, based upon various hourly rates for the personnel employed, depending upon the skills and experience of each of them.[49] There was no price competition in the area of production costs; they were usually loosely estimated in advance, and generally the invoices to the Government for production costs were almost identical to the amount of the estimate. No written estimates were requested from the agency, and no records were kept as to the basis upon which PWGSC calculated the estimates.

In its Inquiry, the Commission discovered no instances in which an agency refused to accept a sponsorship contract on the basis that the remuneration for its services would be inadequate to cover its costs. Everything learned in the course of the Inquiry indicates that the agencies considered the fees and commissions offered to them by PWGSC to be generous. By now we know that the owners of the agencies that handled most sponsorship contracts became very wealthy very rapidly.[50]

5.8
The Agency of Record (AOR)

In the advertising industry, particularly when the advertising agency is engaged to place advertisements for the Government in the media such as newspapers, magazines, television and radio, the usual practice is to use the services of an Agency of Record, described in industry parlance as an AOR, in addition to the advertising agency engaged to design and place the advertising content. The function of an AOR is to receive in advance from the advertiser or client (in this case, the Government) the amount of the contract price and to disburse this amount for the cost of the media placement only after it had been verified to the satisfaction of the AOR that the advertisements had in fact appeared. At that time the commission and any other fees due to the advertising agency would also be paid to it by the AOR, which would retain a 3% commission for its services. In effect, therefore, the advertising agency would receive net commissions of 12%.

Dating back to the previous administration, the Government's AOR had been Genesis Media of Toronto. There was an AOR competition in February 1995. Genesis was the winner, and it was given a three-year contract with an option to renew for two more years.[51] On September 23, 1997, Mr. Guité advised Genesis Media that APORS would not be extending the existing AOR agreement and that a new competition would be held.[52]

Only two agencies, Genesis Media and a consortium in which Groupe Everest had an interest,[53] out of the 24 agencies that had expressed an interest in the competition, were invited to make presentations to the selection committee chaired by Mr. Guité. The consortium was chosen to be the Government's AOR, but the AOR contract was signed with another entity, Média/IDA Vision Inc.[54]

At the outset of the Sponsorship Program, PWGSC did not require the use of an AOR. Each agency employed to manage a sponsorship event was given the responsibility of disbursing, on behalf of the Government, the sum due to the promoter of the sponsored event. However, starting on April 1, 1998, it was decided to use an AOR for sponsorship contracts.[55] The evidence does not disclose who made that decision, or for what reason; probably it was Mr. Guité. From April 1, 1998, until the end of the Sponsorship Program, Média/IDA Vision earned commissions exceeding $3 million for its services as an AOR for sponsorship contracts.

5.9
Selection of Agencies in 1994 and 1995

On November 28, 1994, APORS published a public notice that the Department of Canadian Heritage (hereafter Heritage Canada) was seeking a full-service advertising agency "in support of its mandate to promote Canada's identity and its cultural and natural heritage." The notice specified that to be considered, agencies would have to be Canadian owned and controlled, and able to provide services to the Department's headquarters in Ottawa/Hull and to its regional offices in Vancouver, Calgary, Winnipeg, Toronto, Montreal and Halifax. Agencies would be expected to have ability and experience in advertising, marketing and related communication activities; the qualities required of successful candidates were then enumerated. It may be noted that the public notice did not refer to a selection process leading to the qualification of a number of advertising agencies, and that it indicated that one agency only was being sought.

The notice concluded by inviting interested agencies to mail or fax a one-page letter of intent to Heritage Canada, in return for which agencies would receive a capability questionnaire. "A short list will be developed from the responses received," the notice read.

It should be noted that the notice was silent as to the specific work requirements of the successful agency, how long its services would be required, how candidates would be evaluated and how many agencies were needed; as already noted, the indication is that only one agency was to be selected.

Seventy agencies submitted letters of interest and were sent questionnaires, of which 31 were completed and submitted.[56]

To evaluate the questionnaires, a selection committee was formed. Mr. Guité acted as chairman. The committee was composed of six members, of whom two were representatives of APORS, Andrée LaRose and Mario Parent, who had been designated by Mr. Guité; two were representatives of Heritage Canada; and two were representatives of the private sector.[57] When the committee had completed an evaluation of the questionnaires, ten agencies were put on a short list and were invited to make presentations to the selection committee on either February 2 or February 3, 1995. Four agencies made presentations on February 2 and five on February 3; one agency on the short list decided to drop out of the competition and not make a presentation.[58]

The Heritage Canada representatives on the selection committee on February 2, 1995, were unable to return and continue on February 3, and were not replaced.[59] Uniformity in the evaluation process must necessarily have suffered as a result.

Of the agencies making presentations on February 2, McKim Communications had the best score, but Scott Thornley was within the 10% margin and was also chosen to be on the pre-qualified suppliers list. All five agencies that made presentations on the second day were selected. They were Groupe Everest, BCP Canada, Compass Communications, Palmer Jarvis Communications and Vickers & Benson.[60]

On March 6, 1995, a memorandum was sent to the Minister of Heritage Canada, advising him of the results of the competition. The Minister signed the document, indicating his agreement with the recommendation that seven agencies had been selected to be on the pre-qualified suppliers list.[61]

On an unspecified date following these events, Mr. Guité wrote a memorandum to Andrée LaRose,[62] which appears in Figure V-3.

Figure V-3: Letter from Chuck Guité to Andrée LaRose

MEMO

To: Director of APORS

From: Director General, APORS

Subject: Canadian Heritage agency competition

Please note that the Canadian Heritage agency selection seeking full service agencies in support of its mandate to promote Canada's identity and its cultural and natural heritage has been extended for PWGSC-APORS to support their various sponsorship and partnership programs and other communication initiatives.

The 5 firms selected following the February 3, 1995 presentations (Groupe Everest from Montreal, Quebec, BCP Canada Inc. from Montreal, Quebec, Compass Communications Inc. from Halifax, N.S., Palmer Jarvis Advertising Communications from Vancouver, B.C. and Vickers & Benson Companies Ltd. from Toronto, Ontario) will be included on PWGSC-APORS's qualified supplier list for possible communication/advertising contracts on behalf of APORS.

C. Guité, Director General

In his testimony, Mr. Guité states that the use of the Heritage Canada list of suppliers by PWGSC was decided upon during the pre-referendum period, in consultation with public servants in the Privy Council Office who were working on unity and pre-referendum strategy.[63] Mr. Guité and Ms. LaRose both acknowledge that the conversion of the Heritage Canada list of pre-qualified suppliers into a list to be used by PWGSC was irregular and did not respect the requirements of Appendix Q. No competitive agency-selection procedure whatsoever led to the qualification of suppliers of advertising services to PWGSC.

Neither Mr. Guité nor Ms. LaRose explained why only five of the seven firms on the Heritage Canada list were declared to be qualified as suppliers of advertising services to PWGSC.[64] It may be noted that of the five agencies qualified for PWGSC, three of them (Groupe Everest, BCP Canada and Vickers & Benson) were well known to have been closely associated with the election campaign of the Liberal Party in 1993.

Lafleur Communication Marketing (hereafter Lafleur Communication) was not put on the pre-qualified suppliers list for either Heritage Canada or PWGSC in the competition of February 2-3, 1995. Nevertheless, commencing February 9, 1995, and up to June 30, 1995, Lafleur Communication received an important number of contracts for advertising services from PWGSC, totalling $1,873,998.[65] In his testimony, Mr. Guité could not explain how and why Lafleur Communication would have received contracts without being on a pre-qualified suppliers list.[66] Probably someone woke up to the fact that an unqualified agency was receiving a substantial number of contracts, because an advertising agency competition was announced by a notice requiring letters of interest by March 27, 1995, from agencies wishing to be considered.[67] The notice announces that PWGSC "is seeking a full-service national advertising agency to provide a complete range of advertising services," but is otherwise silent as to the nature of the services to be provided.

Fifty-eight agencies expressed interest in the competition and completed the questionnaires provided to them.[68] Four agencies were placed on a short list and invited to make presentations. They were Allard Communication-Marketing, Cala Human Resources Canada, Lafleur Communication and Day Advertising Group Inc.[69] The Lafleur candidate was in fact a consortium consisting of Compass Communications, Allard Communications, Freeman Rodgers Battaglia, SKS Advertising and Lafleur Communication.[70]

The selection committee's final report indicates that Lafleur Communication (Consortium) was recommended as the agency for PWGSC. This report, dated June 30, 1995, must have received the endorsement of the Minister because Mr. Jean Lafleur was duly advised on July 6, 1995, that his agency had won the competition.[71]

Many questions about this competition remain unanswered. Since the Lafleur agency was already receiving a substantial number of advertising contracts from PWGSC, the suspicion lingers that the objective of the competition was to qualify the Lafleur agency as quickly as possible to remedy, to the extent possible, the irregularity of granting contracts to an unqualified supplier. The 54 out of 58 agencies that completed questionnaires but were not invited to make presentations to the selection committee must have wondered what they had to do to be given a real chance to bid for government advertising business from PWGSC. In the Heritage Canada competition only a few months earlier, ten agencies out of 31 that completed the questionnaires were invited to make presentations.

There is no explanation as to why only one agency was selected in June 1995 when seven were selected for Heritage Canada in March 1995.[72]

It is a reasonable inference from the foregoing that the competition held by PWGSC in June 1995 was a sham and that the result of the competition had been predetermined.

5.10
Selection of Agencies in 1997 and 2001

If the agency-selection process followed in 1995 gives rise to doubts and suspicions about the fairness and legitimacy of the results obtained, the "competition" held in 1997 was even worse.

At the beginning of March 1997, Mr. Guité decided that a new competition was necessary to select agencies to meet the communication and advertising needs of APORS, which was by now involved in awarding an enormous number of sponsorship contracts. It needed the assistance of more communication agencies than it had at its disposal as a result of the previous competitions held in 1995.[73]

A notice was duly published, questionnaires were sent out, completed and evaluated, and a short list of ten agencies resulted. These agencies were scheduled to make presentations before a selection committee on April 22 and 23, 1997, in Toronto, and on April 25, 1997, in Montreal.[74] Mr. Mario Parent had been designated by Mr. Guité to act as chairman of the selection committee and to run the competition, but due to last-minute absences, the selection committee was reduced to only two persons, Mr. Parent and a representative of the private sector, Mr. Louis Cattapan.[75]

Mr. Parent testifies that this was the smallest selection committee he had ever seen. There should normally have been, in addition to the chairman, two representatives of the private sector and two representatives of the department concerned, which in this case was PWGSC itself. When he protested to Mr. Guité that the competition should be postponed to a later date to allow a fully staffed selection committee to be empanelled, he was told that the matter could not be delayed and to proceed to hear the presentations of the agencies on the short list. Reluctantly, Mr. Parent agreed to do so.[76]

The presentations made were carefully evaluated by Mr. Parent and Mr. Cattapan. The scores varied from a high of 179 points for Groupaction

Marketing to a low of 120 for Goodman Communications.[77] Mr. Parent expected that the four or five best candidates would be retained, but when he discussed the results of the competition with Mr. Guité, the latter told him that the needs of the department were such that there would be work for everyone and that all ten agencies should be recommended. Mr. Parent, who was not the sort of person to go against the explicit wishes of his superior, made the recommendation that he had been instructed to make, and all ten firms became qualified to receive communication contracts from PWGSC.[78]

Among the ten firms recommended are names that figure prominently in later revelations concerning the Sponsorship Program, such as Groupaction Marketing, Communication Coffin, and Gosselin and Associates.[79]

What is referred to as the 1997 competition was not in fact a competition at all. All of the agencies making presentations, even those scoring very poorly in comparison to others, became qualified. It may be concluded that Mr. Guité had determined in advance that more assistance from agencies in managing sponsorship contracts was needed, and the fact was overlooked that at least some of the candidates making presentations had relatively poor capabilities. The government policy to ensure that advertising contracts were let through a competitive process was simply disregarded.

In 2001, PWGSC issued a standing offer bid to agencies interested in providing sponsorship or advertising services.[80] Nine responding agencies were invited to make presentations to the selection committee, five of which were involved in the period covered by the 2000 audit.[81] After evaluating the presentations, the committee recommended to Mr. Gagliano that standing offers be issued to all nine, and he approved the recommendation.[82] Of course, a competition where everybody wins is not really a competition at all.

5.11
Advertising Policy Following Cancellation of Appendix Q

During the Commission's hearings, a representative of Communication Canada testified that, before it was dismantled, the organization had tried very hard to bring order to the clearly deficient procurement process for sponsorship and advertising. The problem was compounded by the obscurity of the text of Appendix Q. In fact, the same witness agreed that Appendix Q "was not a model of clarity" and that its text was "a complicated way of saying something that could have been said much more simply."[83] It is reassuring to learn that communication in plain language is a stated objective of the Government's new Communications Policy that came into effect November 29, 2004.[84]

The reforms and initiatives introduced by Communication Canada included the cancellation of Appendix Q in December 2002. The revised Communications Policy includes provisions dealing with advertising activities. The current management of advertising activities represents an attempt by the Government to correct the problems revealed by the Auditor General and the evidence disclosed in the course of this Commission's inquiry.

The success or failure of the new policy will be one of the subjects of study in Phase II of the Commission's work. That reform was needed was obvious, not only within the Government but to the Canadian advertising industry, which wrote to the President of the Treasury Board on July 30, 2002, as follows:

It is timely and critical for the Government to adopt a new system to replace a model that is fraught with problems and abuse and has a reputation in the industry and the public for being subject to inappropriate political influence.[85]

Endnotes to Chapter V

[1] Testimony of Ms. Tremblay, Transcripts vol. 21, pp. 3455-3458 (OF), pp. 3451-3453 (E); Testimony of Mr. Parent, Transcripts vol. 31, pp. 5440-5444 (OF), pp. 5435-5438 (E); Testimony of Ms. LaRose, Transcripts vol. 27, pp. 4640-4642 (OF), p. 4645 (E); vol. 30, pp. 5138-5140 (OF), pp. 5136-5137 (E); Testimony of Mr. Guité, Transcripts vol. 33, p. 5622 (OE), pp. 5624-2625 (F).

[2] Testimony of Mr. Guité, Transcripts vol. 33, pp. 5622-5624 (OE), pp. 5624-5628 (F).

[3] Testimony of Mr. Pelletier, Transcripts vol. 71, p. 12337 (OF), p. 12334 (E); Exhibit P-210(A), p. 9.

[4] Testimony of Mr. Guité, Transcripts vol. 108, pp. 19786-19787 (OE), p. 19800 (F).

[5] Exhibit P-186(A), tab 8, pp. 39-43.

[6] Testimony of Mr. Dingwall, Transcripts vol. 60, pp. 10562-10565 (OE), pp. 10564-10568 (F).

[7] Exhibit P-210(A), pp. 13-36.

[8] Exhibit P-103(A), tab 8.

[9] Exhibit P-186(A), p. 68.

[10] Testimony of Mr. Guité, Transcripts vol. 33, pp. 5658-5659, 5693-5701, 5705, 5741-5742 (OE), pp. 5664-5665, 5705-5714, 5718, 5759 (F); vol. 108, p. 19784 (OE), p. 19797 (F); Exhibit P-103(A), tab 21.

[11] Exhibit P-103(A), pp. 146-147.

[12] Exhibit P-103(A), pp. 141-143.

[13] Testimony of Mr. Dingwall, Transcripts vol. 60, pp. 10574-10575 (OE), pp. 10578-10579 (F).

[14] Testimony of Mr. Guité, Transcripts vol. 108, pp. 19786-19789 (OE), pp. 19799-19800 (F).

[15] Testimony of Mr. Neville, Transcripts vol. 41, pp. 6976-6978 (OE), pp. 6974-6977 (F).

[16] Testimony of Mr. Dingwall, Transcripts vol. 60, p. 10574 (OE), p. 10578 (F).

[17] Testimony of Mr. Neville, Transcripts vol. 41, p. 6977 (OE), p. 6976 (F).

[18] Exhibit 186A, pp. 149, 150.

[19] Testimony of Mr. Dingwall, Transcripts vol. 60, p. 10675 (OE), p. 10579 (F).

[20] Exhibit P-16(A), tab 1, pp. 7-19 (E), pp. 20-32 (F).

[21] Exhibit C-103(B), p. 516.

[22] Exhibit P-16(B), p. 48.

[23] Exhibit P-208(E), p. 84.

[24] Exhibit P-103(B), p. 516. Exhibit P-16(A), p. 172.

[25] Exhibit P-188, p. 49.

[26] Exhibit P-103(B), pp. 462-464, 466, 504, 542, 548, 560.

[27] Exhibit P-428(A), p. 20.

[28] Testimony of Mr. Guité, Transcripts vol. 111, p. 20322 (OE), p. 20327 (F).

[29] For example, see Testimony of Mr. Neville, Transcripts vol. 41, pp. 7028-7029 (OE), pp. 7031-7032 (F); Testimony of Mr. Quail, Transcripts vol. 41, p. 6870 (OE), p. 6870 (F); Testimony of Mr. Stobbe,

Transcripts, vol. 40, p. 6895 (OE), 6896-6897 (F).

30 Exhibit P-210(A), pp. 86-87.

31 Exhibit P-103(B), tab 4, p. 363.

32 Exhibit P-103(B), p. 391.

33 Exhibit P-103(B), p. 445.

34 Reproduced in Appendix B to this Report.

35 Exhibit P-413, p. 2.

36 Exhibit P-413, p. 34, has an example.

37 Exhibit P-424, p. 263.

38 Exhibit P-424, p. 266.

39 Exhibit P-424, pp. 268-269.

40 Exhibit P-424, p. 269.

41 Exhibit P-424, p. 271.

42 Exhibit P-424, pp. 291-292.

43 Exhibit P-424, p. 293.

44 Exhibit 428(A), pp. 176-177.

45 Exhibit C-375, pp. 103-104.

46 Office of the Auditor General of Canada, *Report of the Auditor General to the House of Commons: Government-Wide Audit of Sponsorship, Advertising, and Public Opinion Research* (Minister of Public Works and Government Services Canada 2003), chapter 4, p. 6.

47 Chapters IX, XII and XIII, respectively.

48 Testimony of Mr. Guité, Transcripts vol. 33, pp. 5658-5661 (OE), pp. 5664-5667 (F).

49 See, for example, Exhibit P-219(A), p. 11.

50 Exhibit P-428(A), pp. 86-87, 94-95, 116-117, 125, 130-132, 155-156, 165-166.

51 Exhibit P-55, tab 11.

52 Exhibit P-56, tab 1, p. 2.

53 Testimony of Mr. Guité, Transcripts vol. 33, pp. 5785-5787 (OE), pp. 5808-5810 (F).

54 Exhibit P-56, tabs 15 and 16.

55 Testimony of Ms. LaRose, Transcripts, vol. 29, pp. 5068-5070 (OF), 5067-5069 (E); Exhibit P-428(A), pp. 57-58.

56 Exhibit P-19, tabs 1-3.

57 Testimony of Ms. LaRose, Transcripts, vol. 28, pp. 4862-4863 (OF), pp. 4870-4872 (E).

58 Exhibit P-19, tabs 4-6, 8-10.

59 Testimony of Mr. Parent, Transcripts vol. 32, pp. 5542-5543 (OF), pp. 5527-5528 (E); Testimony of Mr. Guité, Transcripts vol. 33, p. 5795 (OE), p. 5816 (F).

60 Exhibit P-19, tab 14.

61 Exhibit P-19, tab 17.

62 Exhibit P-19, tab 20.

63 Testimony of Mr. Guité, Transcripts vol. 33, p. 5800 (OE), pp. 5823-5824 (F).

64   Testimony of Mr. Guité, Transcripts vol. 33, pp. 5799-5800 (OE), p. 5823 (F); Testimony of Ms. LaRose, Transcripts vol. 28, pp. 4896-4897 (OF), pp. 4887-4888 (E).

65   Exhibit P-107, tab 1.

66   Testimony of Mr. Guité, Transcripts vol. 34, pp. 5805-5806, 5850-5851 (OE), pp. 5805-5807, 5856-5857 (F).

67   Exhibit P-19, tab 21.

68   Exhibit P-19, tab 23.

69   Exhibit P-19, tab 24.

70   Exhibit P-62, pp. 6-7.

71   Exhibit P-19, tabs 25 and 26.

72   Testimony of Ms. LaRose, Transcripts vol. 28, pp. 4896-4897(OF), p. 4888(E); vol. 30, pp. 5130-5131(OE), pp. 5132-5133(F); Testimony of Mr. Guité, Transcripts vol. 33, p. 5799 (OE), p. 5823(F).

73   Testimony of Mr. Guité, Transcripts vol. 34, pp. 5904-5905 (OE), p. 5914 (F).

74   Exhibit P-19, tabs 27, 29, 37 (E).

75   Exhibit P-19, tab 41 (E). Testimony of Mr. Parent, Transcripts, vol. 32, pp. 5546-5550 (OF), pp. 5531-5534 (E).

76   Testimony of Mr. Parent, Transcripts vol. 32, pp. 5546-5550 (OF), pp. 5531-5534 (E).

77   Exhibit P-19, tab 41 (E).

78   Testimony of Mr. Cournoyer, Transcripts vol. 32, pp. 5549-5551 (OF), pp. 5534-5536 (E).

79   Exhibit P-19, tab 41 (E).

80   Exhibit P-57, tab 2.

81   Exhibit P-57, tab 4 (namely, Groupe Everest, Gosselin, Lafleur, Groupaction and Coffin); Testimony of Mr. Lauzon, Transcripts vol. 26, pp. 4380-4384 (OF), 4374-4377 (E).

82   Exhibit P-57, tab 4.

83   Testimony of Ms. Forand, Transcripts vol. 42, p. 7195 (OE), p. 7196 (F).

84   Exhibit P–409(B1), p. 10.

85   P-196(B), p. 109.

CHAPTER VI

ADMINISTRATION OF THE
SPONSORSHIP PROGRAM

6.1
Non-adherence to Rules and Procedures

Section 32(2) of the *Financial Administration Act*[1] (FAA) stipulates that any person charged with the administration of a program shall establish procedures and maintain records respecting the control of financial commitments to be made in connection with the program. Section 33(1) requires that any charge made against an appropriation shall be made by way of a requisition, leading to the signature of a contract binding upon the Government. In each case the procedures, records and requisitions must be made in the manner prescribed by the Treasury Board, which, to guide public servants, has adopted a voluminous Contracting Policy[2] that is binding upon all persons authorized to enter into contracts on behalf of the Government of Canada. The Contracting Policy is supplemented by Regulations authorized by section 160 of the FAA which have been promulgated and are regularly amended. It takes patience and perseverance to read through and to try to comprehend this mass of law, regulation policy and guidelines, which was, in the case of advertising contracts, further regulated by Appendix Q to the Contracting Policy.[3]

It is beyond the scope of the present Report to make a complete analysis of the Government's contracting regime established by the FAA, Government Contracts Regulations, Contracting Policy, and Policy on Delegation of Authorities. At the risk of oversimplification, its requirements, which are binding upon all public servants who contract to purchase goods and services, include:

- a preliminary assessment of the contract requirements and the probable cost of the goods or services, followed by a call for tenders if the amount of the proposed contract exceeds $25,000; if less than $25,000, there should be a call for tenders whenever it is cost effective to do so and a negotiation of price with the proposed supplier in the event of no call for tenders;[4]

- signature on a requisition or contract, to be made by the person having knowledge of the proposed transaction and possessing the necessary delegated authority to engage the Government in the amount in question;[5]

- a separation of functions, so that different persons negotiate the contract, verify its deliverables and authorize payment;[6]

- certification prior to payment in accordance with section 34 of the FAA, by someone having personal knowledge that the work has been performed, the goods supplied or the services rendered, after verification that the price charged is in accordance with the contract, or reasonable if the contract does not stipulate a final price; and

- decisions, reports and authorizations be on file and in writing.[7]

The objective of sections 26 to 41 of the FAA and of Treasury Board's Contracting Policy is to acquire goods and services and carry out construction in a manner that results in best value to the Crown and Canadians.[8]

As indicated in the Report of the Auditor General, these requirements were not systematically followed by the public servants who handled contracting and payment in relation to the Sponsorship Program. Many of them were systematically *not* followed. The failure to fulfill these requirements is so well documented by the Auditor General, whose Report is substantially unchallenged, that it is unnecessary to review in detail the evidence heard by the Commission on this subject. All of the evidence heard by the Commission tends to confirm the findings of the Auditor General.

6.2
Problems of Accountability and Direction

Of greater importance for the purposes of this Inquiry are the reasons why public servants who were perceived by the Commission to be ordinarily competent and honest repeatedly and systematically failed to observe the elementary requirements of their employment. For the most part, they followed the direct instructions of Mr. Guité; if he instructed a subordinate to sign a contract or approve a payment without paying attention to the requirements of the FAA, the subordinate did so without questioning why he or she was being told to do something they knew was not in conformity with the law or Treasury Board policies.[9]

The only subordinate who challenged Mr. Guité's authority when he was told not to follow required procedures was Mr. Allan Cutler, and the consequences of his defiance were immediate and dramatic; his continued employment in the public service was put in jeopardy,[10] and his prospects for promotion or advancement disappeared. Although Mr. Guité's threat to fire Mr. Cutler received no reprimand or reproach, it should have been obvious to his superiors that Mr. Guité had exceeded his authority. It seemed apparent to everyone working under him that because he was regularly receiving instructions directly from Minister Dingwall or Minister Gagliano, and because he had direct access to persons in the PMO, including the Chief of Staff of the Prime Minister, Mr. Guité was no longer subject to the authority and direction of his immediate superior, either Mr. Neville or Mr. Stobbe, nor was he subject to the authority and oversight of the Deputy Minister. He was, in their eyes and in the eyes of everyone in the public service, in a special category, seemingly exempt from the usual reporting rules, and not obliged to conform to normal practices and procedures.

Indeed, Mr. Guité had acquired a reputation among politicians and senior bureaucrats as the person in the public service able to cut through red tape and achieve results rapidly, without the usual restrictions and paperwork which are characteristic of a normal bureaucracy, but which are generally deemed necessary for the prudent administration of public funds.

From the perspective of the people working under him, he was the person hand-picked by the PMO, with the knowledge and approval of the PCO, to direct the Sponsorship Program. His authority was all the greater because, contrary to the usual practice and in spite of the requirement of section 32(2) of the FAA, no clear directions about the objectives of the Program, about the criteria for admissibility to its benefits, or about the procedures to be followed in its administration had been given to anyone, and in particular to Mr. Guité or his personnel. This left him free to handle the Program and to make decisions as he saw fit.

Mr. Guité's job descriptions include statements that he was "in continual contact with the Minister's Office," and "works with PCO, PMO and TBS to resolve issues."[11] These statements did not relieve Mr. Guité from his duty to report these contacts to his superiors and the Deputy Minister, nor did they authorize him to disregard Treasury Board guidelines and the Government's Contracting Policy. Regardless of the wording in job descriptions, public servants are supposed to respect normal lines of authority. Many public servants provide advice and assistance to their Ministers and exempt staff, and even to the PMO, without bypassing in any way their immediate superiors in the way Mr. Guité did.

6.3
Lack of In-house Expertise in Sponsorship Programs

An additional factor should be mentioned. The Sponsorship Program was like no other in the sense that government officials were procuring the services of communication agencies which were being paid to supervise the administration of sponsored events and projects. The procurement of advertising services was an area of activity with which the people in APORS were familiar, but they had no particular experience or expertise in the procurement of these "other" agency services. The employees of APORS were uncomfortable in this new field of endeavour and would have preferred to receive specialized training and clear directions as to how to proceed.[12]   In their testimony, they say they were confused and uncertain as to their duties and responsibilities; and in the absence of written guidelines to assist them to know what was expected of them, they chose to follow blindly the oral instructions of Mr. Guité, assuming that he knew what he was doing and had authority to proceed as he did. The subordinate personnel in APORS and CCSB failed miserably to perform the tasks assigned to them in conformity with the law and Treasury Board policies, but fairness dictates that, when assessing their conduct, consideration must be given to the above factors.

6.4
Choice of Events, Amounts and Agencies

Next to be considered is the performance of his duties by Mr. Guité himself. Let us begin by reviewing the procedure by which events and activities were either selected to receive sponsorship monies from the Government, or refused. This will necessitate findings with regard to contradictory evidence on a number of questions, including how and by whom communication agencies were selected to administer sponsored events on the Government's behalf. As we already know, prior to his retirement on August 31, 1999, there was no direction in writing given to Mr. Guité or to the public servants working under his direction, by the PMO, the PCO, his Minister, his Deputy Minister Mr. Quail or anyone else on how to select events and amounts for sponsorships.[13] The only guidance he ever received with respect to the selection of agencies to handle sponsorship contracts was Appendix Q, and, as detailed in the preceding chapter, it was simply not followed.

There was no public announcement of the Government's decision to increase its visibility by sponsoring events and activities through PWGSC. It was left up to Mr. Guité to locate promoters of events who would be willing, for a price, to allow the federal government to display the Canadian flag or its wordmark or other advertising material in a prominent way at such events. He also considered other projects, such as the Bluenose project by which the reconstruction of the famous schooner would sail up the St. Lawrence River and Seaway at government expense, to give prominence to a recognized Canadian symbol. In his testimony, Mr. Guité is unclear about the methods he used to seek out willing participants, but it may be deduced from the facts established by the evidence that it was not difficult for him to find prospective "sponsorees." In 1996-97, all the events sponsored, with the exception of the series broadcast on Chinese television (discussed later in this chapter), were managed by Lafleur Communication. Although Mr. Jean Lafleur says that he has no recollection of how it happened that his agency suddenly began to receive millions of dollars of federal government contracts,[14] we may safely assume that at some point in time he had conversations with Mr. Guité, during which those contracts were discussed and negotiated before they were concluded.

6.5
PMO Involvement

It is also apparent that the first list of events, showing the amounts to be paid to the promoter of each event, which must surely have been drawn up by Mr. Guité after discussions with Mr. Lafleur, was submitted by Mr. Guité to Mr. Pelletier before it was put into its final form and annexed to the corresponding Treasury Board submission.[15]

Mr. Pelletier testifies that he had only one face-to-face meeting with Mr. Guité in 1996, on April 16, when Mr. Guité was introduced to him by Mr. Jean Carle, the Prime Minister's Director of Operations, who knew Mr. Guité from the time when Mr. Dingwall was the Minister of PWGSC. Mr. Pelletier says he has no clear recollection of what was discussed at that meeting,[16] but it may fairly be assumed that Mr. Guité informed Mr. Pelletier, then or shortly thereafter, that he was budgeting for sponsorships totalling $17 million for the current year, because that amount appears on the draft Treasury Board submission dated April 22, 1996, signed by Minister Marleau. Because that draft submission included a line for the signature of the Prime Minister,[17] it must have had the approval of Mr. Pelletier, and in order to fix the financial requirements at $17 million, Mr. Guité must have made some sort of a preliminary enumeration of the projects he had in mind, and of the amounts to be allocated to each.

The first list of proposed projects in writing that was produced in evidence is attached to a note dated May 14, 1996, sent to Mr. Carle by Andrée LaRose, reading as follows:

> [Unofficial Translation]
>
> May 14, 1996
>
> Dear Mr. Carle:
>
> Here is a breakdown of the costs in the submission to Treasury Board in the amount of $17 million. The asterisks identify the projects for which funds have already been committed and cannot be changed. These projects are all represented in the First Phase.
>
> Total sponsorship activities figuring in the First Phase amount to $17 million.
>
> We have identified the additional sponsorship activities that figure in the Second Phase. If any of these activities are of greater interest to you, please let me know.
>
> Once you have had a chance to read the document, I would like to discuss it with you. Do not hesitate to contact me...
>
> Thank you,
>
>
> Andrée LaRose
> Encl.

The list attached to the note covers eight pages. The first five pages describe sponsorship projects already agreed to or under consideration totalling $17,022,000, and include several which were subsequently dropped from the list. The three remaining pages describe events for which amounts totalling $6,393,000 are suggested. The same list was sent by Mr. Guité to Minister Marleau's Executive Assistant and to Mr. Stobbe.[18]

On May 29, 1996, Éric Lafleur, the vice-president of Lafleur Communication, the agency which handled all sponsorship contracts for PWGSC in 1996-97, sent by fax to Ms. LaRose a detailed list of sponsored events which were to be managed by Lafleur,[19] some of which were already the subject of contracts with APORS,[20] although funding had not yet been approved. One can reasonably conclude that APORS was under pressure to conclude sponsorship contracts rapidly since many of the events to be sponsored were scheduled to take place during the summer months, and visibility plans and other arrangements with the promoters of the events had to be concluded immediately.

The lists sent by Éric Lafleur to Ms. LaRose include details of the commissions and production costs to be paid to the agency, but there is no evidence that this information was communicated to the PMO.

The first list which exactly corresponds to what was later attached to the Treasury Board Précis of October 1, 1996, is attached to a memo dated August 27, 1996, sent by Mr. Guité to Roger Collet in anticipation of the latter's meeting on that same date with Mr. Pelletier. By that time, over $11 million in sponsorships had been either paid out already or firmly committed.[21] The entire allotment of $17 million was disbursed before March 31, 1997; by that time, planning for the next fiscal year was already well advanced.

In 1997-98, a second allotment of $17 million from the Unity Reserve was supplemented by additional sums of money provided by PWGSC's own budget, by amounts transferred to PWGSC from the Canada Information Office or Heritage Canada, or by amounts transferred from other departments. However, the evidence remains fragmentary as to how the events found their way initially onto Mr. Guité's list, or how the amount to be allotted to each event was determined.

In the years following the initial year of the Program, a pattern developed. Knowledge of the existence of the Sponsorship Program seems to have spread by word of mouth, or as a result of visual evidence of the Government's sponsorships. Mr. Chrétien testifies that as far as he was concerned, it was not necessary to make any public announcement concerning the Program, since its existence was obvious to anyone who could see the federal government's flags and posters at public events;[22] but most of his Ministers testify that they did not become aware of the existence of the Program until it became a subject of public comment and controversy in 2001. Most testified they became aware of some sort of spending on events, but not of the "Sponsorship Program."[23]

There was no shortage of requests for sponsorships. Requests for sponsorships came to APORS or its successor, CCSB, from various sources: from either the promoter of an event or from an agency representing a promoter; from the Minister or someone in his office; or from another Minister or a Member of Parliament. They came directly to Mr. Guité and his personnel or were redirected to APORS from other sources.[24] An annual master list would be prepared, after eliminating requests that were obviously inappropriate or unjustified. Mr. Guité says he took it upon himself to decide on the approval or rejection of most of the smaller requests for less than $25,000, but that all applications for greater amounts were decided in consultation with Mr. Pelletier or Mr. Gagliano. The master list was prepared at the beginning of the fiscal year and would usually exceed the amount of the budget available. It would be modified on a number of occasions as the year progressed. Some proportion of the annual budget for sponsorships would be held in reserve for last-minute additions that were considered important.[25]

Mr. Guité says that periodically he would meet with Mr. Pelletier, sometimes in the presence of Mr. Carle, and they would go over lists of proposed sponsorships, which would be approved after modifications suggested by Mr. Pelletier. Mr. Guité took those suggestions to be instructions.[26] When he returned to his office after a meeting, he gave his staff instructions to amend the master list in accordance with the decisions reached at the meeting.[27]

6.6
Involvement of Minister Gagliano

When Mr. Gagliano became Minister, Mr. Guité's periodic meetings were at first with both Mr. Pelletier and Mr. Gagliano. After a time, Mr. Pelletier attended the meetings less often.[28] He continued to meet fairly frequently with Mr. Guité, as appears from entries in his own agenda[29] and as stated by Mr. Guité. This is evidence that Mr. Pelletier continued to provide guidance to the Sponsorship Program. The meetings with Mr. Gagliano proceeded as they had previously, with Mr. Gagliano making suggestions and giving instructions on events, amounts and the agencies to be used in each instance.[30]

Both Mr. Pelletier and Mr. Gagliano acknowledge that meetings with Mr. Guité to review lists of proposed sponsorships took place from time to time, although they do not agree with Mr. Guité's testimony with respect to the frequency of such meetings. Mr. Guité's testimony concerning the frequency of the meetings is substantially corroborated by the testimony of the persons who worked for him, such as Huguette Tremblay, Andrée LaRose and Mario Parent, all of whom have absolutely no reason or incentive to lie or to mislead the Commission in this respect. They saw Mr. Guité leave his office for these meetings, and they saw him return some time later, telling his subordinates that he had had such meetings, that decisions had been made, and that the lists as revised and approved were now ready to be implemented. It is unlikely that Mr. Guité's subordinates would invent these stories, and even more unlikely that Mr. Guité would have gone through an elaborate pretense of going to a meeting with Mr. Pelletier or Mr. Gagliano so as to mislead his own subordinates, for no purpose whatsoever. Accordingly, Mr. Guité's testimony concerning the number of meetings he had with Mr. Pelletier and Mr. Gagliano is accepted. In particular, Mr. Gagliano's affirmations about the infrequency of his meetings with Mr. Guité are not believed.

There is a more important discrepancy between the versions of Mr. Guité and Mr. Pelletier concerning the former's assertion that his purpose in going to these meetings was not merely to obtain the approval of Mr. Pelletier for the events and amounts on the list. Mr. Guité says that Mr. Pelletier on these occasions also directed him to add or subtract events and to modify the amounts to be granted to certain applicants. Mr. Pelletier denies that he gave approval or disapproval of the lists, or that he gave Mr. Guité such directions, saying that his only function at their meetings was to provide political advice or input with respect to the advisability of a particular sponsorship or amount. Mr. Pelletier testifies that the reason Mr. Guité came to him was only for political input, since Mr. Guité relied upon Mr. Pelletier's superior knowledge of Quebec politics and the need for greater visibility of the federal presence in the location of the proposed event. Mr. Pelletier, however, insists that final decisions were always left to Mr. Guité.[31]

This conflict in the evidence raises the issue of the credibility of Mr. Guité, an issue which consumed a good deal of time during the hearings. The issue comes up again in relation to another contradiction between the testimony of Mr. Pelletier and Mr. Guité. Mr. Guité testifies that Mr. Pelletier not only gave him instructions with respect to events and amounts for sponsorship projects, but also gave him directions with respect to the agencies which would be engaged to act on the Government's behalf. Mr. Guité repeated this assertion on a number of occasions.[32] Mr. Pelletier vigorously denies that he gave Mr. Guité directions about the use of agencies, or even that he made suggestions with respect to agency selection. Agency selection is a delicate subject because much of the public scandal concerning the Sponsorship Program is due to the enormous amount of money paid to communication agencies, reputed to be generous contributors to the Liberal Party of Canada. No one connected to the Liberal Party wants to be identified as the person who directed lucrative government contracts to those agencies.

Mr. Pelletier acknowledges that political input was being offered to Mr. Guité, not only on the question of the admissibility of events and projects seeking sponsorships, but also on the question of the amounts to be paid for sponsored events. The value to the Government of the visibility it might receive at a particular event or as a result of participating in a particular project is a matter of judgment for an expert in advertising, accustomed to evaluating the impact of posters, advertisements and publicity. Mr. Guité was reputed to be such an expert—to a much greater degree than Mr. Pelletier, who has greater expertise in political matters but no particular expertise in advertising. This raises the question of why, if Mr. Pelletier thought it was acceptable for him to offer advice or suggestions on the amounts to be paid to promoters of sponsorships, it was less acceptable for input to be offered on the choice of agencies, and the commissions and fees to be paid to them. Since the Commission accepts that Mr. Guité went to his meetings with Mr. Pelletier to obtain Mr. Pelletier's advice and suggestions about events and the amounts to be paid to sponsor them, it is hardly plausible that he and Mr. Pelletier would have studiously avoided any discussion or mention of the important question of which agency would be hired to manage the event or the project on behalf of the Government.

There is little documentary evidence to corroborate the evidence of either Mr. Guité or Mr. Pelletier with respect to the question of agency selection. According to Mr. Guité, the lists they discussed at their meetings identified the agencies to be used,[33] but none of the lists produced into the record of the Commission that were examined by Mr. Pelletier include the names of agencies. Many of the lists that were discussed at their meetings have been destroyed or cannot be located, but two should be mentioned because they are the only documents which tend to corroborate the testimony of either witness, and they have been the subject of comment.

A list of seven proposed sponsorships was sent by Mr. Guité to Mr. Gagliano, with a copy to Mr. Pelletier, on January 21, 1999, at a time when meetings with both Mr. Pelletier and Mr. Gagliano present were taking place. The list was accompanied by the following note:

[Unofficial Translation]

Dear Sir:

The projects mentioned above were discussed with Mr. Pelletier yesterday. He asked me to send him the list since I am sure that there will be pressure on us to take part in these events. The same list is going to be sent to Mr. Pelletier this morning since he told me he wanted to discuss it with you at noon today. If you wish to talk to me before meeting with Mr. Pelletier, I will be available at...

c.c. Mr. Pelletier

The proposed sponsorships listed were:

Salon du Grand Air – Trois-Rivières	$300,000
Salon du Grand Air – Sherbrooke	$300,000
Almanach	$529,000
Salon National du Grand Air – Montreal	$850,000
Salon National du Grand Air – Quebec City	$450,000
Canada Games – Cornerbrook, Newfoundland	$750,000
Série Maurice Richard	$650,000
GRAND TOTAL	$3,829,000

Clearly, these were projects of great significance financially. The first five were being promoted by Mr. Jacques Corriveau, a personal friend of the Prime Minister, although there is no direct evidence to suggest that Mr. Chrétien knew of his friend's involvement in the promotion of these sponsorships. Nevertheless, the mention in Mr. Guité's note that "nous allons avoir des pressions pour participer à ces événements" (there will be pressure on us to take part in these events) cannot be reconciled with the affirmations of Messrs. Pelletier and Gagliano that Mr. Guité had the sole authority to make decisions in such matters. Mr. Guité was obviously waiting for an indication from Mr. Gagliano as to how these proposed projects were to be treated, once they had been discussed with Mr. Pelletier. It is not clear from the evidence where the pressure was coming from. Mr. Pelletier says that he has no recollection of the five sponsorships in question, although he recalls certain discussions about the other two, which did not involve Mr. Corriveau.[34] Why he remembers only those not involving Mr. Corriveau is curious in light of what the Commission has learned about Mr. Corriveau's lobbying to persuade PWGSC to sponsor these events, and his interest that the agency appointed to manage them be Groupaction Marketing. The lobbying by Mr. Corriveau will be a later subject of this Report, but it may be stated immediately that the Commission considers it unlikely that he would have limited his attempts to influence PWGSC to contacts with Mr. Guité. The latter is unequivocal that he was *not* the decision-maker with respect to Mr. Corriveau's proposals.

The second document is a list in Mr. Pelletier's handwriting which appears as Figure VI-1. It was produced by Mr. Guité as evidence supporting his contention that Mr. Pelletier was suggesting events and amounts to him, and was not passively giving approval to lists already prepared by Mr. Guité. Mr. Pelletier attempts to give another explanation to the document, saying that the list was written out by him as sort of an aide-memoire during a meeting he had with Mr. Guité, and that at the end of the meeting he handed it to Mr. Guité who, according to Mr. Pelletier, had not made notes of what had been discussed.[35] The proposition that Mr. Pelletier would prepare notes to assist Mr. Guité to remember what had transpired at a meeting is improbable and cannot be reconciled with the rest of Mr. Pelletier's evidence. Mr. Pelletier's testimony generally leads one to believe that he did not initiate the consideration of a particular sponsorship project, but the document in his handwriting is clear evidence that the projects mentioned were being discussed for the first time; if they were already on one of Mr. Guité's lists, Mr. Guité had no need of Mr. Pelletier's notes. The list gives credence to Mr. Guité's testimony that Mr. Pelletier was actively promoting certain sponsorships, and suggesting the amounts to be paid in at least some cases. The notations on the document concerning commissions to be paid to unidentified agencies in connection with the events to be sponsored are not in Mr. Pelletier's handwriting; they were added by Mr. Guité after the list was handed to him. Nevertheless, Mr. Pelletier's testimony concerning this document is not credible.

Figure VI-1: Mr. Pelletier's handwritten list.

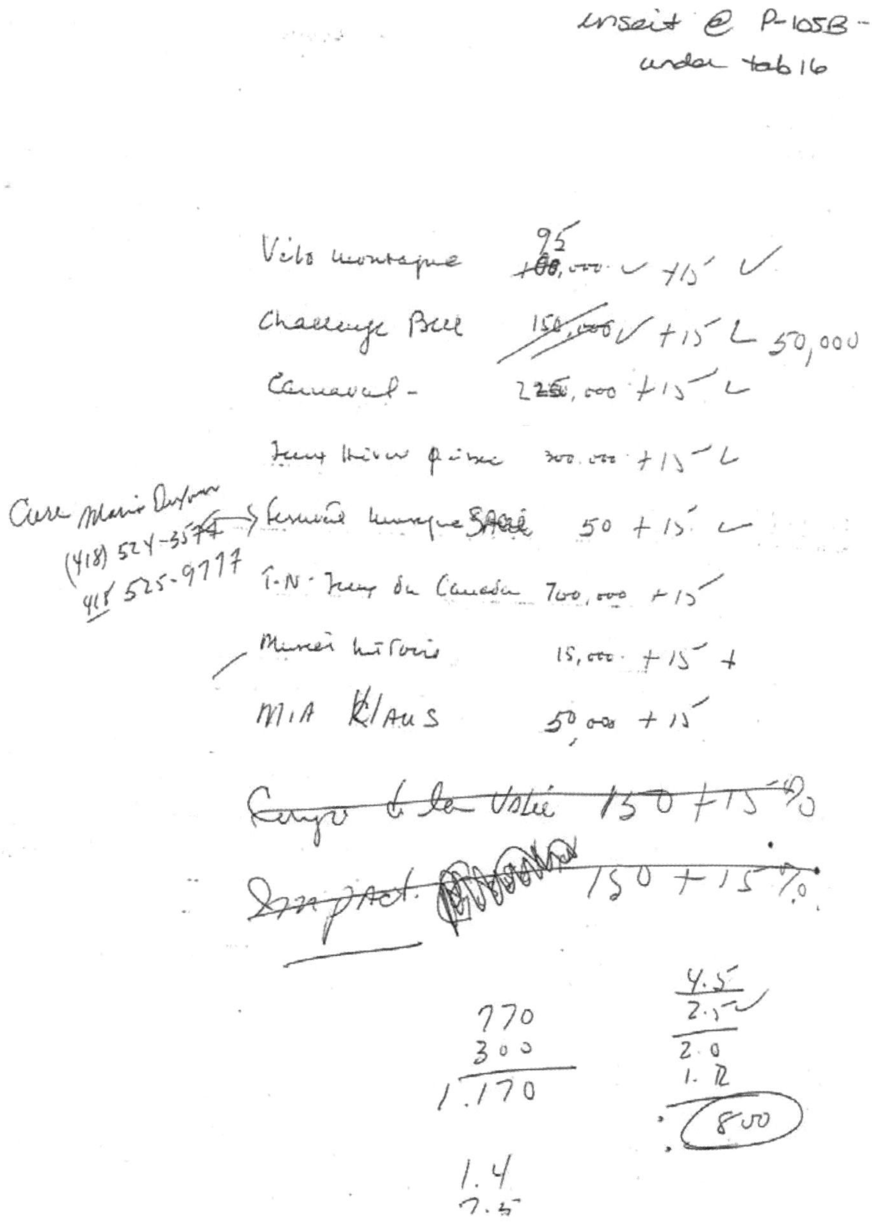

However, although Mr. Guité's testimony concerning the meetings he had with Mr. Pelletier is plausible and is not contradicted by any contemporary documentation, there are reasons to be cautious about accepting his testimony. He made admittedly false statements to Mr. Shahid Minto,[36] a representative of the Auditor General's Office, concerning his role as a decision-maker in the Sponsorship Program—statements which are sharply contradicted by what he said under oath to the Commission. When asked to explain why he had made false statements to Mr. Minto, he gave contradictory answers, saying first that when he made them he had retired and did not have the necessary documents before him; he then amended that answer to say that he had been protecting certain unidentified persons by not telling the truth to Mr. Minto, and then again changed his testimony to say that he had been bound by an obligation of confidentiality.[37] His comments that "a lot of water has gone under the bridge"[38] are of no assistance in understanding why his story has changed. There were other instances in the course of his sworn testimony in which he contradicted himself, and his evidence was in several instances contradicted by more reliable witnesses. On some occasions, especially when testifying about his post-retirement activities, Mr. Guité was evasive or unable to recall fairly recent events.

The Commission is of the opinion, in spite of its reservations about the truthfulness of Mr. Guité on other subjects, that his testimony about Mr. Pelletier's role in the choice of events and the amounts to be disbursed to their promoters is credible, whether Mr. Pelletier's suggestions or input were in the form of directions or worded less directly.

The giving of advice or the making of suggestions by a person in the position of Mr. Pelletier was the equivalent of an order. It is probable that Mr. Guité is telling the truth when he said that he took these suggestions and advice as instructions. He was not in a position to contest or disregard anything that Mr. Pelletier might say, and Mr. Pelletier surely must have known this. It would be a brave public servant indeed who would dare to contradict the Chief of Staff of the Prime Minister or disregard anything that he said, whether what he said was put in the form of an order or only as a suggestion.

6.7
Choice of Agencies

On the question of the choice of agencies, it was apparent that Mr. Pelletier, when testifying, wished to emphasize and re-emphasize that this matter was not discussed with Mr. Guité, to the point that he repeated the denial in answering questions on other subjects. For example, when asked to explain in general terms the nature of the discussions he had with Mr. Guité, Mr. Pelletier replied as follows:

> [Unofficial Translation]
>
> > Mr. Guité received sponsorship requests day in day out. Mr. Guité would make inquiries here and there. He couldn't be expected to know about all the events, the scope, the size of each event seeking sponsorship.
> >
> > So, I imagine that he made inquiries here and there to find out if we should sponsor a certain event in order to increase—if we should use this opportunity—take advantage of the opportunity to raise Canada's visibility. ...
> >
> > [Given the lack of Liberal members in several regions in Quebec]...he frequently consulted the Prime Minister's Office in order to get our opinion, which was perfectly logical for us, because, as I explained earlier, one of the roles of the Prime Minister's Office is to provide relevant political advice.
> >
> > ......
> >
> > So, we gave our opinion. Guité showed up with the lists. The only kind of lists I saw were lists with names of events and the amounts requested. I never saw any lists with the names of agencies or intermediaries who had been designated to handle specific files, let alone details about the payment of the intermediaries.

It should be noted that the question did not relate to the lists Mr. Guité brought to his meetings with Mr. Pelletier, nor to the things that were *not* on the lists.[39]

A few minutes later, Mr. Pelletier again introduced the question of who was choosing the agencies, when asked only if he had been informed by Mr. Guité as to which agencies were to be used for specific events. Mr. Pelletier's reply was as follows:

> [Unofficial Translation]
>
> Mr. Pelletier: Perhaps. That might have happened. I don't specifically remember, in the case of a major file, a very important file, Mr. Guité ever saying, "We won't use a small agency, or that particular agency. We'll use a much more professional agency. We should perhaps give it to…" He might have said that to me, and I, at the time, may have agreed, but, as I said, we never selected an agency at the Prime Minister's Office for what you call the Sponsorship Program.
>
> Mr. Cournoyer: As concerns the payment of agencies
>
> Mr. Pelletier: We had nothing to do with that.
>
> Mr. Cournoyer: …The percentages that went to the agencies—
>
> Mr. Pelletier: Nothing to do with that.[40]

These answers betray a rather nervous mental preoccupation with the issue of the choice of agencies, which is difficult to reconcile with the position taken by Mr. Pelletier's counsel that the matter was simply not part of the discussions with Mr. Guité at all.

When called to testify by his own counsel at the end of the hearings, Mr. Pelletier returned to the question of the choice of agencies, which he treats as a purely administrative matter. His testimony includes the following sentences:

[Unofficial Translation]

> All the administration and financial management of the sponsorship program was up to the Department of Public Works, and the Prime Minister's Office had nothing to do with the administrative and financial area. We didn't choose the agencies. We didn't determine the contract terms and conditions. We didn't sign any contracts, and we saw none of that administrative and financial paperwork. To me, it's very clear.[41]

And yet, when describing how important a priority national unity questions were for the Prime Minister, Mr. Pelletier affirmed that he was expected to follow the file very closely. His testimony includes the following extract:

[Unofficial Translation]

> Look, the national unity file was a very special file. It was the highest-priority file among all the high-priority files, in the eyes of the Prime Minister personally. The Prime Minister had given the instruction, as I said, to his chief officials to be proactive wherever we could be useful and positive in the national unity file. Mr. Chrétien wanted to retain control of that directly. He made decisions reflecting that. So I would say it was no mystery for us that this was a high priority and that he wanted to know what was going on and he wanted us to keep close tabs on it. So that is what we did. We always—we always asked ourselves a lot of questions: was it not a bit—I want to use the word "incongruous" for the Prime Minister's chief of staff to be meeting with an official at the level of Mr. Guité? It wasn't usual, but it wasn't the first or the last time that it was going to happen in the system.[42]

It is not possible to reconcile this testimony with Mr. Pelletier's pretension that the choice of agencies and the fees to be paid to them were never a subject of discussion with Mr. Guité. Mr. Pelletier, probably conscious of the political implications of the awarding of contracts to communication agencies owned, at least in the case of the Lafleur agency, by persons with whom he had social contacts, attempted during his testimony to minimize his involvement in the choice of agencies. I prefer the more logical conclusion that the choice of agencies was a matter in which he offered his "input" to Mr. Guité, just as he gave him advice on other aspects of the Sponsorship Program. The choice of agencies was simply too important a decision to leave entirely to "un fonctionnaire du niveau de Monsieur Guité" (a public servant of Mr. Guité's level)[43]

The meetings between Mr. Guité and Mr. Gagliano were more regular and frequent. As already stated, the Commission does not accept Mr. Gagliano's testimony that his meetings with Mr. Guité to discuss sponsorships were few and far between, and only of a short duration. As corroborated by his subordinates, they were as regular and frequent as Mr. Guité affirms. Like Mr. Pelletier, Mr. Gagliano testifies that he did no more than give political advice and make suggestions; for the same reason that this statement is not accepted in the case of Mr. Pelletier, it is not accepted with respect to Mr. Gagliano. The latter had the apparent authority to impose his decisions upon Mr. Guité, and it is highly improbable that Mr. Guité would not be anxious to accommodate his wishes, however expressed. Mr. Gagliano is not the sort of person who would make suggestions that his subordinate would be free to disregard.

Moreover, the testimony of Ms. Isabelle Roy, who worked as a political assistant in Mr. Gagliano's office and kept a written record ("the MP Log") of the decisions made with respect to sponsorship matters,[44] tends to corroborate Mr. Guité's assertion that many decisions were made by Mr. Gagliano. These included decisions to amend the lists presented to him by Mr. Guité, to add events and amounts to those lists and to reverse decisions which Mr. Guité had already made. Ms. Joanne Bouvier, who succeeded Ms. Roy when the latter went to work at CCSB in 1998 and who inherited the MP Log, also observed the active role of Mr. Gagliano in deciding who would be awarded sponsorships, and in what amounts.[45] In spite of his protestations to the contrary, the evidence is overwhelming that Mr. Gagliano was a hands-on manager who took a great interest in the Sponsorship Program and an active part in its direction.

Throughout his testimony, Mr. Gagliano insisted that Mr. Guité and his successor, Mr. Pierre Tremblay, made all the decisions and that the role of the Minister was limited to giving advice on the political advisability of sponsoring certain events, or what he called "input."[46] Mr. Gagliano recognized that in some instances he made suggestions, and when confronted by documentation such as the entries in the MP Log or letters sent to him by grateful recipients of sponsorships, he was prepared to acknowledge that in some cases his suggestions were strongly worded, and might even be described as recommendations; but he refused to admit that anyone other than Mr. Guité or Mr. Tremblay had the final say.[47]

All the same, Mr. Gagliano admitted that what Mr. Guité was seeking was his endorsement or approval of the lists he brought to the meetings, and that he gave that approval.[48] Messrs. Guité and Tremblay were subordinates coming to their Minister for approval of what they were proposing; it necessarily follows that the person making the ultimate decision is the Minister when he gives the approval, but Mr. Gagliano refuses to see the logic of this proposition. He refuses to accept that he was directly involved in the administration of the Sponsorship Program, not because it was not so, but because he is reluctant to accept responsibility for the errors committed in the course of that administration and the political interference which his decision-making constituted.

Mr. Gagliano was not a good or persuasive witness. He was at times evasive and argumentative, and he did not give the impression that he was as interested in increasing the Commission's understanding of the operation of the Sponsorship Program as he was in seeking his own vindication. In this respect, he compares unfavourably with Mr. Guité. When the latter says that Mr. Gagliano gave him advice, suggestions and instructions concerning the choice of agencies to handle sponsorship contracts, I am inclined to believe him in spite of Mr. Gagliano's denials.

6.8
Reporting Lines and Oversight

The normal practice in the public service is for each public servant to report to an immediate superior, and so on up the line to the Deputy Minister. In this way Mr. Stobbe, as Assistant Deputy Minister, would ordinarily have been kept advised of what Mr. Guité was doing when he was Mr. Guité's immediate superior, and would have been in a position to fulfill his obligation to oversee the activities occurring within his organization. After the formation of CCSB in late 1997, Mr. Guité was to report directly to Mr. Quail, the Deputy Minister.

Not very much of Mr. Quail's time was spent on the sponsorship file. Between 1993 and 1997, he says, he was involved only if there was a funding problem or if he was called upon to assist Mr. Guité and the PCO in putting together a Treasury Board submission.[49] Until 1997, he was entitled to expect that Mr. Stobbe would be keeping track of what Mr. Guité was doing, but in fact Mr. Stobbe was not supervising what was taking place at APORS to any important degree.[50]

The independence of Mr. Guité's section and the lack of reporting on his activities to his immediate superior go back to the time when Mr. Dingwall was Minister of PWGSC. At that time, Mr. Quail was very busy with the problems created by the departmental merger to create PWGSC and with related cutbacks. It was, practically speaking, impossible for him to attend meetings between Mr. Dingwall and Mr. Guité. Mr. Guité, at that time, was having discussions directly with Mr. Dingwall and with Mr. Dingwall's Executive Assistant, Mr. Warren Kinsella, concerning the formulation of the new policy which resulted in Appendix Q.[51] These discussions usually took place in the presence of his superior, who at that time was Mr. Richard Neville. Mr. Quail was not really involved.

When Ms. Marleau became Minister, Mr. Guité began to have meetings with Mr. Pelletier and Mr. Carle concerning the Sponsorship Program, at which Mr. Quail or his representative was not represented.[52] Mr. Guité's communications and contacts with Mr. Quail concerning the Program were limited to related Treasury Board submissions and budgeting considerations.

Mr. Quail recalls that, when Mr. Stobbe became Mr. Guité's superior, he received a telephone call from Mr. Bilodeau of the PCO, who said that he was calling on behalf of the PMO and wanted to know who Mr. Stobbe was, saying that he was reported as asking too many questions about sponsorship matters. Mr. Quail says that he replied that Mr. Stobbe was only doing his job, which was to supervise Mr. Guité's section, but the clear inference from the call was that Mr. Stobbe's supervision and involvement were not welcome and that people in the PMO preferred him not to interfere.[53] Mr. Stobbe learned about the call,[54] and both he and Mr. Quail understood the message that was being communicated: Mr. Guité's direction of the Sponsorship Program was under the direct supervision of the PMO, and no one should intervene.

When Mr. Gagliano became Minister, Mr. Guité's meetings with Mr. Pelletier and Mr. Carle were gradually replaced by meetings directly with Mr. Gagliano.[55] Although Mr. Stobbe insisted that Mr. Guité keep him and the Deputy Minister advised of the results of these meetings by sending them copies of the lists of sponsored events after they had been approved by the Minister's office, the lists were not otherwise discussed with Mr. Quail or with anyone else in the department. Mr. Quail understood that the only purpose in sending the approved lists to him was to enable him to keep a record of what had been spent, for budgeting purposes.[56] His role in the Sponsorship Program had been reduced to ensuring that Mr. Guité's section did not spend more money than it had available.

As a consequence, the authority and oversight that the Deputy Minister would normally have maintained over Mr. Guité's section of his department virtually ceased to exist. Both Mr. Quail and Mr. Stobbe knew that Mr. Guité had direct access to the PMO, which directed his activities and provided funds for the Program he was administering,[57] until they could be included in PWGSC appropriations starting in 1999-2000. The involvement that the Deputy Minister would normally have in the formulation of a new program, its administration and its oversight did not occur, and Mr. Quail's involvement was never sought. The Program commenced when Ms. Marleau was the Minister, but she had not been involved at all. Since Mr. Guité obviously had the support and approval of persons at the highest level of the Government, for whom questions of national unity, including the Sponsorship Program, were matters of the highest priority, he was, in spite of Mr. Quail's obligation to manage his department, untouchable and beyond his control.

6.9
Mr. Guité's Promotions

The special status of Mr. Guité is also reflected in his rapid rise in the bureaucracy.

As director of APORS, in 1993 Mr. Guité was at the level of an EX-01. In the performance rating signed by Mr. Neville in 1994, he was rated as fully satisfactory. The following remarks describe his qualities:

> Mr. C. Guité's expertise is very specialized and as a result he is very autonomous in his dealings internally within the new department of PWGSC. The focus for his responsibilities are mainly with the client departments and outside suppliers. Towards the end of 1993-94 Mr. C. Guité and myself worked very closely with TBS officials to develop the new policy and guidelines on advertising and public opinion research. Mr. C. Guité's advice is often sought by the Minister's office.[58]

On January 25, 1995, Mr. Guité was promoted to the level of EX-02, with an increase in salary of $4,670 per year. The description of his position as Director General of APORS includes the following:

> The director general is in continual contact with senior program and communication managers in all federal government departments and agencies to provide guidance, advice and provide direction regarding the procurement of advertising and public opinion survey products and services. The incumbent is also in continual contact with the Minister's office to provide advice and recommend specific advertising and public opinion research campaigns and projects.[59]

Mr. Guité received this promotion because his position was reclassified as of December 22, 1994, and he was appointed to it without competition.[60]

Mr. Guité testifies that he had intended to retire in 1995, but that when he mentioned this in his conversations with Mr. Pelletier, the latter persuaded him to stay on for a few more years.[61]

On November 23, 1995, Mr. Kinsella, the Executive Assistant of Mr. Dingwall, who was then Minister of PWGSC, wrote a surprising memorandum to Messrs. Quail and Stobbe, which to be appreciated must be reproduced in full:

> Gentlemen, repeated reviews of the management of the federal government's communications apparatus—and recent experience – have established a clear requirement for a centralized delivery system for the procurement and coordination of advertising, public opinion research and communications products. We have discussed this on previous occasions.
>
> There is also obviously a clear requirement to work with the Privy Council Office so that communications initiatives can be tied to overall government priorities. PCO and PMO have recently expressed similar views.
>
> After discussing this with the Minister, it is therefore requested that the following tasks be undertaken;
>
> I.   Create a common delivery system for advertising, research and all communications services products.
>
> II. Develop an information program explaining the role of functions of the integrated organization to departments of government including all regions as well as to communications industry suppliers.
>
> III. Work with the Privy Council Office and other relevant central agencies to develop recommendations for a system that will generate ongoing strategic communications initiatives around government priorities.

IV. Investigate all "out-of-home" advertising and potential sponsorship initiatives that are available to effectively promote government programs.

As the lead agency in the management of government advertising and public opinion research activities, the Advertising and Public Opinion Research Sector (APORS) is clearly best suited to carry out the noted tasks. In my view, Mr. J.C. Guité, current Director General of APORS should be assigned to carry out this review on a full time basis.

It is requested that he be assigned to a position that will allow him to carry out these tasks and that he be provided with the appropriate resources consistent with such an initiative. Central agencies have requested that his current position should be staffed immediately with a permanent and qualified person.

The deliverable will be as follows:

• Develop an action plan to accomplish all of the above-noted tasks by January 15th, 1996.

• Provide a written report(s) on the findings by June 1, 1996.

Thank you for your attention to this matter.[62]

This communication was rightly taken by Mr. Quail to be a highly inappropriate attempt by political staff to interfere in the internal administration of PWGSC, which is entirely within the jurisdiction of the Deputy Minister. The reference to unidentified persons in the PCO and PMO gives the impression that the proposed reorganization of government communications under Mr. Guité was desired by persons at the highest level. To his credit, Mr. Quail resisted the temptation to take offence, and replied by a memorandum reading as follows:

I have your note of Nov 23/95 re: Direction to review the APORS and would make the following observations:

1. In paragraph 2 you mention the recent views of PCO. Would you please provide me the name at PCO—so we don't cross lines.

2. The review that you have outlined in your note suggests this may be seen at the Centre as a Machinery of Government responsibility which as you know is the prerogative of the Prime Minister to assign. My experience indicates that it is necessary to ensure PMO/PCO is aware of the assignment of such issues to a Minister. Will you confirm this is in place?

3. On page 2 you recommend that we use Mr. Guité on this assignment and that the Central Agencies have suggested the position he "vacates" be staffed immediately on a permanent basis. I have 2 points on this:

    a] I am not aware of any such directions; please advise who has recommended this action with respect to Mr. Guité's position, so I can discuss the issues I see arising from this proposal.

    b] On the assignment of Mr. Guité; my concern here is that the action you propose, while attractive in one sense, presents a problem to me in the handling of the EX personnel. There will be a requirement to find an additional EX position to cover the assignment period and secondly, no clear assignment for Mr. Guité once the work is completed...We already have a number of these cases and I have been working over the last two years to get these down to zero. In other words what to do with Mr. Guité at the end when no work exists...

I would like to hear from you before I take any further action.[63]

The matter died there. Mr. Quail decided that Mr. Kinsella's memo was a mistake by an inexperienced political staffer who did not know better than to attempt to give direction to a senior public servant on how to organize his department. Mr. Dingwall testifies that he does not remember the incident, but assumes that he must have instructed Mr. Kinsella to write the memo.[64] As to why he would have wanted Mr. Guité to be given important new responsibilities, the record is unclear.

But we do know that Mr. Guité and his personnel at APORS were given the whole responsibility for the management and administration of the Sponsorship Program when it came into being in the spring of 1996. Sponsorship contracts were considered by all concerned to be a form of advertising, and were so defined in Appendix Q, and Mr. Guité was the government's expert in advertising matters.

When CCSB was created in November 1997, it constituted almost exactly the consolidation of functions that had been advocated by Mr. Kinsella two years previously. At that time, Mr. Guité's position was reclassified from EX-02 to EX-03.[65] Mr. Guité testifies that he had spoken to Mr. Quail and to Mr. Gagliano and told them that he considered that he should be promoted and that his position should be reclassified as Executive Director of CCSB, with the equivalent rank of Assistant Deputy Minister, reporting directly to the Deputy Minister, because of the increased responsibilities that he was assuming with the creation of CCSB. He says that he also brought up the reclassification request with Mr. Pelletier or Mr. Carle and was told that he should deal with the matter at the level of the Deputy Minister. Nevertheless, he assumed that someone would talk to Mr. Gagliano and that his promotion would be facilitated as a result.[66] The promotion and reclassification occurred shortly afterwards. It is interesting to note that in the description of the responsibilities attached to his new position may be found the following sentence:

> When events force the government into a reactive posture, the incumbent brings to bear a capacity for quick response, cutting red tape, influencing key media and other opinion leaders...[67]

The reference to "cutting red tape" certainly corresponds to Mr. Guité's style, but it is not necessarily a desirable attribute of a public servant responsible for allocating discretionary funds with little or no supervision.

With his promotion to the EX-03 level, Mr. Guité received an increase in salary of $9,900 per year.

Mr. Guité was again promoted, this time to an acting EX-04 position, effective April 1, 1998, only a few months after his last promotion, with a corresponding increase in salary of $5,500 per year. This final promotion, which had an effect upon his pension entitlement, was offered to him in February 1999, in spite of the fact that he had already announced his intention of retiring in April, 1999.[68]

Mr. Quail has notes in his records that on two occasions he was made aware of the fact that Mr. Guité had discussed the question of his reclassification or promotion with the Minister or with the PMO.[69] Mr. Quail was not happy that he had done so; promotions, job classifications and salary adjustments are supposed to be exempt from political interference.[70] He does not remember any political interference, but it is difficult to understand why his notes would make reference to the Minister or the PMO if he had not been contacted by someone.

It may be concluded from the foregoing that Mr. Guité used his privileged status and contacts with Mr. Gagliano and the PMO in his successful attempts to gain promotions and salary increases. Although Mr. Gagliano and Mr. Pelletier deny that they assisted Mr. Guité's promotions by intervening with Mr. Quail, the latter knew that they had been spoken to.[71] Mr. Guité's rise from an EX-01 to an acting EX-04 in less than five years was remarkably rapid.

When Mr. Guité made known his intention to retire on August 31, 1999, Mr. Gagliano's Executive Assistant, Mr. Pierre Tremblay, announced that he would like to transfer to the public service and to assume Mr. Guité's position as Executive Director of CCSB.[72] According to public service staffing rules, exempt staff wishing to transfer to the public service and having relevant experience are given priority over applicants for the same position from within the public service. There were some who had reservations about Mr. Tremblay,[73] but Mr. Gagliano fully supported his candidacy for Mr. Guité's position, and in February 1999 his transfer to the public service took place. Although Mr. Guité retired with an acting EX-04 classification, Mr. Tremblay, who replaced him, was classified at the EX-02 level.[74]

Mr. Guité's retirement was preceded by a transition period during which he was still nominally the Executive Director of CCSB while Mr. Tremblay was becoming familiar with his new functions. Mr. Tremblay was already knowledgeable about the Sponsorship Program and about how it was being run under Mr. Guité's direction. Although the Commission heard no testimony from Mr. Tremblay, who passed away before he could testify, it is impossible to believe that he did not know about the irregularities that affected its administration. During the period from February to August 1999, Mr. Tremblay gradually assumed more and more of Mr. Guité's responsibilities, and the latter spent most of his time preparing for his retirement.[75]

Mr. Tremblay brought a different management style to CCSB. He was determined to be more systematic, and asked his personnel to see to proper documentation of sponsorship files. For the first time, computerized lists of pending applications for sponsorship contracts were prepared, as were lists of accepted applications—indicating the communication agencies that had been engaged to handle each contract, and the commissions and fees that would be paid to them.[76] In this way, from the time that Mr. Tremblay began to take charge of CCSB, Mr. Gagliano was made aware of the agencies that were handling sponsorship contracts.

Mr. Tremblay continued the practice established by Mr. Guité of going to the Minister's office on a regular basis to review lists of proposed sponsorships. Mr. Gagliano delegated more responsibility in this area to his new Executive Assistant, Jean-Marc Bard, with whom Mr. Tremblay met more and more frequently. He found Mr. Bard to be prone to interfere in the management of the Sponsorship Program, which he felt fully competent to handle without Mr. Bard's directions and advice, and expressed his frustration about Mr. Bard's interference to his subordinates when he returned from a meeting at the Minister's office.[77]

6.10

Absence of Guidelines and Criteria

Prior to the implementation of any new government program, the usual practice is to develop and make known to interested parties the guidelines which will apply to it. These guidelines would normally explain:

- the objectives of the program;

- a description of the means adopted to achieve these objectives;

- where the program involves the disbursement of public funds on a discretionary basis, the criteria which will guide the decision-maker; and

- the procedure to be followed by applicants for admissibility to the benefits of the program.[78]

Of these, of prime importance are the criteria for eligibility for sponsorships. Prior to September 1, 2001, when Communication Canada took over the administration of the Sponsorship Program, guidelines had never been adopted, and decisions made for access to the Program were almost entirely arbitrary. However, from time to time attempts were made to prepare and develop criteria in the form of policy guidelines.

Mr. Guité testifies that while he was the Director of APORS or CCSB, there was never a formal set of guidelines for selecting sponsorship events. No one ever told him not to draft guidelines, but Mr. Guité cannot remember anyone ever asking him to draft guidelines, either. While Mr. Gagliano or Mr. Pelletier made suggestions to him as to events that should be given funding, they did not tell Mr. Guité on what basis certain events should be selected and others rejected, or ask questions on this subject. Mr. Guité agreed that the absence of a set of guidelines gave everyone a much wider scope of discretion in selecting events and amounts.[79]

On December 13, 1996, in response to a request from Mr. Stobbe, Mr. Guité's assistant, Denise Paquette, sent him an e-mail, presumably as directed by Mr. Guité, citing a long list of the criteria used to evaluate sponsorship opportunities.[80] The list is so vague that it does not really assist an understanding of which opportunities would be admissible and which would be rejected. In any event, those so-called criteria were not published or made available to anyone other than Mr. Stobbe.

Shortly after he became Minister in June 1997, Mr. Gagliano met with Messrs. Guité and Quail to discuss sponsorships generally, and the question of developing selection criteria was raised. Mr. Gagliano says that Mr. Quail told him he was working on a draft set of criteria.[81] It was probably as a result of this discussion that efforts to draft guidelines were made, but from what follows it may be deduced that the task had low priority.

Marie Maltais says that when she arrived at CCSB in May 1998 she found that there were no sponsorship guidelines or criteria. When she suggested to Mr. Guité that they needed guidelines he agreed, and she began to work on drafts.[82] She turned over what she had prepared to Evelyn Marcoux in August 1998, and together they produced a further draft in January 1999. When it was shown to Mr. Guité, he indicated that it was satisfactory, but nothing appears to have been done to approve or implement the document.[83] It was eventually sent to Mr. Quail, who said he wanted to see an example of how the criteria would be applied in practice before proceeding to have them formally approved.[84]

The proposed guidelines were tested in connection with the application for a sponsorship submitted by the Ottawa Tulip Festival in 1999. An evaluation of the application was made by an employee of CCSB using the draft guidelines and criteria, and in February 1999 the employee who had performed the evaluation recommended that the sponsorship request be declined. When this recommendation was communicated to the promoters of the Tulip Festival, they responded by marshalling support from Ottawa area Members of Parliament and Ministers, who wrote letters and otherwise put pressure upon Mr. Gagliano. He reversed the decision of CCSB and the event was sponsored, although for an amount less than what had been requested.[85] This is an example of a direction by the Ministers as to both eligibility for a sponsorship and the amount.

Following this experience, the draft guidelines were set aside and no longer used to evaluate sponsorship requests.

When Isabelle Roy arrived at CCSB in May 1999, she inherited the task of working on the draft guidelines. She briefed Mr. Tremblay, who was in the process of taking over from Mr. Guité, as well as the Minister and his new Executive Assistant, Jean-Marc Bard, on the draft guidelines. She says that she had the impression from these briefings that the guidelines would have to be sufficiently vague to allow interventions from the Minister's office, and adds that the guidelines were finalized as far as she was concerned in April 2000, but were not formally adopted and were used only as a reference tool.[86] She is of the opinion that the main purpose in drafting the guidelines was to have something to show outsiders if requests under the access to information legislation were made concerning the Sponsorship Program.[87]

A copy of the April 2000 draft guidelines was communicated to the communication agencies that were working with CCSB on sponsorship files, but Ms. Roy does not recall ever having received an application from the agencies containing an analysis based upon the guidelines.[88]

From all of this it may be concluded that prior to the administration of the Sponsorship Program by Communication Canada, there was never in effect a set of guidelines which had been formally adopted and approved by the Deputy Minister of PWGSC, or by anyone else in authority, containing criteria to guide the selection of applicants for sponsorship funding. Whether or not they were formally adopted, the evidence shows that no draft guidelines or criteria were ever systematically applied.

The absence of a set of criteria permitted the granting of sponsorships for purposes unrelated to national unity considerations or increased visibility in Canada of the federal presence. There were many examples of this and some of them will be described elsewhere in this Report. Two examples can be cited immediately.

Starting in 1996 and continuing for several years, a series of sponsorship contracts were entered into between PWGSC and the well-known advertising agency Vickers & Benson to finance the costs of a series of television programs, to be broadcast on Chinese television, extolling Canadian institutions and values. This project was the brainchild of the president of Vickers & Benson, John Hayter, who had become enthusiastic about Canada's trade possibilities with China as a result of his participation in a 1994 trade mission to China, spearheaded by the Prime Minister. Mr. Hayter is frank; he was looking for funding for this project from any source available.[89] He does not know the source of the funding, but on the basis of his contacts with Jean Carle and the PCO, it may be deduced that there were interventions from the Prime Minister's Office in favour of funding for the project which permitted it to proceed.[90] A total of approximately $10 million was disbursed by the Government of Canada in the context of the Sponsorship Program for what was known as the China series.[91] It is most unlikely that the broadcasting of a series of television programs in China contributed in any way to considerations of national unity in Canada.

A second example of the use of sponsorship funds for purposes unrelated to enhancing the visibility of the federal presence in Quebec was the modest sum of $6,000 paid as a sponsorship to promoters of a project to have a plaque erected in the village of San Martino in Italy, naming the town square "Plaza Canada." The plaque was to be unveiled on the occasion of a visit to that locality by Mr. Gagliano. It was acknowledged within CCSB at the time that this project had nothing to do with Canadian unity, and instructions were given to Mario Parent, who by this time had left the public service and was working for the Gosselin agency, to conceal the invoicing of this sponsorship in another contract, so that it would not appear upon the public record.[92] Mr. Gagliano tries in his testimony to defend this sponsorship, which he apparently knew about and supported, as a legitimate effort to promote Canadian unity to citizens of Italian descent,[93] but the Commission remains unconvinced that the project had anything to do with the objectives of the Sponsorship Program, and concludes that it was entirely motivated by a desire to promote Mr. Gagliano's political career.

The San Martino sponsorship was one of a number of relatively small projects most often described in CCSB documentation as "unforeseen events." Upon closer examination these projects turn out to be sponsorships of cultural and sporting events almost entirely located either in Mr. Gagliano's constituency or in the region known as la Mauricie, where Mr. Chrétien's riding is to be found.[94] Probably it was virtually impossible for Mr. Gagliano and his staff to refuse to authorize the payment of small amounts to Mr. Gagliano's local supporters, and it was equally impossible to refuse requests from the promoters of events from the region where the Prime Minister periodically sought re-election, but the uses to which the "unforeseen events" file was put illustrate why guidelines and criteria are essential to the administration of a program if the Government genuinely wants to obtain value that corresponds to the reason for making money available in the first place.

In the absence of criteria for access to the Program, the availability of discretionary funding was an almost irresistible temptation to politicians and to persons well connected to the party in power who sought to obtain public funds for purposes and projects that they considered to be desirable or advantageous. Some of these projects were clearly politically desirable. Others were socially and economically legitimate in the sense that they were designed to achieve results that would promote the welfare of Canadian citizens, but many had little connection to considerations of Canadian unity or the visibility of the federal presence. Mr. Hayter's attitude was typical; he thought sincerely that Canada's long-term trade prospects with China would be promoted by a series of television programs providing the population of China with a better understanding of Canadians and their virtues.[95] Perhaps Mr. Hayter was right and perhaps the China series was an excellent investment for the Government of Canada, but it had nothing to do with the objectives, poorly defined as they were, of the Sponsorship Program.

6.11
Commissions, Fees and Production Costs

Personnel at CCSB had only vague ideas as to the services that were to be provided by communication agencies in exchange for the commissions, usually at the rate of 12 to 15% of the sponsorship's value, which they charged when they entered into sponsorship contracts with the Government.

No attempt was ever made to negotiate the commission rate downwards. Mr. Quail recalls that during the period when Mr. Guité was the Executive Director of CCSB he asked Mr. Guité why they were using communication agencies, and whether the rates charged by the agencies were standard. Mr. Guité told him that a 15% commission was the industry standard, and the discussion ended there.[96]

There are indications in the documentation that is part of the record that the possibility of attempting to negotiate more favourable commission rates with the industry could have been explored. On April 19, 1995, Doug Fyfe, Director General of Tourism Canada (a part of Industry Canada), wrote to Mr. Neville to question the assumption that the 15% commission rate was a standard rate that could not be altered. Mr. Fyfe realized that the advertising industry was in favour of a fixed rate of 15%, increasing to 17.65% in certain instances, but pointed out, based upon his own experience, that:

> ...many agencies provide alternate methods of establishing the cost of their services ranging from hourly billing to performance-based remuneration. I had earlier been assured that these methods of payment would be explored with the agencies selected. If this has happened, I am unaware of it and no one from this organization participated in any such discussions.[97]

Mr. Neville referred this correspondence to Mr. Guité, who was not at all interested in exploring the possibility of negotiating lower commission rates.[98] Once again, everyone appears to have considered that because Mr. Guité was the acknowledged expert in advertising matters, his approach, that there should be a non-competitive standard commission rate, was accepted.

The communication agencies retained by PWGSC to handle sponsorship files took the position that they were entitled to invoice the Government for additional sums, described as "production costs," when the agency performed services over and above the standard services to be covered by the fixed commission.[99] However, even today there is no unanimity, among the agencies or at the level of the personnel of CCSB, as to what services were to be supplied by the agencies in exchange for the commission of 15% and what services deserved payment of additional amounts. In the absence of any guidelines on this subject, the production costs provided for on each sponsorship contract, and what those production costs would include, seem to have been established on an *ad hoc* basis. This sometimes produced ludicrous results; there are cases where an analysis of the file reveals that all of the hours recorded by the employees of a communication agency were billed to the Government as a production cost, which meant that no services at all were covered by the 15% commission. Different agencies took varying positions.

Three particularly striking examples of how the concept of production costs came to be abused can be cited. However, before discussing those examples, let us clarify some of the terminology used in sponsorship contracts and invoices. The "sponsorship amount" is the sum of money allocated to the promoters of the event itself. "Production costs" are amounts the communication agency invoices PWGSC for the design, purchase or creation of such things as signage, brochures and similar promotional items. Many invoices bill separately for fees or "honoraria" based on the hours worked by employees multiplied by the rate charged by their agency for each hour worked. Finally, there are "commissions," usually 15% of the sponsorship amount, but at a rate of 17.65% on goods or services purchased by the agency from a third party.

The standard PWGSC contracts used for ordinary advertising procurement are not models of clarity. The Commission heard evidence from several witnesses that the contracts for sponsorships were those used for the procurement of advertising services, and that the forms were not well adapted for sponsorships.[100] Before the use of an Agency of Record (AOR) began in 1998, contracts stated that the agency would be paid the sponsorship amount to be delivered to the promoter of the event, together with an "admin/management fee," which is its commission on the sponsorship amount plus fees for "all creative services…reasonably and properly incurred in the production of advertising material" according to a set hourly rate schedule.[101]

6.12
Montreal Expos Sponsorship

Lafleur Communication had the "Montreal Expos" sponsorship contracts for the baseball seasons of 1995, 1996 and 1997. In 1995 and 1996, the sponsorship amount was about $537,000, so that Lafleur's 12% commission would be approximately $64,500 each year. The puzzle lies in the hourly charges in the invoices sent by Lafleur to PWGSC: 234 employee hours in 1995 and 1,104 in 1996.[102] One would think that the work described in some detail on certain of the 1995 invoices (meetings with PWGSC, meetings with the Expos, negotiating visibility, visiting the event site, managing publicity, production of mock-ups[103] ("maquettes"), reports, administration and finishing and closing the file)[104] would be adequately covered by the $64,500 commission. Figure VI-2 illustrates examples of invoices from 1995 and 1996.

When he testified, the head of Lafleur Communication, Jean Lafleur, was unable to provide any additional detail about this work charged as production costs and hourly fees. Although he proposed that many of the hours invoiced must have been related to the mock-ups, he finally agreed that the mock-ups had been subcontracted to a third party.[105] Logically, the production costs and hourly fees would tend to decrease in the following year, since much of the agency's work would be a repetition of what had been done the year before, even if some signs had to be redesigned or relocated for the 1996 season. Instead, the hours that were billed more than quadrupled. Little credence can be given to Mr. Lafleur's hypothesis (he had almost no recollection of the facts or circumstances of the Expos contracts) that other events included in the main contract might have been mistakenly billed to the Expos file.[106]

Billings in 1996 also included 364 hours (roughly $60,000) and a $5,000 commission billed under a separate contract for a one-day backpack promotion that entitled the promoter, in this case the Expos, to receive a $40,000 sponsorship. PWGSC paid Lafleur more than $195,000 for backpacks given to fans attending that day, which were purchased from the company belonging to Jean Lafleur's son Éric.[107]

The Expos sponsorship increased to almost $800,000 in 1997, entitling Lafleur to a $119,000 commission. Inexplicably, only 64.5 hours of employee time were billed to the file.[108]

We have no evidence of PWGSC questioning or challenging any of Lafleur's hourly invoicing on the Expos sponsorships in 1995 or 1996, or indeed of any of Lafleur's invoices throughout the Sponsorship Program.

6.13
The Bluenose Sponsorship

A second example of extraordinary hourly production fees was Gosselin Communications' handling of the Bluenose sponsorship on behalf of Lafleur Communication. The Bluenose, a reconstruction of the famous Nova Scotia sailing ship, was to make a multi-stop tour from Halifax to a series of ports of call along the St. Lawrence River and Seaway. Gosselin's books show it received almost $542,000 in the 1997 calendar year for work in connection with the Bluenose project. For the 1997-98 fiscal year, PWGSC was invoiced for 3,673 hours of Mr. Gosselin's time, of which 1,117 hours were for the Bluenose project.[109] This was his personal time only—for April through

Figure VI-2: Lafleur Communication invoices.

P34

IRC/CDRE

COMMUNICATION
JEAN LAFLEUR INC.

V.137

'95 JUN 22 PM 2 51

Le 12 juin 1995

G

TRAVAUX PUBLICS ET SERVICES
GOUVERNEMENTAUX CANADA
151, rue Slater, bureau 215
Ottawa (Ontario) K1P 5H3

DOIT A:
COMMUNICATION JEAN LAFLEUR INC.
300, rue du St-Sacrement #114
Montréal (Québec) H2Y 1X4

Dossier EN751-5010201GCA
Expos de Montréal

FACTURE 4705181
TPS: 101069912
TVQ: 1002249835

Rencontres avec le client:
- Précision des stratégies publicitaires

Rencontres avec les Expos:
- Négociation de la visibilité publicitaire
- Visite des lieux et repérage des espaces publicitaires
- Inventaire des panneaux disponibles
- Gestion du programme publicitaire

Identification des messages possibles sur divers
programmes fédéraux;

Concepts et production de 47 maquettes;

Honoraires de coordination et gestion du
programme publicitaire:
    Jean Lafleur
        21 heures x 275 $ 5 775,00 $
    Eric Lafleur
        22 heures x 150 $ 3 300,00 $
    Travail clérical
        24 heures x 40 $ 960,00 $

Production de 47 maquettes:
    47 maquettes @ 2750,00 $ chacune: 129 250,00 $

Certified pursuant to section 34 of the
Financial Administration Act.
Certifié en vertu de l'article 34 de
la Loi sur l'administration financière

Signature   95/06/23
Date

$149,034. 95
of
20

P96

1097886 : Front

INVOICE

Lafleur
COMMUNICATION
MARKETING

Le 30 septembre 1996

'96 OCT 9 AM 9 27

Travaux Publics et Services
Gouvernementaux Canada
107, rue Sparks
4e étage, Édifice Birks
Ottawa (Ontario) K1P 5B5
À l'attention de: M. J.-C. Guité

FACTURE: 96.260

V.293

Dossier:	Expos de Montréal - Commandite		Facture:	96.260
Contrat:	EN771-6-0008/01-ACA		T.P.S.:	101069912
Devis:			T.V.Q.:	1002249835

Description

Commandite du Gouvernement du Canada pour les Expos de Montréal

30% de la commandite (facture annexée):	161,040.00
Commission d'agence (12%):	19,324.80

Frais, coûts

Frais de messagerie:	20.00
Frais de déplacement:	34.20

Concepts

42 maquettes @ 2,750$ ch.:	115,500.00

Honoraires du 4 juillet au 27 septembre 96

		Heures	Taux	
J. Lafleur	Senior Strategic Planning Director	71.0	275.00	19,525.00
E. Lafleur	Account Director	109.0	245.00	26,705.00
S. Guertin	Account Supervisor	95.0	150.00	14,250.00
M. Octeau	Operations Director	87.0	150.00	13,050.00
P. Mayrand	Operations Director	105.0	150.00	15,750.00
E. Octeau	Production Co-ordinator	86.0	75.00	6,450.00
Secrétariat	Clerical Support	62.0	40.00	2,480.00

Certified pursuant to section 34 of the
Financial Administration Act.
Certifié en vertu de l'article 34 de
la Loi sur l'administration financière.

Total:	394,129.00
T.P.S.:	27,589.03
T.V.Q.:	
TOTAL:	421,718.03

Signature   96-10-09

Date *421, 718.03*

500, place d'Armes, bureau 2110, Montréal (Québec), H2Y 2W2
Tél.: (514) 288-9877 • Télec.: (514) 288-2601 • Courrier électr.: lcm@sympatico.ca

October. At least 1,188 hours were invoiced for the services of other Gosselin employees for the Bluenose file.[110] In a nutshell, Mr. Gosselin's testimony was that he took over management of virtually all aspects of the Bluenose tour from the Lafleur agency, which had been awarded the PWGSC contract, personally putting in 13 to 18 hours a day in June, July and August 1997, for which he billed Lafleur on an hourly basis.[111] The services of many other persons were invoiced to Lafleur as if they were Gosselin employees, but the Commission heard evidence that these "employees" had themselves invoiced Gosselin Communications as if they were subcontractors; they invoiced one of Mrs. Gosselin's companies, which then added a markup and billed Gosselin Communications, which then invoiced the Lafleur agency, with another markup. In one instance, Geneviève Proulx, one of the Gosselin employees, was grossing $12 per hour for her work, while Gosselin Communications sent invoices for her work to the Lafleur agency at the rate of $60 per hour.[112] There was no evidence of PWGCS questioning, challenging or verifying the invoicing for the Bluenose project for the number of hours worked, or for the hourly rates being charged.

A third example is Gosselin Communication's management of the $125,000 sponsorship for the City of Ste-Hyacinthe's 250th Anniversary. Gosselin Communications was paid a $15,000 commission, calculated at 12% of the amount of the sponsorship and invoiced 569 hours for work which presumably was over and above what should have been covered by the commission, described as "frais de gestion" (management fees) or "frais de coordination et de gestion" (administration and management fees), for an additional $53,000. This included more than 94 hours claimed on behalf of the Gosselin team manager, Enrico Valente.[113] In his testimony before this Commission, Mr. Valente estimated he had put in not more than 17 to 20 hours on the file.[114] There is no reason to believe that the $15,000 commission would not fully cover the cost of managing this particular sponsorship, which involved no creative work. The Commission concludes that the $53,000 charged by Gosselin Communications on an hourly basis was undeserved. The question of whether it was entitled contractually to charge as it did is left to the courts to decide.

After the first two years, a practice was adopted of including estimated production costs in virtually every contract with a communication agency. The production costs were sometimes determined as a percentage of the total value of the sponsorship, and little effort was made to assess what additional costs might be incurred by the agency.[115] This produced the result that production costs became a more important source of revenue to the communication agencies than the commissions, and the commissions really covered no services at all. In almost every case, the agency charged almost exactly the full amount of the estimated production costs.

6.14
Promotional Items and Free Tickets

Prior to the absorption of PRPCSS by CCSB, the former contracted directly with suppliers to manufacture or purchase promotional items without the intervention of communication agencies to manage the contracts. Once procurement was taken over by CCSB, the practice was to have agencies purchase promotional items and to be paid a commission for doing so. Since the agency would always acquire the promotional items by way of a subcontract, according to the standard contract used by the personnel at CCSB, the commission payable to the agency for handling the subcontract was 17.65%, instead of the standard rate of 12% or 15%. Other than the paperwork involved in the subcontract, in most cases virtually no services were provided by the communication agency in exchange for the commission. of 17.65%.

When Jean Lafleur testified before the Commission, he was pressed to explain the value added by Lafleur Communication when purchasing promotional items, in exchange for the commission paid by PWGSC. Essentially, his testimony was that regardless of whether value was added or not, the PWGSC contract authorized the communication agency to collect a commission on the price of the promotional items purchased from a third party. According to Mr. Lafleur, it was a matter of respecting the contract rather than a question of exactly what and how much work was done in exchange for the commission: "Avec respect, monsieur le commissaire, le contrat ne stipule pas qu'il doit y avoir un peu, beaucoup ou pas de travail." (With respect, Commissioner, the contract does not stipulate that there should be a little work, a lot of work, or no work at all.)[116]

He was unable to provide details of the work done by the agency for any particular promotional items contract, but said that, as a general rule, when the merchandise was delivered it would be verified, looked at, counted and checked for quality and to see if the colours were correct. He said that his son, Éric Lafleur, as vice-president of Lafleur Communication, would check the promotional items delivered by the subcontractor, Publicité Dézert,[117] which Éric Lafleur himself owned and ran for a time from the same premises as Lafleur Communication. In cases where the agency invoices added hourly charges as well, Mr. Lafleur explained that the agency commission related to the receipt and delivery of materials to PWGSC, but that handling, packaging and checking were additional charges.[118]

Mr. Lafleur confirmed that he billed Éric Lafleur's time for this kind of handling and packaging at $245 an hour, whereas the cost to Lafleur Communication for Éric Lafleur's time, as reflected by his salary, was $40 per hour.[119] When asked whether $245 per hour properly reflected the value of the work done by Éric Lafleur, a young man with only four years' experience, Mr. Lafleur relied again on the terms of the PWGSC contract: "Si on avait appliqué...la mauvaise terminologie pour une personne, il y a quelqu'un à Travaux publics qui nous l'aurait dit. Alors, Éric était le Account Director. Alors on a chargé le taux d'un Account Director." (If we had applied the wrong—the wrong terminology for a person, there was someone at Public Works who would have told us that. Éric was the Account Director. So, we charged the rate for an Account Director.)[120] The PWGSC contract specified that the time of an Account Director would be paid at $245 per hour.

Whether or not the Lafleur agency was within its legal rights to charge PWGSC $245 per hour for routine handling of merchandise purchased from the company owned by the same person doing the handling is a question which the Commission will leave to the courts. From the point of view of public administration, the failure of personnel at PWGSC to challenge or question such excessive charges cannot be excused.

There was additional mismanagement due to the fact that the agencies engaged to act on behalf of the Government of Canada failed to seek competing bids for the subcontract as the standard contract stipulation requires. The relevant clause reads as follows:

> For requirements estimated over $30,000 GST included, the agency will, whenever it requires goods and services from outside suppliers or from its affiliated companies or modules, obtain competing bids from no less than three outside suppliers, firms or individuals; and will submit such bids to the <u>Contract Authority</u> for approval together with a rationale for its choice of supplier, before entering into subcontractual arrangements.
>
> This condition may be waived if prior approval is given by the Contract Authority in writing.[121]

Although the Commission takes into account evidence of Lafleur Communication routinely obtaining Mr. Guité's approval to proceed without competing bids, which he says he granted because of "urgency," there was seldom any real urgency. In any event, the Lafleur agency usually assured Mr. Guité that a competitive price would still be obtained from the subcontractor, although there is no evidence that in fact it was doing so.[122]

It must be remembered that in most cases the subcontract was with a related company, such as Lafleur Communication's transactions with Publicité Dézert, or the Gosselin agency's purchases from subcontractors owned by Mr. Gosselin's wife or son. The related company which would itself expected to earn a profit margin on the acquisition and resale of acquisition of the promotional items needed. On average, Publicité Dézert charged a 100% markup.[123] Most of Gosselin's purchases of promotional items for PWGSC were subcontracted to Centre de placement de professionnels en communications, inc. (CPPC), belonging to Mrs. Gosselin. On average, CPPC took a 22% markup on clothing and 96% on all other promotional items.[124] As already mentioned, the Lafleur or Gosselin agencies in turn added a commission when billing PWGSC for the items purchased. This led to what can only be described as blatant overcharging for these items, as appears from the following examples.

6.15
Examples of Overcharging

In August 1997, an amendment to an existing PWGSC contract with Lafleur Communication added a number of sponsorship events and called on the Lafleur agency to purchase "Items Promotionnels" for $680,000.[125] By the time the contract amendment was signed, Lafleur had already invoiced PWGSC for five promotional items under the contract, such as 5,000 Bluenose Christmas ornaments at a cost of $50,000.[126] Publicité Dézert had paid $5 for each ornament, and resold them to Lafleur Communication for $10 per ornament. The Lafleur agency passed the $10 price along to PWGSC, adding a commission of $7,500 and billed PWGSC additional hours for employee time handling the transaction.[127] It is difficult to imagine how any appreciable number of hours of work could be attributed to a simple purchase of Christmas ornaments, or to understand why PWGSC did not itself simply buy the ornaments directly from the supplier. We know that PWGSC employees were experienced in the purchase of goods and services. Mr. Guité testifies that he had limited staff and that acquiring promotional items for the PMO tended to be urgent; however, he had some difficulty explaining the urgency for the Christmas ornaments for which Publicité Dézert invoiced Lafleur Communication in April 1997, and for which Lafleur invoiced PWGSC in June 1997.[128] If any time of the Lafleur agency's employees was actually devoted to this transaction, it was adequately compensated by the commission.

The Commission also heard evidence about 24 "Bluenose jackets" acquired by PWGSC at $675 each plus 15% commission by way of a sponsorship contract with Lafleur Communication. The latter subcontracted the procurement of the jackets to Publicité Dézert, which purchased them from a supplier for no more than $240 each,[129] and then had them embroidered and waterproofed for much less than the $435 added to the final price. When he testified, Éric Lafleur was unable to say what Publicité Dézert's profit had been per jacket, but he agreed that the additional costs would not have been more than $250.[130]

The Commission heard no evidence about who received the Bluenose jackets after they had been delivered to Mr. Guité at PWGSC, or for what purpose they had been acquired. They had been given serial numbers starting with 001. According to Huguette Tremblay and Éric Lafleur, jacket number 001 was reserved by Mr. Guité for the Prime Minister of Canada.[131] Mr. Chrétien testifies that although he might have received a Bluenose jacket, he does not remember receiving one, and is sure that he has never used a Bluenose jacket. He says in his testimony that:

> I have received a lot of jackets because when a Prime Minister will go anywhere, in a college or at a celebration, there would be a jacket distributed to the organizers. There was always a gesture where I received jackets and I have dozens and dozens of them either at home or in the archives.[132]

Exactly how the Bluenose jacket serial number 001 promoted Canadian unity remains unexplained.

Lafleur Communication also invoiced PWGSC $202,800 plus 15% commission for 1,014 copies ($200 per copy) of a fine art lithograph of the Bluenose. Although Lafleur Communication was invoiced for the prints by the Bluenose Trust, the covering letter to Jean Lafleur from the Hon. Wilfred P. Moore, Q.C., the Chairman of the Trust, says that the prints were all shipped directly to Mr. Guité.[133] We have no evidence that the $30,420 commission paid to Lafleur was for anything more than receiving and paying the Bluenose Trust invoice, and then invoicing PWGSC. Nor do we know who were the fortunate recipients of these valuable lithographs, especially the 50 or so copies that were very nicely framed by Mrs. Gosselin at Mr. Guité's request.

The evidence before the Commission shows that PWGSC paid for a wide variety of promotional items: pens, coat-of-arms plaques, garment bags, gift-boxed watches, sports watches, golf caps, polo shirts, denim shirts, coat-of-arms cufflinks, $250 clocks, badges, $62 alarm clocks, golf and other umbrellas, deluxe umbrellas, windbreakers, t-shirts, leather waist-packs, money clips, $650 videos, $50 travel bags, "la vie au Canada en 1880" (Life in Canada in 1880) gift packs, ties, leather photo albums and frames, lanyards (for name tags), sports bags with wheels, briefcases, patio umbrellas, leather card-holders, leather writing cases, golf-tee holders, putter cases, gift-boxed pencils, Mag-lites, gold-buckled belts, decorative teaspoons, key cases, and combination leather and felt jackets and autographed golf balls.[134] However, the Commission heard little evidence of what these items were to be used for. Mr. Guité testified that "60 to 70 per cent of the promotional items went to PMO."

When Huguette Tremblay, who worked as Mr. Guité's assistant, testified, she was shown a list of some 31 "Government of Canada" promotional items for 1997, including the Bluenose jackets.[135] She confirms having received delivery of most of the items, which she then divided according to whether they would stay at PWGSC or be delivered to the Prime Minister's Office. Generally speaking, a certain number of each item would go to the PMO, based on written instructions from Mr. Guité, or, on at least two occasions, Jean Carle's selection. The promotional items were put on display in the PWGSC offices by Éric Lafleur, and Mr. Carle would arrive and make his choices, a process Ms. Tremblay referred to at the time as the "government garage sale."[136] Éric Lafleur testifies that most of the 28 items listed on two October 1996 Publicité Dézert invoices to Lafleur Communication totalling $298,907, were chosen by Mr. Carle.[137] The latter testifies he only went once to the PWGSC offices to choose promotional items, which he describes as:

[Unofficial Translation]

> ...it could be 200 travel alarms, it could be 250 umbrellas, it could be 150 pens, like that, 200 watches, but not expensive watches. So, we're talking about approximately 20 items from a table where there must have been maybe 100 on display...We had rain jackets made, yes, jackets...[138]

Mr. Carle denies having ordered a Bluenose jacket, and says that he has no knowledge of such a jacket being delivered to the Prime Minister's Office.[139]

Ms. Tremblay also tells the Commission that PWGSC warehoused its accumulation of promotional items on its own premises or paid the communication agencies to store the items.[140] We have heard or seen little or no evidence of what PWGSC or the PMO ultimately did with these promotional items. But if they were used outside of Canada in connection with the Prime Minister's travels and trade missions, which would explain Mr. Carle's involvement, then their contribution to the cause of national unity and federal visibility within Canada is most certainly in doubt.

6.16
Example—Grand Prix du Canada Tickets

In some cases, sponsorship contracts were also used to purchase tickets to sponsored events. The most astounding example presented to the Commission was in the context of the management of the 1998 Grand Prix du Canada by Groupaction Marketing Inc. Groupaction had the contract for that year only, after Jacques Villeneuve won the Formula 1 World Championship in 1997. As a result, tickets to the 1998 Grand Prix were in demand like never before or since.

The evidence before the Commission indicates that the original arrangement negotiated between Groupaction and the Grand Prix organizers was for a $700,000 sponsorship, which would have entitled Groupaction to a commission of $105,000, plus $50,000 in production costs.[141] In January 1998, Groupaction indicates initially asked for 74 three-day tickets (passes) for the event, but the number of tickets requested by Groupaction increased periodically during the months prior to the signing of the contract with the promoter on May 26, 1998.[142] Groupaction's letters to the Grand Prix organizers indicate that the additional ticket demands were from Groupaction's "partenaire dans ce dossier" (project partner).[143] The final number requested was 230 three-day tickets, worth $264,000.[144] This was far beyond what the promoter was prepared to supply for free. The May 26, 1998, contract therefore increased the sponsorship amount to $900,000, and increased production costs to $114,000.[145] The increased amounts for sponsorship and production costs were the same as the total ticket price, namely $264,000.

When Jean Laflamme, Grand Prix vice-president for Finance and Administration, testified before the Commission, he agreed that production costs had not increased from $50,000 to $114,000, and that the increases to both the sponsorship amount and the production costs were to cover the price of the tickets.[146]

The most expensive of the three-day event tickets were worth $2,800 or $1,400 each ("paddock club" or "loges restaurant," respectively).

Witnesses appearing before the Commission were unable to say to whom all the tickets were given, but the Commission deduces from the evidence that they were distributed by Mr. Guité to his family and friends, personnel at CCSB, and various Liberal politicians and executives of Crown Corporations. Jean Brault, Groupaction's president, testifies that he had no knowledge of the 230 three-day tickets being delivered to Groupaction; Groupaction had purchased its own tickets.[147] It is probable that they were delivered directly to Mr. Guité and distributed according to his directions. Since Groupaction charged a 17.65% commission on production costs, it earned 17.65% on $64,000 worth of tickets (the increased production costs), and 12% on the sponsorship amount. This means that Groupaction earned a $24,000 commission on the tickets that accounted for the increased sponsorship amount ($200,000). Mr. Brault says that he cannot confirm how the tickets were used by the Government of Canada, but he notes that all the seats were occupied at the event.[148] Mr. Guité agrees that the increased sponsorship amount and production costs were precisely designed to "bury" the costs of the $264,000 in "free" tickets.[149]

The presence at the Grand Prix in 1998 of the beneficiaries of free tickets acquired at the expense of the Government of Canada cannot have contributed in any significant way to the promotion of national unity. The use of the free tickets by the beneficiaries of Mr. Guité's largesse created an advantage or benefit for which the Government of Canada obtained no corresponding compensation.

6.17
Communication Canada

In 1998, responsibility for the Canada Information Office (CIO) was transferred from Heritage Canada to PWGSC, and consideration was given to the possibility of integrating all communication services of the Government, including sponsorships and advertising, under one roof at an expanded CIO. Since this was what is called a "machinery of government" issue requiring the approval of the Prime Minister, discussions of the subject involved not only the Minister of PWGSC but also the PMO and the PCO. The opinion of Mr. Pelletier, according to Mr. Quail, was that any transfer of the Sponsorship Program to new management at the CIO should be delayed until after the retirement of Mr. Guité in August 1999. Mr. Quail would have preferred that the amalgamation of communication services take place sooner rather than later.[150] Mr. Pelletier's wishes seem to have prevailed.

In a memorandum dated April 14, 2000, Mr. Mel Cappe, as Clerk of the Privy Council, wrote to Mr. Chrétien, requesting his approval of the transfer of certain responsibilities formerly exercised by CCSB to the CIO. This was the beginning of a gradual transition that culminated, on September 1, 2001, in the creation of Communication Canada, which assumed all of the responsibilities of the CIO—including those transferred to it from CCSB, which effectively ceased to exist. Communication Canada took over the management of the Sponsorship Program.

Mr. Guy McKenzie was appointed Executive Director of Communication Canada in June 2001. He possessed long experience in government administration generally, including program development and implementation. One of his first decisions in his new position was to advise Pierre Tremblay, who had been acting as interim manager of the Sponsorship Program, that his contract would not be renewed at its expiration on December 31, 2001. Mr. Tremblay understood the message he was being given and resigned on November 16, 2001.[151] This left Mr. McKenzie free to reorganize the Program on a basis consistent with his experience and usual government practices, and to engage personnel with the training and experience needed to accomplish the Program's objectives. None of the former personnel of CCSB handling sponsorship files was retained.[152]

The new team at Communication Canada was aware that many of the problems of the past, which had been revealed in an internal audit conducted in 2000, had been due to the lack of clearly defined policy objectives and guidelines, including the absence of criteria for access to the benefits of the program.[153] A new sponsorship solicitation process had been developed early in 2001, and guidelines governing the management of sponsorship files had been adopted and were in the process of being implemented. On January 25, 2002, the communication agencies which in May 2001 had been selected to manage sponsored events were convened to meet representatives of Communication Canada, who explained to them the requirements of the new guidelines.[154]

All of this, presented in the form of an "action plan," was duly approved by the new Minister of PWGSC, the Honourable Don Boudria, on February 25, 2002. The action plan provided a more precise definition of the objectives and priorities of the Sponsorship Program, imposed new requirements for the contents of a sponsorship proposal, and foresaw closer follow-up and supervision of more rigorous administrative and financial procedures.[155]

It is reasonable to assume that if the guidelines and procedures introduced in 2001 to manage the Sponsorship Program had been in place from its inception, the mismanagement and abuses that occurred from 1996 to 2000 would not have been possible.

In spite of the enthusiasm and strenuous efforts of Mr. McKenzie and his team at Communication Canada to reform the Sponsorship Program, political developments were overtaking their efforts. In May 2002, the

Auditor General made public her first report on the three Groupaction contracts, which became the subject of a police investigation, and announced her decision to audit the entire program. Questions were being addressed to the Government in the House of Commons and in the media that required an immediate response. The Honourable Ralph Goodale, the newly appointed Minister of PWGSC, took only a few hours to conclude on May 27, 2002, that a moratorium of the Sponsorship Program should be ordered to permit him to analyze the situation.[156]

The moratorium lasted five weeks, during which Communication Canada at Mr. Goodale's request, worked out the details of an interim Sponsorship Program to be administered entirely by its own personnel, without the intervention or assistance of communication agencies. Mr. Goodale had come to the conclusion, within 24 hours of being asked by the Prime Minister to "fix" what was wrong with the Sponsorship Program, that the contracting out of the administration of a government program of this kind was "not appropriate in the circumstances." His testimony on this subject is eloquent:

> The Hon. R. Goodale: That night, I met with my political staff to do the necessary disengagement from being House Leader and the engagement to being Minister of Public Works. That all had to be accomplished in a very short span of time. I spent a little time with the officials that night from Public Works and from Communication Canada. I met with them in more detail the next morning, trying to brief myself as rapidly as I could on the detail of the issues before me.
>
> The one administrative issue that stood out very quickly as something, to my mind, that needed correction was the way in which the Sponsorship Program had apparently been managed. In those briefings the night before and the morning of Monday, the 27th, I became familiar with the fact that the administration was effectively contracted out.

. . . . . .

> To third-party communications firms that were paid commissions to administer the program. That struck me, quite frankly, as not appropriate in the circumstances and I immediately began to turn my mind to how to run a program of this nature without the intervention of third parties.[157]

Evidently, what was immediately apparent to Mr. Goodale had not occurred to his predecessors as Minister, nor had it been apparent to Mr. Pelletier when the Program was initiated in 1996.

On July 3, 2002, the Sponsorship Program was resumed on a trial basis, using an increased number of personnel from Communication Canada. Even taking into account the cost of the new personnel, the elimination of communication agencies resulted in substantial savings for the Government.[158]

In the meantime the Prime Minister had asked the Honourable Lucienne Robillard, President of the Treasury Board, to study the Sponsorship Program "to determine how [it] could be better managed to ensure value for money and to make recommendations before the return of the House in September. She reported to him on September 5, 2002, with a series of recommendations for better management, delivery, oversight and transparency, all of which had formerly been, apparently, deficient. She added that in view of the preparation and the Treasury Board approvals required, the earliest launch of the revised program would be four months later. From this it may be deduced that the time required for the launch of a new program is at least four months, to allow for necessary planning and approvals.[159] Mr. Chrétien accepted these recommendations and approved the renewal of the Program for one year. This resulted in an announcement of the Sponsorship Program on December 17, 2002, which appears to be the first time it was made known in a formal way to the general public.

Communication Canada proceeded to manage the Sponsorship Program until it was cancelled in December 2003, much to the regret of the personnel of Communication Canada, who are firmly convinced of the benefits to the people of Canada of a well-defined program of this kind when it is administered properly by trained public servants.[160]

Communication Canada was itself disbanded in March 2004.

Endnotes to Chapter VI

1   RSC 1985, c. F-11.

2   "Contracting Policy," to be found at
    www.tbs-sct.gc.ca/pubs_pol/dcgpubs/contracting/contractingpol_e.asp.

3   "Appendix Q – Supplementary Policy and Guidelines with Respect to Contracting Procedures for Public
    Opinion Research and Advertising Services," Exhibit P-123B, pp. 432-440.

4   Government Contracts Regulations, SOR 87-402, section 6, and Contracting Policy, paras. 10.6.5 to
    10.6.7.

5   Financial Administration Act, s. 34(1)(a); Testimony of Ms. Fraser, Transcripts vol. 1, pp. 136-137
    (OE), pp. 141-143 (F).

6   "Policy on Delegation of Authorities," "Procedural Requirements," section 3 found at www.tbs-
    sct.gc.ca/Pubs_pol"dcgpubs/TBM_142"2-1-1_e.asp.

7   Contracting Policy, section 12.3.1.

8   Contracting Policy, section 1.

9   See, for example, Testimony of Mr. Parent, Transcripts vol. 32, pp. 5500-5502, 5504-5505 (OF); pp.
    5500, 5504 (E); Testimony of Mr. Myer, Transcripts vol. 31, pp. 5297-5298, 5300-5305 (OE), pp.
    5300-5301, 5304-5309 (F). Exhibit P-54, pp. 6-8. Testimony of Mr. Parent, Transcripts vol. 32, pp.
    5504-5505 (OF), pp. 5502-5503 (E); Testimony of Mr. Lauzon, Transcripts vol. 26, pp. 4319-4325,
    4345-4346 (OF), pp. 4319-4324, 4342-4343 (E).

10 Testimony of Mr. Cutler, Transcripts vol. 13, pp. 2146-2147, 2119-2120, 2110 (OE); pp. 2151-2152,
    2121-2123, 2112 (F).

11 Exhibit P-23(A), tab B, p. 4.

12 Testimony of Ms. Marcoux, Transcripts vol. 26, pp. 4455-4456 (OF), pp. 4447-4448 (E); Testimony
    of Ms. Maltais, Transcripts vol. 30, pp. 5207-5208 (OF), pp. 5199-5200 (E).

13 Testimony of Mr. Guité, Transcripts vol. 37, p. 6266 (OE), p. 6270 (F); Testimony of Mr. Guité, Transcripts
    vol. 34, pp. 5920-5921 (OE), pp. 5931-5932 (F).

14 Testimony of Mr. Jean Lafleur, Transcripts vol. 75, pp. 13157-13162 (OF), pp. 13146-13151 (E).

15 Exhibit P-106A, tab 13, pp. 91-98.

16 Testimony of Mr. Pelletier, Transcripts vol. 71, pp. 12361, 12363, 12366 (OF), pp. 12356-12358,
    12361(E).

17 Exhibit P-106(A), tab 12.

18 Exhibit P-106(A), tabs 14, 15.

19 Exhibit P-106(A), tab 16.

20 Exhibit P-216.

21 Exhibit P-106(A), tab 17, p. 124.

22 Testimony of Mr. Chrétien, Transcripts vol. 72, pp. 12592-12594 (OF), pp. 12578-12580 (E).

23 Testimony of Mr. S. Dion, Transcripts vol. 62, p. 10884 (OF), pp. 10883-10884 (E); Testimony of Mr. Coderre, Transcripts vol. 60, pp. 11032-11034 (OF), pp 11025-11026 (E); Testimony of Ms. Robillard, Transcripts vol. 65, pp. 11252-11253, 11248-11249 (OF), pp. 11250-11251, 11246-11247 (E); Testimony of Mr. Massé, Transcripts vol. 64, pp. 11196-11197, 11212 (OF), pp. 11195-11196, 11209 (E); Testimony of Mr. Cauchon, Transcripts vol. 65, pp. 11297-11299, 11301-11302 (OF), pp. 11292-11293, 11295-11296 (E); Testimony of Mr. Pettigrew, Transcripts vol. 66, p. 11337 (OF), p. 11336 (E); Testimony of Mr. Martin, Transcripts vol. 73, pp. 12767-12770 (OF), 12776-12779 (F); Testimony of Mr. Goodale, Transcripts vol. 128, pp. 24079-24081 (OE), pp. 24080-24081 (F).

24 Testimony of Mr. Guité, Transcripts vol. 34, pp. 5937-5938 (OE), pp. 5950-5951 (F).

25 Testimony of Mr. Guité, Transcripts vol. 33, p. 5673 (OE), p. 5682 (F); Exhibit P-87(B), p. 390; Testimony of Ms. Marcoux, Transcripts vol. 26, pp. 4493-4496 (OF), pp. 4482-4485 (E).

26 Testimony of Mr. Guité, Transcripts vol. 33, pp. 5669-5670, 5707-5708 (OE), pp. 5676-5677, 5720-5721 (F).

27 Testimony of Mr. Guité, Transcripts vol. 37, pp. 6302-6303 (OE), pp. 6310-6312 (F).

28 Testimony of Mr. Guité, Transcripts vol. 33, pp. 5674-5675 (OE), pp. 5677-5678 (F).

29 Exhibit P-208(D), p. 115.

30 Testimony of Mr. Guité, Transcripts vol. 33, pp. 5673-5674 (OE), pp. 5681-5682 (F); Testimony of Mr. Guité, Transcripts vol. 33, pp. 5676-5677 (OE), pp. 5685-5686 (F).

31 Testimony of Mr. Pelletier, Transcripts vol. 71, pp. 12390-12393 (OF), pp. 12383-12385 (E).

32 Testimony of Mr. Guité, Transcripts vol. 33, pp. 5669, 5676 (OE), pp. 5677, 5686 (F); Testimony of Mr. Guité, Transcripts vol. 34, pp. 5858, 5861-5862 (OE); pp. 5863-5864, 5868-5869 (F); Testimony of Mr. Guité, Transcripts vol. 35, pp. 5973-5974 (OE), pp. 5975-5976 (F).

33 Testimony of Mr. Guité, Transcripts vol. 33, pp. 5667-5668 (OE), p. 5675 (F).

34 Testimony of Mr. Pelletier, Transcripts vol. 71, pp. 12460-12462 (OF), pp. 12447-12449 (E).

35 Testimony of Mr. Pelletier, Transcripts vol. 71, pp. 12448-12450 (OF), pp. 12436-12438 (E).

36 Testimony of Mr. Guité, Transcripts vol. 35, p. 6116 (OE), p. 6128 (F).

37 Testimony of Mr. Guité, Transcripts vol. 35, p. 6116 (OE), p. 6128 (F); Testimony of Mr. Guité, Transcripts vol. 37, pp. 6460-6461 (OF), pp. 6484-6486 (E); Testimony of Mr. Guité, Transcripts vol. 110, pp. 20250-20252 (OE), pp. 20264-20266 (F).

38 Testimony of Mr. Guité, Transcripts vol. 111, pp. 20320, 20322 (OE), pp. 20325, 20326-20327 (F); Testimony of Mr. Guité, Transcripts vol. 110, p. 20212 (OE), p. 20223 (F).

39 Testimony of Mr. Pelletier, Transcripts vol. 71, pp. 12390-12393 (OF),pp. 12383-12364(E).

40 Testimony of Mr. Pelletier, Transcripts vol. 71, p. 12398 (OF), pp. 12389-12390 (E).

41 Testimony of Mr. Pelletier, Transcripts vol. 129, p. 24496 (OF), p. 24481 (E).

42 Testimony of Mr. Pelletier, Transcripts vol. 71, pp. 12402-12403 (OF), 12393-12394 (E).

43 Testimony of Mr. Pelletier, Transcripts vol. 71, pp. 12402-12403 (OF), pp. 12393-12394 (E).

44 Exhibit P-78.

45 Testimony of Ms. Bouvier, Transcripts vol. 25, pp. 4145, 4159-4160, 4162-4163 (OF), pp. 4142, 4155, 4158-4159 (E).

46 Testimony of Mr. Gagliano, Transcripts vol. 67, pp. 11588-11589, 11639-11640(OF), pp. 11584, 11632(E); p. 11652-11653(OF), pp. 11651-11652 (E).

[47] Testimony of Mr. Gagliano, Transcripts vol. 67, pp. 11594, 11597-11599 (OF), pp. 11589, 11592-11593 (E); Testimony of Mr. Gagliano, Transcripts vol. 68, pp. 11653, 11795-11809 (OF), pp. 11652-11653, 11785-11796 (E).

[48] Testimony of Mr. Gagliano, Transcripts vol. 68, pp. 11814-11817, 11844-11845 (OF), pp. 11804-11805, 11830-11831 (E).

[49] Testimony of Mr. Quail, Transcripts vol. 39, pp. 6706-6707(OE), pp. 6709-6710(F).

[50] Testimony of Mr. Stobbe, Transcripts vol. 40, pp. 6899-6901 (OE), pp. 6901-6904 (E).

[51] Testimony of Mr. Guité, Transcripts vol. 108, p. 19786 (OE), 19799 (F); Testimony of Mr. Dingwall, Transcripts vol. 60, p. 10594-10597 (OE), pp. 10600-10604 (F).

[52] Testimony of Mr. Guité, Transcripts vol. 33, p. 5669 (OE), p. 5677 (F).

[53] Testimony of Mr. Quail, Transcripts vol. 40, pp. 6883-6885 (OE), pp. 6884-6886 (F).

[54] Testimony of Mr. Stobbe, Transcripts vol. 40, pp. 6897-6898 (OE), pp. 6900-6901 (F).

[55] Testimony of Mr. Guité, Transcripts vol. 33, pp. 5674-5675 (OE), pp. 5682-5683 (F).

[56] Testimony of Mr. Quail, Transcripts vol. 39, pp. 6756-6757(OE), p. 6765(F).

[57] Testimony of Mr. Quail, Transcripts vol. 39, pp. 6729, 6844-6847 (OE), pp. 6734, 6865-6867 (F).

[58] Exhibit P-23(A), tab 1A (7121827).

[59] Exhibit P-23(A), tab 1B (7121838).

[60] Exhibit P-104, p. 15.

[61] Testimony of Mr. Guité, Transcripts vol. 38, pp. 6520-6522 (OE), pp. 6524-6525 (F); vol. 108, pp. 19642-19643 (OE), pp. 19642-19644 (F).

[62] Exhibit P-186(B), pp. 216-217.

[63] Exhibit P-186(B), p. 218.

[64] Testimony of Mr. Dingwall, Transcripts vol. 60, pp. 10599-10600 (OE), p. 10605 (F).

[65] Exhibit P-23A tab C (7121915).

[66] Testimony of Mr. Guité, Transcripts vol. 33, pp. 5643, 5653-5655 (OE); pp. 5647-5648, 5658-5661 (F).

[67] Exhibit P-23A, tab C (7121875).

[68] Exhibit P-104, tab 1; Exhibit P23(A), tab D.

[69] Exhibit P-120(C), tabs 12, 18.

[70] Testimony of Mr. Quail, Transcripts vol. 39, pp. 6834-6836 (OE), pp. 6853-6855 (F).

[71] Testimony of Mr. Pelletier, Transcripts vol. 71, pp. 12489-12490 (OF), pp. 12473-12474 (E); Testimony of Mr. Gagliano, Transcripts vol. 68, pp. 11734-11737 (OF), pp. 11728-11731 (E).

[72] Testimony of Mr. Gagliano, Transcripts vol. 68, pp. 11741-11742 (OF), p. 11735 (E).

[73] For example, see Testimony of Mr. Guité, Transcripts vol. 108, pp. 19645-19646 (OE), pp. 19646-19647 (F).

[74] Exhibit P-23A, tab 2A (7122008).

[75] Testimony of Mr. Guité, Transcripts vol. 108, p. 19644 (OE), pp. 19644-19645 (F); Testimony of Mr. Guité, Transcripts vol. 33, pp. 5677-5678 (OE), p. 5687 (F).

[76] Testimony of Mr. Gagliano, Transcripts vol. 67, p. 11590 (OF), p. 11585 (E); Testimony of Mr. Gagliano, Transcripts vol. 68, pp. 11705-11706 (OF), pp. 11701-11702 (E); Testimony of Ms. Roy, Transcripts vol. 22, pp. 3637-3641 (OF), pp. 3637-3641 (E).

77 Testimony of Ms. Roy, Transcripts vol. 23, pp. 3708-3709, 3778-3779 (OF), pp. 3709, 3772-3773 (E).

78 Testimony of Mr. Bilodeau, Transcripts vol. 46, pp. 7917-7918 (OF), pp. 7882-7884 (E).

79 Testimony of Mr. Guité, Transcripts vol. 34, pp. 5920-5923 (OE), pp. 5931-5934 (F).

80 Exhibit P-105B, tab 5.

81 Testimony of Mr. Gagliano, Transcripts, vol. 68, pp. 11783-11784 (OF), pp. 11773-11774 (E).

82 Testimony of Ms. Maltais, Transcripts vol. 30, p. 5196 (OF), pp. 5188-5189 (E).

83 Testimony of Ms. Maltais, Transcripts vol. 30, p. 5196 (OF), p. 5189 (E).

84 Testimony of Mr. Quail, Transcripts vol. 39, pp. 6816-6819 (OE), pp. 6832-6835 (F); Testimony of Ms. Marcoux, Transcripts vol. 26, p. 4478 (OF), pp. 4467-4468 (E).

85 Testimony of Ms. Marcoux, Transcripts vol. 26, pp. 4478-4485 (OF), pp. 4468-4474 (E); Testimony of Mr. Guité, Transcripts vol. 37, pp. 6419-6421 (OE), pp. 6439-6441 (F).

86 Testimony of Ms. Roy, Transcripts vol. 22, pp. 3655-3664 (OF), pp. 3647-3655 (E).

87 Testimony of Ms. Roy, Transcripts vol. 22, pp. 3667-3668 (OF), p. 3659 (E).

88 Testimony of Ms. Roy, Transcripts vol. 23, pp. 3768-3769 (OF), p. 3764 (E).

89 Testimony of Mr. Hayter, Transcripts vol. 122, pp. 22829-22830 (OE), pp. 22836-22837 (F); Testimony of Mr. Hayter, Transcripts vol. 123, p. 23032 (OE), pp. 23036-23037 (F).

90 Testimony of Mr. Hayter, Transcripts vol. 122, pp. 22851-22852 (OE), pp. 22860-22861 (F).

91 Exhibit P-412, p. 213.

92 Testimony of Ms. Tremblay, Transcripts vol. 87, pp. 15368-15370 (OF), pp. 15364-15365 (E); Testimony of Mr. Parent, Transcripts vol. 87, pp. 15388-15390 (OF), pp. 15381-15382 (E).

93 Testimony of Mr. Gagliano, Transcripts vol. 131, pp. 24950-24955 (OF), pp. 24945-24950 (E).

94 Exhibit P-265(A), Index preceding p. 1; Testimony of Mr. Gosselin, Transcripts vol. 82, p. 14685-14687, 14692-14694 (OF), pp. 14666-14668, 14672-14675 (E).

95 Testimony of Mr. Hayter, Transcripts vol. 122, pp. 22847-22848 (OE), pp. 22856-22857 (F).

96 Testimony of Mr. Quail, Transcripts vol. 39, pp. 6804-6805 (OE), pp. 6818-6819 (F).

97 Exhibit P-123(A), p. 322.

98 Testimony of Mr. Neville, Transcripts vol. 41, pp. 7009-7014 (OE), pp. 7011-7016 (F).

99 Testimony of Mr. Lafleur, Transcripts vol. 79, pp. 13852-13858 (OF), pp. 13846-13852 (E); Testimony of Mr. Gosselin, Transcripts vol. 83, pp. 14752-14753, 14761-14765 (OF), pp. 14749-14750, 14758-14761 (E).

100 Testimony of Ms. Cumming, Transcripts vol. 88 (Part I), pp. 15547-15560 (OE), pp. 15549-15565 (F).

101 See, for example, Exhibit P-219(A), pp. 124-131, 129-130.

102 Exhibit P-216(B), p. 10.

103 According to the testimony heard by the Commission, these "maquettes" or "mock-ups" were the models or samples created before the final decision was made on any given sign, brochure or promotional item.

104 Exhibit P-219(A), pp. 34-35, 43.

105 Testimony of Mr. Jean Lafleur, Transcripts vol. 76, p. 13432 (OF), p. 13420 (E).

106 Testimony of Mr. Jean Lafleur, Transcripts vol. 77, pp. 13467-13473 (OF), pp. 13461-13466 (E).

107 Exhibit P-216(B), p. 10; Exhibit P-219(A), pp. 115-116.

108 Exhibit P-216(B), p. 10.

[109] Exhibit P-257(A), pp. 53-57.

[110] Exhibit P-257(B), p. 3; Exhibit P-272, p. 2; Exhibit P-277(A), pp. 6, 8, 21, 33 (for a total of 1,188 hours).

[111] Testimony of Mr. Gilles-André Gosselin, Transcripts vol. 84, pp. 14931-14936 (OF), pp. 14929-14933 (E).

[112] See, for example, Exhibit P-277(A), p. 66; Exhibit P-272, p. 2.

[113] Exhibit P-261, pp. 33, 39, 54, 112, 125; Exhibit P-261, pp. 45-47, 109.

[114] Testimony of Mr. Valente, Transcripts vol. 85, p. 15180 (OF), p. 15167 (E).

[115] Testimony of Mr. Coffin, Transcripts vol. 106, pp. 19325-19327 (OE), pp. 19328-19331 (F).

[116] Testimony of Mr. Jean Lafleur, Transcripts vol. 75, p. 13190 (F), p. 13176 (E).

[117] Testimony of Mr. Jean Lafleur, Transcripts vol. 75, pp. 13195-13196 (F), pp. 13180-13181 (E).

[118] Testimony of Mr. Jean Lafleur, Transcripts vol. 75, pp. 13216-13217 (F), p. 13199 (E).

[119] Testimony of Mr. Jean Lafleur, Transcripts vol. 77, p. 13517 (OF), p. 13508 (E).

[120] Testimony of Mr. Jean Lafleur, Transcripts vol. 78, p. 13764 (OF), 13749-13750 (E).

[121] See, for example, Exhibit P-219(A), p. 10.

[122] Exhibit P-226, pp. 199-202.

[123] Exhibit P-428(A), p. 82.

[124] Exhibit P-428(A), p. 93.

[125] Exhibit P-226, pp. 82-85.

[126] Exhibit P-226, p. 87.

[127] Exhibit P-226, pp. 87-89.

[128] Exhibit P-226, p. 88.

[129] Exhibit P-226, p. 133.

[130] Testimony of Mr. Éric Lafleur, Transcripts vol. 80, p. 14176 (OF), p. 14161 (E).

[131] Testimony of Mr. Éric Lafleur, Transcripts vol. 80, p. 14168 (OF), 14154 (E); Testimony of Ms. Tremblay, Transcripts vol. 20, p. 3220.

[132] Testimony of Mr. Chrétien, Transcripts vol. 72, p. 12669 (OE), p. 12674 (E).

[133] Exhibit P-108, pp. 97, 98.

[134] Exhibit P-266, pp. 23, 24, 155; Exhibit P-351, p. 32; Testimony of Ms. Tremblay, Transcripts vol. 20, pp. 3223-3224 (OF), pp. 3216 (E); vol. 21, pp. 3436-3437 (OE), pp. 3436-3437 (F); Testimony of Mr. É. Lafleur, Transcripts vol. 80, pp. 14185-14186 (OF), pp. 14170-14171 (E); Testimony of Mr. Guité, vol. 110, p. 20087 (OE), pp. 20088-20089 (F).

[135] Exhibit P-64(A), pp. 153-155; Testimony of Ms. Huguette Tremblay, Transcripts vol. 20, pp. 3217-3218 (OF), pp. 3210-3211 (E).

[136] Testimony of Ms. Tremblay, Transcripts vol. 20, pp. 3221-3225 (OF), 3214-3217 (E).

[137] Exhibit P-226, pp. 23-24; Testimony of Mr. Éric Lafleur, Transcripts vol. 80, p. 14087 (OF), p. 14081 (E).

[138] Testimony of Mr. Carle, Transcripts vol. 70, p. 12225 (OF), p. 12215 (E).

[139] Testimony of Mr. Carle, Transcripts vol. 70, pp. 12225-12226 (OF), pp. 12215-12216 (E).

[140] Testimony of Ms. Tremblay, Transcripts vol. 20, pp. 3205-3206, 3214-3215, 3239-3240 (OF), pp. 3200, 3208, 3229-3230 (E).

[141]   Testimony of Mr. Brault, Transcripts vol. 91, pp. 16085-16087 (OF), pp. 16080-16083 (E); Exhibit C-309, p. 255-256.

[142]   Exhibit C-309, pp. 126-127, 132-134, 164.

[143]   Exhibit C-309, pp. 132-134.

[144]   Exhibit C-309, p. 164.

[145]   Exhibit C-309, pp. 33-40.

[146]   Testimony of Mr. Laflamme or Mr. Spalding, Transcripts vol. 101, pp. 18243-18244 (OF), p. 18229 (E).

[147]   Testimony of Mr. Brault, Transcripts vol. 91, pp. 16097-16100 (OF), 16091-16094 (E).

[148]   Testimony of Mr. Brault, Transcripts vol. 91, p. 16109 (OF), 16102 (E).

[149]   Testimony of Mr. Guité, Transcripts vol. 110, pp. 20099-20100 (OE), pp. 20101-20102 (F).

[150]   Testimony of Mr. Quail, Transcripts vol. 39, pp. 6824 (OE), p. 6841 (F).

[151]   Exhibit P-127(A), tab A, para. 17; Exhibit P-127(D), p. 1169-1170.

[152]   Testimony of Ms. Tremblay vol. 20, pp. 3145-3146 (OF), pp. 3144-3145 (E); Testimony of Ms. Larose, Transcripts vol. 27, p. 4642 (OF), pp. 4695-4696 (E); Testimony of Mr. Lauzon, Transcripts vol. 25, pp. 4255, 4257, 4312-4313 (OF), pp. 4244, 4246, 4295; Testimony of Ms. Roy, Transcripts vol. 21, pp. 3465-3466 (OF), pp. 3459-3460 (E); Testimony of Mr. Myer, Transcripts vol. 31, pp. 5267-5268, 5297 (OE), pp. 5267-5268, 5301 (F).

[153]   Testimony of Mr. McKenzie, Transcripts vol. 42, pp. 7229-7231 (OF), pp. 7229-7231 (E); Exhibit P-127(A), tab A, paras. 21, 22; Testimony of Mr. McKenzie, Transcripts vol. 42, pp. 7099-7100 (OF), pp. 7099-7100 (E).

[154]   Testimony of Mr. McKenzie, Transcripts vol. 42, pp. 7124-7126 (OF), pp. 7125-7127 (E).

[155]   Exhibit P-127(D), tab B11, p. 1353.

[156]   Testimony of Mr. Goodale, Transcripts vol. 128, pp. 24086-24088 (OE), pp. 24086-24089 (F).

[157]   Testimony of Mr. Goodale, Transcripts vol. 128, p. 24086 (OE), pp. 24086-24087 (F).

[158]   Testimony of Mr. G. Pelletier, Transcripts vol. 42, p. 7162 (OF), p. 7162 (E).

[159]   Exhibit P-196(B), pp. 231-234.

[160]   Testimony of Mr. McKenzie, Mr. G. Pelletier, and Ms. Viau, Transcripts vol. 42, pp. 7171-7173 (OF), pp. 7171-7173 (E).

Chapter VII

AUDITS and INVESTIGATIONS

7.1
Introduction

It is difficult for an ordinary citizen to understand how gross mismanagement of a government program can remain undetected for more than five years. It is even more difficult to understand how a series of audits and investigations conducted during that period, each of which revealed at least some aspects of the mismanagement, did not provoke a reaction from the public servants who were supposed to supervise the work of the employees implementing the program (sometimes called "oversight") or at least enough of a reaction to prevent the continuation of the problems which had been revealed.

Within Public Works and Government Services Canada (PWGSC) there is an organization named the Audit and Ethics Branch (AEB), which has the function of conducting periodic audits of its various procurement and program management operations. In 1993, the AEB was called the Audit and Evaluation Branch, and in 1996 it was renamed the Audit and Review Branch.

In 2002 it assumed its present name. It is headed by a director general, who reports to the Deputy Minister (DM).

The existence of the AEB confirms that the Government is aware that within a department handling billions of dollars of contracts, the possibility exists of incidents of dishonesty, incompetence and error being committed by public servants. The obvious purpose of periodic audits is to discover and expose such matters, whether systemic or isolated, so that they can be corrected, and so that any incompetent or dishonest government employees can be relieved of their functions, disciplined or retrained, depending on the circumstances.

Audits may be of various kinds. A financial attest audit is designed to give an opinion on financial statements. Compliance audits seek to find out if practices and procedures of the organization being audited comply with the law and Treasury Board policies. Performance audits look into whether value for money is being received. Forensic audits are more detailed and intense, since they seek to uncover mismanagement or wrongdoing. A forensic audit will usually not be ordered unless there has been a serious complaint alleging fraud or wrongdoing, or unless a compliance audit has disclosed circumstances that indicate the real possibility of improper behaviour. No matter what kind of audit has been performed, the opinion and advice of the auditor must be fearless and uncompromising. If anomalies are discovered, they must be reported.

The internal audit function should not be confused with the role played by the Office of the Auditor General (OAG). The OAG is the Government's independent external auditor, reporting directly to Parliament, whereas the AEB reports to the DM about the departmental operations of PWGSC.

With this background, let us examine the various audits and investigations which were carried out over the years, either by the AEB or on its behalf, of the organizations within PWGSC which were handling the Government's advertising activities and sponsorships.

7.2
Management Control Framework Assessment

In March 1995 Richard Neville, the Assistant Deputy Minister (ADM) who was at that time supervising the Advertising and Public Opinion Research Sector (APORS), requested the AEB to carry out an analysis of the management control framework in effect at APORS, then a newly created organization, to ensure that it was starting out on the right foot. The objective was to find out if APORS had made appropriate plans and reporting mechanisms, and if there were proper accountability and performance systems in place. Julia Ginley, an employee of AEB, made the assessment and analysis. She signed a report dated March 25, 1995, which recommended that "at some future date an audit of compliance to the Contracting Policy...should be conducted."[1]

This recommendation was based upon interviews she had conducted with a number of key employees of APORS, including Mr. Guité and Mr. Cutler, who was at that time its manager of contracting. Mr. Cutler made certain troubling statements to her which she recorded in her notes, as "political sensitivities = allegations of bid rigging, or complaints to Minister. Answer is to follow the Rules religiously." She was also concerned to learn that Mr. Guité was meeting the Minister's Chief of Staff (Mr. Kinsella) once a week, and had a shredder beside his desk.[2]

One would think that suggestions of bid-rigging and political interference in the management of an organization charged with administering a huge advertising budget would be enough reason to call for an audit as Ms. Ginley had recommended, but Mr. Neville did not think that an audit was warranted in 1995,[3] and that any deficiencies could be attributed to the fact that APORS had been formed only recently. He decided that an audit could be put off until 1996 or 1997.

7.3
Allan Cutler's Complaint

Prior to 1994 Allan Cutler was a procurement officer for PWGSC, working in the Public Relations and Print Contract Services Sector (PRPCSS) which was not then under Mr. Guité's management. However, on occasion he was called upon to negotiate contracts with advertising agencies that had been selected by APORS. Mr. Guité was very unhappy with any delay in concluding contracts. The minutes of a meeting held on November 17, 1994, to discuss this problem contain the following extracts. The minutes were prepared by Mr. Cutler, but their accuracy is not challenged.

> Chuck stated that clients are disgusted with the normal contracting rules and regulations being applied by PRPCSS to advertising.

> In Chuck's view…PRPCSS should only take two days to get the contract booked. Normal rules and regulations should not apply to advertising. He will talk to the Minister to have these changed.

> Also he can not accept that the normal rules requiring a cost analyst and legal review are acceptable in advertising.

> Chuck stated that the Minister could remove the responsibility for advertising contracting from PRPCSS and delegate authority to clients if we are going to continue to cause problems.

> ……..

> Chuck said that advertising is clearly a competitive process and that we should not consider it non-competitive…

> Chuck stated that it had taken him two weeks to convince Treasury Board that price should not be a factor in the advertising selection process. He objects to any evaluation of cost in PRPCSS preparing and awarding a contract. PRPCSS should just use boiler plate contracts and issue the same contract format to all firms, and not examine cost at all.

> Chuck also stated that if he considers the price fair for advertising, PRPCSS should not dispute this. Creativity can not be costed. Any resulting invoice should just be paid. If he tells

us to issue the contract we should do so. He pointed out that the Minister could delegate the contractual authority to him.

Pierre [a different Pierre Tremblay who was then the director of PRPCSS and Allan Cutler's superior] stated that we could appreciate his concerns but that we are working in a structured environment and are responsible for applying the normal contracting rules and regulations to all contracts. In order for advertising to deviate from normal government contract policy, we would need written direction from higher levels.

Pierre stated that we will not resist any decisions made by our Minister, and will respect these decisions.

Chuck stated that he is going to discuss advertising with the Minister today to get the problem rectified.[4]

It should be noted that this meeting took place four months before Ms. Ginley's assessment described above. The minutes show that in spite of the adoption of Appendix Q by Treasury Board, Mr. Guité was not in agreement with its requirements, or with the Government's Contracting Policy in general, at least to the extent that it applied to contracts with advertising agencies. He was obviously confident of his influence with the Minister's office, and of his ability to persuade the Minister to his point of view.

Subsequent events indicate that Mr. Guité's confidence was well founded. Only weeks after the meeting of November 17, 1994, Mr. Cutler was informed that he and two other employees of PRPCSS were being transferred to APORS, and that from then on contracting for advertising would fall under Mr. Guité's authority.[5]

Shortly after his arrival at APORS, Mr. Cutler became concerned about contracting practices there. They were regularly not in conformity with the normal rules. For example, documents were back-dated; contracts were issued with no financial authority, no preliminary analysis and no legal review; information in contract files was falsified; and commissions were paid for work that was not performed. On February 5, 1995, Mr. Cutler began to keep a computer log to record his concerns, some of which he dared to raise with Mr. Guité. The latter's response was to inform him that he would now be reporting to Mario Parent, who until then had been at a lower level than Mr. Cutler. For all practical purposes, he had been demoted.

Mr. Cutler's concerns about contracting practices at APORS steadily increased and he began to refuse to sign contracts that he considered to be questionable or improper, although he continued to prepare them for signature by others, as instructed. In April 1996, Mr. Parent explicitly ordered him to sign a contract, telling him, apparently on behalf of Mr. Guité, that the latter was tired of his refusal to approve or sign contracts, and that there would be a price to pay for refusing. Mr. Cutler refused to sign.[6]

However, he was sufficiently alarmed by Mr. Parent's vague threat that he wrote to his union representative, detailing the many irregularities which he had observed. The union representative in turn wrote to Mr. James Stobbe, then in charge of dealing with complaints of this kind.[7] Mr. Stobbe did not favour an audit, but felt Mr. Cutler's allegations were sufficiently serious to discuss them with Mr. Norman Steinberg, the Director General of AEB. The latter delegated Ms. Janet Labelle from his office to investigate Mr. Cutler's allegations. After interviewing him and examining the documentary evidence he had accumulated, she concluded they were well founded.[8]

Although Mr. Cutler had not made an allegation that Mr. Guité was motivated by personal gain, an allegation which would certainly have required verification, Mr. Steinberg decided, over Mr. Stobbe's opposition, that there should be an audit of APORS contracting practices, since there were clearly indications of pressure on Mr. Cutler to break rules or to circumvent policies.[9]

While this was going on, Mr. Guité was dealing with Mr. Cutler in his own way. On June 11, 1996, he called him into a meeting and told him he had been declared surplus, which meant, in effect, that he had no functions to perform and no future in the public service. Mr. Cutler believed that it was a necessary preliminary step towards being fired.[10] Mr. Guité says that his decision had nothing to do with Mr. Cutler's complaint to the union,[11] but the coincidence of dates is striking; on June 10, Mr. Cutler had met with Ms. Labelle to provide her with copies of documents supporting his allegations. It might be noted as well that the decision to shelve Mr. Cutler was taken at a time when Mr. Guité had begun to award sponsorship contracts. It may be presumed that he did not want someone like Mr. Cutler, who insisted on observing the rules, to obstruct or delay his method of handling sponsorship files.

On July 17, 1996, Mr. Cutler filed a grievance, alleging that Mr. Guité's behaviour towards him constituted an improper threat to his employment. The grievance was settled more than a year and a half later, on February 24, 1998, by a reassignment of Mr. Cutler to a new position and by a letter of apology to him from an officer of PWGSC, but not from Mr. Guité himself. The letter acknowledges on behalf of the Deputy Minister that senior management of APORS (presumably Mr. Guité) acted "inappropriately" in informing him that his position would be declared surplus, and that "questionable judgment" had been exercised. The letter goes on to say that "steps have been taken to ensure there will be no recurrence." But, in fact, to the best of Mr. Cutler's knowledge, no such steps were taken nor has the Commission been informed of any such steps.[12] Mr. Neville admits that it is surprising that Mr. Guité was not reproached or reprimanded in any way for his behaviour towards Mr. Cutler.

During the hearings, Mario Parent was questioned concerning his complaisant behaviour in signing contracts and certifying payments on the instructions of Mr. Guité, when he knew nothing about the matters he was approving by his signature. Mr. Parent testified emotionally that he had complied blindly with Mr. Guité's instructions because he remembered well what had happened to Mr. Cutler when the latter had dared to refuse to do what he was told.[13] Mr. Parent was simply afraid of losing his job. It is probable that the other employees of APORS and CCSB who did what they were told to do by Mr. Guité were moved by similar sentiments and apprehensions.

If whistleblower legislation is to have any meaning, it must protect public servants from the kind of retaliation to which Mr. Cutler was subjected.

7.4

Ernst & Young Audit of APORS

Mr. Steinberg decided to retain the services of outside auditors to carry out a compliance audit of APORS as a result of Mr. Cutler's complaint and allegations. Ernst & Young, which did work from time to time for PWGSC, was engaged in July 1996 for this purpose. The audit team was composed of Ms. Deanna Monaghan, who was its head, Ms. Madeleine Brillant and Ms. Julie Morin.[14] It was not foreseen that they would carry out a forensic audit, but if in the course of their work they uncovered reasons to suspect situations of personal gain, they would be expected to report them.[15]

At the time of the Ernst & Young audit, a few sponsorship contracts had already been awarded. They were included in the audit sample, but were not distinguished from advertising contracts. The audit report did not draw attention to the fact that in the case of sponsorship files, APORS was both the project authority and the contract authority.

Mr. Cutler, on the advice of his union representative and because of the pending grievance, refused to be interviewed by the auditors. For unexplained reasons, the results of Ms. Labelle's interviews and investigation were not communicated to the auditors, although they knew about Mr. Cutler's allegations.[16] They reviewed a random sample of files as well as the files specifically identified by Mr. Cutler as problematic. They also reviewed 15 out of 32 competitions to select advertising agencies.

On September 13, 1996, Ms. Brillant sent Mr. Raoul Solon, who had been delegated by Mr. Steinberg to be the representative of AEB having a working relationship with the Ernst & Young team, a draft document entitled "Preliminary Survey Report," which contained the following preliminary findings under the heading "Risk Assessment":

- [APORS] could be acting in a manner not in accordance with Treasury Board policies and specific contracting policies;

- Contracts could be awarded unfairly and to the benefit of [selected] contractors;

- The tendering process could be perceived as not being transparent and open therefore potentially resulting in criticism to the government;

- The government could not receive full value for its money.[17]

In a subsequent draft of the same document, these alarming "risk areas" have been eliminated.[18] No one from the Ernst & Young audit team could recall why these preliminary findings had been removed from the "Preliminary Survey Report," or who suggested such removal. These "risk areas" are not mentioned in the final report of the auditors.[19]

The Final Report[20] is a 21-page document delivered by Ernst & Young to AEB in November 1996, after its contents had been discussed with Mr. Solon and others.[21] It constitutes a severe criticism of the advertising competitions conducted by APORS, in which compliance with policy and guidelines was rare. With respect to contracting, instances of irregularities and non-compliance with rules and policies are identified in a high percentage of cases. The section entitled "Audit Conclusions and Recommendations" commences with the following statement:

> Our audit findings indicated instances of non compliance to policies and procedures.[22]

It then goes on to make two recommendations, which are obviously alternatives, "in order to avoid potential problems." The first recommendation is to redirect the procurement process away from APORS to another section of PWGSC, due to the lack of trained personnel in APORS to handle this aspect of their activity. The alternative recommendation is to maintain the status quo but to implement more rigid controls.[23]

When the audit conclusions were first drafted by Ms. Brillant, the opening paragraph was worded much more strongly. The draft read:

> Our audit findings reveal non compliance to policies and procedures on a consistent basis. Fortunately, no legal action or public attention has resulted from the deviations thus far. In order to avoid potential embarrassing situations it is best to address the issues immediately.[24]

The draft report was discussed with Mr. Solon before it was put in its final form,[25] in which "instances of non compliance" replaces the wording "non compliance...on a consistent basis." The audit team does not recall being asked or told to change the language from the original draft,[26] and it is possible they decided to modify it on their own. Certainly, the original draft contains a much stronger warning that immediate remedial work is advisable.

The Final Report is preceded by an Executive Summary of four pages, which includes on the first page a General Assessment which reads as follows:

> The audit of the advertising contracting process determined that APORS' contracting activities generally follow the prescribed contracting policies and procedures but that there are recurring instances of non-compliance with specific contracting policies.
>
> ...With a few exceptions, the overall policies and procedures governing APORS were assessed as being appropriate.
>
> We found no instances where non-compliance might have led to situations of personal gain or benefit.[27]

Mr. Steinberg testified that the General Assessment is not a fair or accurate summary of the report as a whole, and that it gives the impression that APORS was generally following prescribed contracting policies, when in fact the report comes to the contrary conclusion.[28] The reference in the last paragraph to "no instances...of personal gain or benefit" leaves the reader with the impression that the auditors had examined this question, when in fact, being a compliance audit, the question of fraud or impropriety had not been looked into at all.

In their appearance before the Commission, members of the audit team of Ernst & Young were hard pressed to explain the mild wording of the General Assessment contained in the Executive Summary. They recognized that, human nature being what it is, most persons who would be expected to take cognizance of the Final Report would rely upon the Executive Summary, or even upon the General Assessment, and would not bother to read the entire report, or, in many cases, the entire Executive Summary.[29] It was therefore imperative that the General Assessment be an accurate reflection of the entire report. Although Ms. Monaghan of Ernst & Young reluctantly acknowledged that the General Assessment should have been "stronger," she continued to defend it as fair and reasonable.[30] Nonetheless, in seven out of 26 areas examined, APORS failed to comply with the rules, a rate of non-compliance of about 27 per cent. It cannot be seriously argued that that constituted general compliance with the contracting policies.

The established procedure at PWGSC required that the report be sent to Mr. Guité, who was expected to put together an "action plan" to remedy the problems that had been identified. Mr. Stobbe followed this procedure and says that he gave no thought to removing Mr. Guité as head of APORS.[31] Mr. Guité's "management response" was to agree that the procurement function should be transferred out of APORS, in accordance with the first recommendation. This response was communicated by Mr. Stobbe to Mr. Steinberg six months later, on June 5, 1997.[32] No one explains why it took six months to formulate and transmit the management response. Clearly, Mr. Stobbe did not think there was any urgency.

It was also the established procedure that the audit report should be considered by the Audit and Review Committee at PWGSC, which meets, according to Mr. Quail, quarterly.[33] Consideration of the Ernst & Young report and Mr. Guité's management response was done at a meeting of the Committee held on July 28, 1997, at which time the action plan of Mr. Guité was approved. However, the transfer of procurement out of APORS had to be delayed until administrative arrangements could be finalized. In the meantime, the Executive Summary and management response were forwarded to the Treasury Board Secretariat on September 1997.[34] No one alerted Treasury Board that there were serious problems at APORS,[35] and it could not be expected to take any initiatives on the basis of the bland General Assessment in the Executive Summary.

Mr. Quail, as a member of the Audit and Review Committee, saw the audit report, and testifies that he took it for granted that the management response would be implemented. He says that in his experience, public servants who undertake to implement action plans may be trusted to do so. He sees nothing wrong with asking the manager who is the source of administrative problems, such as those identified in the Ernst & Young report, to be in charge of implementing the changes needed to correct those problems.[36]

In fact, the action plan was never implemented. Mr. Stobbe was responsible for supervising its implementation, and he admits that he did nothing.[37] No one from the AEB did a follow-up to ensure that it was implemented. Mr. Quail, although he had noted the conclusion in the report that no one in APORS had training or expertise in procurement now that Mr. Cutler was sidelined, took no action. In fact, in the autumn of 1997, he decided to integrate APORS and PRPCSS into a new organization (CCSB) headed by Mr. Guité, thus giving him more responsibility over contracting and procurement than he had had previously.

Mr. Quail sees no inconsistency in this. His reading of the Ernst & Young report did not indicate to him that there were deficiencies in Mr. Guité's management, but rather a lack of trained personnel available to him, which would be corrected by the integration of PRPCSS into CCSB. He expected Mr. Guité to follow the rules,[38] even if the experience with Mr. Cutler and the audit showed that this particular manager had never been inclined to follow Treasury Board policies. Mr. Quail's position on this subject is summed up in the following extract from his testimony:

| Mr. Quail: | Anyway, you appoint the right people, you give them your trust, you expect them to be able to deliver, expect people to treat people with respect and you expect them to follow the rules. You have a way in which to check some of the work that is going on by way of an audit. You have the audit done, you have some results. The audit results say that you don't have the necessary expertise. I give you |

the necessary expertise. You say that you are going to put it into place. I expect that is going to happen.[39]

For all practical purposes, the Ernst & Young audit was a waste of time, money and bureaucratic effort. No changes within APORS occurred as a consequence, and the creation of CCSB did not serve to correct the issues of non-compliance with policies and regulations, but to concentrate more responsibility and authority in the hands of the same manager whose improper conduct in disciplining Allan Cutler had led to the audit in the first place. The audit report was forgotten and gathered dust until 2000, when it was belatedly remembered in the context of a new compliance audit.

7.5
Internal Audit of 2000

When Mr. Gagliano became Minister of PWGSC in 1997, he was not told there had been an audit of APORS by Ernst & Young, although he was aware that internal audits were routinely conducted of various sections of the department on a rotating basis, or as needed when the Audit Committee decided an audit was warranted.[40] Nor had his predecessor, Ms. Marleau, been informed of the Ernst & Young audit or of the investigation of Mr. Cutler's allegations. Nobody told either her or Mr. Gagliano that there was or had been any problem at APORS.[41]

At the beginning of 2000, as a result of a scandal which erupted concerning Human Resources Development Canada, the Government as a whole became acutely aware of the vulnerability of programs involving what is called "grants and contributions," which is bureaucratic jargon for discretionary spending. Treasury Board recommended to all Ministers responsible for grants and contributions programs that they carry out audits of those programs. Although the Sponsorship Program was not, strictly speaking, a grants and contributions program, Mr. Gagliano thought it was sufficiently comparable to one that an internal audit should be ordered. He says that he expressed this wish to Mr. Quail, who in turn asked AEB to conduct an audit.[42]

Mr. Quail has a different recollection of the sequence of events. He testifies that the idea of the need for an internal audit came from him, that he discussed it with the Minister, and that the latter approved.[43]

The idea to conduct an internal audit may have been provoked by an access to information (ATI) request received by PWGSC on January 11, 2000, from Daniel Leblanc of the Globe and Mail newspaper, who asked for "all records detailing the sponsorship budget within Public Works, since the 1994-1995 fiscal year. The records would include, without being limited to, the events that received federal money such as festivals, hot air balloons and the airing of commercials."[44]

The request was tagged "interesting" by the ATI officer handling the file, meaning that it would be brought to the attention of the Minister and Deputy Minister because of the possibility of publication of the information requested, and because such publication could give rise to questions in the House of Commons, for which the Minister would need to be prepared. Mr. Leblanc had already written news stories about some aspects of the Sponsorship Program, on the basis of previous ATI requests, but the Program had not yet become the object of much media attention.

Mr. Leblanc was contacted and agreed to limit the scope of his request. Ms. Anita Lloyd, who was the ATI officer responsible for the matter, was contacted by the Corporate Secretary of PWGSC, Ms. Dominique Francoeur, who made her aware that the file was politically sensitive, and that she was to be kept advised of its progress. In the meantime, the information and documents required from CCSB were slow in appearing, and Mr. Stobbe was known to be following the matter closely. When the material was finally received, Ms. Lloyd did not feel it responded adequately to the request, particularly with respect to the budget for sponsorships. She says that she was asked by Ms. Francoeur to interpret the request restrictively and not to seek its clarification by contacting the applicant. Ms. Lloyd was reluctant on an ethical basis to comply with this direction. She was so disturbed by what was patently an attempt to improperly limit the Government's response to the ATI request that she consulted her own lawyer to be sure of her legal position.

In the end, the information requested was furnished to Mr. Leblanc to his satisfaction,[45] although processing the request took far longer than normal. The incident illustrates how a large government department may feel uncomfortable with an ATI request, especially when the disclosure of the information requested risks causing embarrassment at senior levels of the administration or possibly even higher.

Regardless of who or what provoked the internal audit, it was conducted in 2000. Mr. Steven Turner was at the time the acting Director General of AEB and took responsibility for the file. The audit resulted in a Report dated August 31, 2000. The key findings, as expressed in the Executive Summary, were:

- The processes used by CCSB to select and contract with the Communications Agencies and Agency of Record did not fully comply with the spirit or the letter of Treasury Board rules and directives. ...

- The sponsorship approval and decision-making process is subjective and based on professional judgement and experience. Because of a lack of documentary evidence, audit activities could not confirm that the described ad hoc processes for sponsorship approval and decision making have been consistently applied. ...

- The management framework for CCSB's sponsorship decision-making process is inadequate and does not ensure that CCSB sponsorship decisions are transparent, compliant with requirements, or appropriate to achieving value-for-money for the Government of Canada. ...[46]

The audit team learned of many of the problems about which the Auditor General was to remark three years later, such as the consistent lack of documentation in the files and the use of sponsorship funds for events having little to do with the visibility of the federal presence. The expenditures related to the celebration of the RCMP's 125th anniversary in 1998-99 were given as an example.[47]

The recommendations of the report to Pierre Tremblay, then the acting Executive Director of CCSB, were as follows:

- Take the necessary steps to ensure that CCSB's contracting processes comply with TB directives, policies and procedures:

- Formally implement appropriate processes and controls over the granting and management of sponsorships to ensure sound management of, control over, and accountability for sponsorship— encompassing due diligence, consistency in approach, transparency of operations and adequate reporting; and

- Implement adequate management controls to ensure that sponsorship amounts are consistently determined (at a minimum level needed to attain expected results) and appropriately documented; and, the application of effective asset management principles including: control over the disposition of interest earned on cash advances, the establishment and control of production budgets and matching expenditures, control over the inventory of promotional items, stronger linkages between the funds provided and the results achieved and sufficient reporting to support a value-for-money evaluation.[48]

Mr. Steinberg briefed Mr. Gagliano on the results of the audit at a presentation made on September 20, 2000. Mr. Gagliano says that when he learned of the mismanagement of the Sponsorship Program, of which he had not previously been aware, he was furious, and immediately asked if he should call the police. He was assured by Mr. Steinberg that there was no evidence uncovered of criminal activity.[49] Next, Mr. Gagliano ordered that although the audit team had reviewed 90% in value of the sponsorship contracts, a further review of the remaining 10% should take place. This was done in the months following and did not change, but tended to confirm, the findings.[50]

Finally, Mr. Gagliano says that he ordered that the Sponsorship Program should be frozen at once until an action plan to correct the problems had been put in place. The action plan, prepared in haste by CCSB, contained 31 measures intended to eliminate the problems disclosed by the audit.[51] As noted in Chapter I, the freeze ordered by Mr. Gagliano does not appear to have lasted very long, if in fact it took effect at all.

Many of the problems with the administration of the Sponsorship Program that were described in the 2000 internal audit were similar, and in some cases identical, to the problems described by Ernst & Young in 1996. For example, there are similar criticisms of non-compliance with the procedure for selecting agencies, and criticisms of the decision-making process for sponsorships, of the lack of transparency and of the lack of control over the processing of payments.

In an early draft of the 2000 internal audit report, these similarities are mentioned, and the draft report includes the following text:

> ...no evidence was found to conclude CCSB management fully implemented the recommendations from that 1996-1997 audit. ...
>
> In our opinion, if management had implemented the recommendations from that 1996/97 audit, the conditions found during this current audit may not have existed. To prevent a similar situation from recurring and to stress the importance of implementing actions to address the deficiencies noted in this report, we suggest the AEB conduct a follow-up audit of the sponsorship activities at CCSB approximately one year following acceptance of this report.[52]

Mr. Steinberg acknowledges that the audit made it apparent that the management of CCSB had not only failed to implement the recommendations of the Ernst & Young report fully, but that it had failed to implement them at all. Nevertheless, the above paragraphs were dropped from the final text of the 2000 Report, which fails to mention in any way the 1996 audit. The reasons given for eliminating all reference to the earlier audit are unconvincing, to say the least; they include arguments that the audit team had not conducted tests to assess the extent to which the Ernst & Young recommendations had been (or had *not* been) implemented.

A more plausible explanation for the omission of all references to the earlier audit is the probable embarrassment they would cause to the persons who had failed to ensure that the earlier recommendations had been implemented. An internal communication dated July 26, 2000, at the time when AEB was debating whether or not to include reference to the Ernst & Young audit in the report, reveals that Mr. Stobbe wished to suppress references to the earlier audit. Mr. Tom Murray, who was one of the persons in AEB in charge of the 2000 audit, told Mr. Pierre Lacasse, who was writing the report, not to look into the question of the implementation of the Ernst & Young recommendations, because that would have delayed conclusion of the audit. Mr. Steinberg, who was their superior, testifies that he was not aware of these instructions and would have reversed them had he known about them.[53]

It should be recalled that the modification of the draft audit report had also occurred in 1996. In each instance, the effect of the modification had been to moderate the severity of the criticisms of management that the auditors were proposing. Such moderation is inconsistent with the obligation of auditors to be fearless in their language. An audit report should not be manipulated to make it more acceptable to the management whose administration is being tested.

7.6
Kroll Lindquist Avey Administrative Review

Kroll Lindquist Avey (Kroll) is a firm of forensic accountants that is well known to the Commission, which retained Kroll's services to assist in its investigation.

In October 2002, long before the Commission came into being, Kroll was retained by the Human Resources Branch of PWGSC to carry out an administrative review of the Sponsorship Program, with the specific objective of determining whether there should be disciplinary action taken against the employees of PWGSC involved in the contracting process.[54] The review was not to constitute an audit.

Kroll knew of the work that had already been done by a Quick Response Team (QRT), which had been created in May 2002 when the full extent of the mismanagement at CCSB was starting to be revealed. The QRT consisted of about a dozen people recruited from various parts of PWGSC, and its primary purpose was to provide quick responses to the Minister to anticipated questions in the House of Commons, where the Minister was facing a daily barrage of questions about the Sponsorship Program. To answer these questions, it was necessary to carry out a systematic review of 721 sponsorship files opened over a period of about four years. The QRT had prepared a comprehensive report detailing many of the problems which have since preoccupied the Auditor General and this Commission.[55]

Kroll was retained to do an independent review and was not given a copy of the QRT report, but had access to the same files and to the internal audits conducted by the AEB. Initially it reviewed only 45 files, with a view to documenting the standards under which the employees of CCSB were supposed to operate. Subsequently, it was asked to extend its work to an additional 91 files. It did not conduct interviews of the management of CCSB or its employees.

Kroll produced a report dated February 4, 2003, which provides an analysis of each of the 136 files studied. In 130 of them, instances of non-compliance with the law or government policies were found. The names of the CCSB employees responsible for each instance of non-compliance are given in a detailed appendix to the report; Mr. Guité's name is mentioned repeatedly, but of course he had retired by this time.

The report deals principally with two areas of non-compliance: first, in no case were competitive bids solicited for sponsorship contracts; and second, the tests required by section 34 of the *Financial Administration Act* for certification for payment of an invoice were routinely disregarded.[56]

7.7
Demers Administrative Review

Upon receiving Kroll's report, PWGSC retained the services of an attorney in private practice, Mr. Jacques Demers, Q.C., who has experience in labour relations matters, to head a committee formed to make recommendations for disciplinary action against those employees who had been held to be responsible for non-compliance with Treasury Board policy. This committee interviewed all such employees except Mr. Guité, who had retired, and produced a detailed report on November 24, 2003. Its conclusions may be summarized as follows:

- Paul Lauzon had demonstrated only "benign negligence," and considering the extenuating circumstances applicable to the files reviewed, should be the subject only of minor disciplinary action.

- Evelyn Marcoux was negligent in only one instance, and her actions should give rise only to minor disciplinary action.

- Andrée LaRose had performed all necessary verifications before signing the invoices in question, and could not be reproached.

- David Myer's actions in certifying invoices for payment constituted serious negligence requiring a commensurate disciplinary measure.

- Pierre Tremblay was held to have demonstrated unacceptable laxity and lack of rigour for a manager at his level; in spite of the explanations he offered, he was found to have been guilty of very serious negligence that called for commensurate disciplinary action.[57] The section from that report relevant to Mr. Tremblay appears as Appendix H to this Report.

Following these findings, David Myer lodged a grievance by which he successfully challenged the recommendation that he be disciplined.[58] Pierre Tremblay retired before he could be disciplined and died before he could be called to testify at the Commission's hearings. Evelyn Marcoux has a legitimate sense of grievance that she was singled out unfairly as negligent.[59]

> The overall result is that as a consequence of all of the faults, irregularities and outright disregard of the imperative prescriptions of section 34 of the FAA that have been committed and documented on numerous occasions, to date only minor disciplinary action has been taken against two public servants of PWGSC, neither of whom played an important role in the mismanagement detailed in the Report of the Auditor General.

> No one in a management position at PWGSC has suffered any consequence, either financial or to his or her career prospects, because of what occurred in the Sponsorship Program.

Endnotes to Chapter VII

1   Exhibit P-3(A), tab 1, p. 6.

2   Exhibit P-3(A), tab 1, document numbers 1034912, 1034914.

3   Testimony of Mr. Neville, Transcripts vol. 41, p. 7055 (OE), pp. 7061-7062 (F).

4   Exhibit P-43(A), tab 2.

5   Testimony of Mr. Parent, Transcripts vol. 31, pp. 5449-5450 (OF), pp. 5443-5444 (E); Testimony of Mr. Cutler, Transcripts vol. 13, pp. 2105-2106 (OE), pp. 2107 (F).

6   Testimony of Mr. Cutler, Transcripts vol. 13, pp. 2108-2109, 2111-2119, 2124, 2134-2135 (OE), pp. 2110, 2120, 2127, 2138-2139 (F); Exhibit P-43(A), tab 4, p. 7001769; Exhibit P-43(B), tab 25(A) p. 104.

7   Exhibit P-43(A), tabs 6, 7.

8   Testimony of Mr. Stobbe, Transcripts vol. 40, pp. 6907-6909 (OE), pp. 6910-6812 (F); Testimony of Ms. Labelle, Transcripts vol. 16, pp. 2510-2511 (OE), pp. 2515-2516 (F); Exhibit P-43(A), tab 23(F).

9   Testimony of Ms. Labelle, Transcripts vol. 16, pp. 2601-2602 (OE), pp. 2618-2619 (F); Exhibit P-43(A), tab 12.

10 Exhibit P-43(A), tabs 10, 11; Testimony of Mr. Cutler, Transcripts vol. 13, pp. 2146-2147, 2150 (OE), pp. 2151-2152, 2155 (F).

11 Exhibit P-43(A), tab 10.

12 Testimony of Mr. Cutler, Transcripts vol. 13, pp. 2148, 2153-2154 (OE), pp. 2154, 2158-2159 (F); Exhibit P-43(A), tab 17.

13 Testimony of Mr. Parent, Transcripts vol. 32, pp. 5505-5507 (OF), pp. 5503-5506 (E).

14 Ms. Morin was "Julie Boisvert" at the time of the audit.

15 Testimony of Mr. Steinberg, Transcripts vol. 16, pp. 2485-2487 (OE), pp. 2486-2488 (F); Testimony of Ms. Monaghan, Transcripts vol. 14, pp. 2219-2220 (OE), pp. 2219-2220 (F); Exhibit P-44, tab 1; Testimony of Ms. Monaghan, Transcripts vol. 14, pp. 2229-2230 (OE), pp. 2229-2230 (F).

16 Testimony of Mr. Cutler, Transcripts vol. 13, p. 2150 (OE), pp. 2155-2156 (F); Testimony of Ms. Brillant, Transcripts vol. 15, pp. 2409-2410 (OE), pp. 2409-2410 (F).

17 Exhibit P-44, tab 7(B), pp. 4-5.

18 Exhibit P-44, tab 7(A).

19 Testimony of Ms. Monaghan and Ms. Brillant, Transcripts vol. 14, pp. 2296-2297 (OE), pp. 2299-2300 (F); Exhibit P-44, tab 11(E).

20 Exhibit P-44, tab 11(E).

21 Testimony of Ms. Monaghan and Ms. Brillant, Transcripts vol. 14, pp. 2296-2297 (OE), pp. 2299-2300 (F).

22 Exhibit P-44, tab 11(E), p. 20.

23 Exhibit P-44, tab 11(E), p. 20.

24 Exhibit P-44, tab 11(A), p. 14.

[25] Testimony of Ms. Monaghan and Ms. Brillant, Transcripts vol. 14, pp. 2296-2297 (OE), pp. 2299-2300 (F).

[26] Testimony of Ms. Brillant, Transcripts vol. 14, pp. 2251, 2262-2263 (OE), pp. 2252, 2264-2265 (F).

[27] Exhibit P-44, tab 11(E), p. i.

[28] Testimony of Mr. Steinberg, Transcripts vol. 16, pp. 2528-2529 (OE), pp. 2536-2537 (F).

[29] Testimony of Ms. Monaghan and Ms. Brillant, Transcripts vol. 14, pp. 2267-2268 (OE), pp. 2269-2270 (F).

[30] Testimony of Ms. Monaghan, Transcripts vol. 14, pp. 2304, (OE), pp. 2306 (F); vol. 15 (revised), pp. 2417-2418 (OE), pp. 2417-2418 (F).

[31] Testimony of Mr. Stobbe, Transcripts vol. 40, pp. 6910-6912, 6914-6915 (OE), pp. 6913-6915, 6918-6920 (F).

[32] Exhibit P-47(A), tab 23.

[33] Testimony of Mr. Quail, Transcripts vol. 40, pp. 6876-6878 (OE), pp. 6877-6878 (F).

[34] Exhibit P-47(A), tab 25.

[35] Testimony of Mr. Steinberg, Transcripts vol. 16, pp. 2556-2557 (OE), pp. 2567-2568 (F).

[36] Testimony of Mr. Quail, Transcripts vol. 39, pp. 6765-6774 (OE), pp. 6775-6785 (F).

[37] Testimony of Mr. Stobbe, Transcripts vol. 40, pp. 6916-6917 (OE), pp. 6920-6922 (F).

[38] Testimony of Mr. Quail, Transcripts vol. 39, pp. 6763-6765, 6778-6779 (OE), pp. 6772-6775, 6789-6790 (F).

[39] Testimony of Mr. Quail, Transcripts vol. 39, p. 6780 (OE), p. 6791 (F).

[40] Testimony of Mr. Gagliano, Transcripts vol. 69, pp. 12029-12031, 12035-12036 (OE), pp. 12030-12032, 12037-12038 (F).

[41] Testimony of Ms. Marleau, Transcripts vol. 62, pp. 10955-10956, 10983 (OE), pp. 10958-10959, 10987-10988 (F); Testimony of Mr. Gagliano, Transcripts vol. 69, p. 12030 (OE), pp. 12030-12031 (F).

[42] Testimony of Mr. Gagliano, Transcripts vol. 67, pp. 11550-11551 (OF), pp. 11549-11550 (E).

[43] Testimony of Mr. Quail, Transcripts vol. 40, p. 6878 (OE), p. 6879 (F); Exhibit P-45, paras. 116-117.

[44] Exhibit P-117, p. 13.

[45] Testimony of Ms. Lloyd, Transcripts vol. 38, pp. 6555-6556, 6564, 6569-6572, 6574-6579, 6598-6599 (OE), pp. 6561-6562, 6571, 6576-6579, 6583-6586, 6608-6609 (F).

[46] Exhibit P-3(A), tab 4, pp. 2-3.

[47] Testimony of Mr. Turner, Transcripts vol. 16, pp. 2562-2568, 2570-2572 (OE), pp. 2574-2580, 2583-2585 (F).

[48] Exhibit P-3(A), tab 4, p. 4.

[49] Testimony of Mr. Gagliano, Transcripts vol. 69, pp. 11976-11978 (OF), pp. 11968-11970 (E); Testimony of Mr. Hamer, Transcripts vol. 16, pp. 2638-2640 (OE), pp. 2660-2662 (F); Exhibit P-47(C), tab 73.

[50] Testimony of Mr. Steinberg, Transcripts vol. 16, pp. 2639, 2643 (OE), pp. 2662, 2667 (F); Exhibit P-47(C), tab 74.

[51] Testimony of Mr. Gagliano, Transcripts vol. 69, pp. 11977-11978, 11983 (OF), pp. 11969-11970, 11974-11975 (E); Testimony of Mr. Steinberg, Transcripts vol. 16, pp. 2644-2645 (OE), pp. 2668-2669 (F).

[52] Exhibit P-46, tab 18, p. 103.

[53] Testimony of Mr. Steinberg, Transcripts vol. 16, pp. 2585-2591 (OE), pp. 2597-2603 (F); vol. 17, pp. 2680-2685 (OE), pp. 2682-2688 (F); Exhibit P-46, tab 18, p. 104.

[54] Exhibit P-3(A), tab 11; Exhibit P-3(B), tab 12; Testimony of Mr. Whitla, Transcripts vol. 17, pp. 2807-2808 (OE), pp. 2828-2829 (F).

[55] Testimony of Mr. McLaughlin, Transcripts vol. 17, pp. 2706-2709, 2712-2713, 2722-2725, 2742-2748 (OE), pp. 2712-2716, 2719-2720, 2731-2734, 2753-2760 (F); Exhibit P-3(A), tab 8.

[56] Testimony of Mr. Whitla, Transcripts vol. 17, pp. 2825-2833, 2835-2836 (OE), pp. 2848-2857, 2859-2860 (F).

[57] Exhibit P-54, pp. 16, 21, 23, 29, 48.

[58] Exhibit P-100, tab 34, p. 231; Testimony of Mr. Myer, Transcripts vol. 31, p. 5326 (OE), p. 5333 (F).

[59] Testimony of Ms. Marcoux, Transcripts vol. 26, pp. 4522-4524 (OF), pp. 4508-4510 (E).

CHAPTER VIII

CROWN CORPORATIONS
AND THE RCMP

8.1
Auditor General's Concerns

In her Report, the Auditor General expresses concerns about the involvement of Crown Corporations and the RCMP in the Sponsorship Program in three respects, which should be examined broadly before dealing with her more specific concerns.

First, it is the Auditor General's opinion that transfers of funds from Public Works and Government Services Canada (PWGSC) to a Crown Corporation or to the RCMP do not conform to the intent of Treasury Board's Policy on Transfer Payments, which is designed to ensure that grants or contributions, which have been compared to sponsorship payments, are not used as substitutes for financing the recipient's operating or capital requirements.[1] Parliament will have established the mode of financing the operations of a Crown

Corporation, either by way of an annual appropriation or as a self-financing entity with the potential of returning dividends to its sole shareholder, the Crown (as is the case for Canada Post). Consequently, any grants or contributions made to a Crown Corporation or agency must have prior Treasury Board approval; otherwise, Parliament risks losing control over the appropriations process since the transferring department in effect subsidizes the transferee.

Second, it is the Auditor General's opinion that Crown Corporations and the RCMP should not be entitled to receive financial encouragement to promote the visibility of the federal presence since they are already obliged to do so by virtue of the Treasury Board Federal Identity Program (FIP).[2] This program establishes standards and requirements for managing the Government's corporate identity. For example, it obliges all Canadian government institutions, which include Crown Corporations, to display the Canada wordmark (the word "Canada" with a small Canadian flag over the last letter) prominently in all of its corporate identity applications. (See Figure VIII-I.) The Canadian flag is also to be displayed prominently at all federal facilities.

Figure VIII-1.

Third, the Auditor General is obviously dismayed to learn that PWGSC agreed to pay fees and commissions to communication agencies for their services in transferring funds from one department or agency of the Government to another, with little in the way of work or services required other than the transmission of a cheque.[3]

Some of the transactions which particularly troubled the Auditor General are well described in Chapter 3 of her Report. None of the evidence heard by the Commission contradicts her findings, and it would be pointless to repeat what she has written, but a few comments are necessary to describe certain matters that were the subject of testimony and submissions at the hearings, and to clarify some issues that have been raised.

8.2
Via Rail

In October 1998, Robert-Guy Scully on behalf of his company, L'Information Essentielle, was attempting to arrange financing for a television series he intended to produce on the hockey career of Maurice Richard. He had already obtained backing to the extent of $1,625,000 from Canada Post, and had persuaded Mr. Guité that this was a project that should be supported by the Sponsorship Program. But Mr. Guité wanted to involve other sponsors and suggested that Mr. Scully approach Via Rail. When he did so, he was told by Marc LeFrançois, Chairman of the board of directors, that it had no funds available for such a project.[4] Two weeks later Mr. Guité contacted Mr. LeFrançois and advised him that PWGSC would contribute 75% of a $1 million contribution to the project by Via Rail; the funds would be reimbursed to Via Rail only in the next fiscal year, since Mr. Guité's budget for the current year had been spent.[5]

At a subsequent meeting with Mr. LeFrançois and Christena Keon Sirsly, Via Rail's Vice-President of Marketing, Mr. Scully persuaded them that Via Rail would receive favourable publicity from its association with the Maurice Richard series, and secured from them Via Rail's commitment for $1 million, which Mr. LeFrançois later negotiated down to $910,000. Mr. LeFrançois says that his agreement to advance this amount was based upon Mr. Guité's oral undertaking that PWGSC would reimburse Via Rail $750,000 in the next fiscal year.[6]

Mr. LeFrançois hardly knew Mr. Guité. He had been introduced to him by Jean Lafleur, who headed the communications firm which looked after Via Rail's account. With no more than Mr. Guité's verbal assurance, during 1999 Mr. LeFrançois authorized the issuance of cheques by Via Rail to Mr. Scully's firm in the amount of $910,000. No contract was signed as evidence of the arrangements concluded with L'Information Essentielle.[7] The television series was produced and broadcast, and Via Rail was shown in the credits as one of the sponsors. The advances of $910,000 appeared on the books of Via Rail as an account receivable from the Government of Canada.[8]

In December 1999, Mr. LeFrançois contacted Pierre Tremblay of CCSB, who had replaced Mr. Guité following the latter's retirement, and asked for repayment of the $750,000 in accordance with the verbal agreement with Mr. Guité. Mr. Tremblay sought instructions from the Minister, Mr. Gagliano, who, after speaking to Mr. LeFrançois, says that he was satisfied that the sum should be paid by PWGSC, and gave the necessary authorization to Mr. Tremblay. The latter informed Mr. LeFrançois that the amount would be paid through the agency of Lafleur Communication.[9]

On March 31, 2000, Éric Lafleur called Via Rail to say that a cheque for $750,000 payable to Via Rail would be delivered against the latter's invoice, addressed to Lafleur Communication, for that amount. The invoice describes the reason for its issuance as *Commandite-Télésérie, the Maurice "Rocket" Richard Story* and includes amounts for GST and PST, giving the false impression that goods or services were involved. The cheque in full payment of the invoice from Lafleur Communication is for the sum of $862,687.50. The remaining $160,000 on the books of Via Rail was changed from being an account receivable to a marketing expense.[10]

This was a very irregular and abnormal transaction, especially for a large Crown Corporation. The disbursement of $910,000, unsupported by a contract, relying upon a verbal undertaking by a public servant, who had no legal right to commit funds from a future fiscal period, that $750,000 would be repaid later, followed by an invoice misrepresenting the transaction, addressed to a communication agency from which Via Rail had no right to claim payment: all of these are improprieties committed by officers of Via Rail, which, it is presumed, wishes never to see repeated. From the point of view of the Canadian taxpayer, the payment by PWGSC of a commission of $112,500 to Lafleur Communication for simply delivering a cheque to Via Rail is an abuse of public funds which cannot be condoned.

Counsel for Via Rail argues that this was an isolated transaction, that Via Rail received good publicity worth much more than the $160,000 net it spent, that "no moneys were lost" and that no personal gain was received by anyone at Via Rail.[11] Unfortunately, even if these were isolated transactions, they are evidence of unacceptable corporate behaviour which the responsible parties seem to be unwilling to acknowledge. If no money was lost by Via Rail, money was surely lost by the Government of Canada in that $112,500 was misspent by PWGSC as an unnecessary and unearned commission paid to a communication agency for which no value was received, after Via Rail had facilitated the payment by issuing a false invoice.

The Auditor General also criticizes Via Rail's use of $205,000, which had originally been provided to fund the publication of *Via Rail Magazine*.[12] In September 2000 the magazine project was cancelled and CCSB, at Via Rail's request, transferred this sum, less a commission of 17.65% paid to Lafleur Communication, to Via Rail to upgrade its signs at train stations across Canada. This was not in accordance with the intent of the Transfer Payments Policy since it subsidized Via Rail's operating costs without Treasury Board authorization. It also involved the payment of a commission of $30,754 for no work whatsoever. The signage should have given visibility to the Canada wordmark without payment to Via Rail because of the Federal Identity Program. The criticism of this transaction by the Auditor General is fully justified.

8.3
Canada Post

In her Report, the Auditor General describes a sponsorship contract whereby Canada Post received from PWGSC in March 1999 an amount of $521,739 as compensation for visibility given to the Government of Canada in connection with a postage stamp contest called "Stampin' the Future."[13] Canada Post had disbursed an equivalent amount to Lafleur Communication for its services related to the contest. In addition to the amount paid to Canada Post, PWGSC paid to Lafleur Communication and Média/IDA Vision agency commissions of $62,609 and $15,652, respectively, apparently only for transmitting the sponsorship amount to Canada Post. The concerns of the Auditor General were multiple: the sponsorship contract was totally undocumented by Canada Post, any subsidization of the latter's commercial activities by PWGSC would be in violation of the Transfer Payments Policy, and if the payment could be qualified as a legitimate sponsorship to enhance the visibility of the federal presence, it would be an unnecessary duplication of what is required by the Federal Identity Program.

It is particularly ludicrous to think that the Government of Canada needed to pay Canada Post to persuade the latter that it should identify itself as a federal institution to Canadians. Surely every Canadian knows that already; the name of Canada Post makes it evident, and every stamp bears the word "Canada."

The Auditor General notes in her Report that the Lafleur agency, which had been engaged by Canada Post to work on the "Stampin' the Future" project, invoiced CCSB for a total of $114,740[14] for mock-ups or layouts to be used in connection with the contest. Micheline Montreuil, Director of Stamp Products for Canada Post from 1996 to 2002 and in charge of its promotions, was not aware that the Lafleur agency was also invoicing the Government either for commissions or for work that was being done for Canada Post, such as the preparation of mock-ups. She testifies that she believed that the invoices Canada Post received from Lafleur were in full payment of its services.[15] The possibility of double-billing for the mock-ups was put to Pierre Michaud, who at the relevant times was working for Lafleur Communication and was the manager of the Canada Post account. He admitted that it appeared from the documentary evidence that the work done in preparing 18 mock-ups had been billed twice, once to PWGSC and again to Canada Post.[16]

Jean Lafleur, although unable to remember the circumstances of the invoicing of this contract in the same way that he was generally unable to remember most of the details of his involvement in the Sponsorship Program, is sure that his agency would not have invoiced twice for the same work.[17] The matter remains unresolved.

At the hearings, officials from Canada Post recognized the waste of government money that the "Stampin' the Future" sponsorship represented. Canada Post has offered to reimburse the Government for the funds it received from the Sponsorship Program. Following the release of the Auditor General's Report, Canada Post commissioned its own audit by external auditors Deloitte & Touche, and since receiving the latter's report, it has implemented the measures recommended to ensure that in the future its marketing and advertising activities conform to government policies and ethical standards.[18]

At the hearings, additional questions arose, of which Ms. Montreuil had not previously been aware, with respect to sponsorship contracts concluded between PWGSC and Lafleur Communication concerning Canada Post's visibility. She learned for the first time that in 1997 Lafleur Communication had been given the mandate by PWGSC to pay sponsorships of $150,000 and $250,000 to Canada Post for visibility at Montreal Expos baseball games and at the 1997 Grand Prix du Canada, respectively.[19] In neither case was the amount which was received on behalf of Canada Post by the Lafleur agency, together with commissions and production costs, actually transmitted to Canada Post.[20] However, there are in the files post-mortem reports that visibility, in the form of posters and advertisements, appears to have been given to Canada Post at the events in question;[21] and it is possible that Lafleur Communication paid out sums to the promoters of these events for the privilege of exhibiting Canada Post's name and logo at their venues. Nevertheless, it is extraordinary that this was done without the knowledge of the person in charge of Canada Post's advertising program.

But it was even more remarkable for Ms. Montreuil to learn for the first time of a sum totalling $275,000 paid to Lafleur for sponsorships in connection with the Series of the Century Stamp Launch. The books of Canada Post disclose that these amounts have never been paid to it, nor have they been paid to anyone else.[22]

Ms. Montreuil managed the Series of the Century Stamp project for Canada Post. It consisted of the issuance of a series of stamps to commemorate the hockey games played between Canada and the Soviet Union in 1972. A number of stamp launches were planned in the Canadian cities where some of the games had been played, all organized by Lafleur Communication. Ms. Montreuil had been vaguely aware of the possibility that some of the costs might be subsidized by PWGSC to the extent of $25,000, but she was completely unaware of an additional sum of $250,000 to be paid to Canada Post as a sponsorship.[23]

An invoice from the Lafleur agency to PWGSC dated November 11, 1997, and paid by the latter, proves that Lafleur received $250,000 on behalf of Canada Post, together with a commission of $37,500, production costs of $5,500 for two mock-ups, and fees for the services of its personnel totalling $169,000.[24] An earlier invoice, dated March 31, 1997, for $25,000 and related commissions and fees,[25] is marked "Annulé" (Void), although it appears to have been paid also.

When questioned on this subject, Jean Lafleur was at first unable to provide any explanation as to why the amount of $275,000 due to Canada Post had not been paid to it. At a later stage of his testimony he said that he had looked into the matter, and that his research had uncovered the possibility that sums were due to his agency by Canada Post which were set off against the $275,000 owed to it.[26] This possible set-off was not established by admissible evidence. At the time Mr. Lafleur was looking into the matter, his books and records were in the possession of the Commission by virtue of a subpoena.

In a further attempt to establish that the $275,000 is not due to Canada Post, Mr. Lafleur produced a document which purports to be an invoice for

$250,000 sent on October 1, 1997, by Canada Post to the Lafleur agency, together with GST and PST, for "Visibilité accordée au gouvernement du Canada dans le cadre de la tournée promotionelle entourant le lancement du timbre commémorant la Série du Siècle de 1972."[27] ("Visibility provided to the Government of Canada during the promotional tour relating to the launching of the 1972 Series of the Century stamp.") It is not clear to the Commission what the production of this document is intended to prove. In any event, Canada Post denies that the invoice emanated from its accounting department; it is not on the form used by it for invoices, and could have been prepared by anyone having access to Canada Post's letterhead.[28]

The Commission, which does not have jurisdiction to settle disputes of this kind, comes to no conclusion as to whether Lafleur Communication owes a sum of money to Canada Post, except to say that Mr. Lafleur has no credibility on this subject.

The Commission heard evidence of instances of mismanagement at Canada Post which can be traced back to the period when André Ouellet became involved in its administration. His decisions and influence were not always in the best interests of Canada Post—although he would vigorously contest that statement—and provide an illustration of the dangers of political appointments to positions with Crown corporations where sound business experience is a better qualification than experience in politics and public administration. I agree with the opinion of the new Chair of Canada Post, Gordon Feeney, who says that the tone at the top of an organization defines its culture.[29]

In January 1996,[30] after a long career as a Liberal politician and Cabinet member, André Ouellet was appointed Chairman of the Board of Canada Post.[31] Three years later he was appointed by the Government to be its President and Chief Executive Officer, first acting on an interim basis for nine months and then on a permanent basis in November 1999, until his resignation in 2004.[32] During the three years that he was Chairman of the Board, the President and CEO was Georges Clermont, and Mr. Ouellet had no administrative responsibilities.[33] This did not prevent him from assuming an increasingly important role in the day-to-day operations of Canada Post. He gave particular attention to the activities of the Stamp Committee, which he chaired.[34] The committee chose stamp designs and organized events known as "stamp launches" at which new stamp designs would be announced, usually at a cocktail reception.[35] Until Mr. Ouellet arrived at Canada Post in 1996, stamp launches were less elaborate affairs that were handled internally, at a relatively minor cost.[36] In order to increase the sale of stamps, particularly to stamp collectors, in 1997 Mr. Ouellet instructed Micheline Montreuil, the Director of Stamp Products, to utilize the consulting services of Lafleur Communication and Gervais, Gagnon, Covington et associés (GGA) specifically for stamp launches.[37] Contracts were awarded on a sole-source basis with Lafleur and GGA.[38] A third agency, Tremblay Guittet Communications (TGC), whose president, Michelle Tremblay, was a long-time personal friend of Mr. Ouellet, was also retained at his request.[39] The cost of stamp launches immediately shot upwards. In the period from August 8, 1997, to May 17, 2002, TGC billed Canada Post fees of $383,671 for services related to the organization of stamp launches;[40] and from August 1997 to April 2004 it billed $1,770,579 for other services, such as speech writing, advice and disbursements.[41]

From December 1996 to July 2001, Lafleur Communication billed Canada Post fees in excess of $2 million for stamp-related activities, excluding the "Stampin' the Future" contest.[42] Jean Lafleur had become a personal friend of Mr. Ouellet in March 1996, and social contacts between them and their wives were frequent.[43] Mr. Ouellet also hired Mr. Lafleur's son, Éric, to act as his advisor for the purpose of the launch of a new stamp during a visit to China in 1997.[44] Nevertheless, Mr. Ouellet would have the Commission believe that he and Mr. Lafleur never discussed business or the sponsorship contracts that the Lafleur agency was managing on behalf of PWGSC for the benefit of Canada Post.[45] Although Ms. Montreuil had the authority to decide which advertising agency should be used in conjunction with the promotion of new stamps, practically speaking it was impossible for her to refuse the wish of Mr. Ouellet. The Lafleur agency became Canada Post's agency without having to go through a tendering process.[46]

As Chairman of the Board, Mr. Ouellet was entitled to attend the meetings of the Sponsorship Committee which decided on the events to be sponsored by Canada Post and the amounts to be paid. Mr. Ouellet testifies that his participation at committee meetings was limited to making recommendations, but the minutes of some of the meetings indicate that in fact he gave unilateral approval to certain projects, including the sponsorship of the Maurice Richard series, another television series known as "Tout écran," *Le Chant de l'eau* (a coffee table book) and le Musée d'art contemporain de Montréal.[47] The other members of the committee were unlikely to contest the "recommendations" of the Chairman, no matter how they were expressed, much less his approvals, and Mr. Ouellet effectively took over decision-making at the Sponsorship Committee. When he became President of the Crown Corporation, he abolished the Sponsorship Committee, and all sponsorship applications were handled by himself and Alain Guilbert, the Vice-President in charge of communications.[48] Although there was, at the time, a sponsorship policy which provided criteria for selection, it was largely ignored, and their decisions were based on subjective considerations.[49]

In general, Mr. Ouellet's actions and administration of the business operations of Canada Post, with respect to sponsorships, advertising and stamp marketing, whether as Chairman or President, were characterized by extravagance. Decisions were made unilaterally, disregarding established procedures and favouring his friends over the interests of the corporation. Contrary to the position taken by Mr. Ouellet's counsel in his brief to the Commission,[50] Canada Post did have a corporate procurement and expenditure policy for goods and services which was clearly predicated on compliance with competitive tendering processes.[51]

Mr. Clermont, as President of Canada Post until 1999,[52] did not approve of Mr. Ouellet's initiatives in arranging elaborate and expensive stamp launches and in engaging the Lafleur agency and Michelle Tremblay to render services at great expense; but he believed that Mr. Ouellet had the support and approval of the shareholder, i.e., the Government.[53] He eventually chose to retire rather than to provoke a rift with the Chairman, who continually interfered in the management of the Corporation.[54]

Some of the decisions made on behalf of Canada Post during Mr. Ouellet's tenure, including those related to the issuance of sole-source contracts to Lafleur, TGC and GGA, were criticized in the Report of the Auditor General, and these criticisms were endorsed and repeated in the July 2004 report of the external auditors of Canada Post, Deloitte & Touche,[55] who were mandated the year before to carry out, *inter alia*, an audit of the firm's sponsorship, marketing and advertising activities. Mr. Ouellet disagrees with the findings of both audit reports, but his criticisms are not justified.[56]

8.4
Business Development Bank of Canada

Three transactions involving the Business Development Bank of Canada (BDC) are the subject of comments in the Report of the Auditor General[57] or of testimony before the Commission.

With respect to the first matter, in 1998 the BDC agreed, without a contract being signed,[58] to contribute $250,000 directly to the cost of producing a television series entitled *Le Canada du Millénaire*, which was a project of Mr. Scully of L'Information Essentielle. This contribution was a legitimate part of the BDC's advertising and marketing program. Any irregularity due to the lack of written documentation supporting this transaction, which a Crown Corporation should obviously have in its files, is not a matter within the mandate of the Commission.

The same television series was also supported financially by the Communication Coordination Services Branch (CCSB), which agreed with Mr. Scully to contribute funding of an additional $250,000 as a sponsorship through the agency of Lafleur Communication.[59] The funding by PWGSC was in two instalments of $125,000, together with commissions paid to Lafleur and the Agency of Record, the first of which was paid in July 1998, via the AOR, to L'Information Essentielle.[60] It was the second instalment that gives rise to questions, because instead of the sponsorship amount being paid to L'Information Essentielle, cheques for a total of $125,000 plus tax were issued by the AOR to the BDC, on instructions to that effect by Pierre Tremblay.[61] These cheques arrived at the BDC's offices in March 2000, just before the fiscal year end, and at first no one knew what to do with them.

Alan Marquis, the Chief Financial Officer of the BDC, was of the opinion that the cheques should be returned or destroyed.[62] By this time, the television series had long ago been produced and broadcast, with the BDC receiving appropriate credits. On March 27, 2000, its Vice-President in charge of public affairs, Christiane Beaulieu, wrote a memo to the accounting department, suggesting that the cheques should be cashed and indicating that she was satisfied that the BDC had received publicity having a value far in excess of its contribution of $250,000.[63] With the benefit of hindsight, we know now that Pierre Tremblay at CCSB preferred to send the amount of the sponsorship to the BDC because he was uneasy about the amounts that had already been paid in the current fiscal year by PWGSC for Mr. Scully's various projects. To resolve the impasse, Jean Carle, First Vice-President of the BDC, after speaking to Pierre Tremblay, intervened to authorize the deposit of the cheques and the issuance of a cheque to L'Information Essentielle, after he had reassured Stefano Lucarelli, the controller of the BDC, that all was in order.[64]

The BDC should not have agreed to accommodate the wish of Mr. Tremblay to disguise in this way a payment made to L'Information Essentielle, and Mr. Carle should have left an accounting matter to be handled by the appropriate BDC officers, Messrs. Marquis and Lucarelli, without his intervention. However, it would be an exaggeration to characterize his role in the matter as comparable to money-laundering, although the evidence shows that Mr. Tremblay meant to conceal the PWGSC payment to L'Information Essentielle by passing it through the BDC.[65] Mr. Carle's cooperation, though improper, was not in any way criminal.

As far as the BDC was concerned, it derived a clear benefit from the fact that the television series was produced with the assistance of public funds,[66] and the Auditor General was correct to criticize this breach of the intent of the Government's Transfer Payments Policy. Although the conduct of Messrs. Lucarelli and Marquis might be questionable under the BDC's internal policies, their conduct is not blameworthy since they relied upon Mr. Carle's instructions.

Internal reforms at the BDC since this incident occurred[67] make it unlikely that it will be repeated.

The third subject of testimony at the hearings of the Commission concerns a coffee table book to be produced by Mr. Scully's company in connection with the Maurice Richard series. The BDC contributed $74,800 towards the total anticipated cost of $149,800; the balance of $75,000 was to be paid by PWGSC as a sponsorship. Once again there was no written agreement to confirm these understandings.[68] When invoices were received from L'Information Essentielle requesting payment of the contribution of the BDC,[69] Mr. Lucarelli questioned the expense but was assured by Mr. Carle and Ms. Beaulieu that it should be paid.[70] In fact, the book had not yet been produced,[71] and has never appeared. It may be concluded that both the BDC and PWGSC acted too hastily in paying for goods and services that had not yet been delivered.

8.5
RCMP

In 1998-99, the Royal Canadian Mounted Police wished to celebrate the founding of Canada's national police force 125 years earlier, but had no money to finance the celebrations. In 1997 Odilon Emond, the Deputy Superintendent for the Quebec Division of the RCMP, had become acquainted with Jean Lafleur, whose name had been suggested to him by Mr. Carle, then working in the PMO, as a result of a request by the RCMP for financial assistance in organizing a golf tournament, with the proceeds going to charity. Mr. Lafleur had provided financial assistance of $30,000 to this charitable endeavour (it was only years later that Mr. Emond learned that the money was paid as a sponsorship, with Lafleur earning a commission).[72] Thinking that Mr. Lafleur might be of assistance again, Mr. Emond contacted him. Mr. Lafleur arranged a meeting in or about April 1997 with Mr. Guité, with a view to seeking government funding for the Quebec Division's projects for events in 1998-99 to celebrate the anniversary.[73]

Mr. Emond was very agreeably surprised by the reception he received from Mr. Guité, who asked him to prepare, with the assistance of Mr. Lafleur, a list of the projects which were being planned or contemplated. Shortly after the "wish list" was delivered, Mr. Guité announced that funding of $500,000 would be made available to the Quebec Division of the RCMP.[74]

Mr. Emond informed Dawson Hovey, the Director of Public Affairs for the RCMP at its headquarters in Ottawa, of the results of his initiative to secure government funding for the 125th anniversary celebrations, and Mr. Hovey in turn got in touch with Mr. Guité, and had similar success. Mr. Guité told him that Gosselin Communications would manage the RCMP's events outside of Quebec, as the representative of PWGSC. Mr. Hovey did not know until much later the details of the arrangements made between PWGSC and Gosselin Communications,[75] and was dismayed to learn how much public money was disbursed by the Government to pay for its services. He and everyone else involved in these projects now feel that there was substantial overcharging.

The Auditor General describes the financial aspects of the sponsorships by PWGSC of the various RCMP projects, and it is unnecessary to repeat them here.[76] Suffice it to say that of more than $3 million disbursed from the public purse, only $1.7 million reached the RCMP, together with non-monetary benefits such as promotional items, the financing of the Musical Ride in various localities, and reimbursement of the price of six horses. The rest of the money, totalling $1,326,290, paid for agency commissions, production costs and work given to subcontractors.

The RCMP has agreed with all of the findings of the Auditor General and has taken steps to comply with government policies in the future. It wishes to clarify one finding: the six horses acquired at a cost of $46,530 in December 1997 to supplement its Musical Ride capacity, were not directly purchased with sponsorship funds, but from available funds resulting from the RCMP's normal appropriations. However, the cost of the horses was later reimbursed to the Crown in 1998 from the bank account maintained by the organizing committee in Quebec to hold and administer the funds advanced to it by PWGSC.[77] The practical result is the same: sponsorship funds were used to finance the cost of acquisition of a capital asset—an asset that continued to exist long after the celebrations of 1998-99 had ended—which is a clear violation of the appropriations process and the Transfer Payments Policy.

One aspect of the evidence presented by the representatives of the RCMP who were heard by the Commission is particularly revealing.

In May 1999, the RCMP was planning a re-enactment of the March West, which occurred long ago when the North-West Mounted Police, which was to become the RCMP, was formed to bring order to the territory and set off across the prairies. Based upon the relative ease with which Mr. Guité had been persuaded in the past to grant sponsorships for events related to its anniversary celebrations, the RCMP had assumed that funding of $200,000, needed to assist in the costs of this event, would be provided as a sponsorship by PWGSC. It learned at the last minute from Wendy Cumming, the representative of Gosselin Communications who was handling the file, that funding for the March West had been refused.[78] André Thouin, who was then the Chief Superintendent of the RCMP, called Mr. Guité to try to persuade him to reverse this decision and certain other adverse decisions of lesser importance. Mr. Thouin testifies that Mr. Guité seemed sympathetic to his request and asked him to provide details of the RCMP's needs for funding, which he would show to Minister Gagliano at a forthcoming meeting.[79] Mr. Thouin prepared a letter as suggested, which concludes: "I wish you success in your discussions with your Minister."[80]

A few days later Mr. Thouin was advised by his staff that they had heard from Mr. Guité, who left the message that he had met the Minister that day and would be seeing him again for supper, and that the subject of Mr. Thouin's letter would be followed up.[81]

Eventually, the RCMP was advised that no funding for the March West would be provided. It went ahead with the event anyway, financing it by registration fees paid by participants, and it was a great success.

The significance of the exchanges between Mr. Thouin and Mr. Guité is that it tends to rebut Mr. Gagliano's repeated assertion that he made no decisions about which events would be sponsored, leaving these questions entirely to Mr. Guité. If this is true, there was no need for Mr. Thouin to write the letter to Mr. Guité, and no need for the latter to discuss its contents with Mr. Gagliano, apparently on two occasions. What is more, there appears to be no doubt that Mr. Guité was inclined to favour the March West project; left alone to decide the question, he would almost certainly have approved the requested funding of the relatively modest sum of $200,000. It was therefore Mr. Gagliano who made the decision to refuse the request.

Endnotes to Chapter VIII

[1] Office of the Auditor General of Canada, Report of the Auditor General to the House of Commons: Government-Wide Audit of Sponsorship, Advertising, and Public Opinion Research (Minister of Public Works and Government Services Canada 2003), chapter 3, para. 3.38.

[2] Office of the Auditor General of Canada, Report of the Auditor General to the House of Commons: Government-Wide Audit of Sponsorship, Advertising, and Public Opinion Research (Minister of Public Works and Government Services Canada 2003), chapter 3, para. 3.40.

[3] Office of the Auditor General of Canada, Report of the Auditor General to the House of Commons: Government-Wide Audit of Sponsorship, Advertising, and Public Opinion Research (Minister of Public Works and Government Services Canada 2003), chapter 3, para. 3.44, and case studies at pp. 10-20.

[4] Exhibit P-154, pp. 165-169; Testimony of Mr. Scully, Transcripts vol. 49, pp. 8497-8498 (OE), pp. 8501-8502 (F).

[5] Testimony of Mr. LeFrançois, Transcripts vol. 53, pp. 9146-9149 (OF), pp. 9142-9144 (E).

[6] Testimony of Mr. LeFrançois, Transcripts vol. 53, pp. 9150-9153, 9156-9157 (OF), pp. 9145-9148, 9150-9152 (E).

[7] Exhibit P-164(B), p. 116 (Declaration of the Officers of Via Rail Canada); Testimony of Mr. LeFrançois, Transcripts vol. 53, pp. 9130, 9165-9167 (OF), pp. 9127, 9158-9161 (E).

[8] Exhibit P-164(B), p. 126, observations, 2,3; Testimony of Mr. LeFrançois, Transcripts vol. 53, p. 9269 (OF), p. 9261 (E).

[9] Testimony of Mr. LeFrançois, Transcripts vol. 53, pp. 9186-9188 (OF), pp. 9178-9180 (E); Testimony of Mr. Gagliano, Transcripts vol. 69, pp. 12001-12003 (OF), 11991-11993 (E).

[10] Exhibit P-164(B), pp. 139-140, 147-148; Testimony of Mr. LeFrançois, Transcripts vol. 53, pp. 9203, 9269 (OF), pp. 9193, 9261 (E).

[11] Arguments of Mr. Campion, Transcripts vol. 133, pp. 25267-25268, 25285, 25292 (OE), pp. 25269-25270, 25290, 25298 (F).

[12] Office of the Auditor General of Canada, Report of the Auditor General to the House of Commons: Government-Wide Audit of Sponsorship, Advertising, and Public Opinion Research (Minister of Public Works and Government Services Canada 2003), chapter 3, pp. 17-18.

[13] Office of the Auditor General of Canada, Report of the Auditor General to the House of Commons: Government-Wide Audit of Sponsorship, Advertising, and Public Opinion Research (Minister of Public Works and Government Services Canada 2003), chapter 3, pp. 16-17.

[14] Office of the Auditor General of Canada, Report of the Auditor General to the House of Commons: Government-Wide Audit of Sponsorship, Advertising, and Public Opinion Research (Minister of Public Works and Government Services Canada 2003), chapter 3, p. 16.

[15] Testimony of Ms. Montreuil, Transcripts vol. 58, pp. 10173, 10176, 10202 (OE), pp. 10176-10177, 10180, 10209 (F).

[16] Exhibit P-175, pp. 106, 109; Testimony of Mr. Michaud, Transcripts vol. 79, pp. 13933-13935 (OF), pp. 13921-13923 (E).

17 Testimony of Mr. Jean Lafleur, Transcripts vol. 78, pp. 13732-13734, 13744-13745 (OF), pp. 13721-13723, 13732 (E).

18 Exhibit P-187, pp. 13-16, paras. 37-60.

19 Testimony of Ms. Montreuil, Transcripts vol. 58, pp. 10148, 10150 (OE), pp. 10149-10152 (F).

20 Exhibit P-474(E), Written Representation of Canada Post, paras. 55, 59.

21 Exhibit P-219(B), p. 416; Exhibit P-251; Testimony of Ms. Montreuil, Transcripts vol. 58, p. 10148 (OE), p. 10150 (F).

22 Exhibit P-474(E), Written Representation of Canada Post, para. 45.

23 Testimony of Ms. Montreuil, Transcripts vol. 57, pp. 10124-10125 (OE), pp. 10129-10131 (F).

24 Exhibit P-181, addendum, p. 82J.

25 Exhibit P-181, addendum, p. 82M.

26 Testimony of Mr. Lafleur, Transcripts vol. 78, pp. 13701-13704 (OF), pp. 13692-13695 (E).

27 Exhibit P-181, addendum, p. 82K.

28 Exhibit P-474(E), Written Representations of Canada Post, paras. 51-52; Exhibit P-471, Affidavit of Ms. Montreuil, paras. 4-5.

29 Testimony of Mr. Feeney, Transcripts vol. 61, p. 10844 (OE), pp. 10844-10845 (F).

30 Testimony of Mr. Ouellet, Transcripts vol. 58, pp. 10215-10216 (OF), p. 10218 (E).

31 Testimony of Mr. Ouellet, Transcripts vol. 58, pp. 10215-10216 (OF), p. 10218 (E).

32 Testimony of Mr. Ouellet, Transcripts vol. 58, p. 10217 (OF), 10219 (E).

33 Testimony of Mr. Ouellet, Transcripts vol. 58, p. 10223 (OF), p. 10225 (E).

34 Testimony of Mr. Ouellet, Transcripts vol. 58, p. 10223 (OF), p. 10224 (E).

35 Testimony of Mr. Ouellet, Transcripts vol. 58, p. 10230 (OF), p. 10231 (E).

36 Testimony of Mr. Ouellet, Transcripts vol. 58, pp. 10231-10233 (OF), pp. 10233-10234 (E).

37 Exhibit P-181, pp. 62-63; Testimony of Mr. Ouellet, Transcripts vol. 58, pp. 10234-10242 (OF), pp. 10234-10243 (E); Testimony of Ms. Montreuil, vol. 57, pp. 10116-10118 (OE), pp. 10120-10123 (F).

38 Exhibit P-181, p. 65.

39 Testimony of Mr. Ouellet, Transcripts vol. 59, pp. 10327-10328, 10343-10345 (OF), pp. 10326-10327, 10341-10342 (E).

40 Exhibit P-178, addenda, pp. 1-2.

41 Exhibit P-178, addenda, pp. 1-7.

42 Exhibit P-177(A), pp. 1-7.

43 Testimony of Mr. Ouellet, Transcripts vol. 58, pp. 10264-10266, 10270-10271, 10316 (OF), pp. 10262-10264, 10268-10269, 10310-10311 (E).

44 Testimony of Mr. Ouellet, Transcripts vol. 59, pp. 10447-10449 (OF), pp. 10437-10438 (E).

45 Testimony of Mr. Ouellet, Transcripts vol. 58, pp. 10296-10300 (OF), pp. 10291-10295 (E).

46 Exhibit P-181, pp. 62-63; Testimony of Ms. Montreuil, Transcripts vol. 57, pp. 10116-10117 (OE), pp. 10120-10122 (F).

47 Exhibit P-183, pp. 39-40; Testimony of Mr. Ouellet, Transcripts vol. 58, pp. 10250-10256 (OF), pp. 10249-10256 (E).

48 Testimony of Mr. Ouellet, Transcripts vol. 58, pp. 10256-10258 (OF), pp. 10255-10256 (E).

49 Exhibit P-173, pp. 97-108.

50 Exhibit P-474(D), pp. 4-6.

51 Exhibit P-8, vol. 13, pp. 7151565-7151572.

52 Testimony of Mr. Clermont, Transcripts vol. 61, p. 10664 (OF), p. 10664 (E).

53 Testimony of Mr. Clermont, Transcripts vol. 61, pp. 10680, 10752-10753 (OF), pp. 10678, 10745-10746 (E)

54 Testimony of Mr. Clermont, Transcripts vol. 61, p. 10753 (OF), p. 10746 (E).

55 Exhibit P-173, p. 132.

56 Testimony of Mr. Ouellet, Transcripts vol. 59, pp. 10389-10427 (OF), pp. 10383-10418 (E).

57 Office of the Auditor General of Canada, Report of the Auditor General to the House of Commons: Government-Wide Audit of Sponsorship, Advertising, and Public Opinion Research (Minister of Public Works and Government Services Canada 2003), chapter 3, pp. 12-15.

58 Office of the Auditor General of Canada, Report of the Auditor General to the House of Commons: Government-Wide Audit of Sponsorship, Advertising, and Public Opinion Research (Minister of Public Works and Government Services Canada 2003), chapter 3, p. 13.

59 Testimony of Mr. Scully, Transcripts vol. 49, pp. 8573-8574, 8581-8582 (OF), pp. 8573-8574, 8581-8582 (E).

60 Exhibit P-152, tab 4.

61 Exhibit P-169, pp. 153-155; Testimony of Mr. Carle, Transcripts vol. 70, pp. 12278-12281 (OF), pp. 12263-12266 (E).

62 Testimony of Mr. Marquis, Transcripts vol. 67, pp. 11498-11499 (OE), pp. 11500-11501 (F).

63 Exhibit P-169, p. 157.

64 Exhibit P-169, p. 157, see handwritten note bottom, right-hand corner. Testimony of Mr. Lucarelli, Transcripts vol. 67, pp. 11466-11469 (OE), pp. 11467-11470 (F).

65 Testimony of Mr. Carle, Transcripts vol. 70, p. 12286 (OF), p. 12271 (E).

66 Exhibit P-474(H), Written Representations of the Business Development Bank of Canada, para. 42.

67 Exhibit P-474(H), Written Representations of the Business Development Bank of Canada, paras. 15-24.

68 Testimony of Mr. Lucarelli, Transcripts vol. 67, pp. 11475-11478 (OE), pp. 11476-11480 (F).

69 Exhibit P-157, p. 159.

70 Exhibit P-157, p. 160.

71 Testimony of Mr. Scully, Transcripts vol. 50, p. 8747 (OF), p. 8747 (E).

72 Testimony of Mr. Émond, Transcripts vol. 51, pp. 8908-8915 (OF), pp. 8908-8915 (E).

73 Testimony of Mr. Émond, Transcripts vol. 51, pp. 8916-8921 (OF), pp. 8916-8921 (E).

74 Testimony of Mr. Émond, Transcripts vol. 51, pp. 8918-8919 (OF), pp. 8918-8919 (E).

75 Testimony of Mr. Hovey, Transcripts vol. 51, pp. 8881-8884 (OE), pp. 8883-8886 (F).

76 Office of the Auditor General of Canada, Report of the Auditor General to the House of Commons: Government-Wide Audit of Sponsorship, Advertising, and Public Opinion Research (Minister of Public Works and Government Services Canada 2003), chapter 3, pp. 19-20.

77 Testimony of Commissioner Zaccardelli, Transcripts vol. 50, pp. 8835, 8858-8865 (OE), pp. 8840, 8866-8874 (F).

[78] Testimony of Mr. Thouin, Transcripts vol. 52, p. 9004 (OF), p. 9004 (E).

[79] Testimony of Mr. Thouin, Transcripts vol. 52, pp. 9015-9017 (OF), pp. 9015-9017 (E).

[80] Exhibit P-160, pp. 187-188.

[81] Exhibit P-160, p. 187.

CHAPTER IX

JEAN BRAULT

9.1
Communication Agencies

In my opening statement delivered on May 7, 2004, I identified the questions which would be examined in Phase IB of the hearings of the Commission to be held in Montreal. Phase IA dealt with the Sponsorship Program and Advertising Activities of the Government of Canada from the point of view of their administration by public servants, according to the policies formulated by the political leaders of the Government. Phase IB intended to deal with the use of public funds once they had been disbursed by PWGSC, and with four related questions:

- whether the Government received value for the money disbursed;

- whether there was political influence on the distribution of funds;

- whether such political influence was related to political contributions or gifts made by the recipients or beneficiaries of the funds; and

- whether there were sufficient monitoring and financial controls over those funds, once disbursed.

Most of the witnesses who were questioned on these subjects were the proprietors, employees and representatives of the communication agencies engaged by PWGSC to manage or execute sponsorship or advertising contracts on behalf of the Government, followed by certain officers and employees of the Liberal Party of Canada (Quebec), referred to as LPCQ.

Dealing first with the communication agencies, the evidence made it apparent that those who were qualified to handle government business were not all treated in the same way. Only a few were awarded sponsorship contracts. Let us review briefly which agencies became qualified, and which of them received contracts.

In Joseph Charles Guité's memorandum to Andrée LaRose in early 1995, five agencies (Groupe Everest, BCP, Compass Communication, Palmer Jarvis, and Vickers & Benson), which had formerly been declared to be qualified to receive contracts from Heritage Canada, were arbitrarily declared to be qualified also to receive contracts from Public Works and Government Services Canada (PWGSC).[1]

On July 6, 1995, a second group of agencies, identified as "Lafleur Communication Consortium" and composed of Compass Communication, Allard Communication-Marketing, Freeman Rodgers Battaglia, SKS Advertising and Communications Jean Lafleur, was added to this list of qualified suppliers.[2] In 1997 another ten agencies became qualified as suppliers of advertising services to PWGSC after what I have already qualified as a sham competition. They were Groupaction, Manifest Communications, Publicité Martin, Scott Thornley, Communication Coffin/SOS Communications, Gosselin et Associés, Freeman Rodgers Battaglia, Delta Media, Sparks Communications and Goodman Communications[3].

In other words, a total of 18 agencies (Compass Communication and Freeman Rodgers Battaglia were qualified twice) were declared qualified to receive sponsorship contracts, although only five of them (Lafleur, Gosselin, Groupaction, Everest and Coffin) ever actually received a significant number of contracts from PWGSC.[4] Those five agencies were, at one time or another, contributors to the Liberal Party of Canada, some with greater enthusiasm and generosity than others.[5] One of them, the Gosselin agency, because of the political convictions of some of its employees and clients and because its owner, Gilles-André Gosselin, has a profound dislike of political involvement, became reluctant to make further political contributions to the Liberal Party of Canada,[6] with the result that its share of sponsorship contracts was sharply diminished; this will be more fully described when we come to review the testimony of Mr. Gosselin.

The above paragraphs seem to indicate that the distribution of sponsorship contracts was, at least in some instances, related to political allegiance and affiliation. The five agencies that received business from PWGSC seemed to be viewed with greater favour by those making decisions about the awarding of sponsorship contracts than the 13 that received nothing. Mr. Chrétien, in his prepared statement to the Commission, declared openly that "separatist friendly" agencies, whatever that means, would not be viewed favourably when it came to awarding sponsorship contracts. He affirmed the following:

> The Sponsorship Program was not partisan. It was not about the Liberal Party. It was about promoting the visibility of Canada in Quebec. A conventional wisdom had nonetheless been created about "Liberal friendly" advertising agencies.
>
> We have to be very careful about labels. In Quebec, there are basically two types of advertising agencies; those who are "separatist friendly" and those who are "federalist friendly".
>
> "Federalist friendly" agencies tended to support the Conservatives when they were in power and the Liberals when they were in power. I do hope the Government of Canada used "federalist friendly" agencies to promote the visibility of Canada in Quebec, not because the agencies contributed to the Liberal

Party until we abolished corporate donations or contributions, but because the only alternative in practical terms was to use "separatist friendly" agencies to promote Canada.[7]

It may be assumed that Mr. Chrétien's opinions carried great weight with his subordinates, including Mr. Guité and any others who had to participate in the making of decisions as to which agency to use for a particular sponsorship. One of the ways an agency could demonstrate that it was "federalist friendly" was by making contributions to the party in power. Certainly the agencies concerned believed that the political contributions they were making were one of the most important reasons why they were awarded sponsorship contracts.[8] In particular, that was the opinion of Jean Brault of Groupaction, the most generous contributor.

Of the evidence given to the Commission by the representatives of the five favoured agencies, by far the most comprehensive and candid testimony came from Mr. Brault, who was at all relevant times the president, controlling shareholder and chief operating officer of the complex of corporations that will be described collectively in this Report as either Groupaction or Groupaction Marketing. The Commission accepts all of Mr. Brault's evidence as credible. If his testimony was on occasion inexact, it was as a result of an involuntary error or a memory lapse rather than caused by an intention to mislead. As a result of his revelations and candour, the Commission was enabled to examine in detail his contributions, whether formal or irregular and whether freely offered or not, to persons acting in various capacities for the LPCQ.

Mr. Brault's testimony also led the Commission to give particular attention to Groupaction's transactions with a group of companies operated by Luc Lemay and under the name of Expour or Polygone, which benefited from sponsorships managed by Groupaction and obtained as a result of representations made by Jacques Corriveau. Mr. Corriveau's reputation, his friendship with the Prime Minister and his position of influence within the LPCQ give reason to believe that these factors were used by him to further the interests of Mr. Lemay's companies, as well as his own interests and the interests of the LPCQ.

The complicated web of interlocking relationships involving Groupaction, Mr. Lemay, Mr. Corriveau, certain persons within the LPCQ, and the Government of Canada is described in considerable detail in Mr. Brault's testimony over a period of six days.

But before summarizing his evidence, let us begin by explaining why I believe Mr. Brault to be a credible witness.

9.2
Credibility of Jean Brault

The key witnesses summoned to testify with respect to the administration of sponsorship contracts by the Lafleur and Gosselin agencies, who were questioned by counsel for the Commission before Mr. Brault was called to testify, chose to be forgetful, evasive and uncooperative when requested to provide details of their management of the events for which their agencies had been generously rewarded. Their testimony was replete with selective memory lapses and repeated instances of failure or inability to give clear and unequivocal answers to simple questions. Some of their answers were flatly contradicted by documentation, or simply made no sense. To avoid being unexpectedly confronted with documentation tending to show that their testimony was untrue, certain witnesses took care to study carefully each piece of paper put before them before answering any question, instead of answering spontaneously. What they said or refused to say, and their demeanour in general, left the Commission with the overwhelming impression that the representatives of the Lafleur and Gosselin agencies who had appeared before it had much to hide, and that they were prepared to disguise, distort or pretend to forget the truth, rather than to frankly disclose their conversations and agreements with the other persons, either at the political level or within the apparatus of government, with whom they had been dealing.

Mr. Brault provided a refreshing contrast to the sorry spectacle offered by the witnesses who preceded him. Generally speaking, he was frank and precise in his testimony. He willingly produced supporting documentation, where it exists, to corroborate his version of the meetings and conversations he had with other persons. The Commission was especially assisted by the production of his agendas[9] and the records that were maintained by his secretary of his telephone calls and messages.[10] Many other witnesses were unable to explain convincingly why this kind of documentation could not be produced by them.[11] Mr. Brault made all such records available, the authenticity of which cannot be doubted.

In his testimony, Mr. Brault makes no attempt to evade his personal responsibility for the mismanagement of many of the sponsorship contracts which his agency handled. He frankly admits that Groupaction overcharged PWGSC in some cases,[12] and that he was motivated by ambition and by a desire for financial gain. He recognizes that the payment by Groupaction of sums of money to officers and representatives of the LPCQ, or the furnishing of employment to certain persons at its request, had as its objective the securing of additional sponsorship contracts from PWGSC.[13] He does not suggest that he was motivated by political ideals and acknowledges that his contributions to the LPCQ were entirely cynical.[14]

It should be remembered that when he testified, Mr. Brault was facing criminal charges of fraud as a result of certain contracts awarded to Groupaction by Mr. Guité. Although Mr. Brault's testimony before the Commission could not be used against him in the criminal courts, counsel for the Commission nevertheless took care not to question him about the particular transactions in relation to which he had been accused. However, his testimony might be used against him in connection with civil proceedings threatened or commenced by the Government of Canada, which seek to recover from him and from others reimbursement of substantial sums allegedly overcharged by Groupaction or otherwise recoverable from it. Mr. Brault made no attempt to protect himself from the consequences of his testimony in other proceedings. It would have been easy for him, in the circumstances, to pretend that he remembers nothing, a tactic employed by other witnesses. Instead, he made a genuine effort to remember the details of events occurring over a period of nearly ten years.

Mr. Brault did not attempt to shield himself from the public embarrassment of having to admit that, once he had embarked on a policy to obtain contracts from the Government by purchasing political influence, he rapidly became the object of ever-increasing demands for gifts and political contributions of various kinds, and was called upon to disburse progressively greater sums of money to maintain the influence which he believed was directly related to the profitable contracts Groupaction was receiving.[15] In the end, not only has his personal reputation been tarnished, but Groupaction has been financially ruined. These are not defeats to which an ambitious and formerly successful businessman likes to admit.

Having had the opportunity to observe Mr. Brault being examined and cross-examined for several days, I am satisfied that he is a fundamentally truthful witness who has decided to make a clean breast of it and to provide to the Commission a full and frank disclosure of what he knows and remembers about all aspects of his involvement in the Sponsorship Program. Many of his revelations, surprising when they were first described, were subsequently corroborated by other evidence. In some instances his testimony about certain events was contradicted by other witnesses, but in each such instance, after analysis of the contradictions, I came to the conclusion that Mr. Brault's version of the facts is more credible and that he is a more reliable witness than those who contradicted him.

9.3
Initial Government Contracts and Political Contributions

After graduating from university in 1976 with a degree in marketing, and after a few lean years, Mr. Brault and his wife, Joanne Archambault, founded Groupaction Marketing in the early 1980s and gradually built up a list of clients in the private sector[16] who valued the services of Groupaction and its employees in the fields of advertising and public relations.

Following the election of a Liberal administration in 1993, Mr. Brault was interested in expanding his business by soliciting contracts for advertising services from the new government. He was encouraged in this ambition by

Alain Renaud, to whom he had been introduced by a mutual friend in 1991. Mr. Renaud was a young entrepreneur, a part owner of a printing business who wanted to sell his printing services to Mr. Brault and his clients. In this he was not successful, but the two men got to know each other and talked fairly often. In their conversations Mr. Renaud told Mr. Brault that he had cultivated valuable contacts with key public servants at PWGSC such as Mr. Guité and Andrée LaRose, and had also, by involving himself in political fundraising activities, become friends with persons in the upper echelons of the LPCQ. He felt he could exploit these contacts to obtain government business for Groupaction.[17] Mr. Brault was prepared to participate in this business promotion, and an informal verbal agreement between them resulted: Groupaction would reimburse Mr. Renaud for the expenses he incurred in his attempts to obtain government business, but no salary or other remuneration would be paid to him until he produced results.[18]

In the meantime, Mr. Brault was pursuing his own attempts to obtain government business for Groupaction by more conventional means. He made several formal presentations, called "pitches" in the industry, to selection committees organized by the Advertising and Public Opinon Research Sector (APORS), by which the latter sought to qualify suppliers for various federal government departments and agencies. His presentations were successful on two occasions, and Groupaction obtained important contracts from the CRTC and the Department of Justice. The latter needed an agency to assist it with advertisements and publicity following the adoption of the Government's firearms legislation. Mr. Brault says that Mr. Renaud had nothing to do with these ventures, but he acknowledges that Mr. Renaud arranged to introduce him to key players in the LPCQ and in government administration, and encouraged him to make himself better known to persons of influence.[19]

As examples of the contacts that Mr. Brault was making on the initiative of Mr. Renaud, he purchased tickets to attend various fundraising functions organized by the LPCQ, such as receptions, cocktail parties and golf tournaments. On these occasions, he was repeatedly told by senior officers of the Party, such as its successive executive directors Roger Légaré, Michel Béliveau and Benoît Corbeil, that Alain Renaud was much appreciated and highly esteemed for the unpaid work he did for the Party.[20] He was also persuaded to join the Club Laurier, which meets about twice a year and gives its members the opportunity to shake hands with the Prime Minister. Groupaction paid the annual membership fees of $1,000 each for Mr. Brault and Mr. Renaud.[21]

Mr. Brault attended the Molson Indy car race in Vancouver in September 1995, accompanied by Alain Renaud. Mr. Guité and Jean Carle were also in attendance.[22] Mr. Brault had first met Mr. Carle in Ottawa about two weeks earlier. Mr. Renaud had arranged a meeting with him at the PMO at which they together made a "pitch," extolling to Mr. Carle the qualities and capacities of Groupaction and plainly asking that it be given a share of government business. Mr. Carle, initially cold, seemed to become more receptive as the meeting went on and told them they should see Mr. Guité and Ms. LaRose at APORS, adding that the Government was like a superhighway with room for vehicles of all sizes.[23]

At the Molson Indy in Vancouver, Mr. Brault learned from Mr. Guité, whom he had also met previously through the efforts of Mr. Renaud, that APORS administered a substantial budget used for subsidizing events such as the one they were attending. Mr. Guité explained to him that communication agencies were engaged by his organization to manage such events on behalf of the Government, and Mr. Brault understood that this could be a profitable area of activity for Groupaction in the future.[24] The word "sponsorship" was not yet in use.

In the spring of 1996, which we know was the period during which the Sponsorship Program was being planned at the highest levels, Mr. Brault had a series of meetings at which it was made plain to him that in order to obtain government contracts for sponsorship initiatives, Groupaction would have to make financial contributions of various kinds to the LPCQ. The first contribution was in the form of a series of payments made by Groupaction to a certain Serge Gosselin, at the request of Jacques Corriveau. These payments, which are the subject of highly contradictory testimony, came about in the following way according to Mr. Brault.

His agenda shows that on April 16, 1996, he had a meeting or a conversation with Jacques Corriveau, who would have asked him to engage the services of Serge Gosselin, a person totally unknown to Mr. Brault, and to pay him a salary of $7,000 per month for a year.[25] At that time or later, Mr. Gosselin may have been working for the LPCQ, under Mr. Corriveau's direction, preparing documentation such as minutes, resolutions and supporting material for one of the Party's upcoming policy meetings.[26] Mr. Brault agreed to assume this very considerable expense, convinced that disbursements of this kind would be well compensated by sponsorship contracts, in spite of the fact that Mr. Gosselin never performed any work for Groupaction and did not even come to its offices.[27]

Mr. Brault testifies that the arrangement to pay for the services rendered by Mr. Gosselin to the LPCQ was confirmed at a dinner meeting on April 25, 1996, which he hosted at the Club Saint Denis.[28] The dinner is recorded in Mr. Brault's agenda[29] (reproduced in Figure IX-1) and in the club's register, which confirms that six persons dined together that night.[30] Mr. Brault says they were Messrs. Corriveau, Guité, Corbeil, Renaud, Serge Gosselin and himself. What is particularly intriguing is the presence of Mr. Guité, because it establishes a direct link between the alleged payments to Gosselin by Groupaction, to the advantage of the LPCQ, and the public servant responsible for the sponsorship contracts that were later awarded to Groupaction. Mr. Corriveau claims that he has no recollection of this dinner meeting or of the arrangement concerning Mr. Gosselin,[31] but Mr. Guité remembers the dinner well and confirms Mr. Brault's testimony about who was there. He specifically remembers the presence of Serge Gosselin.[32] The Commission has no doubt that the dinner occurred, that the persons mentioned by Mr. Brault attended, and that they were there for the reasons and with the results described by Mr. Brault.

Figure IX-1: Jean Brault's agenda, April 22-25, 1996

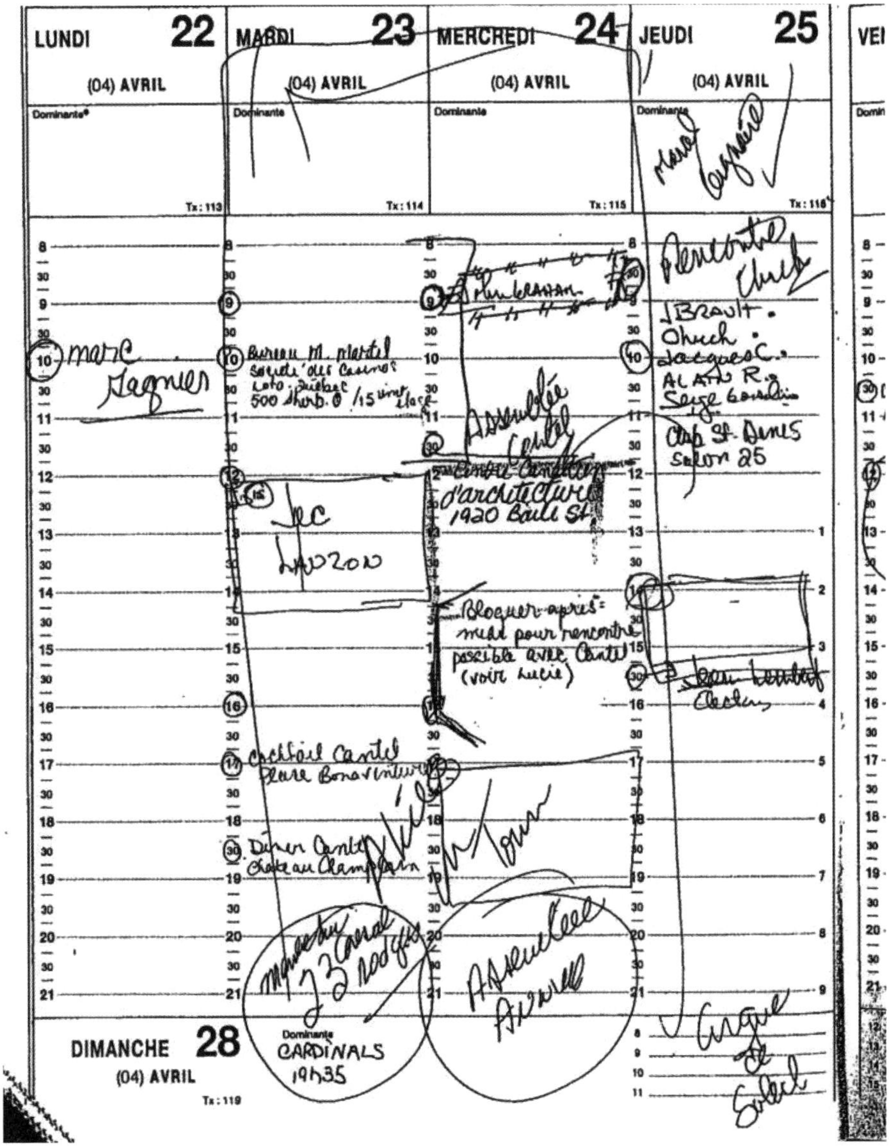

However, there is no documentary evidence of payments made by Groupaction directly to Serge Gosselin in 1996 or 1997. Mr. Gosselin flatly denies that he attended a meeting with Mr. Brault and the others at the Club Saint Denis in April 1996, or that he was paid sums of money during that year or in 1997 as related by Mr. Brault.[33] He acknowledges that he received $42,500 plus taxes in 1999 and 2000 from Groupaction, which he alleges he earned for preparing three studies about voting patterns and polling results in the City of Longueuil, saying that two of the studies were commissioned by Alain Renaud on Groupaction's behalf and one in a brief meeting with Mr. Brault himself.[34] No one, including Mr. Gosselin himself, can explain why Groupaction would agree to pay for such studies.[35]

Serge Gosselin says that he was working in 1996 in the office of the Honourable Stéphane Dion.[36] If this is so, it must be assumed that if he was ever reimbursed for his services rendered to the LPCQ by Groupaction, it was at the time that he started working full-time for the LPCQ in 1997, when it was preparing for the elections held in June of that year. In 1997 and perhaps before, he was working out of Mr. Corriveau's offices[37] and was probably being paid for his services by Mr. Corriveau's company, PluriDesign. It may be that payments made by Groupaction to Mr. Gosselin were routed through PluriDesign.

What is abundantly clear is that the LPCQ did not have the means to pay Mr. Gosselin for his services in 1996 and 1997,[38] and that some third party supplied whatever funds were paid to him. Mr. Gosselin gives the impression that he is not the sort of person to work for nothing. Mr. Brault says he was paid by Groupaction, and however and whenever the payments were made, the substance of his version is to be preferred to the denials by Serge Gosselin that he received sums of money from Groupaction prior to 1999. A reason to doubt Mr. Gosselin's denials—to be added to the improbability of his story about studies for the City of Longueuil and his denial that he attended the dinner at the Club Saint Denis in April 1996—is what he says about the flattering biography of Mr. Gagliano that he wrote in 1996 and 1997, which was published and presented to Mr. Gagliano in June 1997.

According to Mr. Gosselin, the biography was written by him on his own initiative and entirely gratuitously. He states unequivocally that he was not remunerated in any way for this work.[39] However, Joseph Morselli tells a different story. He testifies that a group of friends of Mr. Gagliano had contributed to a fund to finance the printing and publication of the biography, and that out of that fund Mr. Gosselin was paid the sum of $6,000.[40] The Commission has no reason to doubt the truth of Mr. Morselli's testimony on this subject. It must be concluded that on this question and generally, on matters having to do with sums of money paid to him, Mr. Serge Gosselin is not a reliable witness.

Another reason why the Commission is inclined, even in the absence of documentary evidence of payments such as cancelled cheques or receipts, to believe Mr. Brault's testimony that he paid for Mr. Gosselin's services to the LPCQ, is because in two other instances Groupaction paid salaries at the request of the LPCQ to persons whom it would not otherwise have hired or remunerated. In each of these two instances, his testimony is well supported by documentary evidence. His agreement to look after the financial needs of Mr. Gosselin for the benefit of the LPCQ was therefore not an isolated instance of a political contribution in the form of sums paid someone as requested by the LPCQ, but part of a pattern of conduct.

The first of the two instances concerns John Welch who, over the years, has worked on behalf of the Liberal Party, both federally and provincially, in various capacities. Either Benoît Corbeil or Jacques Corriveau (Mr. Brault is not sure which, but Mr. Welch's testimony indicates that it was more likely Mr. Corbeil) asked Mr. Brault to give Mr. Welch employment for a year, starting in April 1999.[41] At that time Mr. Welch was out of work and needed a salary from someone. Mr. Brault did not know Mr. Welch at all but agreed to look after him and supplied him with a small office in Groupaction's premises.[42] Groupaction paid him a salary of $7,000 per month for a year.[43] The only services he rendered in exchange was to represent Groupaction and Mr. Brault at various Liberal Party functions and fundraisers, although Mr. Welch testifies in a most convincing way that he was at all times ready and willing to do any work that Groupaction chose to assign to him.[44] The simple fact is that his services were not needed by Groupaction, and that Mr. Corbeil, on behalf of the LPCQ, for whom Mr. Welch had worked diligently in the past, wanted to assure him a source of income, which Mr. Brault agreed to supply.

The second person put on the payroll by Groupaction was Maria-Lyne Chrétien, a niece of the Prime Minister, who was employed by one of Groupaction's subsidiaries for about eight months in 1998. She was paid an appropriate salary for the work she was doing. Mr. Corriveau had requested Mr. Brault to find her a job, saying she had worked previously for him. Mr. Brault considered that the request was more of a demand than a suggestion. I conclude that he probably would not have hired her if it had not been for Mr. Corriveau's "request."[45]

Other indirect contributions to the LPCQ over the years when Groupaction was receiving sponsorship contracts from PWGSC may be more briefly described.

On three occasions Groupaction paid, as requested by Mr. Renaud, invoices addressed to the LPCQ by the Club de Golf de Verchères in the total amount of $14,100. The evidence indicates that these amounts were due as a result of the annual fundraising golf tournament organized by Tony Mignacca, the chief political organizer for Mr. Gagliano.[46] Persons wishing to meet Mr. Gagliano and to contribute to his election and other expenses could purchase tickets to the golf tournament. The proceeds were deposited with the headquarters of the LPCQ, which paid all expenses including those of the golf club. By paying these invoices, the net proceeds raised by the event were increased by an equivalent amount. Mr. Brault further enhanced the profitability of the event by arranging for bottled water and soft drinks to be donated for consumption by the participants.[47]

Other bills were sent to Groupaction by officials at the LPCQ, some of which Mr. Brault agreed to pay, while refusing others. Groupaction's accounting records show that it paid $8,281.80 for a reception at the Restaurant La Tarentella,[48] for the benefit of the LPCQ, but that other invoices, such as one from Avicor Construction for work contracted by Mr. Mignacca when the LPCQ relocated its offices, were refused.[49] Eventually the LPCQ paid Avicor itself. Similarly, Mr. Brault turned down several invoices due by the LPCQ presented to him by Mr. Morselli.[50]

However, Mr. Brault was more accommodating when the request for payment came directly from Mr. Gagliano. In 1998 and 1999, a television production company named Productions Caméo, belonging to one Thalie Tremblay, was engaged by the LPCQ to film a series of interviews with Liberal Members of Parliament, to be broadcast on a community television network. The programs were called *Vos députés vous parlent*. Mr. Gagliano was very supportive of this project, and when the first invoices from Productions Caméo were received at his office, he had them paid out of his own budget. When four later invoices totalling $45,837.47[51] arrived, his Executive Assistant, Pierre Tremblay, asked Ms. Tremblay to redirect them to Groupaction for payment.[52] Since Mr. Brault was unwilling to have Groupaction pay bills addressed to the LPCQ, he asked Ms. Tremblay to reword and address them to Groupaction.[53] She was puzzled by this request but agreed, and prepared new invoices which falsely described the services rendered as "Analyses, recherches et repérages projet video corporatif, Groupaction…."[54] With these modifications, Groupaction paid the invoices. Mr. Brault testifies that he was asked to do so either by Mr. Renaud, speaking on behalf of Benoît Corbeil, or by Mr. Corbeil himself.[55]

Mr. Gagliano was questioned on this subject and testifies that he was unaware that his Executive Assistant had requested that the bills in question be sent to Groupaction.[56] He agrees that if he did, and Ms. Tremblay's evidence on this subject appears to be irrefutable, it was entirely inappropriate.[57] It is most unlikely that Mr. Tremblay would have taken such an initiative without the authorization of his Minister, and that Mr. Gagliano, who saw to the payment of subsequent invoices from Productions Caméo from his office budget,[58] must have been aware that someone else had looked after earlier invoices. Mr. Tremblay died before testifying, and could not give his side of the story. Whether or not he acted with Mr. Gagliano's authorization, Mr. Gagliano was responsible for him.

Regardless of who asked Groupaction to pay the invoices, someone in authority did and they represent a direct benefit to the LPCQ of $45,837.47 from an agency that was receiving business from the Government.

In the autumn of 1998, Groupaction provided the use of a van to Gaëtano Manganiello, a full-time LPCQ worker who had put too much mileage on his own automobile, travelling to Sherbrooke in connection with the by-election campaign going on there. After the by-election, he asked Mr. Corbeil for help and was told he could pick up the keys to a Dodge Caravan from someone at Groupaction's offices. Mr. Manganiello used the van for at least six months, and when he left the employ of the LPCQ he turned it over to Jean Brisebois, another LPCQ worker who was being paid a salary, like Mr. Manganiello, by PluriDesign.[59]

There is no evidence to establish the value conferred upon the LPCQ by Groupaction's loan of a vehicle to Messrs. Manganiello and Brisebois, but considering that the arrangement lasted at least six months and probably longer, and that the value of a van might be conservatively estimated at $500 per month, the Commission evaluates this benefit conservatively at $3,000.

9.4
Contract with Alain Renaud

Returning to the subject of Mr. Brault's relationship with Mr. Renaud, by mid-1996 it appeared probable that the latter was going to be able to assist Groupaction in obtaining government contracts. He was evidently on familiar terms with influential persons in the LPCQ, the most important of them being Mr. Corriveau, who was perceived not only by Mr. Brault but by almost everyone as a person who had contacts at the very highest levels.[60] Other important persons who obviously were favourably disposed towards Mr. Renaud were Michel Béliveau, the Executive Director at the Montreal Headquarters of the LPCQ in 1997, and his deputy, Benoît Corbeil, who succeeded Mr. Béliveau in that position in 1998.[61]

In 1996, Groupaction received its first contract from PWGSC having to do with sponsorships, as opposed to an advertising contract, and Mr. Brault was satisfied that the time had come to reward Mr. Renaud for what were essentially lobbying activities, although Mr. Renaud was never registered with the Government of Canada as a lobbyist.[62]

Starting on June 1, 1996, Groupaction began to pay Mr. Renaud's personal corporation, Investissements Alain Renaud Inc., $7,143 per month plus taxes against invoices which incorrectly described the work done as "honoraires professionnels pour différents projets."[63] Groupaction continued to reimburse Mr. Renaud for his expenses[64] in spite of the fact that he consistently failed to justify them by receipts or vouchers. The expenses reimbursed to him by Groupaction in 1996 totalled $16,135.74.[65] No written agreement confirmed this arrangement, which lasted until November 1, 1996, when the monthly payments to Investissements Alain Renaud Inc. were increased to $8,500; however, concurrently with that increase, Groupaction stopped reimbursing Mr. Renaud for his expenses.[66]

The parties confirmed their arrangement for the first time by a contract in writing dated September 3, 1997, by which it was agreed that Groupaction would pay 9004-8612 Quebec Inc., which had replaced Investissements Alain Renaud Inc. as Mr. Renaud's personal company, the amount of $10,000 per month for two years, and would reimburse it as well for business expenses up to a maximum of $30,000 per year. The contract foresees the payment of discretionary bonuses to Mr. Renaud's company in the event that Groupaction's billings exceeded certain scheduled levels.[67] As it turned out, substantial bonuses were paid, but there were disagreements between the parties about whether the bonuses paid truly reflected Groupaction's billings.[68] As will be seen later, these disagreements were part of the reason for the termination of the contract in 2000,[69] after it had been extended by a new contract for a third year. From April 1996 to September 2000, Groupaction paid Alain Renaud's personal companies a total of $902,046 in the form of fees, expenses and bonuses, plus applicable taxes.[70]

Obviously in 1997 the value of Mr. Renaud's services to Groupaction had increased, in spite of the fact that he almost never appeared at Groupaction's place of business and spent more of his time at the Headquarters of the

LPCQ.[71] As appears from Table 68 of the Kroll Report, the value of the sponsorship contracts managed by Groupaction on behalf of PWGSC went from $830,000 in 1996-97 to $10,404,058 in 1997-98, and increased again in 1998-99 to $14,809,305. The net revenues and profitability of Groupaction increased proportionately as appears from Tables 72 and 73 of the same Report, even taking into consideration the generous salaries and benefits paid to Mr. Brault and his wife as a cost of doing business.[72]

Mr. Brault recognizes that the sudden avalanche of sponsorship contracts awarded to Groupaction in 1997 and in subsequent years was mostly attributable to the efforts he made, with the guidance and assistance of Mr. Renaud, to ingratiate himself with the LPCQ by the payment to it of contributions of various sorts.[73] He likes to think that the quality of his agency's work was also a reason why government business was directed to it, but he realistically acknowledges that the most important factor was the political connection and, above all, the contributions he was prepared to make to the LPCQ.[74]

In addition to promoting Groupaction's relations with the officials of the LPCQ at its Headquarters in Montreal, Mr. Brault did not neglect elected officials in Ottawa. Mr. Renaud arranged for him to have dinner on July 8, 1996, in a restaurant in Hull with Mr. Gagliano and his Executive Assistant, Pierre Tremblay.[75] At that time Mr. Gagliano was the Minister of Labour, a key member of the Quebec Liberal caucus, and a force to be reckoned with in the LPCQ. Mr. Brault says that at their dinner Mr. Gagliano noted with appreciation the value of Mr. Renaud's work on behalf of the Party. In December 1996, Mr. Gagliano paid an impromptu visit to the Montreal offices of Groupaction.[76] On February 1, 1997 Mr. Renaud arranged for Groupaction to make a carefully prepared presentation of its capacities to the members of the political commission of the LPCQ, which included Mr. Gagliano, and was rewarded for its efforts by being invited to join a consortium of advertising agencies, including BCP and Groupe Everest, generally considered to be "Liberal friendly," to work with them for the LPCQ during the 1997 election campaign.[77]

During the campaign Richard Boudreault, an employee and shareholder of Groupaction, wanted to work full-time for the consortium, and, on paper at least, took an unpaid leave of absence from Groupaction. In fact, he continued to receive his regular remuneration through the cooperation and assistance of Harel Drouin, a firm of chartered accountants that acted as Groupaction's external auditors. Harel Drouin sent monthly invoices to Groupaction for professional services that were not in fact rendered, upon receipt from Mr. Boudreault's personal corporation, Richard Boudreault Inc., of invoices, also false, to Harel Drouin for approximately equivalent amounts.[78] The payment of the invoices by Groupaction and by Harel Drouin permitted them to circumvent the provisions of the *Canada Elections Act*, which forbid anyone to furnish services to a political party during an election campaign for which they are remunerated by anyone other than the political party concerned. Any such remuneration constitutes an illegal campaign contribution since it is not recorded as an election expense.[79] The same provisions were again circumvented when Mr. Boudreault's company paid three supposedly volunteer election workers for their services during the election, on the basis of false invoices that were addressed to his company. Groupaction reimbursed Mr. Boudreault's company for these expenses, again on the basis of false invoices, in the sum of $14,790.[80] Mr. Boudreault testifies that these transactions were handled by Groupaction's accountant, who looked after his bank account while he was absent for the duration of the election campaign.[81]

9.5
Cash Contributions to the Liberal Party of Canada (Quebec)

Mr. Brault testifies that Groupaction, in addition to what has already been described, made unrecorded cash contributions to the LPCQ on at least three occasions.

The first occurred in 1997, which, it should be recalled, was an election year. Mr. Brault says he was approached either by Mr. Renaud, Mr. Corriveau or Mr. Corbeil, speaking on behalf of the LPCQ, asking him for a donation of $100,000. Mr. Brault preferred to make this donation in cash since he was negotiating with the J. Walter Thompson Agency, which was interested in investing in Groupaction, and Mr. Brault did not want Groupaction's books to reflect excessive political contributions. However, he agreed to contribute $50,000 in cash.[82] This amount was remitted in two installments: the first of $15,000 in the weeks immediately preceding the election, and the second of $35,000 in the month of August.[83] To corroborate Mr. Brault's evidence, Bernard Michaud, the comptroller of Groupaction, testifies that Mr. Brault asked him to obtain $15,000 in cash on April 28, 1997, by cashing a cheque drawn on Groupaction's account to Mr. Michaud's order. Mr. Michaud describes the incident in considerable detail, including the tax problem created by his apparent receipt of a cash advance from his employer. Eventually he was reimbursed by Groupaction for the income tax he had to pay as a result.[84] The $15,000 in cash was turned over to Mr. Brault, who says that he delivered it in person to Mr. Renaud.[85]

According to Mr. Brault, the balance of $35,000 was also delivered in cash to Mr. Renaud and its receipt was later confirmed to him by Mr. Corbeil.[86] On Groupaction's books the $35,000 cheque payable to Mr. Brault, which he cashed himself, was treated as a bonus.[87]

Both Mr. Corbeil and Mr. Renaud deny that they received these payments.[88] The Commission does not consider that either of them is a reliable witness and accepts Mr. Brault's testimony. It is corroborated in part by the cancelled cheques which are evidence of the withdrawals from Groupaction's bank account,[89] and by the testimony of Mr. Michaud, in preference to their denials. It is also corroborated by the testimony of Michel Béliveau, who remembers receiving a contribution of $50,000 from Groupaction at about that time.[90]

In February 1998 Mr. Renaud approached Mr. Brault again, at the request of Mr. Béliveau, saying that the LPCQ was in dire financial straits and could not pay its rent and other bills. Mr. Brault was persuaded to have Groupaction remit to Mr. Renaud's company $63,500 in payment of two false invoices, one for $55,000 and another for $8,500, which refer to services rendered that are pure inventions.[91] The sum of $63,500 was then paid by Mr. Renaud's company as a properly recorded political contribution to the LPCQ.[92] Mr. Renaud, confronted by the documentary evidence of these transactions, admits them.[93] In any event, there can be no doubt about the direct relationship between the sums paid by Groupaction to Mr. Renaud's company and the contribution by the latter to the LPCQ.

The third cash contribution was made in the autumn of 1998 when a by-election occurred in Sherbrooke, Quebec, to fill a vacancy in the House of Commons resulting from the decision of the Honourable Jean Charest to resign his seat to head the provincial Liberal Party. Mr. Renaud asked Mr. Brault for a contribution to assist in the payment of campaign expenses, and Mr. Brault gave him $8,000 in cash.[94] Mr. Renaud acknowledges receiving this amount,[95] which was used to pay campaign workers. The contribution is also acknowledged by Mr. Béliveau.[96]

Further contributions to the LPCQ were made by cheque, rather than in cash, but were disguised by using as an intermediary a corporation in Quebec City named Commando Communications, an inactive entity owned and controlled by one Bernard Thiboutot.[97] Mr. Thiboutot worked for Gosselin Communications as the head of its Quebec City office, but in the year 2000, when Groupaction's contributions were made, the assets of Gosselin Communications had already been purchased by Groupaction[98] and Mr. Thiboutot was in effect working for Mr. Brault. He was an active supporter of the LPCQ in the eastern Quebec region.[99]

On January 6, 2000, and again on November 1, 2000, Commando invoiced Groupaction for $10,000 for services rendered,[100] but according to Mr. Brault, these invoices and the cheques in payment of them are evidence of political contributions that he was asked to make, to pay unexplained expenses of the LPCQ in Quebec City.[101] Mr. Thiboutot does not deny the payments or that they were paid to Commando as political contributions.

On October 1, 2000, Mr. Thiboutot sent a further false invoice to a Groupaction subsidiary for $50,000, describing the services rendered by Commando as research and analysis.[102] On October 13, 2000, only a short time before the federal election campaign commenced, the invoice was paid, and Mr. Thiboutot acknowledges that the proceeds were used to pay five employees of the LPCQ for their work in the forthcoming election campaign. Each of the workers sent Commando an invoice for the amount received.[103]

There is contradictory evidence about whether Mr. Brault knew the identity of the persons who were to receive these payments. He says he did not, but acknowledges that he may have transmitted a list of their names to Mr. Thiboutot, saying that the list would have been given to him by Mr. Corbeil, or perhaps by Mr. Corriveau. Obviously, Mr. Brault's recollection on this subject is not clear.[104] Mr. Corbeil testifies that he was the one who provided the list of names. Mr. Thiboutot says the names of the recipients were dictated to him by Mr. Brault, who did not want it to appear that he or one of his companies was making a political contribution.[105] It does not matter a great deal whose recollection is to be retained; what matters is that an illegal and unrecorded campaign contribution of $50,000 was made to the LPCQ by Groupaction by means of false invoices.

9.6
Termination of the Renaud Contract

In September 2000, Groupaction and Alain Renaud came to a parting of the ways. Mr. Brault felt Groupaction was paying too much for Mr. Renaud's lobbying on its behalf, and the latter was unwilling to renegotiate their agreement. There was continuing friction over the calculation of Mr. Renaud's bonuses, and at about the time the contract came up for renewal, Mr. Renaud made a formal demand to have access to Groupaction's financial statements to verify the amounts upon which the bonuses were calculated.[106] Mr. Brault refused this demand but invited Mr. Renaud by letter to renegotiate their agreement, enclosing a cheque for $25,000 as an advance.[107] In the weeks following he learned that the cheque had been cashed, but that Mr. Renaud had agreed to go to work for a competitor, the Armada Bates agency, for which he was trying to obtain sponsorship contracts from PWGSC.[108]

Legal proceedings were threatened by the lawyers for both parties, but Messrs. Brault and Renaud remained in touch with each other and tried to find a solution to the impasse. They agreed to settle Mr. Renaud's claims for bonuses for $25,000.[109] The settlement was made with the cooperation of Communications Art Tellier Inc., a company belonging to Mr. Renaud's brother Benoît, which sent Groupaction five false invoices for a total of $25,000.[110] It may be presumed that this device was utilized by Mr. Renaud for tax purposes.

But the settlement did not foresee the future engagement of Mr. Renaud's services as a lobbyist by Groupaction. It had quickly become apparent to Mr. Renaud that he could not hope to earn as much with Armada Bates as he had been receiving from Groupaction, which had paid him more than $900,000 as salary, commissions and bonuses in the years from 1996 to 2000, inclusively.[111] Although some of this amount had probably been remitted by Mr. Renaud by way of Mr. Corbeil as contributions to the LPCQ, there was no way he could hope to earn as much money representing another agency. Only a few months after leaving Groupaction, Mr. Renaud, without admitting it openly, clearly wished to be rehired, and brought pressure to bear upon Mr. Brault to achieve this objective, saying that Groupaction had made a mistake and should reconsider its position.[112] He was obviously disappointed that his pressure tactic of going to work for someone else had not succeeded in persuading Mr. Brault to pay him more rather than less. When testifying he was unable to disguise his vindictiveness, which he showed by describing Mr. Brault in extremely unflattering terms and by reinventing some of their exchanges after he had left Groupaction's service to make it appear that Mr. Brault was desperate to have him return.[113]

By this time, Groupaction had acquired two of the other agencies which were receiving sponsorship contracts from PWGSC. As of October 1, 1998, one of its subsidiaries purchased the assets of the Gosselin agency,[114] and in January 2001 another subsidiary purchased Lafleur Communication.[115] Both agencies continued to operate as more or less separate entities, but were owned and controlled by Groupaction. The acquisition of the Lafleur agency was stressful and may have contributed to a heart attack that incapacitated Mr. Brault for several weeks and left him in less than robust health.

During May 2001, at a time when he was still recuperating from his illness, Mr. Brault says that Mr. Renaud called him and proposed a dinner at the Restaurant Méditerraneo in Montreal.[116] At the dinner, at which Mr. Renaud continually returned to the topic of being rehired by Groupaction, he received a call on his cell phone from Tony Mignacca, who was known to Mr. Brault as a member of the political entourage of Mr. Gagliano.[117] With the benefit of hindsight it may be deduced that the phone call had been prearranged. Mr. Mignacca asked to speak to Mr. Brault, and asked him if he was going to agree to "look after" Mr. Renaud, mentioning that he had just finished dinner with the "choo-choo man," which Mr. Brault took to refer to a senior executive of Via Rail, one of Groupaction's most important clients. Mr. Mignacca then said he was coming to share a grappa with them. He arrived a short time later and openly pressured Mr. Brault to take Mr. Renaud back, intimating that if he did not, Groupaction's contract with Via Rail would be in jeopardy. Mr. Brault, although he refused to give in to this thinly veiled threat, was upset and angry.[118]

Mr. Renaud denies that this encounter took place at all. He testifies that the only time the three were ever together in a restaurant was in 1999, when Mr. Mignacca joined him and Mr. Brault at the Restaurant Prima Luna, intending to put "a little pressure" on Mr. Brault to conclude a deal with Mr. Renaud.[119] This assertion is improbable, because in 1999 there was already a contract in force between Groupaction and Mr. Renaud's company. But there are more reasons to doubt the truthfulness of Mr. Renaud's testimony when it is compared to Mr. Mignacca's version of the encounter.

Mr. Mignacca is a lifelong close friend of Mr. Gagliano and Joe Morselli, with whom he was in partnership in the 1980s in a company named Migamor. Since 1971 Mr. Mignacca worked for the Jerôme Le Royer School Commission, of which both Mr. Gagliano and Mr. Morselli were president at one time or another. Starting in 1984, when Mr. Gagliano entered federal politics, Mr. Mignacca served as his chief political organizer at the constituency level for many years.[120]

In 1996, Mr. Gagliano requested Mr. Mignacca to take a leave of absence from the school commission and to work full-time for the LPCQ at its headquarters in Montreal, as its regional coordinator. In this capacity he worked closely with Executive Director Michel Béliveau and his deputy Benoît Corbeil, and had frequent contacts with Mr. Renaud, who spent most of his time at the headquarters but had no clearly defined title or functions. They became friends.[121]

In October 1997 Mr. Mignacca had a heart attack and had to convalesce for more than two years, during which he was unable to do work of any kind.[122] This means that Mr. Renaud's statement that he joined him and Mr. Brault for a meal in 1999 is probably untrue. When Mr. Mignacca recovered enough from his illness to seek employment, Mr. Gagliano got him a job working for Canada Lands Corporation, where he worked for about one year before retiring. [123]

When questioned about the alleged encounter with Messrs. Renaud and Brault, Mr. Mignacca acknowledged that he had joined them after dinner at the Restaurant Méditerraneo (not the Restaurant Prima Luna), but said at first that this occurred in 1997, before his illness, conceding later that it might have happened after his recovery in 2000 or 2001.[124] He says that he was invited by Mr. Renaud to meet Mr. Brault, whom Mr. Renaud described as his boss, but could not explain why he would on the spur of the moment leave his dinner companion, whom he reluctantly identified as Mr. Morselli, at another restaurant, to meet someone for no apparent purpose.[125] He describes Mr. Brault as dressed like a biker who appeared to be drunk, and says that there was no conversation about Mr. Renaud's continued employment by Groupaction, or about any other subject of importance.[126] Mr. Mignacca denies that his presence there was to pressure Mr. Brault.[127] This denial and most of the rest of his testimony directly contradicts Mr. Renaud's version of the meeting. He says that he only learned about Mr. Renaud's wish to be rehired by Groupaction a few days or weeks later.[128]

Mr. Mignacca gave the strong impression of being a witness who does not want to tell everything that he knows. His version of his meeting with Mr. Brault is improbable and confused, and serves only to contradict the version of the same meeting related by Mr. Renaud. I have no doubt that Mr. Brault's testimony about the encounter is truthful and accurate; his description of the details of the meeting could not have been invented except by a skilful dramatist. What it demonstrates is the influential position that Mr. Renaud had acquired within the LPCQ. It was evident from his testimony that Mr. Mignacca's first loyalty in political matters has always been to his close friend and patron, Mr. Gagliano. At the time he shared a grappa with Mr. Brault at the Restaurant Méditerraneo, Mr. Gagliano was the Quebec lieutenant of the Party, and when Mr. Mignacca attempted to pressure Mr. Brault into putting Mr. Renaud back on Groupaction's payroll, it is reasonable to deduce that he did so because he understood Mr. Gagliano wanted Groupaction to continue to be generous to Mr. Renaud, and through him to the LPCQ. It is improbable that Mr. Mignacca would have acted as he did only out of a somewhat tenuous friendship with Mr. Renaud.

9.7
Encounters with Joseph Morselli

Mr. Brault's agenda shows that either on April 25 or May 2, 2001, he had dinner at Restaurant Frank with Mr. Morselli.[129] The meeting had been arranged by Mr. Renaud.[130] Mr. Brault had met Mr. Morselli previously at Liberal Party functions, but this was the first time they had a one-on-one encounter.[131]

Mr. Brault says that at their meeting Mr. Morselli expressed the appreciation of the LPCQ for the past work of Mr. Renaud, its thanks for Groupaction's past contributions to the Party, and its hope that its generosity would continue.[132] He offered his assistance to Groupaction in any way he could help.[133] He stated that he had assumed responsibility for the financing of the LPCQ, replacing Mr. Corriveau in that function, and gave Mr. Brault his business card, on which he was described as the Vice-President of the Finance Commission of the LPCQ.[134] (In fact, such a position does not exist.)[135] Mr. Morselli's testimony confirms the substance of the conversation, as recalled by Mr. Brault.[136]

At a subsequent dinner meeting at Restaurant Frank,[137] Mr. Brault says that Mr. Morselli asked him to hire one of his former associates at the LPCQ, Beryl Wajsman, who had lost his employment there as the result of a conflict with the President of the LPCQ. Mr. Morselli described Mr. Wajsman as a valuable contact with the Jewish community in Montreal, and asked Mr. Brault to pay him a salary of $10,000 per month so that he could continue his fundraising efforts on behalf of the LPCQ. Mr. Brault was unwilling to put Mr. Wajsman on his payroll, but proposed that he would pay him $5,000 per month in cash, which Mr. Morselli accepted.

Mr. Brault says that he returned one week later to meet Messrs. Morselli and Wajsman at the same restaurant with $5,000 cash in an envelope, which he left on the table. Mr. Wajsman arrived late, and when Mr. Brault went to the washroom, on his return he noticed the envelope was gone.[138]

Both Mr. Morselli and Mr. Wajsman testify that the meeting took place at the time and place given by Mr. Brault, but both deny that any exchange of money occurred. They both testify that the object of the meeting was to confirm the engagement of Mr. Wajsman by Groupaction, which wished to hire him to obtain business contacts within the circle of Mr. Wajsman's friends. It is most improbable that Groupaction would have been interested in the kind of contacts Mr. Wajsman, whom Mr. Brault had never met, could offer. Moreover, some aspects of the versions of the meeting given by Messrs. Morselli and Wajsman do not correspond. For example, Mr. Wajsman testifies that when Mr. Brault went to the washroom, he said to Mr. Morselli that he could never convince his friends and clients to do business with him because of his haircut, moustache and general appearance. Mr. Morselli has no recollection of this detail, nor does he remember that Mr. Wajsman said that he refused to be hired for less than $10,000 a month, although he had agreed to work for the LPCQ for half that amount.[139]

In general, Mr. Wajsman was a very poor witness, and gave the impression that he was more interested in boasting about his own importance and in attacking the credibility of everyone who disagrees with him than in telling the truth. He had been engaged by Mr. Morselli, with the encouragement of Mr. Gagliano, to assist in fundraising for the LPCQ, but the methods he employed were not acceptable to its new Executive Director, Daniel Dezainde, who had the support of the President of the LPCQ, Françoise Patry.[140] When Mr. Dezainde tried to assert his authority, Mr. Wajsman's reaction was to refuse to report to him on any of his activities, which he justified when testifying by calling Mr. Dezainde a racist.[141] Mr. Dezainde came to the conclusion, with the full concurrence of Ms. Patry, that the only solution to the problem was to dismiss Mr. Wajsman, but in so doing he earned the unrelenting hostility not only of Mr. Wajsman but of Mr. Morselli.[142] The antagonism of Mr. Wajsman towards Mr. Dezainde, his anger at having been dismissed by him, his unqualified support and friendship of Mr. Morselli, and his undisguised contempt for Mr. Brault make his testimony most doubtful.

Mr. Morselli does not come across as a biased witness in the same way that Mr. Wajsman does, but his attempt to usurp the functions of Mr. Dezainde, with the blessing of Mr. Gagliano, does not make him a sympathetic figure. He is disarmingly frank at times. For example, although he denies Mr. Brault's allegations that $5,000 per month in cash was paid for several months by Mr. Brault to Mr. Wajsman,[143] he cheerfully admits that on one occasion he picked up an envelope containing $5,000 from Groupaction's offices and kept the contents for himself, although he knew that the envelope was supposed to be delivered to Mr. Corbeil to assist him with his election campaign expenses at the municipal level.[144] That admission establishes that on one occasion at least, Mr. Morselli participated in the delivery of a cash contribution for political purposes by Groupaction. In other words, he had no compunction about irregularities of this kind. It also establishes that the immorality of appropriating the property of another is of little concern to him. The testimony of such a person when it conflicts with testimony from a basically credible witness is not acceptable. The testimony of Mr. Brault concerning this and other encounters he had with Mr. Morselli is to be preferred to Mr. Morselli's denials.

Their subsequent dealings had to do with Groupaction's contracts with PWGSC on behalf of the Department of Justice, with respect to the Government's advertising activities relating to firearms legislation. Groupaction had been working on the contract since it was first awarded in 1995 to a consortium headed by the Lafleur agency, but including Groupaction. Some of the Groupaction personnel depended for their livelihood on its continuation. Mr. Brault was alarmed in the summer of 2001 to learn that PWGSC was preparing a call for tenders for the future advertising needs of the Department of Justice relating to the firearms file.[145] He knew that the usual outcome of such a call for tenders is to replace the agency which until then had been looking after the matter.

Remembering Mr. Morselli's offer when they first met—to help Groupaction as needed, in recognition of its past contributions to the LPCQ—Mr. Brault called him to propose that if he could successfully intervene to have the call for tenders cancelled or postponed, it would be worth $100,000 to him from Groupaction. Mr. Morselli, according to Mr. Brault, said he would look into it.[146]

A few days later, on September 26, 2001, Mr. Morselli asked Mr. Brault to come to his office in Ville d'Anjou and on his arrival told him that his problem was solved and that he did not need to worry about a new call for tenders. He asked for payment of $100,000. Mr. Brault said he would have to pay in two instalments of $50,000 in the autumn of 2001 and on April 1, 2002. The delay would enable him to confirm that Mr. Morselli had in fact intervened, and that his intervention had been successful.[147] Subsequently, Mr. Brault was informed by Pierre Tremblay at PWGSC that the call for tenders had been postponed to the spring of 2002. Mr. Morselli denies having intervened with anyone on Mr. Brault's behalf.[148] However, Mr. Brault's story explains the Auditor General's observations that the competitive process commenced in mid-1999 to choose an advertising agency for the Department of Justice was "halted without explanation" and the services of Groupaction were retained. We are now able to deduce that the missing explanation might well be related to an intervention by Mr. Morselli which Mr. Brault asked him to make.

Accordingly, Mr. Brault says that he gave $50,000 in cash to Mr. Morselli before the end of 2001 by a series of deliveries, details of which he does not provide. However, he remembers specifically one delivery of $20,000 or $25,000 on the occasion of the LPCQ Christmas cocktail party at the Buffet Le Rizz, on December 20, 2001.[149]

Mr. Brault recalls two other encounters with Mr. Morselli. The first occurred in the spring of 2002, when the first Report of the Auditor General had turned the spotlight of public attention onto the relationship between Groupaction and PWGSC. Mr. Brault invited Mr. Morselli to a private salon at the Club Saint Denis and took the precaution to raise the thermostat to make the salon so warm that Mr. Morselli could be persuaded to remove his jacket. Mr. Brault was concerned that their conversation might be recorded by a body pack. When Mr. Morselli arrived he advised Mr. Brault to lie low and let the media storm pass, and asked him if he wanted "Denis" to intervene on his behalf. Mr. Brault believed he was referring to Denis Coderre.[150]

The second encounter was in August 2002 at the Restaurant La Samaritaine, at the request of Mr. Renaud, who was present. After an exchange of pleasantries, Mr. Morselli asked Mr. Brault for the second instalment of $50,000. Mr. Brault was surprised that he would openly do so in the presence of a third party, and said that the losses he had incurred as a result of the publicity surrounding the Auditor General's first Report made it impossible for him to pay.[151]

Both Messrs. Morselli and Renaud deny that this meeting took place.[152] Of course Mr. Morselli has strong motivations to deny any involvement in the payment of a Liberal Party official for his influence in a call for tenders. Once again, Mr. Brault's testimony is more credible in that he has nothing to gain by lying and is generally a more believable witness than they are.

9.8
Conclusion

As detailed in section 10.3 of the Kroll Report, between the 1996-97 and 2001-02 fiscal years Groupaction and its subsidiaries managed sponsorship contracts for PWGSC having a total value of $89.5 million, increasing Groupaction's gross revenues from $11.4 million in 1994, before it started to receive any significant amount of government business, to over $40 million per year in 2001. The net revenues increased from $314,078 in 1994 to $1,468,745 in 1999, declining to $879,222 in 2001. Most of these increases were due to the Sponsorship Program. During the years from 1992 to 2001 inclusively, Mr. Brault and his wife drew salaries totalling $3,906,104 and received dividends of $2.7 million.

During those same years, Groupaction made recorded political contributions of $170,854 to the Liberal Party of Canada. It also made unrecorded contributions, as detailed in this chapter, in the following amounts:

Salary of John Welch	$84,000
Commando Communication	70,000
Paid to Serge Gosselin	84,000
Productions Caméo	39,850
Richard Boudreault via Harel, Drouin	24,975
Gestions Richard B. Boudreault	14,790
Club de Golf de Verchères	14,100
Restaurant La Tarentella	8,282
Cash contribution in 1997	50,000
Contribution via Alain Renaud	63,500
Cash contribution in 1998 (Sherbrooke)	8,000
Beryl Wajsman	5,000
Loan of van to G. Manganiello	3,000
Total	$469,497

In addition, Groupaction paid other amounts to the personal company of Alain Renaud in exchange for his political lobbying. It may be that some of the amounts so paid were turned over to the LPCQ, but the evidence does not establish this with sufficient precision to enable me to draw that conclusion.

Sums paid by Groupaction to PluriDesign constitute additional contributions to the LPCQ and will be dealt with in Chapter X.

There is no indication that the amount of $50,000 paid by Mr. Brault to Joseph Morselli for his influence in postponing a call for tenders was remitted to the LPCQ or directly benefited it in any way. Probably what he received was retained by Mr. Morselli in the same way that he retained the $5,000 from the Groupaction envelope that was intended to assist in paying Benoît Corbeil's municipal election expenses.

Mr. Brault testified, and his evidence is amply corroborated by documentation, that Groupaction paid Groupe Everest the sum of $50,000 in November 1998.[153] He says that this payment, supported once again by a false invoice, was made as a political contribution to the Liberal Party of Quebec, at the request of Mr. Guité.[154] Claude Boulay, the head of Groupe Everest, denies this and alleges that this sum of money was due to his agency as the result of a real estate transaction.[155] If this is so, it was well disguised by the invoice reading, "Honoraires de développement pour la collaboration de projets spéciaux."[156] If Mr. Boulay wishes to be credible, he should not have prepared and sent a phony invoice to the competitor with whom he was doing business. The invoice is also suspect because Groupe Everest is not entitled to bill for taxes on an invoice for the balance of the price of a real estate purchase. For these reasons, the Commission chooses to believe Mr. Brault's explanation of this transaction.

However, it was not Mr. Brault's intention that the payment of $50,000 be transmitted to the LPCQ, and it therefore had no relationship to the issuance of sponsorship contracts. In other words, this payment is not within the mandate of the Commission.

Similarly, sums of money paid by Groupaction to Georges Farrah ($6,000), Au Printemps Gourmet ($5,168) and Gabriel Chrétien ($4,000) were not, according to the evidence,[157] related to the subject of this Inquiry.

The recorded contributions of Groupaction to the LPCQ totalling $170,854[158] were in accordance with the law and may not be criticized. At the time they were made, there were no restrictions on the amounts Canadian corporations could donate to political parties. The unrecorded contributions are blameworthy, and deserve to be denounced. They were inspired by Mr. Brault's greed and desire for financial gain, which he believed could be achieved by the purchase of political influence resulting in a greater number of lucrative sponsorship contracts being given to Groupaction. These motives were improper. The behaviour of the representatives of the LPCQ who requested and encouraged Mr. Brault to make these surreptitious contributions and who fostered his belief that they were achieving the purpose he desired was equally improper and blameworthy.

Endnotes to Chapter IX

1   Exhibit P-19, tab 20.

2   Exhibit P-19, tabs 25-26; Exhibit P-62, pp. 6-7.

3   Exhibit P-19, tab 41.

4   Exhibit P-428(D), schedules 14-16.

5   Exhibit P-428(A), p. 37.

6   Testimony of Mr. Gosselin, Transcripts vol. 83, pp. 14817-14823 (OF), pp. 14808- 14814 (E).

7   Testimony of Mr. Chrétien, Transcripts vol. 72, pp. 12516-12517 (OE), pp. 12518-12519 (F).

8   Testimony of Mr. Coffin, Transcripts vol. 106, pp. 19386-19389 (OE), pp. 19396-19400 (F); Testimony of Mr. Gilles Gosselin, Transcripts vol. 88 (Part 1 of 2), pp. 15504-15507 (OF), pp. 15502-15505 (E); Testimony of Mr. Brault, Transcripts vol. 89, pp. 15741-15742, 15748, 15832 (OF), pp. 15738-15739, 15744, 15821 (E).

9   Exhibit C-295.

10 Exhibits C-293(A) and C-293(B).

11 Testimony of Mr. Jean Lafleur, Transcripts vol. 79, pp. 13830-13831 (OF), pp. 13825-13827 (E); Testimony of Mr. Thiboutot, Transcripts vol. 85, p. 15124 (OF), pp. 15137-15138 (E); Testimony of Mr. Corriveau, Transcripts vol. 99, p. 17834 (OF), p. 17815 (E); Testimony of Mr. Renaud, Transcripts vol. 96, pp. 17089-17090 (OF), pp. 17080-17081 (E).

12 Testimony of Mr. Brault, Transcripts vol. 92, pp. 16212-16219 (OF), pp. 16211-16216 (E).

13 Testimony of Mr. Brault, Transcripts vol. 89, pp. 15849-15850 (OF), pp. 15836-15838 (E).

14 Testimony of Mr. Brault, Transcripts vol. 89, pp. 15727, 15850 (OF), pp. 15724-15725, 15837 (E).

15 Testimony of Mr. Brault, Transcripts vol. 89, p. 15832 (OF), p. 15821 (E).

16 Testimony of Mr. Brault, Transcripts vol. 88, pp. 15620-15622 (OF), pp. 15621-15622 (E).

17 Testimony of Mr. Brault, Transcripts vol. 88, pp. 15645-15646 (OF), pp. 15643-15644 (E).

18 Testimony of Mr. Brault, Transcripts vol. 88, pp. 15642-15643 (OF), pp. 15640-15641 (E).

19 Testimony of Mr. Brault, Transcripts vol. 88, pp. 15646-15648, 15650, 15653-15654 (OF), pp. 15644-15646, 15647-15648, 15650-15651 (E).

20 Testimony of Mr. Brault, Transcripts vol. 92, pp. 16321-16324 (OF), pp. 16310-16314 (E).

21 Testimony of Mr. Brault, Transcripts vol. 89, pp. 15721-15724 (OF), pp. 15719-15722 (E).

22 Testimony of Mr. Brault, Transcripts vol. 88, pp. 15695-15697 (OF), pp. 15688-15690 (E).

23 Testimony of Mr. Brault, Transcripts vol. 88, pp. 15692-15696 (OF), pp. 15685-15689 (E).

24 Testimony of Mr. Brault, Transcripts vol. 88, pp. 15696-15700 (OF), pp. 15688-15692 (E).

25 Testimony of Mr. Brault, Transcripts vol. 89, pp. 15740-15744 (OF), pp. 15736-15742 (E).

26 Testimony of Mr. Serge Gosselin, Transcripts vol. 113, pp. 20743-20749 (OF), pp. 20741-20746 (E).

27 Testimony of Mr. Brault, Transcripts vol. 89, pp. 15743, 15748 (OF), pp. 15740, 15744 (E).

28 Testimony of Mr. Brault, Transcripts vol. 89, pp. 15745-15748 (OF), pp. 15741-15744 (E).

29 Exhibit C-295, p. 7.

30 Exhibit C-295, p. 22.

31 Testimony of Mr. Corriveau, Transcripts vol. 99, pp. 17834-17836 (OF), pp. 17815-17817 (E).

32 Testimony of Mr. Guité, Transcripts vol. 109, pp. 19899-19908 (OE), pp. 19906-19915 (E).

33 Testimony of Mr. Serge Gosselin, Transcripts vol. 113, pp. 20755-20766 (OF), pp. 20752-20761 (E).

34 Testimony of Mr. Serge Gosselin, Transcripts vol. 113, pp. 20759-20764, 20768-20771, 20788-20791 (OF), pp. 20755-20760, 20763-20766, 20782-20785 (E); Exhibit P-387, pp. 23-25, 28-29, 31, 51-52.

35 Testimony of Mr. Serge Gosselin, Transcripts vol. 113, p. 20764 (OF), pp. 20759-20760 (E).

36 Testimony of Mr. Serge Gosselin, Transcripts vol. 113, pp. 20773-20774 (OF), pp. 20768-20769 (E).

37 Testimony of Mr. Serge Gosselin, Transcripts vol. 113, pp. 20743-20749 (OF), pp. 20741-20746 (E).

38 Testimony of Mr. Corbeil, Transcripts vol. 115, p. 21186 (OF), p. 21181 (E).

39 Testimony of Mr. Serge Gosselin, Transcripts vol. 113, pp. 20775-20781 (OF), pp. 20770-20775 (E).

40 Testimony of Mr. Morselli, Transcripts vol. 127, pp. 23863-23869 (OF), pp. 23861-23866 (E).

41 Testimony of Mr. Brault, Transcripts vol. 89, p. 15753 (OF), pp. 15748-15749; Testimony of Mr. Welch, Transcripts vol. 119, pp. 22388-22390 (OE), pp. 22399-22400 (F).

42 Testimony of Mr. Brault, Transcripts vol. 89, pp. 15752-15755 (OF), pp. 15748-15750 (E).

43 Exhibit C-299, p. 95; Exhibit P-428(A), p. 119.

44 Testimony of Mr. Welch, Transcripts vol. 119, pp. 22391-22400 (OE), pp. 22401-22411 (F).

45 Testimony of Mr. Brault, Transcripts vol. 89, pp. 15756-15757 (OF), pp. 15751-15752 (E).

46 Exhibit. C-299, p. 179; Exhibit P-404, pp. 55, 57.

47 Testimony of Mr. Brault, Transcripts vol. 89, pp. 15862-15863 (OF), p. 15849 (E); Exhibit C-293(A), p. 125.

48 Testimony of Mr. Brault, Transcripts vol. 90, pp. 15947-15949 (OF), pp. 15943-15945 (E); Exhibit C-299, p. 181.

49 Testimony of Mr. Brault, Transcripts vol. 90, pp. 15949-15950 (OF), pp. 15945-15946 (E).

50 Testimony of Mr. Brault, Transcripts vol. 90, pp. 15949-15951 (OF), pp. 15945-15948 (E).

51 Exhibit P-386, pp. 1, 13, 16, 18, 21-22.

52 Testimony of Ms. Tremblay, Transcripts vol. 112, pp. 20712-20717 (OF), pp. 20707-20711 (E).

53 Testimony of Mr. Brault, Transcripts vol. 89, p. 15834 (OF), pp. 15822-15823 (E).

54 Exhibit P-386, pp. 14, 16, 18, 21.

55 Testimony of Mr. Brault, Transcripts vol. 89, p.15831 (OF), p. 15820 (E).

56 Testimony of Mr. Gagliano, Transcripts vol. 131, pp. 24989-24994 (OF), pp. 24981-24986 (E).

57 Testimony of Mr. Gagliano, Transcripts vol. 131, pp. 24993-24994 (OF), pp. 24985-24986 (E).

58 Remarks by Mr. Roy, and testimony of Mr. Gagliano, Transcripts vol. 131, pp. 24991-24992 (OF), pp. 24983-24984 (E); Exhibit P-386, pp. 23-31.

59 Testimony of Mr. Manganiello, vol. 126, pp. 23810-23817 (OE), pp. 23822-23830 (F).

60 Testimony of Mr. Brault, Transcripts vol. 89, pp. 15760-15761 (OF), pp. 15755-15756 (E); Testimony of Mr. Guité, Transcripts vol. 109, p. 19855 (OE), p. 19857 (F).

[61] See, for example, testimony of Mr. Brault, Transcripts vol. 92, pp. 16321-16324 (OF), pp. 16311-16314 (E).

[62] Testimony of Mr. Renaud, Transcripts vol. 96, p. 17149 (OF), pp. 17136-17137 (E).

[63] Testimony of Mr. Brault, Transcripts vol. 88, p. 15674 (OF), p. 15669 (E); Exhibit C-297, pp. 16-18.

[64] Exhibit C-297, pp. 20-24.

[65] Exhibit C-297, p. 3.

[66] Testimony of Mr. Brault, Transcripts vol. 88, p. 15662 (OF), pp. 15658-15659 (E); Exhibit C-297, p. 7.

[67] Testimony of Mr. Brault, Transcripts vol. 88, p. 15670 (OF), p. 15666 (E); Exhibit C-297, pp. 8-10.

[68] Exhibit C-297, pp. 3-5; Testimony of Mr. Brault, Transcripts vol. 88, pp. 15672-15673 (OF), pp. 15667-15668 (E).

[69] Testimony of Mr. Brault, Transcripts vol. 89, pp. 15850-15853 (OF), pp. 15837-15840 (E); Testimony of Mr. Renaud, Transcripts vol. 96, p. 17059 (OF), p. 17051-17052 (E)

[70] This figure is reached by adding the two amounts paid to Alain Renaud's personal services companies, 9004-8612 Québec Inc. and Investissement Alain Renaud ($812,065 and $153,841), and then subtracting the amount that Mr. Renaud transmitted to the LPCQ ($63,500). See Exhibit 428(A), p. 119.

[71] Testimony of Mr. Brault, Transcripts vol. 88 (Part 2 of 2), p. 15658 (OF), p. 15655 (E); Testimony of Mr. Béliveau, Transcripts vol. 113, pp. 20907-20910 (OF), pp. 20891-20894 (E).

[72] Testimony of Mr. Brault, Transcripts vol. 89, pp. 16235-16238 (OF), pp. 16231-13235 (E).

[73] Testimony of Mr. Brault, Transcripts vol. 89, pp. 15849-15850 (OF), pp. 15836-15837 (E).

[74] Testimony of Mr. Brault, Transcripts vol. 89, pp. 15724-15727 (OF), pp. 15722-15725 (E).

[75] Testimony of Mr. Brault, Transcripts vol. 89, pp. 15768-15771 (OF), pp. 15762-15765 (E); Exhibit C-295, p. 7.

[76] Testimony of Mr. Brault, Transcripts vol. 89, pp. 15771-15772 (OF), pp. 15765-15766 (E); Exhibit C-295, p. 8.

[77] Testimony of Mr. Brault, Transcripts vol. 89, pp. 15776-15777 (OF), pp. 15769-15770 (E).

[78] Testimony of Mr. Brault, Transcripts vol. 89, pp. 15784-15788 (OF), pp. 15777-15781.

[79] Canada Elections Act, R.S.C. 1985, c. E-2, section 217, REPEALED by S.C. 2000, c. 9, section 576, effective September 1, 2000 (Canada Gazette Pt. I, Sept. 1, 2000).

[80] Testimony of Mr. Brault, Transcripts vol. 89, pp. 15789-15795 (OF), pp. 15781-15787 (E)

[81] Testimony of Mr. Boudreault, Transcripts vol. 117, pp. 21708-21720 (OF), pp. 21707-21719 (E).

[82] Testimony of Mr. Brault, Transcripts vol. 89, pp. 15869-15870 (OF), pp. 15855-15856 (E).

[83] Testimony of Mr. Brault, Transcripts vol. 89, pp. 15869, 15872-15873 (OF), pp. 15855-15856, 15857-15859 (E); vol. 92, pp. 16342-16343 (OF), pp. 16330-16331 (E); Exhibit C-299, pp. 2-3.

[84] Testimony of Mr. Bernard Michaud, Transcripts vol. 97, pp. 17247-17251 (OF), pp. 17245-17249 (E).

[85] Testimony of Mr. Brault, Transcripts vol. 89, pp. 15869-15870 (OF), pp. 15856-15857 (E).

[86] Testimony of Mr. Brault, Transcripts vol. 89, pp. 15870-15871 (OF), pp. 15856-15857 (E).

[87] Testimony of Mr. Brault, Transcripts vol. 89, pp. 15872-15873 (OF), pp. 15858-15859 (E); Exhibit C-299, pp. 2-3.

[88] Testimony of Mr. Corbeil, Transcripts vol. 115, pp. 21305-21311 (OF), pp. 21289-21295 (E); vol. 116, pp. 21546-21552 (OF), pp. 21536-21442 (E).

[89] Exhibit C-299, pp. 2-3; Exhibit P-321, pp. 3-5.

[90] Testimony of Mr. Béliveau, Transcripts vol. 113, pp. 20916-20922 (OF), pp. 20899-20905 (E).

[91] Testimony of Mr. Brault, Transcripts vol. 89, pp. 15841-15848 (OF), pp. 15829-15836 (E).

[92] Exhibit C-297, p. 143.

[93] Testimony of Mr. Renaud, Transcripts vol. 95, pp. 16933-16938 (OF), pp. 16919-16924 (E).

[94] Testimony of Mr. Béliveau, Transcripts vol. 113, p. 20925.

[95] Testimony of Mr. Renaud, Transcripts vol. 96, pp. 17022-17024(OF); pp. 17019-17021(E); pp. 17077-17081 (OF), pp. 17069-17072 (E).

[96] Testimony of Mr. Béliveau, Transcripts vol. 113, pp. 20925-20926 (OF), pp. 20907-20908 (E).

[97] Testimony of Mr. Brault, Transcripts vol. 90, pp. 15991-15992 (OF), pp. 15984-15985 (E).

[98] Exhibit P-254, para. 59.

[99] Testimony of Mr. Brault, Transcripts vol. 90, p. 15989 (OF), pp. 15982-15983 (E); Testimony of Mr. Thiboutot, Transcripts vol. 85, pp. 15114-15115 (OF), pp. 15107-15108 (E); Testimony of Mr. Côté, Transcripts vol. 116, pp. 21648-21649 (OF), pp. 21627-21628 (E).

[100] Exhibit C-299, pp. 66, 68.

[101] Testimony of Mr. Brault, Transcripts vol. 90, pp. 15993-15994 (OF), pp. 15986-15987 (E).

[102] Exhibit C-299, p. 70.

[103] Testimony of Mr. Thiboutot, Transcripts vol. 85, pp. 15105-15110 (OF), pp. 15099-15103 (E).

[104] Testimony of Mr. Brault, Transcripts vol. 90, pp. 15996-16001 (OF), pp. 15989-15994 (E).

[105] Testimony of Mr. Thiboutot, Transcripts vol. 85, pp. 15105-15106.

[106] Testimony of Mr. Brault, Transcripts vol. 89, pp. 15850-15852 (OF), pp. 15838-15839 (E).

[107] Exhibit C-297, pp. 5, 116.

[108] Testimony of Mr. Brault, Transcripts vol. 89, pp. 15851-15855 (OF), pp. 15838-15842 (E).

[109] Testimony of Mr. Brault, Transcripts vol. 89, p. 15852 (OF), p. 15839 (E).

[110] Exhibit C-297, pp. 120, 132-142.

[111] Exhibit C-297, pp. 2, 5.

[112] Testimony of Mr. Brault, Transcripts vol. 89, pp. 15855-15856 (OF), pp. 15842-15843 (E).

[113] Testimony of Mr. Renaud, Transcripts vol. 95, pp. 16974-16976 (OF), pp. 16957-16959 (E).

[114] Exhibit C-290(A), para. 96.

[115] Exhibit C-290(A), para. 135.

[116] Testimony of Mr. Brault, Transcripts vol. 89, p. 15856 (OF), pp. 15842-15843 (E); vol. 90, pp. 15923-15924 (OF), pp. 15921-15922 (E).

[117] Testimony of Mr. Brault, Transcripts vol. 89, p. 15857 (OF), pp.15843-15844 (E).

[118] Testimony of Mr. Brault, Transcripts vol. 89, pp. 15858-15860 (OF), pp. 15844-15846 (E).

[119] Testimony of Mr. Renaud, Transcripts vol. 95, pp. 16967-16968 (OF), pp. 16951-16952 (E).

[120] Testimony of Mr. Mignacca, Transcripts vol. 118, pp. 22104, 22116 (OF), pp. 22088, 22099 (E).

[121] Testimony of Mr. Mignacca, Transcripts vol. 118, p. 22140 (OF), p. 22121-22122 (E); Testimony of Mr. Mignacca, Transcripts vol. 119, pp. 22198-22199 (OF), pp. 22195-22196 (E).

[122] Testimony of Mr. Mignacca, Transcripts vol. 118, pp. 22107-22108 (OF), pp. 22091-22092 (E).

[123] Testimony of Mr. Mignacca, Transcripts vol. 118, pp. 22108-22109 (OF), pp. 22092-22093 (E).

[124] Testimony of Mr. Mignacca, Transcripts vol. 118, pp. 22148-22159 (OF), pp. 22129-22138 (E).

[125] Testimony of Mr. Mignacca, Transcripts vol. 118, pp. 22149-22161 (OF), pp. 22131-22141 (E).

[126] Testimony of Mr. Mignacca, Transcripts vol. 118, pp. 22160-22162 (OF), pp. 22140-22142 (E).

[127] Testimony of Mr. Mignacca, Transcripts vol. 118, pp. 22161-22162 (OF), pp. 22141-22142 (E).

[128] Testimony of Mr. Mignacca, Transcripts vol. 118, pp. 22167-22168 (OF), pp. 22146-22147 (E).

[129] Exhibit C-295, p. 21

[130] Testimony of Mr. Brault, Transcripts vol. 89, pp. 15877-15878 (OF), 15862-15863 (E).

[131] Testimony of Mr. Brault, Transcripts vol. 89, p. 15878 (OF), p. 15863 (E).

[132] Testimony of Mr. Brault, Transcripts vol. 89, pp. 15877-15880 (OF), pp. 15863-15865 (E).

[133] Testimony of Mr. Brault, Transcripts vol. 89, pp. 15877-15881 (OF), pp. 15863-15866 (E).

[134] Exhibit C-298, p. 133.

[135] Testimony of Ms. Patry, Transcripts vol. 129, pp. 24536-24538 (OF), pp. 24518-24520 (E).

[136] Testimony of Mr. Morselli, Transcripts vol. 127, pp. 23931, 23934-23946 (OF), pp. 23923-23924, 23926-23937 (E).

[137] Exhibit C-295, p. 43.

[138] Testimony of Mr. Brault, Transcripts vol. 89, pp. 15884-15889 (OF), pp. 15869-15874 (E).

[139] Testimony of Mr. Morselli, Transcripts vol. 127, pp. 23985-23991 (OF), pp. 23973-23978 (E); Testimony of Mr. Wajsman, Transcripts vol. 119, pp. 22240, 22289-22295 (OE), pp. 22241, 22296-23303 (F).

[140] Testimony of Mr. Dezainde, Transcripts vol. 117, pp. 21782, 21839-21842 (OF), pp. 21774, 21825-21828 (E).

[141] Testimony of Mr. Wajsman, Transcripts vol. 119, pp. 22260-22263 (OE), pp. 22263-22266 (F).

[142] Testimony of Mr. Dezainde, Transcripts vol. 117, pp. 21863-21867 (OF), pp. 21845-21849 (E); Testimony of Mr. Morselli, Transcripts vol. 127, pp. 23968-23973 (OF), pp. 23958-23962 (E).

[143] Testimony of Mr. Morselli, Transcripts vol. 127, pp. 23986-23988 (OF), pp. 23974-23976 (E).

[144] Testimony of Mr. Morselli, Transcripts vol. 127, pp. 23991-23995 (OF), pp. 23978- 23983 (E).

[145] Testimony of Mr. Brault, Transcripts vol. 89, pp. 15890-15892 (OF), pp. 15874-15876 (E).

[146] Testimony of Mr. Brault, Transcripts vol. 89, pp. 15891-15893 (OF), pp. 15876-15877 (E).

[147] Testimony of Mr. Brault, Transcripts vol. 89, pp. 15893-15895 (OF), pp. 15877-15879 (E).

[148] Testimony of Mr. Brault, Transcripts vol. 89, pp. 15893-15895 (OF), pp. 15877-15879 (E).

[149] Testimony of Mr. Brault, Transcripts vol. 89, pp. 15865-15869 (OF), pp. 15851-15855 (E).

[150] Testimony of Mr. Brault, Transcripts vol. 90, p. 15942 (OF), p. 15939 (E).

[151] Testimony of Mr. Brault, Transcripts vol. 90, pp. 15943-15945 (OF), pp. 15940-15942 (E).

[152] Testimony of Mr. Morselli, Transcripts vol. 127, pp. 24002-24005 (OF), pp. 23989-23991 (E); Testimony of Mr. Renaud, Transcripts vol. 96, pp. 17032-17035 (OF), pp. 17028-17031 (E).

[153] Testimony of Mr. Brault, Transcripts vol. 89, pp. 15873-15876 (OF), pp. 15859-15862 (E); Exhibit C-299, pp. 5-6

[154] Testimony of Mr. Brault, Transcripts vol. 92, pp. 16307-16312 (OF), pp. 16298-16302 (E).

[155] Testimony of Mr. Boulay, Transcripts vol. 104, pp. 18799-18810 (OF), pp. 18799-18809 (E).

[156] Exhibit C-299, pp. 5-6.

157 Testimony of Mr. Brault, Transcripts vol. 90, pp. 15977-15978 (OF), pp. 15972-15973 (E); vol. 93, pp. 16402-16403 (OF), pp. 16402-16403 (E); vol. 89, pp. 15715-15717 (OF), pp. 15713-15715 (E).

158 Exhibit P-428(A), pp. 117-118.

CHAPTER X

JACQUES CORRIVEAU
AND LUC LEMAY

10.1
Influence and Credibility of Mr. Corriveau

Throughout the Montreal phase of the hearings, the Commission heard repeated confirmation that Jacques Corriveau met with various persons at different levels of authority within the government, at which meetings the initiatives later known as the "Sponsorship Program" were discussed. Mr. Corriveau was invariably perceived by others as a person of substantial influence within the Liberal Party of Canada, whether or not he still occupied an official position within the Party. He had been a Vice-President of the Quebec wing in the early 1980s, and the National Vice-President (Francophone) in the same period.[1] He was known as a close personal friend of the Prime Minister.

As an example of the general impression that Mr. Corriveau was a person of great importance, Mr. Guité recalls an incident in 1994 or 1995 when he was summoned to the office of Mr. Dingwall, then Minister of Public Works and Government Services Canada, by the latter's Executive Assistant, Warren Kinsella, who said Mr. Dingwall wanted Mr. Guité to meet someone.[2] On arrival, Mr. Dingwall told him that he was going to meet a gentleman named Corriveau who was "a very very close friend of the Prime Minister," adding, "if ever you find somebody in bed between Jean Chrétien and his wife, it will be Jacques Corriveau," and that Mr. Guité should "look after him." This message was repeated on other occasions: "look after this guy" and "look after this firm," referring to Mr. Corriveau's business.[3]

It is interesting to note that when Mr. Guité was introduced to Mr. Corriveau a few minutes later, he was in the company of Jean Lafleur,[4] although both Mr. Dingwall and Mr. Kinsella testify that they have never met Mr. Lafleur.[5] Mr. Guité has no reason to mislead the Commission about this incident, and his version of it is accepted. It is interesting to speculate about what Mr. Corriveau and Mr. Lafleur may have been discussing, and it is also interesting to wonder why Mr. Dingwall wanted Mr. Guité to "look after" Mr. Corriveau. Whatever the reasons, Mr. Guité took care to follow Mr. Dingwall's instructions.[6]

As a further example of Mr. Corriveau's perceived influence, Jean Brault testified that Jacques Olivier, a person much involved in Liberal Party affairs, said to him when Mr. Corriveau's name was mentioned, "Colle-toi sur Corriveau; ça va t'ouvrir des portes." (Stick to Corriveau; it will open doors for you.)[7]

The evidence establishes that at all times relevant to the Commission's mandate, Mr. Corriveau has been the owner and operator of a graphic design business known as PluriDesign Canada Inc.[8] (PluriDesign), which in 1997 was engaged by the Liberal Party of Canada (Quebec) to prepare posters and printed election campaign material for use in the 1997 election campaign in Quebec. For this work it billed the LPCQ more than $900,000, making it by far PluriDesign's most important client at that time.[9] When some of PluriDesign's invoices for these goods and services were overdue, Mr. Corriveau was able to arrange a meeting with Mr. Pelletier and Mr. Gagliano in December 1997 to discuss the problem.[10] This is not the kind of access that is available to many persons. Whether as a result of the meeting with Mr. Pelletier and Mr. Gagliano or otherwise, the accounts of PluriDesign were paid in due course.[11]

According to Mr. Brault, each year Mr. Corriveau would ask Mr. Guité or his successor, Pierre Tremblay, for approval of a "very special list" of eight or nine sponsorships of events or projects of a cultural or artistic nature, such as Jeunesses Musicales, Chants Libres,[12] L'Orchestre Métropolitain, or a television program known as *Décibel*.[13] These sponsorships were not for large sums of money, and approval of the special list was more or less automatic. Groupaction was always designated to manage them, although little management was necessary since they were really thinly disguised subsidies to organizations in need of financial assistance—favoured by Mr. Corriveau— much more than sponsorships designed to promote and enhance the visibility of the federal presence in Quebec. No one questioned their eligibility because they were known to be the pet projects of Mr. Corriveau and were included in a group of projects known as "Unforeseen Events," which cost the government only from $200,000 to $300,000 per year.[14]

Mr. Corriveau presents himself to the world and to the Commission as a refined and cultured man with a patrician air, interested in and supportive of the arts.[15] He says that as a committed Liberal and as a matter of principle he has worked for 40 years on a gratuitous basis for the LPCQ.[16] It was only when the full extent of his involvement in the Sponsorship Program was revealed as a result of the testimony of Luc Lemay that the Commission learned that Mr. Corriveau was as much motivated by an appetite for financial gain as by principle.

Mr. Corriveau says that his recollection of certain events has been affected by anaesthesia during surgery he underwent in late November 2004,[17] which serves as a convenient excuse for selective memory lapses.[18] He chose not to file a medical assessment or certificate to support his opinion, and the Commission remains skeptical about his explanation for his alleged inability to remember important details of meetings and conversations, either recent or remote. He testified on two occasions, and in some respects contradicted his earlier testimony. I believe that these contradictions cannot be explained by a failure of memory but are due to an intention to mislead the Commission. He admits that he deliberately lied to a journalist when he told him that he had absolutely no involvement in the Sponsorship Program.[19] His testimony frequently comes into conflict with that of more credible witnesses, such as Jean Brault, Luc Lemay and Daniel Dezainde, and in each such instance, after careful reflection, the Commission has come to prefer what they said to the version of the facts put forward by Mr. Corriveau. All in all, he is not a credible witness, and gives the impression that he chooses to take refuge in forgetfulness instead of telling the truth. His motivation to attempt to hide the facts and to mislead the Commission became apparent as the evidence unfolded; he was the central figure in an elaborate kickback scheme by which he enriched himself personally and provided funds and benefits to the LPCQ.

10.2
Salon National du Grand Air de Montréal

Luc Lemay is a respectable businessman who has built up and acquired over the years a number of companies, operating under the names Polygone and Expour. These enterprises arrange and manage shows and exhibitions, usually referred to as "Salons," promoting hunting, fishing and outdoor activities.[20] His companies also publish specialized magazines aimed at enthusiasts in these fields, the most important being *Sentier Chasse et Pêche*,[21] and a book which appears annually, entitled *L'Almanach du Peuple*.[22] These are offered for sale at a booth at every Salon.[23]

In 1996 one of Mr. Lemay's employees was Denis Coderre, a former broadcaster[24] hired to look after public relations for Mr. Lemay's businesses.[25] Mr. Coderre was known to be very involved in the activities of the Liberal Party, and was Deputy Executive Director and Director of Operations of the LPCQ from 1993 to 1996.[26] He had become a personal friend of Mr. Renaud. He was elected as a Member of Parliament in the 1997 election.[27] In August or September 1996, most probably at the initiative of Mr.

Coderre,[28] Messrs. Brault and Renaud were invited to a meal at the Restaurant Le Muscadin to meet Mr. Lemay, his associate Michel Bibeau and Mr. Corriveau. Mr. Lemay wanted to explain to Mr. Brault the idea that he had conceived of promoting, for the first time, a major exhibition at the Olympic Stadium in Montreal, to be held in the spring of 1997 under the name "Salon National du Grand Air de Montréal."[29] Mr. Corriveau's attendance is explained by the fact that PluriDesign had already been engaged by Mr. Lemay to work[30] on the design and organization of the exhibition, its theme, and the physical arrangement of the booths of exhibitors.[31] This has always been the area of Mr. Corriveau's expertise.[32]

At the dinner meeting, Mr. Brault declined an invitation to participate in the advertising and public relations aspect of the venture.[33] The meeting was therefore unsuccessful, except that it introduced Mr. Brault to Mr. Corriveau and Mr. Lemay, with whom he was to have profitable business dealings in the future.

For the 1997 exhibition of the Salon National du Grand Air de Montréal, Mr. Lemay says that Mr. Corriveau put him in touch with Claude Boulay,[34] the head of a competing public relations agency named Groupe Everest, which accepted the contract to handle publicity and public relations.[35] Mr. Corriveau denies that he was the person who put Mr. Lemay in touch with Groupe Everest, but the Commission prefers Mr. Lemay's precise recollection of this detail. Polygone, Mr. Lemay's company, and Groupe Everest[36] then entered into a formal written contract dated November 27, 1996,[37] in which it was agreed that Polygone was giving Everest a three-year exclusive mandate to represent it, and that it would be bound for that period of time to pay Everest a commission of 20% on each new sponsorship which might be awarded to it, reduced to 15% for sponsorship renewals.[38] Although the contract refers specifically to sponsorships, Mr. Lemay says that when he signed it he did not know that the federal government was using sponsorships as a means of increasing its visibility. He was thinking of sponsorships by commercial firms.[39]

Mr. Corriveau testifies that he recalled the meeting at Le Muscadin. However, he only acknowledged having done design work for the project, for which

Polygone agreed to pay PluriDesign a fixed fee of $125,000.[40] He says that he was not instrumental in hiring the services of Groupe Everest,[41] but this testimony is difficult to reconcile with what was revealed by documents produced at the hearings, of which Mr. Lemay had no knowledge,[42] establishing that PluriDesign also billed Groupe Everest $23,950 plus taxes for professional services relating to the same exhibition.[43] Mr. Corriveau, asked to explain his invoice to Groupe Everest, maintains that the services rendered to Groupe Everest were not the same as those for which he was paid by Mr. Lemay's company, but covered the cost of preparing a brochure used to promote the participation in the event of various Crown Corporations.[44] Mr. Lemay, asked to comment on the invoice to Groupe Everest, expresses the opinion that the services described in the invoice appear to be the same services for which Mr. Corriveau's company was paid $125,000.[45]

In January 1997 Mr. Corriveau advised Mr. Lemay that he expected to obtain a subsidy from the federal government, to assist with the costs of the Salon National du Grand Air de Montréal.[46] By that time Mr. Lemay was already committed to the project, and had not thought of seeking financial assistance from anyone, through Mr. Corriveau or otherwise. He had not given a mandate to anyone to apply for a sponsorship from the Government.[47] He was therefore pleasantly surprised to learn a short time later that his company would receive what Mr. Corriveau described as a "subsidy" of $400,000 from PWGSC. In fact, the "subsidy" was the result of a first sponsorship contract that had been awarded to Groupe Everest, dated February 3, 1997.[48] When payment was ultimately received, Mr. Lemay was again surprised to discover that it was for $50,000 more than first indicated.[49] In order to receive the "subsidy," he was instructed by Mr. Boulay to send Groupe Everest two invoices, for $200,000 and $250,000 respectively.[50] Of course he complied.

Mr. Corriveau acknowledges that he was the person responsible for this windfall. He says that he had learned, through his various contacts,[51] that there was a Sponsorship Program administered by Mr. Guité to promote the visibility of the federal government in Quebec, and that he went to see Mr. Guité in Ottawa to explain to him the visibility potential of the Salon being organized by Mr. Lemay.[52] He says that his presentation to Mr. Guité received a very favourable reception.[53]

Groupe Everest subsequently managed two other sponsorship contracts for Mr. Lemay, for Salons held in the spring of 1998, in Montreal and Quebec City.[54]

Although Mr. Corriveau makes no reference to, and has no recollection of, the dinner meeting in April 1996 that he had with Mr. Brault and Mr. Guité at the Club Saint Denis,[55] at which it was arranged for Groupaction to hire Serge Gosselin,[56] that meeting must have been one of the sources of his awareness of the Sponsorship Program and the possibilities it represented. His inability to recall this earlier meeting is difficult to believe. In any event, no matter how or precisely when he learned about the Program, he was part of the inner circle of persons connected to the LPCQ who knew, at a moment in time when the Sponsorship Program had not at all been publicized, that it was available for the promoters of events that could offer visibility of Canadian symbols to the public. Mr. Lemay's enterprises offered Mr. Corriveau, as an insider, a golden opportunity to cash in on his knowledge of the Program.

10.3
1998 Sponsorships

The exhibition in Montreal in 1997 was hugely successful and, in part due to the unexpected and unneeded "subsidy" received from PWGSC, was extremely profitable to Mr. Lemay.[57] He testifies that at about the time the Salon was taking place in the spring of 1997, he was invited to a dinner, suggested and organized by Mr. Corriveau, in a restaurant in Hull, where the other guests were Messrs. Guité, Collet and Corriveau, at which time future events and projects to be organized by Mr. Lemay, and to be sponsored by PWGSC, were discussed.[58] Mr. Lemay remembers specifically that they talked about the possibility of the Government sponsoring three projects: a series of events described as "les Soirées de chasse et pêche," the publication of L'Almanach du peuple, and a series of spot radio announcements ("les capsules").[59] He says that Mr. Guité showed interest in these projects, asked that they be more fully described in writing,[60] and that upon returning to Montreal he and Mr. Corriveau together set to work to prepare a written presentation.[61]

Once again Mr. Corriveau testifies that he does not remember[62] the dinner meeting in Hull described in such detail by Mr. Lemay, although, according to Mr. Lemay, it had been Mr. Corriveau who had arranged the meeting.[63] However, when questioned about details of the proposed projects that were discussed at the meeting, he acknowledges that the substance of Mr. Lemay's testimony is "possible."[64] Considering the corroborating evidence and Mr. Lemay's clear recollection of the meeting, I accept his testimony.

The document submitted to Mr. Guité a short time later proposed a sponsorship of $425,000 for *L'Almanach du peuple*, $925,000 for the radio spots and $725,000 for the "Soirées de chasse et pêche."[65] Mr. Lemay testifies that Mr. Corriveau undertook to take it to Ottawa and to present it to persons whom he did not identify.[66] His assertion that Mr. Corriveau said that he would present the document to more than one person is interesting. Mr. Corriveau denies this affirmation and testifies that Mr. Lemay knew he was to meet only one person and that that person was Mr. Guité.

Mr. Lemay says that in July 1997, Mr. Corriveau advised him that the proposal had been accepted[67] for the amounts proposed, but that Groupaction, and not Groupe Everest, would act as the Government's agent to manage the projects.[68] The reason for the change of agency was not explained to Mr. Lemay, who was surprised since he had been entirely satisfied with the management of the 1997 event by Groupe Everest.[69] The contract signed with Groupe Everest was simply disregarded, and Mr. Boulay did not protest, indicating in his testimony that he was satisfied that Groupe Everest would receive contracts for other events by other promoters as compensation.[70] Mr. Guité testifies that this was one instance where he is certain that the choice of the agency was not made by him alone,[71] in view of the amounts of the sponsorships involved. As will be seen from what follows, Mr. Corriveau had good reasons to prefer that Groupaction be designated to manage the sponsorships that were awarded to Mr. Lemay's projects from then on, which was what occurred. He says that he was able to convince Mr. Guité to change the agency looking after the Montreal Salon that Mr. Lemay was promoting simply by asking Mr. Guité to do so.[72] If this is true, it illustrates how much importance Mr. Guité gave to Mr. Corriveau's preferences.

I prefer to believe that the designation of the Groupaction agency was done at the political level, as Mr. Guité asserts. In either case, Mr. Corriveau's wishes were accommodated.

10.4
Commission Agreements

It was also at about this time, in the spring of 1997, that it was verbally[73] agreed by Mr. Lemay that PluriDesign would be entitled to receive from Mr. Lemay's companies a commission of 17.65% on any amount paid as a sponsorship to one of them as a result of Mr. Corriveau's representations to the Government.[74] This percentage corresponds to the commission payable by Mr. Lemay to his sales staff, who were soliciting advertisements for his publications,[75] but of course the amounts involved in sponsorships were vastly greater and resulted in huge commissions.[76] In spite of his memory lapses with respect to the two dinner meetings with Mr. Guité in 1996[77] and 1997,[78] Mr. Corriveau has a very clear recollection of this unwritten agreement.[79] He acknowledges that it was understood that the commission would cover any consulting services performed by him or PluriDesign.[80]

From 1998 until the end of the Sponsorship Program, Mr. Corriveau was instrumental in obtaining many sponsorships from PWGSC for the benefit of Expour and Polygone. In every case Groupaction managed the project on behalf of the Government of Canada.[81] The invoices sent by PluriDesign to Mr. Lemay's various companies for fees earned or services rendered relating to these events and projects do not make reference in any way to a commission of 17.65%; instead, they contain descriptions of services allegedly rendered by PluriDesign, for which fees are charged.[82] In almost all cases the services described were simply not rendered, and the invoices are pure inventions designed to leave the impression that the contractual arrangement between the parties was other than a commission agreement. Mr. Lemay fails to explain in a satisfactory manner why the fixed commission was camouflaged in this way, but recognizes that the invoices contain an incorrect description of the reasons why sums of money were owing to PluriDesign.[83] He would have us believe that he did not pay attention to the sometimes nonsensical text of the invoices.[84] It is a reasonable inference from the documentary evidence that the parties arranged that the invoices would avoid mentioning a commission so as to hide the fact that Mr. Corriveau was in effect acting, without being registered, as a paid lobbyist.[85] In this regard Mr. Corriveau, who contests this inference without giving another plausible explanation for why the invoices were prepared as they were, states that he was not familiar with the requirements of the law governing lobbyists,[86] a statement that the Commission does not believe, considering his general knowledge and long experience in public administration.[87] It is also possible that Mr. Corriveau preferred that the revenues earned from this source be paid into PluriDesign, rather than be received by him as personal taxable income.

The amounts paid by Mr. Lemay's companies to PluriDesign over the years for the commissions earned by Mr. Corriveau totalled more than $6 million.[88] The fees charged in the invoices do not correspond precisely to their understanding that 17.65% of the amounts received would be paid.[89] Mr. Lemay says that they intended at some undetermined future date to sit down together to calculate exactly what was due to Mr. Corriveau, but failed to do so.[90] When the Sponsorship Program became a subject of public comment in 2003, Mr. Lemay refused for a time to pay some of PluriDesign's most recent invoices, but, according to Mr. Corriveau, finally agreed to pay $100,000 to settle outstanding claims of approximately $300,000.[91] Mr. Lemay denies that such a settlement occurred.

Two of the sponsorship contracts awarded to Groupaction for the benefit of Mr. Lemay's companies deserve special attention, because they illustrate the extent to which Mr. Guité and his successor at CCSB, Pierre Tremblay, were prepared to accommodate the wishes of the promoter, Mr. Lemay, and his representative, Mr. Corriveau, and to disregard the public interest. The two contracts in question concern the Salon National du Grand-Air et Pourvoirie (the "Quebec Salon") to be held in Quebec City in 2000; and the Salon international de la machinerie agricole (the "Salon Agricole"), which was scheduled to take place in the Olympic Stadium in Montreal in the autumn of 2000.

The Quebec Salon was the subject of a contract dated April 1, 1999, which provided for a sponsorship of $333,043, an agency commission payable to Groupaction of $39,965, and an Agency of Record commission of $9,992.[92] It was one of a number of events that were, according to written documentation in the files, the subject of negotiations between PWGSC and the promoters, which were all corporations owned and controlled by Mr. Lemay. These negotiations led to an agreement by which the amount of the sponsorships would be paid to the promoters at the time of signing the contract, well in advance of the events at which visibility would be given to the Government of Canada. In consideration of the advance payment, the promoters agreed to a discount of approximately 25% of the amount of the sponsorship and the commissions payable.[93]

The only explanation given for this agreement was that the promoter wanted his money in advance and PWGSC was interested in paying less money for the same amount of visibility as in previous years.[94] The obvious weakness of the agreement from the point of view of the public administration was that there was no provision for what would happen if the event for some reason did not take place. This is precisely what happened.

Mr. Lemay testifies that the Quebec Salon had to be cancelled because there were not enough exhibitors willing to participate in 2000. Exhibitors were discouraged by the lack of parking at the chosen venue. He says that he offered to Mr. Guité to reimburse the $333,043 that his company had received, but that Mr. Guité was unwilling to take the money back and asked instead that visibility of the federal presence be provided or enhanced at other events.[95] This part of his testimony is corroborated by Mr. Brault and Mr. Guité, and confirmed by a letter from Mr. Guité to Mr. Brault dated June 7 , 1999.[96]

With the benefit of hindsight, Mr. Guité acknowledges that the payment of a sponsorship in advance was "very unusual," and that the decision not to require its reimbursement when the event was cancelled was an error.[97]

Mr. Lemay alleges that he arranged for other publicity to be given to the federal government at other events that was a sufficient compensation for the loss of visibility at the cancelled Quebec Salon,[98] but he failed to persuade me that what was provided was worth more than $300,000. Specifically, the visibility afforded by the purchase of rights at regional salons in St-Jérôme, Drummondville, Baie Comeau and Rouyn-Noranda was probably not worth more than what he paid for them, which amounted to a total of $5,000.

The Salon Agricole was also cancelled because there was a tear in the roof of the Olympic Stadium which could not be repaired in time to save the Salon.[99] In this case as well, the very substantial sponsorship sum of $508,695 had been paid in advance. By the time he realized that the cancellation was inevitable, Mr. Guité had retired, and had been replaced at CCSB by Pierre Tremblay. Mr. Lemay testifies that like Mr. Guité, Mr. Tremblay did not want PWGSC to be reimbursed, saying that a reimbursement would cause problems, without specifying their nature.[100] Mr. Lemay says that he proposed to compensate the government by holding approximately 60 "Soirées de pêche" in different localities. These events consisted of showing fishing films to the local population, giving related talks and providing information about fishing. He says that Mr. Tremblay agreed to this proposition, and that in the spring of 2000 the "Soirées de pêche" took place.[101]

None of this is corroborated in any way. Mr. Lemay admits that nothing in writing confirms the alleged agreement with Mr. Tremblay, that there was no supervision of the events by Groupaction, which had been paid to manage the Salon Agricole, and no post-mortem reports were provided.[102] We have no testimony from Mr. Tremblay.

The evidence, such as it is, does not persuade me that the Government of Canada received equivalent value for the amount paid to Mr. Lemay's company for the Salon Agricole. It would have been more prudent to accept reimbursement of the $508,695, and it would have been an even better decision not to have paid this or any other sponsorship so far in advance.

From 1997 to 2004 the sponsorship contracts awarded by PWGSC for the benefit of Mr. Lemay's companies amounted to over $41 million. They were all solicited by Mr. Corriveau, whose chief qualification was his political connections with the Liberal Party of Canada. What was unknown to Mr. Lemay[103] was that Mr. Corriveau had concluded an agreement with Mr. Brault by which additional commissions would be paid to PluriDesign by Groupaction, calculated at the rate of 10% of what Groupaction earned for managing the contracts on behalf of PWGSC.

Mr. Brault testifies that he agreed to pay these commissions to help what Mr. Corriveau called "the cause,"[104] understood to refer to the LPCQ,[105] which was chronically in debt and having difficulty in meeting its financial obligations.[106] When the agreement was concluded in the spring of 1998,[107] Mr. Brault says that he was being continually requested to make contributions of various sorts to the LPCQ[108] over and above the salary and bonuses being paid to Mr. Renaud, and that he felt that the time had come to attempt to put some order into the cost of doing business.[109] He therefore agreed with Mr. Corriveau that Groupaction would pay PluriDesign 10% of the commission income it was earning as a result of the sponsorship contracts awarded to Mr. Lemay's companies, in the hope and expectation that this would be in lieu of other contributions to the LPCQ.[110]

Mr. Corriveau confirms that the parties agreed that PluriDesign would receive a commission of 10% of the fees and commissions earned by Groupaction on the sponsorship contracts awarded to Expour and Polygone, but claims that Mr. Brault took the initiative to propose this agreement as a way of inducing Mr. Corriveau to have Groupaction designated as the agency to manage Expour and Polygone contracts.[111] He says that the parties arranged that these amounts were to be claimed from Groupaction by way of invoices containing descriptions of professional services that were not in fact rendered, and that the invoices were deliberately false and misleading.[112] Mr. Corriveau testifies that the text of these invoices was dictated to him by Mr. Brault,[113] and that the reason why deliberately false invoices were prepared was that Mr. Brault did not wish Mr. Renaud to learn of the commissions paid to PluriDesign for fear that this would enable Mr. Renaud to claim more commissions or bonuses from Groupaction.[114]

The total amount of the invoices sent by PluriDesign to Groupaction for the period from June 19, 1998, to November 29, 2000, was $425,000 plus taxes.[115]

Mr. Brault gives an entirely different description of the intention of the parties in preparing and paying these invoices. He says that the commissions were payable to PluriDesign on the understanding that the amounts would be remitted to the LPCQ.[116] Obviously this was an improper agreement, and the parties adopted the stratagem of disguising the payments as fees for professional services paid to PluriDesign with reference to various projects. Mr. Brault admitted that it was impossible for him to know if in fact Mr. Corriveau was sending the amounts thus remitted on to the LPCQ, or if he was retaining them for his own benefit.[117] In early 2001, Benoît Corbeil told him that the LPCQ was seriously in debt and needed $1 million,[118] and asked Mr. Brault for a "contribution" of $400,000,[119] which made him suspect that the sums Groupaction had been remitting to PluriDesign had not reached their ultimate destination.[120] The request was later reduced to $200,000, and Mr. Corbeil assured Mr. Brault that sponsorship contracts to be awarded to Groupaction in April 2001 would more than compensate him for such a "contribution."[121] On the strength of these representations, Mr. Brault testifies that he made a further payment of $60,000, although there is no evidence other than his testimony of such a payment.[122] On the subject of this alleged contribution, Mr. Brault's testimony is vague and is, in my view, insufficiently precise to satisfy me that it should be included with the others as amounts that the LPCQ probably received from him.

There is no documentation indicating that PluriDesign sent Groupaction additional invoices after November 29, 2000, although Mr. Brault is of the opinion that additional remittances may have been made to PluriDesign after that date.[123] It should be noted, however, that early in 2001 Mr. Renaud invited Mr. Brault to meet Mr. Morselli at Restaurant Frank,[124] and Mr. Brault says that Mr. Morselli said at their meeting that he was now in charge of the finances of the LPCQ and had replaced Mr. Corriveau in that function. Mr. Morselli added that the party was grateful for his past generosity and hoped it would continue, and that from now on Mr. Brault should deal with him.[125] The message was understood by Mr. Brault to mean that from now on the kickbacks (because that was what they really were) paid to PluriDesign should be paid to Mr. Morselli or to persons designated by him. The meeting explains to my satisfaction why no further amounts were claimed by or paid to PluriDesign.

The Commission accepts Mr. Brault's version of the reason for the payment of these commissions and rejects Mr. Corriveau's explanations as implausible and untrue.

Mr. Brault says that he found that the amounts Groupaction was paying to PluriDesign, added to the contributions of various kinds he was making to the LPCQ, were a heavy financial burden, and that he asked Mr. Lemay through his companies Expour and Polygone, which were receiving very large sponsorships, to share some of the load.[126] Mr. Lemay agreed to help, by way of compensation, to give Groupaction some lucrative contracts for minimal work.[127] Accordingly, Groupaction and some of its affiliates invoiced Expour and Polygone the sum of $2,097,800 over a period of four years, from 1997-98 to 2001-02, for work which Mr. Brault recognizes was extremely well paid.[128]

Mr. Lemay's version of these payments is somewhat different. He recognizes that the invoices in question were on the high side,[129] but says that Mr. Brault told him that he was spending more time than he had originally expected in managing the Polygone and Expour sponsorships, and that this would be reflected in his invoices.[130] Mr. Lemay says that he trusted Mr. Brault and did not ask for further explanations.[131]

Although I found Mr. Lemay to be a credible witness in general, this part of his testimony leaves me incredulous. I prefer the franker and more believable explanation for the invoices of $2,097,800 given by Mr. Brault.

10.5
Meetings with Mr. Dezainde

In May 2001[132] Daniel Dezainde was appointed Executive Director of the LPCQ, replacing Benoît Corbeil, who had decided to go into municipal politics.[133] Mr. Dezainde had been chosen as Mr. Corbeil's successor by Françoise Patry, the President of the LPCQ, with the rather reluctant concurrence of the Honourable Alfonso Gagliano.[134] Upon taking office, Mr. Dezainde immediately ran into difficulties with respect to the Party's finances, which were in a critical state.[135] Mr. Gagliano, as Quebec lieutenant of the Party, had removed the corporate fundraising responsibilities from the Executive Director and conferred them upon his friend Joseph Morselli. Mr. Dezainde says that Mr. Gagliano told him that if he needed funds, he should notify either Mr. Morselli or the Minister's Executive Assistant, Jean-Marc Bard.[136] Mr. Dezainde was uncomfortable with this decision but agreed to it on the condition that Mr. Morselli would keep him fully advised of his activities and of the Party's finances.[137]

Mr. Dezainde had been dismayed to learn that a few months before he became Executive Director, Mr. Morselli had hired Beryl Wajsman to assist him, and had agreed that the LPCQ would pay him a salary of $5,000 per month, an expense which Mr. Dezainde felt the Party clearly could not afford.[138] Mr. Dezainde was also disturbed to learn of certain fundraising techniques employed by Mr. Wajsman which Mr. Dezainde considered improper. When soliciting donations from businessmen, Mr. Wajsman was offering them a written compilation of information about government programs.[139] The implicit connection between donations and access to information about government programs left little to the imagination. He discussed the matter with Ms. Patry, and they appealed successively to Mr. Gagliano and to the Chief of Staff of Mr. Chrétien at the PMO,[140] for support in their efforts to restore control over fundraising activities to Party officials. They received no support or encouragement. After having attempted in vain to settle the matter directly with Mr. Morselli,[141] Mr. Dezainde decided, with Ms. Patry's concurrence, that Mr. Wajsman's contract of employment would have to be terminated, and this was done on June 29, 2001.[142]

Mr. Gagliano was not supportive of Mr. Dezainde's decision and attempted to persuade Ms. Patry to take Mr. Wajsman back.[143] Mr. Morselli was more direct, rudely telling Mr. Dezainde that they were now at war as a result of his actions.[144]

It was in this context that Mr. Dezainde, following the suggestion of Ms. Patry, determined to appeal to Mr. Corriveau for advice and assistance. Ms. Patry had been told by Benoît Corbeil, to whom Mr. Corriveau was like a father, that he had successfully appealed to him in the past for financial assistance to the Party, and Mr. Dezainde also believed that he had always been a faithful supporter of the LPCQ and of its fundraising activities.[145] He also regarded Mr. Corriveau as a trusted advisor and friend.[146] He called him and they arranged to meet at lunch at Magnan's Tavern, where Mr. Dezainde explained to Mr. Corriveau his difficulties, and asked for help in forming a committee to assist him in the grassroots fundraising activities of the LPCQ.[147] Mr. Corriveau was not ready to help, and said, according to Mr. Dezainde, that he was unwilling to become involved in any fundraising activities so long as Mr. Morselli was involved in the Party's finances.[148] Mr. Corriveau also expressed intense dislike for Mr. Bard.[149] When Mr. Dezainde reported the failure of his approach to Ms. Patry and the reasons given for the refusal of Mr. Corriveau, she was very surprised.[150]

Mr. Dezainde says that he had two more lunches[151] with Mr. Corriveau at Magnan's Tavern during the summer of 2001, each time attempting to persuade him to lend his assistance in taking control of the Party's financial administration, and that Mr. Corriveau turned him down each time.[152] On the last of these occasions, towards the end of August 2001, Mr. Corriveau made what was for Mr. Dezainde a startling declaration.[153] He said that he had already done enough for the Party, and that in the past he had organized a system of kickbacks on commissions paid to communication agencies, retaining a portion for himself and putting the rest at the disposal of the LPCQ.[154]

Mr. Corriveau denies that this conversation took place. He recognizes that in the summer of 2001 he had lunch, but on one occasion only, with Mr. Dezainde, and testifies that he made no statement or admission about a system of kickbacks, either then or at any other time.[155]

Mr. Dezainde is an entirely credible witness. Much of his testimony is corroborated and confirmed by Ms. Patry, an equally credible person of obvious integrity. It is implausible that Mr. Dezainde would have invented, for no discernible reason, such a shocking story about a man that at the time he liked, respected and admired. He says that once Mr. Corriveau told him about the kickback system he had arranged, he broke off all contact with him.[156] He chose not to report the conversation to Ms. Patry, and only told the authorities about it shortly before he testified before the Commission.[157]

Perhaps Mr. Dezainde should not have been so surprised. The admission made by Mr. Corriveau had been hinted at by Jean-Marc Bard in a conversation he had with him on or about May 24, 2001, during which Mr. Bard made statements about Benoît Corbeil and Jacques Corriveau to the effect that they had been mixed up in dishonest dealings having to do with the finances of the Liberal Party.

The combination of Mr. Brault's testimony, which I find to be credible, about payments made by Groupaction to PluriDesign for no consideration other than Mr. Corriveau's political influence, with the admission made by Mr. Corriveau to Mr. Dezainde, leaves me with no alternative but to conclude that Mr. Corriveau was at the heart of an elaborate kickback scheme, according to which at least some of the sums of money paid by Groupaction to PluriDesign, on the strength of false invoices, were used by Mr. Corriveau to the advantage of the LPCQ, by salaries paid to its employees, by services rendered by PluriDesign employees to the LPCQ, or otherwise. The consideration for these payments was the influence of Mr. Corriveau in obtaining sponsorship contracts for Mr. Lemay's companies which were, at Mr. Corriveau's request, managed by Groupaction.

One of the ways in which Mr. Corriveau used the sums received from Groupaction for the advantage of the LPCQ was in putting LPCQ employees on the PluriDesign payroll. Documentary evidence forced Mr. Corriveau to admit that three full-time LPCQ workers, Gaëtano Manganiello, Philippe Zrihen and Jean Brisebois, were remunerated a total of $82,812.27 by PluriDesign in the years 1998 to 2000, inclusively. Messrs. Manganiello and Zrihen were on the PluriDesign payroll starting November 1, 1998, and Mr. Brisebois[158] was added on October 4, 1999. None of these people worked in fact for PluriDesign.

Mr. Corriveau recalls that the person who asked him to look after the salaries of these LPCQ workers was Mr. Béliveau,[159] but the evidence indicates that it was probably Mr. Corbeil who made the request. Mr. Manganiello testifies convincingly that Mr. Corbeil made the arrangement to transfer him to the PluriDesign payroll in 1998.[160] On this question, as is too often the case unfortunately, Mr. Corriveau's testimony is not credible.

Mr. Corriveau acknowledges that when Serge Gosselin was employed and remunerated by PluriDesign, from October 20, 1999, to April 1, 2001, at least 50% of his time was devoted to work for the LPCQ.[161] The evidence establishes that he received remuneration of $53,000 from PluriDesign,[162] of which one-half should be attributed to work performed for the benefit of the LPCQ. If this amount is added to the salaries paid to the three LPCQ workers mentioned above, the financial advantage conferred by Mr. Corriveau's company to the LPCQ, at the time it was receiving kickbacks from Groupaction, comes to a total of $109,312.27. I am satisfied that there was a relationship between the financial advantage conferred in this way on the LPCQ by PluriDesign and the kickbacks being paid to it by Groupaction. Mr. Corriveau's description of these advantages as magnanimous[163] and noble gestures on his part makes a mockery of the meaning of those adjectives.

As will be seen from what follows, there is additional evidence that Mr. Corriveau was instrumental in directing cash payments to senior officers of the LPCQ. The source of these payments cannot be determined on the basis of direct evidence presented to the Commission, but the fact of the payments is clearly established, and it may safely be assumed that they did not originate from legitimate fundraising activities by the LPCQ, but from sums of money paid by communication agencies, which were profiting from the Sponsorship Program, to Mr. Corriveau or PluriDesign.

10.6

Testimony of Michel Béliveau

Michel Béliveau has been an active member of the Liberal Party of Canada all his life.[164] Beginning in 1965, he worked tirelessly for Mr. Chrétien in the latter's constituency of St-Maurice in successive election campaigns, becoming his chief organizer in the federal elections of 1984, 1993 and 2000.[165] In 1996, at the request of Mr. Gagliano, he accepted the position of Executive Director of the LPCQ at its headquarters in Montreal,[166] and continued in that position until the spring of 1998, when he was replaced by his Deputy Executive Director, Benoît Corbeil.[167] Mr. Béliveau went on to become the National Vice-President (Francophone) of the Party. After the 2000 federal election, he was Mr. Chrétien's special advisor in his home riding.[168]

In 1996, when Mr. Béliveau started to work out of the Montreal Headquarters, he noted the constant presence there of Mr. Renaud,[169] whom he understood to be an employee of Groupaction,[170] although he was spending most of his time working on Liberal Party activities. Mr. Béliveau describes him as a member of the Liberal family,[171] a friend of Denis Coderre and Benoît Corbeil,[172] and active on various committees and in fundraising activities.[173] It was through Mr. Renaud that Mr. Béliveau was introduced to Jean Brault and became aware of Groupaction's business and its willingness to make contributions to the financial needs of the LPCQ.[174]

Early in 1997, Mr. Béliveau asked Mr. Renaud to solicit a contribution from Groupaction, which resulted in the receipt of $50,000.[175] Mr. Renaud's denial of any knowledge or participation in the obtaining of this contribution is not credible in light of Mr. Béliveau's testimony.[176]

After the election of June 1997, the finances of the LPCQ were once again in difficulty and Mr. Béliveau asked Mr. Renaud to approach Mr. Brault for a further contribution of $50,000.[177] He seemed surprised to learn at about the time he appeared before the Commission that this resulted in a contribution of a greater amount of $63,500 paid to the LPCQ by Mr. Renaud's company, from cash contributions of $55,000 and $8,500 which he had received from Mr. Brault.[178]

Mr. Béliveau recalls a third contribution to the Party's fortunes made by Mr. Brault consisting of $8,000 in cash, received from Mr. Renaud in the autumn of 1998 in an envelope, which he turned over to Mr. Corbeil, to be used for expenses incurred in a by-election in Sherbrooke.[179]

Mr. Béliveau's testimony concerning these contributions received from Mr. Brault corroborates in many respects the latter's testimony concerning payments made by him to the LPCQ in 1997 and 1998.

Mr. Béliveau also testifies concerning the involvement of Mr. Corriveau in the 1997 election campaign. He says that in preparation for the forthcoming election he had asked the regional directors to prepare an analysis of the financial needs of the LPCQ with respect to some 30 ridings that the Liberal Party considered "orphan ridings," since they were not represented by a sitting Liberal Member of Parliament. The analysis was made by his Deputy, Mr. Corbeil, for ridings in the western part of the province, and by Marc-Yvan Côté for the ridings in the eastern regions.[180] He testifies that the needs were established to be a total of $250,000 to $300,000, of which $175,000 to $200,000 was needed in the eastern ridings and $75,000 to $100,000 in the western part of the province, and that he advised Mr. Corriveau of these needs, explaining that he had confidence that Mr. Corriveau had connections with persons and corporations from whom he would be able to obtain financial assistance.[181]

Mr. Béliveau testifies that shortly thereafter he received directly from the hands of Mr. Corriveau, at the Party's headquarters, a thick envelope in which there was $75,000 to $100,000 in bills of $20 and $100, although he did not count them.[182] He says that he turned the envelope over to Mr. Corbeil to be used in the orphan ridings in western Quebec.[183] Later he received a second envelope for the eastern ridings, which he had delivered to Mr. Côté.[184] He says that he does not believe that the second envelope was delivered to him by Mr. Corriveau, but cannot exclude that possibility.[185] He believes that someone else, whom he cannot identify, may have delivered the money. Again he did not verify the contents of the envelope, but was advised by Mr. Côté subsequently that the needs of eastern Quebec had been met.[186]

Mr. Béliveau remembers two other deliveries of cash from Mr. Corriveau, one in 1997 at about the time of the election campaign, amounting to $7,000 or $8,000 which was paid to a volunteer in Quebec City to reimburse him for out-of-pocket expenses incurred in the riding of St-Maurice.[187] He recalls another delivery of cash in the sum of $8,000, which was received at a later date and paid to a businessman in Quebec City who had provided services during the 1997 campaign in the riding of Louis-Hébert.[188]

Mr. Béliveau was very nervous and emotional during his testimony. He was obviously conscious of the explosive nature of his testimony and that by the admissions he was making, his reputation was ruined. He insisted that he alone bears the responsibility for the irregularities that these deliveries of money represented.[189] He insisted that his lifelong friend Mr. Chrétien knew nothing about these matters.[190] Some aspects of his testimony are incongruous and implausible; for example, it is difficult to believe that any reasonable person would not have verified the amount of such an important sum of money received by him in cash, by counting it before delivering it to a third party. The size of the envelopes received was very inadequately explained.[191] I am left with the strong impression that Mr. Béliveau, while making difficult and incriminating admissions of improper conduct, has not told the Commission everything that he knows. However, he has clearly established in a credible manner that Mr. Corriveau was the person to whom he, as the Executive Director of the LPCQ, could turn for money, that Mr. Corriveau did not disappoint him when he was asked for financial assistance, and that the money received in cash came from unrecorded and improper sources.

Mr. Corbeil was questioned about Mr. Béliveau's testimony and flatly denies that at or about the time of the 1997 election campaign the latter delivered to him an envelope containing $75,000 to $100,000.[192] He does acknowledge receiving on one occasion in 1997 the sum of $5,000 in cash, which was used to pay campaign workers in the riding of Bourassa, and an additional amount of $4,000, used for the same purposes in the county of Anjou.[193] He testifies that about three weeks before the date of the election, Mr. Béliveau left the Montreal headquarters and went to work in the riding of St-Maurice, where Mr. Chrétien was involved in a tight battle with Yves Duhaime, leaving Mr. Corbeil to handle matters at the Montreal headquarters.[194]

That left it up to Mr. Côté to corroborate or to deny Mr. Béliveau's testimony. In 1997, Mr. Côté was the chief organizer for the 21 ridings of eastern

Quebec.[195] He testified in a straightforward and frank manner. He says that he and Mr. Béliveau together assessed the financial needs of the orphan ridings in eastern Quebec and came to the conclusion that $170,000 to $200,000 would be needed to meet those needs.[196] Mr. Béliveau told him that the funds would be forthcoming, and in fact three deliveries of cash were made to him.[197] The first, in the sum of $60,000, was delivered to him by Mr. Béliveau in Montreal in two envelopes containing $100 bills[198] which were enclosed in a big yellow envelope. Mr. Côté divided the money into nine envelopes, which he gave to the candidates in need of assistance at the time the Liberal campaign was officially launched in Shawinigan,[199] for payment of their personal expenses. He says that he did not know nor did he ask about the source of the money.[200] Several weeks later, an additional amount of $60,000 was provided to him in instalments of $40,000 and $20,000, respectively, which were picked up in Montreal on Mr. Côté's behalf by messengers.[201]

Mr. Côté's testimony therefore confirms Mr. Béliveau's testimony to the effect that he had come into possession of substantial sums of money in cash which he turned over to Mr. Côté. It is highly improbable that Mr. Béliveau would, for no discernible reason, lie about delivering an envelope to Mr. Corbeil while telling the truth about corresponding deliveries of money to Mr. Côté. Mr. Corbeil acknowledges that he has had close ties over the years to Mr. Corriveau and it may be that he wished to protect him.[202] His credibility is highly suspect as appears from what is written later in this chapter. I reject his denial that he received an envelope full of money from Mr. Béliveau in or about May 1997.

Mr. Corriveau flatly denies that he delivered sums of money in cash to Mr. Béliveau[203] at any time, but this denial, like Mr. Corbeil's, is not credible. Mr. Corriveau repeated many times that all commissions paid to PluriDesign had been declared as revenue and said that at no time did he remit to the LPCQ any of these revenues in one form or another. He made much of the fact that the banking records of his company obtained by the Commission corroborate his testimony. I do not consider that to be a very convincing explanation since the Commission, notwithstanding many efforts, was unable to obtain Mr. Corriveau's personal banking records, which have apparently been destroyed by his bank and which might have provided useful information.[204]

10.7
Source of Funds in 1997

Since Groupaction did not begin to pay PluriDesign's invoices relating to the Expour and Polygone sponsorships until early in 1998, the Commission has been concerned by the lack of direct evidence indicating the source of the funds which were delivered by Mr. Corriveau to Mr. Béliveau in or about May 1997. Of course, it is not always possible to obtain direct evidence of facts which persons prefer not to disclose. However, direct evidence is not the only way to prove facts. In the absence of direct evidence, reasonable inferences may be drawn from established facts which do not support any other logical explanation.

The evidence establishes that in 1996, 1997 and 1998, PluriDesign received very considerable amounts of money from corporations receiving subcontracts from Lafleur Communication such as Publicité Dezert, Yuri Kruk Communication Design (Kruk) and Xylo Concept Graphique Inc. (Xylo).[205] Both Éric Lafleur and Xylo's owner, Pierre Davidson, were also employees of Lafleur Communication. One could infer that these amounts, probably unearned, were applied by Mr. Corriveau to the advantage of the LPCQ—recalling his receipt of kickbacks from Groupaction beginning in 1998 and how some of them were used, according to the admission he made to Mr. Dezainde.

Mr. Corriveau was questioned concerning a series of invoices sent by PluriDesign to Publicité Dezert between September 1, 1996, and May 1, 1997, totalling $452,668, including taxes.[206] None of the invoices has been found in the records of either Publicité Dezert or PluriDesign, but their existence is established from the accounting records of both companies, and Mr. Corriveau acknowledges that they were sent and paid.[207] He says that they were the result of orders for goods and services given by Éric Lafleur, who needed help in fulfilling the subcontracts that Publicité Dezert had received from Lafleur Communication for promotional items.[208]

Five additional invoices totalling $115,830[209] were sent by PluriDesign to Publicité Dezert in 1998, and since copies of them have been found and form part of the evidence, they provide some indication of the kinds of goods and services that PluriDesign may have been called upon to provide in previous years. It may be noted that all five were paid by one cheque on March 20, 1998, although the invoices are dated, respectively, March 2, March 10, March 16, April 15 and April 20th.[210] Mr. Corriveau was unable to provide a satisfactory explanation for the payment of the two April invoices by a cheque issued before the invoices came into existence, according to their dates.[211]

The invoice dated March 2, 1998, for $60,000 plus taxes was not for a purchase of goods already delivered or services already rendered.[212] Rather it was a bill for what is called an "annual consultation agreement," assuring Publicité Dezert of Mr. Corriveau's availability for consultations at any time. He could not remember if in fact he was ever called upon for such consultations.[213] One of the subsequent invoices includes a charge for "consultations stratégiques," (strategic consultations) which, it may be presumed, should ordinarily have been covered by the retainer.[214]

Going back to the list of invoices in 1996 and 1997,[215] where we do not have the advantage of examining the invoices, some details nevertheless emerge. For example, an invoice dated October 1, 1996, is for $60,000. It might be assumed it was for the same annual retainer.

Mr. Corriveau is unable to describe any of the consultations for which the retainer was paid. He denies that any of the invoices was designed to disguise contributions to the LPCQ, although his answer to the question is curious: "Absolument pas. Mes livres comptables démontrent absolument rien de cette nature."[216] (Definitely not. My accounting records show absolutely nothing of this nature.) Obviously his accounting records would not be maintained in such a way as to document a corrupt practice. Persons participating in corrupt practices usually take great care to avoid documenting or recording their illicit activities.

Éric Lafleur was also closely questioned about the $60,000 "retainer" paid by his company and about the identical expense recorded on October 1, 1996.[217] He testifies that he cannot recall if the "annual retainer" paid in 1998 was paid in other years as well,[218] or furnish any details about the very substantial sums paid by Publicité Dezert in 1996, 1997 and 1998. The only fact he is able to recall is that he agreed to pay a fixed sum of $60,000 as a retainer to Mr. Corriveau's company, which had been recommended to him by his father, Jean Lafleur.[219]

It is tempting to draw conclusions from the foregoing, but there is really not sufficient evidence to do so, except to say that Éric Lafleur's testimony, like that of his father, is so full of questions that went unanswered due to alleged failures of memory that the only possible conclusion that may be drawn is that both decided to say that they could not remember relevant facts, in order to avoid giving truthful answers.

Mr. Kruk, whose company worked as a subcontractor to Lafleur Communication and subcontracted in turn to PluriDesign part of what he was engaged to supply to Lafleur Communication, did not appear as a witness before this Commission, and Mr. Corriveau was not questioned on his transactions with Mr. Kruk. Nonetheless, it is curious to note the remarkable similarity of four of the seven PluriDesign invoices dated March 2, March 18, March 27 and April 2, 1998.[220] Despite the four different events (Montreal International Jazz Festival, Ethnic Communities of Canada, the Space Train and the Just for Laughs Festival), and four slightly varying amounts, the text of the invoices is otherwise identical and each one of them refers to work done on promotional material of identical dimensions: one 25.5" x 36" OMNI poster, one 3' x 20' banner, one 3' x 16' panel and one 18" x 42" poster. The four invoices appear as Figure X-1. On their face they are for amounts that exceed the value of the work described, especially considering that the work was probably identical in each case, and that it was performed over a period of about one month, judging from the dates of the invoices. Is it by chance or coincidence that the pre-tax amounts of these four invoices add up to the very tidy sum of $100,000? Xylo, which, like Kruk, received subcontracts from Lafleur Communication without calls for tenders, also engaged the services of PluriDesign,[221] at the suggestion of Jean Lafleur, for part of the work. Ultimately, PluriDesign's invoices were added to or incorporated into Xylo's invoices to Lafleur Communication, which in turn billed the government. The Kroll Report in section 8.4.5 shows that Xylo's invoices to Lafleur Communication included charges from PluriDesign of $120,000, which is coincidentally the amount of the retainers billed to Publicité Dezert.

Figure X-1: Four PluriDesign invoices to Yuri Kruk.

P453

PLURI DESIGN CANADA INC.
Tél.: (514) 938-2040   Internet: pluri@videotron.ca   Fax: (514) 938-1474

FACTURE
INVOICE   2317-98   Date: 2 mars 1998

Vendu à / Bill to :
Monsieur Yuri Kruk
Yuri Kruk Communication-Design Inc.
781 rue William, Bureau 400
Montréal, Québec
H3C 1N8

Livré à:
Ship to:

IDEM

Tél.: (514) 876-8755   Fax: (514) 876-7953   Tél.:   Fax:

QUANTITÉ QUANTITY	Description	Prix unitaire Unit Price	Prix total Total Price
	PROJET: Festival International de Jazz de Montréal		
	Honoraires pour services professionnelles en design graphique		
	- Recherches stratégiques		8 500,00 $
	- Idéation		
	- Conception et design des items suivants:		20 500,00 $
	. Affiche pour support OMNI, format 25 1/2" x 36"		
	. Bannière, format 3' x 20'		
	. Panneau, format 3' x 16'		
	. Affiche, format 18" x 42"		

1. **Cette facture est payable immédiatement. Si vous l'avez acquitée, veuillez ignorer cette requête.**
This invoice is payable immediately on receipt. If you have already made payment no further action is necesssary.

Total partiel Sub-Total	29 000,00 $
TPS / GST R104248505	2 030,00 $
TVQ / GST (7.5%) 1002542761	2 327,25 $
TOTAL	33 357,25 $

P454

PLURI DESIGN CANADA INC.

Tél.: (514) 938-2040   Internet: pluri@videotron.ca   Fax: (514) 938-1474

FACTURE
INVOICE   **2318-98**   Date: 18 mars 1998

Vendu à / Bill to :	Livré à: Ship to:
Monsieur Yuri Kruk Yuri Kruk Communication-Design Inc. 781 rue William, Bureau 400 Montréal, Québec H3C 1N8	I D E M
Tél.: (514) 876-8755 Fax: (514) 876-7953	Tél.: Fax:

QUANTITÉ QUANTITY	Description	Prix unitaire Unit Price	Prix total Total Price
	PROJET: Communauté ethniques du Canada		
	Honoraires pour services professionnelles en design graphique		
	- Recherches stratégiques - Idéation		7 000,00 $
	- Conception et design des items suivants: . Affiche pour support OMNI, format 25 1/2" x 36" . Bannière, format 3' x 20' . Panneau, format 3' x 16' . Affiche, format 18" x 42"		14 000,00 $

1. Cette facture est payable immédiatement. Si vous l'avez acquitée, veuillez ignorer cette requête. This invoice is payable immediately on receipt. If you have already made payment no further action is necesssary.	**Total partiel** Sub-Total	21 000,00 $
	TPS / GST R104248505	1 470,00 $
	TVQ / GST (7.5%) 1002542761	1 685,25 $
	TOTAL	24 155,25 $

P455

PLURI DESIGN CANADA INC.

Tél.: (514) 938-2040   Internet: pluri@videotron.ca   Fax: (514) 938-1474

FACTURE

INVOICE   **2320-98**   Date: 27 mars 1998

Vendu à / Bill to :	Livré à: Ship to:
Monsieur Yuri Kruk Yuri Kruk Communication-Design Inc. 781 rue William, Bureau 400 Montréal, Québec H3C 1N8	I D E M
Tél.: (514) 876-8755 Fax: (514) 876-7953	Tél.: Fax:

QUANTITÉ QUANTITY	Description	Prix unitaire Unit Price	Prix total Total Price
	PROJET: Le Train de l'espace		
	Honoraires pour services professionnelles en design graphique		
	- Recherches stratégiques - Idéation		9 500,00 $

	- Conception et design des items suivants:
	  . Affiche pour support OMNI, format 25 1/2" x 36"
	  . Bannière, format 3' x 20'
	  . Panneau, format 3' x 16'
	  . Affiche, format 18" x 42"
			19 000,00 $

1. Cette facture est payable immédiatement. Si vous l'avez acquitée, veuillez ignorer cette requête.
This invoice is payable immediately on receipt. If you have already made payment no further action is necesssary.

Total partiel Sub-Total	28 500,00 $
TPS / GST R104248505	1 995,00 $
TVQ / GST (7.5%) 1002542761	2 287,13 $
TOTAL	32 782,13 $

P456

PLURI DESIGN CANADA INC.

Tél.: (514) 938-2040   Internet: pluri@videotron.ca   Fax: (514) 938-1474

FACTURE
INVOICE   **2325-98**   Date: 2 avril 1998

Vendu à / Bill to :	Livré à: Ship to:
Monsieur Yuri Kruk Yuri Kruk Communication-Design Inc. 781 rue William, Bureau 400 Montréal, Québec H3C 1N8	I D E M
Tél.: (514) 876-8755 Fax: (514) 876-7953	Tél.: Fax:

QUANTITÉ QUANTITY	Description	Prix unitaire Unit Price	Prix total Total Price
	PROJET: Festival juste pour rire		
	Honoraires pour services professionnelles en design graphique		
	- Recherches stratégiques - Idéation		7 300,00 $
	- Conception et design des items suivants: . Affiche pour support OMNI, format 25 1/2" x 36" . Bannière, format 3' x 20' . Panneau, format 3' x 16' . Affiche, format 18" x 42"		14 200,00 $

1. Cette facture est payable immédiatement. Si vous l'avez acquitée, veuillez ignorer cette requête. This invoice is payable immediately on receipt. If you have already made payment no further action is necesssary.	Total partiel Sub-Total	21 500,00 $
	TPS / GST R104248505	1 505,00 $
	TVQ / GST (7.5%) 1002542761	1 725,38 $
	TOTAL	24 730,38 $

PLURI DESIGN CANADA INC.

Once again it is tempting to draw conclusions from the foregoing, but there is not enough evidence to do so, except to say that PluriDesign derived substantial revenues from the subcontracts emanating from Kruk and Xylo, that in each case Jean Lafleur suggested that the subcontractor use the services of PluriDesign, and that it cost them nothing to do so since the latter's fees and charges were reimbursed to them by Lafleur Communication. Mr. Corriveau denies that these subcontracts were the source of funds paid to the LPCQ,[222] but he also denies that any cash contributions at all were made by him to the LPCQ,[223] and the evidence from other sources contradicts his denial.

The source of the sums of money paid to Mr. Béliveau by Mr. Corriveau in 1997 and 1998 cannot be determined with certainty, but it is probable that they come either from the commissions earned by PluriDesign on the Expour and Polygone sponsorships or from one of the communication agencies which was managing sponsorship contracts in 1996 and 1997, the prime candidate being the Lafleur agency and its subcontractors. The exact amount of money paid in this way in 1997 and 1998 cannot be calculated precisely due to Mr. Béliveau's failure to verify the amount of the cash he remitted to Messrs. Corbeil and Côté, but the Commission believes that the total amount of money delivered in those years by Mr. Corriveau may be conservatively established at $210,000.

10.8
Testimony of Benoît Corbeil

I have already stated, in an earlier section of this chapter in which I review the testimony of Mr. Béliveau, that I do not accept the affirmation of Mr. Corbeil that he did not receive an envelope containing $75,000 to $100,000 from Mr. Béliveau in the period preceding the 1997 federal election.[224]

On May 9 and 10, 2005,[225] Mr. Corbeil testified at length before the Commission, and was subjected to a searching cross-examination. On the basis of the answers he gave during his testimony, and on the basis of the

impressions I received at that time, I have come to the conclusion that Mr. Corbeil is a fundamentally untruthful witness and that nothing that he says is worthy of belief. The following conflicts, contradictions, evasions or improbabilities in his testimony are examples of why I do not give any value whatsoever to his evidence.

Mr. Corbeil denies that in the autumn of 1998 Mr. Béliveau gave him $8,000 in cash, which the latter had received from Mr. Corriveau, to be used in connection with the by-election in Sherbrooke.[226] I have no reason to disbelieve Mr. Béliveau's testimony on this subject.

Mr. Corbeil denies that he ever had a lunch or dinner with Mr. Brault and Mr. Corriveau together,[227] although inscriptions in Mr. Brault's agenda indicate that such encounters took place,[228] at which Mr. Brault says they talked about the financial needs of the LPCQ. I accept the testimony of Mr. Brault on this subject.

Mr. Corbeil affirms that he did not know in 1998 that Mr. Corriveau was paying his best friend, Serge Gosselin, for full-time work the latter performed for the LPCQ.[229] Considering the close relationship between them, it is most improbable that Mr. Gosselin would not have made his friend aware that he was being paid for his work, and by whom.

Mr. Corbeil would have us believe that in the year 2000 he did not know that Groupaction had been receiving contracts for sponsorships and advertising from the Government,[230] in spite of the fact that he and Mr. Renaud were friends and saw each other frequently at Party functions and at the Party headquarters.[231] Mr. Corbeil goes so far as to state under oath, in cross-examination, that he did not even know what functions Mr. Renaud was performing for Groupaction.[232] Mr. Renaud had no reason to keep his solicitation of contracts a secret from Mr. Corbeil, and it is impossible to believe that the latter did not have any idea of what he was doing.

Mr. Corbeil affirms that he received cash amounts of $35,000 and $15,000 from Mr. Brault in the year 2000, just before the federal election that year,[233]

at about the same time that Mr. Brault was making another donation to the LPCQ through Mr. Thiboutot of Commando Communications.[234] First of all, this story conflicts with Mr. Brault's testimony, which is to the effect that these two contributions were made in 1997, not in 2000, and I accept Mr. Brault's testimony.[235] Second, it is illogical to think that Mr. Brault would pay a total of $100,000 to the LPCQ in 2000, but would divide it for no particular reason into amounts of $50,000 each—paid by cheque to Commando Communications, and in cash to Mr. Corbeil. And third, Mr. Corbeil's testimony that the $50,000 he received was then parcelled out by him to various workers in the LPCQ is denied by at least one of the latter, Daniel Dezainde, who, according to Mr. Corbeil, received $3,000 for himself and $2,000 for a friend.[236] Mr. Dezainde denies receiving this payment, and I believe him.[237]

Mr. Corbeil testifies that he had absolutely nothing to do with securing employment for John Welch at Groupaction.[238] This is not only contrary to Mr. Brault's testimony,[239] it is contradicted by Mr. Welch, a most credible witness, who testifies that he asked Mr. Corbeil to help him find a job and gave him his curriculum vitae, which ended up in Mr. Brault's possession.[240]

Mr. Corbeil says he does not remember whether or not he introduced Mr. Dezainde to Mr. Morselli in March or April 2001, but he is certain that he did not refer to Mr. Morselli as "le vrai boss" (the real boss).[241] I accept Mr. Dezainde's version of this incident.[242]

Mr. Corbeil's description of his dealings with his friend Serge Gosselin in the year 2000, shortly before leaving his position as Executive Director, gives reason to suspect Mr. Corbeil's credibility. At a time when the LPCQ was heavily in debt to its banker and desperately seeking funds from any source available, Mr. Corbeil had it pay Mr. Gosselin for studies and research that the latter had allegedly carried out, and at the same time submitted three invoices to Mr. Gosselin for similar work[243] that Mr. Corbeil had allegedly performed earlier in the year, at a time when he would have been very busy preparing for the federal election.[244] Since these peculiar transactions are beyond the mandate of the Commission it is not appropriate to comment upon them further, except to note that they raise doubts about the reliability in general of Mr. Corbeil and his credibility.

At the end of his testimony I concluded that Mr. Corbeil had come before the Commission determined to shield his friend and collaborator Mr. Corriveau from any shadow of impropriety or misconduct, and to settle some scores with certain political adversaries, no matter how much the truth would be made to suffer in the process.

Endnotes to Chapter X

1   Testimony of Mr. Corriveau, Transcripts vol. 99, p. 17783 (OF), p. 17768 (E).

2   Testimony of Mr. Guité, Transcripts vol. 109, p. 19855 (OE), p. 19856 (F).

3   Testimony of Mr. Guité, Transcripts vol. 109, pp. 19855-19856 (OE), pp. 19856-19857 (F).

4   Testimony of Mr. Guité, Transcripts vol. 109, pp. 19861-19862 (OE), p. 19863 (F).

5   Testimony of Mr. Dingwall, Transcripts vol. 60, p. 10608 (OE), pp. 10614-10615 (F); Testimony of Mr. Kinsella, Transcripts vol. 60, p. 10626 (OE), p. 10635 (F).

6   Testimony of Mr. Guité, Transcripts vol. 109, pp. 19856-19868 (OE), pp. 19857-19871 (F).

7   Testimony of Mr. Brault, Transcripts vol. 89, pp. 15760-15761 (OF), p. 15755 (E).

8   Testimony of Mr. Corriveau, Transcripts vol. 99, pp. 17805-17806 (OF), pp. 17788-17789 (E); Exhibit P-332, pp. 10-11.

9   Testimony of Mr. Corriveau, Transcripts vol. 99, pp. 17811-17817 (OF), pp. 17792-17799 (E); vol. 100, p. 18000 (OF), p. 17987 (E); Exhibit P-335, p. 5; Exhibit P-332, p. 211.

10   Testimony of Mr. Gagliano, Transcripts vol. 68 (revised), pp. 11679-11682 (OF), pp. 11677-11679 (E); Testimony of Mr. Corriveau, Transcripts vol. 100, pp. 18005-18008 (OF), pp. 17991-17994 (E); Exhibit P-208(D), p. 114.

11   Testimony of Mr. Corriveau, Transcripts vol. 100, pp. 18007-18008 (OF), p. 17993 (E).

12   Exhibit P-336.

13   Testimony of Mr. Brault, Transcripts vol. 91 (Part 3 of 3), pp. 16154-16158 (OF), pp. 16144-16147 (E); Exhibit C-296, p. 275.

14   Testimony of Mr. Brault, Transcripts vol. 93 (Part 3 of 3), p. 16563 (OF), pp. 16550-16551 (E).

15   Testimony of Mr. Corriveau, Transcripts vol. 99, pp. 17772-17781 (OF), pp. 17758-17766 (E).

16   Testimony of Mr. Corriveau, Transcripts vol. 99, pp. 17781-17784 (OF), pp. 17766-17769 (E); vol. 129, p. 24348 (OF), pp. 24343-24344 (E).

17   Testimony of Mr. Corriveau, Transcripts vol. 129 (revised), p. 24316 (OF), p. 24314 (E).

18   For example, see Testimony of Mr. Corriveau, Transcripts vol. 99, pp. 17790, 17792, 17803, 17840 (OF), pp. 17775, 17777, 17787, 17820-17821 (E); vol. 100, pp. 18039-18040 (OF), pp. 18022-18023 (E).

19   Testimony of Mr. Corriveau, Transcripts vol. 101, pp. 18096-18103 (OF), pp. 18094-18100 (E).

20   Testimony of Mr. Lemay, Transcripts vol. 97, pp. 17307-17318 (OF), pp. 17301-17312 (E); Exhibit P-328(A), pp. 2-8.

21   Testimony of Mr. Lemay, Transcripts vol. 97, p. 17310 (OF), p. 17304 (E).

22   Testimony of Mr. Lemay, Transcripts vol. 97, pp. 17310-17311 (OF), pp. 17304-17305 (E).

23   Testimony of Mr. Lemay, Transcripts vol. 97, p. 17337 (OF), p. 17329 (E).

24   Testimony of Mr. Coderre, Transcripts vol. 62, p. 11009 (OF), p. 11005 (E).

25   Testimony of Mr. Coderre, Transcripts vol. 62, pp. 11009-11012 (OF), pp. 11005-11006 (E); Testimony of Mr. Lemay, Transcripts vol. 97, pp. 17344-17345 (OF), pp. 17335-17336 (E).

26   Testimony of Mr. Coderre, Transcripts vol. 62, 11009 (OF), p. 11004 (E); Testimony of Mr. Corbeil, Transcripts vol. 115, p. 21174 (OF), p. 21169 (E); Testimony of Mr. Béliveau, Transcripts vol. 113, pp. 20901-20902 (OF), pp. 20886-20888 (E).

27   Testimony of Mr. Coderre, Transcripts vol. 62, p. 11007 (OF), p. 11002 (E).

[28] Testimony of Mr. Lemay, Transcripts vol. 97, pp. 17345-17347 (OF), pp. 17337-17339 (E); Testimony of Mr. Brault, Transcripts vol. 91 (Part 3 of 3), p. 16136 (OF), pp. 16127-16128 (E).

[29] Testimony of Mr. Brault, Transcripts vol. 91 (Part 3 of 3), p. 16139 (OF), p. 16130 (E); Testimony of Mr. Lemay, Transcripts vol. 97, pp. 17345-17347 (OF), pp. 17337-17339 (E).

[30] Testimony of Mr. Lemay, Transcripts vol. 97, pp. 17347-17348 (OF), p. 17339 (E).

[31] Testimony of Mr. Lemay, Transcripts vol. 97, pp. 17339-17342 (OF), pp. 17330-17333 (E); Testimony of Mr. Corriveau, Transcripts vol. 100, pp. 17856-17857 (OF), pp. 17854-17855 (E).

[32] Testimony of Mr. Corriveau, Transcripts vol. 99, pp. 17772-17781 (OF), pp. 17758-17766 (E).

[33] Testimony of Mr. Lemay, Transcripts vol. 97, p. 17348 (OF), p. 17340 (E); Testimony of Mr. Corriveau, Transcripts vol. 100, p. 17852 (OF), p. 17851 (E).

[34] Testimony of Mr. Lemay, Transcripts vol. 97, p. 17349 (OF), p. 17340 (E).

[35] Testimony of Mr. Lemay, Transcripts vol. 97, pp. 17350-17352 (OF), pp. 17341-17343 (E); Exhibit C-302, p. 15.

[36] Testimony of Mr. Corriveau, Transcripts vol. 100, p. 17884 (OF), pp. 17880-17881 (E).

[37] Testimony of Mr. Lemay, Transcripts vol. 97, pp. 17350-17351 (OF), pp. 17341-17342 (E); Exhibit C-302, pp. 14-19.

[38] Testimony of Mr. Lemay, Transcripts vol. 97, p. 17355 (OF), pp. 17345-17346 (E); Exhibit C-302, p. 16.

[39] Testimony of Mr. Lemay, Transcripts vol. 97, p. 17354 (OF), pp. 17344-17345 (E).

[40] Testimony of Mr. Lemay, Transcripts vol. 99, p. 17596 (OF), pp. 17595-17596 (E).

[41] Testimony of Mr. Corriveau, Transcripts vol. 100, p. 17884 (OF), pp. 17880-17881 (E).

[42] Testimony of Mr. Lemay, Transcripts vol. 97, pp. 17362-17365 (OF), pp. 17352-17355 (E).

[43] Exhibit C-302, pp. 30-31.

[44] Testimony of Mr. Corriveau, Transcripts vol. 100, pp. 17871-17873, 17879 (OF), pp. 17868-17870, 17875-17876 (E); vol. 101, pp. 18090, 18138-18139 (OF), pp.18088-18089, 18132-18133 (E); Exhibit COR-1.

[45] Testimony of Mr. Lemay, Transcripts vol. 97, pp. 17364-17365 (OF), pp. 17354-17355 (E).

[46] Testimony of Mr. Lemay, Transcripts vol. 97, pp. 17356-17358 (OF), pp. 17347-17349 (E); Testimony of Mr. Corriveau, Transcripts vol. 100, pp. 17868-17869 (OF), pp. 17865-17866 (E).

[47] Testimony of Mr. Lemay, Transcripts vol. 97, pp. 17353-17354, 17357-17359 (OF), pp. 17344-17345, 17347-17348 (E).

[48] Exhibit C-302, pp. 6-12.

[49] Testimony of Mr. Lemay, Transcripts vol. 97, p. 17361 (OF), pp. 17351-17352 (E).

[50] Exhibit C-302, pp. 27-28.

[51] Testimony of Mr. Corriveau, Transcripts vol. 100, pp. 17862-17863, 18012 (OF), pp. 17860-17861, 17997-17998 (E).

[52] Testimony of Mr. Corriveau, Transcripts vol. 100, pp. 17864-17866 (OF), pp. 17862-17863 (E); vol. 101, pp. 18109-18110 (OF), 18105-18106 (E).

[53] Testimony of Mr. Corriveau, Transcripts vol. 100, pp. 17865-17867 (OF), pp. 17863-17865 (E).

[54] Exhibit C-302, pp. 33-41.

[55] Testimony of Mr. Corriveau, Transcripts vol. 99, pp. 17835-17836 (OF), pp. 17816-17817 (E).

[56] Testimony of Mr. Brault, Transcripts vol. 89, pp. 15740-15744 (OF), pp. 15737-15741 (E).

57 Testimony of Mr. Lemay, Transcripts vol. 97, p. 17365 (OF), p. 17355 (E).

58 Testimony of Mr. Lemay, Transcripts vol. 97, pp. 17367-17371 (OF), pp. 17357-17360 (E); vol. 99, p. 17617 (OF), pp. 17615-17616 (E); Testimony of Mr. Guité, Transcripts vol. 109, p. 19869 (OE), p. 19872 (F).

59 Testimony of Mr. Lemay, Transcripts vol. 97, p. 17370 (OF), p. 17359 (E).

60 Testimony of Mr. Lemay, Transcripts vol. 97, p. 17371 (OF), p. 17361 (E).

61 Testimony of Mr. Lemay, Transcripts vol. 97, pp. 17372-17373 (OF), pp. 17361-17362 (E).

62 Testimony of Mr. Corriveau, Transcripts vol. 100, pp. 17893-17897 (OF), pp. 17889-17893 (E).

63 Testimony of Mr. Lemay, Transcripts vol. 97, p. 17367 (OF), p. 17357 (E).

64 Testimony of Mr. Corriveau, Transcripts vol. 100, pp. 17897-17898 (OF), pp. 17892-17893 (E).

65 Testimony of Mr. Lemay, Transcripts vol. 98, p. 17383 (OF), p. 17383 (E).

66 Testimony of Mr. Lemay, Transcripts vol. 98, pp. 17383, 17385-17386 (OF), pp. 17382, 17384-17385 (E).

67 Testimony of Mr. Lemay, Transcripts vol. 98, p. 17386 (OF), p. 17385 (E).

68 Testimony of Mr. Lemay, Transcripts vol. 98, pp. 17386-17387, 17399-17400 (OF), pp. 17386, 17397 (E).

69 Testimony of Mr. Lemay, Transcripts vol. 99, pp. 17612-17613 (OF), pp. 17610-17612 (E).

70 Testimony of Mr. Boulay, Transcripts vol. 103, pp. 18752, 18756 (OF), pp. 18733, 18737 (E).

71 Testimony of Mr. Guité, Transcripts vol. 109, p. 19893 (OE), p. 19899 (F); Vol. 112 (Part 1 of 2), p. 20548 (OE), pp. 20551-20552 (F).

72 Testimony of Mr. Corriveau, Transcripts vol. 100, pp. 17943-17945 (OF), pp. 17934-17936 (E); vol. 101, pp. 18117-18118 (OF), pp. 18113-18114 (E).

73 Testimony of Mr. Lemay, Transcripts vol. 99, p. 17619 (OF), p. 17617 (E); Testimony of Mr. Corriveau, Transcripts vol. 100, p. 17903 (OF), p. 17898 (E).

74 Testimony of Mr. Lemay, Transcripts vol. 97, pp. 17373-17375 (OF), pp. 17363-17364 (E); vol. 98, p. 17484 (OF), p. 17474 (E).

75 Testimony of Mr. Lemay, Transcripts vol. 97, pp. 17374-17375 (OF), pp. 17363-17364 (E).

76 Testimony of Mr. Lemay, Transcripts vol. 97, p. 17375 (OF), p. 17364 (E).

77 Testimony of Mr. Corriveau, Transcripts vol. 99, pp. 17835-17836 (OF), pp. 17816-17817 (E).

78 Testimony of Mr. Corriveau, Transcripts vol. 100, pp. 17893-17898 (OF), pp. 17889-17893 (E).

79 Testimony of Mr. Corriveau, Transcripts vol. 100, pp. 17898-17900 (OF), pp. 17893-17895 (E).

80 Testimony of Mr. Corriveau, Transcripts vol. 100, pp. 17898, 17919 (OF), pp. 17893-17894, 17912-17913 (E).

81 Exhibit C-302, pp. 2-4.

82 Exhibit P-322(A), pp. 2-248; Exhibit P-322(B), pp. 250-429.

83 Testimony of Mr. Lemay, Transcripts vol. 98, pp. 17415-17418, 17483-17484, 17396-17399 (OF), pp. 17412-17415, 17473-17475, 17394-17396 (E).

84 Testimony of Mr. Lemay, Transcripts vol. 98, pp. 17416-17418, 17484 (OF), pp. 17412-17414, 17474 (E).

85 Testimony of Mr. Corriveau, Transcripts vol. 100, p. 17899 (OF), p. 17894 (E).

86 Testimony of Mr. Corriveau, Transcripts vol. 100, pp. 17927-17928 (OF), pp. 17920-17921 (E).

[87] Testimony of Mr. Corriveau, Transcripts vol. 99, pp. 17772-17784 (OF), pp. 17758-17769 (E).

[88] Exhibit P-322(A), p. 2; Exhibit P-326, p. 1.

[89] Testimony of Mr. Lemay, Transcripts vol. 98, pp. 17379-17381 (OF), pp. 17379-17381 (E).

[90] Testimony of Mr. Lemay, Transcripts vol. 98, pp. 17416-17417, 17484-17486 (OF), pp. 17412, 17477-17479 (E).

[91] Testimony of Mr. Corriveau, Transcripts vol. 100, pp. 17926-17927 (OF), pp. 17919-17920 (E).

[92] Exhibit C-306, pp. 6-25; Exhibit C-302, p. 3.

[93] Testimony of Mr. Brault, Transcripts vol. 91, pp. 16158-16159 (OF), pp. 16147-16149 (E); vol. 93, pp. 16459, 16464 (OF), pp. 16454, 16459 (E); Testimony of Mr. Guité, Transcripts vol. 109, pp. 19945-19946 (OE), pp. 19955-19956 (F).

[94] Testimony of Mr. Brault, Transcripts vol. 91, pp. 16158-16159 (OF), pp. 16147-16149 (E); vol. 93, p. 16459 (OF), p. 16454 (E).

[95] Testimony of Mr. Lemay, Transcripts vol. 98, p. 17506 (OF), p. 17495 (E).

[96] Testimony of Mr. Brault, Transcripts vol. 91, p. 16167-16168 (OF), pp. 16156-16157 (E); vol. 93, p. 16477 (OF), p. 16471 (E); Testimony of Mr. Guité, Transcripts vol. 111, p. 20476 (OE), p. 20493 (F). Exhibit C-306, p. 35.

[97] Testimony of Mr. Guité, Transcripts vol. 109, pp. 19956, 19965, (OE), pp. 19967, 19977-19978 (F).

[98] Testimony of Mr. Lemay, Transcripts vol. 98, pp. 17513-17516 (OF), pp. 17501-17503 (E); vol. 99, pp. 17657-17659 (OF), pp. 17652-17654; Testimony of Mr. Guité, Transcripts vol. 111, pp. 20481-20482 (OE), pp. 20499-20500 (F).

[99] Testimony of Mr. Lemay, Transcripts vol. 98, pp. 17516-17518 (OF), pp. 17504-17506 (E).

[100] Testimony of Mr. Lemay, Transcripts vol. 98, p. 17518 (OF), p. 17506 (E).

[101] Testimony of Mr. Lemay, Transcripts vol. 98, pp. 17518-17519 (OF), pp. 17506-17507 (E); vol. 99, pp. 17655-17656 (OF), pp. 17650-17651.

[102] Testimony of Mr. Lemay, Transcripts vol. 98, pp. 17521-17522 (OF), pp. 17508-17509 (E); Testimony of Mr. Brault, Transcripts vol. 91, p. 16176-16177 (OF), pp. 16164-16165 (E).

[103] Testimony of Mr. Lemay, Transcripts vol. 99, pp. 17685-17686 (OF), pp. 17678-17679 (E).

[104] Testimony of Mr. Brault, Transcripts vol. 91 (Part 3 of 3), p. 16189 (OF), p. 16176 (E).

[105] Testimony of Mr. Brault, Transcripts vol. 91 (Part 3 of 3), p. 16190 (OF), p. 16177 (E).

[106] Testimony of Mr. Béliveau, Transcripts vol. 113, p. 20922 (OF), pp. 20904-20905 (E).

[107] Testimony of Mr. Brault, Transcripts vol. 92, pp. 16199-16201 (OF), pp. 16198-16200 (E).

[108] Testimony of Mr. Brault, Transcripts vol. 92, pp. 16200-16201 (OF), p. 16200 (E).

[109] Testimony of Mr. Brault, Transcripts vol. 92, pp. 16200-16201 (OF), p. 16200 (E).

[110] Testimony of Mr. Brault, Transcripts vol. 92, pp. 16199-16201 (OF), pp. 16199-16200 (E).

[111] Testimony of Mr. Corriveau, Transcripts vol. 100, pp. 17935-17936 (OF), pp. 17927-17928 (E).

[112] Testimony of Mr. Corriveau, Transcripts vol. 100, pp. 17967-17968 (OF), pp. 17957-17958.

[113] Testimony of Mr. Corriveau, Transcripts vol. 100, pp. 17936-17937 (OF), p. 17928 (E).

[114] Testimony of Mr. Corriveau, Transcripts vol. 100, pp. 17937-17938, 17968-17969 (OF), pp. 17929-17930, 17958 (E).

[115] Exhibit P-322(B), p. 462.

[116] Testimony of Mr. Brault, Transcripts vol. 91 (Part 3 of 3), pp. 16189-16190 (OF), pp. 16176-16177 (E).

117 Testimony of Mr. Brault, Transcripts vol. 92, pp. 16202-16203 (OF), p. 16202 (E).

118 Testimony of Mr. Brault, Transcripts vol. 92, p. 16204 (OF), pp. 16203-16204 (E).

119 Testimony of Mr. Brault, Transcripts vol. 92, p. 16204 (OF), p. 16203 (E).

120 Testimony of Mr. Brault, Transcripts vol. 92, pp. 16205-16206 (OF), pp. 16204-16205 (E).

121 Testimony of Mr. Brault, Transcripts vol. 92, pp. 16204-16205, 16349-16350 (OF), pp. 16203-16204, 16337-16338 (E).

122 Testimony of Mr. Brault, Transcripts vol. 92, p. 16205 (OF), p. 16204 (E).

123 Testimony of Mr. Brault, Transcripts vol. 91 (Part 3 of 3), p. 16191 (OF), pp. 16177-16178 (E).

124 Testimony of Mr. Brault, Transcripts vol. 89, p. 15878 (OF), p. 15863 (E).

125 Testimony of Mr. Brault, Transcripts vol. 89, pp. 15878-15880 (OF), pp. 15864-15866 (E).

126 Testimony of Mr. Brault, Transcripts vol. 92, pp. 16211-16212 (OF), pp. 16210-16211 (E).

127 Testimony of Mr. Brault, Transcripts vol. 92, pp. 16212-16213 (OF), pp. 16210-16211 (E).

128 Testimony of Mr. Brault, Transcripts vol. 92, p. 16212 (OF), p. 16211 (E); Exhibit C-315, pp. 2, 7.

129 Testimony of Mr. Lemay, Transcripts vol. 98, pp. 17532, 17546 (OF), pp. 17519, 17532 (E).

130 Testimony of Mr. Lemay, Transcripts vol. 98, pp. 17532-17533, 17540 (OF), pp. 17519-17520, 17526 (E); vol. 99, pp. 17640-17641 (OF), p. 17637 (E).

131 Testimony of Mr. Lemay, Transcripts vol. 98, pp. 17533, 17536, 17541 (OF), pp. 17519-17520, 17522, 17527 (E).

132 Testimony of Mr. Dezainde, Transcripts vol. 117, pp. 21749-21750 (OF), pp. 21744-21745 (E).

133 Testimony of Mr. Corbeil, Transcripts vol. 115, pp. 21180, 21399 (OF), pp. 21175, 21374.

134 Testimony of Mr. Gagliano, Transcripts vol. 130, pp. 24828-24832 (OF), pp. 24807-24811 (E).

135 Testimony of Mr. Dezainde, Transcripts vol. 117, p. 21763 (OF), pp. 21756-21757 (E).

136 Testimony of Mr. Dezainde, Transcripts vol. 117, pp. 21758-21760, 21793-21798 (OF), pp. 21752-21754, 21783-21788 (E).

137 Testimony of Mr. Dezainde, Transcripts vol. 117, pp. 21758-21760 (OF), pp. 21752-21753 (E).

138 Testimony of Mr. Dezainde, Transcripts vol. 117, pp. 21781-21786 (OF), pp. 21772-21777 (E); Testimony of Mr. Corbeil, Transcripts vol. 115, pp. 21334-21335 (OF), pp. 21315-21316 (E).

139 Testimony of Mr. Dezainde, Transcripts vol. 117, pp. 21788-21790 (OF), pp. 21779-21780 (E).

140 Testimony of Mr. Dezainde, Transcripts vol. 117, pp. 21849-21861 (OF), pp. 21834-21845 (E); Testimony of Ms. Patry, Transcripts vol. 129 (revised), pp. 24557-24563 (OF), pp. 24537-24542 (E).

141 Testimony of Mr. Dezainde, Transcripts vol. 117, pp. 21862, 21786 (OF), pp. 21845, 21777 (E).

142 Testimony of Mr. Dezainde, Transcripts vol. 117, pp. 21839-21849 (OF), pp. 21824-21834 (E); Testimony of Ms. Patry, Transcripts vol. 129 (revised), pp. 24563-24566 (OF), pp. 24542-24545 (E); Exhibit P-398, p. 135.

143 Testimony of Ms. Patry, Transcripts vol. 129 (revised), p. 24566 (OF), p. 24545 (E).

144 Testimony of Mr. Dezainde, Transcripts vol. 117, pp. 21863-21867 (OF), pp. 21846-21849 (E).

145 Testimony of Mr. Dezainde, Transcripts vol. 117, pp. 21825-21826 (OF), pp. 21812-21813 (E).

146 Testimony of Mr. Dezainde, Transcripts vol. 117, pp. 21803-21804, 21825-21826 (OF), pp. 21792-21793, 21812-21813 (E).

147 Testimony of Mr. Dezainde, Transcripts vol. 117, pp. 21825-21829 (OF), pp. 21812-21815 (E).

[148] Testimony of Mr. Dezainde, Transcripts vol. 117, p. 21827 (OF), p. 21814 (E).

[149] Testimony of Mr. Dezainde, Transcripts vol. 117, p. 21827 (OF), p. 21814 (E).

[150] Testimony of Mr. Dezainde, Transcripts vol. 117, p. 21829 (OF), pp. 21815-21816 (E).

[151] Testimony of Mr. Dezainde, Transcripts vol. 117, pp. 21829, 21867 (OF), pp. 21815-21816, 21849 (E).

[152] Testimony of Mr. Dezainde, Transcripts vol. 117, pp. 21829-21833 (OF), pp. 21815-21820 (E).

[153] Testimony of Mr. Dezainde, Transcripts vol. 117, pp. 21834-21836 (OF), pp. 21821-21822 (E).

[154] Testimony of Mr. Dezainde, Transcripts vol. 117, pp. 21833-21838 (OF), pp. 21819-21824 (E).

[155] Testimony of Mr. Corriveau, Transcripts vol. 128, pp. 24264-24267 (OF), pp. 24260-24262 (E).

[156] Testimony of Mr. Dezainde, Transcripts vol. 117, pp. 21835-21838 (OF), pp. 21821-21824 (E).

[157] Testimony of Mr. Dezainde, Transcripts vol. 117, p. 21838 (OF), p. 21824 (E).

[158] Testimony of Mr. Corriveau , Transcripts vol. 128, p. 24289 (OF), pp. 24281-24282 (E); Testimony of Mr. Manganiello, Transcripts vol. 126, pp. 23801, 23807 (OE), pp. 23812-23813, 23819 (F); Exhibit P-463, pp. 4, 11, 29-30; Exhibit P-460, p. 90.

[159] Testimony of Mr. Corriveau, Transcripts vol. 129 (revised), pp. 24332-24339 (OF), pp. 24329-24335 (E); vol. 128, pp. 24298-24299 (OF), pp. 24289-24290 (E).

[160] Testimony of Mr. Manganiello, Transcripts vol. 126, pp. 23801-23805, 23826 (OE), pp. 23813-23817, 23840 (F).

[161] Testimony of Mr. Corriveau, Transcripts vol. 128, pp. 24296-24298 (OF), pp. 24289-24290 (E).

[162] Exhibit P-387, p. 3.

[163] Testimony of Mr. Corriveau, Transcripts vol. 128, p. 24289 (OF), pp. 24281-24282 (E); vol. 129 (revised), p. 24386 (OF), p. 24378 (E).

[164] Testimony of Mr. Béliveau, Transcripts vol. 113, pp. 20872-20882 (OF), pp. 20861-20871 (E).

[165] Testimony of Mr. Béliveau, Transcripts vol. 113, pp. 20879-20882 (OF), pp. 20868-20871 (E).

[166] Testimony of Mr. Béliveau, Transcripts vol. 113, pp. 20876-20879 (OF), pp. 20866-20868 (E).

[167] Testimony of Mr. Béliveau, Transcripts vol. 113, p. 20875 (OF), pp. 20864-20865 (E).

[168] Testimony of Mr. Béliveau, Transcripts vol. 113, p. 20884 (OF), p. 20872 (E).

[169] Testimony of Mr. Béliveau, Transcripts vol. 113, pp. 20906-20909 (OF), pp. 20890-20893 (E).

[170] Testimony of Mr. Béliveau, Transcripts vol. 113, pp. 20911-20912 (OF), pp. 20895-20896 (E).

[171] Testimony of Mr. Béliveau, Transcripts vol. 113, pp. 20906-20911 (OF), pp. 20891-20895 (E).

[172] Testimony of Mr. Béliveau, Transcripts vol. 113, p. 20907 (OF), p. 20891 (E).

[173] Testimony of Mr. Béliveau, Transcripts vol. 113, pp. 20906-20911 (OF), pp. 20891-20895 (E).

[174] Testimony of Mr. Béliveau, Transcripts vol. 113, pp. 20915-20925, 20912 (OF), pp. 20898-20907, 20895-20896 (E).

[175] Testimony of Mr. Béliveau, Transcripts vol. 113, pp. 20916-20922 (OF), pp. 20899-20904 (E).

[176] Testimony of Mr. Renaud, Transcripts vol. 96, pp. 17001-17002 (OF), pp. 17000-17001 (E).

[177] Testimony of Mr. Béliveau, Transcripts vol. 113, pp. 20922-20923 (OF), pp. 20904-20905 (E).

[178] Testimony of Mr. Béliveau, Transcripts vol. 113, pp. 20923-20925 (OF), pp. 20905-20907 (E).

[179] Testimony of Mr. Béliveau, Transcripts vol. 113, pp. 20925-20927 (OF), pp. 20907-20909 (E).

[180] Testimony of Mr. Béliveau, Transcripts vol. 113, pp. 20927-20931 (OF), pp. 20909-20912 (E).

181 Testimony of Mr. Béliveau, Transcripts vol. 113, pp. 20930-20942, 20946-20947 (OF), pp. 20912-20922, 20926-20927 (E).

182 Testimony of Mr. Béliveau, Transcripts vol. 114, pp. 21130-21133 (OF), pp. 21109-21112 (E).

183 Testimony of Mr. Béliveau, Transcripts vol. 113, pp. 20932-20942 (OF), pp. 20914-20922.

184 Testimony of Mr. Béliveau, Transcripts vol. 113, pp. 20942-20946 (OF), pp. 20922-20926 (E).

185 Testimony of Mr. Béliveau, Transcripts vol. 113, pp. 20943-20945 (OF), pp. 20922-20925 (E); vol. 114, pp. 21095-21097 (OF), pp. 21077-21079 (E).

186 Testimony of Mr. Béliveau, Transcripts vol. 113, pp. 20944-20945 (OF), pp. 20923-20925 (E); vol. 114, pp. 20959-20960 (OF), pp. 20959-20960 (E).

187 Testimony of Mr. Béliveau, Transcripts vol. 113, pp. 20951-20952 (OF), pp. 20930-20931 (E).

188 Testimony of Mr. Béliveau, Transcripts vol. 113, pp. 20948-20951 (OF), pp. 20928-20930 (E).

189 Testimony of Mr. Béliveau, Transcripts vol. 113, pp. 20925-20926, 20930-20931 (OF), pp. 20907-20908, 20911-20913 (E).

190 Testimony of Mr. Béliveau, Transcripts vol. 113, pp. 20952-20953 (OF), pp. 20931-20932 (E).

191 Testimony of Mr. Béliveau, Transcripts vol. 114, pp. 21125-21128 (OF), pp. 21105-21108 (E).

192 Testimony of Mr. Corbeil, Transcripts vol. 115, pp. 21199-21201 (OF), pp. 21192-21194 (E).

193 Testimony of Mr. Corbeil, Transcripts vol. 115, pp. 21194-21199 (OF), pp. 21187-21192 (E).

194 Testimony of Mr. Corbeil, Transcripts vol. 115, pp. 21197-21198, 21202-21203 (OF), pp. 21191, 21195-21196 (E).

195 Testimony of Mr. Côté, Transcripts vol. 116, pp. 21610-21611 (OF), pp. 21595-21596 (E).

196 Testimony of Mr. Côté, Transcripts vol. 116, pp. 21623-21628 (OF), pp. 21605-21610 (E).

197 Testimony of Mr. Côté, Transcripts vol. 116, pp. 21627-21628 (OF), pp. 21609-21610 (E).

198 Testimony of Mr. Côté, Transcripts vol. 116, pp. 21629-21630, 21682-21683 (OF), pp. 21611-21612, 21660 (E).

199 Testimony of Mr. Côté, Transcripts vol. 116, pp. 21679-21684 (OF), pp. 21656-21660 (E).

200 Testimony of Mr. Côté, Transcripts vol. 116, pp. 21632-21633 (OF), pp. 21613-21614 (E).

201 Testimony of Mr. Côté, Transcripts vol. 116, pp. 21633-21634, 21678 (OF), pp. 21614-21615, 21655 (E).

202 Testimony of Mr. Côté, Transcripts vol. 116, p. 21515 (OF), pp. 21507-21508 (E).

203 Testimony of Mr. Corriveau, Transcripts vol. 128, pp. 24263-24264 (OF), pp. 24259-24260 (E).

204 Testimony of Mr. Corriveau, Transcripts vol. 128, pp. 24264-24271 (OF), pp. 24259-24266 (E).

205 Exhibit P-332, p. 211.

206 Exhibit P-322(B), p. 445.

207 Exhibit P-322(B), p. 445.

208 Testimony of Mr. Corriveau, Transcripts vol. 100, pp. 18011-18016 (OF), pp. 17997-17801 (E); Exhibit P-322(B), pp. 446-450.

209 Exhibit P-249; Exhibit P-322(B), pp. 445-450.

210 Exhibit P-249; Exhibit P-322(B), pp. 446-450.

211 Testimony of Mr. Corriveau, Transcripts vol. 100, pp. 18015-18017 (OF), pp. 18000-18002 (E).

212 Exhibit P-249; Exhibit P-322(B), p. 450.

213 Testimony of Mr. Corriveau, Transcripts vol. 100, pp. 18019-18021 (OF), pp. 18004-18005 (E).

[214] Exhibit P-249; Exhibit P-322(B), p. 449.

[215] Exhibit P-322(B), p. 445.

[216] Testimony of Mr. Corriveau, Transcripts vol. 100, pp. 18020-18021 (OF), p. 18005 (E).

[217] Exhibit P-322(B), p. 445.

[218] Testimony of Mr. Éric Lafleur, Transcripts vol. 81, pp. 14268-14269, 14273-14275, 14284-14290 (OF), pp. 14268-14269, 14272-14274, 14282-14288 (E).

[219] Testimony of Mr. Éric Lafleur, Transcripts vol. 81, pp. 14282, 14290 (OF), pp. 14280, 14287 (E).

[220] Exhibit P-322(B), pp. 452-456.

[221] Testimony of Mr. Davidson, Transcripts vol. 79, pp. 13958-13959 (OF), 13944-13946 (E).

[222] Testimony of Mr. Corriveau, Transcripts vol. 129 (revised), pp. 24341-24345, 24351 (OF), pp. 24336-24341, 24346 (E); Exhibit P-332, p. 211.

[223] Testimony of Mr. Corriveau, Transcripts vol. 128, pp. 24264, 24271, 24273 (OF), pp. 24259, 24266-24267 (E).

[224] Testimony of Mr. Corbeil, Transcripts vol. 115, pp. 21199-21201 (OF), pp. 21192-21194 (E).

[225] Testimony of Mr. Corbeil, Transcripts vols. 115 and 116.

[226] Testimony of Mr. Corbeil, Transcripts vol. 115, pp. 21364-21373 (OF), pp. 21341-21351 (E).

[227] Testimony of Mr. Corbeil, Transcripts vol. 115, pp. 21252-21254 (OF), pp. 21241-21243 (E).

[228] Exhibit C-293(A), pp. 184, 192.

[229] Testimony of Mr. Corbeil, Transcripts vol. 115, p. 21271 (OF), p. 21258 (E); vol. 116, pp. 21453-21454 (OF), p. 21452 (E).

[230] Testimony of Mr. Corbeil, Transcripts vol. 116, p. 21508 (OF), p. 21501 (E).

[231] Testimony of Mr. Corbeil, Transcripts vol. 116, p. 21545 (OF), p. 21535 (E).

[232] Testimony of Mr. Corbeil, Transcripts vol. 116, pp. 21473-21477, 21543-21546 (OF), pp. 21469-21473, 21533-21536 (E).

[233] Testimony of Mr. Corbeil, Transcripts vol. 115, pp. 21272-21276 (OF), pp. 21259-21265 (E).

[234] Testimony of Mr. Corbeil, Transcripts vol. 115, pp. 21239-21243 (OF), pp. 21229-21233 (E).

[235] Testimony of Mr. Brault, Transcripts vol. 89, pp. 15869-15873 (OF), pp. 15854-15859 (E); Exhibit C-299, pp. 2-3.

[236] Testimony of Mr. Corbeil, Transcripts vol. 115, pp. 21281-21285 (OF), pp. 21267-21271 (E).

[237] Testimony of Mr. Dezainde, Transcripts vol. 117, pp. 21895-21899 (OF), pp. 21873-21877 (E).

[238] Testimony of Mr. Corbeil, Transcripts vol. 115, pp. 21363-21364 (OF), pp. 21342-21343 (E).

[239] Testimony of Mr. Brault, Transcripts vol. 89, pp. 15752-15753 (OF), pp. 15748-15749 (E); vol. 92, pp. 16335-16337 (OF), pp. 16324-16326 (E).

[240] Testimony of Mr. Welch, Transcripts vol. 119, pp. 22387-22389 (OE), pp. 22398-22400 (F).

[241] Testimony of Mr. Corbeil, Transcripts vol. 116, pp. 21517-21518 (OF), pp. 21509-21510 (E).

[242] Testimony of Mr. Dezainde, Transcripts vol. 117, pp. 21764-21770 (OF), pp. 21757-21763 (E).

[243] Exhibit P-397, pp. 23-25.

[244] Testimony of Mr. Corbeil, Transcripts vol. 115, pp. 21266-21273 (OF), pp. 21253-21260 (E); Exhibit P-397, pp. 15, 55.

CHAPTER XI

JEAN LAFLEUR

11.1
Introduction

For the years from 1984 until he sold the business to Groupaction in January 2001,[1] Jean Lafleur was the sole shareholder, director and president of Jean Lafleur Communication Marketing Inc. (hereafter Lafleur Communication) and its affiliates.[2]

On June 30, 1995 Lafleur Communication, as the lead member of a consortium of communication agencies taking part in a competition,[3] was declared qualified with the other members of the consortium to receive advertising contracts from PWGSC.[4] It handled a number of events and projects during the 1995-96 fiscal year,[5] such as the Montreal Grand Prix, the government publicity at home games played by the Montreal Expos, and the purchase of a large number of Canadian flags. These were not called sponsorships, but rather "special programs"[6] designed to enhance the federal government's visibility. We should remember that the Sponsorship Program only came into being in the spring of 1996.

With the birth of the Sponsorship Program in the 1996-97 fiscal year, Lafleur Communication received an avalanche of sponsorship contracts, having a total value of $16,362,872.[7] In that year, only one other agency, Vickers & Benson, received a sponsorship contract, and that was for the very special China series[8] (discussed in Chapter VI). When other agencies became qualified on April 28, 1997 to receive sponsorship contracts,[9] Lafleur Communication saw the number and value of its sponsorship contracts diminish, but it continued to receive a substantial proportion of the total.[10] By the time the Program came to an end in 2003, it had handled on the Government's behalf contracts having a total value of $65,464,314.[11]

Out of this amount, Lafleur Communication received as agency commissions $3,556,146 and the astounding total of $28,451,038 as production costs and fees.[12] In other words, in the process of paying to promoters of various events and projects a little more than $26 million, PWGSC paid to Lafleur Communication more than $36.5 million in agency commissions, fees and costs.[13] No other agency charged PWGSC anything quite like this in terms of production costs and fees, as a proportion of the total amount disbursed.

Mr. Lafleur was questioned at length concerning his involvement in the Sponsorship Program and the administration of contracts by his agency. I judged him to be evasive throughout his testimony. He says that he can recall very few details of most of the subjects of interest to the Commission, and I was forced to conclude at an early stage of his testimony that he was a witness determined to disclose as little useful information as possible. He left me with the impression that he had come to fear that a full and frank disclosure of what he knew would result in unpalatable consequences for himself and the members of his family, all of whom were on the Lafleur Communication payroll.[14] It is impossible to accept that an intelligent businessman such as Mr. Lafleur would be unable to remember, either with precision or in a general manner, such important facts as the content of the discussions he must have had with Mr. Guité prior to signing the contracts awarded to his agency in the spring of 1996.[15] Mr. Lafleur says that he is not only unable to remember the content of these discussions, but he cannot recall if any discussions at all occurred, although he presumes that they did.[16] Questioned about the meetings he must have had with Mr. Guité, he replies as follows:

[Unofficial Translation]

> I am trying to clarify things for the Commission by saying it's possible and highly probable that there were meetings, that there were exchanges of information, that there were meetings at my office, at Mr. Guité's office, that lists were probably provided. But I'm sorry, I don't have the memory today to be able to tell you what happened ten years ago.[17]

Obviously there must have been meetings and discussions with Mr. Guité in 1996 prior to the signature of contracts involving the expenditure by PWGSC of more than $16 million dollars, and the receipt by Lafleur Communication of millions of dollars in fees and commissions. Mr. Lafleur's complete absence of memory about these dealings with Mr. Guité is nicely contrasted with his testimony that Mr. Guité gave him permission to subcontract without obtaining bids.[18] (Mr. Guité said, "Order them, it's urgent, it's a rush." Mr. Guité also said, "Don't bother with paperwork. Go ahead. Organize yourselves so that it works. I want results.")[19] When this was compared to his claims that he could not remember any of the details of how he came to be awarded contracts by Mr. Guité or of their prior discussions, it was obvious that the Commission was hearing a witness who was prepared to appear to be slow-witted rather than to give truthful answers.

On May 29, 1996, Mr. Lafleur's son Éric sent a fax message to Andrée LaRose,[20] attaching detailed lists of the sponsorship contracts which Lafleur Communication was already handling for PWGSC, and the events which it expected to handle in 1996 that were not yet the subject of a government contract. The lists are very detailed and include the amounts of commissions and production costs which Lafleur Communication anticipated it would receive.[21] Although Mr. Lafleur and Éric agree that only the father had authority to conclude and sign contracts with PWGSC,[22] Jean Lafleur professes to have no recollection of the list or of how it might have come to be prepared.[23] Éric has a better memory, and testifies that the list was prepared following meetings and discussions between Mr. Lafleur and Mr. Guité, and that he sent the list to Ms. LaRose at the request of his father.[24] Mr. Lafleur's inability to remember anything about this cannot possibly be explained by a faulty memory. The benefit of the doubt and the presumption of good faith that are usually granted to a witness who says that he or she is unable to remember certain facts do not apply to Mr. Lafleur.

To sum up, Mr. Lafleur did not impress me as a credible witness.

II.2
Culture of Entitlement

Mr. Lafleur obviously believes that entertaining lavishly is good for business. Throughout the Sponsorship Program Lafleur Communication spent what must have been a lot of money on business promotion, buying tickets for its clients for hockey games and other sporting events, entertaining them on these occasions and at the Grand Prix, paying for salmon fishing excursions to the Gaspé Peninsula[25] and picking up the tab at lunch or dinner.[26] Mr. Lafleur was known as a host who entertained sumptuously, either at his home in St-Adolphe-d'Howard[27] or at the better restaurants in Montreal and Ottawa. It may safely be assumed that he thought that these expenses were useful and would pay dividends.

Of course there are few limits on what can be spent to solicit private sector clients—although deductions from income are limited by tax law and policy —but it is highly improper and indeed unethical to entertain politicians and public servants involved in the procurement of goods and services from the person or persons doing the entertaining. It is discouraging to note that no one appears to have questioned the propriety of receiving favours from Mr. Lafleur. He was generous with everybody involved in the administration of the Sponsorship Program, starting with Mr. Guité and the public servants working under him, and including persons at the political level who were participating in making decisions about which promoters would receive sponsorships, and who would handle the contracts, such as Jean Pelletier and Jean Carle. He cultivated his friendships with the political establishment at Lafleur Communication's loge at the Bell Centre in Montreal, to which were invited Messrs. Pelletier,[28] Carle,[29] Gagliano,[30] Coderre[31] and Cauchon,[32] and officers of Crown Corporations such as Messrs. Ouellet[33] and LeFrançois.[34]

Some of these same persons were members of an informal "club des cigares" (cigar club) and would meet a few times a year to eat, smoke cigars and talk.[35] Mr. Lafleur was the only representative of an advertising agency to attend meetings of the "club."[36]

Other politicians less directly involved in the Sponsorship Program did not hesitate to accept Mr. Lafleur's hospitality. There was, throughout the period when sponsorship funds were being freely handed out by PWGSC, a sort of culture of entitlement according to which persons enjoying Mr. Lafleur's largesse apparently did not feel that there was anything wrong in being entertained by someone who was receiving, and hoped to continue to receive, obviously lucrative federal contracts.

11.3
Political Contributions

Lafleur Communication was a generous and regular contributor to the Liberal Party. It made donations of $8,000, $14,400, $28,800 and $15,250 in the years 1997, 1998, 1999 and 2000, respectively.[37] Jean Lafleur made additional personal gifts, as did his son Éric.

Mr. Lafleur says that he does not remember asking his employees to make donations to the election campaign of Yolande Thibault, a Liberal candidate in St-Lambert in the 1997 election.[38] However, three of his employees, Pierre Michaud,[39] Pierre Davidson[40] and Stéphane Guertin,[41] say they were asked by him to contribute, and did so, to the tune of $1,000 each. Two of them[42] were reimbursed by Lafleur Communication for these contributions.

Mr. Lafleur acknowledges that at the request of Mr. Morselli and Mr. Corbeil, he also lent his efforts to the sale of tickets to Liberal Party fundraising events, such as golf tournaments and cocktail parties.[43] He remembers in particular being involved in the financing of the annual golf tournament in Mr. Gagliano's riding.[44] Curiously, although Mr. Morselli remembers the fundraising assistance of Mr. Lafleur,[45] Mr. Corbeil says that he does not, but recalls that Mr. Lafleur attended one meeting of the finance committee of the LPCQ.[46]

It may be concluded that Mr. Lafleur, by his contributions to the Liberal Party of Canada and his active participation in its activities, wished to ingratiate himself with its inner circle. Judging from the sponsorship contracts allocated to him starting in 1996, to the extent they were influenced by political considerations, he succeeded.

II.4
Relationship with Jean Pelletier

Because of the important role that Jean Pelletier, the Prime Minister's Chief of Staff, played in the initiation and management of the Sponsorship Program, both he and Mr. Lafleur were questioned about their relationship and were asked specific questions about when they met for the first time. Their answers to these questions cannot be reconciled, and it must be concluded that at least one of them has not been truthful.

Mr. Pelletier testifies that the first meeting he had with Mr. Lafleur was on the occasion when the latter came to the PMO to thank him for hiring his son Éric Lafleur, who had been engaged by the PMO to take part in a trade mission to South America[47]. He explains that Éric Lafleur had asked Jean Carle to allow him to participate in the trade mission, and was prepared to pay his own way, but Mr. Pelletier preferred that he be given a contract of employment.[48] It is fair to conclude that Mr. Pelletier, even if he had not yet met Éric's father, knew that the latter was doing business with the Government, and wished to avoid any appearance of impropriety. Documents show that the trade mission took place in January 1998,[49] so his first encounter with Mr. Lafleur, according to Mr. Pelletier's testimony, must have been around that time.

Mr. Lafleur was extremely careful when testifying not to commit himself to any fact or detail such as meetings or dates, unless he could remember them "precisely" or if he was confronted with the fact or detail in the documentary evidence. Nonetheless, he testifies that in the summer or autumn of 1997,[50] he invited Mr. Pelletier to have the first of several meals they would share over the years. He is specific in testifying that this first meal took place before their meeting in the PMO, at which he thanked Mr. Pelletier for hiring Éric.[51] He insists that at their meal they did not discuss the Sponsorship Program[52] in any detail, but in answer to another question, he says that they may have had a general discussion on the topic.[53] Later still he testifies that he does not remember discussing the Program with Mr. Pelletier at their meals.[54] Mr. Pelletier also denies having discussed advertising and sponsorships with Mr. Lafleur.[55]

The evidence leaves two possibilities. The first is that the two had no meal together in 1997, as Mr. Pelletier says. I am not prepared to give serious consideration to this possibility since it is most unlikely that Mr. Lafleur, with his selective memory lapses, would pretend to recollect a meeting which did not in fact occur. This leaves me with the intriguing question of why Mr. Pelletier would prefer not to recall a meal with Mr. Lafleur if nothing compromising was discussed by them. The second possibility is that they indeed met for a meal and discussed the Sponsorship Program in general, but not in any detail. We can safely disregard Mr. Lafleur when he contradicts himself and says he cannot remember whether or not they discussed the Program.

Mr. Lafleur says that the conversations he had at this and subsequent meals with Mr. Pelletier were generally about politics, federalism and current events; that they discussed nothing in particular.[56] However, Mr. Pelletier describes himself as an exceedingly busy man, working very long hours.[57] It is highly improbable that in the summer or fall of 1997 he had time for meals with a virtual stranger for no purpose other than to have a pleasant conversation about nothing in particular other than the political situation in Quebec. It is even more improbable that these two persons would not have talked about the Sponsorship Program, considering that it had suddenly become by far the most important source of businesss for Mr. Lafleur's agency, which, as always, paid for the meal.[58]

The testimony of Mr. Lafleur must also be considered in the light of a memorandum he sent to Mr. Pelletier on June 11, 1998.[59] Mr. Pelletier testifies that prior to that date the two men met by chance on an Ottawa street and that Mr. Lafleur used the encounter to bemoan the fact that the volume of sponsorship contracts he was receiving from PWGSC had diminished sharply, asking Mr. Pelletier if he would do something about it. Mr. Pelletier did not say No to the request, and says that he suggested that Mr. Lafleur send him details of the problem in writing.[60] The memorandum arrived a few days later. Mr. Lafleur essentially confirms this testimony about their chance encounter and the reason why he wrote to Mr. Pelletier.[61]

It includes a very detailed list of the sponsorship contracts, totalling more than $12 million, awarded to Lafleur Communication in the 1997-98 fiscal year, and the contracts awarded to date in the current year of 1998-99, which amount to only $2,532,200. Those two lists are reproduced in Figure XI-1. Added to the lists of past and current contracts are lists of other projects and events that had been proposed, presumably by Lafleur Communication, for the current year, and several pages of written material indicating how desirable they would be from the point of view of the visibility they would give to the federal government. The last page is another list of proposed projects, describing their advantages.

Nothing resulted from this communication. Mr. Pelletier did not act upon it,[62] and no additional sponsorship contracts can be shown to have been awarded to Lafleur Communication as a result of it. However, the mere fact that it was sent establishes that in the opinion of Mr. Lafleur, Mr. Pelletier was a central figure making decisions about which events to sponsor, and that he was a good person to speak to on the question of which agency would receive sponsorship contracts. Mr. Lafleur did not direct his plea for more business or send the memo to Mr. Guité or to Mr. Gagliano. It is fair to conclude that he had formed his opinion on the basis of his past contacts with Mr. Pelletier, which were, according to both men, limited to their lunches together. From all of this the conclusion is inescapable that at their lunches they discussed, in much more than a general way, the Sponsorship Program.

Figure XI-1: Memo to Jean Pelletier—Lafleur sponsorship contracts.

PROJETS RÉALISÉS PAR LAFLEUR POUR TPSGC
L'ANNÉE DERNIÈRE
Année fiscale 1er avril 1997 au 31 mars 1998.

DOSSIERS	MONTANT TOTAL
Aboriginal Day Toronto	235 750,00
Bluenose Tour Ontario, Québec et Atlantic	2 300 000,00
Concours équestre de Blainville	125 000,00
Concours hippique de Québec	71 500,00
Emission Bluenose	245 836,00
Expo 2005 Calgary	292 500,00
Expos de Montréal	1 223 760,00
F1 Montréal	649 750,00
Jeux du Québec – Montréal	769 000,00
Mardis Cyclistes de Lachine	101 500,00
Maurice Richard – Film et statue	235 000,00
Meligarde & Capitales	300 000,00
Molson Indy Toronto	496 358,00
Molson Indy Vancouver	354 647,00
Musée Grande Cascapédia	235 660,00
Promotion Items	680 000,00
Promotion Via Étudiants	656 450,00
Rafales de Québec	231 000,00
Série du Siècle	310 000,00
Internationaux de Tennis Junior du Canada	93 000,00
Centre interprétation Saumon – Causapscal	35 500,00
Promotion Golf	12 500,00
Bell Canadian Open TV	35 500,00
Unityfest	17 750,00
Festival des couleurs de St-Donat	12 000,00
Club Aviron Montréal	19 250,00
Il Citadino	59 000,00
Golf Maladies infantiles	17 750,00
Souper bénéfice GRC	17 750,00
Budget développement Tour Canada	41 500,00
Promotion Groupes ethniques	71 250,00
Promotion philatélique écoles Canada	82 250,00
Via Canada "On Board Promotion"	79 500,00
Festival de Jazz et Festival Juste pour rire	76 750,00
Train de l'Espace	74 000,00
Expos de Mtl - Caravane	54 750,00
Canadiens de Montréal	345 000,00
Promotion Vite sur tes patins – Canadiens	240 000,00
Magazine Publicité	373 750,00
125e GRC	170 000,00
Items promotionnels	367 500,00
Concours équestres	46 000,00
Expos & Blue Jays	68 000,00
Promotion Mont-Tremblant	68 750,00
Causapscal	29 000,00
Photographie italienne	6 000,00
Promotion Canadiens-Toronto	100 000,00
TOTAL	12 127 711,00

PROJETS EN COURS EN DATE DU 10 JUIN 1998
(Année fiscale du 1er avril 1998 au 31 mars 1999)

Canadien de Montréal	297 200$
Promotion & Logo Canada – Via	500 000$
Hockey Amateur	10 000$
Commandite Dîner Saumon – Timbre	36 250$
Internationaux de Tennis Junior du Canada	59 750$
125e Anniversaire GRC	1 120 000$
Publicité Magazine Via	500 000$
Télésérie – Le Millénaire	10 000$
TOTAL :	**2 532 200$**

PROJETS EN COURS A PAREILLE DATE L'ANNÉE DERNIÈRE (2 juin 1997)	**8 328 711$**
ÉCART NÉGATIF À CE JOUR	**(5 796 511$)**

11.5
The Lafleur Invoices

Mr. Lafleur and several Lafleur Communication employees (Éric Lafleur, Pierre Michaud, Pierre Davidson and Stéphane Guertin) were examined at the Commission's hearings regarding their administration of several sponsorship contracts handled by the Lafleur agency and the resulting invoices sent to PWGSC. Many of the invoices needed a lot of explaining, and the explanations were not always satisfactory. As the evidence accumulated, it established that there had been repeated instances of irregularities and overcharging, although according to the evidence no invoice was ever challenged or questioned by the personnel at PWGSC.

Taken as a whole, it is possible to identify at least eight categories of consistent overbilling by Lafleur Communication:

1. There was no clear idea, even among the officers and employees of Lafleur Communication, of what agency services were covered by the 12% commission, and what work could be invoiced as production costs and fees.[63] This made it possible for the Lafleur agency, in almost every case, to invoice all of the recorded time worked on a contract as production costs, with the result that the commission of 12% was paid to and received by the company in consideration for nothing more than opening the file. When Mr. Lafleur was questioned about this, he took the position that if the contract authorized him to receive a commission, he was legally entitled to it even if no services were rendered in exchange.[64] The problem would have been avoided if PWGSC had provided to the agencies handling sponsorship contracts a clear definition of those services for which the 12% commission would be paid.

2. Mock-ups ("maquettes") were billed by Lafleur Communication at a flat rate of $2,750 each. Mr. Lafleur testifies that the flat rate was in accordance with industry standards and a verbal agreement he reached with Mr. Guité, and represented an approximate average cost for the preparation of a mock-up.[65] However, his own employee, Pierre

Michaud, expresses the opinion that the approximate cost for the company to produce a mock-up was between $275 and $300.[66] Gaëtan Sauriol, who worked as a graphic technician for PluriDesign and prepared a number of mock-ups, testifies that the cost of producing one varies enormously, depending upon the complexity of the project.[67] The Commission concludes that the billing of all mock-ups at $2,750 each constituted blatant overcharging.

3. In many instances, hours of work attributed to Mr. Lafleur were charged on projects where he had little or nothing to do. Generally his functions were limited to meetings with Mr. Guité to secure contracts from PWGSC, for which he should not have been charging, and overseeing the work of others, including those in the accounting department of Lafleur Communication who prepared the bills.[68] His son Éric, asked to explain 78 hours billed for his father's work on the Expos file, admitted that he could not explain them and that the number of hours seemed high.[69] He was also surprised to see that his father had charged 27 hours for work on the production of promotional items, which was a file Éric looked after without his father's participation.[70] Supervisory work would, in almost anybody's interpretation of what should usually be covered by the 12% commission, not be treated as production costs.

4. The charges for hours worked were sometimes billed at a higher rate than the work justified. One particularly outrageous example occurred when 29 hours of work devoted by Éric Lafleur to packaging and shipping promotional items was billed to PWGSC at the rate of $245 an hour, a fee normally applied to an account director.[71] Packaging and shipping work could better be put in the category of clerical work, to be billed at $40 an hour.

5. It was shown that the amount foreseen in the contract as an allowance for production costs was almost invariably billed in full to PWGSC, although the allowance fixed at the time the contract was negotiated with PWGSC[72] could only predict in an approximate way what the actual production costs would be. The Commission is left with the

impression that even when the work was less time-consuming than had been originally foreseen, the invoice would be adjusted upwards.

6. There were inexplicable variations in the hours billed for the same event when it was sponsored for more than one year.[73] It is reasonable to presume that to provide the Government with equivalent visibility in the second year, Lafleur Communication employees would be required to spend fewer hours to work out and execute the visibility plan (assuming that there was one), even considering that there may have been variations in the project from year to year. For example, a sponsorship of $536,800 paid to the Montreal Expos in 1995 was renewed for the same amount in 1996, but the number of hours of work of the Lafleur agency employees on the contract increased from 234 to 1,105 in 1996.[74] Even taking into account special promotions that occurred in 1996,[75] the increase in the number of hours charged to PWGSC cannot be justified. Sample invoices of this nature are reproduced in Figure VI-2.

7. Three persons who were on the books of Lafleur Communication as employees, Pierre Davidson, Daniel Lévesque and Stéphane Guertin, considered themselves independent contractors and had formed their own companies, which billed the Lafleur agency for the work they performed.[76] (Mr. Guertin later became a Lafleur Communication employee.)[77] The accounts they sent the Lafleur agency were in turn billed to PWGSC.[78] Where they billed for their time, Lafleur Communication rebilled that time at a rate that greatly exceeded what the agency had paid. Where they billed a flat rate for work done, Lafleur Communication billed for production, plus a percentage markup. If this were not bad enough, Lafleur Communication also billed for that person's hours as if he were an employee, again at a much higher rate.[79] The net result was that PWGSC was charged twice for the same work, sometimes at exaggerated rates, and also paid unearned markups on the so-called subcontracts.

8. Work was subcontracted by Lafleur Communication without competitive bids as required by the conditions of the standard PWGSC contract. The most flagrant examples of this were subcontracts given by the Lafleur agency to Éric Lafleur's company, Publicité Dezert,[80] which for a time operated out of the same premises as Lafleur Communication.[81] Jean Lafleur justified this practice by asking for Mr. Guité's approval of an exemption from the contract condition, on the grounds of time constraints and an alleged urgency in having the contract completed.[82] There was in fact no real urgency. The participation of Messrs. Lafleur and Guité in this stratagem to get around the intent of the Government's Contracting Policy cannot be excused. The Commission heard no evidence that PWGSC saved any money or time, or gained any expertise, when Lafleur Communication subcontracted sponsorship work to Publicité Dezert. As an employee of Lafleur Communication, Éric Lafleur, its vice-president,[83] could just as easily have done this work directly for Lafleur Communication rather than by subcontracting it to his own firm. The transparent purpose of the subcontract was twofold: it permitted Publicité Dezert to charge Lafleur Communication a markup on the price it paid to obtain the goods or services it procured from others,[84] and it permitted Lafleur Communication to charge a commission of 17.65% on the amount of the Publicité Dezert invoice. These two surcharges were in addition to the cost to PWGSC of having the subcontract given to a related company without competitive bidding. The effect of all of this was the payment by PWGSC of vastly greater amounts than would have been paid otherwise for the same goods and services.

From the many sponsorship contracts which were the subject of evidence presented to the Commission in the course of the hearings, three will be examined as examples of the abuses, mismanagement and overcharging described in general terms in the preceding paragraphs.

11.6
RCMP Anniversary Celebration

Mr. Lafleur solicited and obtained from Mr. Guité a sponsorship of $500,000 to assist the Quebec Division of the RCMP in celebrating its 125th anniversary. This amount was employed in various ways, two of which will be examined in some detail.

The RCMP planned to hold a regimental ball in Montreal as part of the anniversary activities. Originally it had expected that this event would be self-financed by the sale of tickets and beverages.[85] Nevertheless, Lafleur Communication set to work to assist the RCMP in planning this activity, and gave a subcontract to Xylo Concept Graphique Inc., the company owned and operated by its sometime employee Pierre Davidson, to prepare a report on where the ball should take place.[86] Mr. Davidson, at the suggestion of Mr. Lafleur, engaged Mr. Corriveau of PluriDesign to work on this project.[87] Mr. Corriveau looked at three possible locations: a tent at the Old Port, Windsor Station and Bonsecours Market. He came to the conclusion that the Windsor Station location was preferable.[88] He testifies that to come to this conclusion, he had to make studies of all three locations and to map out how the spaces would be best used and decorated, and then prepare a report.[89] For this work, on December 3, 1997, PluriDesign billed Xylo $35,000 plus taxes.[90]

No matter how carefully Mr. Corriveau studied the three possibilities, $35,000 seems to be a very high price to pay for advice as to where a ball would best be held, but the story does not end there.

On December 8, 1997, Xylo billed Lafleur Communication $41,500 for the same work, although the invoice refers to a fourth possible location at the Marriott Château Champlain.[91] In effect, Mr. Davidson added $6,500 to the PluriDesign bill. He testifies that this charge was for his "co-ordination" of the project.[92] On April 15, 1998, Xylo sent a supplementary bill to Lafleur Communication for $6,000 for additional work such as designing the layout of the space at Windsor Station, and preparing sketches.[93]

Of course the RCMP did not see any of this money, but it is fair to assume they were assisted in planning the ball by the advice and plans prepared for them at taxpayers' expense by PluriDesign and Xylo. We do not know precisely how Lafleur Communication recovered from PWGSC the amounts it paid to Xylo, or the amount paid by Xylo to PluriDesign, because none of the invoices sent to PWGSC which have turned up in its files refer to the subcontracts or the amounts paid to subcontractors.[94]

Five invoices sent by Lafleur Communication to PWGSC refer to the RCMP anniversary project.[95] They are dated March 5, April 1, July 1, September 17 and December 15, 1998. They total, without taxes, $469,845, of which $88,000 is for 32 mock-ups at $2,750 each. The remainder is for time recorded by different Lafleur Communication employees, some of whom testified about the work they performed on the RCMP file. The testimony of Mr. Davidson is particularly revealing.

Mr. Davidson testifies that the only work he performed in the RCMP file had to do with the selection of the site for the regimental ball, which was essentially subcontracted to PluriDesign, and the design of various promotional items that were distributed by the RCMP as part of its anniversary activities.[96] These designs, together with the plans for the regimental ball locations, are probably the basis of the charge for mock-ups. Mr. Davidson does not believe that any other Lafleur Communication employee or subcontractor produced mock-ups related to the RCMP file.[97] He adds that all of his time and charges for his work in the file were billed to Lafleur Communication by Xylo in the two accounts already referred to and an additional account dated March 24, 1998, for $28,070 plus taxes.[98] He says categorically that he worked on the file only as an employee of Xylo, for which he was compensated by Xylo's accounts to Lafleur Communication, and that he did not record time as an employee of Lafleur Communication in connection with the RCMP file.[99]

For this reason, Mr. Davidson was surprised to learn about charges that appear on the Lafleur Communication invoices to PWGSC for hours worked by P. Davidson, described in the invoice as a "creative director."[100] On the first three invoices PWGSC is charged for 115 hours,[101] 240 hours[102] and 119.5 hours[103] of Mr. Davidson's time, billed at the rate of $180 per hour, amounting to a total of $85,410. As far as Mr. Davidson is concerned, no part of this amount is justified.[104]

It is possible that Lafleur Communication, which as already noted does not show any amounts paid to subcontractors on its invoices, intended to mask such payments by billing as it did, and that Xylo's three accounts to Lafleur Communication, which total $75,570[105] plus taxes, are buried within the $85,410 of hourly charges on its invoices. If this is so, questions remain as to why it was considered necessary to falsify Lafleur Communication invoices in this way, and for what reason Xylo's accounts give rise to a markup of approximately $10,000. Whatever answers to these questions might be given, the least that can be said is that the Lafleur Communication invoices are false, misleading and excessive.

11.7
Encyclopédie du Canada 2000

Since late 1997, Les Éditions Alain Stanké had been looking for financial assistance to enable it to complete the publication and printing of 15,000 copies of the *Encyclopédie du Canada 2000*, to be distributed free of charge to schools across Canada.[106] The project was enthusiastically supported by a Liberal Senator,[107] and on September 1, 1999, Mr. Tremblay confirmed to Mr. Lafleur that Lafleur Communication would be awarded a contract to manage the sponsorship of the project,[108] according to which Éditions Stanké would receive a sponsorship of $1.2 million.[109] The contract stipulates that the commission payable to Lafleur Communication for managing the contract would be 12% of that amount, or the sum of $144,000, and an additional sum of $36,000 would be paid to the Agency of Record, Média IDA/Vision.[110] Mr. Lafleur was unable to tell the Commission exactly what work his agency would be obliged to perform to earn its commission of $144,000.[111] On the face of it, no work was required, other than to assure PWGSC that the required visibility of Canada, in the form of an inscription on the jacket, cover and bookmark and in the preface, had been provided.

Nearly a year later, on August 22, 2000, a second contract was awarded to Lafleur Communication in connection with the same project.[112] This time the services expected of Lafleur Communication were specified; it would be paid $9 per copy, $135,000 in total, to see to the distribution of the 15,000 copies of the encyclopedia to Canadian schools, and would receive an additional $100,000 to pay for the printing cost of written material which would accompany each copy.[113] The sum of $100,000 was duly paid to Éditions Stanké, which looked after the printing part of the contract.[114] Mr. Guertin of Lafleur Communication was given responsibility for the other aspects of the file, working under the supervision of Éric Lafleur.

Most of the difficulties concerning this matter come from confusion surrounding the delivery of the encyclopedias. The publisher, Mr. Stanké, had hoped that distribution could be entrusted to a non-profit organization called Travail sans frontières, which gave employment to young persons attempting to gain entry to the labour market,[115] but Lafleur Communication did not seem interested in the economies that would result from such an arrangement, and instead had the encyclopedia delivered by Canada Post, at a cost of $43,185.40, to which Lafleur Communication added an agency commission of $7,622.22.[116] The total amount billed to PWGSC was $134,382.49,[117] coming within $1,000 of the amount estimated ($135,000) when the contract was awarded.[118] The difference between $134,382.49 and what was paid to Canada Post and for other disbursements was charged as fees for time spent on the file by Lafleur Communication employees. It is difficult to imagine that there is any justification for fees of more than $69,000 for what was a very simple project. Mr. Guertin's testimony did little to enlighten the Commission about the hours of work charged to the file. Compounding the problem, apparently no work or services by any employee was covered by the commission of $144,000. The Canadian taxpayer ended up compensating Lafleur Communication more than $213,000 for its services plus over $65,000 in disbursements for arranging the delivery of 15,000 encyclopedias.

To make matters worse, after paying to warehouse these volumes for a few months (the cost of storage was duly billed to PWGSC), the delivery was not successfully accomplished. Approximately 300 copies of the encyclopedia were not delivered for a variety of reasons, such as an incorrect address, a move by the addressee, or a refusal to accept delivery. Ultimately someone decided the books should be disposed of in a landfill site. No one is able or willing to say who made the decision.[119]

11.8
Grand Prix du Canada 1996

The Lafleur agency was chosen by PWGSC to manage the sponsorship of the Formula I race known as the Grand Prix du Canada in every year except 1998[120] when, for reasons that no one has been able to explain in a satisfactory manner, it was given to Groupaction. Mr. Guité proposes that it was appropriate from time to time to change agencies for important events; but if this was the true reason for the introduction of a new agency in 1998, the event should not have reverted to Lafleur Communication in 1999,[121] but should have been assigned to another agency altogether. Mr. Guité testifies that the agency change in 1998 was decided by the Minister's office.

Be that as it may, Lafleur Communication received the contract in 1996,[122] after having managed a similar contract in 1995[123] when the amount paid to the organizers of the Grand Prix was to entitle advertising by the Government at the event, rather than to enhance its visibility. The amount of the sponsorship payable to the promoter was fixed at $325,000,[124] compared to $300,000[125] in 1995, and the total amount to be disbursed by PWGSC, including the sponsorship payment and all agency fees and commissions, was fixed at a maximum of $536,000,[126] compared to $501,000[127] in the previous year.

Two invoices were sent by Lafleur Communication to PWGSC, on June 12[128] and 28, 1996,[129] for amounts of $110,280 and $425,703, respectively. They add up to $535,983,[130] which is exactly $17 less than the amount foreseen in the contract to be the maximum the Government would be called upon to disburse. Either PWGSC was extraordinarily accurate in its estimates, or this is an indication that the invoices sent by Lafleur Communication to

PWGSC were tailored to fit the fees and production costs allowed. Let us examine the invoices more closely to see which of these possibilities is the more probable.

The invoice of June 12 includes a charge of $68,750 for 25 mock-ups at $2,750 each.[131] No witness was able to explain what these mock-ups were for, or who prepared or designed them.[132] Usually the preparation of mock-ups was work done by Pierre Davidson, but he testifies that he does not remember working on the Grand Prix project in 1996, and that if he did, it would have only been to design the cover page of the activity report, which would not have necessitated more than 30 minutes of his time.[133] Éric Lafleur, who was in charge of the Grand Prix project in 1996 and other years, was unable to remember why so many mock-ups would have been necessary, saying that he agrees that 25 mock-ups seem to be a large number ("un nombre important de maquettes") (a significant number of mock-ups).[134]

The second amount charged in the June 12 invoice represents fees for nine employees of Lafleur Communication, charged at their respective hourly rates ranging from $275 per hour for Jean Lafleur to $40 per hour for clerical support. The charges, which represent hours worked in the period from April 9 to May 31, come to a total of $41,530.[135] The individual who worked the most hours in that period was, understandably enough, Éric Lafleur, whose hourly rate as "account director" was $245, which I consider to be an excessive rate for a young man who had been in the labour market for less than four years and had not yet completed his MBA.

The invoice of June 28 includes $325,000 for the amount of the sponsorship to be paid to the promoter, $39,000 for the agency commission of 12% of $325,000, $8 for delivery costs and $61,695 as fees for the time of Lafleur Communication employees during the period from June 3 to 28,[136] when the project had been completed. Of the last amount, the 102 hours of work on the file by Éric was the most important, accounting for $24,990. He testifies that the number of hours charged by other employees, such as Pierre Michaud and Philippe Mayrand, were surprisingly high.[137] Looking at both invoices together, they reveal that a total of 593.5 hours were billed to the client.[138]

Éric Lafleur himself, in charge of the project, considered that to be surprising.[139] The Commission shares his opinion.

If he had said that the hours charged to the file were surprisingly low, it might be possible to argue, as Jean Lafleur did when testifying about this and other invoices where the amount charged almost exactly corresponds to the maximum anticipated production costs, that his accounting staff might have actually reduced the recorded time charges to make them correspond to the production costs predicted.[140] What is more probable is that the hours were arbitrarily increased by someone when the account was prepared.

11.9
Financial Results

Sponsorship and advertising contracts awarded to Lafleur Communication by the Government of Canada had an enormous effect upon its revenues and the personal incomes of Mr. Lafleur and the members of his family who worked for the agency and Publicité Dezert.

In 1993 and 1994, before the sudden increase in government business occurred, Lafleur Communication had gross revenues of approximately $1 million per year,[141] of which less than 25% was distributed to its employees as salaries and bonuses.[142] Starting in 1995 its revenues zoomed upwards to a high of more than $22 million in 1996, decreasing slightly to $21 million in 1997.[143] In those same years Publicité Dezert had gross revenues, mostly due to subcontracts from Lafleur Communication, of $1.1 million and $3.4 million, respectively.[144]

Most of the net revenues earned by Lafleur Communication and Publicité Dezert were paid out to Mr. Lafleur and his wife and children in the form of salaries and bonuses.[145] These amounted to a total of more than $12 million for the taxation years from 1995 to 2000, inclusively, an average of about $2 million per year. In January 2001, Mr. Lafleur's holding company sold its shares in Lafleur Communication to a company controlled by Jean Brault for a price of not less than $1.1 million and not more than $3.2 million, depending upon the financial performance of the newly acquired subsidiary.[146]

All in all, it may be concluded that his cultivation of close relationships with certain members of the Liberal Party, combined with the contracts awarded to his agency as a result of the Sponsorship Program, contributed to what might be described as a financial bonanza for Jean Lafleur and his family.

Endnotes to Chapter XI

1   Exhibit P-215(A), pp. 21-57; Exhibit P-229, p.1.

2   Exhibit P-229, pp. 1-3; Exhibit P-215(A), p. 2.

3   Exhibit P-233, pp. 14, 17, 67.

4   Exhibit P-233, pp. 1-4, 10-12.

5   Exhibit P-216, pp. 5-9.

6   Exhibit P-65(B).

7   Exhibit P-216, pp. 2, 9-12.

8   Testimony of Mr. Guité, Transcripts vol. 33, pp. 5767-5768 (OE), pp. 5788-5789 (F); Exhibit P-112, tab 12.

9   Exhibit P-19, tab 41.

10 Exhibit P-216, p. 2; Exhibit P-428(A), p. 24.

11 Exhibit P-216, p. 2.

12 Exhibit P-216, p. 2.

13 Exhibit P-216, p. 2.

14 Exhibit P-216, pp. 106-107; Exhibit P-428(A), pp. 92-93.

15 Testimony of Mr. Jean Lafleur, Transcripts vol. 75, pp. 13157-13162 (OF), pp. 13145-13151(E).

16 Testimony of Mr. Jean Lafleur, Transcripts vol. 75, pp. 13157-13162 (OF), pp. 13145-13151 (E).

17 Testimony of Mr. Jean Lafleur, Transcripts vol. 75, p. 13134 (OF), pp. 13124-13125 (E).

18 Testimony of Mr. Jean Lafleur, Transcripts vol. 76, pp. 13258-13260 (OF), pp. 13257-13260 (E).

19 Testimony of Mr. Jean Lafleur, Transcripts vol. 76, pp. 13274-13276 (OF), p. 13263-13264 (E).

20 Exhibit P-106(A), tab 16.

21 Exhibit P-106(A), tab 16.

22 Testimony of Mr. Jean Lafleur, Transcripts vol. 75, pp. 13162-13164 (OF), p. 13150-13151 (E); Testimony of Mr. Éric Lafleur, Transcripts vol. 80, pp. 14076-14077, 14081-14082 (OF), pp. 14071-14073, 14074-14076 (E).

23 Testimony of Mr. Jean Lafleur, Transcripts vol. 75, pp. 13158-13165 (OF), pp. 13146-13153 (E).

24 Testimony of Mr. Éric Lafleur, Transcripts vol. 80, pp. 14076-14079 (OF), pp. 14071-14074 (E).

25 Testimony of Mr. Jean Lafleur, Transcripts vol. 75, pp. 13077-13078 (OF), pp. 13074-13076 (E).

26 Testimony of Mr. Jean Lafleur, Transcripts vol. 75, pp. 13072-13073 (OF), pp. 13070-13071 (E); Testimony of Mr. Jean Lafleur, Transcripts vol. 76, p. 13321 (OF), p. 13315 (E).

27 Testimony of Mr. Jean Lafleur, Transcripts vol. 75, pp. 13074-13075 (OF), pp. 13072-13074 (E).

28 Testimony of Mr. Pelletier, Transcripts vol. 71, pp. 12437-12438 (OF), pp. 12426-12427 (E); Exhibit P-202, pp. 41, 43.

29 Testimony of Mr. Carle, Transcripts vol. 70, pp. 12239-12240 (OF), pp. 12228-12229 (E); Exhibit P-202, pp. 41, 43; Testimony of Mr. Jean Lafleur, Transcripts vol. 79, p. 13809 (OF), pp. 13806-13807 (E).

30 Testimony of Mr. Gagliano, Transcripts vol. 68, pp. 11767-11768 (OF), pp. 11758-11759 (E); Exhibit P-202, pp. 41, 43; Testimony of Mr. Jean Lafleur, Transcripts vol. 79, p. 13808 (OF), pp. 13805-13806 (E).

31 Testimony of Mr. Jean Lafleur, Transcripts vol. 79, p. 13808 (OF), p. 13806 (E).

32 Testimony of Mr. Cauchon, Transcripts vol. 65, p. 11319 (OF), p. 11311 (E); Exhibit P-202, pp. 41, 43.

33 Testimony of Mr. Jean Lafleur, Transcripts vol. 79, p. 13809 (OF), pp. 13806-13807 (E); Exhibit P-202, p. 41.

34 Testimony of Mr. LeFrançois, Transcripts vol. 53, p. 9216 (OF), pp. 9205-9206 (E); Exhibit P-202, pp. 41, 43.

35 Testimony of Mr. Jean Lafleur, Transcripts vol. 75, pp. 13075-13076 (OF), pp. 13073-13074 (E).

36 Testimony of Mr. Jean Lafleur, Transcripts vol. 75, p. 13076 (OF), p. 13074 (E).

37 Exhibit P-428(D), p. 780.

38 Testimony of Mr. Jean Lafleur, Transcripts vol. 75, pp. 13238-13240 (OF), pp. 13219-13221 (E); vol. 79, pp. 13799-13802 (OF), pp. 13798-13801 (E).

39 Testimony of Mr. Michaud, Transcripts vol. 79, pp. 13895-13898 (OF), pp. 13886-13889 (E); Exhibit P-232(A), p. 2.

40 Testimony of Mr. Davidson, Transcripts vol. 79, pp. 13959-13962 (OF), pp. 13946-13949 (E); Exhibit P-232(A), p. 2; Exhibit P-243(A), p. 5.

41 Testimony of Mr. Guertin, Transcripts vol. 81, pp. 14421-14425 (OF), pp. 14408-14411 (E).

42 Testimony of Mr. Michaud, Transcripts vol. 79, pp. 13896-13897 (OF), p. 13888 (E); Testimony of Mr. Guertin, Transcripts vol. 81, p. 14423 (OF), pp. 14409-14410 (E).

43 Testimony of Mr. Jean Lafleur, Transcripts vol. 75, pp. 13086-13089 (OF), pp. 13082-13085 (E).

44 Testimony of Mr. Jean Lafleur, Transcripts vol. 75, p. 13086 (OF), pp. 13082-13083 (E).

45 Testimony of Mr. Morselli, Transcripts vol. 127, pp. 23878-23880 (OF), pp. 23875-23876 (E).

46 Testimony of Mr. Corbeil, Transcripts vol. 115, pp. 21396-21397 (OF), pp. 21371-21372 (E).

47 Testimony of Mr. Pelletier, Transcripts vol. 71, p. 12429 (OF), pp. 12418-12419 (E).

48 Testimony of Mr. Pelletier, Transcripts vol. 71, pp. 12429-12430 (OF), pp. 12418-12419 (E).

49 Exhibit P-247; Exhibit P-248.

50 Testimony of Mr. Jean Lafleur, Transcripts vol. 76, pp. 13317-13321 (OF), pp. 13310-13315 (E).

51 Testimony of Mr. Jean Lafleur, Transcripts vol. 76, pp. 13315-13316 (OF), p. 13309 (E).

52 Testimony of Mr. Jean Lafleur, Transcripts vol. 76, p. 13318 (OF), pp. 13311-13312 (E).

53 Testimony of Mr. Jean Lafleur, Transcripts vol. 76, p. 13319 (OF), pp. 13312-13313 (E).

54 Testimony of Mr. Jean Lafleur, Transcripts vol. 76, pp. 13319, 13322 (OF), pp. 13312-13313, 13315-13316 (E).

55 Testimony of Mr. Pelletier, Transcripts vol. 71, pp. 12436-12437 (OF), pp. 12425-12426 (E).

56 Testimony of Mr. Jean Lafleur, Transcripts vol. 76, pp. 13319-13320 (OF), pp. 13313-13314 (E).

57 Testimony of Mr. Pelletier, Transcripts vol. 71, pp. 12326-12327 (OF), pp. 12324-12326 (E).

58 Testimony of Mr. Jean Lafleur, Transcripts vol. 76, p. 13321 (OF), p. 13315 (E).

59 Exhibit P-208(A), pp. 119-129.

60 Testimony of Mr. Pelletier, Transcripts vol. 71, pp. 12434-12436 (OF), pp. 12423-12424 (E).

61 Testimony of Mr. Jean Lafleur, Transcripts vol. 76, pp. 13323-13325 (OF), pp. 13317-13318 (E).

62 Exhibit P-216, p. 86; Testimony of Mr. Jean Lafleur, Transcripts vol. 76, pp. 13323-13325 (OF), pp. 13317-13318 (E).

63 Testimony of Mr. Éric Lafleur, Transcripts vol. 80, pp. 14134-14138 (OF), pp. 14123-14127 (E); Testimony of Mr. Guertin, Transcripts vol. 82, pp. 14596-14600 (OF), pp. 14584-14588 (E); Testimony of Mr. Michaud, Transcripts vol. 79, pp. 13920-13925 (OF), pp. 13909-13915 (E).

64 Testimony of Mr. Jean Lafleur, Transcripts vol. 75, pp. 13189-13192 (OF), pp. 13173-13176 (E).

65 Testimony of Mr. Jean Lafleur, Transcripts vol. 77, pp. 13461-13463 (OF), pp. 13455-13457 (E); vol. 78, pp. 13743-13744 (OF), pp. 13730-13732 (E).

66 Testimony of Mr. Michaud, Transcripts vol. 79, p. 13931 (OF), pp. 13919-13920 (E).

67 Testimony of Mr. Sauriol, Transcripts vol. 101, pp. 18203-18205 (OF), pp. 18192-18193 (E).

68 Testimony of Mr. Éric Lafleur, Transcripts vol. 80, pp. 14236-14237, 14065-14067, 14070 (OF), pp. 14216-14217, 14061-14063, 14065-14066 (E).

69 Testimony of Mr. Éric Lafleur, Transcripts vol. 81, pp. 14333-14334 (OF), pp. 14325-14326 (E).

70 Testimony of Mr. Éric Lafleur, Transcripts vol. 80, pp. 14182-14183 (OF), pp. 14167-14168 (E); Exhibit P-226, p. 173.

71 Testimony of Mr. Éric Lafleur, Transcripts vol. 80, pp. 14140-14142 (OF), pp. 14129-14131(E).

72 Testimony of Mr. Jean Lafleur, Transcripts vol. 75, pp. 13101-13103 (OF), 13096-13097 (E); vol. 78, pp. 13762-13763 (OF), pp. 13748-13749 (E).

73 Exhibit P-216(B), pp. 19-20, 10-11.

74 Exhibit P-216(B), pp. 10-11.

75 Testimony of Mr. Éric Lafleur, Transcripts vol. 81, p. 14337 (OF), p. 14329 (E).

76 Testimony of Mr. Davidson, Transcripts vol. 79, p. 13953 (OF), pp. 13940-13941 (E); Testimony of Mr. Jean Lafleur, Transcripts vol. 75, pp. 13174-13183 (OF), pp. 13161-13170 (E); Testimony of Mr. Guertin, Transcripts vol. 81, pp. 14408-14410 (OF), pp. 14396-14398 (E).

77 Testimony of Mr. Guertin, Transcripts vol. 81. pp. 14403-14404 (OF), pp. 14391-14393 (E); Testimony of Mr. Guertin, Transcripts vol. 82, pp. 14579-14580 (OF), p. 14568 (E).

78 Testimony of Mr. Jean Lafleur, Transcripts vol. 75, p. 13177 (OF), p. 13164 (E); Exhibit P-428(A), pp. 81-83.

79 Testimony of Mr. Jean Lafleur, Transcripts vol. 78, pp. 13644-13645 (OF), pp. 13640-13642 (E).

80 Testimony of Mr. Jean Lafleur, Transcripts vol. 75, p. 13187 (OF), pp. 13171-13172 (E); vol. 76, pp. 13258-13260 (OF), pp. 13257-13259 (E).

81 Testimony of Mr. Jean Lafleur, Transcripts vol. 76, pp. 13248-13250 (OF), pp. 13248-13249 (E); Testimony of Mr. Éric Lafleur, Transcripts vol. 80, p. 14041 (OF), pp. 14039-14040 (E).

82 Testimony of Mr. Jean Lafleur, Transcripts vol. 76, pp. 13264-13276 (OF), pp. 13263-13273 (E).

83 Testimony of Mr. Éric Lafleur, Transcripts vol. 80, pp. 14021-14022 (OF), pp. 14021-14022 (E).

84 Testimony of Mr. Éric Lafleur, Transcripts vol. 80, pp. 14088-14092, 14112-14118 (OF), pp. 14104-14109 (E).

85 Testimony of Mr. Émond, Transcripts vol. 51, pp. 8949-8952 (OF), pp. 8949-8952 (E).

86 Testimony of Mr. Davidson, Transcripts vol. 79, pp. 13971-13972 (OF), p. 13957 (E); Exhibit P-243(B), p. 167; Exhibit P-243(C).

87 Testimony of Mr. Davidson, Transcripts vol. 79, p. 13958 (OF), p. 13945 (E).

88 Testimony of Mr. Davidson, Transcripts vol. 79, pp. 13973-13974 (OF), p. 13959 (E).

89 Testimony of Mr. Davidson, Transcripts vol. 79, p. 13976 (OF), pp. 13958-13959 (E).

90 Exhibit P-243(B), p. 167.

91 Exhibit P-243(C), p. 1.

92 Testimony of Mr. Davidson, Transcripts vol. 79, p. 1396 (OF), p. 13961 (E).

93 Exhibit P-243(B), p. 171.

94 Exhibit P-243(B), pp. 155-157, 159.

95 Exhibit P-243(C), pp. 1, 6; Exhibit P-243(B), pp. 155-157, 159.

96 Testimony of Mr. Davidson, Transcripts vol. 79, pp. 13971-13978, 13984-13987 (OF), pp. 13956-13961, 13968-13971 (E).

97 Testimony of Mr. Davidson, Transcripts vol. 79, pp. 13983-13984 (OF), pp. 13968-13969 (E).

98 Testimony of Mr. Davidson, Transcripts vol. 79, p. 13985 (OF), p. 13969 (E); Exhibit P-243(B), p. 168.

99 Testimony of Mr. Davidson, Transcripts vol. 79, pp. 13956-13957, 13983 (OF), pp. 13943-13944, 13967-13968 (E).

100 Testimony of Mr. Davidson, Transcripts vol. 79, p. 13983 (OF), pp. 13967-13968 (E); Exhibit P-243(B), pp. 155-159.

101 Exhibit P-243(B), p. 155.

102 Exhibit P-243(B), p. 156.

103 Exhibit P-243(B), p. 157.

104 Testimony of Mr. Davidson, Transcripts vol. 79, pp. 13986-13987 (OF), pp. 13970-13971 (E).

105 Exhibit P-243(B), pp. 166, 168, 171.

106 Exhibit P-217, pp. 155, 158.

107 Exhibit P-217, p. 178.

108 Exhibit P-217, pp. 2-24.

109 Exhibit P-217, pp. 2-24.

110 Exhibit P-217, p. 24.

111 Testimony of Mr. Jean Lafleur, Transcripts vol. 77, pp. 13548-13555 (OF), pp. 13533-13542 (E).

112 Exhibit P-217, p. 60.

113 Exhibit P-217, p. 60.

114 Exhibit P-217, pp. 77-78.

115 Exhibit P-217, pp. 243, 181.

116 Exhibit P-217, pp. 103-105.

117 Exhibit P-216(B), p. 4. The contract allowed Lafleur Communication to bill PWGSC $100,000 for printing and up to $135,000 for distribution. Exhibit P-217, p. 60.

118 Exhibit P-217, p. 60.

[119] Testimony of Mr. Guertin, Transcripts vol. 82, pp. 14488-14497, 14580-14581 (OF), 14486-14494, 14569 (E); Exhibit P-217, addenda inserted after p. 327.

[120] Exhibit P-225(A), pp. 120-131.

[121] Exhibit P-225(A), pp. 138-155.

[122] Exhibit P-225(A), pp. 52-64.

[123] Exhibit P-225(A), pp. 2-13.

[124] Exhibit P-225(A), p. 66.

[125] Exhibit P-225(A), p. 36.

[126] Exhibit P-225(A), p. 64.

[127] Exhibit P-225(A), p. 25.

[128] Exhibit P-225(A), p. 67.

[129] Exhibit P-225(A), p. 66.

[130] Exhibit P-216(B), p. 19.

[131] Exhibit P-225(A), p. 67.

[132] See, for example, Testimony of Mr. Jean Lafleur, Transcripts vol. 78, pp. 13763-13764 (OF), p. 13749 (E); Testimony of Mr. Éric Lafleur, Transcripts vol. 81, pp. 14299-14303 (OF), pp. 14295-14299 (E).

[133] Testimony of Mr. Davidson, Transcripts vol. 79, pp. 14009-14010 (OF), pp. 13991-13992 (E).

[134] Testimony of Mr. Éric Lafleur, Transcripts vol. 80, p. 14255 (OF), pp. 14232-14233 (E); vol. 81, pp. 14301-14302 (OF), pp. 14297-14298 (E).

[135] Exhibit P-225(A), p. 67.

[136] Exhibit P-225(A), p. 66.

[137] Testimony of Mr. Éric Lafleur, Transcripts vol. 81, p. 14315 (OF), pp. 14309-14310 (E).

[138] Exhibit P-216(B), p. 20.

[139] Testimony of Mr. Éric Lafleur, Transcripts vol. 81, p. 14316 (OF), p. 14310 (E).

[140] Testimony of Mr. Jean Lafleur, Transcripts vol. 75, pp. 13101-13103 (OF), 13096-13097 (E); vol. 78, pp. 13762-13763 (OF), pp. 13748-13749 (E).

[141] Exhibit P-215(A), p. 108.

[142] Exhibit P-428(A), p. 84.

[143] Exhibit P-428(A), p. 84.

[144] Exhibit P-428(A), p. 86.

[145] Exhibit P-428(A), p. 87.

[146] Exhibit P-428(A), p. 88; Exhibit P-215(A), p. 21.

XII
————

Chapter XII

GILLES-ANDRÉ GOSSELIN

12.1
Introduction and Early PWGSC Contracts

In 1993 Gilles-André Gosselin and his wife, Andrée Côté, incorporated a communication agency under the name Gosselin & Associés Communications Stratégiques Inc. (Gosselin Associés), with the intention of operating it out of their residence in Outremont, a Montreal suburb.[1] Mr. Gosselin had been working for almost two years as Director of Communications for the Canadian Space Agency and had decided to try to earn a living from his own business. [2]

At the beginning, Gosselin Associés had only modest revenues from a few clients of about $250,000 gross per year[3]. Its only personnel were three members of the Gosselin family[4]. But the revenues of its successor corporation, Gosselin Communications Stratégiques Inc. (Gosselin Communications), shot up dramatically in 1997, when it was hired by Public Works and Government Services Canada to manage sponsorship contracts[5]. This increased business arrived on April 28, 1997[6], only one month after the Gosselin agency moved

353

its offices to Ottawa[7] and on the same day that PWGSC announced the agency was qualified to manage advertising and sponsorship contracts on behalf of the Government.[8] On that same day, Gosselin Associés transferred its assets to Gosselin Communications.[9] Given the dramatic increase in business, Mr. Gosselin was also persuaded to open a branch office in Quebec City in July 1998, which operated under the direction of Mr. Thiboutot, whose dealings with Mr. Brault were discussed in Chapter XI.[10] The Quebec City office was largely autonomous, except that the Ottawa office did the invoicing for the first six months.[11]

Mr. Gosselin has known Mr. Guité since 1985, when they were both federal public servants working in the Department of Supply and Services.[12] They lost touch with each other for a few years but became reacquainted in 1991.[13] When Mr. Gosselin formed Gosselin Associés in 1993, he offered its services to Mr. Guité,[14] who by then had become the Director of the Advertising and Public Opinion Research Sector, and was rewarded for his efforts by a first contract in June 1994 for advice on federal government communications.[15] A second contract, signed in September 1994, retained the services of Gosselin Associés to develop questionnaires for APORS to use in selecting or qualifying advertising and communication agencies for government work. It began as an $18,000 contract and was amended twice to increase its value to $76,750.[16] A third mandate was for a $22,500 study of the Government's method of payment to agencies of record.[17] A fourth contract was in May 1995 for $47,500 for more questionnaires and participation on selection committees as an "independent expert."[18]

Mr. Gosselin's first Sponsorship Program work was in 1996 as a subcontractor to the Lafleur agency, taking over most aspects of the sponsorship contract for the summer 1997 trip of the Bluenose II up the St. Lawrence River and Seaway.[19] Mr. Guité "suggested" to Jean Lafleur that due to the complexity of the project he should seek the assistance of Mr. Gosselin's agency,[20] which at that time was not qualified to handle PWGSC contracts directly.[21] It is most likely that the suggestion of Mr. Guité was understood by Mr. Lafleur to be more of a directive which he probably would not have followed if he had had any choice in the matter, since the personal relationship between Messrs. Lafleur and Gosselin is described by the latter as complicated and difficult.[22]

The Bluenose project turned out to be both demanding and lucrative. In the fiscal year 1996-97, ending before the Bluenose tour began, the Lafleur agency billed PWGSC for 1,043.5 hours of work performed by Mr. Gosselin at $245 per hour for a total of $255,657.50.[23] Mr. Gosselin had billed the Lafleur agency at $110 per hour,[24] for a total of $114,785.[25] The summer tour generated another 1,117 hours of work performed by Mr. Gosselin. The Lafleur agency billed a total of 3,549 hours for the project in the name of the Gosselin agency.[26]

During the planning for the Bluenose tour, Mr. Gosselin met Mr. Guité in Halifax, and in his testimony relates the content of a significant conversation they had there.[27] He says that Mr. Guité told him he should move his agency's offices to Ottawa, that he would not be sorry if he did, and that "tu vas avoir plein de contrats" (you'll have lots of contracts).[28] Mr. Gosselin takes care to add that Mr. Guité did not indicate that Mr. Gosselin would owe him anything in return.[29] Mr. Guité does not deny that they had the conversation or that the question of a move to Ottawa was discussed, but denies that he ever promised Mr. Gosselin that he would be awarded contracts if he moved to Ottawa.[30] The version of the conversation given by Mr. Gosselin is more convincing.

Although Mr. Gosselin testifies that the move of his agency's offices to Ottawa was not motivated by what Mr. Guité said to him in Halifax,[31] there are just too many coincidences and contradictions to make this a credible statement. The evidence is that Ms. Côté was most reluctant to move away from Montreal.[32] Nonetheless, on March 26, 1997, Gosselin Associés signed a lease for premises in Ottawa even though it was not then qualified to receive sponsorship contracts from PWGSC. It qualified on April 28, 1997,[33] at the conclusion of a selection process begun in February 1997 by PWGSC's call for tenders.[34] Mr. Guité had called Mr. Gosselin to inform him about the call for tenders before it was issued.[35] Although Mr. Gosselin does not say so, the decision to relocate the Gosselin agency to Ottawa must have been based on an expectation of sponsorship contracts, once it became qualified.

When he testified, Mr. Gosselin was confronted with documentary evidence indicating that during April 1997, before receiving a letter informing him of the qualification of his agency,[36] he was already working on at least two sponsorship contracts, although they had not yet been signed: one for the Ottawa Tulip Festival, and the other for the Trans Canada Trail project. He attempted at first to deny that work was performed on these projects before April 28,[37] and then faced with invoices indicating the contrary, abruptly broke off his testimony, complaining that his health did not permit him to continue. [38] He returned to continue his testimony at a later date and finally admitted that work on the two projects had begun well before the qualification letter was received.[39]

It must be concluded that Mr. Gosselin had been advised by someone, almost surely his friend Mr. Guité, that as soon as his agency was qualified to contract with PWGSC it would be awarded those two contracts. This is exactly what happened—the contracts dated April 28, 1997, are part of a batch of contracts in the total amount of $985,000 awarded to Gosselin Communications, which began its legal existence on that exact date.[40] Also on April 28, 1997, Gosselin Communications sent several invoices to PWGSC for work already performed on some of these projects—including the Tulip Festival, which was already under way.[41]

Mr. Gosselin's initial reluctance to admit that sponsorship contracts had been promised to him in advance must be understood to indicate that he had had discussions about them with Mr. Guité, which he knows were inappropriate. Mr. Guité also refuses to admit to the discussions, including the promises he made in Halifax that Mr. Gosselin acknowledges.[42]

12.2
Contract and Billing Irregularities

As mentioned earlier, Gosselin Communications began as a three-person operation, and no permanent employees were added until the end of 1997. [43] Additional personnel were obtained by contracting with Ms. Côté's placement agency (CPPC)[44]. Nevertheless, Gosselin Communications invoiced PWGSC for its personnel according to the hourly rates fixed by the sponsorship contract and did not disclose it had subcontracted the work, or the much lower rates it paid CPPC or what the individual was actually paid.[45] Both CPPC and Gosselin Communications profited from this irregular billing practice. For example, Geneviève Proulx billed CPPC at $12 or $15 per hour. CPPC billed Gosselin Communications $25 or $35 per hour; and Gosselin Communications billed Ms. Proulx's time at $60 per hour.[46]

In late 1997, CPPC branched out into promotional items as "Uni-Com," subcontracting to Gosselin Communications.[47] Since Ms. Côté already worked for Gosselin Communications, there was no valid reason for this work to be done by subcontract rather than by Gosselin Communications directly. Although Mr. Gosselin testified that he required that competitive bids be secured from other suppliers for contracts over $25,000, he is contradicted by his own employees. Only two such instances are established by documentary evidence. In any case, the other bids were invariably higher, and Uni-Com always won the subcontract. It is fair to conclude that the search for competitive prices was half-hearted. Uni-Com earned a 20% to 40% markup on the promotional items supplied to Gosselin Communications,[48] giving CPPC $526,833 of its gross revenues of $617,833 for January 1, 1998, to October 1, 1998, when its shares were sold by Ms. Côté.[49]

The many sponsorship contracts awarded to Gosselin Communications in 1997-98 totalled $7,066,293.[50] In the next fiscal year, prior to its October 1998 sale, Gosselin Communications received $14,094,976 in sponsorship contracts.[51] Although there were many instances of improper invoicing, most often related to falsified or exaggerated records of the time spent on a file, it should be noted that Mr. Gosselin made an effort to fulfill his agency's sponsorship contracts in a more systematic manner than was the case of the Lafleur agency. For example, he took care to sign an agreement with the promoter of each event. He had a clear conception of what services should be covered by the agency commission of 12%, and did not attempt to charge for the time spent in preparing post-mortem reports to the client, or for routine inspections of the visibility given to the Government at the event being sponsored.[52]

The testimony of Josée Thibeau-Carrier, the accountant who prepared the Gosselin agency accounts for the Ottawa office and the Quebec City office for its first six months,[53] is most revealing. She was hired as an independent contractor in July 1997.[54] She says that all invoicing was done under Mr. Gosselin's supervision.[55] Ms. Thibeau-Carrier says that records of the time spent by Mr. and Mrs. Gosselin on the various sponsorship contracts were not maintained on a daily basis, and it was left to her to complete time sheets for them based on their agendas or what they told her, sometimes several days later.[56] When two new vice-presidents, Wendy Cumming and Enrico Valente, first joined the firm, they did not bother to fill out time sheets either. [57] However, time records were maintained on a more systematic basis in 1998, at the request of someone at PWGSC.[58]

The absence of accurate time records may not have complicated the billing process, since Ms. Thibeau-Carrier testifies that sometimes the hours worked on a file were increased to match the full amount allowed by the PWGSC contract.[59] She gives specific examples, and says that her instructions came from Mr. Gosselin and the vice-presidents.[60] She would also increase the hours recorded to cover the costs of restaurant meals which could not otherwise be billed.[61] Mr. Gosselin admits this latter practice, and says that he was explicitly told to do so by Mr. Guité.[62]

Ms. Thibeau-Carrier also testifies that she would transfer excess time charges from one file to another, based on the maximum amount allowed on each file.[63] She says this was done with the knowledge and consent of Huguette Tremblay at PWGSC.[64] Mr. Gosselin denies that his agency billed improperly or that it exaggerated time actually worked,[65] but his credibility on these issues is adversely affected by his admission that he recorded and billed PWGSC for the astounding total of 3,673 hours in 1997-98, more than ten hours for each day in the year.[66] Considering the additional time that would have been required to move his business to Ottawa and for non-billable administration on client files,[67] his serious illness for part of the year,[68] that the PWGSC contracts began April 28, 1997, a month after the start of the fiscal year, and that that some of his time should have been covered by the 12% commission earned on every sponsorship contract,

Mr. Gosselin's claim that those 3,673 hours were actually worked and legitimately billed is rejected as incredible.[69] It is an obvious exaggeration and serves as confirmation that the agency regularly billed PWGSC for hours which had not in fact been worked.

There is no evidence that the personnel at PWGSC ever questioned any of the invoices of Gosselin Communications, or required validation of the hours of work which it was charging.

12.3
The Ottawa Senators Contract

Like Mr. Lafleur, Mr. Gosselin lent his cooperation to the culture of entitlement that fails to see that there is something wrong when politicians and public servants benefit personally from the expenditure of public funds for which they are responsible.

On October 1, 1997, PWGSC mandated Gosselin Communications to manage the sponsorship of the Ottawa Senators hockey team, which was, according to the contract, to receive $355,000 for the visibility given to the federal government in various ways at games played at the Corel Centre.[70] The agency commission of 12% foreseen by the contract was $42,600, together with fees and production costs estimated at $190,000.[71]

Mr. Gosselin immediately commenced negotiations with the owners of the hockey club to confirm the sponsorship and to work out a mutually acceptable visibility plan. When the resulting contract dealing with these matters was signed on October 16, 1997,[72] a second contract bearing the same date confirmed the lease by Gosselin Communications of one-third of what is usually referred to as a "luxury box" for two seasons, together with related catering services.[73] Although the lease does not stipulate the cost of the rental, later invoices show it to be $33,000.[74] The catering cost, also billed to PWGSC, is $27,000.[75]

Mr. Gosselin testifies that the actual cost of the visibility purchased by PWGSC for $350,000 (there is no explanation for the difference of $5,000 between the price given in the sponsorship contract and what is stipulated in the visibility plan) was $290,000[76] and that the remainder of $60,000 was to cover the cost of the seats in the box and catering.[77] In other words, PWGSC, through Gosselin Communications, was purchasing seats in the box and treating the cost as part of the sponsorship. His testimony is corroborated by documentation prepared by the hockey club prior to the signature of the visibility plan, which indicates clearly that the cost to be paid by the Government for the visibility it was to receive in the 1997-98 season was $290,000, to increase to $310,000 in the following season of 1998-99,[78] when it was anticipated the sponsorship would be fixed at $370,000.[79]

Mr. Gosselin testifies that it was Mr. Guité's explicit request that seats at the Senators hockey games be made available to him and to his guests in this manner.[80] Other evidence supports his testimony; for example, the schedule of the games to be played (see Figure XII-1) at the Corel Centre was sent to Mr. Guité and he was given first choice for tickets.[81] It was only when Mr. Guité did not want the tickets or did not give the tickets to guests of his choosing, that guests selected by Gosselin Communications would use them. [82]

Figure XII-1: Fax from Mr. Gosselin regarding Corel Centre events

```
┌────────────────────────────────────────────┐
│          1997-1998 OTTAWA SENATORS           │
│           THIRD SEASON PACKAGES              │
└────────────────────────────────────────────┘
```

PACKAGE E

SEPT(pre season)
FRI   26   BUFFALO   7:30

OCT
SUN   19   DALLAS   7:30
THUR 23   FLORIDA   7:30

NOV
SAT   8   PHILADELPHIA   7:30
MON   17   BOSTON   7:30
SAT   22   EDMONTON   7:30

DEC
THUR   4   LOS ANGELES   7:30
THUR 18   CAROLINA   7:30

JAN
MON   26   TAMPA BAY   7:30
THUR 29   NYR   7:30

FEB
MON   2   NEW JERSEY   7:30
SAT   7   PITTSBURGH   7:30

MAR
SAT   7   CALGARY   7:30
WED   18   NYI   7:30

APR
THUR 16   MONTREAL   7:30

Handwritten note:

Other events: (MAJOR)

Elton - 4 tix Nov 7th

Lord of the Dance
Dec. 1st

Backstreet Boys Jan. 2

Post-it Fax Note:

Feuillets de transmission par télécopieur   Date   # of pages
Post-It™ Fax Note   71B   / Nbre de pages ▶   /

To / A   J.C. Guité   From / De   G-A Gosselin
Co./Dept. / Car/Service   Co. / Cie

Phone # / N° de tél.   Phone # / N° de tél.

Fax # / N° de télécopieur   Fax # / N° de télécopieur
        952 - 1003

What is clearly established, beyond any serious possibility of contradiction, is that the Government of Canada paid for the cost of free tickets in luxury boxes to hockey games at the Corel Centre, together with refreshments and food, and that the tickets were used either by guests designated by Mr. Guité or for business promotion by Gosselin Communications, and the personal pleasure of its employees. No objective of the Sponsorship Program was achieved by the distribution and use of these free tickets.

The abuse of public funds at the Corel Centre was increased in the 1998-99 season. Mr. Gosselin says that Mr. Guité asked that a full box be leased, in a more prestigious location.[83] This was accomplished by leasing to Gosselin Communications the box that in the previous season had been used by the owners of the hockey team themselves.[84] The cost of the lease increased to $100,000 and was again disguised as part of the amount paid to the Ottawa Senators as a sponsorship.[85]

It became customary to have a representative of Gosselin Communications present in the box to receive the ticket-holders and to see that their comfort was assured.[86] In the 1998-99 season, Mario Parent, who by now had left the public service to work for Gosselin Communications shortly before it was purchased by Groupaction,[87] was assigned this task.[88] He testifies that he was on duty at the Corel Centre box throughout the hockey season and charged the hours spent there as time worked.[89] Those hours were in due course invoiced to PWGSC as fees or production costs.[90]

Mr. Guité categorically denies that the box at the Corel Centre was leased and paid for by PWGSC or that he had anything to do with the arrangements described by Mr. Gosselin.[91] He acknowledges that he and members of his family used the box on a few occasions,[92] and that some of the personnel at CCSB were given tickets to hockey games by Gosselin Communications,[93] but he says that the box and the tickets were bought and paid for by Gosselin Communications,[94] and that when he and his friends and family went to the Corel Centre, they did so as guests of Mr. Gosselin.[95]

The documentary evidence supporting Mr. Gosselin's testimony, and the corroborating testimony of Mr. Parent and Mr. Valente, who replaced Mr. Parent on a few occasions, are decisive. Mr. Guité's claims are rejected. He used sponsorship funds to make hockey tickets in a luxury box at the Corel Centre available to himself and to his guests, including PWGSC personnel, senior public servants such as Roger Collet, and politicians such as Don Boudria and Denis Coderre.

The distribution of favours in this way is not in accordance with the ethical principles which Treasury Board expects public servants to follow.

12.4
Politics and Friendship

There is no evidence that political considerations influenced the awarding of sponsorship contracts to Gosselin Communications. Indeed, the evidence shows that although Mr. Gosselin reluctantly made a few modest contributions to the Liberal Party,[96] in general he resisted pressures put upon him to make political contributions to the party in power as a means of currying favour, a practice that he disliked intensely.[97] In fact, when he began to hire employees in 1998 because of the flood of new business, he says he had to hide from them the essentially political objective of the Sponsorship Program, namely influencing voters to favour the federalist option by giving them a better perception and understanding of the federal role, particularly in Quebec.[98] He testifies that if this objective had been openly stated, two-thirds of his personnel would have resigned.[99] Mr. Gosselin clearly did not think of his agency as one that was "Liberal friendly."

However, at about the time the Gosselin agency was awarded the 1994 and 1995 contracts, the relationship between Mr. Guité and Mr. Gosselin and their wives had evolved into a warm friendship. The two couples shared meals at their respective residences about ten times a year, according to Ms. Côté. [100] It is safe to conclude that their friendship was at least one of the reasons for the sudden prosperity of Gosselin Communications and the Gosselin family starting in 1997, another being Mr. Gosselin's willingness to cooperate in the making of dubious arrangements like the PWGSC luxury box included in the Ottawa Senators sponsorship. In exchange, Mr. Gosselin and his wife earned revenues in a short period of time greater than anything they could have ever imagined.

It is therefore improbable that the reason contracts were awarded to Gosselin Communications was the skill and expertise of Mr. Gosselin and his employees, or that these factors were important considerations, in spite of the fact that they should have been. In fact, Mr. Gosselin learned a few years later that his friendship with Mr. Guité would, once Mr. Guité had left the Communication Coordination Services Branch, be insufficient to ensure the continuation of contracts directed to his agency. On September 15, 1999, after Mr. Gosselin had sold his agency to Jean Brault's company, he had breakfast at the Château Laurier in Ottawa with Jean-Marc Bard, who was Mr. Gagliano's Executive Assistant.[101] The purpose of their meeting was to discuss the drop in the volume of business given by PWGSC to the Gosselin agency, which affected the bonus arrangements Mr. Gosselin had negotiated with Mr. Brault.[102] Mr. Gosselin had earlier raised the subject with Pierre Tremblay, who had just replaced Mr. Guité at CCSB, and Mr. Tremblay had told him to speak to Mr. Bard, who was, according to him, the person making all the decisions.[103]

At their breakfast meeting, Mr. Bard was characteristically blunt. Mr. Gosselin, who has a very clear recollection of their meeting, quotes him as follows:

> Tes adversaires t'ont cassé la gueule et si tu continues comme ça là, c'est la mâchoire qu'ils vont t'arracher.

[Unofficial Translation]

> Listen, your opponents have punched you in the face. Okay? And if you continue what you're doing, they're going to rip it off.[104]

Mr. Gosselin interpreted these words to mean that he was not a Liberal insider, and that to be an insider he would have to be a supporter of the Liberal Party,[105] something that he had resisted except when he surrendered to Diane Deslauriers' repeated telephone requests to purchase a table at a 1998 fundraiser,[106] and the February 1999 $10,000 contribution arranged by Groupaction on his behalf. [107]

What is worth noting is that Mr. Bard did not say that the drop in Mr. Gosselin's fortunes was related to any lack of expertise in handling sponsorship contracts. Instead, he attributed the drop to the machinations of his adversaries. It is also worth noting that Mr. Bard did not protest that he had nothing to do with the allocation of sponsorship contracts, or that he was ignorant of the factors that led to one agency receiving contracts rather than another. One may conclude that the factors were known by Mr. Bard to be mainly political.

12.5
Commissions for Little or No Work

Let us review two examples of the Gosselin agency accepting PWGSC mandates for substantial sums of money for little or no work.

The first example, the television series produced by Robert-Guy Scully's firm L'Information Essentielle and based upon the life of the hockey legend Maurice Richard, is the subject of a detailed analysis in the Report of the Auditor General. It will not be repeated here, but it may be useful to describe what was done or not done by Gosselin Communications to earn a commission of $132,000.

Mr. Gosselin testifies that he was advised by PWGSC by a fax dated December 18, 1997 (confirmed by a contract bearing the same date), that his agency had been retained to manage a $600,000 sponsorship to be given to L'Information Essentielle.[108] It would receive a commission for doing so of $72,000, and would be entitled to charge production costs and fees up to $10,000 for related work.[109] At the time of receiving the contract, Mr. Gosselin says that he knew nothing about the project.[110] He contacted Mr. Scully, but was unsuccessful in working out the terms of the sponsorship agreement and a visibility plan, and says that Mr. Scully was not interested. [111] This story is consistent with the attitude displayed by Mr. Scully during his own testimony before the Commission.

A second mandate was given to Gosselin Communications relating to the same project on April 1, 1998, the beginning of a new fiscal year.[112] This time the sponsorship was, after a series of amendments, for the additional sum of $575,000, including a commission of $60,000 and additional production costs and fees.[113]

Gosselin Communications billed PWGSC and was paid $132,000 in commissions and $19,000 in related fees. Mr. Gosselin was understandably defensive when he was asked what work was done, as he had to admit that his agency's sole contribution to the Maurice Richard series was viewing the television programs to confirm that the Government was recognized properly in the credits, and organizing a cocktail reception at the time the series was launched. He tries to justify the commission paid by saying, "ma compagnie, on était bien disposé à faire un bon travail honnête pour être rémunéré convenablement et que le client nous a dit que ce n'était pas nécessaire" (I was—and my firm, we were quite willing to do a good, honest job and be paid properly for it, but the client told us it wasn't necessary).[114] Mr. Scully testifies that Gosselin Communications performed no work at all in the production of the series.[115] Whether or not this denial excludes the viewing and the reception, we cannot blame Mr. Gosselin for accepting commissions for little or no work. However, we certainly can criticize the organization of a government program that allowed the payment of commissions for no work. Mr. Guité administered the program, but it was conceived and organized at a higher level in the PMO and Mr. Gagliano's office, and there was simply no oversight of what was going on.

The second example is the January 23, 1998, advertising contract awarded to Gosselin Communications to work with Industry Canada on an advertising campaign in relation to the potential effects on computer systems associated with the arrival of the year 2000.[116] The contract foresees the expenditure of $1,284,000,[117] of which $1,110,000 was nominally for the sponsorship[118] but was really for media purchases related to the advertising campaign.[119] The sum of $90,000[120] was provided for a commission payable to Gosselin Communications, and $84,000 was for taxes.[121] These amounts were duly billed by Gosselin Communications to Industry Canada on February 23, 1998, exactly one month after the date of the contract.[122]

Mr. Gosselin testifies that in fact he had nothing to do with the advertising campaign that had been agreed to by Industry Canada and Cossette Communication.[123] The problem was that Industry Canada could not contract directly with Cossette because it was not 100% Canadian owned.[124] Mr. Gosselin says that Mr. Guité was consulted and "solved" the problem by arranging for a contract with Gosselin on the understanding that all the work would be done by Cossette without a formal subcontract.[125] Cossette billed Gosselin Communications for the media purchases and its commissions,[126] and Gosselin billed PWGSC as though it had handled the matter itself.

The contract gave Gosselin Communications a fixed amount of $90,000 as commission even though no work or services were required other than preparation of invoices and the examination of proofs of publication.[127] Mr. Gosselin maintains he also corrected the texts of the advertisements which he felt were not up to his standards, and says that the people at Cossette were irritated by his revisions.[128] While we cannot blame Mr. Gosselin for accepting this commission for little or no work, he certainly cooperated with Mr. Guité's plan to circumvent Treasury Board's 100% Canadian-owned policy, keeping a substantial portion of the $90,000 commission for his agency.

The evidence does not disclose whether anyone at Industry Canada was aware that Cossette Communication was ineligible, or was aware of or condoned how Mr. Guité manoeuvred around the problem. The evidence does show that there were problems in processing the Gosselin invoices for payment, that questions were asked about why the contract was for sponsorship rather than advertising, and that Industry Canada was sent a number of Cossette invoices showing that it, and not the Gosselin agency, did the media placement work.[129]

12.6
Financial Results

Effective October 1, 1998, Gosselin Communications sold all of its business and assets to 3522610 Canada Inc.,[130] a newly created corporation controlled by Jean Brault. For all practical purposes, Mr. Gosselin was employed within Mr. Brault's expanding network of companies until he retired in September 2000, principally due to health problems.[131] At the same time, Ms. Côté sold all of her CPPC shares to the same buyer for $510,000.[132] The evidence shows that the buyer made no use of CPPC[133] - the sale had nothing to do with CPPC's intrinsic value and was clearly tied to the larger sale.

During the relatively short period when Gosselin Communications was operating autonomously, from April 28, 1997, to October 1, 1998, it handled over $21 million of sponsorship contracts on behalf of PWGSC, earning $1.4 million in agency commissions and $8.2 million in production costs and fees, and was awarded two advertising contracts having a value of $1.5 million.[134] This enabled it to pay salaries and bonuses to Mr. Gosselin, his wife and his son in excess of $3.3 million.[135] When it sold its assets to Mr. Brault's company in 1998,[136] Gosselin Communications received a down payment of $223,979 and the right to participate in future profits, for which Mr. Gosselin received bonuses in the next two years totalling $281,500.[137] He was given a contract of employment by which he was entitled to earn a salary of $200,000 per year.[138] Clearly, the Sponsorship Program had presented a financial bonanza to Mr. Gosselin and his wife.

Endnotes to Chapter XII

1   Exhibit P-254, p. 1; Exhibit P-256(A), p. 13.

2   Testimony of Mr. Gosselin, Transcripts vol. 82, p. 14621 (OF), p. 14608 (E); Exhibit P-256(A), p. 3.

3   Exhibit P-428(A), p. 89; Exhibit P-259, p. 206; Exhibit P-254, para. 15.

4   Exhibit P-254, para. 16.

5   Exhibit P-257(A), p. 2; Exhibit P-428(A), p. 90.

6   Exhibit P-257(A), p. 4.

7   Exhibit P-254, para. 18.

8   Exhibit P-259, pp. 223-226, 229.

9   Exhibit P-254, paras. 19, 21.

10   Testimony of Mr. Thiboutot, Transcripts vol. 85, pp. 15059-15062 (OF), pp. 15057-15060 (E).

11   Testimony of Mr. Thiboutot, Transcripts vol. 85, pp. 15062, 15093 (OF), pp. 15060, 15088 (E).

12   Testimony of Mr. Gosselin, Transcripts vol. 82, pp. 14619-14620 (OF), p. 14607 (E).

13   Testimony of Mr. Gosselin, Transcripts vol. 82, pp. 14622-14624 (OF), pp. 14609-14610 (E).

14   Testimony of Mr. Gosselin, Transcripts, vol. 82, p. 14623 (OF), p. 14610 (E).

15   Exhibit P-267.

16   Exhibit P-288, pp. 13, 16, 22.

17   Exhibit P-288, p. 37.

18   Exhibit P-257(A), p. 3; Exhibit P-256(A), p. 239.

19   Exhibit P-254, para. 12.

20   Testimony of Mr. Lafleur, Transcripts vol. 75, pp. 13109-13111 (OF), pp. 13103-13105 (E); Testimony of Mr. Gosselin, Transcripts vol. 83, p. 14841 (OF), pp. 14830-14831 (E); Exhibit P-216, p. 45.

21   Exhibit P-259, pp. 223-226, 229.

22   Testimony of Mr. Gosselin, Transcripts vol. 83, p. 14846 (OF), p. 14835 (E).

23   Exhibit P-257(B), pp. 2-3.

24   Exhibit P-277(A), pp. 6, 8, 21, 33.

25   Exhibit P-257(B), p. 3.

26   Exhibit P-257(B), p. 3.

27   Testimony of Mr. Gosselin, Transcripts vol. 83, 14838-14840 (OF), pp. 14828-14830 (E).

28   Testimony of Mr. Gosselin, Transcripts vol. 83, p. 14839 (OF), p. 14828 (E).

29   Testimony of Mr. Gosselin, Transcripts vol. 83, p. 14840 (OF); pp. 14829-14830 (E); Testimony of Mr. Gosselin, Transcripts vol. 88 (Part 1), pp. 15505-15506 (OF), pp. 15503-15504 (E).

30   Testimony of Mr. Guité, Transcripts vol. 110, pp. 20111-20112 (OE), pp. 20113-20114 (F); Testimony of Mr. Guité, Transcripts vol. 112 (Part 1), pp. 20557-20662 (OE), pp. 20562-20567 (F).

[31] Testimony of Mr. Gosselin, Transcripts vol. 82, pp. 14660-14662 (OF), pp. 14644-14645 (E); Testimony of Mr. Gosselin, Transcripts vol. 83, pp. 14838-14839 (OF), pp. 14828-14829 (E).

[32] Testimony of Mr. Gosselin, Transcripts vol. 82, p. 14662 (OF), p. 14645 (E); Testimony of Mr. Gosselin, Transcripts vol. 83, pp. 14838-14840 (OF), pp. 14828-14829 (E).

[33] Exhibit P-259, pp. 223-226, 229.

[34] Exhibit P-259, p. 23.

[35] Testimony of Mr. Gosselin, Transcripts vol. 82, pp. 14654, 14658-14660 (OF), pp. 14638-14639, 14641-14644 (E).

[36] Exhibit P-259, p. 229.

[37] Testimony of Mr. Gosselin, Transcripts vol. 82, pp. 14662-14665 (OF), pp. 14646-14648 (E).

[38] Testimony of Mr. Gosselin, Transcripts vol. 84, pp. 14939-14959 (OF), pp. 14928-14955 (E); Exhibit P-277, pp. 87, 89-99.

[39] Testimony of Mr. Gosselin, Transcripts vol. 87, pp. 15416-15418 (OF), pp. 15406-15408 (E).

[40] Exhibit P-257(A), p. 4.

[41] Exhibit P-272, pp. 7-9.

[42] Testimony of Mr. Guité, Transcripts vol. 110, pp. 20111-20112 (OE), pp. 20113-20114 (F); Testimony of Mr. Guité, Transcripts, vol. 112 (Part 1), pp. 20557-20662 (OE), pp. 20562-29567 (F).

[43] Exhibit P-428(A), p. 92; Exhibit P-254, para. 54.

[44] Testimony of Mr. Gosselin, Transcripts vol. 82, p. 14668 (OF), p. 14651 (E); Exhibit P-254, para. 55.

[45] Exhibit P-428(A), p. 93.

[46] Exhibit P-277(A), pp. 6, 59-79.

[47] Testimony of Mr. Gosselin, Transcripts vol. 83, pp. 14795-14796 (OF), pp. 14789-14790 (E); Testimony of Ms. Côté-Gosselin, Transcripts vol. 84, p. 14982 (OF), pp. 14975-14976 (E); Exhibit P-281, para. 4.

[48] Testimony of Ms. Côté-Gosselin, Transcripts vol. 84, pp. 14983-14984 (OF), pp. 14976-14977 (E).

[49] Exhibit P-275, p. 6; Exhibit P-281, Testimony of Ms. Côté-Gosselin, Transcripts vol. 84, p. 14981 (OF), p. 14974-14975 (E).

[50] Exhibit P-257(A), p. 2.

[51] Exhibit P-257(A), p. 2.

[52] Testimony of Mr. Gosselin, Transcripts vol. 83, pp. 14736-14748 (OF), pp. 14735-14746 (E).

[53] Testimony of Ms. Thibeau-Carrier, Transcripts vol. 87, p. 15343 (OF), p. 15340 (E).

[54] Testimony of Ms. Thibeau-Carrier, Transcripts vol. 87, p. 15321 (OF), p. 15320 (E).

[55] Testimony of Ms. Thibeau-Carrier, Transcripts vol. 87, pp. 15327, 15343 (OF), pp. 15326, 15340 (E); Testimony of Mr. Gosselin, Transcripts vol. 83, p. 14812 (OF), p. 14805 (E).

[56] Testimony of Ms. Thibeau-Carrier, Transcripts vol. 87, pp. 15323-15327 (OF), pp. 15322-15325 (E).

[57] Testimony of Ms. Thibeau-Carrier, Transcripts vol. 87, pp. 15323-15324 (OF), p. 15323 (E).

[58] Testimony of Ms. Thibeau-Carrier, Transcripts vol. 87, pp. 15324-15326 (OF), pp. 15323-15324 (E).

[59] Testimony of Ms. Thibeau-Carrier, Transcripts vol. 87, pp. 15326-15328 (OF), pp. 15326-15327 (E).

[60] Testimony of Ms. Thibeau-Carrier, Transcripts vol. 87, pp. 15327-15328 (OF), pp. 15326-15327 (E).

[61] Testimony of Ms. Thibeau-Carrier, Transcripts vol. 87, pp. 15338-15340 (OF), pp. 15336-15337 (E).

62 Testimony of Mr. Gosselin, Transcripts vol. 87, p. 15469 (OF), p. 15456 (E).

63 Testimony of Ms. Thibeau-Carrier, Transcripts vol. 87, pp. 15340-15342 (OF), pp. 15338-15340 (E).

64 Exhibit P-286, p. 17; Testimony of Ms. Thibeau-Carrier, Transcripts vol. 87, pp. 15341-15342 (OF), pp. 15337-15340 (E).

65 Testimony of Mr. Gosselin, Transcripts vol. 87, p. 15469 (OF), p. 15456 (E).

66 Exhibit P-257(B), p. 2.

67 Testimony of Mr. Gosselin, Transcripts vol. 84, pp. 14934-14936 (OF), pp. 14931-14933 (E).

68 Testimony of Mr. Gosselin, Transcripts vol. 84, pp. 14937-14941 (OF), pp. 14934-14937 (E).

69 Testimony of Mr. Gosselin, Transcripts vol. 84, pp. 14937-14941 (OF), pp. 14934-14937 (E).

70 Exhibit P-287(A), pp. 2-10.

71 Exhibit P-287(A), p. 10.

72 Exhibit P-287(A), pp. 13-14.

73 Exhibit P-287(A), p. 19.

74 Exhibit P-287(A), pp. 19, 28.

75 Exhibit P-287(A), pp. 19, 28, 31-32.

76 Testimony of Mr. Gosselin, Transcripts vol. 87, p. 15421 (OF), p. 15411 (E); Exhibit P-287(A), p. 65.

77 Testimony of Mr. Gosselin, Transcripts vol. 87, pp. 15426, 15437-15438 (OF), pp. 15416, 15426-15427 (E).

78 Exhibit P-287(A), p. 65.

79 Testimony of Mr. Gosselin, Transcripts vol. 87, pp. 15437-15438 (OF), pp. 15426-15427 (E).

80 Testimony of Mr. Gosselin, Transcripts vol. 87, pp. 15427-15428 (OF), pp. 15417-15418 (E).

81 Exhibit P-287(A), pp. 21-22.

82 Testimony of Mr. Gosselin, Transcripts vol. 87, pp. 15445-15446 (OF), pp. 15434-15436 (E).

83 Testimony of Mr. Gosselin, Transcripts vol. 87, pp. 15435-15436 (OF), pp. 15425-15426 (E).

84 Testimony of Mr. Gosselin, Transcripts vol. 87, pp. 15435-15436 (OF), pp. 15425-15426 (E); Exhibit P-287(A), pp. 118-137.

85 Exhibit P-287(A), p. 141.

86 Testimony of Mr. Gosselin, Transcripts vol. 87, p. 15431 (OF), pp. 15420-15421 (E).

87 Exhibit P-428(A), p. 96.

88 Testimony of Mr. Gosselin, Transcripts vol. 87, pp. 15392-15393 (OF), pp. 15384-15385 (E).

89 Testimony of Mr. Parent, Transcripts vol. 87, pp. 15396-15407 (OF), pp. 15388-15398 (E).

90 Exhibit P-257(B), pp. 21-22.

91 Testimony of Mr. Guité, Transcripts vol. 110, pp. 20063-20064 (OE), p. 20064 (F).

92 Testimony of Mr. Guité, Transcripts vol. 110, pp. 20073-20075 (OE), pp. 20074-20076 (F).

93 Testimony of Mr. Guité, Transcripts vol. 110, pp. 20075-20080 (OE), pp. 20077-20081 (F).

94 Testimony of Mr. Guité, Transcripts vol. 110, p. 20068 (OE), p. 20069 (F).

95 Testimony of Mr. Guité, Transcripts vol. 110, pp. 20075, 20085 (OE), pp. 20076, 20086-20087 (F).

[96] Exhibit P-256(A), pp. 274-275; Testimony of Mr. Gosselin, Transcripts vol. 83, pp. 14814-14821 (OF), pp. 14806-14813 (E).

[97] Testimony of Mr. Gosselin, Transcripts vol. 83, p. 14817 (OF), p. 14809 (E).

[98] Testimony of Mr. Gosselin, Transcripts vol. 83, pp. 14741-14742 (OF), p. 14740 (E).

[99] Testimony of Mr. Gosselin, Transcripts vol. 83, p. 14741 (OF), p. 14740 (E).

[100] Testimony of Ms. Côté-Gosselin, Transcripts vol. 84, p. 15013 (OF), pp. 15002-15003 (E).

[101] Testimony of Mr. Gosselin, Transcripts vol. 83, pp. 14822, 14825-14826 (OF), p. 14814, 14816-14817 (E).

[102] Testimony of Mr. Gosselin, Transcripts vol. 83, pp. 14823-14824 (OF), pp. 14814-14815 (E).

[103] Testimony of Mr. Gosselin, Transcripts vol. 83, pp. 14824, 14830 (OF), pp. 14815, 14821 (E).

[104] Testimony of Mr. Gosselin, Transcripts vol. 83, p. 14826 (OF), p. 14817 (E).

[105] Testimony of Mr. Gosselin, Transcripts vol. 83, p. 14827 (OF), p. 14819 (E).

[106] Testimony of Mr. Gosselin, Transcripts vol. 83, pp. 14814-14818 (OF), pp. 14806-14809 (E); Exhibit P-256(A), p. 274.

[107] Testimony of Mr. Gosselin, Transcripts vol. 83, pp. 14818-14821 (OF), pp. 14809-14813 (E); Exhibit P-256(A), p. 275.

[108] Testimony of Mr. Gosselin, Transcripts vol. 83, pp. 14857-14858 (OF), pp. 14844-14846 (E); Exhibit P-154, pp. 4-11.

[109] Exhibit P-154, p. 11.

[110] Testimony of Mr. Gosselin, Transcripts vol. 83, p. 14858 (OF), pp. 14845-14846 (E).

[111] Testimony of Mr. Gosselin, Transcripts vol. 83, pp. 14857-14860 (OF), pp. 14844-14848 (E).

[112] Exhibit P-154, p. 19.

[113] Exhibit P-154, p. 21.

[114] Testimony of Mr. Gosselin, Transcripts vol. 83, p. 14886 (OF), pp. 14871-14872 (E).

[115] Testimony of Mr. Scully, Transcripts vol. 49, pp. 8549-8550 (OF), pp. 8549-8550 (E).

[116] Exhibit P-277(B), pp. 3-9.

[117] Exhibit P-277(B), p. 3.

[118] Exhibit P-277(B), p. 7.

[119] Exhibit P-277(B), pp. 15-23, 39-57.

[120] Exhibit P-277(B), p. 7.

[121] Exhibit P-277(B), p. 11.

[122] Exhibit P-277(B), p. 11.

[123] Testimony of Mr. Gosselin, Transcripts vol. 87, pp. 15471-15473 (OF), pp. 15458-15460 (E).

[124] Testimony of Mr. Gosselin, Transcripts vol. 87, p. 15472 (OF), p. 15458 (E).

[125] Testimony of Mr. Gosselin, Transcripts vol. 87, pp. 15472-15474 (OF), pp. 15459-15460 (E).

[126] Exhibit P-277(B), pp. 15-25, 29-37, 39-57, 59-60, 67.

[127] Testimony of Mr. Gosselin, Transcripts vol. 87, pp. 15472-15473 (OF), pp. 15458-15460 (E).

[128] Testimony of Mr. Gosselin, Transcripts vol. 87, p. 15473 (OF), pp. 15459-15460 (E).

[129] Exhibit P-277(B), pp. 26-27.

[130] Exhibit P-254, paras. 25-26.

[131] Testimony of Mr. Gosselin, Transcripts vol. 84, pp. 14914-14915 (OF), pp. 14913-14914 (E); Exhibit P-256(A), p. 2.

[132] Exhibit P-256(A), p. 65.

[133] Testimony of Ms. Côté-Gosselin, Transcripts vol. 84, p. 15005 (OF), pp. 14995-14996 (E); Exhibit P-281, para. 23.

[134] Exhibit P-428(A), pp. 91-92; Exhibit P-254, para. 38.

[135] Exhibit P-428(A), pp. 94-95; Exhibit P-254, paras. 52-53; Exhibit P-257(A), pp. 126-127; Testimony of Mr. Gosselin, Transcripts vol. 82, pp. 14653-14654 (OF), pp. 14637-14638 (E).

[136] Exhibit P-458, pp. 93-129.

[137] Exhibit P-428(A), p. 96.

[138] Exhibit P-458, pp. 85-91.

Chapter XIII

PAUL COFFIN

13.1
Communication Coffin

After working for other agencies since the mid-1960s, in 1992 Paul Coffin incorporated a numbered company (2794101 Canada Inc.) which carried on business as a graphic design and advertising agency under the name of Communication Coffin (the Coffin agency). It was and remained a small operation with only two full-time employees, Paul Coffin and his son Charles. It employed contract workers and freelancers for its remaining personnel needs, although in its invoices these workers were regularly described as employees, and Public Works and Government Services Canada was billed for their services in that way. As will be seen, this was only one of many irregularities in the billing practices of Communication Coffin.

The Coffin agency became qualified to manage advertising and sponsorship contracts on behalf of PWGSC in the 1997, agency-selection process which culminated, on April 28, 1997, with the declaration that ten agencies were so qualified. In the completed questionnaire submitted to the selection committee, Mr. Coffin made a number of deliberately false statements about the size of his agency, the number of persons it employed, and the revenues earned in previous years.[1] These responses probably did not deceive Mr. Guité, if he bothered to review the material, because he already knew about the small size of Mr. Coffin's agency from their social and business contacts.[2]

Probably the Coffin agency was destined to be qualified, no matter how well or badly it presented itself, because it was already working on a sponsorship contract, named "On the Road to Atlanta," which in 1996 had been given to the Lafleur agency. The Coffin agency did all the work as a subcontractor. More will be said about this contract later. As well, prior to April 28, 1997, the Coffin agency was already supplying consulting services to PWGSC,[3] and on the very date it was qualified, it was awarded five sponsorship contracts having a total value of $665,000.[4] It may be assumed that the agency knew this work was coming.

Mr. Coffin and Mr. Guité were good friends and had an active social relationship.[5] Their friendship, more than any other factor, is almost surely the reason why the Coffin agency was kept busy handling sponsorship and advertising contracts for the next few years,[6] since it had no particular qualifications to justify why it was selected over any other agency. After Mr. Guité left the public service, Mr. Coffin continued to be awarded contracts by Pierre Tremblay until the Sponsorship Program came to an end in 2003. In total, the Coffin agency looked after sponsorship contracts having a total value of more than $8.5 million in the years from 1997 to 2003.[7]

What is most remarkable about the contracts awarded to the Coffin agency is the amount of production costs and fees they foresaw and allowed. Although the promoters of events and projects received a total of $5,392,500 as sponsorships, the Coffin agency received in commissions, fees and costs a total of over $3 million. In some years (1998-99 and 1999-2000), the revenues earned by the Coffin agency were almost exactly equivalent to the amounts paid to the events being sponsored.[8] No other agency's fees attained this proportion. Figure XIII-1 reproduces a summary table submitted as evidence regarding these various sponsorships and fees.

COMMISSION OF INQUIRY INTO THE SPONSORSHIP PROGRAM AND ADVERTISING ACTIVITIES

COMMUNICATION COFFIN

Summary by fiscal year of sponsorship contracts for series EN771, EP043 et 6C523 submitted by PWGSC and/or CCSB to Communication Coffin and/or Média-I.D.A. Vision Inc. [1] for fiscal years ended March 31, 1995 to 2003

Fiscal Year	Submitted Amounts [2]					
	Media Placement	Sponsorship	CA Fee	AOR Fee	Production / Professional Fees	Total
1994-1995	-	-	-	-	25,855	25,855
1995-1996	-	-	-	-	105,000	105,000
1996-1997	-	-	-	-	46,750	46,750
1997-1998	-	835,000	100,200	-	516,800	1,452,000
1998-1999	-	565,000	67,800	16,050	494,750	1,143,600
1999-2000	-	630,000	75,600	18,000	571,950	1,295,550
2000-2001	-	1,157,000	138,840	33,000	526,975	1,855,815
2001-2002	-	1,775,500	213,060	53,265	228,519	2,270,344
2002-2003	-	430,000	51,600	12,900	6,320	500,820
TOTAL	-	5,392,500	647,100	133,215	2,522,918	8,695,733

Notes:

[1] The summary includes sponsorship contracts of series EN771 and/or EP043 and/or 6C523 submitted by PWGSC-APORS and/or CCSB, for whom Communication Coffin was the communication agency. This summary is including instructions given to Média-I.D.A Vision Inc. for whom Communication Coffin was acting as a communication agency.

[2] There are amounts which transited by Communication Coffin and/or Média-I.D.A. Vision Inc. to finally be given to publicities (re. Media Placement) or events (re. Sponsorship).

Figure XIII-1: Communication Coffin Sponsorships and Fees

In his testimony before the Commission, Mr. Coffin was remarkably candid about the billing practices of his agency and admitted the falsification of its accounting records and invoices. His candour was all the more remarkable because he was, when he testified, about to go to trial on 18 criminal charges of fraud relating to invoices to PWGSC, which were not an issue before the Commission. Before his criminal trial started, he pleaded guilty to the charges and submitted to the Court an agreed statement of facts preparatory to sentencing submissions. In the statement, Mr. Coffin acknowledges many of the practices which are the subject of the following section of this chapter.[9]

13.2
Billing Irregularities

In his testimony, and in the agreed statement of facts,[10] Mr. Coffin acknowledges that the Coffin agency regularly and consistently overcharged PWGSC in its invoices relating to sponsorship files in the following ways:

- Production costs and fees were billed for work which was not performed.

- Hours were billed for the work of persons who were subcontractors and not employees of the agency, at hourly rates far in excess of what the subcontractors charged for their services.

- Production costs and fees were billed for work that was performed, but which should normally have been compensated from the agency commission. For example, PWGSC was charged for time spent meeting with the organizers of sponsored events, for visits of a routine nature to the site, or for preparing post-mortem reports, all services that should not be the subject of time charges.

- The hours worked by employees were, until 2000, not recorded at all, and were billed by estimating the number of hours, regularly exaggerating them to bring the total charges up to the amount of production costs and fees fixed by the sponsorship contract.

- Generally, the hours worked by Coffin agency personnel or subcontractors were exaggerated, both in number and value.[11]

Mr. Coffin says that these billing practices were explicitly authorized and even encouraged verbally by Mr. Guité.[12] Mr. Guité denies this allegation.[13] Considering the frank manner in which Mr. Coffin testified and the finding I have already made that Mr. Guité's testimony in general is a good deal less than credible, on this issue I prefer the testimony of Mr. Coffin.

Two of the contracts handled by the Coffin agency deserve more detailed attention.

13.3
On the Road to Atlanta—Sponsorship Contract

In 1996, Robert St-Onge, who did subcontract work of a creative nature fairly often for Mr. Coffin, conceived the idea of producing a series of radio spot announcements about Canadian athletes who were preparing to compete in the Olympic Games in Atlanta. He discussed the possibility of government funding for such a project with Mr. Coffin, and the two men went to Ottawa to meet Mr. Guité and to try to convince him to sponsor it. Mr. Guité was interested but told them that the sponsorship contract would have to be directed to Lafleur Communication since it was the only Quebec agency qualified for such work in 1996, but that all the work could be done by Communication Coffin.[14] As has already been shown, Mr. Guité often resorted to this kind of subcontracting arrangement to circumvent the requirements of Appendix Q to the Government's Contracting Policy.

The amount of the sponsorship was based on an estimate of the costs, which was accepted by Mr. Guité at $225,000,[15] to which agency fees of $27,000 would be added as a commission. The contract with Lafleur Communication is dated May 13, 1996.[16]

The radio spot announcements were produced by Mr. St-Onge. His personal company billed the Coffin agency $13,400 for his work. The media placement costs and other expenses came to a total of $96,065. The Coffin agency billed Lafleur Communication for $225,000, turning a neat profit of $115,534[17] on the project. Obviously no thought was given to billing for the actual time spent and expenses incurred; the contract was treated as though it were a fixed-price agreement. The Lafleur agency billed PWGSC for the $225,000 it paid to the Coffin agency plus the commission of $27,000,[18] for which it did no work at all, other than to send its invoices.[19] Poor Mr. St-Onge, who conceived the project and did almost all of the work, was the least remunerated of all. At the hearings he remarked ruefully, when told how others had profited from his idea and his work, that he had most certainly been taken advantage of.[20]

13.4
The *Clarity Act*—Advertising Contract

A contract for advertising services related to publicity that the Government wanted in the context of the *Clarity Act* was given to Communication Coffin on December 7, 1999,[21] because Mr. Coffin understood that someone in the Government (the evidence does not disclose this person's identity) did not wish the agency that was really handling the file to be publicly identified. That agency was BCP, generally considered to be "Liberal friendly."

The cost to the taxpayer of this subterfuge was the fees charged by Communication Coffin to act as the billing agency without rendering any other services.

Mr. Coffin testifies that in 1999 he was asked by Pierre Tremblay or by David Myer at the Communication Coordination Services Branch to act as the agency purporting to handle the contract, it being understood that the services would be done by others and that they were already well under way. It was agreed that the Coffin agency would receive a commission for doing so of $30,000, and would be entitled to charge, in addition, a 17.65% commission on all subcontracts.[22] The contract foresees a total expenditure by PWGSC of $642,000, of which $214,000 would be for creative services, fees and commissions, and $428,000 would be for media placement.[23]

John Parisella of BCP testifies that, in fact, BCP had not been engaged to work on the *Clarity Act* contract, and could not assist in the work at that time due to a lack of resources. He says that BCP suggested that the work be done by a small agency called Éminence grise Inc., owned and operated by a former BCP employee named Luc Mérineau.[24]

The evidence shows that Mr. Mérineau worked on the project, and that the invoices for his services and the services of those who worked for and with him on the project were addressed to Communication Coffin in the name of Éminence grise Inc., but most of Mr. Mérineau's work was performed using BCP's studio with the assistance of BCP's employees.[25] This contradicts Mr. Parisella's testimony that no BCP employees were available to work on the project.

Regardless of who really did the creative work on the project and when the work was started (it appears unlikely that the Government would have left the public relations work to be done until the last minute), the involvement of Communication Coffin was not useful, and very costly. It billed PWGSC fees of $36,135, a commission of $35,596 on media placement and additional commissions on subcontracted work of $14,753, for a grand total of $86,484.[26] The fees charged were based upon hours worked that were simply invented.[27] The personnel at PWGSC who had awarded the contract to the Coffin agency in the first place must have known that it was not in fact spending time on the project, but authorized payment of the invoices anyway.

The failure of the personnel at CCSB to monitor the work and the invoices of the agency selected to handle an advertising campaign on behalf of the Government is particularly scandalous in this case. It may be explained in part by the expressed desire of the Government to handle what they considered to be a politically sensitive matter without appearing to use an advertising agency publicly perceived to have a political bias. As Mr. Coffin says in his testimony:

> They were looking for a small low-profile Montreal-based agency to handle a project that was highly sensitive and...they were asking me to help them facilitate this contract that was being prepared by another firm.[28]

Of course, the more honest and appropriate way to place such a contract would have been by a call for tenders. There was no public interest issue or urgency sufficient to justify awarding the contract without going through a public tendering process.

13.5
Relationship with Mr. Guité

Shortly after Mr. Guité's retirement on August 31, 1999, Mr. Coffin had dealings with him which will be reviewed in Chapter XV of this Report. One transaction should be mentioned immediately because it appears probable that it was discussed and negotiated while Mr. Guité was still a member of the public service, although it was concluded only afterwards.

Mr. Guité was, prior to his retirement, the owner of a 26-foot pleasure boat known as a Bayliner Cruiser, on which he and Mr. Coffin together went for a couple of cruises. In 1999 Mr. Guité decided to sell the boat, and after he had put it in the hands of a broker, Mr. Coffin offered Mr. Guité $27,000 for it, which was accepted. The price was paid by two cheques for $13,500 each, dated September 20 and November 1, 1999, respectively as reproduced in Figure XIII-2. No documents record the transactions.[29]

If the negotiation or the sale of the boat preceded Mr. Guité's retirement, questions could be raised about their propriety, in view of the ongoing business dealings of Communication Coffin with the CCSB, of which Mr. Guité was the Executive Director.

Figure XIII-2: Paul Coffin cheques to Chuck Guité.

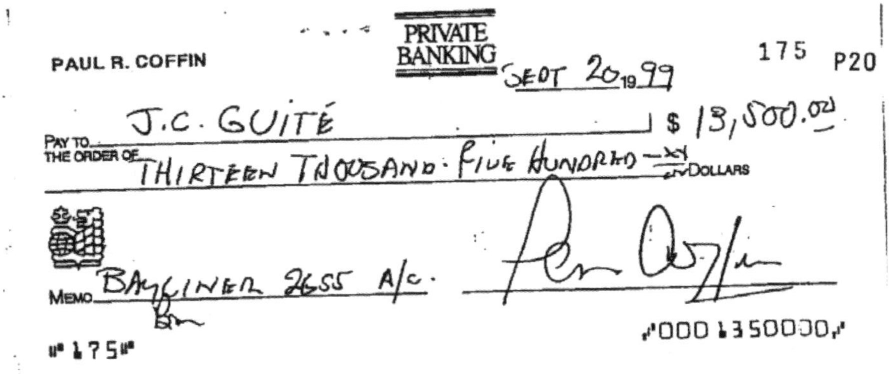

PAUL R. COFFIN

PRIVATE BANKING

SEPT 20 19 99

175 P20

PAY TO THE ORDER OF J.C. GUITÉ $ 13,500.00

THIRTEEN THOUSAND · FIVE HUNDRED — xx/xx DOLLARS

MEMO BAYLINER 2655 A/C.

⑈000 1350000⑈

⑆175⑆

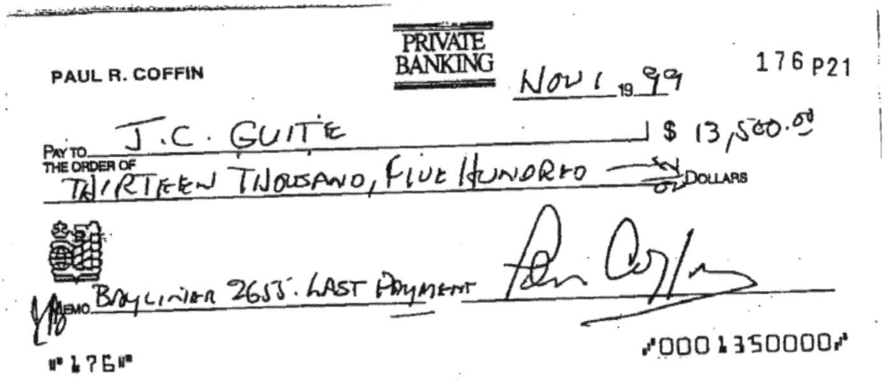

PAUL R. COFFIN

PRIVATE BANKING

NOV 1 19 99

176 P21

PAY TO THE ORDER OF J.C. GUITÉ $ 13,500.00

THIRTEEN THOUSAND, FIVE HUNDRED — xx/00 DOLLARS

MEMO BAYLINER 2655. LAST PAYMENT

⑈000 1350000⑈

⑆176⑆

Endnotes to Chapter XIII

1. Testimony of Mr. Coffin, Transcripts vol. 106, pp. 19296, 19302-19315, 19401-19403 (OE), pp. 19296-19318, 19412-19415 (F); Exhibit C-370, pp. 38-47; Exhibit C-369, p. 75.

2. Testimony of Mr. Guité, Transcripts vol. 108, pp. 19810-19811 (OE), p. 19826 (F).

3. Exhibit C-371, pp. 3-5; Testimony of Mr. Coffin, Transcripts vol. 106, pp. 19391, 19397-19400 (OE), pp. 19402, 19408-19412 (F).

4. Exhibit C-371, p. 6.

5. Testimony of Mr. Guité, Transcripts vol. 108, pp. 19673, 19803 (OE), pp. 19676, 19818 (F); Testimony of Mr. Coffin, Transcripts vol. 106, p. 19344 (OE), pp. 19348-19349 (F).

6. Testimony of Mr. Coffin, Transcripts vol. 106, p. 19495 (OE), p. 19514 (F).

7. Exhibit C-368, p. 1; Exhibit C-371, p. 2.

8. Exhibit C-371, p. 2.

9. Exhibit P-475.

10. Exhibit C-368.

11. Testimony of Mr. Coffin, Transcripts vol. 106, pp. 19306-19313, 19328-19334 (OE), pp. 19307-19315, 19332-19338 (F); vol. 107, pp. 19533-19541 (OE), pp. 19535-19544 (F); Testimony of Mr. St-Onge, Transcripts vol. 107, pp. 19608-19613 (OF), 19602-19607 (E).

12. Testimony of Mr. Coffin, Transcripts vol. 106, pp. 19461-19466, 19498 (OE), pp. 19477-19482, 19517 (F); Vol. 107, pp. 19518-19525 (OE), pp. 19520-19527 (F).

13. Testimony of Mr. Guité, Transcripts vol. 108, pp. 19808, 19825-19826, 19820 (OE), pp. 19823-19824, 19842-19843 (F).

14. Testimony of Mr. Coffin, Transcripts vol. 106, pp. 19428-19430 (OE), pp. 19442-19444 (F); Testimony of Mr. St-Onge, Transcripts vol. 107, pp. 19603-19605 (OF), pp. 19598-19600 (E).

15. Testimony of Mr. Coffin, Transcripts vol. 106, pp. 19432-19434 (OE), pp. 19447-19449 (F).

16. Exhibit P-239, pp. 1, 5-17.

17. Exhibit C-374, p. 2.

18. Exhibit P-239, pp. 25-27.

19. Testimony of Mr. Coffin, Transcripts vol. 106, p. 19433 (OE), p. 19448 (F); Testimony of Mr. St-Onge, Transcripts vol. 107, p. 19605 (OF), p. 19600 (E).

20. Testimony of Mr. St-Onge, Transcripts vol. 107, pp. 19612-19613 (OF), pp. 19606-19607 (E).

21. Exhibit C-373, pp. 8-35.

22. Testimony of Mr. Coffin, Transcripts vol. 106, pp. 19440-19448 (OE), pp. 19455-19463 (F).

23. Exhibit C-373, pp. 29-30.

24. Testimony of Mr. Parisella, Transcripts vol. 130, pp. 24708-24717, 24719-24721 (OF), pp. 24694-24703, 24705-24706 (E).

25. Exhibit C-373, pp. 41-81; Testimony of Mr. Mérineau, Transcripts vol. 123, pp. 23080-23082 (OF), pp. 23076-23078 (E).

26 Exhibit C-373, p. 3.

27 Exhibit C-373, pp. 67, 74, 79; Testimony of Mr. Coffin, Transcripts vol. 106, pp. 19458-19467 (OE), pp. 19474-19484 (F).

28 Testimony of Mr. Coffin, Transcripts vol. 106, pp. 19440-19441 (OE), p. 19456 (F).

29 Exhibit C-370, pp. 20, 21; Testimony of Mr. Coffin, Transcripts vol. 106, pp. 19344-19346 (OE), pp. 19349-19351 (F).

XIV

Chapter XIV

CLAUDE BOULAY

14.1
Corporate Organization

After operating an advertising agency in Quebec's Eastern Townships with his partner Jean-Pierre Belisle for five or six years, Claude Boulay and Mr. Belisle opened an office in Montreal in 1982 and started to expand their business across Canada under the name Groupe Everest. Over the years, other partners joined the firm, but Mr. Boulay continued to be its president and principal shareholder. A web of interrelated corporations was created, but for the sake of simplicity they will be described collectively as Groupe Everest, the name by which the businesses were known to the Government and under which advertising and sponsorship contracts were administered.

In 1996, Mr. Boulay's wife, Diane Deslauriers, started to carry on business with and for Groupe Everest through her personal corporation, Caliméro Partenariat Inc. (Caliméro), which sought out and administered sponsorship contracts on behalf of Groupe Everest for both public and private clients.[1]

14.2
Selection as Agency of Record (AOR)

Groupe Everest was one of the agencies qualified by the February 1995 competition to receive advertising contracts from Heritage Canada.[2] Since it immediately began to receive sponsorship contracts from Public Works and Government Services Canada once Mr. Guité "extended" the Heritage Canada list of qualified suppliers to cover suppliers to PWGSC, Groupe Everest did not need to involve itself in either the March 1995 or the 1997 competitions which led to the qualification of ten other advertising and communication agencies.[3]

However, on October 29, 1997, when PWGSC announced its intention to hold a competition to select a new AOR,[4] Groupe Everest allied itself with two other agencies to form a consortium under the name Média Vision, to present its candidacy and to make a presentation to the selection committee chaired by Mr. Guité.[5] Groupe Everest's role in the consortium is not disclosed in the application, although its presentation document refers to certain federal government accounts including the Attractions Canada file. Mr. Boulay's name does not appear anywhere.[6] He may have been concerned that an entity controlled by Groupe Everest might have been disqualified from acting as an AOR because of the potential for a conflict of interest.

On December 15, 1997, following the competition, Mr. Guité informed a representative of MédiaVision that it had been chosen as the new AOR.[7] A contract was prepared for signature, and it was in that context that it was revealed that the contracting party was to be a corporation named Média/IDA Vision Inc., whose obligations would be guaranteed by Groupe Everest.[8] Mr. Boulay must have revealed to Mr. Guité that Média/IDA Vision Inc. was a wholly owned subsidiary of Groupe Everest.

Evidently the presentation of the representatives of MédiaVision to the selection committee had been misleading, to say the least. It is impossible to know if the selection committee would have made the same choice if it had been made aware of the ownership and the true identity of the candidate.

Nevertheless, the contract engaging Média/IDA Vision Inc. as the Government's AOR for a five- year period was signed on March 31, 1998, in spite of the irregularity.[9] From then on it earned a 3% commission on all sponsorship contracts for its services.

14.3
The Business of Groupe Everest

Although sponsorship contracts and advertising became an important source of revenue for Groupe Everest in the years from 1995 to 2002, it also had significant revenues from its private sector clients. It was never as dependent on government business as were the agencies operated by Jean Brault, Jean Lafleur, Gilles-André Gosselin and Paul Coffin. Leaving aside the fees earned as an AOR, government sources accounted for 28% of its total revenues over the period.[10]

It should also be noted that the Commission saw no evidence of the abusive practices that have been described in the preceding chapters, such as recording and billing hours that were not worked, the exaggeration of time charges and overbilling generally, in the contracts managed by Groupe Everest.

Nevertheless, as will be seen from what follows, the pursuit for profit led Mr. Boulay and his associates to manage their business in ways which, although they may not have been illegal, were at best dubious and at worst unethical.

14.4
Relationship with Paul Martin and the Liberal Party

Mr. Boulay and Ms. Deslauriers and the corporations they own or control have overtly been strong supporters of the Liberal Party of Canada.[11] In the years from 1996 to 2003 inclusive, they made political contributions to the Party totalling $194,832. In the election year of 2000 alone, their contributions totalled $68,593.[12] Mr. Boulay also worked actively for Paul Martin in 1991 as a volunteer supporting his unsuccessful campaign for the federal Liberal leadership.[13]

During the election campaign of 1993, both Mr. Boulay and Ms. Deslauriers contributed their time and efforts for about 40 days, assisting the organizers in Mr. Martin's riding. They participated in speech-writing, telephone solicitation, door-to-door campaigning, and advising on strategy and communications. During this period they had occasion to meet Mr. Martin frequently, as did other election workers.[14]

Following the election, Ms. Deslauriers continued to be active in fundraising activities in Mr. Martin's riding on one occasion for the LPCQ and for the Quebec provincial Liberal Party.[15] She acquired a formidable reputation as a seller of tickets for fundraising events.

Again in 1997, Groupe Everest and Mr. Boulay personally rendered services to the LPCQ in developing and implementing campaign strategy, for which Groupe Everest was remunerated the sum of $118,950.[16]

In the course of these activities, a social friendship developed between the Boulays and Mr. Martin. This having been said, there is no evidence that that friendship or the well-documented ties of the Boulay couple to the Liberal Party of Canada were ever invoked by Mr. Boulay in an attempt to influence government officials to direct business or contracts to Groupe Everest, nor is there any credible evidence that Mr. Martin ever had a hand in the awarding of contracts to Mr. Boulay's agency.[17]

In his testimony Alain Renaud alleged, in a transparent attempt to discredit Prime Minister Martin, that he had overheard a conversation in which Mr. Boulay would have discussed the Attractions Canada dossier (discussed later in this chapter) with Mr. Martin.[18] I was satisfied that no credence at all could be given to his allegation, which is firmly denied by Mr. Boulay.[19]

14.5
Canvassing Commissions

In a number of instances Groupe Everest entered into agreements with its clients, who were promoting sponsored events, by which it would be entitled to receive a commission paid by the promoter as a reward for its efforts in securing the sponsorship from PWGSC ("a canvassing commission").[20] The commission was usually stipulated to be 20% of the amount of the sponsorship obtained in the first year, decreasing to 15% in subsequent years. It would be received from the sponsoree in addition to the usual 12% commission payable by PWGSC to the communication agency managing a sponsorship contract on behalf of the Government. The latter commission would nowhere be mentioned in Groupe Everest's agreement with the promoter.

Such double commissions were collected, for example, with respect to the sponsorship contracts awarded to Groupe Everest for the Société du parc des Îles ("the Société"), which operated an amusement park at which the Government wished to have visibility.[21] They were also paid in connection with the Jeux de Québec in 2001.[22] Although a canvassing commission was not in fact paid by Luc Lemay's company, Polygone, for the Salons held in Montreal and Quebec City, it was foreseen in the contract dated late 1996 by Polygone and Groupe Everest.[23]

In the case of parc des Îles, the Société received sponsorships for five years starting in 1997, totalling $2,625,000. The usual agency commission of 12% payable by PWGSC to Groupe Everest brought in revenues of $315,000, to which were added production fees of $57,910. From the evidence, it may be concluded that the total of $371,910 very adequately remunerated Groupe Everest for its time and efforts devoted to the management of the five sponsorship contracts.[24]

However, by virtue of its agreement with the Société, Groupe Everest also received from it in the first four years commissions totalling $343,750[25] for the solicitation of the sponsorships. These commissions were not disclosed to PWGSC.[26] In the fifth year, 2001, Pierre Tremblay heard that some agencies were charging such commissions. He promptly sent a letter to all sponsorees, explaining that the agency handling the sponsorship was adequately paid for its services by the Government, and that no additional remuneration was warranted.[27] Probably as a result of that letter in the fifth year the Société did not pay Groupe Everest a canvassing commission.

Despite Pierre Tremblay's intervention, Mr. Boulay and Ms. Deslauriers saw nothing wrong with the practice of collecting a commission from both the promoter of a sponsored event and the client paying the sponsorship money. They say that in the private sector the payment of a commission by the sponsoree, who of course is usually very happy to receive money of this kind, is normal practice.[28] Their explanation fails to recognize the fundamental difference between what might take place in the private sector and what occurred in the Sponsorship Program.

In the private sector, when a commercial enterprise pays the promoter of an event for the privilege of being able to announce its financial participation, and to advertise its products, it is perfectly logical for the canvasser who solicited the sponsorship to receive a commission as a reward for the successful solicitation. The sponsor does not pay the canvasser, who has only one client, the sponsoree, and is loyal only to its interests.

In the case of sponsorship contracts awarded by the Government, the loyalty of the communication agency is supposed to be to its client, which, in the case of the Sponsorship Program, is PWGSC. The contract obliges the agency to look after the Government's interests, for example by ensuring that the visibility for which it is paying is given in accordance with the visibility plan negotiated with the sponsoree at the outset. If the sponsoree, by carelessness or by a disregard of its engagements, fails to fulfill its obligations, the duty of the communication agency is to advise the Government of this breach, so that it might protect the public interest by withholding the sponsorship money or by seeking redress in some other way.

When Groupe Everest was arranging to collect commissions from both sides, it put itself in a conflict of interest because of its divided loyalties. It could not objectively represent the interests of both sides at once.[29] The fact that its representatives do not understand the concept of a conflict of interest demonstrates that they were not fully aware of their contractual responsibilities to the Government of Canada. The case of the Société du parc des Îles is a good example of a conflict of interest and the receipt by Groupe Everest of very substantial commissions, far in excess of what was necessary as fair remuneration for the work accomplished.

What is most revealing is that Ms. Deslauriers, who through her personal corporation, Caliméro, handled this file on behalf of Groupe Everest, did not disclose to Pierre Bibeau, the Executive Director of the Société, that Groupe Everest was paid by the Government to manage the sponsorship. Mr. Bibeau testifies that he had no idea that Groupe Everest was being remunerated for its work other than by the very substantial commissions it was receiving from his own enterprise.[30] If Ms. Deslauriers truly had a clear conscience that collecting a commission from both sides of a transaction was entirely appropriate, surely she would have let both her clients know that she was doing so. Keeping this information from them was a tacit admission that what she was doing could be criticized.

The public servants in PWGSC are not blameless with respect to the payment of double commissions. Some realities should have been faced. In a market economy such as ours, commercial enterprises such as communication agencies are operated by their owners and managers with one overriding objective, to make profits. The greater the profits, the more successful the business. Government officials should be conscious that the business enterprises with which they contract will be motivated in this way, and will not be inclined to safeguard the public interest at their own expense. It is accordingly one of the functions of the bureaucracy to protect the public purse against the desire for excessive profit of the private sector. This function was totally neglected in the file of the Société du parc des Îles. A telephone call or other simple verification with Mr. Bibeau concerning the arrangements he had made with Groupe Everest would have revealed that he was paying it a second commission. Clearly the Government paid $343,750 more for the visibility obtained than it was worth to Mr. Bibeau's business, since that was the amount redirected to Groupe Everest as a canvassing commission.

14.6
Art Tellier Contract

In the Art Tellier file, a substantial commission was paid to Groupe Everest in spite of the fact that it performed no services and failed to fulfill its obligations to the Government under the sponsorship contract in question.

In February 1999, Alain Renaud put Mr. Guité in contact with his brother Benoît Renaud, who operated a small business called Art Tellier, which was producing and procuring promotional articles such as t-shirts. Mr. Guité, on behalf of PWGSC, was interested in acquiring a quantity of such articles. He visited the Art Tellier premises to examine samples, and asked Benoît Renaud to prepare a quotation. There was no price negotiation or solicitation of competing bids.[31]

Almost immediately after Mr. Guité's visit, Art Tellier received a purchase order from Groupe Everest[32] in all respects identical to its quotation. Mr. Guité explained to Benoît Renaud that it was necessary to proceed through the agency of Groupe Everest because Art Tellier was not a pre-selected supplier.[33] Of course, this was nonsense. Nothing prevented PWGSC from procuring the articles directly from this supplier if it had taken time to follow normal contracting procedures, if it had sought competing bids, and if this supplier had won the bid. Instead, Mr. Guité issued a contract to Groupe Everest.[34]

Art Tellier filled the order, and the articles were delivered directly to Mr. Guité's office.[35] It sent a bill to Groupe Everest for $390,000, and Groupe Everest in turn invoiced PWGSC for that amount, adding a commission of 17.65%, or $68,835.[36]

Vincent Cloutier of the Groupe Everest subsidiary which handled this matter says that no work was performed by his agency.[37] This confirms Benoît Renaud's testimony on this issue. The usual services for which a commission of 17.65% is charged consist of seeking out at least three bids from potential suppliers of the goods to be procured by the subcontractor, and verifying that the goods supplied are in conformity with the specifications of the purchase order. Failure to perform these services[38] was a failure to fulfill the terms of the contract between PWGSC and Groupe Everest. It follows that it did not earn its commission of $68,835.

When Mr. Boulay learned of this transaction, he was conscious of its irregularity and made an investigation. He says that his staff showed him a letter from Mr. Guité, saying that a call for tenders had taken place and that Art Tellier had been chosen as the low bidder. However, neither Mr. Boulay nor PWGSC was able to produce a copy of that letter for the Commission.[39] In any event it was the responsibility of Groupe Everest, not Mr. Guité or PWGSC, to call for tenders, and this was not done.

14.7
Attractions Canada Contracts

The Attractions Canada project was conceived in 1996 by Mr. Boulay himself, and consisted of a publicity campaign aimed at Canadians to make them aware of the tourist attractions available to them in Canada. It was financed by the tourist industry in partnership with the federal government, which sought to gain greater visibility in print advertisements and in radio and television announcements.[40]

The project had been proposed in 1996 by Mr. Boulay to Roger Collet of the Canada Information Office, which agreed to sponsor it for an initial term of three years.[41] A contract with Groupe Everest was signed, engaging its services to act as its coordinator, to supply creative services, and to organize media placement. This was a major undertaking and involved disbursements by the Government of more than $27 million[42] over the five-year lifetime of the project, of which about $3 million was earned as fees and commissions by Groupe Everest. Nothing suggests that there was any impropriety in the administration of the project, which was generally considered to be a success.

The initial sponsorship contract was extended to 2001, but in that year the question of its further renewal became a cause for concern for Mr. Boulay,[43] since several of his employees worked full-time on the Attractions Canada file and would be out of work if the project were to be discontinued. On February 2, 2001, he wrote to Mr. Gagliano asking that the contract be extended and that the Government commit itself to disburse an additional $3.5 million on the project.[44] Mr. Boulay testifies that he wrote the letter on the recommendation of Pierre Tremblay, then the Executive Director of the Communication Coordination Services Branch.[45] Jean-Marc Bard, who was the Executive Assistant of Mr. Gagliano's office, recalls having received telephone calls from Mr. Boulay about the problem,[46] although Mr. Boulay says he has no recollection of making any such calls.[47]

On April 1, 2001, the contract between Groupe Everest and PWGSC, which had inherited the file from the CIO, was signed for exactly the amount requested in Mr. Boulay's letter.[48]

What is significant about these facts is the direct involvement of the Minister's office. Such involvement contradicts Mr. Gagliano's assertions that such matters were left to the sole discretion of the bureaucrat in charge of administering the Program, in this case Pierre Tremblay. Mr. Boulay's testimony about why he wrote to Mr. Gagliano is credible. Pierre Tremblay's advice to Mr. Boulay demonstrates that Mr. Tremblay did not consider that he had the authority to renew the contract without the concurrence of the Minister, a belief shared by Mr. Boulay. We have no evidence that Mr. Gagliano redirected this inquiry, or similar inquiries, to departmental officials, indicating that he would not participate in the decision-making process. It would have been a simple matter for him to do so.

14.8
Financial Results

Because of the significant revenues which Groupe Everest continued to earn from its clients in the private sector during the years when it was also deriving revenues from the Sponsorship Program and from government advertising, it is not possible to determine with precision the extent to which it profited from the latter sources, but there can be no doubt that they were lucrative. The net revenues from the operations of Média/IDA Vision Inc. alone between 1998 and 2003 were $1,709,441.[49]

It should be noted, however, that when the Attractions Canada contract was renewed in 2002, following Mr. Goodale's temporary suspension of the Sponsorship Program, the commission payable for media placement was reduced from 17.65% to 11.75% and the AOR commission was reduced from 3% to 2%.[50] Such reductions could have been requested and negotiated years earlier for this contract and indeed for all sponsorship contracts administered by PWGSC. It was incumbent upon Mr. Guité or Pierre Tremblay to attempt to procure goods or services at the lowest prices available, but they did not initiate such efforts. It is too much to expect the private sector to voluntarily reduce its profits unless the Government negotiates a lower price or the contract stands to be lost to a competitor offering the Government better value for its money.

Endnotes to Chapter XIV

[1] Testimony of Ms. Deslauriers, Transcripts vol. 104, p. 18951 (OF), p. 18939 (E).

[2] Exhibit P-19, Tab 15.

[3] Exhibit P-19, Tab 20.

[4] Exhibit P-56, Tab 3.

[5] Exhibit P-56, Tab 13; Testimony of Mr. Boulay, Transcripts vol. 104, pp. 18872-18873 (OF), pp. 18866-18867 (E).

[6] Exhibit P-56, Tab 13.

[7] Exhibit P-56, Tab 15.

[8] Exhibit P-56, Tab 16.

[9] Exhibit P-56, Tab 16.

[10] Exhibit P-428(A), p. 153.

[11] Testimony of Mr. Boulay, Transcripts vol. 104, pp. 18898-18899 (OF), p. 18891 (E); Testimony of Ms. Deslauriers, Transcripts vol. 104, pp. 18963, 18965-18968, 18972-18973 (OF), pp. 18950, 18952-18954, 18958-18959 (E).

[12] Exhibit P-340(B), p. 74.

[13] Testimony of Mr. Boulay, Transcripts vol. 102, pp. 18492-18493 (OF), pp. 18473-18474 (E).

[14] Testimony of Mr. Boulay, Transcripts vol. 102, p. 18492 (OF), p. 18473 (E); Testimony of Mr. Boulay, Transcripts vol. 104, pp. 18828-18829 (OF), pp. 18826-18827 (E); Testimony of Ms. Deslauriers, Transcripts vol. 104, pp. 18958-18959 (OF), pp. 18945-18946 (E).

[15] Testimony of Ms. Deslauriers, Transcripts vol. 104, pp. 18952-18956, 18963-18968 (OF), pp. 18940-18944, 18950-18954 (E).

[16] Exhibit PL-3. Remarks of Mr. Mitchell, Transcripts vol. 103, pp. 18555-18557 (OF), pp. 18555-18557 (E).

[17] Testimony of Mr. Martin, Transcripts vol. 73, pp. 12784-12798 (Original transcript; testimony of Mr. Martin in both English and French), pp. 12783-12798 (F), pp. 12783-12798 (E); Testimony of Mr. Boulay, Transcripts vol. 102, pp. 18495-18504 (OF), pp. 18474-18483 (E).

[18] Testimony of Mr. Renaud, Transcripts vol. 96, pp. 17065 (OF), pp. 17058 (E).

[19] Testimony of Mr. Boulay, Transcripts vol. 102, pp. 18500-18504 (OF), pp. 18480-18484 (E).

[20] Testimony of Mr. Boulay, Transcripts vol. 102, p. 18395 (OF), p. 18388 (E).

[21] Exhibit P-357, addenda, p. 2 of the agreement; Testimony of Mr. Boulay, Transcripts vol. 103, p. 18696 (OF), p. 18682 (E); Testimony of Ms. Deslauriers, Transcripts vol. 104, p. 19019 (OF), pp. 18999-19000 (E); Testimony of Mr. Bibeau, Transcripts vol. 105, p. 19192 (OF), pp. 19179-19180 (E).

[22] Exhibit P-355, pp. 62-67, 155; Testimony of Mr. Boulay, Transcripts vol. 103, pp. 18729-18730 (OF), p. 18712 (E).

[23] Exhibit C-302, pp. 14-19; Testimony of Mr. Boulay, Transcripts vol. 103, pp. 18751-18752 (OF), pp. 18732-18733 (E).

[24] Exhibit P-357, p. 2.

25 Exhibit P-357, p. 2.

26 Testimony of Mr. Guité, Transcripts vol. 109, pp. 19851-19852 (OE), pp. 19852-19853 (F).

27 For example, Exhibit P-357, addenda (letter from Pierre Tremblay to Pierre Bélanger).

28 Testimony of Mr. Boulay, Transcripts vol. 103, pp. 18688-18691, 18719-18725 (OF), pp. 18674-18678, 18703-18709 (E); Testimony of Ms. Deslauriers, Transcripts vol. 105, pp. 19033-19034 (OF), p. 19033 (E).

29 Testimony of Mr. Polevoy, Transcripts vol. 105, p. 19162 (OF), p. 19152 (E); Testimony of Mr. Bibeau, Transcripts vol. 105, pp. 19198-19199 (OF), pp. 19185-19186 (E).

30 Testimony of Ms. Deslauriers, Transcripts vol. 105, pp. 19033-19034 (OF), p. 19033 (E); Testimony of Mr. Bibeau, Transcripts vol. 105, pp. 19198-19199 (OF), pp. 19185-19186 (E).

31 Testimony of Mr. Benoît Renaud, Transcripts vol. 105, pp. 19230-19237 (OF), pp. 19214-19221 (E).

32 Exhibit P-351, pp. 31-35; Testimony of Mr. Benoît Renaud, Transcripts vol. 105, p. 19242 (OF), p. 19224 (E).

33 Testimony of Mr. Benoît Renaud, Transcripts vol. 105, pp. 19235-19236 (OF), pp. 19218-19219 (E).

34 Exhibit P-351, pp. 10-27.

35 Exhibit P-351, pp. 57-63.

36 Exhibit P-351, pp. 37-38.

37 Testimony of Mr. Cloutier, Transcripts vol. 105, p. 19132 (OF), p. 19124-19125 (E).

38 Testimony of Mr. Cloutier, Transcripts vol. 105, pp. 19123-19124 (OF), p. 19116 (E).

39 Exhibit P-367; Testimony of Mr. Boulay, Transcripts vol. 104, pp. 18841-18843 (OF), pp. 18839-18840 (E).

40 Testimony of Mr. Boulay, Transcripts vol. 103, pp. 18617-18622 (OF), pp. 18612-18616 (E).

41 Testimony of Mr. Boulay, Transcripts vol. 103, pp. 18626-18627, 18638-18640 (OF), pp. 18619-18621, 18631-18632 (E).

42 Exhibit P-90(A)

43 Testimony of Mr. Boulay, Transcripts vol. 103, p. 18641 (OF), p. 18633 (E).

44 Exhibit P-90(C), pp. 34-35.

45 Testimony of Mr. Boulay, Transcripts vol. 103, pp. 18643-18644 (OF), pp. 18635-18636 (E).

46 Testimony of Mr. Bard, Transcripts vol. 63, pp. 11110-11111 (OF), p. 11105 (E).

47 Testimony of Mr. Boulay, Transcripts vol. 102, pp. 18469-18475 (OF), pp. 18453-18458 (E).

48 Exhibit P-90(C), pp. 17-29.

49 Exhibit P-340(A), p. 28.

50 Testimony of Mr. Boulay, Transcripts vol. 103, p. 18649 (OF), p. 18640 (E); Exhibit P-90(C), p. 54.

Chapter XV

JOSEPH CHARLES GUITÉ
in RETIREMENT

15.1
Credibility

Throughout this Report I have had to assess the credibility of Mr. Guité's testimony on a number of subjects. In general, I have come to the conclusion that he is not always a reliable witness, and that any affirmations made by him should be accepted with caution. This being said, some of the statements of even the most unreliable witness may prove to be true. For example, if a statement is corroborated by the evidence of other witnesses or by documentation, or if it is made against the interests of the witness, or if it corresponds to a logical or plausible explanation of the surrounding circumstances, it may be accepted, even if the statement has been made by an otherwise untruthful person.

In the closing submissions made on behalf of the Attorney General of Canada[1] and Jean Pelletier,[2] the reasons why Mr. Guité should not be treated as a credible witness are set out in detail. I have considered these submissions with care as I have all of the written and oral representations presented at the final stage of the hearings, but I am not persuaded that Mr. Guité's testimony about what transpired during his meetings with Mr. Pelletier and Mr. Gagliano should be disregarded. As I indicated earlier in this Report when analyzing that evidence, considering the evidence as a whole, taking into account simple logic, plausibility, and elements of corroboration by independent witnesses such as Isabelle Roy and Joanne Bouvier, it is improbable that the question of the selection of agencies was never discussed during those meetings. Accordingly, in spite of the many instances where Mr. Guité contradicted himself and was not truthful on other subjects, his testimony with respect to the subjects discussed at his meetings with Messrs. Pelletier and Gagliano was accepted, notwithstanding the denials of these two witnesses who, in general, were more credible.

When Mr. Guité appeared before the Commission at the Montreal hearings, he was testifying for the second time.[3] Many of the questions put to him on that occasion concerned his actions following his retirement from the public service on August 31, 1999,[4] when he immediately offered his services as a consultant, lobbyist or intermediary to the persons and corporations in the private sector with whom he had been contracting on behalf of Public Works and Government Services Canada.[5] This gave rise to obvious suspicions that there may have been a connection between the benefits accruing to Mr. Guité from his post-retirement activities and the contracts that he dispensed while he was working for the Government. Mr. Guité's testimony provided him with an opportunity to dispel these suspicions.

There were already serious doubts about Mr. Guité's credibility concerning some of his evidence of facts occurring prior to his retirement, and these doubts were intensified by the implausibility of what he said about the remuneration paid to him for his services after retirement. He gave no evidence of any concern about the possible impropriety of what he was doing after his retirement, just as he was unconcerned about the way in which he failed to fulfill his responsibilities as a public servant prior to his retirement. To be fair to him, he does not in his testimony attempt to disguise the fact that, to use the expression coined by Sheila Fraser, he broke all the rules. Mr. Guité's frankness is shocking. He systematically failed to follow the requirements of Appendix Q with respect to calling for tenders or competing bids, he blatantly failed to observe the law with respect to certifications for payment in section 34 of the *Financial Administration Act*, he made deliberately false reports to Treasury Board about the observance, or should I say non-observance, of the rules respecting competitive bidding and he told Mr. Coffin to overbill PWGSC and tolerated obvious cases of overbilling by other agencies. The examples of his misconduct and maladministration could go on and on. Mr. Guité in his testimony reveals himself to be a man without scruples, and if he was unscrupulous in his actions, it may be inferred that he would be equally unscrupulous about telling the truth about those actions.

Accordingly, with respect to what he says about what he did following his retirement, Mr. Guité is not only an unreliable witness—he simply has no credibility on these issues.

15.2
Oro Communications Inc.

Mr. Guité's last day in the federal public service was August 31, 1999.[6] Oro Communications Inc. ("Oro") was incorporated the following day.[7] Mr. Guité was at all relevant times the principal actor directing Oro's activities; its shareholders were Mr. Guité and his immediate family.[8] Oro's office was in Mr. Guité's Ottawa home,[9] and it had no employees other than Mr. Guité and his wife.[10] From its financial statements, revenues from consulting fees for fiscal years ending July 31, 2000, 2001 and 2002, were $261,200, $402,400 and $375,831, respectively—a total of $1,039,431.[11] Questions come to mind at once how a former mid-level public servant could command such substantial fees for his accumulated expertise and advice—roughly three times his departing salary[12]—and whether there were reasons other than his expertise for which these amounts were paid.

It will be recalled that several of the persons representing communication agencies with whom Mr. Guité, in his capacity as the Director of APORS and CCSB, entered into sponsorship and advertising contracts, were noticeably reticent about testifying on the subject of their conversations and discussions with him in 1996 and 1997. Jean Lafleur professed to have no recollection whatsoever of any of the discussions with Mr. Guité that immediately preceded the avalanche of sponsorship contracts awarded to his agency in 1996, although he acknowledged that there must have been such discussions.[13] His total memory failure was not credible, and the Commission deduces that Mr. Lafleur's pretended memory lapses were used as a means of avoiding incriminating testimony and admissions.

Gilles-André Gosselin was so anxious to avoid testifying about his discussions with Mr. Guité prior to being awarded a series of contracts dated April 28, 1997, that he falsely affirmed that his agency was not working on the contracts prior to that date, even when he was confronted with documentary evidence that conclusively established the contrary.[14] He later admitted that his earlier testimony had been incorrect,[15] but little was learned from him about what had been said to him by Mr. Guité prior to the date when the contracts were awarded. Obviously he had been told they were coming to his agency, but no contextual details were provided. It must be concluded that Mr. Gosselin feels that there is something to hide.

Although Mr. Guité's testimony about the frequency and timing of his many meetings with Mr. Corriveau is credible,[16] he was vague about the substance of the conversations he had with him concerning the sponsorship contracts given by PWGSC to Groupaction for sponsorships to Mr. Lemay's enterprises, saying only that these matters were decided upon "upstairs."[17] We do not know from him how much he knew or might have suspected about Mr. Corriveau's kickback scheme.

In spite of sustained efforts to learn more about the meetings and conversations involving Mr. Guité following the communication to him by persons unknown of the Government's decision to launch the Sponsorship Program, the Commission remains largely in the dark. We know that APORS was given the mandate to administer the Program, that it was directed by Jean Pelletier, and that Mr. Guité enjoyed a degree of autonomy in allocating small sponsorship contracts to agencies he favoured, but no representative of an agency or subcontractor has been prepared to testify in any detail about their first contacts with Mr. Guité, even though it is fair to assume that he must have given the agencies concerned some sort of explanation about how each contract was to be administered, and how the agency was to be remunerated for its work.

The conclusion is unavoidable that no one who was questioned on this topic was willing to disclose openly the details of the early discussions between Mr. Guité and the communication agencies which later handled sponsorship and advertising contracts on behalf of PWGSC because some parts of those discussions involve seriously improper conduct by the participants.[18]

Oro's records identify 14 clients paying consulting fees for its 2000, 2001 and 2002 fiscal years, the most substantial being Groupaction, PacCanUS and the Institute of Canadian Advertisers. Also included are Communication Coffin, Jean Lafleur's Gescom and Groupe Everest International.[19] Table XV-I provides a breakdown of the consulting fees received by Oro in the three fiscal periods following Mr. Guité's retirement.

Table XV-1: Consulting Fees Received by Oro Communications Inc.[a]

Client	2000[b]	2001	2002	Total
Groupaction	$76,200	$1,400	$50,131	$127,731
PacCanUS[c]	56,000	168,000	147,600	371,600
Serdy Video Inc./Serge Arsenault	50,000	15,000	-	65,000
Compass Communications Inc./Tony Blom[d]	47,900	-	-	47,900
Communication Coffin	20,600	-	-	20,600
Essential Information Inc./Claudette Theoret	10,500	5,000	-	15,500
Institute of Canadian Advertising	-	100,000	90,000	190,000
Le Festival de la Santé Inc.	-	35,000	49,000	84,000
Wallding International Inc.[e]	-	30,000	10,000	40,000
Toronto 2008 Olympic Bid	-	20,000	-	20,000
Gescom[f]	-	15,400	22,100	37,500
Radio Marketing Bureau Inc.	-	7,000	-	7,000
Groupe Everest International	-	5,600	-	5,600
Palm Publicité Marketing Inc.	-	-	7,000	7,000
Total	$261,200	$402,400	$375,831	$1,039,431

[a] Data compiled by Kroll Lindquist Avey found at Exhibit C-375, p. 40.

[b] Oro Communications Inc.'s fiscal year was August 1-July 31.

[c] PacCanUS is the name of a company affiliated with, or the parent of, Vickers & Benson.

[d] Compass Communications is an agency based in Halifax which received most if not all sponsorship contracts with respect to events or projects occurring in the Atlantic Provinces.

[e] Wallding International Inc. is the consulting and lobbying firm formed by David Dingwall following his defeat in the 1997 general election.

[f] Gescom is a name of a corporation belonging to Jean Lafleur which was not acquired by one of Jean Brault's corporations when Lafleur Communication Marketing was sold to him in 2000.

The Commission notes at once that virtually all of the clients, with the principal exception of the Institute of Canadian Advertising, received direct benefits from sponsorship or advertising contracts, either as sponsorees or as communication and advertising agencies, during Mr. Guité's tenure at PWGSC. In more direct language, each of them had reasons to be grateful to Mr. Guité, to the extent that he had been influential in allocating those contracts.

15.3
Groupaction and Jean Brault

Mr. Brault testifies that in the fall of 1999, Groupaction was interested in expanding its business through acquisitions.[20] He knew of Mr. Guité's experience in the communications industry and, following his retirement, agreed to hire him as a consultant.[21] An agreement dated October 1, 1999, was signed between Oro and 9054-0337 Quebec Inc., a corporation belonging to Mr. Brault,[22] which stipulates that Oro will be paid $15,000 on signing and $10,000 per month plus expenses for 11 months, in exchange for Mr. Guité's consulting services and marketing advice.[23] The agreement notes that Mr. Guité cannot represent its client to the Government of Canada until August 31, 2000, because of "a post-employment clause as a senior public servant."[24]

This was not the first time Mr. Brault had sought and obtained Mr. Guité's advice. He says that in 1998, when Groupaction was contemplating the possibility of opening an office in Ottawa, Mr. Guité had told him that Gilles-André Gosselin's agency might be for sale due to Mr. Gosselin's health problems, and had given him assurances about the volume of business that would follow an acquisition.[25] However, Mr. Brault says that no remuneration was paid to Mr. Guité at that time for his advice or services relating to the Gosselin transaction.[26]

In accordance with the agreement of October 1, 1999,[27] Mr. Brault's numbered company paid Oro $35,000 in the period from October 1, 1999, to December of that year.[28] He says that Mr. Guité advised him about the possibility of the acquisition of, or amalgamation with, two other advertising agencies, Compass Communications and Vickers & Benson.[29] Another avenue that was explored in a preliminary way was the possibility of a transaction with Palmer Jarvis.[30] However, on November 30, 1999, Mr. Brault wrote a long letter to Mr. Guité[31] explaining why he had decided to put a premature end to their agreement, and offering him an indemnity of $30,000, equivalent to three months' notice.[32] This amount was paid in three instalments of $10,000 each over the next three months.[33]

In spite of the fact that the agreement had been cancelled, in April 2000 Groupaction paid Oro $11,984, said to be for consulting services concerning possible sales or mergers.[34]

On April 19, 2001, one of Mr. Brault's companies, Société Immobilière Alexsim Inc., paid Mr. Guité $25,000 personally by cheque.[35] Mr. Brault testifies that this cheque represents a loan to Mr. Guité, which Mr. Guité undertook to repay with interest at 3% per year one year later, evidenced by a promissory note.[36] The loan was never repaid.[37] Mr. Brault testifies that the $25,000 was an advance against future fees to be earned by Oro, and cannot explain why the cheque and the note are in the name of Mr. Guité personally.[38] His testimony on this subject could fairly be described as incoherent. Mr. Guité is much clearer; he says the loan was made to him to enable him to purchase a boat.[39]

On October 10, 2001, a second agreement with Oro was signed, this time by Mr. Brault on behalf of Groupaction,[40] which foresees payments in a total amount of $87,500 for "services to develop markets in Eastern and Western Canada."[41] The agreement is in the form of a one-page letter, which does not set out the services to be rendered in any detail. Mr. Brault testifies that the true nature of the services to be rendered by Oro had to do with continuing negotiations to sell or merge his agency with another.[42] There is no explanation as to why the letter agreement incorrectly describes the services to be rendered. Groupaction paid Oro, by cheques dated October 17, 2001,[43] and February 28, 2002,[44] the sums of $28,756.25 and $24,743.75, respectively, presumably pursuant to the agreement of October 10, 2001.

These payments, together with the loan or advance that was never reimbursed, are difficult to reconcile with the complete lack of any evidence of tangible results obtained for the benefit of Mr. Brault, as a result of the efforts and interventions allegedly made by Mr. Guité. There is no doubt that Mr. Guité was very experienced in the field of advertising and communications. His expertise was recognized by the Institute of Canadian Advertising, which engaged his services in August 2000 and paid him $10,000 per month until April 2002 to act as a lobbyist.[45] In October 2002 he resigned[46]due to the unfavourable publicity which followed the first report of the Auditor General.[47] However, the sum of $127,731[48] is out of proportion with the value of the services allegedly rendered to Mr. Brault, especially considering the lack of results. Mr. Brault is an experienced businessman and it is unlikely that he would repeatedly engage the services of a "consultant" and pay him very substantial fees when nothing in the way of results is ever produced.

While Mr. Guité was still a public servant, there is evidence that on two occasions Mr. Brault provided him with substantial non-monetary benefits that were highly inappropriate. In 1997, Groupaction bought and paid for a set of Pirelli tires for Mr. Guité's 1997 Mustang at a cost in excess of $1,000;[49] and in September 1998, it purchased four tickets to the Grand Prix of Italy in Monza at a cost of $12,537, which were provided as a gift to Mr. Guité.[50]The tickets were used by Mr. Guité and his wife, son and daughter-in-law on a trip to Italy.[51]

15.4
PacCan US

Oro's most important client was PacCanUS Inc.,[52] a corporation closely related to Vickers & Benson. During the period from September 1, 2000, when Mr. Guité became eligible to do business with the Government, until March 2002, Oro billed PacCanUS consultation fees of $371,600 and expenses of $29,794.[53] An abbreviated agreement in the form of a letter dated March 1, 2000, stipulates that Oro will be paid for its services to PacCanUS at the rate of $1,400 per day, and notes that it will be entitled in addition to a commission, in an amount to be determined, in the event of the sale of the Vickers & Benson business to a third party.[54]

Mr. Guité and John Hayter, the president of Vickers & Benson, knew each other well, and had had dealings with respect to the China series and Tourism Canada files.[55] Mr. Hayter testifies that Mr. Guité offered his services to PacCanUS as early as January 2000, but that Oro was retained only in March of that year when the possibility of a sale of the business to Havas, a corporation owned by interests in France, became realistic.[56] The principal reason that Mr. Guité's services were retained stemmed from Mr. Hayter's concern that because of the 100% Canadian rule, if Vickers & Benson should be acquired by Havas, it might no longer be eligible to receive advertising contracts from the Government of Canada.[57] He hoped that Mr. Guité would be able to find a solution to the problem.[58]

Mr. Guité says that in March 2000 he met Mr. Gagliano in an Ottawa restaurant and asked him for assurances that the sale of the Vickers & Benson business to Havas would not be a bar to future government contracts.[59] He thought this could be accomplished by a proposed corporate structure whereby the corporate vehicle doing business with the Government would be, at least nominally, wholly Canadian-owned.[60] Mr. Guité believed that such a structure had previously been used so that the ownership of BCP could be sold to foreign interests without compromising its business with the Government.[61] According to Mr. Guité's testimony, Mr. Gagliano said that he would have to discuss the matter with others, and would get back to him.[62] A short time later, Mr. Guité allegedly received a telephone call from Pierre Tremblay, who told him that Mr. Gagliano had spoken to Ministers Martin and Manley and that the volume of government business to Vickers & Benson would be maintained notwithstanding the proposed sale to Havas.[63] Mr. Guité says that he then informed Mr. Hayter that he had obtained the desired assurances.[64]

Mr. Hayter denies not only that Mr. Guité spoke to him about his alleged conversation with Mr. Gagliano, but also that he had ever asked Mr. Guité to seek the assurances that he said he had obtained.[65]

What is established by the evidence beyond any doubt is that the transaction with Havas took place on September 14, 2000,[66] that it did not cause any diminution of the business received by Vickers & Benson from the Government, and that Mr. Guité subsequently received from PacCanUS a commission of $100,000 for whatever role he played in facilitating the transaction.[67] It was arranged between the parties that this commission would be paid to him by way of monthly instalments of $14,000 each,[68] although Mr. Guité does not admit that the purpose of this arrangement was to disguise the fact that a commission was being paid.[69] He maintains that the payments of $14,000 were a monthly retainer for consultations. He continued to receive them until April 2002,[70] by which time he had received a total of $336,000 (24 months at $14,000 per month).

On April 25, 2002, Mr. Guité wrote to PacCanUS and attached to his letter a "financial reconciliation"[71] in which it is clearly stated that part of what he had been paid was the commission of $100,000 on the Vickers & Benson sale. In the letter (reproduced in Figure XV-1) he asks for a balance claimed to be due to Oro of $21,600.[72]

Figure XV-1: "Financial reconciliation letter"

April 25, 2002

Mr. Jim Satterthwaite
Paccanus Inc.
1920 Yonge Street
Toronto, Ontario
M4S 3E4

Dear Jim,

Thank you for your letter dated April 22, 2002 advising me that you are suspending our agreement due to further acquisitions being put on hold.

As you are aware, I was concentrating my efforts with a firm in Montreal and I have advised them accordingly. Should you decide to pursue these initiatives in the future, please feel free to call as I have made some important progress on this file.

Please find attached a financial reconciliation of our account. This summarizes the value of services against a monthly retainer paid to date. Once you've had a chance to review and agree with the attached, I will invoice Paccanus accordingly. Should you require clarification, please call and we can discuss in more details.

Finally, I would like to thank you for the assignment and we have been very successful over the last 2 years.

Looking forward to work with you in the near future.

Best regards,

J.C. Guité

FINANCIAL RECONCILIATON

April to December 2000

General assistance in the sale of V&B and ongoing advice regarding government relations. Provided professional advice on the sale to Havas.

Total days spent from April to December 2000:

80 days @ $1,400/day	=	**$112,000**
Commission on sale of V&B	=	**$100,000**
TOTAL		$212,000

January to December 2001

Ongoing advice on government relations. Search and preliminary discussion with Quebec based agencies.

Total days spent for 12 months:

88 days @ $1,400/day	=	**$123,200**

January to March 2002

Continued detailed negotiations with Quebec agencies and provided ongoing governmental relations.

Total days for 3 months:

16 days @ $1,400/day	=	**$22,400.00**

GRAND TOTAL	**$357,600.00**
AMOUNT BILLED (24 months @ $1,400/mo)	**$336,000.00**
AMOUNT DUE	**$21,600.00 + GST**

This "financial reconciliation," which was explicitly accepted by PacCanUS when it paid Oro the balance of $21,600, tends to corroborate Mr. Guité's testimony that he had been engaged to facilitate the sale in some way for which he was paid a commission of $100,000.[73] The document makes it probable that his recollection of the mandate he received from Mr. Hayter, and of the manner in which he accomplished it, is accurate. Mr. Hayter would have had no reason to pay him the commission otherwise.

With respect to the additional amounts paid to Mr. Guité, in excess of $250,000, after hearing the testimony of Mr. Hayter and Mr. Guité, I come to the conclusion that there was probably a relationship between what Mr. Guité was paid after his retirement and the contracts that Vickers & Benson received from PWGSC prior to his retirement. There is no other plausible explanation for the excessive amount of those payments, which greatly exceeded any rational evaluation of the time and services that Oro rendered to its client.

Finally, Mr. Guité admits that his approach to Mr. Gagliano in March 2000 was a contravention of the law regulating lobbying, since he has never been registered as a lobbyist, and that it was also a breach of his obligation not to carry out any form of government solicitation during the first year after his retirement.[74]

15.5
Communication Coffin

According to Paul Coffin, on January 4, 2000, he agreed with his friend Mr. Guité that Oro would be engaged by Communication Coffin to seek out financial partners for the Grand Prix de Trois Rivières, an event sponsored annually by PWGSC through contracts managed by Coffin.[75] As consideration for its services, he agreed to pay Oro $5,000 per month for three months.[76] Mr. Guité effectively confirms what Mr. Coffin says, although there are some details in the testimony of the two witnesses that do not correspond. The sum of $15,000 was paid to Oro for its efforts, if in fact there were any, which produced no results whatsoever.[77]

Oro invoiced Communication Coffin for an additional $5,600 in July 2000,[78]but this time the explanations given for the invoice are entirely contradictory. Mr. Coffin testifies that the $5,600 was due to Mr. Guité as the price of accessories of the boat purchased from him by Mr. Coffin the previous summer.[79] Since the boat purchase was a private transaction between two individuals, the invoice from one corporation to another for consulting fees cannot be readily reconciled with this explanation. Mr. Guité testifies that the invoice was for consultation services in relation to one of Mr. Coffin's clients.[80] One or both of the witnesses is clearly not telling the truth.

I am satisfied beyond doubt that both men are not to be believed about the consideration for any of the payments made by Communication Coffin to Oro, and that the total of $20,600 paid by Communication Coffin to Oro was a thinly disguised payoff for favours received from Mr. Guité while he was a public servant.

15.6
Gescom

At the time relevant to what follows, Jean Lafleur owned Gescom, a corporation which assists its clients in crisis management.[81] During the years when Mr. Guité was a public servant, Mr. Lafleur was not only the person who owned and directed the communication agency which received many lucrative sponsorship contracts from Mr. Guité's branch at PWGSC, but he was also a friend with whom Mr. Guité went salmon fishing and had a fairly frequent social relationship at dinners and hockey games.[82]

Starting in May 2001 and continuing until November 2001,[83] Oro sent monthly invoices to Gescom for "strategic consultations." There was an additional payment in January 2002 for which no invoice has been found. The total amount paid was $37,500.[84] No document records the reason for these payments. According to Mr. Guité's testimony, the $37,500 represented half of the consulting fee to which he was entitled as a result of the sale of the Lafleur agency to Groupaction, which occurred in January 2001;[85] he had expected to receive the other half from Groupaction, but he did not, and decided not to insist upon payment.[86] A little while later, he changed this testimony, and said that two of the invoices sent to Groupaction, dated October 12, 2001, and January 7, 2002, each for $25,000, represented the Groupaction share of the fee he earned for his participation in the Lafleur sale.[87]

Mr. Brault is simply unable to recall whether he had paid Mr. Guité anything in connection with the Lafleur sale,[88] whereas Mr. Lafleur says first that he cannot remember what amount was paid to Mr. Guité for his services relating to the sale, and then mentions that perhaps it was $10,000 or $20,000.[89]

It is impossible to reconcile these contradictory and confusing testimonies, and the credibility of all three witnesses on this subject is minimal. I am satisfied that the main reason they are unable to give coherent and believable answers to questions about the sums paid to Mr. Guité's company is that in all probability there never was a clear understanding about what would be paid to him, if anything, pursuant to the sale of the Lafleur agency. What is abundantly clear is that both Mr. Brault and Mr. Lafleur were grateful to Mr. Guité for the business he directed their way while he was the Director of APORS and CCSB, and were willing to pay him sums of money in recognition of his largesse. The sale of the Lafleur agency provided a convenient pretext for such payments.

15.7
Groupe Everest

According to the testimony of Messrs. Guité and Boulay, they only became friends after Mr. Guité retired from PWGSC.[90] From then on they and their wives saw each other socially, and they went on fishing trips together.[91] Of course, they had had frequent contacts professionally while Mr. Guité was a public servant.[92]

In 2001, according to Mr. Boulay, Mr. Guité offered to construct and stock a wine cellar at the Boulay residence, for which he was paid exactly $25,000.[93] No written documentation exists to support Mr. Boulay's version of this transaction, but it is confirmed by Mr. Guité.[94]

Also according to Mr. Boulay, in the fall of the year 2000, Groupe Everest retained the services of Oro to do a market study,[95] for which it was billed $5,600 on September 16, 2000, representing four days' work at $1,400 per day.[96] Mr. Guité says that he helped Everest prepare a pitch but has no recollection of to whom the pitch was to be made.[97]

In 2001, according to Mr. Boulay's testimony, Oro gave Groupe Everest a verbal mandate to carry out a study of the perception Canadian advertisers had of the advertising industry, at a cost of $60,000.[98] Related to the study, he says that Mr. Guité sought his advice concerning transactions involving the sale of Canadian advertising agencies to foreign firms.[99] However, the study was not completed and the only invoice from Groupe Everest to Oro is dated October 29, 2001, for an advance of $20,000.[100] In spite of the fact that no work was performed, and that Groupe Everest did not apparently send other invoices, the full amount of $60,000 was paid by Oro.[101]

Mr. Guité confirms that the original mandate was not fulfilled and that Oro paid Groupe Everest $60,000 anyway, explaining that Mr. Boulay gave him valuable advice on other subjects and projects.[102] His explanations are totally unconvincing.

All of these transactions are suspect, and both witnesses are obviously unwilling to disclose to the Commission the true nature and rationale of their financial relationships. Mr. Guité must have had some motivation for paying Groupe Everest $60,000, but it cannot have been for the verbal advice alleged to have been given by Mr. Boulay, leaving the Commission to conclude that something of an improper or illicit nature was the consideration for the sums paid, just as were the payments to Mr. Guité ostensibly for the construction and stocking of a wine cellar and a non-existent market study.

15.8
Conclusion

If one were to examine Mr. Guité's post-retirement dealings with each of these agencies one at a time, it would be dangerous to draw conclusions of impropriety. However, there is evidence of many transactions involving several different agencies and proof of payment of substantial sums of money for alleged "consultations," but virtually no proof of the services provided in exchange.

There is no direct evidence that there were understandings concluded with these agencies while Mr. Guité was still in the public service, but the reluctance of witnesses to reveal the substance of their conversations with Mr. Guité at the time when the first contracts were being allocated, combined with the evidence of the payments made to Oro after he retired, permits me to draw the reasonable inference that there had been such understandings, and that Mr. Guité relied upon them to persuade people like Messrs. Brault, Hayter, Lafleur, Coffin and Boulay to enrich him, under the guise of consulting services, once he had retired.

Mr. Guité, like Mr. Corriveau, seized upon the opportunity that the Sponsorship Program presented, with its complete lack of guidelines, criteria and oversight. He exploited it to enrich himself by obtaining or arranging payoffs and kickbacks from the communication and advertising agencies to which the PWGSC contracts were directed.

Endnotes to Chapter XV

1   Exhibit P-474(GG).

2   Exhibit P-474(S), pp. 33-35.

3   Testimony of Mr. Guité, Transcripts vols. 108-112 (Part 1).

4   Testimony of Mr. Guité, Transcripts vol. 108, pp. 19640 (OE), p. 19640 (F); Exhibit C-375 (Addenda), p. 106.

5   Exhibit C-376(A) pp.1-5.

6   Testimony of Mr. Guité, Transcripts vol. 108, p. 19640 (OE), p. 19640 (F); Exhibit C-375 (Addenda), p. 106.

7   Exhibit C-375, p. 2; Testimony of Mr. Guité, Transcripts vol. 108, p. 19652 (OE), p. 19654 (F).

8   Testimony of Mr. Guité, Transcripts vol. 108, pp. 19652-19653 (OE), p. 19654 (F).

9   Testimony of Mr. Guité, Transcripts vol. 110, pp. 20177-20178 (OE), pp. 20184-20186 (F).

10   Testimony of Mr. Guité, Transcripts vol. 108, pp. 19652-19653 (OE), p. 19654 (F); vol. 110, p. 20177 (OE), p. 20184 (F).

11   Exhibit C-375, p. 40; Testimony of Mr. Guité, Transcripts vol. 108, p. 19653 (OE), p. 19655 (F).

12   Exhibit P-104, tab 1.

13   Testimony of Mr. Lafleur, Transcripts vol. 75, pp. 13157-13162 (OF), pp. 13145-13150 (E).

14   Testimony of Mr. Gosselin, Transcripts vol. 82, pp. 14662-14665 (OF), pp. 14645-14648 (E).

15   Testimony of Mr. Gosselin, Transcripts vol. 87, pp. 15416-15418 (OF), pp. 15406-15408 (E).

16   Testimony of Mr. Guité, Transcripts vol. 109, pp. 19867-19868 (OE), pp. 19870-19871 (F).

17   Testimony of Mr. Guité, Transcripts vol. 109, p. 19951 (OE), p. 19962 (F).

18   Mr. Brault was not asked about possible discussions with Mr. Guité because such evidence could have compromised Mr. Brault's pending criminal trial for fraud and conspiracy to defraud (the latter allegations involving Mr. Guité.) The Commissioner is explicitly directed by his mandate "to ensure that the conduct of the inquiry does not jeopardize any ongoing criminal investigation or criminal proceedings" (paragraph k).

19   Exhibit C-375, p. 40.

20   Testimony of Mr. Brault, Transcripts vol. 91 (Part 3), pp. 16038-16039 (OF), pp. 16036-16038 (E).

21   Testimony of Mr. Brault, Transcripts vol. 91 (Part 3), pp. 16032, 16039 (OF), pp. 16031, 16037-16038 (E).

22   Exhibit C-299, after p. 9 (Addenda).

23   Exhibit C-299, after p. 9 (Addenda).

24   Exhibit C-299, after p. 9 (Addenda).

25   Testimony of Mr. Brault, Transcripts vol. 91 (Part 3), pp. 16034-16037 (OF), pp. 16033-16036 (E).

26   Testimony of Mr. Brault, Transcripts vol. 91 (Part 3), p. 16037 (OF), p. 16036 (E).

27   Exhibit C-299, after p. 9 (Addenda).

28 Exhibit C-299, pp. I0-I5.

29 Testimony of Mr. Brault, Transcripts vol. 9I (Part 3), pp. I604I-I6042 (OF), pp. I6040-I6042 (E).

30 Testimony of Mr. Brault, Transcripts vol. 9I (Part 3), pp. I6043-I6046 (OF), pp. I604I-I6045 (E).

31 Exhibit C-299, pp. I6-I9.

32 Exhibit C-299, p. I9; Testimony of Mr. Brault, Transcripts vol. 9I (Part 3), pp. I6040-I6042 (OF), pp. I6039-I604I (E).

33 Exhibit C-299, pp. 20-24.

34 Exhibit C-299, pp. 25-26.

35 Exhibit C-299, p. 39; Testimony of Mr. Brault, Transcripts vol. 9I (Part 3), pp. I6048-I605I (OF), pp. I6046-I6049 (E); Exhibit C-376(A), p. 293; Testimony of Mr. Guité, Transcripts vol. I08, p. I97I0 (OE), p. I97I6 (F).

36 Exhibit C-376(A), p. 293.

37 Testimony of Mr. Brault, Transcripts vol. 9I (Part 3), pp. I6050-I605I (OF), pp. I6048-I6050 (E).

38 Testimony of Mr. Brault, Transcripts vol. 9I (Part 3), pp. I6049-I6050 (OF), pp. I6048-I6049 (E).

39 Testimony of Mr. Guité, Transcripts vol. I08, pp. I97I0-I97I6 (OE), pp. I97I6-I9722 (F).

40 Exhibit C-299, pp. 35-36.

41 Exhibit C-299, p. 35.

42 Testimony of Mr. Brault, Transcripts vol. 9I (Part 3), pp. I6046-I6048 (OF), pp. I6044-I6046 (E).

43 Exhibit C-299, p. 37.

44 Exhibit C-299, p. 38.

45 Exhibit C-376(B), pp. I8, I9, 22-56, I22-I38.

46 Exhibit C-376(B), p. I45.

47 Testimony of Mr. Guité, Transcripts vol. I08, pp. I9769-I9774 (OE), pp. I0780-I9786 (F).

48 Exhibit C-375, p. 40.

49 Testimony of Mr. Brault, Transcripts vol. 9I (Part 3), pp. I6053-I6058 (OF), pp. I605I-I6055 (E); Exhibit C-3I3, pp. 78, II6; Testimony of Mr. Brault, Transcripts vol. 92, pp. I6286-I6288 (OF), pp. I6278-I628I (E).

50 Testimony of Mr. Brault, Transcripts vol. 9I (Part 3), pp. I6I09-I6II4 (OF), pp. I6I02-I6I07 (E); Exhibit C-309, pp. 222-228.

51 Testimony of Mr. Guité, Transcripts vol. II0, pp. 20I06-20I09 (OE), pp. 20I09-20II2 (E).

52 Exhibit C-375, pp. 40-57; Exhibit C-376(A), pp. I68-239.

53 Exhibit C-375, pp. 40-57; Exhibit C-376(A), pp. I68-239.

54 Exhibit C-376(A), pp. I49-I50; Testimony of Mr. Guité, Transcripts vol. I08, pp. I9744-I9745 (OE), pp. I9752-I9754 (F).

55 Testimony of Mr. Guité, Transcripts vol. I08, pp. I9745-I9746 (OE), p. I9754 (F); Testimony of Mr. Hayter, Transcripts vol. I22, p. 22857 (OE), pp. 22866-22867 (F).

56 Testimony of Mr. Hayter, Transcripts vol. I22, pp. 22858-22859 (OE), pp. 22867-22869 (F).

57 Testimony of Mr. Hayter, Transcripts vol. I22, pp. 22866-22869 (OE), pp. 22876-22879 (F).

58 Testimony of Mr. Hayter, Transcripts vol. I22, pp. 22866-22869 (OE), pp. 22876-22879 (F).

59 Testimony of Mr. Guité, Transcripts vol. I08, pp. I975I-I9756 (OE), pp. I976I-I9766 (F); Exhibit P-377, p. I.

60 Testimony of Mr. Guité, Transcripts vol. 108, p. 19757 (OE), p. 19767 (F).

61 Testimony of Mr. Guité, Transcripts vol. 108, pp. 19749-19751 (OE), pp. 19758-19760 (F).

62 Testimony of Mr. Guité, Transcripts vol. 108, pp. 19754-19755 (OE), p. 19764 (F).

63 Testimony of Mr. Guité, Transcripts vol. 108, pp. 19755-19757 (OE), pp. 19764-19766 (F).

64 Testimony of Mr. Guité, Transcripts vol. 108, pp. 19757-19759 (OE), pp. 19767-19769 (F).

65 Testimony of Mr. Hayter, Transcripts vol. 122, pp. 22906-22911 (OE), pp. 22920-22926 (F).

66 Exhibit C-376(B), pp. 249-252.

67 Exhibit C-376(A), p. 236; Testimony of Mr. Guité, Transcripts vol. 108, pp. 19760-19761 (OE), pp. 19769-19771 (F).

68 Testimony of Mr. Guité, Transcripts vol. 108, pp. 19761-19765 (OE), pp. 19771-19776 (F); Exhibit C-376(A), pp. 154A-229.

69 Testimony of Mr. Guité, Transcripts vol. 108, pp. 19764-19765 (OE), pp. 19775-19776 (F).

70 Exhibit C-376(A), p. 227.

71 Exhibit C-376(A), pp. 235-236.

72 Exhibit C-376(A), p. 236.

73 Exhibit C-376(A), pp. 238-239.

74 Testimony of Mr. Guité, Transcripts vol. 108, pp. 19760-19761 (OE), pp. 19769-19771 (F).

75 Exhibit C-370, p. 11; Testimony of Mr. Coffin, Transcripts vol. 106, pp. 19349-19350 (OE), pp. 19354-19355 (F).

76 Testimony of Mr. Coffin, Transcripts vol. 106, pp. 19350-19351 (OE), pp. 19354-19355 (F).

77 Testimony of Mr. Guité, Transcripts vol. 108, pp. 19803-19806 (OE), pp. 19818-19822 (F).

78 Exhibit C-370, pp. 17, 17A.

79 Testimony of Mr. Coffin, Transcripts vol. 106, pp. 19356-19357, 19470-19474 (OE), pp. 19363, 19488-19492 (F).

80 Testimony of Mr. Guité, Transcripts vol. 108, pp. 19805-19808 (OE), pp. 19820-19824 (F).

81 Testimony of Mr. Lafleur, Transcripts vol. 74, p. 12904 (OF), p. 12901 (E); Exhibit P-229, p. 3.

82 Testimony of Mr. Guité, Transcripts vol. 108, pp. 19675-19676 (OE), pp. 19678-19679 (F).

83 Exhibit C-376(A), pp. 240-253; Exhibit C-375, pp. 49, 54.

84 Exhibit C-375, p. 40.

85 Testimony of Mr. Guité, Transcripts vol. 109, pp. 19981-19986 (OE), pp. 19994-20000 (F).

86 Testimony of Mr. Guité, Transcripts vol. 109, pp. 19986-19992 (OE), pp. 20000-20006 (F).

87 Testimony of Mr. Guité, Transcripts vol. 109, pp. 19990-19992 (OE), pp. 20004-20006 (F); Exhibit C-376(A), pp. 301, 306.

88 Testimony of Mr. Brault, Transcripts vol. 91 (part 3), pp. 16037-16038 (OF), pp. 16035-16036 (E); Testimony of Mr. Brault, Transcripts vol. 92, pp. 16294-16296 (OF), pp. 16286-16288 (E).

89 Testimony of Mr. Lafleur, Transcripts vol. 79, pp. 13822-13825 (OF), pp. 13819-13821 (E).

90 Testimony of Mr. Boulay, Transcripts vol. 102, pp. 18456-18461 (OF), pp. 18443-18446 (F); Testimony of Mr. Guité, Transcripts vol. 108, pp. 19676-19677 (OE), pp. 19679-19680 (F).

91 Testimony of Mr. Boulay, Transcripts vol. 102, p. 18460 (OF), pp. 18445-18446 (E).

92 Exhibit C-295, pp. 24-27.

[93] Testimony of Mr. Boulay, Transcripts vol. 102, pp. 18439-18441 (OF), pp.18428-18429 (E).

[94] Testimony of Mr. Guité, Transcripts vol. 109, pp. 19839-19843 (OE), pp. 19840-19843 (F).

[95] Testimony of Mr. Boulay, Transcripts vol. 102, pp. 18418-18420, 18438-18439 (OF), pp. 18409-18411, 18451-18452 (E); Exhibit P-359, Addenda, p. 7.

[96] Exhibit C-376(B), pp. 160-161.

[97] Testimony of Mr. Guité, Transcripts vol. 109, pp. 19838-19839 (OE), pp. 19838-19839 (F); Testimony of Mr. Boulay, Transcripts vol. 102, pp. 18418-18420, 18438-18439 (OF), pp. 18408-18410, 18427-18428 (E); Exhibit P-359, Addenda, p. 7; Exhibit P-376(B), pp. 160-161.

[98] Testimony of Mr. Boulay, Transcripts vol. 102, pp. 18406-18408 (OF), pp. 18397-18399 (E).

[99] Testimony of Mr. Boulay, Transcripts vol. 102, pp. 18407-18408 (OF), pp. 18398-18399 (E).

[100] Testimony of Mr. Boulay, Transcripts vol. 102, pp. 18408-18418 (OF), pp. 18399- 18409 (E); Exhibit P-359, p. 3.

[101] Testimony of Mr. Boulay, Transcripts vol. 102, pp. 18409-18410 (OF), pp. 18400-18401 (E).

[102] Testimony of Mr. Guité, Transcripts vol. 108, pp. 19827-19834 (OE), pp. 19843-19851 (F).

CHAPTER XVI

ASSIGNING RESPONSIBILITY

As noted in the Introduction to this Report, I heard oral arguments at the conclusion of the hearings. They lasted five days and included representations from 21 participants, intervenors and interested parties, all of whom had previously filed written submissions. Fifteen others filed written submissions, but chose not to argue orally.

Many of the arguments put forward are dealt with elsewhere in the Report. Where that has occurred, I will try not to repeat what has already been said. The names of some of the persons who made submissions are either not mentioned anywhere in the Report, or are not the subject of any critical comments. Nothing adverse has been said about those persons because I came to the conclusion that their involvement in the matters which are the subject of the Report was not blameworthy, or was of such little significance that it was not worth mentioning.

This Report is not a judgment, and the present conclusions do not establish the legal responsibility, either civil or criminal, of the persons and organizations singled out for critical comment or a finding of misconduct. The paragraphs that follow should not be read in isolation, but form part of the overall conclusions of the Report, which are to be found throughout the text. The fact that only certain persons or organizations are mentioned in this chapter does not absolve the others assigned blame earlier in this Report.

When the Commission received its mandate more than 18 months ago, a body of opinion expressed the view that the Inquiry would be a waste of time and money because the essential facts of what was being described as the "sponsorship scandal" were already known and had been fully exposed in Chapters 3 and 4 of the Report of the Auditor General of Canada. According to these opinions, the scandal was due to the improper and illegal actions of a small number of public servants in PWGSC working under the direction of Mr. Guité, who was perceived to have been directing lucrative contracts to certain "Liberal friendly" advertising and communication agencies. There was no point in looking for responsibility elsewhere. These propositions were reflected in many of the submissions. No one, at any level within the federal government and bureaucracy, was prepared to accept blame for his or her actions or omissions in the development, management, operation and oversight of the Sponsorship Program, or for irregularities in government advertising disclosed by the Auditor General and the evidence before this Commission.

The results of the Inquiry have shown how erroneous were the predictions that it would be a waste of time and money. Although there has never been any doubt that the maladministration of the Sponsorship Program by Mr. Guité, Pierre Tremblay and a few of the public servants who were working under them was at the heart of the problem, it has become apparent that they were not the sole cause of the "sponsorship scandal," nor were they its principal beneficiaries. They should not be the only persons held responsible for the errors committed in its administration. Other factors and the actions taken and decisions made by other persons not only made it possible for them to act as they did, but made it probable and predictable that public funds would be mismanaged and misappropriated. I do not need to repeat what has been said in preceding chapters about the character and actions of

Mr. Guité, nor is it useful to reiterate all of the administrative errors and inadequacies of the personnel at the Advertising and Public Opinion Research Service and the Communication Coordination Services Branch. The purpose of this closing chapter is to highlight, summarize and put into context what I consider to be the Report's most significant findings with a view to identifying the other persons who should share the responsibility for allowing the "sponsorship scandal" to occur.

On the basis of the evidence, I have been able to identify three main factors that caused or contributed to the problems described in the Report of the Auditor General:

- the unprecedented decision to direct the Sponsorship Program from the PMO, bypassing the departmental procedures and controls which the Deputy Minister of PWGSC would normally have been expected to apply and enforce;

- the failure of the Deputy Minister of PWGSC to provide oversight and administrative safeguards against the misuse of public funds;

- the deliberate lack of transparency on how the Program was initiated, financed and directed.

16.1
The Responsibility of Messrs. Chrétien and Pelletier

The evidence establishes that in order to give effect to the Cabinet resolution of February 1-2, 1996, which adopted the recommendations of the Massé Report, Prime Minister Chrétien delegated to Jean Pelletier the responsibility for a new program of sponsorships. Mr. Pelletier initiated the program and directed it himself. In order to implement the new program, Mr. Pelletier met with and gave instructions to Mr. Guité without the participation of the Deputy Minister of PWGSC or any other senior official. The program was commenced in haste without a public announcement of any kind, and without clearly defined objectives, administrative guidelines or criteria.

Mr. Pelletier, with his many years of experience in public administration, must have known that such a program of discretionary spending would be open to error and abuse unless provided with rules, guidelines, controls, safeguards and oversight specific to that program. He was not entitled to assume that the mandatory rules stipulated in the *Financial Administration Act* and by Treasury Board policies would provide sufficient protection against the possibility of dishonesty, error and incompetence, or that Mr. Guité and his staff could be trusted to administer such an unprecedented program with perfect competence and probity. The opportunities for misappropriation of public funds and personal gain offered by an unstructured program of grants and contributions such as the Sponsorship Program are enormous, and the opportunities they offer to unscrupulous persons to profit personally or grant favours to others are temptations almost impossible to resist. The rules and guidelines prescribed by Treasury Board policies and oversight by deputy ministers and their staff ordinarily provide the procedural framework for honest and competent public servants. However, such policies and oversight are also meant to create an obstacle to dishonesty and incompetence. By choosing to give direction to Mr. Guité personally, Mr. Pelletier bypassed the normal methods of administration of government programs by public servants, and effectively eliminated the oversight that would otherwise have been provided by Mr. Quail and his department.

Counsel for Mr. Pelletier, Mr. Chrétien and Mr. Gagliano all argue that it was entirely legitimate for Messrs. Pelletier and Gagliano to meet with Mr. Guité and to provide him with "political input," since the Sponsorship Program was of a political nature. They argue that experienced politicians from Quebec were best able to assess where and how much money would most effectively be spent to achieve the objectives of the Program. This argument presupposes that administrative officials, provided with appropriate guidelines and criteria, would not have been able to make such assessments, and this has not been shown. But the argument is also dangerously flawed for another reason. If it is accepted as valid, it opens the door to political interference in all government programs where there is discretion in the allocation of money or benefits, for example on a regional basis. All such programs may well be described as political in the sense that they may be said to rely on the expertise and input of elected representatives who initiated the programs, and they have the potential to confer electoral advantage to the governing party. In our Canadian system, the administration of the programs, which includes choosing the persons and organizations that will benefit from them, is better left to the bureaucracy. It is only in that way that the Government can avoid the appearance and the reality of arbitrary handouts to the governing party's present or potential friends and supporters, for partisan considerations.

The notion that Mr. Pelletier and Mr. Gagliano could provide "political input" without strongly influencing the decision-making process is nonsense and ignores the obvious reality that the expression of an opinion to a subordinate official by the Prime Minister's Chief of Staff or the Minister amounts to an order.

Mr. Pelletier said during his testimony how much he was impressed by Mr. Chrétien's speech to his deputy ministers shortly after the 1993 election, when he announced how policy-making and bureaucratic administration were to be kept separate and distinct; but his actions in meeting with Mr. Guité in the absence of Mr. Quail or his representative ran directly counter to that principle. It constituted political encroachment into the administrative domain, and was a dangerous precedent that should not be condoned.

Counsel for Mr. Pelletier argues that there were no norms or standards of performance for the direction of a program like the Sponsorship Program, and that, without such norms or standards, there is no basis for finding fault on the part of Mr. Pelletier. However, there were two major flaws in the Program from the beginning, of which an experienced politician or public administrator should have been aware. First, having the Program administered on behalf of the Government by private sector communication agencies was an open invitation to unscrupulous persons within those agencies to reap unjustified or exaggerated profits; and second, initiating a program of this kind without first developing rules, guidelines and criteria, and without ensuring effective bureaucratic oversight, left the door open to error, abuse and careless administration. These two flaws were immediately recognized by Mr. Goodale when he was suddenly appointed Minister of PWGSC in 2002. Within 24 hours of his appointment, on the basis of briefings from the Deputy Minister and departmental officials, he realized that the Program was being run badly, and froze it at once. When it recommenced a few months later, Mr. Goodale discontinued the use of communication agencies, which he found to be inappropriate, in favour of administration by public servants equipped with the proper tools and resources including newly established guidelines. The abuses that had characterized the Program when it was first initiated, and during the time when Mr. Gagliano had been the responsible Minister, stopped immediately.

These elementary measures should have been applied from the beginning. The standard of performance which the Commission is applying is the common sense standard illustrated by Mr. Goodale's corrective measures.

There is no evidence or indication that Mr. Pelletier was in any way involved in Mr. Corriveau's kickback scheme, or that he knew about it, although it would have been more prudent for him to investigate the general suspicions that he says he communicated to the Prime Minister when, according to his testimony, he had a "hunch" that there was something not quite right about Mr. Corriveau. However, the absence of any evidence of direct involvement in Mr. Corriveau's wrongdoing entitles both Mr. Pelletier and Mr. Chrétien to be exonerated from blame for Mr. Corriveau's misconduct.

But they are to be blamed for omissions. Since Mr. Chrétien chose to run the Program from his own office, and to have his own exempt staff take charge of its direction, he is accountable for the defective manner in which the Sponsorship Program and initiatives were implemented. Mr. Pelletier, for whom Mr. Chrétien was responsible, failed to take the most elementary precautions against mismanagement. There is ample evidence of an appalling lack of preparation for the introduction of a new program involving the discretionary disbursement of millions of dollars of public money by Mr. Guité's organization, without supervision or guidelines. What Mr. Chrétien and Mr. Pelletier should have done in 1996 was what Mr. Goodale did in 2002.

They should also have done precisely what Ms. Bourgon counselled the Prime Minister to do, which was to postpone making decisions about sponsorship initiatives until a formal process had been adopted for evaluating them. It would have been more prudent for Mr. Chrétien to have accepted her suggestion that responsibility for the administration of the Program be transferred to the PCO or to a Minister, instead of being retained within the PMO. He chose to disregard this advice, and since he is directly responsible for errors committed by Mr. Pelletier, he must share the blame for the mismanagement that ensued.

Good intentions are not an excuse for maladministration of this magnitude. The Prime Minister and his Chief of Staff arrogated to themselves the direction of a virtually secret program of discretionary spending to selected beneficiaries, saying that they believed in good faith that those grants would enhance Canadian unity. Whether or not their belief in that outcome was justified is not for the Commission to judge. However, each has testified that he believed that the Program would be properly administered by Mr. Guité and his organization. They did not verify this assumption even though they had created a program lacking all of the normal safeguards against maladministration. The assumption was naïve, imprudent and entirely unfounded.

16.2
The Responsibility of Mr. Gagliano

In June 1997 Mr. Gagliano became Minister of PWGSC. He chose to perpetuate the irregular manner of directing the Sponsorship Program that had been adopted by Mr. Pelletier, and with him, met with and gave directions in person to Mr. Guité, excluding Mr. Quail from the direction and supervision of the activities of a public servant within his department. When he became involved in the direction of the Program, Mr. Gagliano, like Mr. Pelletier, failed to give sufficient attention to the adoption of guidelines and criteria, and failed to provide oversight to what Mr. Guité and his successor, Pierre Tremblay, were doing, all the while systematically bypassing the Deputy Minister from whom oversight would normally be forthcoming. Contrary to his testimony to the effect that his participation was limited to providing political input and making recommendations about events and projects to be sponsored, Mr. Gagliano became directly involved in decisions to provide funding to events and projects for partisan purposes, having little to do with considerations of national unity.

Finally, just as Mr. Chrétien must accept responsibility for the actions of his exempt staff such as Mr. Pelletier, Mr. Gagliano must accept responsibility for the actions and decisions of his exempt staff including Pierre Tremblay, when Mr. Tremblay was serving as his Executive Assistant, and Jean-Marc Bard.

16.3
The Responsibility of Other Ministers

On the evidence there is no basis for attributing blame or responsibility for the maladministration of the Sponsorship Program to any other Minister of the Chrétien Cabinet, since they, like all Members of Parliament, were not informed of the initiatives being authorized by Mr. Pelletier, and their funding from the Unity Reserve. Mr. Martin, whose role as Finance Minister did not involve him in the supervision of spending by the PMO or PWGSC, is entitled, like other Ministers in the Quebec caucus, to be exonerated from any blame for carelessness or misconduct. Ministers are not responsible for what they do not know about the actions and decisions of the PMO or other Ministers, or about the administration of departments other than their own. Sponsored events that took place in a Member's riding, or that may have been supported or advocated by the riding association, do not create a presumption that the MP in question was familiar with the Sponsorship Program as a whole.

Mr. Chrétien, Mr. Pelletier and Mr. Gagliano, apparently motivated by a belief that their political adversaries in Quebec would exploit information about the Sponsorship Program to the disadvantage of the federalist cause, chose to keep it a secret, even from Mr. Chrétien's colleagues in the Cabinet, at least to the extent that that was possible, and for as long as possible. This strategy eventually backfired, since the public tends to assume the worst when transparency in government spending is lacking. The lack of information made available to Parliament about the administration of the Prime Minister's special Unity Reserve, which was accessed without parliamentary approval, raises questions about the legitimacy of such reserves in a parliamentary democracy. The evidence demonstrates Treasury Board approval of the use of the Unity Reserve was virtually automatic because the Treasury Board submission was expressly endorsed by the Prime Minister. When the Sponsorship Program spending was finally listed in the PWGSC appropriations submitted to Parliament for 1999-2000, no questions were asked. Even then, few parliamentarians were aware of the Program, which had still not been announced publicly.

Public disclosure of the Sponsorship Program was the result of efforts by a diligent journalist whose access to information requests resulted in knowledge about the Program, to the public and parliamentarians alike, for the first time. This serves to illustrate the role that an effective access to information regime can play, enabling a more informed public and a vigilant opposition in Parliament.

According to the doctrine of ministerial responsibility as it has been expounded in some of the submissions, Diane Marleau, who was the Minister of PWGSC at the time the Sponsorship Program was initiated in 1996, would bear ministerial responsibility for the Program because she was the Minister of the department where Mr. Guité was working, and because she was made aware of the funds which were made available to him as the result of the Treasury Board submissions which she signed jointly with Mr. Chrétien in 1996 and 1997. I disagree with that interpretation of the doctrine. Ms. Marleau played no part in the conception and implementation of the Program, other than to obligingly sign the Treasury Board submissions in question. She had already decided not to meet Mr. Guité directly because this would circumvent proper reporting channels. She had reservations about him dating back to Mr. Guité's handling of an agency competition when she was Minister of Health. She rightly believed that the performance of his functions was subject to supervision by his superiors in the department, and that he, as part of the chain of command, should not be allowed to act independently. When she expressed concerns about reports that Mr. Guité was having meetings with Mr. Pelletier, Mr. Quail reacted strangely, warning her not to make allegations about such meetings without proof, although Mr. Quail knew perfectly well that such meetings were taking place. This exchange effectively foreclosed any further attempt by Ms. Marleau to inform herself about what Mr. Guité was doing.

For ministerial responsibility to have any real meaning, it must be based upon knowledge of the actions for which the Minister is to be held responsible. When that knowledge is deliberately withheld from the Minister by someone else, it is the latter person who must bear responsibility, not the Minister who has been kept in the dark. The secrecy with which the Sponsorship Program was being implemented prevented Ms. Marleau from learning about it, and Mr. Quail, who should have known better, did not assist her in learning of Mr. Guité's activities. In these circumstances, it would be unfair to assign Ms. Marleau any degree of responsibility for Mr. Guité's faults.

16.4
The Responsibility of the Deputy Minister of PWGSC

Mr. Quail knew that Mr. Guité was meeting with the PMO and later with Mr. Gagliano, and he knew that in the course of those meetings, decisions were being made about the administration of a program for which Mr. Quail, as Deputy Minister, was responsible. He says that he decided to tolerate a situation which he acknowledges was abnormal and unprecedented, in the belief that the decisions being made were essentially political and best left to the politicians. This acceptance constituted an abdication of his responsibility to control, direct and oversee the actions of officials in his department.

Although Mr. Quail could not be expected to keep track of all of the activities of all the personnel in his huge department, there were many reasons why he should have given particular attention to Mr. Guité and his organization.

First of all, it was imprudent for him not to know details of what was being discussed at Mr. Guité's meetings with Mr. Pelletier and Mr. Gagliano. The usual rule that a representative of the Deputy Minister should be present when a departmental official meets with a Minister or his or her exempt staff exists for a good reason: the Deputy Minister is supposed to be aware of everything that is going on in the department—and if Mr. Quail did not take steps to inform himself of what was going on, he must accept the consequences if it is subsequently learned that irregularities were occurring.

Second, Mr. Guité's reputation as a public servant oriented to obtaining results by cutting through red tape should have alerted Mr. Quail to the possibility that he was not administering the Sponsorship Program according to Treasury Board rules and policies. Mr. Quail knew or should have known about Mr. Guité's reputation and the dangers that went with the administration of a politically directed program by a public servant with that attitude and mentality, but he made only belated and inadequate attempts to assure himself that there were guidelines and criteria in place to regulate the Sponsorship Program. The nature of the Program, with discretionary spending for political objectives, was such that guidelines and criteria were of particular importance.

Third, the telephone call from Mr. Bilodeau requesting information about Mr. Stobbe, with its implied wish to discourage his attempts to be kept abreast of Mr. Guité's activities, should have aroused suspicions that if someone in the PMO did not want Mr. Stobbe to follow Mr. Guité's activities, there was something about the activities that needed investigation.

Fourth, the report of the Ernst & Young audit included an unambiguous reference to significant non-compliance with Treasury Board policies. The follow-up was slow and resulted in no changes whatsoever except to confer additional responsibilities to Mr. Guité as Executive Director of the newly formed CCSB.

Each of these elements included indications that Mr. Guité was not administering the Sponsorship Program in accordance with the required standards. Taken individually they might not have given Mr. Quail reason to be alarmed, but together they should have provoked a reaction. The duty of Mr. Quail was to make inquiries, personally or through his ADM, to better inform himself of the situation, and to call Mr. Guité to account for his deficient administration. He should have acted to correct any inadequacies, and if necessary to replace Mr. Guité if he continued to fail to comply with the rules. Mr. Quail took none of these steps.

There are mitigating factors which should be mentioned, in fairness to Mr. Quail. He was, in 1996 and 1997, very busy and preoccupied with the enormous problems associated with program review and had little time for anything else. In addition, it is evident that he was reluctant to interfere in the Sponsorship Program, a matter of public policy and administration which, to the knowledge of everyone in government, was a priority of the Prime Minister.

The concentration of power in the office of the Prime Minister is a phenomenon of modern Canadian government which has been noted with concern by academics and commentators. The dangers created by that concentration are demonstrated by the "sponsorship scandal." As shown by the evidence, if a proposal or program is perceived as being supported by the PMO, politicians and public servants alike, mindful of the effect that opposition might have upon their careers, hesitate to object to it in any fashion, no matter how ill-conceived or poorly administered it may be. This undermines the whole concept of a professional and non-partisan public service, fearlessly giving objective advice to its political masters.

Mr. Guité took full advantage of the general perception, solidly based on the signature of Mr. Chrétien on several Treasury Board submissions, that the Sponsorship Program was a high priority for the Prime Minister. He was, rightly or wrongly, viewed by those dealing with him as being a public servant in a special category, not subject to the usual chain of command, and free from the normal restraints limiting his ability to act as he pleased. Mr. Guité's easy access to the offices of Messrs. Pelletier and Gagliano lent him an authority and status well beyond his rank, and made everyone in PWGSC, including Mr. Quail himself, hesitate to enquire about, to question or to oppose what he was doing. The fate of Allan Cutler, who dared to insist on contracting according to the rules, was an abject lesson to Mr. Guité's subordinates that they should do as they were told.

Nonetheless, it was Mr. Quail's duty to assert control over the personnel in his department. There were more than adequate reasons for him to be concerned about Mr. Guité and his organization, and he failed to do what he should have done to satisfy himself that public funds were not being wasted. He was being bypassed, he knew he was being bypassed, and he failed to complain. One of the qualities required of a senior public servant is fearlessness. If Mr. Quail was concerned about the possible reaction of the PMO or the Minister's office if he dared to complain about their interaction with Mr. Guité, he always had recourse to the Clerk of the Privy Council.

16.5
The Responsibility of the Liberal Party of Canada (Quebec)

The method of providing for the financial needs of the Quebec wing of the Liberal Party of Canada, using kickbacks obtained by Jacques Corriveau from persons deriving benefits from the Sponsorship Program such as Jean Brault (and probably others), is described elsewhere in this Report. The venality of the scheme makes Mr. Corriveau's participation particularly blameworthy.

The persons who accepted contributions in cash and other improper benefits from Mr. Corriveau and Mr. Brault on behalf of the LPCQ have brought dishonour upon themselves and the political party they were supposed to serve. For this reason Michel Béliveau, Marc-Yvan Côté, Benoît Corbeil, and Joseph Morselli deserve to be blamed for their misconduct, whether or not they derived personal profit from the money which passed through their hands. They disregarded the relevant laws governing donations to political parties, and contributed to the all too common perception that many of those participating in the democratic exercise of political activism are dishonest and disreputable persons.

The LPCQ as an institution cannot escape responsibility for the misconduct of its officers and representatives. Two successive Executive Directors were directly involved in illegal campaign financing, and many of its workers accepted cash payments for their services when they should have known that such payments were in violation of the *Canada Elections Act*.

According to evidence presented on behalf of the LPCQ, reforms to the Party's management and systems make it less likely that such irregularities will reoccur. At the political level, only one elected Member of Parliament has been shown to have been involved in these irregularities. At the time that Mr. Corriveau decided to discontinue his support of the LPCQ, Mr. Gagliano was the head of its administrative structure. In 2001 he needed to find a replacement for Mr. Corbeil, who was about to resign as Executive Director. During his tenure Mr. Corbeil had been able to take advantage of the financial assistance to the party provided by Mr. Corriveau, and both men had had regular recourse to Mr. Brault for illegal financial contributions and other assistance such as jobs for party workers.

Mr. Gagliano accepted the nomination of Mr. Dezainde as the new Executive Director of the LPCQ, although he was not his first choice, but specifically relieved him from responsibility for looking after the Party's financial requirements, a task that he chose to confer upon Mr. Morselli. It is significant that Mr. Morselli at once announced to Mr. Brault that he would be replacing Mr. Corriveau. The only possible interpretation that can be given to that declaration is that Mr. Brault should henceforth pay the financial contributions and kickbacks, that he had until then been giving to the LPCQ through Mr. Corriveau, to Mr. Morselli.

Concurrently, Mr. Gagliano told Mr. Dezainde that in case of financial need he could also turn to Mr. Gagliano's Executive Assistant, Jean-Marc Bard, implying that Mr. Bard would be able to find money for him by means which Mr. Gagliano himself could not employ.

Although there is no direct evidence that Mr. Gagliano was aware of Mr. Corriveau's improper methods of providing financial assistance to the LPCQ, the facts and circumstances just related permit me to infer that he must have known something about Mr. Corriveau's activities, and arranged that the responsibility for fundraising would be taken away from the Executive Director so that those same activities could be continued by Mr. Morselli. He must have known that Mr. Dezainde was not the sort of person to tolerate what Mr. Corriveau, in conjunction with Mr. Corbeil, had been doing. In spite of Mr. Gagliano's protestations to the contrary, he must accept a share of the blame for tolerating the improper methods employed to finance the activities of the LPCQ during the years when he was the Quebec lieutenant of the Liberal Party of Canada.

16.6
The Responsibility of the Communication Agencies

The Commission has heard abundant evidence of irregularities and improprieties committed by the five communication and advertising agencies specifically identified in this Report, which were employed by PWGSC to manage sponsorship contracts on behalf of the Government. Their misconduct, more fully described in the preceding chapters, consisted of systematic overbilling, failure to fulfill contractual obligations, charging for work not performed, conflicts of interest, assigning work to subcontractors without justification and without competitive bids, and very dubious contracting practices. The list could go on.

The negligent administration of the Sponsorship Program by PWGSC opened the door wide to profiteering by those five agencies and their owners, and they took full advantage of the opportunity. They exploited the Sponsorship Program by unethical and highly improper business practices that have resulted in great harm not only to the public purse but also to the reputation of the communication and advertising industry.

All of the agencies mentioned in this Report contributed in one way or another to the financing of the Liberal Party of Canada, although to a varying extent. Whether those contributions were in conformity with the law or illicit, it is difficult to avoid the conclusion that there was at least an implicit link between the contributions and the expectation that government contracts would be awarded to those agencies. If the agency-selection process had been, as once intended, open, transparent and competitive, the public concern that such links existed would certainly have been diminished. With very few exceptions, the legal and illegal contributions made to the LPCQ had the entirely cynical objective of promoting the business interests of the donors, and nothing to do with political idealism.

16.7
Conclusion

Many factors contributed to what has been described as the "sponsorship scandal": inappropriate political interference in administrative matters, acceptance by public servants of such interference, excessive concentration of power in the Prime Minister's Office, carelessness and incompetence and blatant disregard of Treasury Board policies, greed and venality. The public trust in its system of government was subverted and betrayed, and Canadians were outraged, not only because public funds were wasted and misappropriated, but also because no one was held responsible or punished for his misconduct.

Citizens are entitled to be fully informed when public monies are spent on programs having political objectives. Such programs may be entirely legitimate, when appropriately defined and managed, and when value for money is assured. Their legitimacy is undermined when details of the programs are not made public and their administration is biased by partisanship. The atmosphere of secrecy surrounding the implementation of the Sponsorship Program contributed to its failure.

The Government has had great difficulty in devising and implementing a system for allocating its advertising work in a fair, open and competitive manner, free of political influence. If these obstacles are overcome, government advertising can be conducted in a legitimate manner.

This Report marks the completion of the first part of my double mandate, and I am commencing the second phase of the Inquiry as this volume goes to press. In my second Report I will endeavour, after consultations with my expert advisory panel and taking into consideration the views of Canadian citizens, to find solutions to some of the problems discussed in this Report. In the recommendations that I am called upon to make, I intend to propose measures to help the Government of Canada improve its administrative and accountability system, so that advertising and sponsorship programs can in the future be managed efficiently, free of inappropriate political influence, and in an administrative structure where the public interest is the first consideration.

A

Annex A

INDEX OF NAMES

- **Joanne Archambault**, wife of Jean Brault

- **Jean-Marc Bard**, EA to Alfonso Gagliano (replaced Pierre Tremblay in January 1999)

- **Christiane Beaulieu**, Vice President, BDC (in charge of public affairs)

- **Michel Béliveau**, Executive Director, Liberal Party of Canada (Quebec) from 1996-1998

- **Ron Bilodeau**, Deputy Clerk of the Privy Council and Associate Secretary to the Cabinet

- **Lucien Bouchard**, Premier of Quebec, 1996-2001 (following Jacques Parizeau)

- **Richard Boudreault**, employee and shareholder of Groupaction

- **Hon. Don Boudria**, Minister PWGSC, January 2002-May 2002

- **Claude Boulay**, President of Group Everest

439

- **Jocelyne Bourgon**, Clerk of the Privy Council, 1994-1999

- **Joanne Bouvier**, succeeded Isabelle Roy as Minister Gagliano's political assistant in May 1999

- **Jean Brault**, President of Groupaction Marketing

- **Jean Brisebois**, LPCQ worker

- **Mel Cappe**, Clerk of the Privy Council, 1999-2002

- **Jean Carle**, Director of Operations, PMO, October 1993-February 1998/ First Vice President, BDC, February 1998-August 2001

- **Louis Cattapan**, representative of the private sector on 1997 PWGSC selection committee

- **Hon. Martin Cauchon**, Minister of Regional Development in Quebec

- **Maria-Lyne Chrétien**, niece of PM, employed by Groupaction

- **Right Honourable Jean Chrétien**, Prime Minister of Canada, 1993-2003.

- **Janice Cochrane**, DM, PWGSC, April 2001-June 2003

- **Denis Coderre**, Deputy Executive Director and Director of Operations of the LPCQ, 1993-1996

- **Paul Coffin**, President, Communication Coffin

- **Roger Collet**, ADM Canadian Heritage, 1992-1996, and Executive Director of CIO, 1996-1998

- **Hon. Sheila Copps**, Minister, Canadian Heritage, 1996-2003

- **Benoît Corbeil**, Executive Director, Liberal Party of Canada (Quebec), Deputy to Michel Béliveau (subsequently replaced Mr. Béliveau in 1998)

- **Jacques Corriveau**, Vice-President, PluriDesign

- **Andrée Côté**, wife of Gilles-Andrée Gosselin/partner in Gosselin Communications Stratégiques Inc.

- **Wendy Cumming**, Vice President, Gosselin Communications Stratégiques Inc.

- **Allan Cutler**, Manager of contracting at APORS

- **Daniel Dezainde**, Executive Director LPCQ

- **Hon. David Dingwall**, Minister, PWGSC, November 1993-January 1996

- **Hon. Stéphane Dion**, Minister of Intergovernmental Affairs and President of the Privy Council, January 1996-December 2003

- **Hon. Arthur C. Eggleton**, President of Treasury Board, November 1993-January 1996

- **Odilon Emond**, Deputy Superintendent for the Quebec Division of the RCMP

- **Gordon Feeney**, Chair, Canada Post, September 2004 to present

- **Dominique Francoeur**, Corporate Secretary of PWGSC

- **Hon. Alfonso Gagliano**, Minister PWGSC, 1997-2002

- **Hon. Ralph Goodale**, Minister, PWGSC, May 2002-September 2003

- **Gilles-André Gosselin**, partner in Gosselin Communications Stratégiques Inc./married to Andrée Côté

- **Serge Gosselin**, LPCQ worker

- **Yves Gougoux**, president of BCP

- **Joseph Charles Guité**, Executive Director, CCSB,1997-1999, Director APORS (APORD), 1993-1997, head, Oro Communications

- **John Hayter**, President of Vickers & Benson

- **Alex Himelfarb**, Clerk of the Privy Council, May 2002 to present

- **Dawson Hovey**, Director of Public Affairs, RCMP, Ottawa

- **Jim Judd**, Secretary Treasury Board Secretariat, April 2002-November 2004

- **Warren Kinsella**, EA to Minister Dingwall, November 1993-January 1996

- **Éric Lafleur**, Vice President of Lafleur Communication

- **Jean Lafleur**, Head of Lafleur Communication

- **Marc Lafrenière**, Head of CIO following Mr. Collet, July 27, 1998

- **Andrée LaRose**, APORS/CCSB, 1993-1999

- **Paul Lauzon**, CCSB employee, handling contracts

- **Daniel Leblanc**, Globe and Mail reporter

- **Marc LeFrançois**, Chair of the Board of Directors, Via Rail, February 1993-September 2001

- **Roger Légaré**, Executive Director LPCQ

- **Luc Lemay**, Owner Expour and Polygone

- **Anita Lloyd**, access to information official, PWGSC

- **Stefano Lucarelli**, Controller of BDC

- **Marie Maltais**, Director General of Strategic Communications Coordination, May 1998-January 1999

- **Gaëtano Manganiello**, LPCQ worker

- **Hon. John Manley**, Minister of Industry Canada, 1993-2000

- **Evelyn Marcoux**, Charles Guité's second in command, CCSB

- **Hon. Diane Marleau**, Minister of PWGSC, January 1996-June 1997

- **Alan Marquis**, Chief Financial Officer of BDC

- **David Marshall**, DM PWGSC, 2003-present

- **Right Honourable Paul Martin**, former Minister of Finance, Prime Minister of Canada, December 2003 to present

- **Hon. Marcel Massé**, Minister of Intergovernmental Affairs, 1993-1996, President of TB and Minister responsible for infrastructure, 1996-1999

- **Guy McKenzie**, Head of Canada Information Office, June 2001-September 2001, then head of Communication Canada

- **Pierre Michaud**, Lafleur Communication, manager of the Canada Post account

- **Tony Mignacca**, political organizer for Alfonso Gagliano

- **Shahid Minto**, a representative of the Auditor General's Office

- **Deanna Monaghan**, Head Ernst & Young audit team

- **Micheline Montreuil**, Director of Stamp Products for Canada Post

- **Hon. Wilfred P. Moore**, Q.C., the Chairman of the Bluenose Trust

- **Joe Morselli**, LPCQ party worker

- **Senator Lowell Murray, Head**, Cabinet Committee on Communications, prior to 1993 Liberal government

- **David Myer**, Director General of Procurement, CCSB, June 1998

- **Richard Neville**, ADM, Corporate Services of PWGSC, June 1993-July 1995

- **André Ouellet**, Chair of Canada Post, January 1996-August 2004, CEO, November 1999-August 2004

- **Denyse Paquette**, Assistant to Chuck Guité

- **Mario Parent**, CCSB employee, later employee of Gosselin Communications Stratégiques Inc.

- **Jacques Parizeau**, Premier of the Province of Québec, September 1994-January 1996

- **Françoise Patry**, President LPCQ

- **Jean Pelletier**, Chief of Staff to Prime Minister Jean Chretién, 1993-2001

- **Tom Penney**, Tourism Canada, PWGSC Selection Committee

- **Hon. Pierre Pettigrew**, Minister of International Cooperation and Minister responsible for the Francophonie

- **Ranald Quail**, DM PWGSC June 1993-April 2001

- **Alain Renaud**, Businessman

- **Hon. Lucienne Robillard**, Minister of Citizenship and Immigration, 1996-1999

- **Isabelle Roy**, political assistant in Minister Gagliano's office

- **Robert-Guy Scully**, broadcaster/producer and shareholder in L'Information Essentielle

- **John Sinclair**, President of the Institute of Canadian Advertising

- **Christena Keon Sirsly**, Vice President of Marketing, Via Rail

- **Jim Stobbe**, ADM, PWGSC, 1990-2001

- **Bernard Thiboutot**, Head of Gosselin Communications Stratégiques Inc., Quebec City office

- **André Thouin**, Chief Superintendent, RCMP

- **Huguette Tremblay**, PWGSC, in charge of agency selection procedure

- **Pierre Tremblay**, EA to Alfonso Gagliano/Executive Director, CCSB, 1999 following Mr. Guité's retirement

- **Thalie Tremblay**, owner Productions Caméo

- **Enrico Valente**, Gosselin Communications Stratégiques Inc.

- **Beryl Wajsman**, LPCQ

- **John Welch**, LPCQ

ANNEX B

CHRONOLOGY OF EVENTS

Before November 1993, government advertising handled by Advertising Management Group (AMG)

At some point, AMG became known as Advertising and Public Opinion Research Directorate (APORD), later renamed Advertising and Public Opinion Research Sector (APORS), and then Advertising and Public Opinion Research Branch (APORB)

1993

- **1993**, Rt. Hon. Jean Chrétien becomes PM, Paul Martin becomes Finance Minister, and David Dingwall becomes Minister of PWGSC; Ranald Quail is Deputy Minister of PWGSC

1994

- **April 14, 1994** Cabinet approves new advertising policy

- **July 6, 1994** Appendix Q of Treasury Board Contracting Policy with respect to advertising comes into effect

- **September 1994** Jacques Parizeau elected Premier of the Province of Quebec

- **November 21, 1994** J. C. ("Chuck") Guité writes letter to ADM Richard Neville regarding slowness of contract processing by Public Relations and Print Contract Services Sector (PRPCSS)

- **December 1994** Allan Cutler and two others in PRPCSS transferred to APORS

- **December 6, 1994** Draft sovereignty legislation tabled in Quebec National Assembly

1995

- **January 25, 1995** Mr. Guité promoted to EX-02

- **February 2, 1995** Government makes policy decision that only 100% Canadian-owned and -controlled companies will be considered for advertising contracts

- Mr. Guité writes memo to Andrée LaRose advising that the five agencies declared qualified by Heritage Canada on February 3, 1995, would also be qualified to receive contracts from PWGSC-APORS

- **February 5, 1995** Mr. Cutler begins keeping computer log to record his concerns about contracting practices at APORS

- **February 1995** Lafleur Communication begins to receive contracts for advertising services from PWGSC (though not on qualified suppliers list)

- **March 20, 1995** Clerk of the Privy Council Jocelyne Bourgon advises

PM Chrétien on the disbursement of $100,000 to two ad agencies (BCP and Groupe Everest) for pre-referendum strategy

- **March 25, 1995** PWGSC Audit and Ethics Branch (AEB) reports that audit of compliance to the Contracting Policy should be conducted

- **June 30, 1995** PWGSC selection committee issues final report recommending Lafleur Communication

- **July 6, 1995** Second group of agencies added to list of PWGSC qualified suppliers

- **July 19, 1995** Advice to Mr. Chrétien from Ms. Bourgon to approve purchase of billboard space for $2,600,000 for Quebec Referendum strategy

- **September 1995** Jean Brault attends Molson Indy with Alain Renaud and learns from Mr. Guité that APORS subsidized the event

- **October 30, 1995** Quebec referendum

- **November 23, 1995** Warren Kinsella, Executive Assistant to PWGSC Minister David Dingwall, writes memo to DM Quail and ADM Jim Stobbe regarding internal administration of PWGSC

1996

- **January 1996** Hon. Diane Marleau becomes PWGSC Minister

- **February 1-2, 1996** Cabinet discusses Massé Committee Report on national unity which recommends initiatives to raise federal visibility

- **April 1996** PWGSC identifies need for $17 million for sponsorships for national unity initiatives

- **April 1996** Mr. Cutler refuses to sign contracts; Mr. Guité threatens his position

- **April 16, 1996** first meeting between Mr. Guité and Jean Pelletier,

PM Chrétien's Chief of Staff

- **May 29, 1996** Eric Lafleur, VP of Lafleur Communication, sends Ms. LaRose detailed list of sponsored events to be managed by Lafleur Communication

- **June 1, 1996** Groupaction begins paying Investissements Alain Renaud Inc., for representation

- **June 10, 1996** Mr. Cutler provides AEB with documents supporting his allegations

- **June 11, 1996** Mr. Guité declares Mr. Cutler's position surplus

- **June 19, 1996** PM Chrétien authorizes provisional draw on Unity Reserve for communications-related activities of PWGSC

- **July 8, 1996** Mr. Renaud arranges for Mr. Brault to have dinner with the Hon. Alfonso Gagliano and his Executive Assistant (EA) Pierre Tremblay

- **July 1996** Ernst & Young engaged to perform audit of APORS

1997

- **March 1997** Mr. Guité decides new competition necessary to select ad agencies for APORS

- **April 22 & 23, 1997** Ad agencies make presentations before PWGSC selection committee; all 10 presenting agencies become qualified suppliers of advertising services to PWGSC

- **April 1997** Groupaction makes first unrecorded cash contributions to LPCQ

- **June 10, 1997** Hon. Alfonso Gagliano becomes PWGSC Minister

- **July 28, 1997** PWGSC Audit and Review Committee meets to discuss Ernst & Young Report

- **September 1997** Executive Summary of Ernst & Young Report forwarded to Treasury Board

- **September 30, 1997** Second memo to PM Chrétien from Ms. Bourgon regarding management of the Unity Reserve

- Mr. Guité promoted to EX-03

- **November 1997** APORS and PRPCSS consolidated to form Communication Coordination Services Branch (CCSB)

1998

- **February 1998** Mr. Brault approached by Mr. Renaud, saying LPCQ in financial straits (Groupaction remits $63,500 to Renaud's company)

- **April 1, 1998** Agency of Record to be used for sponsorship contracts

- **April 1, 1998** Mr. Guité appointed Acting EX-04

- **Fall 1998** Third cash contribution from Groupaction to LPCQ

- **October 1, 1998** Groupaction acquires Gosselin agencies

- **1998-99** $35 million from Unity Reserve allocated to PWGSC for Sponsorship Program

1999

- **January 1999** Draft sponsorship guidelines and criteria provided to Mr. Guité by CCSB staff

- **January 21, 1999** Mr. Guité sends list of seven proposed sponsorships to Messrs. Gagliano and Pelletier

- **February 1999** Min. Gagliano's EA, Pierre Tremblay, commences employment at CCSB

- **August 31, 1999** Mr. Guité retires from public service—Pierre Tremblay succeeds him

- **September 1999** first requests by *Globe and Mail* for information about Sponsorship Program

2000

- **2000** Treasury Board recommends that Ministers responsible for grants and contributions programs carry out audits of programs; PWGSC considers sponsorship as such a program

- **January 11, 2000** *Globe and Mail* requests all records detailing sponsorship budget with PWGSC since 1994 -95

- **February 2000** decision to order internal audit of the Sponsorship Program

- **April 2000** Sponsorship guidelines finalized but not formally adopted

- Draft guidelines forwarded to communication agencies working with CCSB on sponsorship files

- **July 26, 2000** Internal communication reveals Mr. Stobbe's wish to suppress references to 1996 audit in Ernst & Young Report of 2000

- **August 31, 2000** Internal Audit report prepared

- **September 2000** Groupaction terminates contract with Alain Renaud

- **September 20, 2000** Min. Gagliano briefed on results of audit and orders audit team to review remaining 10% of sponsorship contracts

2001

- **January 2001** Groupaction subsidiary purchases Lafleur Communication

- **April 2001** Janice Cochrane becomes DM of PWGSC

- **2001** PWGSC invites bids from agencies interested in providing sponsorship and advertising services

- **November 16, 2001** Pierre Tremblay resigns as interim Manager of Sponsorship Program

2002

- **January 2002** Hon. Don Boudria becomes Minister of PWGSC

- **January 25, 2002** Communication agencies convened to meet representatives from Communication Canada regarding requirements of new guidelines

- **February 25, 2002** Min. Boudria approves "action plan" for Sponsorship Program

- **March 2002** Min. Boudria asks Auditor General to investigate three PWGSC contracts

- **May 6, 2002** Auditor General advises Min. Boudria of complete audit of Sponsorship Program from 1997 to 2001

- **May 23, 2002** PM Chrétien announces eight-point action plan to restore confidence in government integrity

- **May 26, 2002** Hon. Ralph Goodale appointed Minister of PWGSC

- **May 27, 2002** Sponsorship Program suspended by Min. Goodale

- **September 2002** Sponsorship Program resumed after a trial period

- **October 2002** Kroll Lindquist Avey retained by Human Resources Branch of PWGSC to carry out administrative review of Sponsorship Program

- **December 17, 2002** First public announcement of Sponsorship Program

2003

- **February 4, 2003** Kroll produces report providing analysis of 136 files studied

- PWGSC retains lawyer Jacques Demers to head committee to recommend disciplinary action against certain employees

- **June 2003** David Marshall becomes Deputy Minister of PWGSC

- **December 2003** Rt. Hon. Paul Martin takes office as PM and cancels Sponsorship Program

2004

- **February 10, 2004** Report of the Auditor General made public

- **February 19, 2004** PCO appoints Justice John Gomery as Commissioner of the Inquiry into the Sponsorship Program and Advertising Activities

- **May 7, 2004** Commissioner makes public opening statement

- **September 7, 2004** Public hearings commence in Ottawa

2005

- **February 28, 2005** Phase I-B of public hearings commences in Montréal

- **May 18, 2005** Forensic report presented by Kroll Lindquist Avey to Commission

- **June 17, 2005** Hearings conclude

APPENDIX A

TERMS OF REFERENCE

The Committee of the Privy Council, on the recommendation of the Prime Minister, advise that a Commission do issue under Part I of the *Inquiries Act* and under the Great Seal of Canada appointing the Honourable John Howard Gomery, a judge of the Superior Court of Quebec, as Commissioner

a. to investigate and report on questions raised, directly or indirectly, by Chapters 3 and 4 of the November 2003 Report of the Auditor General of Canada to the House of Commons with regard to the sponsorship program and advertising activities of the Government of Canada, including

    i. the creation of the sponsorship program,

    ii. the selection of communications and advertising agencies,

    iii. the management of the sponsorship program and advertising activities by government officials at all levels,

    iv. the receipt and use of any funds or commissions disbursed in connection with the sponsorship program and advertising activities by any person or organization, and

v. any other circumstance directly related to the sponsorship program and advertising activities that the Commissioner considers relevant to fulfilling his mandate, and

b. to make any recommendations that he considers advisable, based on the factual findings made under paragraph (a), to prevent mismanagement of sponsorship programs or advertising activities in the future, taking into account the initiatives announced by the Government of Canada on February 10, 2004, namely,

i. the introduction of legislation to protect "whistleblowers", relying in part on the report of the Working Group on the Disclosure of Wrongdoing,

ii. the introduction of changes to the governance of Crown corporations that fall under Part X of the *Financial Administration Act* to ensure that audit committees are strengthened,

iii. an examination of

A. the possible extension of the *Access to Information Act* to all Crown corporations,

B. the adequacy of the current accountability framework with respect to Crown corporations, and

C. the consistent application of the provisions of the *Financial Administration Act* to all Crown corporations,

iv. a report on proposed changes to the *Financial Administration Act* in order to enhance compliance and enforcement, including the capacity to

A. recover lost funds, and

B. examine whether sanctions should apply to former public servants, Crown corporation employees and public office holders, and

v. a report on the respective responsibilities and accountabilities of Ministers and public servants as recommended by the Auditor General of Canada,

and the Committee do further advise that

c. pursuant to section 56 of the *Judges Act*, the Honourable John Howard Gomery be authorized to act as a Commissioner on the inquiry;

d. the Commissioner be directed to conduct the inquiry under the name of the Commission of Inquiry into the Sponsorship Program and Advertising Activities;

e. the Commissioner be authorized to adopt any procedures and methods that he may consider expedient for the proper conduct of the inquiry, and to sit at any times and in any places in Canada that he may decide;

f. the Commissioner be authorized to grant to any person who satisfies him that he or she has a substantial and direct interest in the subject-matter of the inquiry an opportunity during the inquiry to give evidence and to examine or cross-examine witnesses personally or by counsel on evidence relevant to the person's interest;

g. the Commissioner be authorized to conduct consultations in relation to formulating the recommendations referred to in paragraph (b) as he sees fit;

h. for purposes of the investigation referred to in paragraph (a), the Commissioner be authorized to recommend funding, in accordance with approved guidelines respecting rates of remuneration and reimbursement and the assessment of accounts, to a party who has been granted standing at the inquiry, to the extent of the party's interest, where in the Commissioner's view the party would not otherwise be able to participate in the inquiry;

i. the Commissioner be authorized to rent any space and facilities that may be required for the purposes of the inquiry, in accordance with Treasury Board policies;

j. the Commissioner be authorized to engage the services of any experts and other persons referred to in section 11 of the *Inquiries Act*, at rates of remuneration and reimbursement that may be approved by the Treasury Board;

k. the Commissioner be directed to perform his duties without expressing any conclusion or recommendation regarding the civil or criminal liability of any person or organization and to ensure that the conduct of the inquiry does not jeopardize any ongoing criminal investigation or criminal proceedings;

l. the Commissioner be directed to submit, on an urgent basis, one or more reports, interim or final, of his factual findings made pursuant to paragraph (a) in both official languages, to the Governor in Council, and to submit a separate report of his recommendations made pursuant to paragraph (b), in both official languages, to the Governor in Council; and

m. the Commissioner be directed to file the papers and records of the inquiry with the Clerk of the Privy Council as soon as reasonably possible after the conclusion of the inquiry.

APPENDIX B

REPORT OF THE
AUDITOR GENERAL OF CANADA

Government-Wide Audit of Sponsorship, Advertising, and Public Opinion Research

Overall Main Points—Chapters 3,4 and 5

1. We found that the federal government ran the Sponsorship Program in a way that showed little regard for Parliament, the *Financial Administration Act*, contracting rules and regulations, transparency, and value for money. These arrangements—involving multiple transactions with multiple companies, artificial invoices and contracts, or no written contracts at all—appear to have been designed to pay commissions to communications agencies while hiding the source of funding and the true substance of the transactions.

2. We found widespread non-compliance with contracting rules in the management of the federal government's Sponsorship Program, at every

stage of the process. Rules for selecting communications agencies, managing contracts, and measuring and reporting results were broken or ignored. These violations were neither detected, prevented, nor reported for over four years because of the almost total collapse of oversight mechanisms and essential controls. During that period, the program consumed $250 million of taxpayers' money, over $100 million of it going to communications agencies as fees and commissions.

3.   Public servants also broke the rules in selecting communications agencies for the government's advertising activities. Most agencies were selected in a manner that did not meet the requirements of the government's contracting policy. In some cases, we could find no evidence that a selection process was conducted at all.

4.   The government's communications policy states that federal institutions must suspend their advertising during general federal elections. We noted that the policy was properly implemented.

5.   Overall, public opinion research was managed transparently, with roles and responsibilities clearly defined. However, there were some cases in which departments did not establish a clear statement of the need to undertake a public opinion research project. In a small number of troubling cases, we noted that the government had failed to follow its own guidelines in effect at the time and had paid for syndicated research that monitored, among other things, voting behaviour and political party image.

6.   While these chapters contain the names of various contractors, it must be noted that our conclusions about management practices and actions refer only to those of public servants. The rules and regulations we refer to are those that apply to public servants; they do not apply to contractors. We did not audit the records of the private sector contractors. Consequently, our conclusions cannot and do not pertain to any practices that contractors followed.

The Privy Council Office, on behalf of the government, has responded. The entities we audited agree with the findings contained in chapters 3, 4, and 5. Our recommendations and the detailed responses follow.

Recommendations

The observations contained in chapters 3, 4, and 5 of our Report are serious. Action is required in many areas, both in Crown corporations and across government departments.

Recommendation. The government should ensure the development of an action plan for sponsorship, advertising, and public opinion research activities that addresses all of the observations in the three chapters.

As noted in the report the government has undertaken a number of actions to strengthen the management of the sponsorship, advertising, and public opinion research activities. Continued effort is required by the government to ensure that these improvements are sustained. In particular the government should continue to ensure that

- public servants understand their obligations and comply with the *Financial Administration Act*, and

- public servants who are given responsibility for managing advertising activities have the necessary specialized expertise in the subject matter.

In addition, the action plan should include details of actions the government will take to ensure that

- any operating units established to undertake new activities do so with proper control, accountability, and transparency;

- public servants discharge their contracting responsibilities in a manner that complies with the Government Contracts Regulations and Treasury Board policies and that Public Works and Government Services Canada complies with its own policies and stands the test of public scrutiny in matters of prudence and probity, facilitates access, encourages competition, and reflects fairness in the spending of public funds;

- parliamentary appropriations are respected;

- any transfers of funds between government entities are conducted with transparency and efficiency;

- arm's-length relationships are maintained between Crown corporations and government departments; and

- action is taken on issues raised in any other review or investigation conducted by the government or by other agencies.

The action plan should specify time frames, accountabilities, and any recovery action or sanctions that the government decides to impose.

The government's response. The Government of Canada is deeply concerned about the findings contained in these audits and takes the issues raised in them very seriously. The government has taken action on most of the issues and will take action on any new issues raised.

The government has been working over the past several years to address the issues observed in these audits. The government is committed to excellence in management, and it continues to make significant progress in modernizing and strengthening its management practices, based on a strong partnership between Treasury Board Secretariat and government departments. It has implemented a broad-based government-wide agenda to strengthen and modernize management, including a new Management Accountability Framework for the public service, Guidance for Deputy Ministers, and a new Values and Ethics Code for the Public Service.

The government's commitments are reflected in its leadership in undertaking the Public Works and Government Services Canada 2000 internal audit of sponsorships and by acting on its findings. When it became apparent that there were further issues, the Minister of Public Works and Government Services requested that the Auditor General examine three specific contracts awarded in 1996, 1998, and 1999. The Minister also imposed a moratorium on any new sponsorships in May 2002, and then set up an interim program to eliminate the use of communication agencies. These efforts were followed by a complete and detailed review of sponsorship program files, and remedial actions including withholding and recovering monies, in bringing issues to the attention of the appropriate authorities, and in addressing program design and management issues.

While these efforts were underway, in 2002 the Treasury Board Secretariat, in collaboration with Public Works and Government Services Canada and Communication Canada, conducted a comprehensive review of the sponsorship, advertising and public opinion research programs.

In response to the recommendations of that review, the government looked to the future by implementing a completely new management and accountability regime for the Sponsorship Program as of 1 April 2003, and which requires a complete review before any extension beyond 31 March 2004.

A comprehensive action plan was also put in place with respect to advertising management practices guided by the objectives of transparency, accountability, value for money and increased competition. Communication Canada has established a core centre of expertise which continues to implement the plan that the Minister of Public Works and Government Services announced on 28 April 2003.

Beyond the other two programs, there were also recommendations made with respect to the management of public opinion research in government. Since that time, Communication Canada has been working to fulfill and to meet the recommendations of the reviews.

In May 2002, the Secretary of the Treasury Board wrote to each Deputy Minister regarding expenditures related to the three activities which are the focus of these chapters, along with a request for an assessment of management capacity and adherence to the *Financial Administration Act*. A copy of the letter, as well as the departmental replies, were provided to the Office of the Auditor General in the course of the audits which follows.

The government's actions to date are fully outlined in a detailed and comprehensive response to the Tenth Report of the Standing Committee on Public Accounts, which can be found at:

http://www.tbs-sct.gc.ca/report/gr-rg/grtr-rgdr_e.asp

The government will review further these audits to ensure that any additional issues are addressed. This includes ensuring that departments have appropriate management regimes in place when undertaking initiatives with Crown corporations.

The government has demonstrated by its actions the seriousness with which it takes any evidence of alleged misconduct or mismanagement of public funds, by responding to all reviews and investigations, by government or by other agencies, including efforts to recover any misappropriated funds, and employee discipline ranging from reprimands to loss of employment, including involving the appropriate authorities where warranted.

The government is committed to continuing to work diligently on the implementation of specific measures to address these issues.

Chapter 3: The Sponsorship Program

Main Points

3.1   From 1997 until 31 August 2001, the federal government ran the Sponsorship Program in a way that showed little regard for Parliament, the *Financial Administration Act*, contracting rules and regulations, transparency, and value for money:

- Parliament was not informed of the program's objectives or the results it achieved and was misinformed as to how the program was being managed.

- Those responsible for managing the program broke the government's own rules in the way they selected communications agencies and awarded contracts to them.

- Partnership arrangements between government entities are not unusual in programs of mutual benefit. However, some sponsorship funds were transferred to Crown corporations using unusual methods that appear designed to provide significant commissions to communications agencies, while hiding the source of funds and the true nature of the transactions.

- Documentation was very poor and there was little evidence of analysis to support the expenditure of more than $250 million. Over $100 million of that was paid to communications agencies as production fees and commissions.

- Oversight mechanisms and essential controls at Public Works and Government Services Canada failed to detect, prevent, or report violations.

3.2 Since Communications Canada's creation in September 2001, there have been significant improvements in the program's management, including better documentation and more rigorous enforcement of contract requirements.

Background and other observations

3.3 A new sponsorship program has been announced that, if properly implemented, will improve transparency and accountability. For example, the program will be delivered using contribution agreements with event organizers directly rather than contracts with communications agencies. Whatever mechanisms are used, Parliament needs to be assured that public funds are being administered in compliance with the rules and in a manner that ensures fairness, transparency, and the best possible value for money.

3.4 While this chapter includes the names of various contractors, it must be noted that our conclusions about management practices and actions refer only to those of public servants. The rules and regulations we refer to are those that apply to public servants; they do not apply to contractors. We did not audit the records of the private sector contractors.

Consequently, our conclusions cannot and do not pertain to any practices that contractors followed.

The Privy Council Office, on behalf of the government, has responded. The entities we audited agree with the findings contained in chapters 3, 4 and 5. Our recommendations and the detailed responses appear in the Overall Main Points at the beginning of this booklet.

Introduction

Origins of the Sponsorship Program

3.5 In November 1997, a new branch of Public Works and Government Services Canada (PWGSC) was created as a result of concerns about the federal presence and visibility across Canada, the effectiveness of the federal government's communications activities, and the need for an integrated structure to deliver those activities. The mandate of the new Communications Co-ordination Services Branch (CCSB) was to co-ordinate, promote, advise, and facilitate federal communications initiatives.

3.6 One vehicle for delivering that mandate was the Sponsorship Program, created in 1997. Sponsorships were arrangements in which the Government of Canada provided organizations with financial resources to support cultural and community events. In exchange, the organizations agreed to provide visibility by, for example, using the Canada wordmark and other symbols such as the Canadian flag at their events, and on promotional material.

3.7 Sponsorships were intended to encourage a positive perception of the government through its association with popular events and organizations in fields such as sports and culture. They would also increase the federal presence and visibility in communities across Canada. From 1997 until 31 March 2003, the Government of Canada spent about $250 million to sponsor 1,987 events (Exhibit 3.1). Over $100 million of that (40 percent of total expenditures) was paid to communications agencies as production fees and commissions.

3.8   Sponsorships were to be managed in two distinct ways, depending on their dollar value. Those valued at less than $25,000 were to be managed only by a communications agency contracted by CCSB; for sponsorships over $25,000, CCSB was to contract both with an agency of record to provide financial management services on behalf of CCSB and with a communications agency.

3.9   In March 2002, the Minister of Public Works and Government Services asked the Office of the Auditor General to audit the government's handling of three contracts totalling $1.6 million that had been awarded to Groupaction Marketing (Groupaction), a communications agency based in Montréal. The audit report, presented to the Minister on 6 May 2002, revealed significant shortcomings at all stages of the contract management process.

3.10   The nature of the findings was such that the Auditor General referred the matter to the RCMP and also decided to undertake a government-wide audit of the Sponsorship Program (as well as the public opinion research and advertising activities of the Government of Canada, including those of Crown corporations—see chapters 4 and 5 of this Report).

Focus of the audit

3.11   Our audit examined the management of the Sponsorship Program by CCSB up to 31 August 2001, when Communication Canada was created by the amalgamation of CCSB and the Canada Information Office; we examined the subsequent management of the program by Communication Canada. We looked at whether the program complied with the federal government's regulations and policies that govern contracting and the proper handling of public money. We assessed the program's design, the management of individual sponsorship projects, and the measurement of project and program results. We also assessed the quality of documentation in the files. We selected a sample of sponsorship projects and reviewed them in detail. We also interviewed staff and former staff of the Sponsorship Program.

3.12   Further, we selected a sample of transactions involving payments by CCSB to Crown entities, including Crown corporations. We audited the way both CCSB and the Crown entities managed the transactions. At the conclusion of the audit, we also interviewed two former ministers and a former deputy minister of PWGSC who had been involved in the Sponsorship Program. Further details are found at the end of Chapter 4 in "About the Audit".

3.13   It must be noted that our conclusions about the management practices and actions for contracting refer to those of public servants. The rules and regulations we refer to are those that apply to public servants; they do not apply to contractors. We did not audit the records of the private contractors. Consequently, our conclusions cannot and do not pertain to any practices that contractors followed.

Observations

Parliament was not informed of the Sponsorship Program's true objectives

3.14   When it created the Sponsorship Program, the federal government did not inform Parliament of the program's real objectives; nor has it ever reported the results. Former officials of CCSB told us that after the 1995 Quebec referendum, the government wanted to raise its profile in Quebec by sponsoring local events and so it set up the Sponsorship Program. However, we saw no such direction from the government and no formal analysis or strategic plan. In the absence of any written direction from the Deputy Minister or the Executive Committee of PWGSC and any written decision by the Cabinet or the Treasury Board, it is not clear to us how the decision to create the program was made, and by whom. Nor is it clear why the decision was not communicated in writing.

3.15   However, the Treasury Board approved increased funding for PWGSC's communications activities in order to promote the government's programs and services following the Quebec referendum. PWGSC had to ensure that initiatives conformed to Treasury Board policies and guidelines; that all communications services would be competitive, as required; and that contracts would be issued appropriately.

3.16   We found that PWGSC failed to ensure that before allocating funds, it had established an adequate control and oversight framework for the Sponsorship Program. Even though communication was a ministerial priority, the *Financial Administration Act* still applied.

3.17   We were informed that the program was promoted in Quebec but not elsewhere in Canada. As people outside Quebec became aware of the program, the government received some applications and approved some sponsorships of some events in other provinces. However, from 1997 to 2000, the vast majority of regional events sponsored were in Quebec.

3.18   We reviewed PWGSC's performance reports. None of them mentioned the program until 2001, even though sponsorships accounted for more than half of CCSB's annual spending. The 2001 *Performance Report* discussed the Sponsorship Program but made no reference to its objectives and its emphasis on events in Quebec. It simply stated that 291 events had been sponsored across Canada. Parliament was not informed that the primary focus of the program was on Quebec.

3.19   Given the importance of the objectives described to us by officials and the significance of the program's spending (more than $250 million from 1997 to March 2003), we would have expected the government to provide Parliament with at least a description of the program, its objectives, its expenditures, and the results it achieved.

Program controls and oversight

Few people involved in delivering the program

3.20   Normally, central divisions of PWGSC manage the procurement and financial activities of that Department's branches. For the Sponsorship Program, however, contracting and financial management were handled by the CCSB and not a central division. CCSB's Executive Director reported to the Deputy Minister of PWGSC and had direct access to the Minister and his staff, which further reduced normal control and oversight provisions.

3.21   Staff of CCSB told us that an Executive Director had not involved them in making decisions on sponsorships. They described to us the following process (much of this was confirmed to us by a former Minister of Public Works and Government Services):

- CCSB contracted with a communications agency to identify potential sponsorship opportunities in Quebec. The agency provided some information verbally, but there are no written records of that information.

- CCSB received unsolicited sponsorship proposals from a number of sources, including other government departments, event/activity/project organizers, communications agencies, community groups, and non-governmental organizations. Some requests were made to the Minister and forwarded to CCSB.

- The Executive Director of CCSB reviewed the requests and decided which events would be sponsored and which communications agency would get the contract. Project files were discussed with the Minister's office at various times.

- At the request of the Executive Director, program staff prepared the requisition and forwarded it to CCSB's procurement staff, who completed the contract.

- The Executive Director approved the payments to the contracted communications agencies.

These procedures violate two fundamental principles of internal control: segregation of duties and appropriate oversight.

Weak control environment

3.22   In *Results for Canadians*, the management framework for the federal government, the Treasury Board states that departments and agencies are responsible for ensuring that they have adequate management frameworks to achieve results and manage resources. This means, among other things, that they must maintain robust internal controls and be vigilant to detect early any conditions that could lead to a control failure. The Sponsorship Program operated in a weak control environment: procurement and financial activities were handled within CCSB with little oversight by PWGSC's central services, communications agencies and events to be sponsored were selected by only a few individuals, and the same individuals who approved the projects also approved invoices for payment. Roles and responsibilities were not segregated to eliminate, as far as possible, any opportunities for fraud and misstatement or an override of controls by management.

3.23 **No written program guidelines.** Written guidelines can be a key tool for delivering any program consistently, fairly, and transparently: they can provide clear criteria for eligibility, set out the conditions attached to financial support, and in this case, provide guidance on levels of sponsorship. We noted that the Sponsorship Program operated with no guidelines from its inception in 1997 until 1 April 2000, resulting in ad hoc selection and approval of projects and decisions on levels of sponsorship funding. In our review of files, we found it impossible in most cases to determine why an event was selected for sponsorship, how the dollar value of a sponsorship was determined, or what federal visibility the sponsorship would achieve.

Lack of transparency in decision making

3.24 To understand how decisions had been made, given that they were rarely documented, we interviewed staff who had been involved in the Sponsorship Program. Apparently only a handful of people had participated in decision making, and those who remain at PWGSC, Communication Canada, and other government departments were unable to tell us why certain decisions had been made.

3.25 They noted that the Executive Director had discussed sponsorship issues with the Minister. A retired Executive Director told us that his discussions with the Minister were only to provide information. He said that he and his staff had decided what events would be sponsored and at what level. He told us that he had also relied on verbal advice from a communications agency but had not documented that advice.

3.26 The former Minister stated that his office had not decided which events to sponsor. He confirmed that there had been no written objectives or guidelines but also stated that the program had been part of the national unity strategy.

3.27 We found a memo in one file indicating that the Minister's office had overturned a decision by program staff not to sponsor an event; the memo said the Minister's office would inform the event's organizer. The file did not show who in the Minister's office had made the decision and why, or how the level of sponsorship funding had been determined.

3.28 Another recipient of funding said his request had been denied initially. At the Executive Director's suggestion, he discussed the matter with the Minister's office. The decision was reversed, and funding was approved. We found no documentation in the files to support this change of decision.

3.29 It is clear from our discussions with a former Minister and the retired Executive Director that there were discussions from time to time between the Executive Director, the Minister, and the Minister's staff. The absence of documentation prevents us from determining the extent or the appropriateness of those discussions; the files did not indicate their results.

Sponsorship funds to Crown entities

Transactions designed to hide sources of funding to Crown entities

3.30 In the course of our audit, we noted that CCSB and subsequently Communication Canada had paid sponsorship funds to certain Crown corporations. We selected all such transactions that related to Business Development Bank of Canada, Canada Mortgage and Housing Corporation, Canadian Tourism Commission, Old Port of Montreal Corporation Inc., National Arts Centre Corporation, National Capital Commission, and VIA Rail Canada Inc. Our observations on Canada Mortgage and Housing Corporation and Canadian Tourism Commission are reported in Chapter 4 of this Report.

3.31   We also audited transactions involving Canada Lands Company Limited/Parc Downsview Park Inc. and the Royal Canadian Mint. In these two Crown corporations and in the National Arts Centre and the National Capital Commission, we noted no significant observations to report to Parliament.

3.32   Through an order-in-council, we were able to audit selected sponsorship transactions at Canada Post Corporation. However, our Office did not audit the sponsorship/marketing program of Canada Post Corporation in its entirety. Given the nature of our findings in a small sample, we have suggested to Canada Post Corporation that it undertake an audit of its full sponsorship/marketing program and report the results of the audit to its Board of Directors.

3.33   In addition, we audited transfers of money by CCSB to other federal entities.

3.34   Partnership arrangements between government entities are not unusual in programs of mutual benefit. Normally an agreement states the roles and responsibilities of each entity, the limits of its financial commitment, and the benefits it expects to achieve. The required funds are usually transferred between entities through a journal voucher or paid directly by cheque.

3.35   Many of the transfers by CCSB to Crown entities were made through communications agencies, who were paid commissions to move the money. We believe that none of the agencies was selected properly, and in many cases there is little evidence of the value the Crown received.

3.36   Our audit found that CCSB had no agreements or partnership arrangements with the Crown corporations whose programs it sponsored. It used highly complicated and questionable methods to transfer sponsorship funds. Some payments were based on artificial invoices and contracts; others were subsidies—sponsorship money used by the Crown corporations to cover their normal operating costs.

3.37   CCSB made payments to Crown corporations through communications agencies with whom it had to contract, rather than transferring the funds to the corporations directly. If the Sponsorship Program had been framed under the transfer payments policy as a contribution, an approved program framework including specific eligibility criteria, terms and conditions, and a more structured approach to providing information to Parliament would have been required. We believe that it was inappropriate for such transfers to be undertaken through communications agencies or using procurement contracts.

3.38   The Treasury Board's Policy on Transfer Payments stipulates that "where a department is considering a grant, contribution, or other transfer payment to a Crown corporation…, there must be prior consultation with the Treasury Board Secretariat… to ensure that a grant, contribution or other transfer payment is not, and does not become, a substitute for financing a corporation's operating or capital requirements."

3.39   Irrespective of the transfer mechanism used, almost none of the Crown corporation transfers were supported by a business case. CCSB should have sought appropriate legislative authority and transferred the funds directly, by means of a contribution agreement. This would have eliminated the payment of significant commissions and would have required that CCSB obtain authority from the Treasury Board to make the transfers. Treasury Board Secretariat's officials stated that since the money was transferred using a contract, the transfer payments policy is not the applicable audit standard for the Sponsorship Program. However, in our view, the policy not only covers grants and contributions but also "other transfer payments." In our opinion, CCSB violated the intent of the transfer payments policy.

Questionable value for money

3.40   In exchange for receiving sponsorship funds, Crown corporations and departments were to provide visibility for the Government of Canada. In 1998, the Treasury Board's policy on the Federal Identity Program was amended to require Crown corporations (which previously had been exempted) to apply the Canada wordmark prominently on all their corporate identity applications. Given that requirement, we question why

CCSB needed to pay Crown corporations for providing visibility, particularly in those cases where we found no documented evidence of any additional visibility purchased with sponsorship funds.

3.41   In several of the transactions we audited, we found that CCSB officials had contravened rules, regulations, and the *Financial Administration Act*. They also displayed a lack of concern for obtaining the best value for the Crown. The cases in "Transactions with Crown entities are cause for concern" elaborate on these findings. They also illustrate that some officials of Crown entities participated in the mismanagement of public funds. Each case is presented with a diagram that shows the flow of money to explain the nature of the transaction.

The transactions with Crown entities are cause for concern

3.42   Our work indicates that the Sponsorship Program was used mainly for community, cultural, and sports events. However, as the case studies show, it was also used for funding certain other events, television series, commercial activities, and capital acquisitions by Crown entities, including Crown corporations.

3.43   Communications agencies were paid significant commissions by CCSB to simply deliver cheques to the corporations. Many of the transactions we examined had violated one or more of the Government Contracts Regulations, the *Financial Administration Act*, financial and contracting policies of Crown corporations, and the intent of the Treasury Board's Policy on Transfer Payments.

3.44   What is particularly disturbing about these sponsorship payments is that each involved a number of transactions with a number of companies, sometimes using false invoices and contracts or no written contracts at all. These arrangements appear designed to provide commissions to communications agencies, while hiding the source of funds and the true nature of the transactions. The parliamentary appropriation process was not respected. Senior public servants in CCSB and some officials of the Crown corporations were knowing and willing participants in these arrangements. The former Minister of Public Works and Government Services told us he was aware that CCSB's Executive Director had entered into transactions with the Crown corporations; the Executive Director had informed him that moving money between entities in this way was appropriate.

Mismanagement of sponsorships

3.45 Our audit work in Crown corporations covered only a part of the Sponsorship Program. The majority of transactions under the program involved the payment of funds by the Government of Canada to support organizations that were staging sports and cultural events. This section discusses the management of the program by CCSB up to 31 August 2001, when Communication Canada assumed the responsibility for the program.

Widespread failure to comply with contracting policies and regulations

3.46 Starting in April 2000, PWGSC conducted one audit and several reviews of sponsorship files, in each case uncovering serious problems. Our findings were consistent with those of PWGSC.

3.47 Those who managed the Sponsorship Program were responsible for

- complying with the *Financial Administration Act*,

- exercising due diligence in selecting events for sponsorship and determining the level of financial support to each,

- ensuring that the process of selecting and awarding contracts to communications agencies complied with the government's policies and regulations on contracting,

- enforcing the terms and conditions of the contracts, and

- ensuring that the government received the best possible value for the public funds it spent.

3.48   We observed that from 1997 to 31 August 2001, there was a widespread failure to comply with the government's contracting policies and regulations, a pervasive lack of documentation in the files, and little evidence in many cases that the government had received value for its sponsorship—in some cases, no evidence.

Selection of communications agencies broke the rules

3.49   Section 5 of the Government Contracts Regulations requires the contracting authority to solicit bids before entering into any contract; competitive bidding should therefore be the norm.

3.50   The Sponsorship Program used communications agencies from three pre-established lists of qualified suppliers identified in three separate selection processes (for details see section "Selection of agencies" in Chapter 4).

3.51   In the first process, five firms were selected in early 1995 to provide advertising services to the Advertising and Public Opinion Research Sector (APORS) of PWGSC. However, the selection process did not comply with the Government Contracts Regulations. We saw no evidence that the specific requirements of the work were ever advertised or documented. The selected firms had been identified earlier in a selection process for other work in another department. Other potential suppliers were never given a chance to compete for this work.

3.52   In the second selection process, carried out in 1995, a consortium was selected to provide a complete range of advertising services. In the third process, in 1997, 10 companies were selected to develop and administer national or regional marketing campaigns to supplement advertising initiatives. Many of these companies were later awarded contracts to manage sponsorship events.

3.53   In each of the latter two selection processes, the government posted a letter of interest on MERX, its electronic bidding system, to inform suppliers about its needs and allow them to apply as potential suppliers.

In each case, the letter of interest did not specify in what period the services were needed, which of the stated requirements were mandatory and which would be rated, and how the suppliers would be selected or the pass mark (score) they had to obtain. All of this information was required under CCSB's own procedures.

3.54   In our opinion, none of the companies on the three lists of qualified suppliers was selected through the competitive process that the government's contracting policies and regulations require.

Selection of the agency of record contravened contracting rules

3.55   In March 1998, the government contracted with a firm to be its agency of record and provide financial management services for sponsorships. Again, the letter of interest was posted for less than the 30 days required by the Contracting Policy, Appendix Q. It did not say when the services would be required, what the mandatory and the rated requirements were, and how suppliers would be selected or the score they would need to be considered in the next stage of the selection process.

3.56   The company chosen was given a contract for the next five years to act as sole purchaser of all media placements that the government needed to support its advertising activities. The advertising aspects of this contract are addressed in Chapter 4 of this Report.

Contracts awarded for specific events without following contracting policies

3.57   Appendix Q of the government's contracting policy states that if the contracting authority creates a list of qualified suppliers of a type of service, then each time it wants to award a contract for that type of service it must invite all suppliers on the list to submit a proposal. The contracting authority must also post an annual notice that the list of qualified suppliers exists, and it must give other suppliers an opportunity to qualify for inclusion on the list. We saw no evidence that CCSB or PWGSC ever posted an annual notice of the list of qualified suppliers or gave other potential suppliers an opportunity to qualify.

3.58 Furthermore, in the contracts we audited, we found that CCSB had never invited proposals from the suppliers who did get on the list. Nor did the files show on what basis each contract was awarded and why one agency and not another was chosen for a given project.

Lack of due diligence in selecting and approving events to sponsor

3.59 We expected that in recommending an event for sponsorship, program staff would indicate how the event would contribute to achieving the program's objectives. We expected to find analyses showing that program managers had assessed proposed events for their potential to provide federal visibility and presence and that they had recommended sponsorship funding at a corresponding level.

3.60 Most of the 53 files in our audit sample contained no assessment of the project's merits or even any criteria for assessing merit. No file contained the rationale supporting the decision to sponsor the event. Furthermore, in 64 percent of the files we reviewed, there was no information about the event organizers, no description of the project, and no discussion of the visibility the Government of Canada would achieve by sponsoring the event.

3.61 We found a list of events that CCSB had declined to sponsor, but its officials informed us that no files had been maintained on declined projects so we could not determine why the requests for sponsorship funds had been declined. We noted seven projects that had been declined initially and were later approved—but the files contained no reasons for the changed decisions. In one case a soccer team, Impact de Montréal, received $150,000 in sponsorship funds for its indoor season in 1998-99. The following year, an almost identical proposal from the Edmonton Drillers Soccer Club was declined on the grounds that no funds were available. After the Minister of Public Works and Government Services was contacted by a member of Parliament and by the Edmonton Drillers, a sponsorship of $30,000 was approved. The Montreal team received $30,000 in sponsorship funds that year as well.

3.62 Some aspects of this case are troubling. First, given that a note in the file said the Edmonton proposal was initially declined because no funds were available, it is not clear why funds were available for other projects that were approved at that time.

3.63 Second, while it is clear that the Minister was approached, there was little evidence that new facts were provided or additional criteria used to support a reversal of the initial decision.

No analysis of sponsorship amount for each event

3.64 We expected files to be properly documented and, as recommended in the government's contracting policy, to provide a complete audit trail containing details on matters such as options considered, decisions, approvals, and amendments to contracts. In addition, the Supply Manual of PWGSC states that a current file on a contract serves as a historical record and an accurate audit trail in the event of a financial review, subsequent legal action, or an official complaint.

3.65 In the sample of sponsorship files that we audited, not one had any documented rationale to support the level of funding approved; nor, in fact, was there a record of any discussion at all about the level of funding (see "Tour Cyclist Trans Canada").

Little evidence of the value received by the Crown for the money spent

3.66 Having entered into a contract with a communications agency to manage the sponsorship of a specific event, CCSB and PWGSC were expected to show due diligence in managing the spending on the contracted services and ensure accountability for the public funds spent. Good contract management would have ensured that the contract terms and conditions were met and payments made in accordance with them, and that the invoices and post mortem reports submitted to PWGSC or CCSB were verified as reliable. As well, we expected management to have reasonable assurance that funding was used for the intended purposes, that post mortem reports were reviewed against the objectives and expected results outlined in the visibility plan, and that site visits were made.

3.67   CCSB's contract with each communications agency for one or more sponsorship projects specified that the communications agency was to submit details of a visibility plan, execute the sponsorship agreement with the event organizer, monitor the terms of that agreement, obtain proof that the event organizer had performed according to the agreement's terms, and reconcile all relevant documentation.

3.68   **Absence of visibility plans.** Almost half the files in our sample contained no visibility plan describing in any detail the visibility the government could expect to gain. In one case, for example, a member of Parliament received a request for $5,000 from a college in Quebec for financial support for its foundation. The MP forwarded the request to the Minister of Public Works and Government Services. A special assistant in the Minister's office sent the request to CCSB, which entered into a contract with a communications agency for $5,600 that included commission fees of 12 percent. CCSB approved a visibility plan by the agency that consisted solely of putting the name of the member of Parliament on a mural in the college. In this case, the Government of Canada did not receive any visibility for the $5,600 it paid, but the member of Parliament did.

3.69   **Little documentation of what was delivered.** There was little evidence that any communications agency had analyzed the results of sponsored events in our sample. Communications agencies were required to submit post mortem reports summarizing the visibility benefits, with relevant documentation, photos, and examples of visibility such as brochures and press clippings. In 49 percent of our files, there was no post mortem report and therefore no evidence that the government had obtained the visibility it had paid for.

3.70   In December 1996, for example, PWGSC's Advertising and Public Opinion Research Sector (APORS)—which subsequently became CCSB—signed a $330,000 advertising contract with Groupaction to develop a communications strategy related to the new firearms legislation. APORS received invoices for the full amount of the contract and approved the payments. However, there was no evidence that APORS received anything for the money it paid to Groupaction under this contract. The contract said this was a Justice Canada project, but Justice officials have stated that they had not requested the contract and received none of the services outlined in it.

3.71   In another case, a $465,000 contract with Groupaction in April 1997 covered the sponsorship of Série Hermez Racing and Classique du Parc/Parc Équestre de Blainville, as well as advertising-related services described as Promotion de la culture canadienne française and Surveillance et documentation de sites et de groupes d'intérêts/Armes à feu.

3.72   Invoices were received and payments approved by APORS for the full $465,000. However, the file contained no evidence that APORS received the deliverables specified in the contract. There was also no evidence on file to indicate how public servants satisfied themselves that goods and services had been received before approving payments.

3.73   Even the files that did contain post mortem reports had no evidence that CCSB program staff had compared the reported results with the objectives stated in the visibility plan. A report by a communications agency on an event in one city contained photographs of a similar event in another city. CCSB program staff did not identify the inaccuracy or ask the agency why it had used photographs of the wrong event.

Work subcontracted without competition

3.74   The contracts with communications agencies stipulated that before subcontracting any work estimated at more than $25,000, the agencies were to obtain bids from no fewer than three other suppliers, firms, or individuals and submit the bids to CCSB.

3.75   In the 26 percent of sampled files involving subcontracts for amounts greater than $25,000, we saw no evidence that the communications agency had solicited bids from suppliers. Nor did we see evidence of any effort by CCSB to determine that this condition had been met.

3.76 The contracts also state that a communications agency may not receive a commission on work that it subcontracts to a "member of the Strategic Alliance" but they did not define strategic alliance. However, an official of PWGSC told us that the expression "strategic alliance" referred to the companies that had been listed as affiliates on the agencies' responses to the qualification questionnaire during the selection process. Over the years, communications agencies have merged, changed their names, or been bought. CCSB did not maintain up-to-date records of members of the "strategic alliance."

3.77 We observed in some cases that the communications agency had subcontracted work to a company with whom it clearly had a close relationship and had invoiced CCSB for a commission. Some companies had the same address and even the same fax number. We saw no evidence that CCSB ever questioned invoices for subcontracted work before paying them. We saw no evidence that it ever attempted to require compliance with this contract condition.

3.78 The contracts also required that CCSB approve production costs in advance. The majority of the 53 files in our sample show that CCSB was billed for production costs and there was no evidence that it had approved the production costs in advance or subsequently verified them.

3.79 Furthermore, we saw no evidence that on receiving the invoices, CCSB officials had questioned the costs before approving payments or reminded the communications agency that costs were to have been approved in advance. We found a general lack of documentation of production costs. Many of the invoices for production costs lacked support such as a description of the work that had been done or the number of hours it had taken.

Contracts amended without documented support

3.80 We found in 21 percent of the sampled files that contracts had been amended without any explanation. As already noted, one amendment added $400,000 to the contract four months after the event. The rationale for this amendment was stated in one line—it was for "added visibility." There was no evidence that CCSB had requested any added visibility, and no evidence that any had been achieved. Further, we found no analysis to support the contract's initial value of $1.4 million.

3.81   We expected that the public servants responsible for managing these files would have taken reasonable steps to protect the interests of the Crown. Those steps would have included showing due diligence in the spending of public funds, ensuring that government contracting policies and regulations were respected, and enforcing the terms and conditions of the contracts.

3.82   In the files that we audited, we saw very little evidence that the public servants responsible had made any such efforts.

Lack of compliance with relevant financial authorities

3.83   Public servants are expected to take appropriate steps to ensure that they discharge their responsibilities with prudence and probity. The *Financial Administration Act* (FAA) sets out precise conditions that govern payments. Specifically,

> No contract or other arrangement providing for a payment shall be entered into with respect to any program for which there is an appropriation by Parliament or an item included in estimates then before the House of Commons to which the payment will be charged unless there is a sufficient unencumbered balance available out of the appropriation or item to discharge any debt that, under the contract or other arrangement, will be incurred during the fiscal year in which the contract or other arrangement is entered into (section 32).

> No charge shall be made against an appropriation except on the requisition of the appropriate Minister of the department for which the appropriation was made or of a person authorized in writing by that Minister. Every requisition for a payment out of the Consolidated Revenue Fund shall be in such form, accompanied by such documents and certified in such manner as the Treasury Board may prescribe by regulation. No requisition shall be made for a payment that (a) would not be

a lawful charge against the appropriation; (b) would result in an expenditure in excess of the appropriation; or (c) would reduce the balance available in the appropriation so that it would not be sufficient to meet the commitments charged against it (section 33).

No payment shall be made in respect of any part of the public service of Canada, unless in addition to any other voucher or certificate that is required, the deputy of the appropriate Minister, or another person authorized by that Minister, certifies that: (i) the work has been performed, the goods supplied or the service rendered, as the case may be, and that the price charged is according to the contract or, if not specified in the contract, is reasonable; (ii) and where, pursuant to the contract, a payment is to be made before the completion of the work, delivery of the goods or rendering of the service, as the case may be, that the payment is according to the contract (section 34).

3.84   We observed that many of the files contained no signature indicating compliance with section 32 of the FAA.

3.85   We also noted in the sample of payments we audited that requisitions had been authorized by the appropriate financial officers under section 33 of the FAA.

3.86   All files contained the signatures required under section 34. However, none of the files had evidence that the signing officer had fulfilled the obligations and met the requirements of the *Financial Administration Act*. There was insufficient evidence that the work had been performed according to the requirements of the contract. For example, some payments were made on the basis of a lump sum invoice with no supporting documentation, no record of the work performed, no record of who performed the work, and no post mortem report showing that the sponsored event had taken place and that the government had received the visibility for which it had paid.

3.87   In our view, the public servants involved in administering the Sponsorship Program did not discharge their responsibilities with due care and diligence. There was little evidence that anyone had verified the reliability of the data on the invoices submitted by the communications agencies. Furthermore, the files often lacked evidence showing what work the communications agencies had done and therefore had little support for invoices paid.

How was this allowed to happen?

3.88   We are disturbed not only by the widespread circumvention of the competitive contracting process and the consistent breaking of rules essential to ensuring the proper handling of public funds but also by the fact that this was permitted to occur at all.

3.89   Two factors allowed this regime of mismanagement to occur and persist over a period of several years: departmental oversight and essential controls at PWGSC were bypassed, and the role of Parliament was not respected.

Oversight and essential controls were bypassed

3.90   PWGSC is a large department, with annual revenues of over $100 million, expenditures of over $2 billion, and 14,000 employees. It is involved in many lines of business, including providing other government entities with expertise in procurement and related common services. It manages the operations of the federal treasury, including issuing cheques from the Receiver General; and it prepares the Public Accounts of Canada and the government's monthly financial statements.

3.91   To achieve its objectives, PWGSC has established a fairly sophisticated system of internal controls and accountability reporting. While our previous audits have found some weaknesses in contracting and other management processes, we have also found that the Department's systems of internal controls are generally reliable.

3.92   Throughout our current examination we were disturbed not only by actions of Sponsorship Program managers but also by the unexplained and continual failure of oversight mechanisms and essential controls to detect, deter, and report flagrant violations of rules, regulations, and policies. The funding for sponsorships came from PWGSC's appropriations. The small number of officials in CCSB were employees of PWGSC. The authorities they exercised had been delegated to them by the Minister, through the Deputy Minister.

3.93 Senior officials at PWGSC have stressed to us that our observations on CCSB are not indicative of how the vast majority of PWGSC employees discharge their responsibilities. From our previous audits of PWGSC, we would agree. We have not observed such widespread violation of the rules elsewhere in PWGSC.

3.94 The Department has not provided us with an adequate explanation for the almost complete collapse of its essential controls and oversight mechanisms in the management of the Sponsorship Program for the four years preceding 31 August 2001. As already noted, the program consumed $250 million of taxpayers money, over $100 million of it paid to communications agencies in fees and commissions.

3.95 Once audits were begun, the problems were not difficult to find. In 2000, PWGSC's internal audit reported numerous shortcomings in the management of the Sponsorship Program. In 2001 certain improvements were carried out, including a new solicitation process and improvements in the agreement with the agency of record. A follow-up audit by PWGSC in 2002 noted that the documentation on file had improved. However, the follow-up audit did not address issues of value for money.

3.96 In our Report in May 2002 we raised significant concerns about three contracts relating to the Sponsorship Program. Following that Report, PWGSC undertook a review of all 721 files and examined 126 of them in detail. The work was done initially by a Quick Response Team consisting of PWGSC experts from appropriate areas of the Department.

3.97 That review found in most of the files significant problems with documentation, use of affiliated communications companies, overbilling, subcontracting, and potential breaches of the *Financial Administration Act*, Treasury Board policies, and departmental policies. The findings were such that the Department referred a number of files to the RCMP for review and initiated recovery actions. At the completion of our audit, the RCMP's review was still under way.

3.98   In 2003, the Department retained a private sector firm of forensic auditors to do a more in-depth review of sponsorship files on 136 events. The auditors reported that in a significant number of cases, "We note what appear to be clear issues of non-compliance with either the FAA, PWGSC-delegated authorities, or Treasury Board Contracting Policies/Government Contracts Regulations. In relation to a number of events, we have noted multiple issues of non-compliance."

3.99   The audit function worked to identify problems after the fact. What failed were the controls and oversight that should have prevented these problems from occurring in the first place. Although PWGSC's Internal Audit Branch published its report in 2000, some important subsequent management actions—for example, initiating recovery and referring matters to the RCMP—were not undertaken before 2002.

The role of Parliament was not respected

3.100   Not only was Parliament not informed about the real objectives of the Sponsorship Program, it was misinformed about how the program was being managed. The parliamentary process was bypassed to transfer funds to Crown corporations. Funds appropriated by Parliament to PWGSC were used to fund the operations of Crown corporations and of the RCMP.

3.101   PWGSC's 1999-2000 *Report on Plans and Priorities*, signed by the Minister and the Deputy Minister, contained the following statement about CCSB:

> The CCSB business line will focus on the following strategies and key activities over the planning period… provide core communications procurement and project coordination services to federal departments that are useful, timely and value added while ensuring prudence, probity and transparency throughout the process.

3.102   More than half of CCSB's spending was on sponsorships. Prudence and probity in the delivery of the program were certainly not ensured.

Recent improvements in management

Treasury Board Secretariat initiatives

3.103   In May 2002, the Secretary of the Treasury Board wrote to deputy ministers reinforcing the importance of respecting the provisions of the *Financial Administration Act* and the Treasury Board's contracting policies. He asked departments to undertake three specific activities in the areas of sponsorship, advertising, and public opinion research: first, to assess whether appropriate controls and procedures were in place; second, to review current contracts and ensure their compliance with the *Financial Administration Act* as well as government contracting policies and regulations; and third, to ensure that people exercising delegated authorities were properly trained and informed of their responsibilities. He also asked deputy ministers to transmit his request through their ministers to Crown corporations, asking them to conduct a similar exercise.

3.104   We reviewed the responses received by the Treasury Board Secretariat and they indicate that departments have started corrective action in the areas they acknowledged were weak.

3.105   The Treasury Board Secretariat in conjunction with PWGSC and Communication Canada also undertook a study to review the structure and design of the Sponsorship Program. That study resulted in the announcement of a new sponsorship program in December 2002 (as noted in paragraph 3.116).

Changes have been made under Communication Canada

3.106   In September 2001, the CCSB was amalgamated with the Canada Information Office to form Communication Canada, which assumed responsibility for the Sponsorship Program. It made a number of changes aimed at strengthening the implementation of the program, most notably creating a new management structure and program framework and new program guidelines (effective February 2002 and revised in May 2002). Meanwhile, responsibility for contracting was transferred to the Supply Operations Service Branch of PWGSC, the main procurement arm of the Department. More significant changes were announced later and began to be implemented on 1 April 2003.

3.107   In May 2002, a moratorium on sponsorships was imposed in order to take steps toward improving the program. The intent was to ensure that the program could operate in the public interest and on a sound basis in the future. The moratorium was brief and, pending the results of the review, an interim program was launched using in-house resources rather than contracting with communications agencies—that is, Communication Canada entered into sponsorship contracts directly with event organizers.

3.108   We audited a sample of 25 project files from September 2001 to March 2003. We found that in general these files were managed better. Although in some cases its documenting of decisions was still deficient, in most files we found enough documentation to understand the rationale behind decisions to sponsor specific events. Unlike the earlier sample we audited, all of these files contained the appropriate visibility plans and post mortem reports.

3.109   **Some circumvention of contracting rules continued.** Communication Canada improved its documenting of the use of criteria in selecting events to sponsor. However, in the period prior to July 2002 it still had not invited the qualified suppliers on the pre-established list to submit proposals each time a contract was to be awarded. In addition, we found no evidence that Communication Canada posted an annual notice of the list of qualified suppliers or gave others an opportunity to qualify for the list.

3.110   However, effective 3 July 2002, the date on which the moratorium was lifted, communications agencies were no longer used as intermediaries. This was a significant change in the way the Sponsorship Program was managed.

3.111 **Improvements in selecting and approving individual projects.** In the 25 files we reviewed at Communication Canada, we saw an improvement in the rationale for sponsoring events. All files contained proposals from event organizers, so we were able in every case to determine the nature of the event.

3.112 **Better analysis of the level of sponsorship for each event.** Communication Canada developed an analysis sheet that considered the objectives and priorities of the Sponsorship Program, the clientele, the regional distribution of sponsorships, and the participation of other sponsors. Although there were exceptions, we did see some analysis in most of the files. For example, in some cases Communication Canada had compared an event to be sponsored with a similar event sponsored previously, as a basis for deciding what level of funding to provide. In addition, Communication Canada maintained files on projects it had declined to sponsor and included analysis to support those decisions.

3.113 **Better enforcement of the terms and conditions of contracts.** The visibility plan was called a sponsorship plan in the interim program. Under Communication Canada, the sponsorship plans were based on templates prepared by Communication Canada that varied according to the amount of sponsorship money provided. This allowed for relatively consistent degrees of visibility in all events receiving similar amounts. All the Communication Canada files we reviewed included sponsorship plans, and we were able to follow the approval process.

3.114 **Improved compliance with relevant authorities.** Compliance with the *Financial Administration Act* improved considerably under Communication Canada. The required certifications under sections 32, 33, and 34 of the FAA were signed off properly.

3.115 In all of the Communication Canada files we reviewed, staff had waited for a post mortem report and compared the reported results with the objectives set out in the visibility/sponsorship plans before they made the final payment.

A new sponsorship program has been launched

3.116 A new sponsorship program was announced in December 2002 by the President of the Treasury Board, the Minister of Public Works and Government Services, and Communication Canada, effective 1 April 2003. The program is now delivered through a contribution program. Its key features include the following:

- There will be no contracting with third parties.

- Payments are to be made under contribution agreements instead of contracts.

- Written guidelines will be issued for use by program staff.

- Transparency is to be achieved through nationwide publicizing of the program, its objectives, the selection criteria, the events that have been approved, and the funds each event will receive.

- Audits are to be conducted, event sites visited, and compliance with contribution agreement terms and conditions demonstrated before final payments will be made.

The announcement also stated that the program will be in place for 2003-04, during which time the government will assess its value and viability for the long term and publicly report the results. While we are encouraged by the announcement, we have not audited this new program.

3.117 It is important to stress that even while the previous Sponsorship Program was being mismanaged, there were sound rules in place. The *Financial Administration Act* spelled out the requirements and obligations of public servants. The government's own contracting policies articulated quite clearly the steps that public servants were to follow. Yet public servants consistently failed to follow the rules.

3.118 While the new program may provide an opportunity to correct the weaknesses we identified, Parliament and Canadians need assurance that this time, all of the rules will be followed.

Conclusion

3.119   In its 2000 *Report on Plans and Priorities* to Parliament, PWGSC stated that it was managing the Sponsorship Program in a manner that ensured prudence and probity. This was clearly not the case.

3.120   Until 1 September 2001, the government ran the Sponsorship Program in a way that showed little regard for Parliament, the *Financial Administration Act*, contracting rules, transparency, or value for money. There was little evidence of prudence and probity. In May 2002, the Treasury Board wrote to the departments reinforcing the importance of respecting the provisions of the *Financial Administration Act* and contracting policies and regulations. In addition, the government announced a new sponsorship program, effective April 2003.

3.121   Since Communication Canada was formed in September 2001, there have been significant improvements in the Sponsorship Program. The current Executive Director has informed his staff that he expects these improvements to be sustained. He has stated that a thorough internal audit will be conducted by 2005. We hope that this will indeed be a thorough and comprehensive audit, one on which we will be able to rely. We hope that the results of the internal audit will be reported to Parliament in a timely manner.

3.122   It remains of great concern, however, that the Sponsorship Program was ever allowed to operate in the way it did. Considerable amounts of public funds were spent, with little evidence that obtaining value for money was a concern. The pattern we saw of non-compliance with the rules was not the result of isolated errors. It was consistent and pervasive. This was how the government ran the program. Canadians have a right to expect greater diligence in the use of public funds.

3.123   Public servants need to ensure that funds spent on communications, whether for sponsorship or for advertising, require no less attention to the *Financial Administration Act* and no less attention to contracting rules than all other spending of public funds, and as much concern about getting value for the taxpayer's money.

Chapter 4: Advertising Activities

Main Points

4.1   The Communications Coordination Services Branch (CCSB) of Public Works and Government Services Canada failed to meet its obligation to allow suppliers equitable access to government business and obtain best value in selecting advertising agencies. Most agencies were selected in a manner that did not meet the requirements of the government's contracting policy. In some cases, we could find no evidence that a selection process was conducted at all. CCSB officials disregarded the same rules and selected the same agencies as those in Chapter 3 of this Report, on the Sponsorship Program.

4.2   The government needs to ensure that officials in all departments possess the skills they need to meet their obligations and manage their advertising expenditures responsibly. Our audit found that some departments did poorly at carrying out their responsibility for ensuring that agencies complied with the requirements of contracts; other departments met their obligations without difficulty. Some departments did not require that communications agencies seek competitive bids on work they wanted to subcontract, nor did the departments challenge commissions charged by agencies or invoices submitted without adequate support.

4.3   The government's communications policy states that federal institutions must suspend their advertising during federal general elections. We noted that this aspect of the policy was properly implemented.

Background and other observations

4.4   Unlike the Sponsorship Program, for which CCSB was fully responsible, advertising responsibilities were shared. CCSB was responsible for selecting the agencies; individual departments were responsible for managing the advertising campaigns and ensuring that the contract terms and conditions were met.

4.5   The Privy Council Office provides strategic oversight and coordination for government advertising.

4.6   While this chapter includes the names of various contractors, it must be noted that our conclusions about management practices and actions refer only to those of public servants. The rules and regulations we refer to are those that apply to public servants; they do not apply to contractors. We did not audit the records of the private sector contractors. Consequently, our conclusions cannot and do not pertain to any practices that contractors followed.

The Privy Council Office, on behalf of the government, has responded. The entities we audited agree with the findings contained in chapters 3, 4, and 5. Our recommendations and the detailed responses appear in the "Overall Main Points" at the beginning of this booklet.

Introduction

Advertising allows the government to inform Canadians about its programs and initiatives

4.7   Advertising is a way for the government to speak directly to citizens, whether informing them about services, programs, initiatives, and government policies; about their rights and responsibilities; or about dangers or risks to public health, safety, and the environment.

4.8   In recent years, for example, the Canada Customs and Revenue Agency has advertised the use of its Web site for filing tax returns electronically. National Defence has used advertising as a recruiting tool. Health Canada has advertised its anti-tobacco initiative, and the Department of Finance has promoted Canada Savings Bonds.

4.9   Between 1998-99 and 2002-03, the federal government ran more than 2,200 advertising activities with contracts valued at about $793 million, making it one of the larger advertisers in the country.

4.10   The Government of Canada contracts with communications agencies
        to develop concepts and plan its advertising campaigns, produce
        advertising material, and plan all ad placements in the media. It also has
        a service agreement with an agency of record, which buys space and time
        in the media for all government advertising and negotiates the payment
        rates. Communications agencies receive hourly rates and a 17.65 percent
        commission on production work they subcontract out. For planning media
        placements, they also receive, through the agency of record, a commission
        of 11.75 percent on media space and time purchased by the agency of
        record. For placing ads and making payments to the media and the
        communications agencies, the agency of record receives a 3.25 percent
        commission.

4.11   **A corporate approach.** Until 1998, there was no unified approach to
        government advertising. Most federal departments and agencies had
        their own logos and promoted their programs and services individually.
        Then the government decided on a corporate approach to advertising.
        It wanted to ensure that it spoke with one voice when advertising its
        programs and services. To help departments develop and implement
        communications plans and strategies, particularly for advertising, in
        2001 the Privy Council Office (PCO) developed a communications
        framework and marketing plan based on the priorities set out in the Speech
        from the Throne. In concert with the Treasury Board Secretariat, the PCO
        also launched a brand rationalization process, with about 800 brands
        and logos ultimately replaced by a common look and the Canada
        wordmark.

4.12   The PCO's Communications and Consultation Secretariat advises
        Cabinet on communications strategies, including advertising. As Chair
        of the Government Advertising Committee, the PCO provides advice
        and guidance to departments on planning and developing major
        advertising campaigns. It advises and supports the Cabinet Committee
        on Government Communications, which is chaired by the Minister of
        Public Works and Government Services and oversees the government's
        corporate communications strategy and approach, including advertising.

Advertising activities are the responsibility of individual departments but are centrally co-ordinated

4.13 Individual departments identify their advertising needs based on their program priorities and the government's key priorities; they must use Public Works and Government Services Canada (PWGSC) to contract for all advertising services and public opinion research (see Chapter 5 of this Report), after obtaining authorization from Communication Canada.

4.14 Departments identify the funds to be used for advertising and they plan, develop, and implement advertising campaigns. Major campaigns must be submitted for review to the Government Advertising Committee, chaired by the Privy Council Office.

4.15 Departments have to pre-test and evaluate all major campaigns and forward the results to Communication Canada. Each department manages its own contracts with the advertising agencies and ensures when it pays for services that the terms and conditions of the contracts have been respected.

4.16 Until September 2001, the Communications Coordination Services Branch (CCSB) of PWGSC was responsible for collecting and reviewing departments' advertising plans; issuing a registration number for each advertisement (referred to as an "ADV" number); gathering and analyzing departments' advertising and public opinion research plans; and informing the Privy Council Office of these activities. In September 2001, co-ordination of advertising was assumed by Communication Canada, an organization created by the amalgamation of CCSB with the Canada Information Office.

4.17 Public Works and Government Services Canada is responsible for ensuring the integrity of the contracting process in the federal government's advertising activities. Until September 2001, its Communications Coordination Services Branch was responsible for selecting advertising agencies and the agency of record and for issuing contracts to them on behalf of all federal departments. CCSB handled contracting for advertising services itself rather than using PWGSC's central contracting service. When CCSB ceased to exist in September 2001, all contracting for advertising services was assumed by the Communication Procurement Directorate, a group in PWGSC's procurement arm, thereby separating the procurement of advertising from the management of the program.

Focus of the audit

4.18   Our objective was to determine whether, in contracting for advertising services, the federal government ensured that it obtained best value for the Crown in a process that was transparent and gave equitable access to suppliers of advertising services. We also wanted to determine whether departments ensured that their advertising campaigns were designed to achieve the expected results. Finally, we wanted to assess whether the systems and procedures in place allowed for a corporate approach to advertising activities and their co-ordination, as required by the Treasury Board's policy on communications. Further details are found at the end of the chapter in "About the Audit".

4.19   It must be noted that our conclusions about the management practices and actions for contracting refer to those of public servants. The rules and regulations we refer to are those that apply to public servants; they do not apply to contractors. We did not audit the records of the private contractors. Consequently, our conclusions cannot and do not pertain to any practices that contractors followed.

Observations

Selection of agencies

Competitive process was not used in the selection of several advertising agencies

4.20   As the only contracting authority for advertising services, PWGSC is responsible for selecting the advertising agencies used by all federal organizations. In the period covered by this audit, the Department's Advertising and Public Opinion Research Sector, or APORS (1994-97) and subsequently CCSB was responsible for selecting agencies.

4.21 The objective of government contracting is to acquire goods and services in a manner that enhances suppliers' access to government business, encourages competition and fairness, and results in the best value to the Crown or the optimal balance of overall benefits to the Canadian people. It was CCSB's responsibility to ensure that the process for selecting advertising agencies was transparent. We expected the files to be properly documented and, as recommended by the government's contracting policy, to provide a complete audit trail containing details on matters such as options considered, decisions, approvals, and amendments to contracts. We audited the selection of advertising agencies for 10 departments and one Crown corporation, Canada Mortgage and Housing Corporation.

4.22 In the cases described in "Contracts awarded without competitive bids", we noted contracts that had been awarded to companies without a proper competitive process. Other potential suppliers were not given the opportunity to compete for the work.

A competitive process that was used broke the contracting rules

4.23 The government's contracting policy requires that the acquisition of goods and services through contracting follow a process that enhances access, competition, and fairness and obtains the best value possible. From 1998-99 to 2002-03, the Government of Canada issued advertising contracts valued at over $793 million. In our sample of 14 files on selection processes that occurred during that period, we found that most of the agencies were selected in a manner that did not comply with the government's own contracting policy.

4.24 Between 1994 and 2001, PWGSC conducted selection processes on behalf of about 36 departments and agencies and some Crown corporations. Through a selection process in 1997, CCSB selected Media/I.D.A. Vision, a company related to Groupe Everest, as the government's agency of record. We reviewed 14 selection processes, including the one used to select the agency of record.

4.25   The selection process started with CCSB's posting of a Notice of Planned Procurement, called a request for "letters of interest," on the government's Open Bidding System (later known as MERX). The notice followed a client department's request to PWGSC to obtain general advertising services.

4.26   In most of the files we examined, we did not see evidence that APORS, and later CCSB, had specified which requirements were mandatory and which would be rated, how bidders would be rated, the method that would be used to select the suppliers, or the pass mark (score) they had to obtain. All of this information was required under PWGSC's own procedures.

4.27   In 12 of the 14 selection processes, including the one for the agency of record, the request for letters of interest did not specify how long the services would be required. In the selection of agencies for Department of Finance Canada and the Canada Mortgage and Housing Corporation (CMHC), both in 2001, the request for letters of interest mentioned that the winning agency would be retained for a period of three years with an option to renew twice, each time for an additional year.

4.28   In seven cases, including the selection of the agency of record, the requests for letters of interest were posted for periods ranging from 12 to 18 days, although the government's policy on contracting for advertising required that they be posted on the MERX system for 30 days.

4.29   Competing agencies had to respond to a qualification questionnaire sent to them by PWGSC after they had indicated an interest in competing for the advertised work. From responses it received to the questionnaire, PWGSC compiled short lists of usually four or five agencies. These agencies were then invited to make a presentation and were rated on that basis.

4.30   In most cases, we did not see evidence that the questionnaires completed by the competing agencies were evaluated. As a result, it is impossible to determine how the requirements were scored or short lists arrived at, or how and by what criteria the majority of interested communications agencies were screened out in the first rounds of the processes.

4.31   Our review of selection processes for advertising agencies found in most cases that the letter advising the successful agency of its selection did not mention the duration of the contract.

Failure to fulfil contractual obligations and ensure appropriate oversight of the agency of record

4.32   The March 1998 agreement with Media/I.D.A. Vision, making it the agency of record for the next five years, stated that the agency had a "material obligation to negotiate and obtain from the media suppliers the best possible prices, rates or fees charged by these suppliers" for the placement of government ads. The statement of work specified that the agency of record had "to co-ordinate and, where necessary, to adjust all media plans to ensure optimum scheduling and impact and to achieve the most favourable reach and frequency at optimum cost."

4.33   The agreement stipulated that the government had a specific responsibility: "To periodically verify if the contractor has fulfilled his material obligation, the Minister will conduct audits of the Contractor's records pertaining to this Contract." The agreement described the actions that the Minister would take should an audit discover specified deficiencies, such as a failure by the agency of record to obtain the best possible prices in an advertising campaign. In the five years that the contract has been in place, no audit of the agency has been conducted.

4.34   The Government of Canada issued contracts over $435 million on media placement purchases during the five years covered by its agreement with Media/I.D.A. Vision, its agency of record. The agreement with Media/I.D.A. Vision stipulated that once the gross media billings in a fiscal year reached $50 million, the fee that departments paid would be reduced from 3.25 percent to 2.5 percent depending on the level of billing. We would expect the government to ensure that the fee was reduced as appropriate.

4.35   Officials told us they had monitored the cumulative total of expenditures on media placements and had informed Media/I.D.A. Vision when the fee was to change. However, they could not give us any documentation to support this claim.

4.36   While we saw no evidence that CCSB ever instructed departments to reduce the rate they paid to the agency of record, we did see evidence that Media/I.D.A. Vision credited departments' accounts to reflect some reduction in the commission. However, there is no evidence that CCSB ever verified that the amounts credited reflected the correct reduction.

4.37   From Media/I.D.A. Vision's invoices, it was difficult for departments to verify how much had been paid to media outlets for ad placements. The invoices billed gross amounts, including commissions to both the agency of record and the communications agency. That practice was changed in July 2002 at the request of PWGSC, after some departments asked for more detailed information. Media/I.D.A. Vision then started to show the breakdown of commissions in its invoices.

Management of contracts by departments

4.38   Once CCSB had selected an advertising agency for a client department, it issued contracts between the two parties for the specific advertising services requested by the department. Departmental officials were responsible for ensuring not only that the contract requirements were met but also that the *Financial Administration Act* was respected. We audited 34 contracts for advertising services.

Unwritten contracts exposed the Crown to undue risk

4.39   Signed contracts with detailed terms and conditions outline the responsibilities of each party. Written contracts are important because they serve to limit the Crown's liability while specifying what the contractor must do to be paid.

4.40 We found cases in which contracts had been issued verbally by CCSB on behalf of Health Canada. The government's contracting policy allows for this practice, but it also states that a written contract should be signed as soon as possible after the notice of the award has been given to the successful bidder.

4.41 In some cases, however, the contractor worked for several weeks before terms and conditions were specified and a contract signed. In one case at Health Canada, the National Organs and Tissues Awareness campaign, a $1.52 million contract signed with BCP on 28 March 2002 stated that the work was to be completed by 31 March 2002-three days later. In fact, the work had already been completed and the campaign had been airing since 4 March.

4.42 Another case at Health Canada involved a contract valued at $414,405 for the development of an anti-tobacco campaign. We observed that the contractor's proposal was dated 25 March 2002; the contract was issued on 28 March 2002 and was in effect until 31 March 2002, three days later. Of particular concern to us is that invoices totalling $179,570 had been approved for payment, one as early as 15 February—more than five weeks before the contract was signed. Without a written contract, it was impossible for Health Canada to ensure before it paid the invoices that terms and conditions of the contract had been respected.

4.43 The files show that Health Canada and CCSB did begin the contracting process before the work started. Health Canada officials told us that although work began before a written contract existed, they had never intended (nor was it the intent of the contracting policy) that the work would be completed before the contract was signed.

Departments did not ensure that contract terms and conditions were respected

4.44 Once a contract was issued by CCSB, the client department was responsible for ensuring that the contract terms and conditions and the relevant provisions of the *Financial Administration Act* were respected. We expected that departments would do so before approving payments to the agencies.

4.45 We also expected that invoices would be approved by authorized persons in the department in accordance with section 34 of the *Financial Administration Act*. Section 34 says the authorized person must ensure that

> the work has been performed, the goods supplied or the service rendered, as the case may be, and that the price charged is according to the contract or, if not specified in the contract, is reasonable; and

> where, pursuant to the contract, a payment is to be made before the completion of the work, delivery of the goods or rendering of the service, as the case may be, that the payment is according to the contract.

4.46 In many cases, departmental staff did not take adequate steps to ensure that the contractor had met the requirements of the contract.

No challenge of commissions on work subcontracted to affiliated companies

4.47 The contracts prohibited the payment of a commission for overhead or profit to a "member of the Strategic Alliance" but did not define strategic alliance. An official of PWGSC told us that the expression referred to the companies that agencies had listed as affiliates on their responses to the qualification questionnaire during the selection process. Over the years, communications agencies have merged, changed their names, or been bought. We saw no evidence that departments and PWGSC had enforced the contract clause on strategic alliances or verified the lists of strategic alliance members.

4.48 In three departments in our sample (CCRA, PWGSC, and Department of Justice Canada), we found invoices showing that they had been charged a commission of 17.65 percent on work subcontracted by the agency to a supplier affiliated with it. The invoices gave some indication that the companies had a close relationship—for example, both the agency and the subcontractor had the same logo on their letterhead, the same telephone number, or closely similar names. We saw no evidence that the departments had challenged any of the invoices. For example, on six invoices totalling $47,465 under a contract with CCSB, Groupe Everest charged the government a commission of 17.65 percent or $8,378 for subcontracting work to Everest-Estrie. We saw no evidence that CCSB ever challenged these invoices.

Subcontracted work was not tendered competitively

4.49   In each of the departments we reviewed, we found cases with no evidence that the contractor had obtained three bids on subcontracted work over $25,000 or had justified its choice of subcontractor to the department, as required in the contract.

4.50   For example, under a $3 million contract managed by CCSB for Attractions Canada in 2000-01, Groupe Everest subcontracted work valued at $274,735 to one company and $150,000 to another without submitting evidence that it had obtained three bids.

4.51   Under a $1.9 million contract managed by Department of Justice for an advertising activity in 2000, Groupaction subcontracted work valued at $355,999 to Alleluia Design without submitting evidence that it had obtained three bids. Of particular concern is that Groupaction was affiliated with Alleluia. Groupaction and Alleluia Design invoices showed the same phone number and the same departmental reference number, yet the Department did not question the companies' relationship and approved the payment of a 17.65 percent commission.

Departments approved payment of invoices with incomplete or no supporting documentation

4.52   Before approving payments, departments were to ensure that the invoices had all the documentation required by the contracts to support the amounts claimed. In several cases, we found that supporting documentation was incomplete or absent.

4.53   For example, CCSB approved an invoice for $800,000 submitted by Groupe Everest in October 1997 that gave only a short description of the items charged, with no supporting documentation. The Canada Information Office approved an invoice for $1.2 million from Media/I.D.A. Vision with insufficient documentation to support it. On a contract valued at $856,000 related to its 1999-2000 annual anti-racism campaign, the Department of Canadian Heritage approved payments to its agency, Scott Thornley Company Inc. of Toronto, for invoices totalling $250,000 with insufficient documentation.

4.54   Invoices that we reviewed at the Department of Finance, the Department of Canadian Heritage, Human Resources Development Canada, and CCSB were for lump sums, with no breakdown of hours worked by each category of employee, as required by the contracts. There was insufficient information for officials to determine that the charges were acceptable. Nonetheless, the invoices were approved for payment.

4.55   The contracts required that each invoice contain the contractor's certification that the work had been done and that the charges were consistent with the contract terms. Many of the invoices from communications agencies lacked the required certification. Nor did we see any evidence of follow-up by departmental officials.

Estimates were not always approved by departments before work started

4.56   The contracts we reviewed required the agencies to submit written estimates to the departments for approval before beginning any work. If the cost of the completed work exceeded the approved estimates, the Crown would not have to pay more than 10 percent over the estimate.

4.57   Many files we reviewed contained no approved estimates—for example, contracts managed by CCSB for Attractions Canada. In the majority of invoices for the Department of Canadian Heritage's $1.9 million millennium anti-racism campaign in 1999-2000, the Department used the initial global budget as the estimate. We could not establish whether this initial budget had been approved in the first place. The Department has since changed its practices and was able to demonstrate that for the 2002-03 anti-racism campaign, a detailed budget and the scope of work had been approved and were attached to the contract.

4.58   In one case, the Department of Finance approved an invoice for $294,593 from Vickers and Benson before it had approved the related estimate. Our review of the documentation showed that the services were delivered in early fall and the invoice was dated 16 November 2000. The related estimates ($766 and $315,012 respectively) were dated 5 January and 14 February 2001. Although the invoice was not paid until 26 February 2001 after the Department had received the estimates, we are concerned that it did not receive them until three months after the work was completed and the invoice sent.

4.59   Our audit also found similar and other contract management problems in the Canadian Tourism Commission (see case study "Management of advertising contracts awarded by the Canadian Tourism Commission"), and in the Canada Mortgage and Housing Corporation (see case study "Poor management of contractual arrangements").

Obligations under the Financial Administration Act were not always met

4.60   Many of the files we audited contained no evidence that departmental officials had met their obligations under the *Financial Administration Act*. Some public servants, for example,

- approved payments without reference to the work to be performed, normally set out in the contract;

- did not verify that commissions charged were consistent with contract terms; and

- approved the payment of invoices without supporting documentation showing what services had been received and that the charges were consistent with contract terms.

4.61   In our opinion, public servants in those cases did not meet their obligations under the *Financial Administration Act*.

Some good practices and some problems corrected

4.62   We also found that in some cases, departments appeared to have no difficulty managing contracts properly. We saw evidence that HRDC had good controls and had reconciled payments with approved estimates. At the Canada Customs and Revenue Agency and the departments of Finance, Health, and Justice, invoices from advertising agencies contained the contractor's certification as required by the contracts.

4.63   We found that National Defence had taken several measures to correct significant problems identified in 2003 by an internal audit of contracting for advertising services. For example, it now ensures that production estimates are signed by the head of operations after review by project officers. To help project officers assess the accuracy of production estimates and challenge them if necessary, the Department conducted a "job shadowing" experience, taking staff to the advertising agency's premises to become familiar with each step of the production process. We saw evidence that invoices had been revised following challenges by the Department.

4.64   National Defence also adopted a system to track estimates against invoices. It has provided advertising training to its staff and, at the time of our audit, four employees had just completed the Communications and Advertising Accredited Professional (CAAP) program and obtained certification.

4.65   The selection processes conducted by CCSB in mid-2001 for the Department of Finance and for CMHC appeared to be more rigorous than in the past. Files were better documented, and the duration of the assignment was mentioned in the request for letters of interest. In addition, CMHC concluded a more detailed agreement with its agencies Gervais, Gagnon Associés Communications, and Publicité Martin Inc., with clear terms and conditions.

4.66   We found that staff in some departments did not always understand the terms and conditions of advertising contracts. However, other departments had attracted staff with significant advertising expertise, and some departments had ensured that staff undertook specialized training.

4.67   **The Canadian Tourism Commission (CTC) selected a new agency in 2002.** In November 2002, CTC selected a new advertising agency, Palmer Jarvis. We did not audit that selection process; as a Crown corporation since January 2001, CTC was subject to the requirements of its own contracting policy and not those of the Treasury Board. CTC's internal audit team reviewed the process and concluded that it "complied with CTC's contracting policy and was characterized by a high degree of competition and transparency." However, the internal auditors also identified weaknesses in the quality of the documentation rating the proposals submitted by bidders for the contract.

Departmental management of advertising campaigns

4.68   To examine how departments have managed advertising campaigns, we selected campaigns run by Health Canada, Human Resources Development Canada (HRDC), and the former Canada Information Office, now Communication Canada. The three campaigns are described in the case study "Three advertising campaigns managed by three departments."

4.69   We expected to find that departments had followed the requirements of the government's communications policy and

- reflected the government's key priorities and their own program priorities in the campaigns,

- sent their advertising plan to Communication Canada,

- pre-tested and evaluated the campaigns,

- submitted their campaign proposals to the Government Advertising Committee and sought the advice of the Committee and/or the Privy Council Office during the process, and

- obtained a registration (ADV) number from Communication Canada before placing ads in the media.

4.70 We also looked for evidence that each department had followed practices commonly used in the advertising industry and

- presented to the assigned agency a creative briefing with clear and measurable objectives for the campaign, a description of the target audience, and a summary of the desired effect;

- obtained from the agency a media plan for reaching and persuading the target audience, including a budget outline, a summary of the target audience's media habits, and a description of the effort (spending/reach) required by region, week, and type of medium;

- monitored the development of creative content, from the design of the concept through final copy and production, including testing of the advertisements; and

- evaluated the performance of the campaign in producing the expected results.

4.71 How well each organization met these criteria in managing their advertising campaigns is summarized in Exhibit 4.1.

Co-ordination of advertising activities

4.72 The Privy Council Office (PCO) advises departments and agencies on government priorities and themes to ensure that they reflect them in their strategic communications plans. As Chair of the Government Advertising Committee, which reviews and advises departments on their advertising plans, the PCO also helps to ensure that the plans are consistent with key government priorities and the government's advertising plan.

A move led by the Privy Council Office toward a corporate approach to advertising

4.73　In the 2001-02 Communications Framework and Marketing Plan, the Privy Council Office established key priorities for government advertising and provided guidelines to departments for reflecting them in their own advertising activities. It encouraged departments to focus on key priorities and to communicate them in a way that would address citizens' interests and concerns. It also called for better integration of advertising campaigns by departments.

4.74　The PCO measured the impact of the 2001-02 marketing plan and of major campaigns, and it integrated the results in the 2002-03 marketing plan and an annual advertising plan. It identified the need for a longer planning cycle (two years) and more systematic evaluations of advertising campaigns. In 2002, with Communication Canada, the PCO developed an advertising campaign evaluation tool to be used by all federal entities. The PCO holds monthly meetings with departmental directors general of communications to share information and good practices.

Review of major campaigns lacked transparency

4.75　The Government Advertising Committee's records of decisions from January 2001 to May 2003 show that the Committee reviewed about 100 advertising campaigns. The records suggest that in many cases, the Committee challenged departments' proposed campaigns and refused to approve their ads without specified changes. However, the Government Advertising Committee keeps no minutes of its meetings and we were provided no criteria by which it approved or rejected campaigns. Further, because what constitutes the criteria for a major campaign has not been defined, we could not determine that all major campaigns were submitted to the Committee as the communications policy requires.

Communication Canada authorized ads without the required documentation

4.76   As noted, the communications policy calls for departments to submit their advertising plans to Communication Canada (until September 2001, to CCSB), which summarizes the plans in order to assist the PCO in establishing the government's annual advertising plans. Communication Canada officials provided us with consolidated advertising plans for the last five years, but they told us that the plans were not completely reliable because departments had not always complied with the requirements.

4.77   A department that submits a major campaign for review by the Government Advertising Committee is advised verbally when it can request an ADV number from Communication Canada to place the campaign. This is a key control step to ensure that all government ads are co-ordinated and monitored centrally. Guidelines issued in 2000 listed key documents that must accompany a request for an ADV number, including results of campaign pre-testing, a complete media plan, ad samples, and production and media placement costs.

4.78   We found that Communication Canada on several occasions issued an ADV number at a department's request without having received the required accompanying documents. For example, we rarely found results of ad campaign pre-testing. Officials told us they checked mainly for evidence that the ad was in both official languages and advertised a policy, service, or program rather than promoting a minister or a department. We saw some examples of requests that CCSB/Communication Canada had denied, demonstrating a certain degree of control. To issue the ADV number for a major campaign, officials also relied on the Government Advertising Committee's verbal approval of the campaign.

Withdrawal of advertising during elections worked as intended

4.79   The government's communications policy states that federal institutions must suspend their advertising during federal general elections. Suspending all media placements for an organization the size of the Government of

Canada requires a quick and well co-ordinated response to an election call. For the general election in November 2000, we found evidence that the system reacted swiftly and that ads were pulled off the air in time.

Lack of up-to-date information on the extent of advertising activities

4.80   Communication Canada maintains a database of departments' requisitions for advertising contracts. PWGSC maintains a database of the contracts. Because bills are paid by individual departments, Communication Canada's and PWGSC's databases do not have a record of actual expenditures. As a result, the available data on advertising expenditures are not reliable: they capture only the value of the requisitions of the contracts.

New measures for renewal of advertising practices

4.81   On 28 April 2003, after an extensive review of advertising practices and policies by the President of the Treasury Board and consultations with the advertising industry, the Minister of Public Works and Government Services (who is also the minister responsible for Communication Canada) announced extensive changes in the federal government's advertising practices. (See the section "Treasury Board Secretariat initiatives" in Chapter 3 of our Report.)

4.82   The new measures include the following:

- Eliminating long-term partnerships between advertising agencies and individual departments and using specific procurement tools according to the value of each assignment. For example, contracts for less than $75,000 would be assigned to agencies selected through standing offers; for contracts from $75,000 to $750,000, agencies would be selected from a list of qualified suppliers. Campaigns worth more than $750,000 would be subject to open competition.

- Moving from paying agencies commissions to paying hourly rates and fees, as the private sector does. Agencies no longer receive the 17.65 percent commission on subcontracted work but instead are reimbursed only for their out-of-pocket costs.

- Introducing a new scope of work and new method of payment for the agency of record, with several measures to ensure accountability and evaluation, including a formal third-party audit of the agency's performance after two years. In July 2003, the government issued a request for proposals to find a new agency of record. It included strict evaluation and audit clauses.

- Providing training for public servants in all aspects of advertising and creating a centre of expertise at Communication Canada to offer exchanges and seminars with outside agencies.

- Issuing a first annual report on government advertising, including expenditures, a review of some campaigns, and a description of the system and the roles of key players.

- Providing for an audit to be conducted in 2005.

These new measures have the potential to strengthen the management of advertising activities—only, however, if the government ensures that public servants not only understand the rules but also follow them.

Conclusion

4.83   The Communications Coordination Services Branch broke the rules in most of the selection processes that we audited. In some cases, we found no evidence that a competitive process was conducted at all. In the selection of agencies and awarding of contracts, we observed problems similar to those reported in Chapter 3 of this Report, on sponsorship: with few exceptions, the same public servants broke the same rules in awarding contracts to the same companies. In breaking the rules, CCSB did not ensure best value for the Crown.

4.84   Individual departments did not ensure that terms and conditions of the contracts were respected. Overall, we observed a lack of attention to the contracting rules and an absence of rigour in the enforcement of contract terms and conditions. Departments did not require agencies to seek bids for subcontracted work, nor did they challenge commissions charged and invoices that were not adequately supported. Departmental officials who approved payments were not provided with enough supporting documentation in many cases to adequately discharge their responsibilities under the *Financial Administration Act*. We found a wide range of practices in the way three major advertising campaigns were managed. We noted some good practices in the management of advertising contracts, demonstrating that the rules can be followed. These rules must be followed consistently.

4.85   The Government of Canada issued contracts over $435 million on media placement purchases during the five years covered by its agreement with Media/I.D.A. Vision, its agency of record. The government did not properly monitor the performance of its agency of record or audit it as required. Until the fourth year of the five-year agreement, the agency of record did not provide departments with the information they needed to properly verify individual billings. The government did not ensure that it received best value for media placements.

4.86   Key aspects of the government's co-ordinated approach to advertising appear to work. Government priorities are communicated to those responsible for developing advertising strategies. The system worked to ensure that advertising ceased when the 2000 general election was called. However, there are several areas that need improvement, particularly ensuring greater transparency and improving the quality of information available on the government's advertising activities.

4.87   The government has announced significant changes to the management of advertising activities and has started implementing them. If implemented properly, these changes could provide a basis to address the weaknesses we observed during our audit. However, adherence to the rules already in place must become a priority not only for Communications Canada but also for each government department.

About the Audit

Objectives - Our audit objectives were to determine

- whether the government exercised adequate control over its Sponsorship Program,

- whether the results of these activities have been measured and reported them to Parliament, and

- to what extent the government has taken corrective action as a result of previous audits or reviews.

Scope and approach-chapter 3 - We examined a risk-based sample of 38 project files and a random sample of 15 project files from 1997 to 31 August 2001, managed by the Communication Coordination Services Branch (CCSB) of Public Works and Government Services Canada (PWGSC); and a random sample of 25 files from 1 September 2001 to 31 March 2003, managed by Communication Canada. We reviewed the work performed by PWGSC's Internal Audit and its Quick Response Team. They reviewed 580 files and 126 files respectively. We interviewed officials of PWGSC, the Treasury Board Secretariat, and Communication Canada. We also interviewed some former officials and former ministers responsible for CCSB.

Scope and approach-chapter 4 - We examined the systems and practices used in managing advertising activities. We examined a risk-based sample of 14 selection processes for advertising agencies for 10 departments and 1 Crown corporation, conducted by the Communications Coordination Services Branch (CCSB) of Public Works and Government Services Canada (PWGSC) between 1994 and 2001. We examined a risk-based sample of 34 advertising contracts. We examined three major advertising campaigns.

We conducted interviews with officials in PWGSC, the Treasury Board Secretariat, Communication Canada, and in departments. We conducted our work in the following departments and Crown corporations: Canada Information Office, Communication Canada, Public Works and Government Services Canada, Canada Customs and Revenue Agency, Canadian Heritage, Department of Finance Canada, Health Canada, Human Resources Development Canada, Justice Canada, National Defence, Privy Council Office, Canadian Tourism Commission, and Canada Mortgage and Housing Corporation.

Criteria - We expected that the government would do the following:
- comply with authorities;
- ensure that sponsorship activities were designed to achieve expected results;
- exercise due diligence in approving individual projects;
- ensure due diligence in spending and account for public funds spent;
- have reasonable assurance that funding was used for the intended purposes;
- appropriately manage the risks inherent in third-party delivery, where applicable;
- have a clearly communicated accountability framework in place, including performance management and reporting; and
- conduct periodical review and appropriate follow-up.

Crown corporations-chapter 3

Objectives - The objectives and criteria for our audit of sponsorship funding to Crown corporations varied slightly from those used in our examination of the departments. We set out to determine whether selected Crown corporations had exercised adequate control over sponsorship activities involving funds received from the government or disbursed to the government to promote government objectives. We also wanted to determine the extent to which the selected Crown corporations had taken corrective actions as a result of previous audits or reviews.

Scope and approach - We selected 10 Crown corporations: two on a risk basis and eight from the Sponsorship Program database. We examined all 46 transactions from the Sponsorship Program database for those eight Crown corporations. We also looked at transactions from 1997 to 2003 that we selected from the Crown corporations' databases. We interviewed officials of the Crown corporations, PWGSC, the Treasury Board Secretariat, and Communication Canada.

Criteria - We expected that the Crown corporations would do the following:
- comply with relevant authorities;
- ensure that sponsorship activities were designed to achieve the expected results;

- exercise due diligence in approving individual projects;

- ensure due diligence in spending and account for public funds spent;

- have reasonable assurance that funds were used for the intended purposes;

- appropriately manage the risks inherent in third-party delivery, where applicable; and

- periodically review sponsorship activities and follow up as appropriate.

Audit team

Assistant Auditor General: Shahid Minto
Principal: Ronnie Campbell
Directors: Louise Bertrand, Johanne McDuff, and Sue Morgan

Nadine Cormier
Andréanne Élie
Marc Gauthier
Vincent Gauthier
Roberto Grondin
Marilyn Jodoin
Joyce Ku
Lucia Lee
Rosemary Marenger
Sophie Miller
Brian O'Connell
Lucie Talbot
Casey Thomas

For information, please contact Communications at
(613) 995-3708 or
1-888-761-5953 (toll-free).

Definition:

CCSB - In this chapter CCSB refers to the former branch of PWGSC and not to any other branch of the same name in other departments.

C

OPENING STATEMENT

The Honourable John H. Gomery,
Justice, Superior Court of Quebec

May 7, 2004

1. Introduction

By the present opening statement I am commencing the public proceedings of
the Commission of Inquiry established by Order in Council P.C. 2004-110
which was promulgated on February 19, 2004 pursuant to Part I of the
Inquiries Act.

According to the terms of reference which are contained in the Order in Council, the Commission is given a double mandate. The first requires the Commission to make a factual inquiry, to investigate and report on questions raised, directly or indirectly, by Chapters 3 and 4 of the November 2003 Report of the Auditor General of Canada, which, as you may recall, was tabled in the House of Commons on February 10, 2004. Chapters 3 and 4 deal with the sponsorship program and advertising activities of the Government of Canada, and the terms of reference go on to detail particular aspects of the sponsorship program and advertising activities which are to be examined, and conclude with a sub-paragraph giving the Commission a broad discretion to investigate any circumstances it considers relevant to fulfilling its mandate.

The second mandate calls upon the Commission to make recommendations to the Government of Canada, based upon its findings of fact, to prevent mismanagement of sponsorship programs and advertising activities in the future, taking into account certain initiatives announced by the Government on February 10, 2004 which are enumerated in the terms of reference, a copy of which you will find attached as Appendix I to the written text of this opening statement.

This Inquiry has arisen as a result of the significant concerns raised in the Report of the Auditor General to the House of Commons with respect to the sponsorship program and advertising activities of the Government of Canada. According to her Report, there were failures of internal control systems, a lack of appropriate documentation justifying material expenditures of public money, the payment of large sums of money to private parties with no apparent value being received in return, a systematic disregard of the applicable rules including those contained in the *Financial Administration Act*, a lack of competition in the selection of advertising agencies, and a general bypassing of Parliament.

These are serious issues, which have been the subject of much debate in and out of the House of Commons and intense media attention. The hearings before the Public Accounts Committee of the House of Commons have supplied important evidence, but have raised additional questions and concerns. The public is entitled to know what happened, and this Commission will look for the answers.

Let me say at once that although the Commission of Inquiry has been created by a decision of Cabinet, it has by law an almost complete independence of the Government of Canada. Its only obligations are to comply with the terms of reference, and to abide by the legal requirement to act fairly. As Commissioner, I have no preconceived notions as to the conclusions to which I will eventually come. In reaching those conclusions, I will be guided only by the evidence, documentation and representations presented to me in the course of our hearings. I will in no way be influenced by political considerations, and I will not tolerate any attempt by anyone to interfere with the work of the Commission, for political or other reasons.

The Commission will carry out its investigations and hearings separately from any others which may currently be ongoing. For example, the House of Commons Public Accounts Committee has been holding public as well as closed hearings for some time into activities and programs which are related to those referred to in the Commission's terms of reference. While the Commission intends to take into consideration the evidence, documents and other information provided by those hearings as part of its own factual review, it is independent of the Public Accounts Committee and is not involved in any way in its work.

The processes and procedures which will be followed by the Commission will be, of course, different from those used by the House of Commons Public Accounts Committee. For example, before the Committee, while a witness may have a lawyer present to advise him or her privately, the witness may not be asked questions for the record by the lawyer in question, and that lawyer is not permitted to cross-examine other witnesses who may give evidence which impacts upon his or her client's credibility or conduct. In effect, no person whose conduct or credibility may be impugned has the right to defend himself or herself other than through his or her direct testimony, if indeed that person is called as a witness. As you will see later, the

Commission's rules and procedures will provide safeguards in these matters, and it will be more thorough in its examination of the facts. While I will be conscious of the need for expedition, counsel will not be subject to arbitrary time limits. Further, through the process of questioning by Commission counsel, cross-examination by parties with standing and questioning by a witness' own counsel, I expect that relevant and material information will come to light.

Similarly, this Inquiry is neither connected to nor involved with ongoing police investigations, although it will seek to have access to relevant material resulting from such investigations to the extent it is not precluded, by law, from doing so, always taking care not to jeopardize any ongoing criminal investigation or criminal proceedings.

Let me now introduce myself and the persons who I have appointed to work for the Commission.

2. Composition and Schedule of the Commission of Inquiry

I am John Gomery, and have been a Justice of the Superior Court of Quebec for more than 21 years. My Chief Justice has relieved me from my assignments and responsibilities as a judge until this mandate has been completed. As of April 1st, 2004, I have resigned from the Copyright Board of Canada, of which I had been the Chairman as a part-time position for five years.

To handle the administrative needs of the Commission, I have appointed Ms. Sheila-Marie Cook as Executive Director and Secretary of the Commission. She is in the process of engaging such administrative staff as we require, always keeping in mind the most efficient use of public money. As to location of the Commission, the practical effect of the terms of reference requires that public hearings be held in Ottawa, where the programs and activities at issue were created and managed, and Montreal, where most contracts were awarded and funds distributed. Consequently, the Commission has set up premises and arranged hearing facilities in both cities. In Ottawa our premises are located at 222 Queen Street, and hearings will take place in the Conference Centre where we are at present. In Montreal the Commission occupies offices in Suite 608, in the East Wing of the Guy-Favreau Complex, 200 René-Lévesque Boulevard West. In that same complex there is a Conference Centre where hearings will take place.

As Commission counsel, I will benefit from the advice and assistance of senior lawyers from both Quebec and Ontario. Mr. Bernard Roy, Q.C., has been appointed as lead Commission Counsel. Mr. Roy is a senior litigation partner of the Montreal office of Ogilvy Renault. He has extensive experience as counsel to other Commissions of Inquiry, and is knowledgeable about the complex operations of the Government of Canada. He will have the primary responsibility as lead Commission counsel for preparing the Commission's legal, research and investigative activities, and will, assisted by others, present evidence before it.

Mr. Neil Finkelstein has been appointed as Co-Counsel to the Commission. Mr. Finkelstein is a senior litigation partner based in the Toronto office of Blake, Cassels & Graydon. He is an experienced litigator with an impressive national reputation, and has recognized expertise in public law matters.

Mr. Guy Cournoyer has been appointed as Associate Commission Counsel. Mr. Cournoyer is a partner in the Montreal law firm of Shadley, Battista, and specializes in criminal law. He has had valuable experience as counsel to previous Commissions of Inquiry, being the Poitras Commission and the Arbour Commission.

Messrs. Roy, Finkelstein and Cournoyer will assist and guide the Commission throughout the Inquiry, in accordance with my directions, and will see to the orderly presentation of evidence. They have the primary responsibility for representing the public interest at the Inquiry, and for ensuring that all matters relevant to the terms of reference are brought to my attention.

Assisted by their legal staff, they are already hard at work in our partly-completed premises in Montreal, where the Commission has been located for several weeks, and where a massive documentation is being accumulated, organized and studied.

The presentation of evidence will be subject to *Rules of Procedure and Practice* a draft of which is attached as Appendix II. I invite interested parties to send comments on these draft Rules, in writing, to Counsel for the Commission not later than May 31st. It should be noted immediately that the normal procedure and practice in a civil or criminal trial will not apply to our investigation and hearings since this is not a trial, but rather an inquiry. For example, at the hearing of witnesses, Commission counsel may ask leading questions and have a discretion to refuse to call or present certain evidence. Their role is neutral, not adversarial. As Commissioner I may circumscribe the right to cross-examination.

The Commission has retained the services of Mr. Serge Roy to act as its Registrar and Court Clerk during its hearings.

Given the voluminous documentation and evidence that has to be organized and analysed, the need for research into legal questions that will inevitably arise, and to assist senior counsel, I have appointed additional attorneys to assist in the work of the Commission: they are Mr. Gregory Bordan, Ms. Charlotte Kanya-Forstner, Ms. Sophie Nunnelley, Mr. Simon Richard and Ms. Véronique Robert-Blanchard.

As investigators and forensic experts, the Commission has engaged the reputable firm of Kroll, Lindquist, Avey.

The Commission has retained the services of Mr. François Perreault of BDDS/Weber Shandwick as its communications advisor. He will be responsible for media relations and is well-known in that field. He is the only person who will speak on behalf of the Commission.

Now, let me make a few comments about our schedule.

Many people have asked me how long it will take for the Commission to complete its mandate. This is a difficult question to answer at this stage since we can only guess at how long the hearing of witnesses will be; much will depend upon the number of persons and organizations that will ask to participate, and the duration of the examination and cross-examination of each of the many witnesses to be heard. At this moment in time we cannot even predict with accuracy how many witnesses will have relevant evidence to offer. The terms of reference do not impose a deadline for the submission of the Commission's report or reports, but directs us to act on an urgent basis and to conclude the work of the Commission as soon as reasonably possible. We intend to do that.

This having been said, to provide some sort of an idea of the estimated duration of the Inquiry, we have prepared a Tentative Schedule which is attached as Appendix III.

As you will see from that Appendix, the Commission will be receiving motions for standing during the month of May, which will be the subject of hearings in June. This will be followed by written submissions for funding in early July, which will be the subject of a decision to be handed down not later than July 19th. The rest of the summer of 2004 will be devoted to preparations for public hearings which will commence here in Ottawa on September 7, 2004. The public hearings will be in two phases; the first phase, IA, will deal with the creation, purpose and objectives of the sponsorship program, the means by which it was administered, and the extent to which it met the standards of good management. Phase IA is anticipated to last 80 days or so, and will occupy the Commission until the end of January 2005. Phase IB will consider where the sponsorship and advertising funds went, the extent to which there was value for money, and whether there was political influence and involvement. Phase IB will take place in Montreal and is expected to last until April 30, 2005. Closing submissions would be made in June 2005.

As the Tentative Schedule indicates, I propose to submit two Reports to the Governor in Council. The first would deal with the factual findings on the issues set out in paragraph (a) of the terms of reference, and should be submitted by November 1, 2005. A second Report, containing the recommendations required in accordance with paragraph (b) of the terms of reference, should be ready by December 15, 2005.

3. The Nature and Procedure of the Inquiry

The purpose of the Commission is not to conduct a trial or to express any conclusion regarding the civil or criminal liability of any person or organization. That limitation is expressly articulated in paragraph (k) of the terms of reference which I take the liberty of reading aloud, because of its importance:

> (k) the Commissioner be directed to perform his duties without expressing any conclusion or recommendation regarding the civil or criminal liability of any person or organization and to ensure that the conduct of the inquiry does not jeopardize any ongoing criminal investigation or criminal proceedings;

Accordingly, the Commission may not establish either criminal culpability or civil responsibility for sums of money lost or misspent, or damages; it does not have the capacity nor does it intend to do so. The Inquiry is an investigation into the issues and events referred to in the terms of reference. Its future findings of fact and statements of opinion will be unconnected to normal legal criteria, and will be intended to serve as the basis for the recommendations which I will be making as required by paragraph (b) of the terms of reference. It follows that there will be no legal consequences arising from the Commission's findings and Reports, and they will not be enforceable in, and will not bind either civil or criminal courts which might consider the same subject matters.

Nevertheless, although the Commission will not, and indeed cannot, express conclusions or recommendations in relation to the potential civil or criminal liability of anyone, it is part of its mandate to assess the evidence and to make findings of fact, such as findings with respect to the credibility of witnesses. According to s.13 of the *Inquiries Act*, which will be discussed in more detail later, I am entitled to draw conclusions as to whether there has been misconduct and who may be responsible for it. Such findings will be the focus of the Inquiry only to the extent that they are necessary to carry out the mandate in the terms of reference. In the course of the Inquiry's hearing process, evidence may emerge in support of a factual finding which, broadly construed, might be perceived as adverse or unfavourable to the reputation of a person or organization. Given that possibility, it is of paramount importance that the Inquiry's process be scrupulously fair. With this in mind, the Commission intends to conduct its hearings in accordance with the following principles and procedures.

First, consistent with the generally accepted criteria for Commissions of Inquiry of this nature, all those with a direct and substantial interest in the proceedings, or having a clearly ascertainable interest or perspective that would enhance the work of the Commission, will be granted standing to participate appropriate to their interests. Parties wishing to participate are invited to apply for standing by way of a motion in writing on or before May 31, 2004. The motion should set out, giving reasons in support of its position:

i.   whether the person or organization seeks full or special standing, and for what portion of the Inquiry;

ii. those areas and issues where the prospective party is directly and substantially affected, or where the party has a clearly ascertainable interest, or a perspective which would enhance the work of the Commission, and the reasons therefore; and

iii. the specific scope of participation sought.

Applicants who have made written motions will be permitted to make oral submissions not exceeding 15 minutes at a public Standing Hearing which will take place here in Ottawa from June 21 - 23, 2004.

The Commission will recognize two types of standing, full standing or partial standing, depending upon the party's interest. Parties may be granted full or partial standing for all or a portion of Phases IA and IB of the Inquiry. Parties who obtain standing under sections 12 or 13 of the *Inquiries Act* will be granted full standing to the extent of their interests.

The participation of a party with full standing will include:

1. access to documents collected by the Commission subject to the *Rules of Procedure and Practice;*

2. advance notice of documents which are proposed to be introduced into evidence by Commission counsel;

3. advance provision of will-say statements, if any, relevant to the party's or witness' interest;

4. a seat at counsel table;

5. the opportunity to suggest witnesses to be called by Commission counsel, or an opportunity to apply for an order that a particular witness be summoned to appear;

6. the right to cross-examine witnesses on matters relevant to the basis upon which standing was granted; and

7. the right to make closing submissions.

Parties who are not granted full standing may, at my discretion, be granted partial standing, which will include any or all of the following:

1. numbers 1, 2, 3, 5 and 7 above; and

2. the opportunity to suggest areas for examination of a certain witness by Commission counsel, failing which, the opportunity to request leave to examine the witness on such areas.

Some of the principles for determining full or partial standing should be mentioned:

- there must be relevance to the issues described in the Order in Council;

- applicants may be granted standing only for those portions of the Inquiry that relate to their particular interest or perspective;

- to avoid repetition and unnecessary delay, I may decide to group certain applicants into coalitions where there are similar interests or perspectives, where there is no apparent conflict of interest, and where the relevant interest or perspective will be fully and fairly represented by a single grant of standing to the parties as a group.

Once standing has been determined, I am given authority by paragraph (h) of the terms of reference to recommend funding by the Government for the purposes of the factual investigation in paragraph (a) where, in my view, the party would not otherwise be able to participate. I invite parties, once they have been granted standing, to seek funding by motion in writing filed with the Commission on or before July 2, 2004. There will be no oral hearing with respect to funding, and my recommendations in accordance with paragraph (h) of the terms of reference will be made not later than July 16, 2004. To qualify for a funding recommendation, a party must demonstrate that it would not be able to participate in the Inquiry without funding, and must also present a satisfactory plan showing how it intends to use the funds and account for them. I will also take into consideration the party's:

- interest and proposed involvement in the Inquiry;

- established record of concern for and a demonstrated commitment to the interest it seeks to represent;

- special experience or expertise with respect to the Commission's mandate;

- explanation as to why no reasonable alternative means of funding is available to enable the party to participate.

At this stage of the proceedings, I do not intend to recommend payment for experts to be called by those with standing in Phase IA or IB. The primary responsibility for calling experts lies with Commission counsel, who will be open to suggestions from parties as to the types and names of experts to be called. Experts called by Commission counsel will be paid by the Commission.

I shall not consider Phase II funding at the present time, although I may do so in the months to come.

Next, still on the issue of fairness, s. 13 of the *Inquiries Act* provides that no report may be made in relation to misconduct by any person without notice and an opportunity to be heard. s. 13 reads as follows:

> 13. No report shall be made against any person until reasonable notice has been given to the person of the charge of misconduct alleged against him and the person has been allowed full opportunity to be heard in person or by counsel.

The content and dates of s. 13 notices, and the identity of the persons to whom such notices are sent, will be confidential. All persons who receive s. 13 notices will be granted full standing to the extent of their interest at the time they seek such standing.

The purpose of s. 13 of the *Inquiries Act* is to ensure that, where evidence may support a factual finding that may adversely affect a person's reputation, that person is granted procedural fairness. I intend to take a broad view of the meaning of "misconduct" for the purposes of s. 13 so that no person who may reasonably be expected to be adversely affected by a finding is denied a full opportunity to be heard. On this question I will be following the broad principles outlined in Canada (A.G.) v. *Canada Commission of Inquiry on Blood Systems*, [1997] S.C.R. 440. With respect to the scope of the term "misconduct", I will be guided by what was said in *The Report of the Walkerton Inquiry* at p. 160; Mr. Justice O'Connor said there, and I am paraphrasing his comments, that:

> where the evidence might support a factual finding which, broadly construed, might be perceived as unfavourable or adverse to a person's reputation, including conduct that might

be described as careless or an oversight, it would be most fair to the person to provide notice. This was so the person would be put on notice, could avail himself or herself of procedural protections, and could respond. Upon receipt of notice, a person automatically gains limited standing for the purposes of that notice. This gives certain procedural protections to the person.

Accordingly, Commission counsel will send s. 13 notices to persons or organizations from time to time throughout this Inquiry when they reasonably anticipate at that time that the evidence could lead to a factual finding which may adversely affect a person's reputation. I recognize that s. 13 notices have been sent by other Commissions of Inquiry at the end of the public hearings. At that time, the notices can be more detailed and the parties may then wish to apply to have additional witnesses called. However, when notices are sent at the end of the public hearings, the recipient may have committed himself or herself in the way he or she conducted the evidence phase of the hearing. Therefore, in this Inquiry Commission counsel propose to send more generalized s. 13 notices as soon as they, in their judgment, reasonably anticipate that one is appropriate to enable recipients to respond earlier.

The draft *Rules of Procedure and Practice*, attached as Appendix II, are intended to ensure that the public hearings in Ottawa and Montreal into the factual matters raised in paragraph (a) of the terms of reference are conducted fairly. To summarize them, without going into all the details, they provide that:

i. all parties and all witnesses have the right to counsel both at the Inquiry and at any pre-testimony interviews;

ii. each party may cross-examine any witness on matters which are the basis for their grant of standing;

iii. Commission counsel, who, I repeat, are neutral and non-partisan, will call and question witnesses. Any party may apply to the Commissioner for leave to have any witness called whom Commission counsel elects not to call;

iv. each witness and party shall be provided with copies, in paper or electronic form, of documents, evidence, information and will-say statements, if any, which are relevant to the party's or witness' interest, to the extent it is appropriate to do so, together with the documents which Commission counsel expects to put to him or her in the course of his or her testimony, and will have the right to introduce their own documentary evidence;

v. all hearings will be held in public, and will be televised, unless an application is granted for a publication ban or for a portion of the hearing to be held *in camera* in order to preserve the confidentiality of information or the identities of informants (including whistleblowers), witnesses or other persons;

vi. parties are encouraged to provide to Commission counsel the names and addresses of all witnesses they feel ought to be heard, and to provide all relevant documents, at the earliest opportunity;

vii. all witnesses are entitled to have counsel present, who may object to questions put to them;

vii. athough evidence may be presented that might not ordinarily be admissible in a court of law, I shall be mindful of the danger of admitting such evidence and, in particular, its possible effect on someone's reputation;

ix. parties may make closing submissions only on matters relevant to the basis upon which standing was granted to them.

The hearings will be bilingual; witnesses and their counsel are entitled to speak either of Canada's official languages, and to be examined and cross-examined by counsel in the official language of their choice. Simultaneous translation services will be provided throughout. The Commission's written decisions and reports will be in both official languages.

4. The Commission's Mandate and the Issues List

The scope of the Commission's mandate is established by the terms of reference. I interpret these as directing me to perform two separate, but related, functions.

First, in what has been referred to as Phase I, paragraph (a) directs me to determine essentially how and why the sponsorship program and advertising activities considered in Chapters 3 and 4 of the Auditor General's November 2003 report to the House of Commons were created, implemented and managed, and where the money went. As already mentioned, Phase I will consist of public hearings in Ottawa and Montreal, culminating in a report which I hope to submit to the Governor in Council no later than November 1, 2005.

Second, paragraph (b) of the terms of reference directs me to make recommendations based upon my factual findings from Phase I about how to prevent future problems. This will be Phase II, during which I expect to commission papers from experts on various subjects and to hear or receive submissions from persons or organizations who have been granted standing in Phase II. In addition I propose to conduct some form of public hearings so as to receive the views of ordinary citizens. I hope to submit to the Governor in Council my second Report, containing recommendations, on December 15, 2005.

The issues to be considered in Phases IA and IB as I interpret the terms of reference, are set out in the following Issues Lists:

Issues List of Phase IA

1. the creation, purpose and objectives of the sponsorship program;

2. the role and responsibility of elected and non-elected public office holders and others in the Government and Parliament of Canada, including Crown entities (collectively the "Government of Canada"), as well as others outside the Government of Canada, in the creation of the sponsorship program, the selection of communications and advertising agencies (including the creation, purpose and objectives

of the advertising program), and the management of the sponsorship program and advertising activities of the Government of Canada (collectively the "activities");

3. whether Parliament was bypassed and, if so, by whom and on what basis;

4. whether there was political influence involved in the activities and, if so, by whom, to what purpose, and to what effect;

5. whether any person or organization in the Government of Canada gained an advantage financially, politically or otherwise from the activities and, if so who, to what purpose, and to what effect;

6. whether the procedures, structures, reporting lines, systems for approvals and internal controls which were implemented by the Government of Canada, in the activities were sufficient and, if not, why not and to what purpose and effect. This will involve an assessment of the normal procedures, structures, reporting lines, systems for approvals and internal controls, or other potentially applicable standards, for procurement programs and selections of service providers for activities of a similar nature, and whether there were deviations in the activities from normal procedures, structures, reporting lines, systems for approvals and internal controls;

7. whether there was compliance with normally applicable rules, regulations, standards and guidelines, including the *Financial Administration Act* and other relevant instruments and, if not, in what manner was there non-compliance, and to what effect;

8. whether the culture and structure in the Government of Canada discouraged whistleblowing;

9. the path of the funds, including the approvals and procedures in relation thereto, within the Government of Canada to the point that these funds were disbursed to non-Government of Canada sources.

Issues List of Phase IB

1. the identity of those who received the sponsorship, communications and advertising funds, including any commissions or fees payable with respect to them, (hereinafter "the funds") the purpose for which the funds were disbursed, and the extent of value for money received in return by the Government of Canada, the latter term as defined in the Issues List for Phase IA, item 2;

2. whether there was political influence on the distribution of the funds, including questions relating to whether there were direct or indirect political contributions or gifts made by recipients of the funds;

3. whether there were sufficient external monitoring and financial controls used by fund recipients described in I above; if not, why not and to what effect.

5. Conclusion

Without repeating what I have already said concerning the Tentative Schedule for the Commission of Inquiry as set out in Appendix III, a few additional remarks on the subject of the time needed to fulfil this mandate may be necessary.

Paragraph (1) of the terms of reference directs me to submit my reports on an "urgent" basis. I take this direction very seriously, being cognizant of the public outcry which accompanied the release of the Auditor General's Report, which led to the establishment of this Commission. There have been calls from many quarters to begin public hearings promptly and to "get to the bottom of this" as soon as possible. I recognize these concerns, which are perfectly legitimate.

However, I am also cognizant of the fact that my mandate is extremely broad and complex. It will involve hearing from numerous witnesses, reviewing voluminous documentation, and considering a wide variety of evidence.

While I do not intend to track down every point, no matter how immaterial or remotely related, I also do not intend to carry out a superficial examination. The investigation must be thorough. This takes time. A too rapid approach might be construed on the one hand as superficial, intended to absolve certain parties of blame, or on the other hand, as negligent and intended to attach blame too readily. Obviously this must be avoided.

I am also well aware that this Inquiry may tarnish the reputations of some people. A person's reputation may be his or her most important possession. As I said before, I intend to ensure that every person or organization receives appropriate procedural fairness. That also takes time. No one should be railroaded.

Everyone wants answers quickly, and I shall attempt to provide these answers to the best of my ability as promptly as I can. However, to do that, the work of the Inquiry must also be thorough and fair to all concerned. The public interests of expedition, thoroughness and fairness must be balanced.

As I stated at the outset, I have no pre-conceived notions or understandings. I shall prepare my Reports based on the evidence. I intend to conduct the Inquiry based on the five principles to which I have already referred, namely independence, fairness, thoroughness, expedition and efficiency.

I will not express conclusions or recommendations in relation to civil or criminal liability, but I shall investigate and report on the facts to the full extent of my powers under the *Inquiries Act* and the terms of reference, and to make my recommendations accordingly. At the conclusion of my mandate, my hope is that the public will consider that the issues have received a full and fair examination.

Appendix D

SCHEDULE of WITNESSES

PHASE 1A
Bytown Pavilion (Former City Hall), Ottawa

September 7, 2004

   1.   Office of the Auditor General of Canada (panel)
- Sheila Fraser, Auditor General of Canada
- Shahid Minto, Assistant Auditor General
- Ronald Campbell, Assistant Auditor General
- Louise Bertrand, Audit Principal

September 20, 2004

   2.   Treasury Board of Canada, Secretariat (panel)
- Jim Judd, Secretary of the Treasury Board of Canada
- Mike Joyce, Assistant Secretary, Expenditure Operations and Reporting Sector

- Susan Cartwright, Assistant Secretary, Government Operations Sector
- Jane Cochran, Executive Director, Procurement and Project Management Policy Directorate
- Jim Libbey, Executive Director, Strategic Systems Infrastructure Directorate, Office of the Comptroller General

3. Public Works and Government Services Canada (panel)
    - David Marshall, Deputy Minister, Public Works and Government Services Canada
    - Yvette Aloïsi, Assistant Deputy Minister, Corporate Services, Human Resources and Communications
    - Myra Conway, Director General, Financial Operations
    - George A. Butts, A/Director General, Policy, Risk, Integrity and Strategic Management Sector
    - Gerry Thom, Director, Classification, Compensation and Business Systems, Corporate Services, Human Resources and Communications

September 27, 2004

4. Privy Council Office (panel)
    - Alex Himelfarb, Clerk of the Privy Council and Secretary to the Cabinet
    - Michael Wernick, Deputy Secretary to the Cabinet, Plans and Consultation
    - Kathy O'Hara, Deputy Secretary to the Cabinet, Machinery of Government

5. Allan Cutler, Former Manager, Public Relations and Print Contract Services, Public Works and Government Services Canada

6. Ernst & Young (panel)
    - Deanna Monaghan, C.A.
    - Madeleine Brillant, C.A.
    - Julie Morin, C.A.

October 4, 2004

7.   Public Works and Government Services Canada (PWGSC), Audit and Ethics Branch (panel)
     - Norman Steinberg, Director General, Audit and Ethics Branch, PWGSC
     - Jim Hamer, Audit and Review Principal, PWGSC
     - Janet Labelle, Investigations Manager, Fraud Investigations and Internal Disclosure Directorate, PWGSC
     - Steven Turner, Retired Public Servant
     - Raoul Solon, Consultant

8.   Quick Response Team (panel)
     - Steven McLaughlin, Director Payment, Products and Services Public Works and Government Services Canada
     - Rod Monette, Assistant Deputy Minister Finance and Corporate Services Department of National Defense
     - André Auger, Director Assurance, Accounting and Audit Services Consulting and Audit Canada
     - Myra Conway, Director General Financial Operations Public Works and Government Services Canada

9.   Kroll Lindquist Avey (panel)
     - Steven Whitla
     - Guillaume Vadeboncoeur

10. Finance Canada (panel)
     - Kevin G. Lynch, Deputy Minister of Finance, Finance Canada
     - Jeremy Rudin, Director General, EFP - Assistant Deputy Minister's Office, Economic and Fiscal Policy Branch

11. Demers Administrative Review Committee (panel)
     - Jean-Claude Demers, Q.C., Lawyer who chaired the Demers Administrative Review Committee
     - Jean Quevillon, Labour Relations Program Manager, Labour Relations, Public Works and Government Services Canada

- Normand Masse, Senior Director (Contract Expert), Logistics, Electrical, Fuel and Transportation Directorate, Public Works and Government Services Canada

October 12, 2004

12. Advertising and Public Opinion Research Sector (APORS) /Communications Coordination Services Branch (CCSB), Public Works and Government Services Canada (PWGSC)
    - Huguette Tremblay, Chief, Special Projects, CCSB, PWGSC

October 18, 2004

- Isabelle Roy, Former Special Assistant, Minister Gagliano's Office, PWGSC Communications and Strategic Planning Officer, CCSB, PWGSC
- Joanne Bouvier, Former Special Assistant, Minister Gagliano's Office, PWGSC
- Ghislaine Ippersiel, Former Special Assistant, Minister Gagliano's Office, PWGSC Analyst, Communications Canada
- Paul Lauzon, Director, Advertising and Project Management, CCSB, PWGSC
- Evelyn Marcoux, Director General, Client Services and Industry Relations, CCSB, PWGSC

October 25, 2004

- Andrée LaRose, Acting Director General, Public Access Programs, CCSB, PWGSC
- Marie Maltais, Director General, Strategic Communications Coordination, CCSB, PWGSC

November 1, 2004

- David Myer, Director General, Communications Procurement, CCSB, PWGSC

- Patrick Lebrun, Former Special Assistant, Minister Gagliano's Office, PWGSC
- Mario Parent, Coordinator, Advertising Program, APORS, PWGSC Coordinator, Advertising Program, CCSB, PWGSC

November 8, 2004

- Joseph Charles Guité, Executive Director, CCSB, PWGSC

November 15, 2004 - Hearings are in Recess

November 22, 2004

* Joseph Charles Guité, Executive Director, CCSB, PWGSC

13. Anita Lloyd, Access to Information and Privacy, Public Works and Government Services Canada

14. Dominique Francoeur, Corporate Secretary, Public Works and Government Services Canada

15. Ranald Quail, Former Deputy Minister, Public Works and Government Services Canada

16. James Stobbe, Former Assistant Deputy Minister, Public Works and Government Services Canada

November 29, 2004

17. Richard Neville, Former Assistant Deputy Minister, Public Works andGovernment Services Canada

18. Communications Canada (panel)
    - Guy McKenzie
    - Guy Bédard
    - Diane Viau

- Gilles Pelletier
- Liseanne Forand

19. Roger Collet, Former Executive Director, Canada Information Office

December 6, 2004

20. Denyse Paquette, Project Coordinator, Communications Coordination Services Branch, Public Works and Government Services Canada

21. Marc Lafrenière, Former Executive Director, Canada Information Office

22. Ron Bilodeau, Former Deputy Clerk, Privy Council Office

23. Jocelyne Bourgon, Former Clerk and Secretary to the Cabinet (1994-1999), Privy Council Office

24. Michelle d'Auray, Former Director General, Communications, Intergovernmental Affairs, Privy Council Office

December 13, 2004

25. Robert-Guy Scully, Journalist, TV producer, representative of l'Information Essentielle Inc.

26. Giuliano Zaccardelli, Commissioner, Royal Canadian Mounted Police

27. Dawson Hovey, Chief Superintendant, Royal Canadian Mounted Police

28. Odilon Emond, Assistant Commissioner, Commanding Officer, "C" Division, Royal Canadian Mounted Police

29. Allen Burchill, Former Assistant Commissioner, Royal Canadian Mounted Police

30. André Thouin, Public Affairs Director, Royal Canadian Mounted Police

31. William Beahan, Director, Strategic Partnership, Royal Canadian Mounted Police

December 20, 2004 - Hearings are in Recess

January 11, 2005

32. Marc LeFrançois, Former President and Chief Executive Officer, VIA RailCanada Inc.

33. Christena Keon Sirsly, Former Vice President,Marketing and Vice President, Information Services;currently Chief Strategy Officer, VIA Rail Canada Inc.

34. Anthony Rumjahn, Corporate Comptroller, VIA Rail Canada Inc.

35. Christiane Beaulieu, Former Vice President, Public Affairs, Business Development Bank of Canada

36. Richard Morris, Vice President, Audit and Inspection, Business Development Bank of Canada

37. Guy G. Beaudry, Senior Vice President, Corporate Affairs and Chief Planning Officer, Business Development Bank of Canada

38. François Beaudoin, Former President and Chief Executive Officer, Business Development Bank of Canada

January 17, 2005

39. Daniel Sawaya, Former Vice President Marketing and Product Management, Canada Post Corporation

40. Alain Guilbert, Vice President, Communications, Canada Post Corporation

41. Stewart Bacon, Senior Vice President, Customer Relationship Management, Canada Post Corporation

42. Micheline Montreuil, Director, Stamp Products, Canada Post Corporation

43. The Honourable André Ouellet, Former Chairman and Former President and Chief Executive Officer, Canada Post Corporation

44. Anne Buston, Director, Public Relations, Canada Post Corporation

45. Lily Sioris, Manager, Public Relations, Canada Post Corporation

46. The Honourable David Dingwall, Former Minister, Public Works and Government Services Canada

47. Warren Kinsella, Former Executive Assistant, Public Works and Government Services Canada

January 24, 2005

48. Georges Clermont, Former President and Chief Executive Officer, Canada Post Corporation

49. Gordon Feeney, Chairman of the Board of Directors, Canada Post Corporation

50. The Honourable Diane Marleau, Former Minister, Public Works and Government Services Canada

51. The Honourable Stéphane Dion, Minister of Environment

52. The Honourable Denis Coderre, Former Minister of Citizenship and Immigration and Former Secretary of State (Amateur Sport)

53. Jean-Marc Bard, Former Senior Special Assistant and Executive Assistant to Alfonso Gagliano (Former Minister, Public Works and Government Services Canada)

54. The Honourable Marcel Massé, Former Minister of Intergovernemental Affairs

55. The Honourable Lucienne Robillard, President of the Queen's Privy Council for Canada, Minister of Intergovernmental Affairs and Minister of Human Resources and Skills Development

56. The Honourable Martin Cauchon, Former Minister of Justice and Secretary of State (Federal Office of Regional Development-Quebec)

January 31, 2005

57. The Honourable Pierre Pettigrew, Minister of Foreign Affairs Canada

58. Stefano Lucarelli, Former Corporate Comptroller, Business Development Bank of Canada

59. Alan Marquis, Senior Vice President, Finance and Chief Financial Officer, Business Development Bank of Canada

60. The Honourable Alfonso Gagliano, Former Minister of Public Works and Government Services Canada

61. Jean Carle, Former Chief of Operations to Jean Chrétien and First Vice President, Corporate Affairs, Business Development Bank of Canada

February 7, 2005

62. Jean Pelletier, Former Chief of Staff to Jean Chrétien and Chairman of VIA Rail Canada Inc.

63. The Right Honourable Jean Chrétien, Former Prime Minister of Canada

64. The Right Honourable Paul Martin, Prime Minister of Canada

February 14, 2005- Hearings are in Recess

PHASE 1B
Conference Centre, Guy-Favreau Complex, Montreal

February 28, 2005

For the facts pertaining to Jean Lafleur Communications:
65. Jean Lafleur

* Alex Himelfarb, Clerk of the Privy Council and Secretary to the Cabinet, Privy Council Office

For the facts pertaining to Jean Lafleur Communications:
* Jean Lafleur

March 7, 2005

* Jean Lafleur

66. Pierre Michaud

67. Pierre Davidson

68. Éric Lafleur

69. Stéphane Guertin

March 14, 2005

* Stéphane Guertin

For the facts pertaining to Gosselin Communications Stratégiques:
70. Gilles-André Gosselin

71. Andrée Côté Gosselin

72. Nicolas Gosselin

73. Bernard Thiboutot

74. Enrico Valente

March 21, 2005

Applications

March 22, 2005- Hearings are in Recess

March 29, 2005

75. Josée Thibeau-Carrier

* Huguette Tremblay, Chief, Special Projects, CCSB, PWGSC

* Mario Parent, Coordinator, Advertising Program, APORS, PWGSC
Coordinator,Advertising Program, CCSB, PWGSC

For the facts pertaining to Gosselin Communications Stratégiques:
* Gilles-André Gosselin

76. Wendy Cumming

For the facts pertaining to Groupaction:
77. Jean Brault

April 4, 2005

* Jean Brault

78. Jean Lambert

79. Alain Renaud

April 11, 2005

* Alain Renaud

80. Roger Desjeans

81. Bernard Michaud

For the facts pertaining to Groupe Polygone / Expour:
82. Luc Lemay

For the facts pertaining to PluriDesign Canada:
83. Jacques Corriveau

April 18, 2005

* Jacques Corriveau

For the facts pertaining to Groupe Polygone/Expour:
84. Gaëtan Mondoux

For the facts pertaining to PluriDesign Canada:
85. Gaëtan Sauriol

For the facts pertaining to Groupaction:
86. GPFI Inc. (panel)
     • Martin Spalding
     • Jean Laflamme

For the facts pertaining to Groupe Everest—Media IDA Vision:
87. Claude Boulay

88. Diane Deslauriers

April 25, 2005

* Diane Deslauriers

89. Vincent Cloutier

90. Alex Polevoy

91. Pierre Bibeau

92. Benoît Renaud

For the facts pertaining to Coffin Communications:
93. Paul Coffin

94. Robert St-Onge

95. Jacques Guérin

* Joseph Charles Guité, Executive Director, CCSB, PWGSC

May 2, 2005

* Joseph Charles Guité, Executive Director, CCSB, PWGSC

For the facts pertaining to Liberal Party of Canada and/or Liberal Party of Canada (Quebec):
96. Louis Pichette

97. Guy Bisson

98. Jacques Roy

99. Franco Iacono

100. Thalie Tremblay

101. Serge Gosselin

102. Monique Thomas

103. Carolina Gallo-Laflèche

104. Michel Béliveau

105. Claire Brouillet

May 9, 2005

106. Benoît Corbeil

107. Marc-Yvan Côté

108. Richard Boudreault

109. Daniel Dezainde

110. Antonio Mignacca

111. Beryl Wajsman

112. John Welch

May 16, 2005

* Office of the Auditor General of Canada (panel)
   • Sheila Fraser, Auditor General of Canada
   • Ronald Campbell, Assistant Auditor General
   • Louise Bertrand, Audit Principal

113. Privy Council Office, Treasury Board, Department of Public
     Works and Government Services Canada (panel)
   • Richard Robesco, Acting Senior Director, Communications
     Procurement Directorate, Public Works and Government
     Services Canada
   • Laurent Marcoux, Director General, Public Opinion
     Research and Advertising Coordination, Public Works and
     Government Services Canada
   • Jodi Redmond, Director, Strategic Communications
     Planning, Privy Council Office
   • Stephen Wallace, Assistant Secretary, Treasury Board of
     Canada Secretariat

114. John Hayter, Vickers & Benson

115. Luc Mérineau, Éminence Grise

116. Yves Gougoux, BCP Ltd.

May 24, 2005

117. Kroll Lindquist Avey (panel)
   - Robert Macdonald
   - Pierre St-Laurent
   - Steven Whitla *

For the facts pertaining to Liberal Party of Canada and/or Liberal Party of Canada (Quebec):
118. Gaetano Manganiello

119. Giuseppe Morselli

120. The Honourable Ralph Goodale, Minister of Finance

121. The Honourable Don Boudria, Former Minister of Public Works and Government Services Canada

For the facts pertaining to PluriDesign Canada:
* Jacques Corriveau

May 30, 2005

* Jacques Corriveau

For the facts pertaining to Groupe Polygone/Expour:
122. Monique Carle

123. Michel Bibeau

* Jean Pelletier, Former Chief of Staff to Jean Chrétien and Chairman of VIA Rail Canada Inc.

For the facts pertaining to Liberal Party of Canada and/or Liberal Party of Canada (Quebec):
124. Françoise Patry

125. John Parisella, BCP Ltd.

For the facts pertaining to Liberal Party of Canada and/or Liberal Party of Canada (Quebec) (panel):

126. Liberal Party of Canada and/or Liberal Party of Canada (Quebec) (panel)
    - Steven MacKinnon
    - Hervé Rivet

* The Honourable Alfonso Gagliano, Former Minister of Public Works and Government Services Canada

* Returning Witness

E

APPENDIX E

PARTY LAWYERS APPEARING
BEFORE THE COMMISSION

1. **For the Association des agences de publicité du Québec**
    - Daniel Rochefort
    - Mélanie Viguié-Bilodeau

2. **For the Attorney General of Canada**
    - François Couture
    - Sylvain Lussier
    - Marie Marmet
    - Donald Rennie
    - Brian Saunders
    - Joe Wild

3. **For the Office of the Auditor General**
    *   Richard G. Dearden
    *   Anne-Marie Smith

4. **For BCP Ltd.**
    *   François Grondin
    *   Michel Massicotte
    *   Gérald R. Tremblay
    *   Tommy Tremblay

5. **For the Bloc Québécois**
    *   Katty Duranleau
    *   Clément Groleau
    *   Estelle Desfossés *

6. **For Jean S. Brault**
    *   Danielle Barot
    *   Harvey Yarosky

7. **For the Business Development Bank of Canada (BDC)**
    *   Guy Beaudry
    *   William Brock
    *   Mélanie Joly
    *   Louise Paradis
    *   George Pollack
    *   Maria Reit

8. **For Canada Post Corporation**
    *   Phillip Dempsey
    *   Julia Holland
    *   John A. Terry

9. **For Jean Carle**
    *   Pierre La Traverse

10. **For the Right Honourable Jean Chrétien**
    - Peter K. Doody
    - Jean-Sébastien Gallant
    - David W. Scott

11. **For Paul Coffin and Coffin Communications**
    - Pierre Emile Dupras
    - Raphaël Schachter

12. **For the Conservative Party of Canada**
    - Arthur Hamilton
    - Laurie Livingstone
    - Brian Mitchell
    - Jean Fortier **

13. **For Jacques Corriveau and PluriDesign Inc.**
    - Gilles Pariseau
    - Richard Phaneuf

14. **For Ernst & Young**
    - James O'Grady

15. **For the Honourable Alfonso Gagliano**
    - Anouk Fournier
    - Magali Fournier
    - Pierre Fournier

16. **For Charles Guité**
    - Richard Auger
    - Katherine Huot
    - Julio Peris

17. **For Jean Lafleur**
    - Jean-C. Hébert

18. **For Marc LeFrançois**
    - Claude-Armand Sheppard

19. **For the Liberal Party of Canada**
    - Charles B. Côté
    - Doug Mitchell

20. **For Malcom Média Inc. & Luc Lemay**
    - Louis Bélanger
    - Mélanie Joly

21. **For the Honourable André Ouellet**
    - Raymond Doray

22. **For Jean Pelletier**
    - Stéphane Chatigny
    - Guy J. Pratte

23. **For the Public Service Integrity Officer**
    - Jean-Daniel Bélanger
    - Martine Nantel

24. **For Ranald Quail**
    - George D. Hunter

25. **For Via Rail Canada**
    - John A. Campion
    - Marc-André Fabien
    - James Katz
    - Gérald R. Tremblay

* Representative of the Bloc Québécois.

** Representative of the Conservative Party of Canada

F
_____

APPENDIX F
LIST OF EXHIBITS

Cote / Filing number	Description de la pièce / Exhibit description	Date de dépôt / Filing
P-1 (a) + edit	Office of the Auditor General of Canada, Statement of Evidence; Bureau du vérificateur général du Canada, Énoncé de la preuve	2004.09.07
P-1 (b)	French version of Exhibit P-1(a) Enclosed in a thin green binder.	2004.09.07
P-2 (a)	Office of the Auditor General of Canada, Memorandum of Evidence (Supporting Documents) Volume 1.	2004.09.07
P-2(a) tab11	Rapport au ministre des Travaux publics et des Services gouvernementaux sur trois contrats attribués à Groupaction	2004.10.04
P-2(a) tab17	Letter dated November 12, 2003 from Mr. Minto to Mr. Judd.	2004.09.07
P-2 (b)	Office of the Auditor General of Canada, Memorandum of Evidence (Supporting Documents) Volume 2.	2004.09.07
P-2(b)(gc)	Tab 18 of Exhibit P-2(b)	2004.09.08
P-2(c)	Office of the Auditor General of Canada, Memorandum of Evidence (Supporting Documents) Volume 3.	2004.09.07
P-2(d)	Office of the Auditor General : Additional Sponsorship Cases.	2004.09.07
P-3(a)	"Inventory of Audits and Investigations" Volume 1	2004.09.07
P-3(b)	"Inventory of Audits and Investigations" Volume 2	2004.09.07
P-3(c)	"Inventory of Audits and Investigations" Volume 3	2004.09.07
P-3(c) Tab18	2003 Report of the Auditor General of Canada, Government-wide Audit of Sponsorship, Advertising, and Public Opinion Research, chapters 3-5 – VERSION FRANÇAISE	2004.10.25
P-4(a)	Main Authorities (English version) Volume 1	2004.09.07
P-4(b)	Main Authorities (English Version) Volume 2	2004.09.07
P-4(c)	Main Authorities (English Version) Volume 3	2004.09.07
P-4(d)	Main Authorities (English Version) Volume 4	2004.09.07
P-4(e)	Main Authorities (English Version) Volume 5	2004.09.07
P-5(a)	Main Authorities (version française) Volume 1	2004.09.07
P-5(b)	Main Authorities (version française) Volume 2	2004.09.07
P-5(c)	Main Authorities (version française) Volume 3	2004.09.07
P-5(d)	Main Authorities (version française) Volume 4	2004.09.07
P-5(e)	Main Authorities (version française) Volume 5	2004.09.07
P-6	PWGSC service contract with Lafleur Communication Marketing April 1, 1998; and related documents	2004.09.08
P-7(a)	RCMP documentary package re: 125th Anniversary Celebration	2004.09.08
P-8	Substantiation files for Government-wide Audit of the Sponsorship Program OAG	2004.09.08
P-9	Documentary package concerning Health Canada case.	2004.09.08
P-10	Narrative prepared by the TB Secretariat that describes how Treasury Board operates, what it does, matters that it considers to be of relevance to this Commission with a summary of certain of the Treasury Board policies, including annexes in addition to the Statement of Evidence. Also included is a two-page document entitled "Errata".	2004.09.13
P-10(a)	French version of Exhibit 10	2004.09.13
P-10 B	Meeting the Expectations of Canadians - Review of the Governance Framework for Canada's Crown Corporations – Treasury Board of Canada / Répondre aux attentes des Canadiennes et des Canadiens – Examen du cadre de gouvernance des Sociétés d'État du Canada	2005.03.14
P-11	Treasury Board Secretariat Witness Brief, prepared by Commission counsel.	2004.09.13
P-12(a)	Documentary binder entitled "Allocations for Sponsorship, volume 1", prepared by Commission counsel.	2004.09.13
P-12(b)	Documentary binder entitled "Allocations for Sponsorship, volume 2", prepared by Commission counsel.	2004.09.13
P-13	Binder on Frozen Allotments.	2004.09.13
P-14	Document consisting of 14 tabs entitled Treasury Board Secretariat Additional Documents for Witness Brief (redacted version).	2004.09.15

P-14(a)	Documents additionnels portant sur les Réunions du conseil du trésor, du 15 juin 1995, du 19 octobre 1995, du 14 décembre 1995 sur les modalités du nouveau Programme de commandite.	2004.09.20
P-15	Response to undertakings	2004.09.15
P-16(a)	"Treasury Board Secretariat, Documents Related to Appendix "U/Q" to the Government Contracting Policy", Volume 1.	2004.09.20
P-16(b)	"Treasury Board Secretariat, Documents Related to Appendix "U/Q" to the Government Contracting Policy", Volume 2.	2004.09.20
P-17	Response to TBS undertaking to Mr. Hunter on September 15, 2004 (5 affidavits)	2004.09.20
P-18	TBS Response to the Commissioner's question (Number of Internal Audit Reports filed 1997/98 - 2003/04)	2004.09.20
P-19	"Selection of Agencies"	2004.09.20
P-19	ADDENDUM (Supplément d'information)	2005.04.18
P-20	"Statement of Evidence of the Department of Public Works and Government Services" English version.	2004.09.20
P-20(a)	"Énoncé de la preuve du ministère des Travaux publics et des Services gouvernementaux"	2004.09.20
P-21(a)	"Additional PWGSC Documents (1)	2004.09.20
P-21(a)-1	Contract dated August 29, 1996 dealing with the Tradewinds program and referred to in relation to P-21(a), Tab 1.	2004.09.23
P-21(b)	"Additional PWGSC Documents (2)	2004.09.20
P-22	Statement of Evidence of the Department of Public Works and Government Services, Appendix A, Supporting Documents	2004.09.20
P-22(a)	Énoncé de preuve du Ministère des travaux publics et services gouvernementaux.	2004.10.04
P-23(a)	Classification and Staffing Documents pertaining to J.C. Guité and P.G. Tremblay, Volume 1	2004.09.20
P-23(b)	Classification and Staffing Documents pertaining to J.C. Guité and P.G. Tremblay, Volume 2	2004.09.20
P-23(b)	ADDENDUM – (ajouter après p. 7122068) - Note from Linda Gaucher, Director, Learning and Renewal	2005.05.04
P-24	Functional Review of the Integration of PRPCSS and APORS - July 1995	2004.09.20
P-25	Audit and review committee minutes of the meeting of July 28, 1997	2004.09.21
P-26	Email from Evelyn Marcoux to Michael Calcott with handwritten date of June 3, 1999 with an attached email, which in turn attaches an email.	2004.09.22
P-26(a)	Feuilles diverses concernant Evelyn Marcoux	2004.10.20
P-27	Series of emails beginning with one dated June 16, 1999 re: "Achat d'espace publicitaire"	2004.09.22
P-28(a)	PWGSC Response to Undertakings	2004.09.22
P-28(b)	PWGSC Response to Undertakings	2004.09.22
P-29	Memorandum to J.C. Guité from the Assistant Director of the Audit Review Branch with respect to the audit dated July 19th, 1996.	2004.09.22
P-30	Audit and Review Committee Meetings	2004.09.22
P-30 (a)	Minutes of the Audit Review Committee from three separate meetings.	2004.09.23
P-31	List of the institutions that were members of the Institute of Communications and Advertising.	2004.09.22
P-32	Memorandum from Christian Bouvier to Ralph Sprague dated March 31, 1999 with an attached "Delegation of authorities" in respect of Mr. Guité, as well as a memorandum from Mr. Stobbe to Mr. Quail attaching the Schedule 1 and Schedule 3 delegations.	2004.09.23
P-33	One-page document dated December 22, 1994, memorandum from N. Nurse, Assistant Deputy Minister, Human Resources Branch, to Mr. Quail entitled "Executive Reclassification"	2004.09.23
P-34(a)	Statement of Evidence prepared by the Privy Council Office	2004.09.27
P-34(b)	Preuve documentaire préparée par le Bureau du Conseil Privé	2004.09.27
P-34(a +b)	Biographies de Alex Himelfarb, Michael Wernick et Kathy O'Hara - Biographies of Alex Himelfarb, Michael Wernick and Kathy O'Hara.	2004.09.27
P-34(c)	Outstanding PCO Undertakings -- September 27, 2004 / Liste des engagements du BCP - le 27 septembre 2004.	2004.12.02
P-35	Publication du gouvernement du Canada "Gouverner de façon responsable - Le guide du ministre et du ministre d'État 2003 " - Government of Canada publication entitled "Governing Responsibly, a Guide for Ministers and Ministers of State 2003"	2004.09.27
P-36	Guide du sous-ministre - Guidance for Deputy Ministers - BILINGUAL. www.pco-bcp.gc.ca	2004.09.27
P-37(a)	1994: Volume #1	2004.09.28
P-37(b)	1994: Volume #2	2004.09.28
P-38	Documents related to the Cabinet Planning Session held on February 1 and 2, 1996	2004.09.28

P-39	Document consisting of the minutes of a Treasury Board meeting held on June 12, 1995 and accompanying documents.	2004.09.28
P-40	Memorandum to Ms. Bourgon from Ms. Cardinal dated January 1997 with attached report entitled "Trends and Advertising Expenditures".	2004.09.28
P-41	A page from the Treasury Board of Canada Secretariat web site in respect of the Unity Reserve and attached to it a chart from that web site printed out in PDF form so that it could be printed on two pages.	2004.09.28
P-42	Article by Gordon Robertson. "The Changing Role of the Privy Council Office"	2004.09.28
P-43(a)	Allan Cutler Document Brief, Volume 1.	2004.09.28
P-43(b)	Allan Cutler Document Brief, Volume 2.	2004.09.28
P-44	Ernst & Young Document Brief	2004.09.29
P-45	Statement of Evidence to the Commission of Inquiry into the Sponsorship Program and Advertising Activities, submitted by the Audit and Ethics Branch of Public Works, dated September 30, 2004.	2004.10.04
P-45(a)	Énoncé de preuve à la Commission d'enquête sur le programme de commandites et les activités publicitaires, présenté par la Direction générale de la vérification et de l'éthique, le 30 septembre 2004.	2004.10.04
P-45(b)	Responses to Additional Undertakings of the Internal Audit Committee of Public Works and Government Services – November 2004 Volume 1.	2004.12.02
P-45(c)	Responses to Additional Undertakings of the Internal Audit Committee of Public Works and Government Services – November 2004 Volume 2.	2004.12.02
P-46	PWGSC Internal Audit Document Brief	2004.10.04
P-47(a)	Statement of Evidence of the Department of Public Works and Government Services", dated October 2004, Appendix "A" - Supporting Documents, Volume 1.	2004.10.04
P-47(b)	Statement of Evidence of the Department of Public Works and Government Services", dated October 2004, Appendix "A" - Supporting Documents, Volume 2.	2004.10.04
P-47(c)	Statement of Evidence of the Department of Public Works and Government Services", dated October 2004, Appendix "A" - Supporting Documents, Volume 3.	2004.10.04
P-48	Statement of Evidence of the Department of Public Works and Government Services Quick Response Team	2004.10.05
P-48(a)	Énoncé de la prevue du ministère des Travaux publics et des Services gouvernementaux.	2004.10.05
P-49	Memorandum of Understanding between Public Works and Government Services Canada and Consulting and Audit Canada for Assistance in File Reviews, prepared by Consulting and Audit Canada project No.: 310-2001.	2004.10.05
P-50	Document Brief of Kroll Lindquist Avey	2004.10.05
P-51	Document prepared by Finance Canada for the Commission of Inquiry into the Sponsorship Program and Advertising Activities/Document préparé par Finances Canada à l'intention de la Commission d'enquête sur le programme des commandites et les activités publicitaires.	2004.10.06
P-51(a)	Response to undertakings from the Ministry of Finance taken October 6, 2004 (English version) / Réponses aux engagements du panel du ministère des Finances pris le 6 Octobre 2004 (version française)	2004.12.02
P-52	Commission of Inquiry into the Sponsorship Program and Advertising Activities/Commission d'enquête sur le programme de commandites et les activités publicitaires. Budget Records of Decision (Unity) 1996 to 2000 - October 4, 2004, le 4 octobre 2004.	2004.10.06
P-53	Documents au soutien du témoignage du panel de témoins du Comité de révision administrative (Rapport Demers)/Supporting documents for the testimony of the panel of witnesses of the Administrative Review Committee (Demers Report)	2004.10.07
P-54	Rapport Demers/Demers Report	2004.10.07
P-55	Selection of Agency of Record for the Year 1995 / Sélection de l'Agence de coordination pour l'année 1995.	2004.10.12
P-56	Agency of Record Selection - 1997 - Brief of Documents.	2004.10.12
P-56	ADDENDUM (insérer après la page 305)	2005.04.21
P-57	PWGSC Selection - 2001 - Brief of Documents.	2004.10.12
P-58	Organization Charts - PWGSC from July 1993 to July 2001 / Organigrammes - TPSGC de juillet 1993 à 2001.	2004.10.12
P-59	Notebooks of Huguette Tremblay (1-5) / Cahiers de notes de Huguette Tremblay (1-5)	2004.10.12
P-60(a)	Correspondance interne et externe & Documentation (GGP à Communication Canada) INDEX DES VOLUMES 1 À 5 / Internal and External correspondence & documentation (AMG to Communication Canada) - INDEX TO VOLUMES 1 TO 5.	2004.10.12
P-60(b)	Correspondance interne et externe & Documentation (GGP à Communication Canada) - 1991-1995 - Volume 1/5 / Internal and External correspondence & documentation (AMG to Communication Canada) - 1991-1995 - Volume 1/5	2004.10.12
P-60(c)	Correspondance interne et externe & Documentation (GGP à Communication Canada) - 1996-1997 - Volume 2/5 / Internal and External correspondence & documentation (AMG to Communication Canada) - 1996-1997 - Volume 2/5	2004.10.12

P-60(d)	Correspondance interne et externe & Documentation (GGP à Communication Canada) - 1998 - Volume 3/5 / Internal and External correspondence & documentation (AMG to Communication Canada) - 1998 - Volume 3/5	2004.10.12
P-60(e)	Correspondance interne et externe & Documentation (GGP à Communication Canada) - 1999 - Volume 4/5 / Internal and External correspondence & documentation (AMG to Communication Canada) - 1999 - Volume 4/5	2004.10.12
P-60(f)	Correspondance interne et externe & Documentation (GGP à Communication Canada) - 2000-2003 + divers - Volume 5/5 / Internal and External correspondence & documentation (AMG to Communication Canada) - 2000-2003 + miscellaneous - Volume 5/5	2004.10.12
P-61(a)	Correspondance interne et externe & Documentation (GGP à Communication Canada) - ADDENDA - INDEX DES VOLUMES 1 ET 2 / Internal and external correspondence & Documentation (AGM to Communication Canada) - ADDENDA - INDEX TO VOLUMES 1 AND 2	2004.10.12
P-61(b)	Correspondance interne et externe & Documentation (GGP à Communication Canada) - ADDENDA - 1994 - 1998 Volume 1 / Internal And external correspondence & documentation (AMG to Communication Canada) - ADDENDA - 1994 - 1998 Volume 1.	2004.10.12
P-61(c)	Correspondance interne et externe & Documentation (GGP à Communication Canada) - ADDENDA - 1999 - 2004 + divers/miscellaneous Volume 2 / Internal And external correspondence & documentation (AMG to Communication Canada) - ADDENDA - 1999 - 2004 + divers / miscellaneous Volume 2.	2004.10.12
P-61(c)	ADDENDUM – List of Assistants and Policy Advisors to the Minister of Public Works and Government Services Canada from June 11, 1997 to January 15, 2002 (page 1122A)	2005.03.17
P-62	Série Maurice Richard - Documents Sélectionnés - DGSCC / Maurice Richard Series - selected documents - CCSB.	2004.10.12
P-63	Encyclopédie du Canada - 1999-2000 - Documents sélectionnés / Encyclopédie du Canada - 1999-2000 - Selected Documents	2004.10.12
P-64(a)	Documentation relative aux items Promotionnels - Volume 1 / Supporting Documents pertaining to promotional Items - Volume 1.	2004.10.12
P-64(b)	Documentation relative aux items Promotionnels - Volume 2 / Supporting documents pertaining to promotional Items - Volume 2.	2004.10.12
P-64(c)	Documentation relative aux items Promotionnels - Volume 3 / Supporting documents pertaining to promotional Items - Volume 3.	2004.10.12
P-65(a)	SPROP - chiffres budgétisés et actuels - pour la période du 1er avril 1995 au 31 mars 1996 / APORS - Budget and Actual - for the period from April 1, 1995 to March 31, 1996	2004.10.12
P-65(b)	ADDENDA - pour la période du 1 avril 1995 au 31 mars 1996 / ADDENDA - for the period from April 1, 1995 to March 31, 1996.	2004.10.12
P-66	SPROP - chiffres budgétisés et actuels - pour la période du 1 avril 1996 au 31 mars 1997 / APORS - Budget and Actual - for the period from April 1, 1996 to March 31, 1997.	2004.10.12
P-67	CD Volume EXH-CON01(1994-95; 1995-96; 1996-97; 1997-98; 1998-99) / CD Volume EXH-CON01 (1994-95; 1995-96; 1996-97; 1997-98; 1998-99)	2004.10.12
P-68	CD VOLUME EXH-CON01 (1999-2001) / CD VOLUME EXH-CON01 (1999-2001)	2004.10.12
P-69	Contrat de commandites - 1994-1995/ Sponsorship contracts - 1994-1995	2004.10.12
P-70	Contrat de commandites - 1995-1996/ Sponsorship contracts - 1995-1996	2004.10.12
P-71(a)	Contrat de commandites - 1996-1997 Volume 1 / Sponsorship contracts - 1996-1997, Volume 1	2004.10.12
P-71(b)	Contrat de commandites - 1996-1997 Volume 2 / Sponsorship contracts - 1996-1997, Volume 2	2004.10.12
P-72	Contrat de commandites - 1997-1998 / Sponsorship contracts - 1997-1998	2004.10.12
P-73(a)	Contrat de commandites - 1998-1999 Volume 1 / Sponsorship contracts - 1998-1999, Volume 1	2004.10.12
P-73(b)	Contrat de commandites - 1998-1999 Volume 2 / Sponsorship contracts - 1998-1999, Volume 2	2004.10.12
P-74(a)	Contrat de commandites - 1999-2000 Volume 1 / Sponsorship contracts - 1999-2000, Volume 1	2004.10.12
P-74(b)	Contrat de commandites - 1999-2000 Volume 2 / Sponsorship contracts - 1999-2000, Volume 2	2004.10.12
P-74(c)	Contrat de commandites - 1999-2000 Volume 3 / Sponsorship contracts - 1999-2000, Volume 3	2004.10.12
P-74(d)	Contrat de commandites - 1999-2000 Volume 4 / Sponsorship contracts - 1999-2000, Volume 4	2004.10.12
P-74(e)	Contrat de commandites - 1999-2000 Volume 5 / Sponsorship contracts - 1999-2000, Volume 5	2004.10.12
P-74(f)	Contrat de commandites - 1999-2000 Volume 6 / Sponsorship contracts - 1999-2000, Volume 6	2004.10.12
P-74(g)	Contrat de commandites - 1999-2000 Volume 7 / Sponsorship contracts - 1999-2000, Volume 7	2004.10.12
P-74(h)	Contrat de commandites - 1999-2000 Volume 8 / Sponsorship contracts - 1999-2000, Volume 8	2004.10.12
P-75(a)	Contrat de commandites - 2000-2001 Volume 1 / Sponsorship contracts - 2000-2001, Volume 1	2004.10.12
P-75(b)	Contrat de commandites - 2000-2001 Volume 2 / Sponsorship contracts - 2000-2001, Volume 2	2004.10.12
P-75(c)	Contrat de commandites - 2000-2001 Volume 3 / Sponsorship contracts - 2000-2001, Volume 3	2004.10.12

P-75(d)	Contrat de commandites - 2000-2001 Volume 4 / Sponsorship contracts - 2000-2001, Volume 4	2004.10.12
P-75(e)	Contrat de commandites - 2000-2001 Volume 5 / Sponsorship contracts - 2000-2001, Volume 5	2004.10.12
P-75(f)	Contrat de commandites - 2000-2001 Volume 6 / Sponsorship contracts - 2000-2001, Volume 6	2004.10.12
P-75(g)	Contrat de commandites - 2000-2001 Volume 7 / Sponsorship contracts - 2000-2001, Volume 7	2004.10.12
P-76	Lignes directrices concernant les Commandites - chronologie - 1998-2002 / Sponsorship guidelines - chronology - 1998-2002	2004.10.12
P-76(a)	Canada Sponsorship Program, Sponsorship Guidelines, 2002-2003, March 2002	2004.10.20
P-77	1998-04-27 : Lettre de Eleni Bakopanos re Allard et Associés & correspondance jointe / 1998-04-27 : Letter from Eleni Bakopanos re: Allard et Associés & attached correspondence	2004.10.12
P-78	Fichier <<mplog>> Bureau du ministre Alfonso Gagliano /"mplog" file, office of Minister Alfonso Gagliano	2004.10.13
P-79	PWGSC/TPSGC Departmental mail / Courrier institutionnel. Doc. :80658, Date : 98/12/22, consisting of 7 pages	2004.10.14
P-79(a)	Article du 23 novembre 1998 publié dans le Edmonton Journal / Clipping dated November 23, 1998, published in the Edmonton Journal.	2005.02.01
P-80	Courriel de Pierre Tremblay en date du 25 avril 2001 adressé à Isabelle Roy, Régis Gagné, Donna Achimov, Gerry Thom, Paul Lauzon, David Myer.	2004.10.18
P-81	Procès-verbal d'une rencontre qui a eu lieu le 21 septembre 2000 au Lac Carling/Minutes from Carling retreat identified as Minutes from the information session between PWGSC and presidents of communication agencies - September 21, 2000	2004.10.18
P-82	Télécopies/Fax de Stéphane Guertin à Michel Raffie daté du 8 juin 2001	2004.10.18
P-83	PWGSC Responses to Additional Undertaking By Public Works and Government Services Canada Panel, Audit and Ethics Branch Panel and Quick Response Team Panel dated October 18, 2004	2004.10.18
P-83(a)	Version française des engagements du Panel de Travaux publics et services Gouvernementaux Canada, de la Direction Générale de la vérification et de l'éthique et du Groupe d'intervention rapide.	2004.10.27
P-84(a)	Cahiers de notes de Joanne Bouvier (#1 à 4), Volume 1 / Notebooks of Joanne Bouvier (#1 to 4), Volume 1.	2004.10.19
P-84(b)	Cahiers de notes de Joanne Bouvier (#5 à 7), Volume 2 / Notebooks of Joanne Bouvier (#5 to 7), Volume 2.	2004.10.19
P-84(c)	Cahier de notes #8 de Joanne Bouvier / Notebook #8 of Joanne Bouvier.	2004.10.19
P-85	Documents au soutien du témoignage de Paul Lauzon/Supporting documents for the Testimony of Paul Lauzon	2004.10.20
P-86	Contrats de commandites signés par Paul Lauzon/Sponsorship contracts signed by Paul Lauzon	2004.10.20
P-87(a)	Documents au soutien du témoignage de Evelyn Marcoux, Volume 1 / Supporting Documents for the testimony of Evelyn Marcoux, Volume 1	2004.10.21
P-87(b)	Documents au soutien du témoignage de Evelyn Marcoux, Volume 2 / Supporting Documents for the testimony of Evelyn Marcoux, Volume 2	2004.10.21
P-88(a)	Index des Volumes 1 à 5 des documents Au soutien du témoignage de Andrée LaRose / Index of Volumes 1 to 5 of Supporting documents for the testimony of Andrée LaRose.	2004.10.25
P-88(b)	Documents au soutien du témoignage de Andrée LaRose, Volume 1 / Supporting Documents for the testimony of Andrée LaRose, Volume 1.	2004.10.25
P-88(c)	Documents au soutien du témoignage de Andrée LaRose, Volume 2 / Supporting documents for the testimony of Andrée LaRose, Volume 2.	2004.10.25
P-88(d)	Documents au soutien du témoignage de Andrée LaRose, Volume 3 / Supporting Documents for the testimony of Andrée LaRose, Volume 3.	2004.10.25
P-88(e)	Documents au soutien du témoignage de Andrée LaRose, Volume 4 / Supporting Documents for the testimony of Andrée LaRose, Volume 4.	2004.10.25
P-88(e)	Addenda (Insérer après P1011)	2004.10.25
P-88(e)	Addenda (Insérer après P1014)	2004.10.25
P-88(f)	Documents au soutien du témoignage de Andrée LaRose, Volume 5 / Supporting Documents for the testimony of Andrée LaRose, Volume 5.	2004.10.25
P-88(f)	Addenda (Insérer avant la page 1)	2004.10.25
P-88(f)	Addenda (Insérer après P92)	2004.10.25
P-89(a)	Documentation relative au contrat EN771-5-U100 / Documentation pertaining To contract EN771-5-U100.	2004.10.25
P-89 (a)	ADDENDUM (Insérer après la page P279) (p.280 à 292) Documentation relative au contrat EN771-5-U100 / Documentation pertaining to contract EN771-5-U100	2005.05.19
P-89(b)	Documentation relative aux contrats EN771-5-U136, EN771-5-U117, EN771-5-U117, EN771-5-U136, EN771-5-U117, / Documentation pertaining to contracts EN771-5-U136, EN771-5-U117, EN771-5-0093.	2004.10.25
P-89(c)	Note de Howard R. Balloch à l'intention de Lucienne Robillard re : publicité Ministérielle et activités connexes.	2004.10.25
P-90(a)	Liste des contrats octroyés à Groupe Everest dans le dossier ou le programme Attractions Canada.	2004.10.25

C-90 (a)	ADDENDUM (remplace la page P90A)	2005.04.18
P-90(b)	Série de contrats octroyés portant sur le Programme Attractions Canada avec un tableau synoptique portant sur les montants des contrats qui ont été octroyés.	2004.10.25
P-90 (c)	Contrats concernant Attractions Canada - Supplément d'information à la pièce P-90(b)	2005.04.18
P-91(a)	Contrats concernant Attractions Canada, Volume 1 / Contracts pertaining to Attractions Canada, Volume 1.	2004.10.25
P-91(b)	Contrats concernant Attractions Canada, Volume 2 / Contracts pertaining to Attractions Canada, Volume 2.	2004.10.25
P-91(c)	Document intitulé 'Groupe Everest' comprenant 21 pages et daté du 15 octobre 1996.	2004.10.28
P-93	L'agence de coordination du gouvernement Fédéral – AOR Design & Competition – Décembre 1994 – présenté à TPSGC par QUAD Consulting Group / The Federal Government's Agency of Record – AOR Design & Competition – December 1994 – presented To PWGSC by QUAD Consulting Group.	2004.10.25
P-94	Trois courriels : courriel de Marie Maltais à Andrée LaRose, David Myer et Evelyn Marcoux du 26 octobre 1998, Courriel d'Andrée LaRose à Gilles Allen du 9 octobre 1998 et courriel d'Andréa Paravey à DGSCC du 18 novembre 1998.	2004.10.25
P-95	Contrat EN771-5-U199, réquisition de biens et de services et une facture 32658 certifiée par Andrée LaRose / Contract EN771-5-U199, requisition for goods and services and invoice 32658 certified by Andrée LaRose.	2004.10.25
P-96	Lettre de Monsieur Judd, secrétaire du Conseil du Trésor / Letter from Mr. Judd, Secretary of the Treasury Board	2004.10.25
P-97	Documents au soutien du témoignage de Andrée LaRose – Addendum :Fondation Charles Bronfman -- / Supporting Documents for the testimony of Andrée LaRose – Addendum : Charles Bronfman Foundation	2004.10.26
P-98(a)	Sélection d'une Agence de publicité provenant du Bureau fédéral de développement régional (Québec) comportant 52 pages / Advertising Agency Selection' emanating from the Federal Office of Regional Development (Quebec) consisting of 52 pages.	2004.10.28
P-98(b)	élection d'une agence de publicité BUREAU FÉDÉRAL DE DÉVELOPPEMENT RÉGIONAL(QUÉBEC) / Advertising agency selection FEDERAL OFFICE OF REGIONAL DEVELOPMENT (QUEBEC) Volume 2	2004.10.28
P-99(a)	Supply and Services Canada: Specimen Signature Financial, Contractual & Other Authorities and Specimen Signature Spending Authority - Marie Maltais, June 4, 1998.	2004.10.28
P-99(b)	Une série de documents liés au Bureau d'information du Canada comprenant 18 pages	2004.10.28
P-99(c)	Lettre de Monsieur Guité à Madame Maltais	2004.10.28
P-99(d)	Lettre de Monsieur Guité à Madame Maltais datée du 9 avril 1999	2004.10.28
P-99(e)	Une série d'autorisations et de signatures en vertu de l'article 34 de la Loi sur l'administration financière signées par Madame Maltais.	2004.10.28
P-100	"David Myer Document Brief	2004.11.01
P-101	Documents au soutien du Témoignage de Mario Parent/Supporting Documents for the Testimony of Mario Parent	2004.11.01
P-102	Contrats de commandites signés par Mario Parent/Sponsorships contracts signed by Mario Parent	2004.11.01
P-102	Addenda (Insérer après la page 5)	2004.11.01
P-103(a)	Guité Witness Brief - Structural Change and Contracting Policy, Volume 1 of 3	2004.11.03
P-103(b)	Guité Witness Brief - Structural Change and Contracting Policy, Volume 2 of 3	2004.11.03
P-103(c)	Guité Witness Brief - Structural Change and Contracting Policy", Volume 3 of 3.	2004.11.03
P-104	Additional Employment Documents relating to Mr. Guité	2004.11.03
P-105(a)	Guité Witness Brief - Program Management", Volume 1 of 2.	2004.11.03
P-105(b)	Guité Witness Brief - Program Management", Volume 2 of 2.	2004.11.03
P-106(a)	Guité Witness Brief - Involvement in Funding", Volume 1 of 2.	2004.11.03
P-106(b)	Guité Witness Brief - Involvement in Funding", Volume 2 of 2.	2004.11.03
P-107	Summary of Agencies - Receiving Contracts	2004.11.03
P-108	Guité Witness Brief - Promotional Items Documents	2004.11.03
P-109	Guité Witness Brief - Attactions Canada Documents	2004.11.03
P-110	Audit Documents Relevant to J.C. Guité	2004.11.03
P-111	Document entitled "Guité's witness brief - Relationships	2004.11.03
P-112	Document entitled "Treasury Board Précis And Contract Documents	2004.11.03

P-113	Bank of Canada, Canada Savings Bonds - Advertising Agency Selection Committee - Final Report April 25, 1994; Canada Retail Debt Agency, Department of Finance Canada - Advertising Agency Selection Committee - Final Report May 22, 1996; Department of Finance Canada, Advertising Agency Selection - Committee - Final Report August 8, 1995	2004.11.04
P-114(a)	Acts, Regulations and Policies on Access to Information and Privacy, English Version	2004.11.23
P-114(b)	Lois, règlements et politiques au sujet de l'accès à l'information et la protection des renseignements personnels	2004.11.23
P-115	ATI 1999-00450/AM Case Actions – complete file	2004.11.23
P-116	ATI 1999-00713/AM Case Actions – complete file	2004.11.23
P-117	ATI 1999-00747/AM Case Actions – complete file	2004.11.23
P-118	Extracts from agendas and notebooks by Ms. Anita Lloyd.	2004.11.23
P-119	Documentary package including unofficial 1999-2000 Organizational Chart.	2004.11.23
P-120(a)	Ranald Quail Witness Brief, Volume 1 of 3.	2004.11.24
P-120(b)	Ranald Quail Witness Brief, Volume 2 of 3.	2004.11.24
P-120(c)	Ranald Quail Witness Brief, Volume 3 of 3.	2004.11.24
P-120(d)	Additional Documents Relating to Ranald Quail.	2004.11.24
P-121	Jim Stobbe Witness Brief	2004.11.25
P-122	Statement of Evidence of James Stobbe	2004.11.25
P-123(a)	Document pertaining to the testimony of Richard Neville, Volume 1 of 2 / Documents au soutien du témoignage de Richard Neville, Volume 1 de 2.	2004.11.29
P-123(b)	Document pertaining to the testimony of Richard Neville, Volume 2 of 2 / Documents au soutien du témoignage de Richard Neville, Volume 2 de 2.	2004.11.29
P-124	Document entitled "COMMANDITES et PUBLICITÉ RESTRUCTURATION" – rapports d'août et juin 2002 - / SPONSORSHIP and ADVERTISING REDESIGN – August and June 2002 reports.	2004.11.29
P-124 (a)	Guidelines for Effective Advertising / Agency Remuneration	2005.05.17
P-124 (b)	"- Formulaire re demande d'adhésion – AAPQ - Advertising Agency Remuneration ICA Report – September 2001 (Payment by Result 2)	2005.05.31
P-125	Politiques sur les paiements de Transfert/Policy on Transfer Payments.	2004.11.29
P-126	Memorandum to R.J.Neville from Mr. J.C. Guité dated June 9, 1995.	2004.11.29
P-127(a)	Déclaration de faits de Communication Canada pour la Commission d'enquête sur le programme des commandites et activités publicitaires, Novembre 2002, Volume 1.	2004.11.30
P-127(b)	Déclaration de faits de Communication Canada pour la Commission d'enquête sur le programme des commandites et activités publicitaires, Novembre 2002, Volume 2.	2004.11.30
P-127(c)	Déclaration de faits de Communication Canada pour la Commission d'enquête sur le programme des commandites et activités publicitaires, Novembre 2002, Volume 3.	2004.11.30
P-127(d)	Déclaration de faits de Communication Canada pour la Commission d'enquête sur le programme des commandites et activités publicitaires, Novembre 2002, Volume 4.	2004.11.30
P-127(e)	Déclaration de faits de Communication Canada pour la Commission d'enquête sur le programme des commandites et activités publicitaires, Novembre 2002, Volume 5.	2004.11.30
P-127(f)	Déclaration de faits de Communication Canada pour la Commission d'enquête sur le programme des commandites et activités publicitaires, Novembre 2002, Volume 6.	2004.11.30
P-127(g)	Déclaration de faits de Communication Canada pour la Commission d'enquête sur le programme des commandites et activités publicitaires, Novembre 2002, Volume 7.	2004.11.30
P-128	Document ayant comme première page une lettre de Christiane Beaulieu à Guy McKenzie datée du 4 septembre 2001.	2004.11.30
P-129(a)	Sélection de renseignements confidentiels du Conseil privé concernant le Bureau d'information du Canada, Volume 1 de 2 / Selected Cabinet Confidences pertaining to the Canada Information Office Volume 1 of 2.	2004.12.01
P-129(b)	Sélection de renseignements confidentiels du Conseil privé concernant le Bureau d'information du Canada, Volume 2 de 2 / Selected Cabinet Confidences pertaining to the Canada Information Office Volume 2 of 2.	2004.12.01

Exhibit	Description	Date
P-130	Documentation pertinente au témoignage de Roger Collet – Patrimoine canadien - 1994-1996 / Documentation pertaining to the testimony of Roger Collet – Canadian Heritage – 1994–1996.	2004.12.01
P-131(a)	Documentation pertinente au témoignage de Roger Collet – Bureau d'information du Canada – 1996-1998 / Documentation pertaining to the testimony of Roger Collet – Canada Information Office - 1996-1998.	2004.12.01
P-131(b)	Liste de contrats octroyés par le Bureau d'information du Canada 1997-2000 / List of contracts of the Canadian Information Office for 1997-2000	2004.12.01
P-132	Transfert Bureau d'information du Canada et TPSGC – 1996 – 1998 / Transfers Canada Information Office and PWGSC – 1996 – 1998	2004.12.01
P-133	Projets du Bureau d'information du Canada et de L'Information Essentielle / Projects of the Canada Information Office and l'Information Essentielle.	2004.12.01
P-134	Documents concernant le logo du Bureau d'information du Canada / Documents pertaining to the logo of the Canada Information Office.	2004.12.01
P-134	ADDENDUM (Insérer après la page P33) (P.33A à P33Q) Documents concernant le LOGO du Bureau d'information du Canada / Documents pertaining to the LOGO of the Canada Information Office	2005.05.19
P-135	Documents au soutien du témoignage de Marc Lafrenière – Bureau d'information du Canada 1998-2001 / Document pertaining to the Testimony of Marc Lafrenière – Canada Information Office – 1998-2001	2004.12.06
P-136	Documents au soutien du témoignage de Marc Lafrenière – Affaires intergouvernementales 1994-1996 / Documents pertaining to the Testimony of Marc Lafrenière – Intergovernmental Affairs – 1994-1996	2004.12.06
P-137	Documents au soutien du témoignage de Marc Lafrenière – Action partenariat – 1999-2001 / Project of the Canada Information Office – Partnership Initiatives – 1999-2001.	2004.12.06
P-138	Documents au soutien du témoignage de Marc Lafrenière – Sélection de contrats reliés à la Réserve pour l'unité canadienne / Documents pertaining to the testimony of Marc Lafrenière - Selected contracts pertaining the Unity Fund.	2004.12.06
P-139	Projet du Bureau d'information du Canada - L'Appui à l'engagement civique – 1998 / Project of the Canada Information Office – L'Appui à l'engagement civique – 1998	2004.12.06
P-139	ADDENDUM (Insérer après la page P31) (P.31A à P31H) Projet du Bureau d'information du Canada - L'APPUI À L'ENGAGEMENT CIVIQUE – 1998 / Project of the Canada Information Office - L'APPUI À L'ENGAGEMENT CIVIQUE – 1998	2005.05.19
P-140	Projet du Bureau d'information du Canada - Citizens Information Initiative – 2000 / Project of the Canada Information Office – Citizens Information Initiative – 2000	2004.12.06
P-141	Contrat entre le Bureau d'information du Canada et Infras Inc. – 1998 / Contracts between the Canada Information Office and Infras Inc. – 1998.	2004.12.06
P-142	Transferts Bureau d'information du Canada et TPSGC – 1998-2000 / Transfers Canada Information Office and PWGSC – 1998-2000	2004.12.06
P-143	Memorandum dated July 19, 1995 from Ms. Bourgon to Prime Minister Jean Chrétien / Note de service en date du 19 juillet 1995 de Madame Bourgon au Premier ministre Jean Chrétien.	2004.12.06
P-144 (a)	Lettre de Monsieur Himelfarb à la Commission d'enquête accompagnée de trois documents révisés. 1- Une note interne du Bureau du Conseil privé de Monsieur Michael Horgan à Monsieur George Anderson en versions anglaise et française avec pièces jointes. 2- Une note de service de Madame Bourgon au Premier ministre Chrétien en date du 18 décembre 1996 avec pièces jointes. 3- Une note de service de Madame Bourgon au Premier ministre Chrétien en date du 30 septembre 1997.	
P-144 (b)	Documents dans leur forme originale comprenant une note interne du Bureau du Conseil privé de Monsieur Michael Horgan à Monsieur George Anderson en versions anglaise et française avec pièce jointes, un note de service de Madame Bourgon au premier ministre Chrétien en date du 18 décembre 1996 avec pièces jointes et une note de service de Madame Bourgon au Premier ministre Chrétien en date du 30 septembre 1997.	2004.12.06
P-145 (a)	Documents au soutien du témoignage de Ronald Bilodeau, Volume 1 / Supporting documents for the testimony of Ronald Bilodeau, Volume 1.	2004.12.07
P-145 (b)	Documents au soutien du témoignage de Ronald Bilodeau, Volume 2 / Supporting documents for the testimony of Ronald Bilodeau, Volume 2.	2004.12.07
P-146	Memorandum for the Prime Minister - Accessing funds set aside for Unity / Note à l'intention du Premier ministre – Mode d'accèe aux fonds réservés à l'Unité.	2004.12.07
P-147	RAPPORT DE DÉCISION DU CABINET – Le comité du Cabinet chargé de l'union sociale – Réunion du 21 mars 2000 – CONFIRMATION PAR LE CABINET, LE 28 MARS 2000 / RECORD OF CABINET DECISION – The Cabinet Committee for the social Union – Meeting of March 21, 2000 CONFIRMED BY THE CABINET ON MARCH 28, 2000.	2004.12.07
P-148 (a)	Documents au soutien du témoignage de Jocelyne Bourgon, Volume 1 / Supporting documents for the testimony of Jocelyne Bourgon, Volume 1.	2004.12.07
P-148 (b)	Documents au soutien du témoignage de Jocelyne Bourgon, Volume 2 / Supporting documents for the testimony of Jocelyne Bourgon, Volume 2.	2004.12.07

Exhibit	Description	Date
P-148 (c)	Documents confidentiels du Cabinet (extraits de P-148(a) et (b) – Nouvelles versions transmises par le Bureau du Conseil Privé / Cabinet Confidences (extracts from P-148 (a) and (b)) – New Versions transmitted by the Privy Council Office.	2005.01.27
P-148 (d)	Lettre du Commissaire John H. Gomery à M. Alex Himelfarb en date du 21 janvier 2005.	2005.01.27
P-149	Contrat en date du 25 avril 1996 avec Gary Breen Associates / Contract dated April 25, 1996 with Gary Breen Associates.	2004.12.08
P-150	Contrat en date du 31 octobre 1995, à Communication Jean Lafleur / Contract dated October 31, 1995 with Communication Jean Lafleur.	2004.12.08
P-151	Documents produits au soutien du témoignage de madame Michelle d'Auray	2004.12.09
P-152	Information Essentielle / Télémission Information – Organigramme corporatif, Flux des fonds et documents divers / Corporate Flowchart, Cash flow and Various documents.	2004.12.13
P-152 (a)	ADDENDA. -- Page en remplacement de la page 4 de l'onglet 2 de la pièce P-152 / Replacement for page 4 of Tab 2 in Exhibit P-152.	2004.12.13
P-153	Information Essentielle / Télémission Information – Fondation CRB / CRB Foundation.	2004.12.13
P-154	Information Essentielle / Télémission Information – Maurice Richard.	2004.12.13
P-154	ADDENDA – (Insérer après la page P225) Information Essentielle/Télémission Information – MAURICE RICHARD	2005.02.28
P-154	ADDENDA – (Insérer après la page P298) Information Essentielle/Télémission Information – MAURICE RICHARD	2005.02.28
P-154	ADDENDA – (insérer après la page 302) Information Essentielle/Télémission Information – MAURICE RICHARD	2005.03.10
P-154	ADDENDUM Information Essentielle/Télémission Information / MAURICE RICHARD (insérer après la page P51) (P51A et P51B)	2005.04.18
P-154 (a)	Notes relatives à une rencontre à laquelle a participé Monsieur André Scully avec Monsieur André Ouellet le 2 février 1999 / Notes relating to a meeting between Mr. Scully and Mr. André Ouellet of February 2, 1999.	2004.12.13
P-154 (b)	Dossier original interne de la Série Maurice Richard de l'agence Lafleur Communication TPS-20009 / Original File on Maurice Richard Series of Lafleur Communication TPS-20009.	2005.02.28
P-154 (c)	Dossier original interne de la Série Maurice Richard de l'agence Lafleur Communication TPS-20010 / Original File on Maurice Richard Series of Lafleur Communication TPS-20010.	2005.02.28
P-155	Information Essentielle / Télémission Information – Canada du Millénaire.	2004.12.13
P-155	ADDENDUM À P-155 – insérer la page 12(a) – Facture de l'Information Essentielle datée du 27 novembre 1998	2005.02.01
P-155	ADDENDA – (Insérer après la page P45) Information Essentielle/Télémission Information – CANADA DU MILLÉNAIRE	2005.02.28
P-156	Information Essentielle / Télémission Information – Innovation	2004.12.13
P-157	Information Essentielle / Télémission Information – Autres projets / Other projects.	2004.12.13
P-158	Giuliano Zaccardelli Witness Brief	2004.12.14
P-159 (a)	Documents concernant le 125ième anniversaire de la GRC / Documents pertaining to the RCMP 125th Anniversary, Volume 1.	2004.12.15
P-159 (b)	Documents concernant le 125ième anniversaire de la GRC / Documents pertaining to the RCMP 125th Anniversary, Volume 2.	2004.12.15
P-159 (c)	Documents concernant le 125ième anniversaire de la GRC / Documents pertaining to the RCMP 125th Anniversary, Volume 3.	2004.12.15
P-160	GRC - Documents Additionels/RCMP Additional Documents	2004.12.15
P-161	Contrats – GRC – 125ième Anniversaire / Contracts – RCMP – 125th Anniversary Celebrations.	2004.12.15
P-162	Note de service en date du 26 février 1996 de Dawson Hovey à tous les commandants divisionnaires et directeurs / Memorandum dated February 26th, 1996 from Dawson Hovey to all Commanding Officers and Directors.	2004.12.15
P-163	Historique de l'achat de six chevaux de la GRC pour le 125ième anniversaire / History of purchase of six RCMP horses for the 125th Anniversary Celebrations.	2004.12.15
P-164 (a)	VIA Rail Canada - Documents – Volume 1 de 3	2005.01.11
P-164 (b)	VIA Rail Canada - Documents – Volume 2 de 3	2005.01.11
P-164 (c)	VIA Rail Canada - Documents – Volume 3 de 3	2005.01.11
P-165 (a)	VIA MAGAZINE, Volume 1 de 2	2005.01.11
P-165 (b)	VIA MAGAZINE, Volume 2 de 2	2005.01.11
P-166	Consolidated By-Law No.1 and By-Laws #3 - 12 - 27A dated April 1993 / Règlement No.1 Consolidé et Règlements # 3 -12 -27A en date de Avril 1993.	2005.01.11
P-167	Invoice from L'Information Essentielle inc. for $325,000 dated June 29, 1999 / Facture provenant de L'Information essentielle inc. au montant de 325,000$ en date du 29 juin 1999.	2005.01.11

P-168	Memo to Marc LeFrançois from Rod Morrison dated 14 January 1999 / Mémo envoyé à Marc LeFrançois par Rod Morrison en date du 29 juin 1999.	2005.01.11
P-168 (a)	Sponsorship Agreement dated December 23, 2002.	2005.01.12
P-169	Documents relatifs au témoignage des représentants de la BDC – Volume 1 / Documents pertaining to the testimony of BDC representatives – Volume 1	2005.01.12
P-170	Documents relatifs au témoignage des représentants de la BDC – Volume 2 / Documents pertaining to the testimony of BDC representatives – Volume 2	2005.01.12
P-171	Accord de partenariat entre Communication Canada et la BDC signé par Christiane Beaulieu le 12 octobre 2001 / Partnership agreement between Communication Canada and BDC signed on October 12, 2001 by Christiane Beaulieu	2005.01.12
P-172	Lettre et présentation (22 mars 2000) de KPMG / Letters and presentation (March 22, 2000) from KPMG.	2005.01.17
P-173	Documents pertaining to the testimony of Canada Post Corporation representatives - Dossier Général v. 1	2005.01.20
P-173	Documents relatifs au témoignage des représentants de la Société Canadienne des Postes, Dossier Général, Volume 1 - ADDENDUM – inséré après page 205 à 241	2005.01.20
P-173	Documents relatifs au témoignage des représentants de la Société Canadienne des Postes, Dossier Général, Volume 1 - ADDENDUM – inséré après page 241 à 251	2005.01.20
P-173	Documents relatifs au témoignage des représentants de la Société Canadienne des Postes, Dossier Général, Volume 1 - ADDENDUM – Inséré après la page 58 (58A à 58D) (Distribué mais non produit)	2005.01.24
P-173	Documents relatifs au témoignage des représentants de la Société Canadienne des Postes, Dossier Général, Volume 1 - ADDENDUM – inséré après page 251 (252 à 259)	2005.01.24
P-174	Volume 2, Série Maurice Richard et Série Jean Béliveau	2005.01.17
P-174 (a)	ERRATUM (inséré après la page P25) Série – MAURICE RICHARD – Volume 2 Série – JEAN BÉLIVEAU	2005.05.17
P-175	Volume 3 Concours de création de timbres	2005.01.17
P-175	ADDENDA – (Insérer après la page P323) Documents relatifs au témoignage des représentants de la Société Canadienne des Postes	2005.02.28
P-176	Volume 4 Request for Proposal December 2000	2005.01.17
P-177 (a)	Volume 5, Partie I, Lafleur - Factures et Contrats	2005.01.17
P-177 (a)	ADDENDUM (Insérer après la page P12) LAFLEUR COMMUNICATION MARKETING FACTURES ET CONTRATS – Volume 5 (Partie I)	2005.05.17
P-177(b)	Volume 5, Partie II, Lafleur - Factures et Contrats	2005.01.17
P-178	Volume 6 Tremblay Guittet - Factures et Contrats	2005.01.17
P-179(a)	Volume 7 Daniel Sawaya Partie I	2005.01.17
P-179(b)	Volume 7 Daniel Sawaya Partie II	2005.01.17
P-180	Volume 8 Stewart Bacon	2005.01.17
P-181	Volume 9 Micheline Montreuil	2005.01.19
P-181	Addenda (Insert after page P82K)	2005.01.19
P-181 (a)	Micheline Montreuil Partie II Volume 9	2005.01.17
P-182	Volume 10 Alain Guilbert	2005.01.17
P-183	Volume 12 Programme des Commandites	2005.01.17
P-184	Documents pertaining to the testimony of Canada Post Corporation representatives – Groupe Everest – Volume 13 / Documents relatifs aux témoignages des représentants de la Société Canadienne des Postes – Groupe Everest – Volume 13	2005.01.18
P-185 (a)	Documents relatifs au témoignage des représentants de la Société Canadienne des Postes, Volume 11 – André Ouellet, Partie I / Documents pertaining to the testimony of Canada Post Corporation representatives, Volume 11 – André Ouellet, Part I.	2005.01.19
P-185 (b)	Documents relatifs au témoignage des représentants de la Société Canadienne des Postes, Volume 11 – André Ouellet, Partie II / Documents pertaining to the testimony of Canada Post Corporation representatives, Volume 11 – André Ouellet, Part II.	2005.01.19
P-186 (a)	Documents pertaining to the testimony of the Honourable David Dingwall and Mr. Warren Kinsella, Volume 1 of 2 / Documents relatifs au témoignages de l'Honorable David Dingwall et monsieur Warren Kinsella Volume 1 de 2.	2005.01.20
P-186 (b)	Documents pertaining to the testimony of the Honourable David Dingwall and Mr. Warren Kinsella, Volume 2 of 2 / Documents relatifs au témoignages de l'Honorable David Dingwall et monsieur Warren Kinsella Volume 2 de 2.	2005.01.20
P-187	Documents pertaining to the testimony of Gordon Feeney / Documents relatifs au témoignage de monsieur Gordon Feeney.	2005.01.24

P-188	Document entitled "Documents sustaining the testimony – Diane Marleau" Document intitulé "Documents au soutien du témoignage de Diane Marleau"	2005.01.24
P-188	ADDENDUM – page 35(a) – Note de breffage daté du 21 mai 1996 au Ministre de R.A. Quail re rencontre avec la Fondation Charles R. Bronfman en date du 27 mai 1996	2005.01.25
P-189 (a)	Document entitled "Documents sustaining the testimony of Ministers and former ministers – Volume 1 / Document intitulé "Documents au soutien du témoignage des ministres et anciens ministres – Volume 1"	2005.01.24
P-189 (b)	Document entitled "Documents sustaining the testimony of Ministers and former ministers – Volume 2"/Document intitulé "Documents au soutien du témoignage des Ministres et anciens ministres – Volume 2"	2005.01.24
P-190	Documents au soutien du témoignage de Stéphane Dion / Documents pertaining to the testimony of Stéphane Dion.	2005.01.25
P-191 (a)	Documents au soutien du témoignage de Denis Coderre, Volume 1 / Documents pertaining to the testimony of Denis Coderre, Volume 1.	2005.01.25
P-191 (b)	Documents au soutien du témoignage de Denis Coderre, Volume 2 / Documents pertaining to the testimony of Denis Coderre, Volume 2.	2005.01.25
P-192	Extraits du registraire des entreprises, Le système CIDREQ.	2005.01.25
P-193	Extrait du « mplog » concernant Monsieur Coderre	2005.01.25
P-194 (a)	Documents pertaining to the testimony of Jean-Marc Bard, Volume 1 / Documents au soutien du témoignage de Jean-Marc Bard, Volume 1.	2005.01.26
P-194 (b)	Documents pertaining to the testimony of Jean-Marc Bard, Volume 2 / Documents au soutien du témoignage de Jean-Marc Bard, Volume 2.	2005.01.26
P-195	Extrait du « mplog » se rapportant à Jean-Marc Bard / Excerpts from « mplog » pertaining to Jean-Marc Bard.	2005.01.26
P-196 (a)	Documents pertaining to the testimony of the Honorable Lucienne Robillard, Volume 1 of 2 / Documents relatifs au témoignage de l'Honorable Lucienne Robillard, Volume 1 de 2.	2005.01.28
P-196 (b)	Documents pertaining to the testimony of the Honorable Lucienne Robillard, Volume 2 of 2 / Documents relatifs au témoignage de l'Honorable Lucienne Robillard, Volume 2 de 2.	2005.01.28
P-197	Extrait du procès-verbal du cabinet tenu le 13 décembre 2003.	2005.01.28
P-198 (a)	Documents au soutien du témoignage de Martin Cauchon, Volume 1 / Documents pertaining to the testimony of Martin Cauchon, Volume 1.	2005.01.28
P-198 (b)	Documents au soutien du témoignage de Martin Cauchon, Volume 2 / Documents pertaining to the testimony of Martin Cauchon, Volume 2.	2005.01.28
P-198 (b)	Documents au soutien du témoignage de Martin Cauchon, Volume 2 – ADDENDUM – Insérer après la page P329 (329A à 329B)	2005.01.28
P-198 (c)	Documents au soutien du témoignage de Martin Cauchon, Volume 3 / Documents pertaining to the testimony of Martin Cauchon, Volume 3.	2005.01.28
P-199	Extraits du « mplog » concernant Martin Cauchon / Excerpts from the « mplog » pertaining to Martin Cauchon.	2005.01.28
P-200	Documents relatifs au témoignage de M. Alfonso Gagliano / Documents pertaining to the testimony of Mr. Alfonso Gagliano. Déclarations diverses, financement du programme, vérification interne et documents divers / Various declarations, Program funding, intern audit and miscellaneous documents.	2005.02.01
P-200 (a)	Extraits de l'agenda de Jean Pelletier.	
P-201	Documents relatifs au témoignage de M. Alfonso Gagliano / Documents pertaining to the testimony of Mr. Alfonso Gagliano. Interventions de M. Alfonso Gagliano ou de son bureau (Interventions directes) / Involvement of Mr. Alfonso Gagliano or his Office (Direct involvement).	2005.02.02 2005.02.01
P-202	Documents relatifs au témoignage de M. Alfonso Gagliano / Documents pertaining to the testimony of Mr. Alfonso Gagliano relations de M. Alfonso Gagliano avec les agences et les sociétés d'état / Mr. Alfonso Gagliano's relationship with Agencies and Crown Corporations.	2005.02.01
P-203	Documents relatifs au témoignage de M. Alfonso Gagliano / Documents pertaining to the testimony of Mr. Alfonso Gagliano notes manuscrites de M. Ranald Quail / Handwritten notes by Mr. Ranald Quail.	2005.02.01
P-204	Facture de Groupaction à Travaux publics re : les Jeux olympiques à Nagano / Invoice from Groupaction to Public Works re: Olympic Games in Nagano	2005.02.01
P-205	Documents ayant trait à la période de questions relative à la vérification interne de Ernst & Young en 1996 / Documents pertaining to the 1996 internal audit by Ernst & Young.	2005.02.01
P-206	Documents au soutien du témoignage de Jean Carle / Documents pertaining to the testimony of Jean Carle.	2005.02.04
P-207	Jean Carle - handwritten notes on BDC personalized stationary.	2005.02.04
P-208(a)	Documents pertaining to the testimony of Jean Pelletier – sponsorship projects – Volume 1 / Documents au soutien du témoignage de Jean Pelletier – projets de commandites – Volume 1.	2005.02.07
P-208(b)	Documents pertaining to the testimony of Jean Pelletier – sponsorship projects – Volume 2 / Documents au soutien du témoignage de Jean Pelletier – projets de commandites – Volume 2.	2005.02.07

P-208(c)	Documents pertaining to the testimony of Jean Pelletier – sponsorship projects – Volume 3 / Documents au soutien du témoignage de Jean Pelletier – projets de commandites – Volume 3.	2005.02.07
P-208(d)	Documents pertaining to the testimony of Jean Pelletier – miscellaneous – Volume 4 / Documents au soutien du témoignage de Jean Pelletier – divers – Volume 4.	2005.02.07
P-208 (d)	ADDENDA Insérer à l'exhibit P-208(d). après la page 262, la page 262(a)	2005.02.07
P-208(e)	Documents pertaining to the testimony of Jean Pelletier – miscellaneous – Volume 5 / Documents au soutien du témoignage de Jean Pelletier – divers – Volume 5.	2005.02.07
P-208(f)	Documents pertaining to the testimony of Jean Pelletier – Addendum - Miscellaneous documents – Volume 6 / Documents au soutien du témoignage de Jean Pelletier – Documents divers – Volume 6.	2005.02.07
P-209	TPSGC – Réponse aux engagements pris lors de l'interrogatoire de M. J.C. Guité au sujet des Unforeseen Events / Response to undertaking given during the examination of M. J. C. Guité regarding Unforseen Events.	2005.02.07
P-210(a)	Documents au soutien du témoignage de Jean Chrétien, Volume 1 / Documents supporting the testimony of Jean Chrétien, Volume 1	2005.02.08
P-210(b)	Documents au soutien du témoignage de Jean Chrétien, Volume 2 / Documents supporting the testimony of Jean Chrétien, Volume 2	2005.02.08
P-210(c)	Documents au soutien du témoignage de Jean Chrétien, Volume 3 / Documents supporting the testimony of Jean Chrétien, Volume 3	2005.02.08
P-210(d)	Documents au soutien du témoignage de Jean Chrétien, Volume 4 / Documents supporting the testimony of Jean Chrétien, Volume 4	2005.02.08
P-211	Letter from Jean-Pierre Kingsley dated February 10, 2005 addressed to the Honourable John H. Gomery, Commissioner / Lettre de Jean-Pierre Kingsley en date du 10 février 2005 adressé à l'Honorable John H. Gomery, Commissaire	2005.02.10
P-212	Documents relevant to Prime Minister Paul Martin/ Livre rouge intitulé Documents relatifs au Premier Ministre Paul Martin	2005.02.10
P-213	Statement of Evidence of Prime Minister Paul Martin /Énoncé de preuve du Premier Ministre Paul Martin	2005.02.10
P-214	Documents au soutien du témoignage de ALEX HIMELFARB / Documents sustaining the testimony of ALEX HIMELFARB.	2005.02.28
P-214	ADDENDUM – Documents au soutiens du témoignage de Alex Himelfarb / Documents Sustaining the testimony of Alex Himelfarb (pages 1 to 9)	2005.02.28
P-214	ADDENDUM – Page 2A – Lettre de Ursula Menke à Marie Marmet en date du 21 Février.	2005.02.28
P-215 (a)	Documents relatifs aux témoignages des représentants de Lafleur Communication Marketing, Volume 1 de 2 / Documents relating to the testimony of Lafleur Communication Marketing representatives, Volume 1 of 2.	2005.02.28
P-215 (b)	Documents relatifs aux témoignages des représentants de Lafleur Communication Marketing, Volume 2 de 2 / Documents relating to the testimony of Lafleur Communication Marketing representatives, Volume 2 of 2.	2005.02.28
P-216	Documents relatifs au témoignage des représentants de Lafleur communication Marketing / Documents pertaining to the testimony of representatives of Lafleur Communication Marketing – TABLEAUX ET ANALYSES	2005.02.28
P-216 (b)	Documents relatifs au témoignage des représentants de Lafleur communication Marketing / Documents pertaining to the testimony of representatives of Lafleur Communication Marketing - TABLEAUX ET ANALYSES (SUPPLEMENT D'INFORMATION)	2005.03.02
P-216 (b)	ADDENDA (remplacez la page P28 – 2 pages) (remplacez la page P29) – VIA Magazine et Logos Canada – VIA	2005.03.07
P-216 (b)	ADDENDA (remplacez la page P19) – Grand Prix du Canada (Formule 1)	2005.03.07
P-216 (b)	ADDENDA – (remplacez la page P25)	2005.03.08
P-217	Documents relatifs au témoignage des représentants de Lafleur communication Marketing / Documents pertaining to the testimony of representatives of Lafleur Communication Marketing – ENCYCLOPEDIE DU CANADA.	2005.02.28
P-217	ADDENDA – (insérer après la page 327) Lafleur Communication Marketing - Encyclopédie du Canada	2005.03.10
P-218	Documents relatifs au témoignage des représentants de Lafleur communication Marketing / Documents pertaining to the testimony of representatives of Lafleur Communication Marketing – MUSÉE GRANDE CASCAPEDIA	2005.02.28
P-219 (a)	Documents relatifs au témoignage des représentants de Lafleur communication Marketing / Documents pertaining to the testimony of representatives of Lafleur Communication Marketing – EXPOS DE MONTRÉAL – VOLUME 1 DE 2.	2005.02.28
P-219 (b)	Documents relatifs au témoignage des représentants de Lafleur communication Marketing / Documents pertaining to the testimony of representatives of Lafleur Communication Marketing – EXPOS DE MONTRÉAL – VOLUME 2 DE 2.	2005.02.28
P-219 (b)	ADDENDA – (Insérer après la page P145) Au Volume 2 de 2 (pages 416 à 442)	2005.02.28

P-220	Documents relatifs au témoignage des représentants de Lafleur communication Marketing / Documents pertaining to the testimony of representatives of Lafleur Communication Marketing – SANTÉ CANADA – 01-CA H5301-0012	2005.02.28
P-221	Documents relatifs au témoignage des représentants de Lafleur communication Marketing / Documents pertaining to the testimony of representatives of Lafleur Communication Marketing – SÉRIE DU SIÈCLE	2005.02.28
P-222	Documents relatifs au témoignage des représentants de Lafleur communication Marketing / Documents pertaining to the testimony of representatives of Lafleur Communication Marketing – DIRECTIVE EN771-5-U117 GENESIS MEDIA / LAFLEUR OUTDOOR MEDIA TO PROMOTE GOVERNMENT PROGRAMS	2005.02.28
P-223	Documents relatifs au témoignage des représentants de Lafleur communication Marketing / Documents pertaining to the testimony of representatives of Lafleur Communication Marketing – INTERNATIONAUX DE TENNIS JUNIOR DE REPENTIGNY	2005.02.28
P-224	Liste des Post mortem de 1995 à mai 2002	2005.02.28
P-224 (2)	ADDENDA – Liste des post mortems.	2005.03.01
P-224 (a)	CD – Post mortem, Lafleur Communication Marketing, Volume 1	2005.02.28
P-224 (b)	CD – Post mortem, Lafleur Communication Marketing, Volume 2	2005.02.28
P-224 (c)	CD – Post mortem, Lafleur Communication Marketing, Volume 3	2005.02.28
P-224 (d)	CD – Post mortem, Lafleur Communication Marketing, Volume 4	2005.02.28
P-224 (e)	CD – Post mortem, Lafleur Communication Marketing, Volume 5	2005.02.28
P-224 (f)	CD – Post mortem, Lafleur Communication Marketing, Volume 6 - Addenda	2005.03.01
P-225 (a)	Documents relatifs au témoignage des représentants de Lafleur communication Marketing / Documents pertaining to the testimony of representatives of Lafleur Communication Marketing – GRAND PRIX DU CANADA – VOLUME 1 DE 2	2005.02.28
P-225 (b)	Documents relatifs au témoignage des représentants de Lafleur communication Marketing / Documents pertaining to the testimony of representatives of Lafleur Communication Marketing – GRAND PRIX DU CANADA – VOLUME 2 DE 2	2005.02.28
P-226	Documents relatifs au témoignage des représentants de Lafleur communication Marketing / Documents pertaining to the testimony of representatives of Lafleur Communication Marketing – ITEMS PROMOTIONNELS	2005.02.28
P-226 (A)	Analyse des montants facturés par Lafleur Communication Marketing à TPSGC dans le cadre de certains contrats pour l'achat d'items promotionnels.	2005.03.01
P-227	Documents relatifs au témoignage des représentants de Lafleur communication Marketing / Documents pertaining to the testimony of representatives of Lafleur Communication Marketing - SOCIETE DU VIEUX PORT CENTRE ISCI	2005.03.01
P-228 (a)	Rapport d'activités de Lafleur Communication Marketing déposés à la Commission 1998-2000	2005.02.28
P-228 (b)	Boîte de rapports d'activités	2005.02.28
P-228 (c)	Boîte de rapports d'activités	2005.02.28
P-229	Déclaration de Preuve de Jean Lafleur / Statement of Evidence of Jean Lafleur	2005.02.28
P-230	Documents pertaining to the testimony of representatives of Lafleur Communication Marketing – GRC 125e ANNIVERSAIRE	2005.03.01
P-230 (A)	Épinglettes du 125e anniversaire de la GRC	2005.03.01
P-231	Documents relatifs au témoignage des représentants de Lafleur Communication Marketing / Documents pertaining to the testimony of Lafleur Communication Marketing - VIA MAGAZINE ET LOGOS CANADA	2005.03.01
P-232 (A)	Contributions et dépenses déclarées par les candidats et les partis politiques enregistrés	2005.03.01
P-232 (B)	Rapports financiers contributions reçues par une entité politique: www.elections.ca	2005.03.01
P-233	PUBLIC WORKS AND GOVERNMENT SERVICES CANADA ADVERTISING AGENCY SELECTION COMMITTEE - FINAL REPORT – June 30, 1995	2005.03.02
P-234 (a)	Documents relatifs au témoignage des représentants de Lafleur Communication Marketing / Documents pertaining to the testimony of representatives of Lafleur Communication Marketing - GESTION DE COMMUNICATION DE CRISE GESCOM INC.	2005.03.02
P-234 (a)	ADDENDA – Contrat de service de consultations –VIA RAIL Canada et Gescom Inc. (insérer après page 4 de P-234(a), pages P-4(a) à P-4(c))	2005.03.02
P-234 (b)	Documents relatifs au témoignage des représentants de Lafleur Communication Marketing / Documents pertaining to the testimony of representatives of Lafleur Communication Marketing - GESTION DE COMMUNICATION DE CRISE GESCOM INC. (SUPPLEMENT D'INFORMATION)	2005.03.02
P-235	Livre de MAURICE RICHARD /MAURICE RICHARD Story	2005.03.03
P-236	Lettre datée du 15 avril 2004 adressée à Me Jean-C. Hébert de M. Gerard Power de Postes Canada	2005.03.03
P-237	Registre Informatique de la Société Canadienne des Postes.	2005.03.07

P-238	Documents relatifs au témoignage des représentants de Lafleur Communication Marketing / Documents pertaining to the testimony of representatives of Lafleur Communication Marketing - CONTRAT No. EN771-6-0008 - Supplément d'information	2005.03.08
P-239	Documents relatifs au témoignage des représentants de Lafleur Communication Marketing / Documents pertaining to the testimony of representatives of Lafleur Communication Marketing - CONTRAT No. EN771-6-0030 - Supplément d'information (P1 à P27)	2005.03.08
P-240	Memorandum daté du 23 février 2005 de Me J. A. Montigny et Me J.C. Hébert. Re: contribution faites par M. Lafleur et ses compagnies	2005.03.08
P-241	Boîte de documents – Cassettes VHS & CD Rom	2005.03.08
P-242	CV – Pierre Michaud	2005.03.08
P-243 (a)	Documents au soutien du témoignage de PIERRE DAVIDSON / Documents sustaining the testimony of PIERRE DAVIDSON - Volume 1	2005.03.08
P-243 (b)	Documents au soutien du témoignage de PIERRE DAVIDSON / Documents sustaining the testimony of PIERRE DAVIDSON - Volume 2	2005.03.08
P-243 (c)	ADDENDA - Documents au soutien du témoignage de PIERRE DAVIDSON / ADDENDUM – Documents sustaining the testimony of PIERRE DAVIDSON - Volume 2 (remplacez pp. 148 à 150) pp.1 de 4 ainsi que 2 factures : 98.428 et 98.077	2005.03.08
P-244	Déclaration de preuve de Éric Lafleur / Statement of Evidence of Éric Lafleur	2005.03.09
P-245	Documents relatifs au témoignage des représentants de Lafleur Communication Marketing / Documents pertaining to the testimony of representatives of Lafleur Communication Marketing - TABLEAUX ET ANALYSES - Publicité Dezert Inc.	2005.03.09
P-245	Analyse de la facturation de Publicité Dezert à JLCM relative au Programme de commandites pour les exercices financiers terminés le 31 août 1996 à 2000 – (remplacez la page 14 déjà produite)	2005.03.09
P-246	Documents relatifs au témoignage des représentants de Lafleur Communication Marketing / Documents pertaining to the testimony of representatives of Lafleur Communication Marketing - Éric Lafleur et Publicité Dézert Inc.	2005.03.09
P-247	Lettre de Ursula Menke du Bureau du Conseil Privé adressée à Me André Lespérance datée du 28 février 2005 re Demande de documents #59 du 8 février 2005-03-09	2005.03.09
P-248	Lettre de Ursula Menke du Bureau du Conseil Privé adressée à Me André Lespérance datée du 8 février 2005 re Demande de documents #59 du 8 février 2005-03-09	2005.03.09
P-249	Série de factures de PLURI DESIGN	2005.03.10
P-250	Federal Presence List of Events June to September 1995 – Executive Summary	2005.03.14
P-251	Groupaction – Post Mortem 1997 – Grand Prix du Canada	2005.03.14
P-252	Contrat – Grand Prix 1997 - $53,500 accordé à Groupaction	2005.03.10
P-253	Encyclopédie du Canada – Édition 2000	2005.03.14
P-254	Déclaration de la Preuve Gilles-André Gosselin / Statement of Evidence – Gilles-André Gosselin	2005.03.14
P-255	Advertising and Public Opinion Research Directorate (A & PORD) AOR Payment System Study – November 1994 (Ebauche)	2005.03.14
P-256 (a)	Documents relatifs au témoignage des représentants de Gosselin Communications Stratégiques / Documents Pertaining to the testimony of Representatives of Gosselin Communications Stratégiques – Dossier General.	2005.03.14
P-256 (a)	ADDENDA – Dossier général (Insérer après la page P63)	2005.03.14
P-256 (a)	ADDENDA – Dossier général (Insérer après la page P274)	2005.03.14
P-256 (a)	ADDENDA – Dossier général (Insérer après la page P275)	2005.03.14
P-256 (b)	Documents relatifs au témoignage des représentations de Gosselin Communications Stratégiques / Documents Pertaining to the testimony of Representatives of Gosselin Communications Stratégiques – Dossier General – (Supplément d'Information)	2005.03.14
P-257 (a)	Documents relatifs au témoignage des représentants de Gosselin Communications Stratégiques / Documents Pertaining to the testimony of Representatives of Gosselin Communications Stratégiques – Tableaux et Analyses	2005.03.14
P-257 (a)	ADDENDA – (insérer après la page P137)	2005.03.15
P-257 (b)	Documents relatifs au témoignage des représentants de Gosselin Communications Stratégiques / Documents Pertaining to the testimony of Representatives of Gosselin Communications Stratégiques – Tableaux et Analyses – (Supplément d'Information)	2005.03.14
P-257 (b)	ADDENDA (remplace la page P27) (insérer après la page P27)	2005.03.16

P-258	Documents relatifs au témoignage des représentants de Gosselin Communications Stratégiques / Documents Pertaining to the testimony of Representatives of Gosselin Communications Stratégiques – Résumé des Projets 1998	2005.03.14
P-259	Documents relatifs au témoignage des représentants de Gosselin Communications Stratégiques / Documents Pertaining to the testimony of Representatives of Gosselin Communications Stratégiques – Dossier General – Sélection des Agences Mars 1995 et Février 1997	2005.03.14
P-260	Documents relatifs au témoignage des représentants de Gosselin Communications Stratégiques / Documents Pertaining to the testimony of Representatives of Gosselin Communications Stratégiques – Items Promotionnels	2005.03.14
P-260 (b)	Documents relatifs au témoignages des représentants de Gosselin Communications Stratégiques / Documents pertaining to the testimony of representatives of Gosselin Communications stratégiques – ARTICLES PROMOTIONNELS (Supplément d'Information)	2005.03.29
P-261	Documents relatifs au témoignage des représentants de Gosselin Communications Stratégiques / Documents Pertaining to the testimony of Representatives of Gosselin Communications Stratégiques – Les Fêtes du 250e de Saint-Hyacinthe.	2005.03.14
P-261	ADDENDA – (Remplacer l'Index) – Les Fêtes du 250e de Saint-Hyacinthe.	2005.03.14
P-262 (a)	Documents relatifs au témoignage des représentants de Gosselin Communications Stratégiques / Documents Pertaining to the testimony of Representatives of Gosselin Communications Stratégiques – Parc des Champs de Bataille – Volume 1 de 4	2005.03.14
P-262 (b)	Documents relatifs au témoignage des représentants de Gosselin Communications Stratégiques / Documents Pertaining to the testimony of Representatives of Gosselin Communications Stratégiques – Parc des Champs de Bataille – Volume 2 de 4	2005.03.14
P-262 (c)	Documents relatifs au témoignage des représentants de Gosselin Communications Stratégiques / Documents Pertaining to the testimony of Representatives of Gosselin Communications Stratégiques – Parc des Champs de Bataille – Volume 3 de 4	2005.03.14
P-262 (d)	Documents relatifs au témoignage des représentants de Gosselin Communications Stratégiques / Documents Pertaining to the testimony of Representatives of Gosselin Communications Stratégiques – Parc des Champs de Bataille – Volume 4 de 4	2005.03.14
P-263 (a)	Documents relatifs au témoignage des représentants de Gosselin Communications Stratégiques / Documents Pertaining to the testimony of Representatives of Gosselin Communications Stratégiques – Rendez-vous Canada – Ville de Québec	2005.03.14
P-263 (b)	Documents relatifs au témoignage des représentants de Gosselin Communications Stratégiques / Documents Pertaining to the testimony of Representatives of Gosselin Communications Stratégiques – Rendez-vous Canada – Ville d'Ottawa	2005.03.14
P-263 (c)	Documents relatifs au témoignage des représentants de Gosselin Communications Stratégiques / Documents Pertaining to the testimony of Representatives of Gosselin Communications Stratégiques – Rendez-vous Canada – Ville d'Halifax	2005.03.14
P-263 (d)	Documents relatifs au témoignage des représentants de Gosselin Communications Stratégiques / Documents Pertaining to the testimony of Representatives of Gosselin Communications Stratégiques – Rendez-vous Canada – Ville de Calgary	2005.03.14
P-263 (e)	Documents relatifs au témoignage des représentants de Gosselin Communications Stratégiques / Documents Pertaining to the testimony of Representatives of Gosselin Communications Stratégiques – Rendez-vous Canada – Ville de Toronto	2005.03.14
P-264	Documents relatifs au témoignage des représentants de Gosselin Communications Stratégiques / Documents Pertaining to the testimony of Representatives of Gosselin Communications Stratégiques – GRC – 125e Anniversaire	2005.03.14
P-265 (a)	Documents relatifs au témoignage des représentants de Gosselin Communications Stratégiques / Documents Pertaining to the testimony of Representatives of Gosselin Communications Stratégiques – Unforseen Events – Volume 1 de 2	2005.03.14
P-265 (a)	ADDENDA – Unforseen events Volume 1 de 2 (Insérer après la page P68)(p.68A & p.68B)	2005.03.14
P-265 (b)	Documents relatifs au témoignage des représentants de Gosselin Communications Stratégiques / Documents Pertaining to the testimony of Representatives of Gosselin Communications Stratégiques – Unforseen Events – Volume 2 de 2	2005.03.14
P-266	Documents relatifs au témoignage des représentants de Gosselin Communications Stratégiques / Documents Pertaining to the testimony of Representatives of Gosselin Communications Stratégiques – Wendy Cumming	2005.03.14
P-267	Lettre de Gilles-André Gosselin à M. Charles Guité datée du 26 juillet 1994	2005.03.14
P-268	Documents relatifs au témoignage des représentants de Gosselin Communications Stratégiques / Documents pertaining to the Testimony of representatives of Gosselin Communications Stratégiques – Documents relatifs à l'entente d'avril 2002	2005.03.15
P-269	Documents relatifs au témoignage des représentants de Gosselin Communications Stratégiques / Documents pertaining to the Testimony of representatives of Gosselin Communications Stratégiques – CMHC – SCHL - Items Promotionnels	2005.03.15

P-270	Documents relatifs au témoignage des représentants de Gosselin Communications Stratégiques / Documents pertaining to the testimony of representatives of Gosselin Communications Stratégiques – DOSSIER GENERAL – Gosselin Relations Publiques Inc.	2005.03.15
P-271	Documents relatifs au témoignage des représentants de Gosselin Communications Stratégiques / Documents pertaining to the testimony of representatives of Gosselin Communications Stratégiques – TRABLEAUX ET ANALYSES – Gosselin Relations Publiques Inc.	2005.03.15
P-271	ADDENDA – (insérer après la page P125)	2005.03.15
P-272	Factures pour des événements divers de G.A. Gosselin - Avril 1997	2005.03.15
P-273	Original du dossier de l'Agence Gosselin Re la génératrice	2005.03.15
P-274	Memo de R.E. Cardinal à Jocelyne Bourgon daté du 22 août 96	2005.03.15
P-275	Documents relatifs au témoignage de Gosselin Communications Stratégiques / Documents pertaining to the testimony of representatives of Gosselin Communications Stratégiques – Tableaux et Analyses – CPPC Inc. – Centre de Placement de Professionnels en Communications Inc. - Portage Promotion Inc.	2005.03.16
P-276	Documents relatifs au témoignage des représentants de Gosselin Communications Stratégiques / Documents pertaining to the testimony of representatives of Gosselin Communications Stratégiques – Items Promotionnels – Gosselin Relations Publiques Inc.	2005.03.16
P-277	Documents relatifs au témoignage des représentants de Gosselin Communications Stratégiques / Documents pertaining to the testimony of representatives of Gosselin Communications Stratégiques – ÉVÉNEMENT DIVERS	2005.03.16
P-277 (b)	Documents relatifs au témoignages des représentants de Gosselin Communications Stratégiques / Documents pertaining to the testimony of representatives of Gosselin Communications stratégiques - ÉVÉNEMENTS DIVERS (Supplément d'information)	2005.03.29
P-278	Documents relatifs au témoignage des représentants de Gosselin Communications Stratégiques / Documents pertaining to the testimony of representatives of Gosselin Communications Stratégique – ENRICO VALENTE	2005.03.16
P-279	CD-ROM (3) Post Mortem	2005.03.16
P-280	Vidéocassettes et audiocassettes de Post Mortem	2005.03.16
P-281	Déclaration de la Preuve/Statement of Evidence – ANDRÉE CÔTÉ-GOSSELIN	2005.03.16
P-282	Déclaration de la Preuve/Statement of Evidence – NICOLAS GOSSELIN	2005.03.16
P-283	Documents relatifs au témoignage des représentants de Gosselin Communications Stratégiques / Documents pertaining to the testimony of representatives of Gosselin Communications Stratégiques - BERNARD THIBOUTOT	2005.03.17
P-284	Documents relatifs au témoignages des représentants de Gosselin Communications Stratégiques / Documents pertaining to the testimony of representatives of Gosselin Communications stratégiques - SPONSORSHIP STUDY 98/99	2005.03.29
P-285	Documents relatifs au témoignages des représentants de Gosselin Communications Stratégiques / Documents pertaining to the testimony of representatives of Gosselin Communications stratégiques DOCUMENTS DIVERS	2005.03.29
P-286	Documents relatifs au témoignages des représentants de Gosselin Communications Stratégiques / Documents pertaining to the testimony of representatives of Gosselin Communications stratégiques JOSÉE THIBEAU-CARRIER	2005.03.29
P-287 (a)	Documents relatifs au témoignages des représentants de Gosselin Communications Stratégiques / Documents pertaining to the testimony of representatives of Gosselin Communications stratégiques SÉNATEURS D'OTTAWA – Volume 1 de 2	2005.03.29
P-287 (a)	ADDENDUM (Insérer après la page P33) (Page 33-1)	2005.03.29
P-287 (a)	ADDENDUM (Insérer après la page P36) (Page P36-1 à P36-8)	2005.03.29
P-287 (a)	ADDENDUM (Insérer après la page P41) (Pages P41-1 à P41-40)	2005.03.29
P-287 (a)	ADDENDUM (Insérer après la page P144) (Page P144a)	2005.03.29
P-287 (a)	ADDENDUM (Insérer après la page 184)	2005.05.02
P-287 (b)	Documents relatifs au témoignages des représentants de Gosselin Communications Stratégiques / Documents pertaining to the testimony of representatives of Gosselin Communications stratégiques SÉNATEURS D'OTTAWA – Volume 2 de 2	2005.03.29
P-287 (b)	ADDENDUM (Insérer après la page P347) (Page P347-1 à P347-5)	2005.03.29
P-288	Documents relatifs au témoignages des représentants de Gosselin Communications Stratégiques / Documents pertaining to the testimony of representatives of Gosselin Communications stratégiques CONTRATS EN771-4-0037 & EN771-4-0052	2005.03.29
P-289	En liasse – photocopies de 5 photos (Place du Canada en Italie / Piazza du Canada - Panorama)	2005.03.29

P-289 (a)	En liasse – photocopie – photo d'une plaque	2005.03.29
P-316	Lettre de André J. Noreau en date du 6 avril 2005 adressée au Juge John H. Gomery re demande de John Welch d'être entendu.	2005.04.07
P-317	Lettre de Marie Malavoy du Partie Québécois en date du 7 avril 2005 adressée au Juge John H. Gomery.	2005.04.07
P-318 (a)	Documents relatifs au témoignage des représentants de Groupaction Marketing Inc. / Documents pertaining to the testimony of representatives of Groupaction Marketing Inc. JEAN LAMBERT (20 pages)	2005.04.07
P-318 (b)	Documents relatifs au témoignage des représentants de Groupaction Marketing Inc. / Documents pertaining to the testimony of representatives of Groupaction Marketing Inc. JEAN LAMBERT (58 pages)	2005.04.07
P-319	Documents relatifs au témoignage des représentants de Groupaction Marketing Inc. / Documents Pertaining to the testimony of Representatives of Groupaction Marketing Inc. ALAIN RENAUD – DOCUMENTS DIVERS	2005.04.08
P-320	Documents relatifs au témoignage des représentants de Groupaction Marketing Inc. / Documents pertaining to the testimony of representatives of Groupaction Marketing Inc. - ROGER DESJEANS	2005.04.11
P-321	Documents relatifs au témoignage des représentants de Groupaction Marketing Inc. / Documents pertaining to the testimony of representatives of Groupaction Marketing Inc. - BERNARD MICHAUD	2005.04.12
P-322 (a)	Documents relatifs au témoignage des représentants de Groupe Polygone/Expour et PluriDesign Canada Inc. / Documents pertaining to the Testimony of representatives of Groupe Polygone/Expour and PluriDesign Canada Inc. AUTRES TRANSACTIONS D'INTÉRÊT VOLUME 1 DE 2	2005.04.12
P-322 (a)	ADDENDUM (remplace les pages P91 à P106)	2005.04.12
P-322 (b)	Documents relatifs au témoignage des représentants de Groupe Polygone/Expour et PluriDesign Canada Inc. / Documents pertaining to the Testimony of representatives of Groupe Polygone/Expour and PluriDesign Canada Inc. AUTRES TRANSACTIONS D'INTÉRÊT VOLUME 2 DE 2	2005.04.12
P-323	Documents relatifs au témoignage des représentants de Groupe Polygone/Expour / Documents pertaining to the testimony of representatives of Groupe Polygone/Expour Soirées régionales de pêche, magazines régionaux, capsules radio, bulletins de la circulation et conditions routières, rendez-vous Autochtones – DOCUMENTS SÉLECTIONNÉS	2005.04.12
P-324	Documents relatifs au témoignage des représentants de Groupe Polygone/Expour et PluriDesign Canada Inc. / Documents pertaining to the Testimony of representatives of Groupe Polygone/Expour and PluriDesign Canada Inc. CONTRATS D'APPROVISIONNEMENT ENTRE PLURIDESIGN CANADA ET EXPOUR	2005.04.12
P-325	Documents relatifs au témoignage des représentants de Groupe Polygone/Expour et PluriDesign Canada Inc. / Documents pertaining to the Testimony of representatives of Groupe Polygone/Expour and PluriDesign Canada Inc. LISTE DES REPAS DE LUC LEMAY – MARS 2000 À JANVIER 2003	2005.04.12
P-326	Documents relatifs au témoignage des représentants de Groupe Polygone/Expour / Documents pertaining to the testimony of representatives of Groupe Polygone/Expour DOCUMENTS DIVERS	2005.04.12
P-326	ADDENDUM (Insérer après la page 99)	2005.04.12
P-327	Contrat 6C501-1-0051 – Information Guide 2001/2002	2005.04.12
P-328 (a)	Documents relatifs au témoignage des représentants de Groupaction Marketing Inc. et Groupe Polygone/Expour / Documents pertaining to the testimony of representatives of Groupaction Marketing Inc. and Groupe Polygone/Expour VOLUME 1 DE 2	2005.04.15
P-328 (b)	Documents relatifs au témoignage des représentants de Groupaction Marketing Inc. et Groupe Polygone/Expour / Documents pertaining to the testimony of representatives of Groupaction Marketing Inc. and Groupe Polygone/Expour VOLUME 2 DE 2	2005.04.15
P-329	Information financière sélectionnée du Groupe Polygone et Expour Inc.	2005.04.12
P-330	Liste des contributions politiques au Parti Libéral du Canada - Rapports financiers - Contributions et dépenses - Détails – contributions	2005.04.13
P-331	Documents relatifs au témoignage des représentants de Groupe Polygone/Expour et PluriDesign / Documents pertaining to the testimony of representatives of Groupe Polygone/Expour and PluriDesign Canada Inc. INTERPÔLES DESIGN COMMUNICATION MARKETING	2005.04.13
P-332	Documents relatifs au témoignage des représentants de PluriDesign Canada Inc. / Documents pertaining to the testimony of representatives of PluriDesign Canada Inc. - DOSSIER GÉNÉRAL - JACQUES CORRIVEAU ET PLURIDESIGN CANADA INC.	2005.04.14

P-333	Documents relatifs au témoignage des représentants de PluriDesign Canada Inc. / Documents pertaining to the testimony of representatives of PluriDesign Canada Inc. - EXTRAITS DU REGISTRE D'APPELS TÉLÉPHONIQUES - BUREAU DU PREMIER MINISTRE - 1996-2003	2005.04.14
P-334	Documents relatifs au témoignage des représentants de PluriDesign Canada Inc. / Documents pertaining to the testimony of representatives of PluriDesign Canada Inc. - ÉLECTIONS DE 1997	2005.04.14
P-335	Documents relatifs au témoignage des représentants de PluriDesign Canada Inc. / Documents pertaining to the testimony of representatives of PluriDesign Canada Inc. - LISTE DES FACTURES DE PLURIDESIGN AU PARTI LIBÉRAL DU CANADA ÉLECTION DE 1997	2005.04.18
P-335 (a)	Lettres de PluriDesign re Non paiement de factures envoyées par M. Jacques Corriveau	2005.04.18
P-335 (a)	Documents relatifs au témoignage des représentants de PLURIDESIGN CANANDA INC. / Documents pertaining to the testimony of representatives of PLURIDESIGN CANADA INC. LISTE DES FACTURES DE PLURIDESIGN AU PARTI LIBÉRAL DU CANADA – ÉLECTIONS DE 1997 (81 pages – document identique produit le 18 avril sous la même côte (8 pages))	2005.04.19
P-336	Documents relatifs au témoignage des représentants de PluriDesign Canada Inc. / Documents pertaining to the testimony of representatives of PluriDesign Canada Inc. – CHANTS LIBRES	2005.04.14
P-337	Documents relatifs au témoignage des représentants de PluriDesign Canada Inc. / Documents pertaining to the testimony of representatives of PluriDesign Canada Inc. – THÉÂTRE LYRICHOREGRA	2005.04.14
P-338	Série de Factures de PluriDesign # 2109-97 – 2122-97 – 2123-97	2005.04.14
P-340 (a)	Déclaration de la preuve de CLAUDE BOULAY / Statement of evidence of CLAUDE BOULAY	2005.04.19
P-340 (b)	Documents relatifs au témoignage des représentants de Groupe Everest / Documents pertaining to the testimony of representatives of Groupe Everest DOSSIER GÉNÉRAL CLAUDE BOULAY	2005.04.18
P-341	Documents relatifs au témoignage des représentants de Groupe Everest / Documents pertaining to the testimony of representatives of Groupe Everest ÉTATS FINANCIERS – SOCIÉTÉS DU GROUPE EVEREST VOLUME 1 DE 5	2005.04.18
P-342	Documents relatifs au témoignage des représentants de Groupe Everest / Documents pertaining to the testimony of representatives of Groupe Everest ÉTATS FINANCIERS – SOCIÉTÉS DU GROUPE EVEREST VOLUME 2 DE 5	2005.04.18
P-343	Documents relatifs au témoignage des représentants de Groupe Everest / Documents pertaining to the testimony of representatives of Groupe Everest ÉTATS FINANCIERS – SOCIÉTÉS DU GROUPE EVEREST VOLUME 3 DE 5	2005.04.18
P-343	ADDENDUM – VOLUME 3 DE 5 (Remplacer les pages P513 et P514)	2005.04.18
P-344	Documents relatifs au témoignage des représentants de Groupe Everest / Documents pertaining to the testimony of representatives of Groupe Everest ÉTATS FINANCIERS – SOCIÉTÉS DU GROUPE EVEREST VOLUME 4 DE 5	2005.04.18
P-345	Documents relatifs au témoignage des représentants de Groupe Everest / Documents pertaining to the testimony of representatives of Groupe Everest ÉTATS FINANCIERS – SOCIÉTÉS DU GROUPE EVEREST VOLUME 5 DE 5	2005.04.18
P-346	Documents relatifs au témoignage des représentants de Groupe Everest / Documents pertaining to the testimony of representatives of Groupe Everest TABLEAUX ET ANALYSES	2005.04.18
P-346	ADDENDUM – TABLEAUX ET ANALYSES (Remplace la page P134)	2005.04.18
P-346	ADDENDUM (remplaces les pages 52 à 64) Documents relatifs au témoignage des représentants de Groupe Everest / Documents pertaining to the testimony of representatives of Groupe Everest TABLEAUX ET ANALYSES	2005.04.20
P-347	Documents relatifs au témoignage des représentants de Groupe Everest / Documents pertaining to the testimony of representatives of Groupe Everest TABLEAUX ET ANALYSES (Supplément d'information) (Comparaison de montants inscrit au contrat avec ceux facturés)	2005.04.18
P-348	Documents relatifs au témoignage des représentants de Groupe Everest / Documents pertaining to the testimony of representatives of Groupe Everest DOSSIER GÉNÉRAL MEDIA I.D.A. VISION	2005.04.18
P-349	Documents relatifs au témoignage des représentants de Groupe Everest / Documents pertaining to the testimony of representatives of Groupe Everest MEDIA I.D.A. VISION TABLEAUX DES COMMANDITES ET COMMISSIONS REÇUES ET VERSÉES	2005.04.18
P-350	Documents relatifs au témoignage des représentants de Groupe Everest / Documents pertaining to the testimony of representatives of Groupe Everest DIVERSES ET AUTRES DOCUMENTS – CLAUDE BOULAY ET DIANE DESLAURIERS	2005.04.18

P-350	ADDENDUM (Insérer après la page P74) CORRESPONDANCES DIVERSES ET AUTRES DOCUMENTS (SUPPLÉMENT D'INFORMATION)	2005.04.19
P-350	ADDENDUM (insérer après la page P89) (pp. 90 à 104) Documents relatifs au témoignage des représentants de Groupe Everest / Documents pertaining to the testimony of representatives of Groupe Everest CORRESPONDANCES DIVERSES ET AUTRES DOCUMENTS (SUPPLÉMENT D'INFORMATION)	2005.04.21
P-351	Documents relatifs au témoignage des représentants de Groupe Everest / Documents pertaining to the testimony of representatives of Groupe Everest ITEMS PROMOTIONNELS – COMMUNICATIONS ART TELLIER INC.	2005.04.18
P-351 (a)	ADDENDUM (remplace pages P233 à P235A-P235K) (insérer après la page P258(P258A à P263A)	2005.04.18
P-351 (a)	ADDENDUM (Insérer après la page P263(a))	2005.04.25
P-352	Documents relatifs au témoignage des représentants de Groupe Everest / Documents pertaining to the testimony of representatives of Groupe Everest CONTRATS RÉFÉRENDAIRES	2005.04.18
P-353	Documents relatifs au témoignage des représentants de Groupe Everest / Documents pertaining to the testimony of representatives of Groupe Everest FÊTE DU CANADA – 1996	2005.04.18
P-354	Documents relatifs au témoignage des représentants de Groupe Everest / Documents pertaining to the testimony of representatives of Groupe Everest RIOPELLE	2005.04.18
P-355	Documents relatifs au témoignage des représentants de Groupe Everest / Documents pertaining to the testimony of representatives of Groupe Everest JEUX DU QUÉBEC	2005.04.18
P-356	ADDENDUM (insérer après la page P50) JEUX DU QUÉBEC.	2005.04.18
P-357	Documents relatifs au témoignage des représentants de Groupe Everest / Documents pertaining to the testimony of representatives of Groupe Everest SOCIÉTÉ DU PARC DES ILES	2005.04.25
P-357	ADDENDUM (Insérer après la page P250) (P251)	2005.04.25
P-357	ADDENDUM (Insérer après la page 18) (18A)	2005.04.18
P-358	Documents relatifs au témoignage des représentants de Groupe Everest / Documents pertaining to the testimony of representatives of Groupe Everest SOCIÉTÉ DES INTERNATIONAUX DU SPORT DE MONTRÉAL – VOLUME 1 DE 2	2005.04.18
P-358 (a)	Documents relatifs au témoignage des représentants de Groupe Everest / Documents pertaining to the testimony of representatives of Groupe Everest SOCIÉTÉ DES INTERNATIONAUX DU SPORT DE MONTRÉAL – VOLUME 2 DE 2	2005.04.18
P-359	Documents relatifs au témoignage des représentants de GROUPE EVEREST / Documents pertaining to the testimony of representatives of GROUPE EVEREST ORO COMMUNICATIONS INC.	2005.04.19
P-359	ADDENDUM (Insérer après la page P6)	2005.04.19
P-360	Documents relatifs au témoignnage des représentants de Groupe Everest / Documents pertaining to the testimony of representatives of Groupe Everest - CONTRAT EP043-0-0026 (ARTICLES PROMOTIONNELS)	2005.04.20
P-361	Mosaïcultures Internationales	2005.04.20
P-362	Documents relatifs au témoignage des représentants de Groupe Everest / Documents pertaining to the testimony of representatives of Groupe Everest DOSSIER GÉNÉRAL (SUPPLÉMENT D'INFORMATION)	2005.04.21
P-363	Documents relatifs au témoignage des représentants de Groupe Everest / Documents pertaining to the testimony of representatives of Groupe Everest DEBT PROGRAM (CONTRAT 60074-5-1404)	2005.04.21
P-364	Documents relatifs au témoignage des représentants de Groupe Everest / Documents pertaining to the testimony of representatives of Groupe Everest RETAIL CALIMERO PARTENARIAT	2005.04.21
P-364	ADDENDUM (Insérer après la page P-135)	2005.04.25
P-365	Documents relatifs au témoignage des représentants de Groupe Everest / Documents pertaining to the testimony of representatives of Groupe Everest TRADEWINDS/UNIVERS INC.	2005.04.25
P-366	Factures de Groupe Everest et Coffin Communication	2005.04.25
P-367	Lettre de Myra Conway de Travaux Publics en date du 25 avril 2005 Re :Demande de document #69 (Everest Estrie Publicité)	2005.04.26
P-381	Documents relatifs au témoignage des représentants du Parti Libéral du Canada (Québec) / Documents pertaining to the testimony of representatives of the Liberal Party of Canada(Québec) ÉTATS FINANCIERS	2005.05.04

Exhibit	Description	Date
P-382	Documents relatifs au témoignage des représentants du Parti Libéral du Canada (Québec) / Documents pertaining to the testimony of representatives of the Liberal Party of Canada (Québec) FACTURES DE PLURIDESIGN	2005.05.04
P-383	Documents au soutien du témoignage de GUY BISSON / Documents sustaining the testimony of GUY BISSON	2005.05.04
P-384	Documents au soutien du témoignage de JACQUES ROY / Documents sustaining to the testimony of JACQUES ROY	2005.05.04
P-385	Documents au soutien du témoignage de FRANCO IACONO / Documents sustaining to the testimony of FRANCO IACONO	2005.05.04
P-386	Documents au soutien du témoignage de THALIE TREMBLAY / Documents sustaining to the testimony of THALIE TREMBLAY	2005.05.04
P-387	Documents au soutien du témoignage de SERGE GOSSELIN / Documents sustaining to the testimony of SERGE GOSSELIN	2005.05.04
P-387	ADDENDUM (remplace la page P3) (insérer après la page P20) Documents au soutien du témoignage de SERGE GOSSELIN / ADDENDUM (replace page P3) (insert after page P20) Documents sustaining to the testimony of SERGE GOSSELIN	2005.05.04
P-387	ADDENDUM (Insérer après les pages P65 et P68)	2005.05.11
P-387	ADDENDUM (insérer après la page P70) (pp. 71 à 74)	2005.05.26
P-387 (a)	Documents concernant une note d'honoraires de Serge Gosselin datée du 28 janvier 2000 de $5,950, et autres documents, étude et compilation concernant la campagne électorale fédérale de 2000	2005.05.26
P-388	Originaux des documents concernant Le Parti Libéral du Canada	2005.05.04
P-388(a)	En liasse = 1- Parti libéral du Canada : Sa philosophie, son histoire et sa structure / 2- Le Parti libéral du Canada (Québec) Guide pratique des communications / 3- Guide des communi-cations – libéral / 4- Un avenir à partager : règles de procédures et règles d'élection, constitution et amendements (Congrès Biennal du Parti libéral du Canada (Québec) – Hull 26, 27, 28 novembre 1999) / 5- Un avenir à partager : cahier des résolutions (Congrès biennal du Parti Libéral du Canada(Québec) – Hull 26, 27, 28 novembre 1999) / 6- Bienvenue 2000 : Rapport sur les consultations populaires dans les régions du Québec	2005.05.04
P-389	Liste des factures émises par Groupe de Consultants Corbeil au Groupe Gosselin et Associés	2005.05.05
P-390	3 chèques – Serge Gosselin	2005.05.05
P-390	ADDENDUM (complète la pièce P-390) (P5 à P16)	2005.05.11
P-391	Registraire des entreprises Système CIDREQ – Groupe de Consultants Corbeil Inc.	2005.05.05
P-392	Documents au soutien du témoignage de Carolina Gallo-Laflèche / Documents sustaining the testimony of Carolina Gallo-Laflèche	2005.05.05
P-393 (a)	Documents relatifs au témoignage des représentants du Parti Libéral du Canada (Québec) / Documents pertaining to the testimony of representatives of the Liberal Party of Canada (Québec) ÉVÉNEMENTS ORGANISÉS PAR LE PARTI LIBÉRAL DU CANADA (QUÉBEC) – VOLUME 1 DE 2	2005.05.06
P-393 (b)	Documents relatifs au témoignage des représentants du Parti Libéral du Canada (Québec) / Documents pertaining to the testimony of representatives of the Liberal Party of Canada (Québec) ÉVÉNEMENTS ORGANISÉS PAR LE PARTI LIBÉRAL DU CANADA (QUÉBEC) – VOLUME 2 DE 2	2005.05.06
P-394	Documents relatifs au témoignage des représentants du Parti Libéral du Canada (Québec) / Documents pertaining to the testimony of representatives of the Liberal Party of Canada (Québec) COCKTAIL BÉNÉFICE – MONTRÉAL	2005.05.06
P-395	Documents relatifs au témoignage des représentants du Parti Libéral du Canada (Québec) / Documents pertaining to the testimony of representatives of the Liberal Party of Canada (Québec) RAPPORTS DES FIRMES DELOITTE ET PRICEWATERHOUSE COOPERS	2005.05.06
P-396	Documents relatifs au témoignage des représentants du Parti Libéral du Canada (Québec) / Documents pertaining to the testimony of representatives of the Liberal Party of Canada (Québec) TABLEAUX ET ANALYSES	2005.05.06
P-397	Documents relatifs au témoignage des représentants du Parti Libéral du Canada (Québec) / Documents pertaining to the testimony of representatives of the Liberal Party of Canada (Québec) BENOIT CORBEIL	2005.05.09
P-398	Documents relatifs au témoignage des représentants du Parti Libéral du Canada (Québec) / Documents pertaining to the testimony of representatives of the Liberal Party of Canada (Québec) BERYL WAJSMAN	2005.05.09
P-398	ADDENDUM (Insérer après la page P137) (P138)	2005.05.11
P-398	ADDENDUM (remplace p. P42 à 45 et insérer après la page P137)	2005.05.12
P-399	Notes manuscrites de M. Michel Béliveau	2005.05.09
P-400	Documents relatifs au témoignage des représentants du Parti Libéral du Canada (Québec) / Documents pertaining to the testimony of representatives of Liberal Party of Canada (Québec) MARC-YVAN CÔTÉ	2005.05.10
P-401	Documents relatifs au témoignage des représentants du Parti libéral du Canada (Québec) / Documents pertaining to the testimony of representatives of the Liberal Party of Canada (Québec) LES GESTIONS RICHARD B. BOUDREAULT	2005.05.11

P-402	Documents au soutien du témoignage de DANIEL DEZAINDE / Documents pertaining to the testimony of DANIEL DEZAINDE DOCUMENTS DIVERS	2005.05.11
P-403	Documents au soutien du témoignage de DANIEL DEZAINDE, Cahiers de notes 2001 et 2001-2002 / Documents pertaining to the testimony of DANIEL DEZAINDE, Notebook 2001 and 2001-2002	2005.05.11
P-403	ADDENDUM (Insérer avant la page 1) (i-ii) Documents au soutien du témoignage de DANIEL DEZAINDE, Cahiers de notes 2001 et 2001-2002 / Documents pertaining to the testimony of DANIEL DEZAINDE, Notebook 2001 and 2001-2002	2005.05.11
P-403 (a)	ADDENDUM (Corrections – Cahiers de notes - Pages manquantes) Documents au soutien du témoignage de DANIEL DEZAINDE, Cahiers de notes 2001 et 2001-2002 / Documents pertaining to the testimony of DANIEL DEZAINDE, Notebook 2001 and 2001-2002	2005.05.12
P-403 (b)	Nouvelle version d'extraits sélectionnés	2005.05.11
P-404	Documents relatifs au témoignage des représentants du Parti libéral du Canada (Québec) / Documents pertaining to the testimony of representatives of the Liberal Party of Canada (Québec) SUPPLÉMENT D'INFORMATION	2005.05.11
P-404	ADDENDUM (Insérer après la page P30) (P31 à P33)	2005.05.12
P-404	ADDENDUM (Insérer après la page P33) (P34 à P59) SUPPLÉMENT D'INFORMATION (CLUB DE GOLF DE VERCHÈRES)	2005.05.11
P-405	Constitutions du Parti liberal du Canada et du Parti libéral du Canada(Québec)	2005.05.11
P-406	Letter from Joanne Perry of ExecEspace (Montreal) Inc. dated November 23, 2001 Memorandum from Hélène L'Écuyer to Beryl Wajsmann dated November 23, 2001	2005.05.13
P-407 (a)	Bureau de la vérificatrice générale du Canada, documents concernant la publicité (chapitre 4) / Office of the Auditor General of Canada, supporting documents on Advertising (Chapter 4) VOLUME 1	2005.05.16
P-407 (b)	Bureau de la vérificatrice générale du Canada, documents concernant la publicité (chapitre 4) / Office of the Auditor General of Canada, supporting documents on Advertising (Chapter 4) VOLUME 2	2005.05.16
P-407 (b)	ADDENDUM (Insérer après la page P198) Supporting documents on advertising (Chapter 4) VOLUME 2	2005.05.16
P-407 (c)	Bureau de la vérificatrice générale du Canada, documents concernant la publicité (chapitre 4) / Office of the Auditor General of Canada, supporting documents on Advertising (Chapter 4) VOLUME 3	2005.05.16
P-407 (d)	Bureau de la vérificatrice générale du Canada, documents concernant la publicité (chapitre 4) / Office of the Auditor General of Canada, supporting documents on Advertising (Chapter 4) VOLUME 4	2005.05.16
P-407 (d)	ADDENDUM (Insérer après la page P156) VOLUME 4	2005.05.16
P-407 (e)	Documents concernant l'annonce le 25 octobre 1994 de la mise sur pied de la Commission cana-dienne du tourisme / Documents pertaining to the October 25, 1994, announcement of the esta-blishment of the Canadian Tourism Commission	2005.05.16
P-407 (e)	ADDENDUM (Insérer après les pages P13, P14 et P15) Documents concernant l'annonce le 25 octobre 1994 de la mise sur pied de la Commission canadienne du tourisme / Documents pertaining to the October 25, 1994 announcement of the esta-blishment of the Canadian Tourism Commission	2005.05.17
P-408	Advertising Management Renewal within the Government of Canada, Statement of Evidence prepared for the Commission of Inquiry into the Sponsorship Program and Advertising Activities Submitted by the Privy Council Office, Public Works and Government Services Canada and the Treasury Board of Canada Secretariat - MAY 2005 – English and French Versions.	2005.05.16
P-408 (a)	ERRATUM (remplacer la 2e partie de la deuxième phrase du paragraphe 16)	2005.05.17
P-409 (a-1)	Renouveau dans la gestion de la publicité au sein du Gouvernement du Canada, documentation reliée à l'énoncé de la preuve établie à l'intention de la commission d'enquête sur le programme de commandites et les activités publicitaires - Mai 2005 – VOLUME 1/2	2005.05.16
P-409 (a-2)	Renouveau dans la gestion de la publicité au sein du Gouvernement du Canada, documentation reliée à l'énoncé de la preuve établie à l'intention de la commission d'enquête sur le programme de commandites et les activités publicitaires - Mai 2005 – VOLUME 2/2	2005.05.16
P-409 (b-1)	Advertising Management Renewal within the Government of Canada background documentation to the statement of evidence prepared for the Commission of Inquiry into the Sponsorship Program and Advertising Activities - May, 2005 – VOLUME 1/2	2005.05.16
P-409 (b-2)	Advertising Management Renewal within the Government of Canada background documentation to the statement of evidence prepared for the Commission of Inquiry into the Sponsorship Program and Advertising Activities - May, 2005 – VOLUME 2/2	2005.05.16
P-410	Critères Obligatoires / Mandatory Requirements	2005.05.17
P-411	Statement of Evidence of JOHN HAYTER/ Déclaration de preuve de JOHN HAYTER	2005.05.18

Exhibit	Description	Date
P-412	Documents relatifs au témoignage des représentants de Vickers & Benson / Documents pertaining to the testimony of representatives of Vickers & Benson GENERAL FILE	2005.05.18
P-412	ADDENDUM (Remplace plusieurs pages) VICKERS & BENSON – GENERAL FILE	2005.05.18
P-412	ADDENDUM (Insérer après la page 256) (pp. 257 à 261) GENERAL FILE	2005.05.19
P-412	ADDENDUM (Remplace la page 210)	2005.05.25
P-412 (a)	Documents relatifs au témoignage des représentants de Vickers & Benson documents pertaining to the testimony of representatives of Vickers & Benson PURCHASE AGREEMENT	2005.05.19
P-413	Documents relatifs au témoignage des représentants de Vickers & Benson / Documents pertaining to the testimony of representatives of Vickers & Benson SELECTION PROCESSES	2005.05.18
P-414	Documents relatifs au témoignage des représentants de Vickers & Benson / Documents pertaining to the testimony of representatives of Vickers & Benson ORO COMMUNICATION INC. AND WALDING INTERNATIONAL INC.	2005.05.18
P-415	Documents relatifs au témoignage des représentants de Vickers & Benson / Documents pertaining to the testimony of representatives of Vickers & Benson CHINA SÉRIE – CONTRACT BRIEF – VOLUME 1	2005.05.18
P-415	ADDENDUM (Insérer après la page P9) (P9A à P9D) – CHINA SÉRIE – VOLUME 1	2005.05.18
P-415 (a)	Documents relatifs au témoignage des représentants de Vickers & Benson / Documents pertaining to the testimony of representatives of Vickers & Benson CHINA SÉRIE – VOLUME 2	2005.05.18
P-415 (b)	Documents relatifs au témoignage des représentants de Vickers & Benson / Documents pertaining to the testimony of representatives of Vickers & Benson CHINA SÉRIE – VOLUME 3	2005.05.18
P-416 (a)	Summary of Agency Selection Competitions VOLUME 1/2	2005.05.18
P-416 (b)	Summary of Agency Selection Competitions VOLUME 2/2	2005.05.18
P-417	Documents relatifs au témoignage des représentants de Vickers & Benson / Documents pertaining to the testimony of representatives of Vickers & Benson GENESIS	2005.05.18
P-418	DÉCLARATION DE LA PREUVE YVES GOUGOUX ET JOHN PARISELLA STATEMENT OF EVIDENCE YVES GOUGOUX AND JOHN PARISELLA	2005.05.19
P-419 (a)	Dossier général – Volume 1 de 2	2005.05.19
P-419 (b)	Dossier général – Volume 2 de 2	2005.05.19
P-420	Documents relatifs au témoignage des représen-tants de BCP LTÉE / Documents pertaining to the testimony of representatives of BCP LTD. CONTRATS PRÉRÉFÉRENDAIRES (EN77105-0032 et EN771-5-U100)	2005.05.19
P-421	Documents relatifs au témoignage des représentants de BCP LTÉE / Documents pertaining to the testimony of representatives of BCP LTD. OPTION CANADA – CONTRAT DE PUBLICITÉ	2005.05.19
P-422	Documents relatifs au témoignage des représentants de BCP LTÉE / Documents pertaining to the testimony of representatives of BCP LTD. CONTRATS DE PUBLICITÉ PARTI LIBÉRAL CAMPAGNES ÉLECTORALES – 1997 ET 2000	2005.05.19
P-423	Documents relatifs au témoignage des représentants de BCP LTÉE / Documents pertaining to the testimony of representatives of BCP LTD. AUTRES CONTRATS DE COMMANDITES - EN771-5-U205 - EN771-6-0186 - EN771-7-0092 - EN771-8-0030	2005.05.19
P-424	Documents relatifs au témoignage des représentants de BCP LTÉE / Documents pertaining to the testimony of representatives of BCP LTD. TOURISME CANADA CONTRATS DE PUBLICITÉ	2005.05.19
P-424	ADDENDUM (Insérer après la page P4) (P4A à P4K) Documents relatifs au témoignage des représentants de BCP LTÉE / Documents pertaining to the testimony of representatives of BCP LTD TOURISME CANADA – CONTRATS DE PUBLICITÉ	2005.05.19
P-424	ADDENDA(insérer après la page P93) (93A à 93UU)	2005.05.31
P-424 (a)	En Liasse - Deux communiqués de BCP	2005.05.31
P-425	Documents relatifs au témoignage des représentants de BCP LTÉE / Documents pertaining to the testimony of representatives of BCP LTD. SANTÉ CANADA – CONTRATS DE PUBLICITÉ	2005.05.19

P-426	Documents relatifs au témoignage des représentants de BCP LTÉE / Documents pertaining to the testimony of representatives of BCP LTD. CONTRATS DE PUBLICITÉ AVEC LA SOCIÉTÉ CANADIENNE DES POSTES	2005.05.19
P-427	Documents relatifs au témoignage des représentants de BCP LTÉE / Documents pertaining to the testimony of representatives of BCP LTD. CONTRATS DE PUBLICITÉ AVEC LA BDC	2005.05.19
P-428 (a)	The Commission of Inquiry into the Sponsorship Program and Advertising Activities - KROLL LINDQUIST AVEY REPORT - May 18, 2005 – English	2005.05.24
P-428 (a)	ADDENDUM (replace various pages) (pp. 13-25-29-37-68)	2005.05.24
P-428 (b)	The Commission of Inquiry into the Sponsorship Program and Advertising Activities - Schedules to be read with the - KROLL LINDQUIST AVEY REPORT dated May 18, 2005 – VOLUME 1 OF 3	2005.05.24
P-428 (c)	Schedules to be read with the KROLL LINDQUIST AVEY REPORT dated May 18, 2005 - VOLUME 2 OF 3	2005.05.24
P-428 (c)	ADDENDUM (Remplace la page P337)	2005.05.24
P-428 (d)	Schedules to be read with the KROLL LINDQUIST AVEY REPORT dated May 18, 2005 - VOLUME 3 OF 3	2005.05.24
P-428 (d)	ADDENDUM (Remplace la page P341)	2005.05.24
P-429 (a)	RAPPORT KROLL – VERSION FRANÇAISE	2005.05.27
P-429 (b)	Commission d'enquête sur le programme de commandites et les activités publicitaires - Tableaux devant être lus en conjonction avec le rapport Kroll du 18 mai 2005 - Volume 1 de 3	2005.05.27
P-429 (c)	Commission d'enquête sur le programme de commandites et les activités publicitaires - Tableaux devant être lus en conjonction avec le rapport Kroll du 18 mai 2005 - Volume 2 de 3	2005.05.27
P-429 (d)	Commission d'enquête sur le programme de commandites et les activités publicitaires - Tableaux devant être lus en conjonction avec le rapport Kroll du 18 mai 2005 - Volume 3 de 3	2005.05.27
P-430 (a)	Kroll Lindquist Avey Report Presentation - May 24, 2005 - CD-ROM	2005.05.24
P-430 (b)	Présentation du rapport Kroll Lindquist Avey – 24 mai 2005 – CD-ROM	2005.05.24
P-431 (a)	Kroll – Summary of Financial Statements by agency – CD ROM	2005.05.24
P-431 (b)	Kroll – Sommaire des états financiers par agence – CD ROM	2005.05.24
P-432 (a)	Production Analysis Working Papers Volume 1 – Lafleur Communication Marketing	2005.05.24
P-432 (b)	Production Analysis Working Papers Volume 2 – Groupaction Marketing Inc.	2005.05.24
P-432 (c)	Production Analysis Working Papers Volume 3 – Groupaction/Gosselin Communications Stratégiques	2005.05.24
P-432 (d)	Production Analysis Working Papers Volume 4 – Compass	2005.05.24
P-432 (e)	Production Analysis Working Papers Volume 5 – Gosselin	2005.05.24
P-432 (f)	Production Analysis Working Papers Volume 6 – Groupe Everest	2005.05.24
P-432 (g)	Production Analysis Working Papers Volume 7 – Vickers & Benson	2005.05.24
P-432 (h)	Production Analysis Working Papers Volume 8 – Communication Coffin	2005.05.24
P-432 (i)	Production Analysis Working Papers Volume 9 – BCP Group	2005.05.24
P-432 (j)	Production Analysis Working Papers Volume 10 – Palmer Jarvis Communications	2005.05.24
P-433 (a)	Advertising Analysis Working Papers Volume 1 – BCP Group	2005.05.24
P-433 (b)	Advertising Analysis Working Papers Volume 2 – Compass	2005.05.24
P-433 (c)	Advertising Analysis Working Papers Volume 3 – Groupe Everest	2005.05.24
P-433 (d)	Advertising Analysis Working Papers Volume 4 – Gosselin	2005.05.24
P-433 (e)	Advertising Analysis Working Papers Volume 5 – Communication Coffin	2005.05.24
P-433 (f)	Advertising Analysis Working Papers Volume 6 – Groupaction Marketing Inc.	2005.05.24
P-433 (g)	Advertising Analysis Working Papers Volume 7 – Groupaction/Gosselin Communications Stratégiques	2005.05.24
P-433 (h)	Advertising Analysis Working Papers Volume 8 – Lafleur Communications Marketing	2005.05.24
P-433 (i)	Advertising Analysis Working Papers Volume 9 – Vickers & Benson	2005.05.24
P-433 (j)	Advertising Analysis Working Papers Volume 10 – The Gingko Group LTD.	2005.05.24

P-433 (k)	Advertising Analysis Working Papers Volume 11 – Ensemble Consortium	2005.05.24
P-433 (l)	Advertising Analysis Working Papers Volume 12 – Armada Agence de Publicité Inc.	2005.05.24
P-434 (a)	Documents supportant le témoignage de Kroll / Documents supporting the testimony of Kroll – Special programs and Sponsorship Contracts – Source of funds / Programmes Spréciaux et commandites – Sources des Fonds – Volume 1 of 4	2005.05.24
P-434 (b)	Documents supportant le témoignage de Kroll / Documents supporting the testimony of Kroll – Special programs and Sponsorship Contracts – Source of funds / Programmes Spréciaux et commandites – Sources des Fonds – Volume 2 of 4	2005.05.24
P-434 (c)	Documents supportant le témoignage de Kroll / Documents supporting the testimony of Kroll – Special programs and Sponsorship Contracts – Source of funds / Programmes Spréciaux et commandites – Sources des Fonds – Volume 3 of 4	2005.05.24
P-434 (d)	Documents supportant le témoignage de Kroll / Documents supporting the testimony of Kroll – Special programs and Sponsorship Contracts – Source of funds / Programmes Spréciaux et commandites – Sources des Fonds – Volume 4 of 4	2005.05.24
P-435	Documents supportant le témoignage de Kroll / Documents supporting the testimony of Kroll – Additionnal documents – Documents additionnels	2005.05.24
P-436 (a)	Lafleur Communication Marketing – Analysis of Production Invoices for 1996-1997 Contracts – Binder 1 of 3	2005.05.24
P-436 (b)	Lafleur Communication Marketing – Analysis of Production Invoices for 1996-1997 Contracts – Binder 2 of 3	2005.05.24
P-436 (c)	Lafleur Communication Marketing – Analysis of Production Invoices for 1996-1997 Contracts – Binder 3 of 3	2005.05.24
P-436 (d)	Lafleur Communication Marketing – Analysis of Production Invoices for 1997-1998 Contracts – Binder 1 of 3	2005.05.24
P-436 (e)	Lafleur Communication Marketing – Analysis of Production Invoices for 1997-1998 Contracts – Binder 2 of 3	2005.05.24
P-436 (f)	Lafleur Communication Marketing – Analysis of Production Invoices for 1997-1998 Contracts – Binder 3 of 3	2005.05.24
P-436 (g)	Lafleur Communication Marketing – Analysis of Production Invoices for 1998-1999 Contracts – Binder 1 of 2	2005.05.24
P-436 (h)	Lafleur Communication Marketing – Analysis of Production Invoices for 1998-1999 Contracts – Binder 2 of 2	2005.05.24
P-436 (i)	Lafleur Communication Marketing – Analysis of Production Invoices for 1999-2000 Contracts – Binder 1 of 1	2005.05.24
P-436 (j)	Lafleur Communication Marketing Analysis of Production Invoices for 2000-2001 Contracts – Binder 1 of 4	2005.05.24
P-436 (k)	Lafleur Communication Marketing Analysis of Production Invoices for 2000-2001 Contracts – Binder 2 of 4	2005.05.24
P-436 (l)	Lafleur Communication Marketing Analysis of Production Invoices for 2000-2001 Contracts – Binder 3 of 4	2005.05.24
P-436 (m)	Lafleur Communication Marketing Analysis of Production Invoices for 2000-2001 Contracts – Binder 4 of 4	2005.05.24
P-437 (a)	Gosselin Communications – Analysis of Production invoices for 1994-1995, 1995-1996, 1996-1997, 1997-1998 Contracts - Binder 1 of 2	2005.05.24
P-437 (b)	Gosselin Communications – Analysis of Production invoices for 1994-1995, 1995-1996, 1996-1997, 1997-1998 Contracts - Binder 2 of 2	2005.05.24
P-437 (c)	Gosselin Communications – Analysis of Produc-tion invoices for 1998-1999 contracts – Binder 1 of 6	2005.05.24
P-437 (d)	Gosselin Communications – Analysis of Produc-tion invoices for 1998-1999 contracts - Binder 2 of 6	2005.05.24
P-437 (e)	Gosselin Communications – Analysis of Produc-tion invoices for 1998-1999 contracts - Binder 3 of 6	2005.05.24
P-437 (f)	Gosselin Communications – Analysis of Produc-tion invoices for 1998-1999 contracts - Binder 4 of 6	2005.05.24
P-437 (g)	Gosselin Communications – Analysis of Produc-tion invoices for 1998-1999 contracts - Binder 5 of 6	2005.05.24
P-437 (h)	Gosselin Communications – Analysis of Produc-tion invoices for 1998-1999 contracts - Binder 6 of 6	2005.05.24
P-438 (a)	Groupaction Marketing – Analysis of Production invoices for 1997-1998 contracts – Binder 1 of 1	2005.05.24
P-438 (b)	Groupaction Marketing – Analysis of Production invoices for 1998-1999 contracts– Binder 1 of 1	2005.05.24
P-438 (c)	Groupaction Marketing – Analysis of Production invoices for 1999-2000 contracts – Binder 1 of 2	2005.05.24
P-438 (d)	Groupaction Marketing – Analysis of Production invoices for 1999-2000 contracts – Binder 2 of 2	2005.05.24
P-438 (e)	Groupaction Marketing – Analysis of Production invoices for 2000-2001 & 2001-2002 contracts - Binder 1 of 2	2005.05.24
P-438 (f)	Groupaction Marketing – Analysis of Production invoices for 2000-2001 & 2001-2002 contracts - Binder 2 of 2	2005.05.24
P-439 (a)	Groupaction/Gosselin Communications - Analysis of production invoices for 1998-1999 contracts – binder 1 of 3	2005.05.24
P-439 (b)	Groupaction/Gosselin Communications - Analysis of production invoices for 1998-1999 contracts – binder 2 of 3	2005.05.24
P-439 (c)	Groupaction/Gosselin Communications - Analysis of production invoices for 1998-1999 contracts – binder 3 of 3	2005.05.24
P-439 (d)	Groupaction/Gosselin Communications - Analysis of production invoices for 1999-2000 contracts – binder 1 of 8	2005.05.24
P-439 (e)	Groupaction/Gosselin Communications - Analysis of production invoices for 1999-2000 contracts – binder 2 of 8	2005.05.24
P-439 (f)	Groupaction/Gosselin Communications - Analysis of production invoices for 1999-2000 contracts – binder 3 of 8	2005.05.24

P-439 (g)	Groupaction/Gosselin Communications - Analysis of production invoices for 1999-2000 contracts – binder 4 of 8	2005.05.24
P-439 (h)	Groupaction/Gosselin Communications - Analysis of production invoices for 1999-2000 contracts – binder 5 of 8	2005.05.24
P-439 (i)	Groupaction/Gosselin Communications - Analysis of production invoices for 1999-2000 contracts – binder 6 of 8	2005.05.24
P-439 (j)	Groupaction/Gosselin Communications - Analysis of production invoices for 1999-2000 contracts – binder 7 of 8	2005.05.24
P-439 (k)	Groupaction/Gosselin Communications - Analysis of production invoices for 1999-2000 contracts – binder 8 of 8	2005.05.24
P-439 (l)	Groupaction/Gosselin Communications - Analysis of production invoices for 2000-2001 contracts – binder 1 of 7	2005.05.24
P-439 (m)	Groupaction/Gosselin Communications - Analysis of production invoices for 2000-2001 contracts – binder 2 of 7	2005.05.24
P-439 (n)	Groupaction/Gosselin Communications - Analysis of production invoices for 2000-2001 contracts – binder 3 of 7	2005.05.24
P-439 (o)	Groupaction/Gosselin Communications - Analysis of production invoices for 2000-2001 contracts – binder 4 of 7	2005.05.24
P-439 (p)	Groupaction/Gosselin Communications - Analysis of production invoices for 2000-2001 contracts – binder 5 of 7	2005.05.24
P-439 (q)	Groupaction/Gosselin Communications - Analysis of production invoices for 2000-2001 contracts – binder 6 of 7	2005.05.24
P-439 (r)	Groupaction/Gosselin Communications - Analysis of production invoices for 2000-2001 contracts – binder 7 of 7	2005.05.24
P-440 (a)	Groupe Everest – Analysis of Production Invoices for 1996-1997 contracts - Binder 1 of 1	2005.05.24
P-440 (b)	Groupe Everest – Analysis of Production Invoices for 1997-1998 contracts - Binder 1 of 3	2005.05.24
P-440 (c)	Groupe Everest – Analysis of Production Invoices for 1997-1998 contracts - Binder 2 of 3	2005.05.24
P-440 (d)	Groupe Everest – Analysis of Production Invoices for 1997-1998 contracts - Binder 3 of 3	2005.05.24
P-440 (e)	Groupe Everest – Analysis of Production Invoices for 1998-1999 contracts - Binder 1 of 3	2005.05.24
P-440 (f)	Groupe Everest – Analysis of Production Invoices for 1998-1999 contracts - Binder 2 of 3	2005.05.24
P-440 (g)	Groupe Everest – Analysis of Production Invoices for 1998-1999 contracts - Binder 3 of 3	2005.05.24
P-440 (h)	Groupe Everest – Analysis of Production Invoices for 1999-2000 contracts - Binder 1 of 3	2005.05.24
P-440 (i)	Groupe Everest – Analysis of Production Invoices for 1999-2000 contracts - Binder 2 of 3	2005.05.24
P-440 (j)	Groupe Everest – Analysis of Production Invoices for 1999-2000 contracts - Binder 3 of 3	2005.05.24
P-440 (k)	Groupe Everest – Analysis of Production Invoices for 2000-2001 contracts - Binder 1 of 4	2005.05.24
P-440 (l)	Groupe Everest – Analysis of Production Invoices for 2000-2001 contracts - Binder 2 of 4	2005.05.24
P-440 (m)	Groupe Everest – Analysis of Production Invoices for 2000-2001 contracts - Binder 3 of 4	2005.05.24
P-440 (n)	Groupe Everest – Analysis of Production Invoices for 2000-2001 contracts - Binder 4 of 4	2005.05.24
P-441 (a)	Communication Coffin – Analysis of Production invoices for 1997-1998 Contracts – Binder 1 of 1	2005.05.24
P-441 (b)	Communication Coffin – Analysis of Production Invoices for 1998-1999 Contracts – Binder 1 of 1	2005.05.24
P-441 (c)	Communication Coffin – Analysis of Production Invoices for 1999-2000 Contracts – Binder 1 of 1	2005.05.24
P-441 (d)	Communication Coffin – Analysis of Production invoices for 2000-2001, 2001-2002 contracts – Binder 1 of 3	2005.05.24
P-441 (e)	Communication Coffin – Analysis of Production invoices for 2000-2001, 2001-2002 contracts – Binder 2 of 3	2005.05.24
P-441 (f)	Communication Coffin – Analysis of Production invoices for 2000-2001, 2001-2002 contracts – Binder 3 of 3	2005.05.24
P-442	Vickers & Benson – Analysis of production of invoices for 1996-1997, 1997-1998, 1998-1999, 1999- 2000 contracts – Binder 1 of 1	2005.05.24
P-443	Groupe BCP – Analysis of Production Invoices for 1997-1998 and 1998-1999 Contracts – Binder 1 of 1	2005.05.24
P-444	Palmer Jarvis Communications – Analysis of Production Invoices for contracts years 1996-1997 and 1997-1998 – Binder 1 of 1	2005.05.24
P-445 (a)	Compass Communications Inc. – Analysis of production invoices for 1997-1998 Contracts – Volume 1 of 1	2005.05.24
P-445 (b)	Compass Communications Inc. – Analysis of production invoices for 1998-1999 Contracts – Volume 1 of 3	2005.05.24
P-445 (c)	Compass Communications Inc. – Analysis of production invoices for 1998-1999 Contracts – Volume 2 of 3	2005.05.24
P-445 (d)	Compass Communications Inc. – Analysis of production invoices for 1998-1999 Contracts – Volume 3 of 3	2005.05.24
P-445 (e)	Compass Communications Inc. – Analysis of production invoices for 1999-2000 Contracts – Volume 1 of 6	2005.05.24
P-445 (f)	Compass Communications Inc. – Analysis of production invoices for 1999-2000 Contracts – Volume 2 of 6	2005.05.24
P-445 (g)	Compass Communications Inc. – Analysis of production invoices for 1999-2000 Contracts – Volume 3 of 6	2005.05.24
P-445 (h)	Compass Communications Inc. – Analysis of production invoices for 1999-2000 Contracts – Volume 4 of 6	2005.05.24
P-445 (i)	Compass Communications Inc. – Analysis of production invoices for 1999-2000 Contracts – Volume 5 of 6	2005.05.24

P-445 (j)	Compass Communications Inc. – Analysis of production invoices for 1999-2000 Contracts – Volume 6 of 6	2005.05.24
P-446	Lafleur Communication – Analysis of Invoices for 1997-1998 Advertising Contracts – Health Canada – Volume 1/1 / Analyse des factures de 1997-1998 pour les contrats de publicité – Santé Canada – Volume 1/1	2005.05.24
P-447	Gosselin Communications Stratégiques – Analysis of invoices for 1997-1998 Advertising contracts – Industry Canada – Volume 1/1 / Analyse des factures de 1997-1998 pour les contrats de publicité – Industrie Canada – Volume 1/1	2005.05.24
P-448 (a)	Groupaction – Analysis of invoices for 1999-2000 Advertising Contracts – PWGSC- Volume 1/1 / Analyse des factures de 1999-2000 pour les contrats de publicité - TPSCG – Volume 1/1	2005.05.24
P-448 (b)	Groupaction – Analysis of Invoices for 1999-2000 advertising contracts – Canada Firearms Center, Justice Canada – Volume 1/2 / Analyse des factures de 1999-2000 Pour les contrats de publicité – Centre Armes à feu Canada, Ministère de la Justice Canada – Volume 1/2	2005.05.24
P-448 (c)	Groupaction – Analysis of Invoices for 1999-2000 advertising contracts – Canada Firearms Center, Justice Canada – Volume 2/2 / Analyse des factures de 1999-2000 Pour les contrats de publicité – Centre Armes à feu Canada, Ministère de la Justice Canada – Volume 2/2	2005.05.24
P-448 (d)	Groupaction – Analysis of invoices for 2000-2001 Advertising Contracts – PWGSC – Volume 1/1 / Analyse des factures de 2000-2001 pour les contrats de publicité - TPSCG – Volume 1/1	2005.05.24
P-448 (e)	Groupaction – Analysis of invoices for 2000-2001 Advertising Contracts – PWGSC/CIO - Volume 1/2 / Analyse des factures de 1999-2000 pour les contrats de publicité - TPSCG/BIC – Volume 1/2	2005.05.24
P-448 (f)	Groupaction – Analysis of invoices for 2000-2001 Advertising Contracts – PWGSC/CIO - Volume 2/2 / Analyse des factures de 1999-2000 pour les contrats de publicité - TPSCG/BIC – Volume 2/2	2005.05.24
P-448 (g)	Groupaction Marketing – Analysis of Invoices for Advertising Contracts Volume 1/7 / Analyse des factures pour les contrats de publicité Volume 1/7	2005.05.24
P-448 (h)	Groupaction Marketing – Analysis of Invoices for Advertising Contracts Volume 2/7 / Analyse des factures pour les contrats de publicité Volume 2/7	2005.05.24
P-448 (i)	Groupaction Marketing – Analysis of Invoices for Advertising Contracts Volume 3/7 / Analyse des factures pour les contrats de publicité Volume 3/7	2005.05.24
P-448 (j)	Groupaction Marketing – Analysis of Invoices for Advertising Contracts Volume 4/7 / Analyse des factures pour les contrats de publicité Volume 4/7	2005.05.24
P-448 (k)	Groupaction Marketing – Analysis of Invoices for Advertising Contracts Volume 5/7 / Analyse des factures pour les contrats de publicité Volume 5/7	2005.05.24
P-448 (l)	Groupaction Marketing – Analysis of Invoices for Advertising Contracts Volume 6/7 / Analyse des factures pour les contrats de publicité Volume 6/7	2005.05.24
P-448 (m)	Groupaction Marketing – Analysis of Invoices for Advertising Contracts Volume 7/7 / Analyse des factures pour les contrats de publicité Volume 7/7	2005.05.24
P-449	Groupaction/Gosselin – Analysis of Invoices for 1999-2000 & 2000-2001 Advertising Contracts – PWGSC – Volume 1/1 / Analyse des factures de 1999-2000 et 2000-2001 pour les contrats de publicité - TPSGC – Volume 1/1	2005.05.24
P-450 (a)	Groupe Everest – Analysis of Invoices for 1996-1997 Advertising Contracts – Federal Office of regional Development(Québec) - Volume 1/1 / Analyse des factures de 1996-1997 pour les contrats de publicité - Bureau federal de développement Regional (Québec) – Volume 1/1	2005.05.24
P-450 (b)	Groupe Everest – Analysis of Invoices for 2000-2001 Advertising contracts – CIO - Volume 1/1 / Analyse des factures de 2000-2001 pour des contrats de publicité - BIC – Volume 1/1	2005.05.24
P-451	Coffin Communication – Analysis of Invoices for 1999-2000 & 2000-2001 Advertising Contracts – PWGSC/CIO – Volume 1/1 / Analyse des factures de 1999-2000 & 2000-2001 pour les contrats de publicité - TPSGC/BIC – Volume 1/1	2005.05.24
P-452 (a)	Vickers & Benson – Analysis of Invoices for 1996-1997 Advertising contracts – Canada Tourism Commission – Volume 1/1 / Analyse des factures de 1996-1997 pour les Contrats de publicité – Commission Canadienne de Tourisme – Volume 1/1	2005.05.24
P-452 (b)	Vickers & Benson – Analysis of Invoices for 1997-1998 Advertising contracts – Canada Tourism Commission – Volume 1/1 / Analyse des factures de 1997-1998 pour les Contrats de publicité – Com-mission Canadienne de Tourisme – Volume 1/1	2005.05.24
P-452 (c)	Vickers & Benson – Analysis of Invoices for 1997-1998 Advertising contracts – Department of Finance Canada – Volume 1/2 / Analyse des factures de 1997-1998 pour les Contrats de publicité – Commission Canadienne de Tourisme – Volume 1/2	2005.05.24
P-452 (d)	Vickers & Benson – Analysis of Invoices for 1997-1998 Advertising contracts – Department of Finance Canada – Volume 2/2 / Analyse des factures de 1997-1998 pour les Contrats de publicité – Commission Canadienne de Tourisme – Volume 2/2	2005.05.24
P-452 (e)	Vickers & Benson – Analysis of Invoices for 1998-1999 & 1999-2000 Advertising contracts – Human Resources Development Canada – Volume 1/1 / Analyse des factures de 1998-1999 & 1999-2000 pour les Contrats de publicité – Ministère du développement des ressources humaines Canada – Volume 1/1	2005.05.24
P-453 (a)	BCP Analysis of Invoices for 1996-1997 Advertising contracts – Canada Tourism Commission – Volume 1/1 / Analyse des factures de 1996-1997 pour les contrats de publicité – Commission canadienne de Tourisme – Volume 1/1	2005.05.24

P-453 (b)	BCP Analysis of Invoices for 1997-1998 Advertising Contracts – Heritage Canada - Volume 1/1 / Analyse des factures 1997-1998 pour les contrats de publicité - Patrimoine Canadien – Volume 1/1	2005.05.24
P-453 (c)	BCP Analysis of Invoices for 2001-2002 Advertising Contracts – Health Canada - Volume 1/1 / Analyse des factures 2001-2002 pour les contrats de publicité - Santé Canada – Volume 1/1	2005.05.24
P-454 (a)	Compass Communications – Analysis of Invoices for 1997-1998 & 1998-1999 Advertising Contracts – Revenue Canada - Volume 1/1 / Analyse des factures de 1997-1998 & 1998-1999 pour les contrats de publicité – Agence du revenu du Canada - Volume 1/1	2005.05.24
P-454 (b)	Compass Communications – Analysis of Invoices for 2001-2002 Advertising Contracts - PWGSC – Volume 1/1 / Analyse des factures de 2001-2002 pour les contrats de publicité - TPSGC – Volume 1/1	2005.05.24
P-455 (a)	Armada Advertising – Analysis of Invoices for 2001-2002 advertising contracts – CIO - Volume 1/1 / Analyse des factures 2001-2002 pour les contrats de publicité BIC – Volume 1/1	2005.05.24
P-455 (b)	Armada Advertising – Analysis of Invoices for 2001-2002 Advertising Contracts - Economic Develop-ment Canada – Volume 1/2 Analyse des factures de 2001-2002 pour les contrats de publicité – Développement Économique Canada – Volume 1/2	2005.05.24
P-455 (c)	Armada Advertising – Analysis of Invoices for 2001-2002 Advertising Contracts - Economic Develop-ment Canada – Volume 2/2 / Analyse des factures de 2001-2002 pour les contrats de publicité – Développement Économique Canada – Volume 2/2	2005.05.24
P-456	Ensemble Consortium – Analysis of Invoices 2001-2002 Advertising Contracts – CIO - Volume 1/1 / Analyse des factures de 2001-2002 pour les contrats de publicité - BIC – Volume 1/1	2005.05.24
P-457	The Gingko Group Ltd. – Analysis of Invoices for 1998-1999 Advertising Contracts – Industry Canada – Volume 1/1 / Analyse des factures de 1998-1999 pour les contrats de publicité – Industrie Canada – Volume 1/1	2005.05.24
P-458	Documents relatifs au témoignage des représentants de Gosselin Communications Stratégiques / Documents pertaining to the testimony of representatives of Gosselin Communications Stratégiques - AFFIDAVIT CIRCONSTANCIÉ DE GILLES-ANDRÉ GOSSELIN	2005.05.25
P-459	Lettre de Me Valier Boivin de Boivin O'Neil datée du 24 mai 2005 à M. Pierre St-Laurent re BCP Ltée	2005.05.25
P-460	Documents au soutien du témoignage de GAETANO MANGANIELLO / Documents pertaining to the testimony of GAETANO MANGANIELLO	2005.05.25
P-461	Documents concernant la faillite de 9004-8612 Québec Inc. / Documents pertaining to the bankruptcy of 9004-8612 Québec Inc.	2005.05.26
P-462	Documents au soutien du témoignage de GIUSEPPE MORSELLI / Documents pertaining to the testimony of GIUSEPPE MORSELLI	2005.05.26
P-463	Documents relatifs au témoignage des représentants de PLURI DESIGN CANADA INC. / Documents pertaining to the testimony of representatives of PLURI DESIGN CANADA INC. extrait sélectionné du registre des salaires de Pluri Design Canada	2005.05.27
P-463	ADDENDUM (remplace la page P2) Documents relatifs au témoignage des représentants de PLURI DESIGN CANADA INC. / Documents pertaining to the testimony of representatives of PLURI DESIGN CANADA INC. - Extrait sélectionné du registre des salaires de Pluri Design Canada	2005.05.30
P-464	Documents au soutien du témoignage de FRANÇOISE PATRY / Documents sustaining the testimony of FRANÇOISE PATRY	2005.05.30
P-465	7 Volumes provenant du Secrétariat du Conseil du Trésor (bilingues) (sauf pour l'année 1995) et concernant les lignes directives à l'intention des cabinets des ministres pour les années 1992, 1993, 1995, 1997, 2001, 2003, 2004.	2005.05.31
P-466	Documents relatifs au témoignage des représentants de BCP Ltée / Documents pertaining to the testimony of representatives of BCP ltd – Dossier General – Supplément d'information	2005.05.31
P-467 (a)	Réflexions personnelles sur des listes de réformes possibles par John Parisella – mai 2005	2005.05.31
P-467 (b)	Version anglaise de P-467(a) (7 pages) Intitulé 'Some personal thoughts for potential change' by John Parisella - May 2005	2005.05.31
P-468	Affidavit – Claire Brouillet	2005.05.31
P-468 (a)	Documents au soutien du témoignage de Claire Brouillet / Documents pertaining to the testimony of Claire Brouillet	2005.05.31
P-469	Affidavit de Carolina Gallo-Laflèche	2005.05.31
P-470	Affidavit – Monique Thomas	2005.05.31
P-471	Affidavit – Micheline Montreuil	2005.05.31
P-472	Affidavit – Daniel Carrier	2005.05.31
P-473 (a)	Issues List – Version Anglaise	2005.06.02
P-473 (b)	Liste des Questions à Examiner - version française	2005.06.02
P-474 (a)	Représentations écrites par Malcom Media Inc. et Luc Lemay	2005.06.13

P-474 (b)	Représentations écrites de Jacques Corriveau et PluriDesign Canada Inc.	2005.06.13
P-474 (c)	Représentations écrites de BCP	2005.06.14
P-474 (d)	Argumentation écrite soumise par l'honorable André Ouellet	2005.06.14
P-474 (e)	Written representations of Canada Post Corporation	2005.06.14
P-474 (f)	Written submissions VIA RAIL CANADA INC.	2005.06.14
P-474 (g)	Représentations de Monsieur Marc Lefrançois	2005.06.14
P-474 (h)	Written representations of the Business Development Bank of Canada	2005.06.14
P-474 (i)	Représentations écrites – Association des Agences de Publicité du Québec	2005.06.14
P-474 (j)	Présentation sur la phase 1A de l'enquête par L'Agent de l'intégrité de la Fonction publique - M. Edvard Keyserlingk, Ph.D / Submission on Phase 1A of the Inquiry by Public Service Integrity Officer - Dr. Edward Keyserlingk	2005.06.15
P-474 (k)	Représentations du Bloc Québécois	2005.06.15
P-474 (l)	Written submissions – The Conservative Party of Canada / Présentation écrite du Parti Conservateur du Canada	2005.06.15
P-474 (m)	Mémoire du Parti Libéral du Canada et du Parti libéral du Canada (Québec) amendé	2005.06.15
P-474 (n)	Written submissions on behalf of Charles Guité	2005.06.15
P-474 (o)	Written representations of Mr. Ranald Quail	2005.06.15
P-474 (p)	Représentations de l'honorable Alfonso Gagliano	2005.06.15
P-474 (q)	Submissions ERNST & YOUNG LLP	2005.06.16
P-474 (r)	Représentations écrites au nom de M. Jean Carle	2005.06.16
P-474 (s)	Représentations écrites de Jean Pelletier	2005.06.16
P-474 (t)	Written representations of the Right Honourable Jean Chrétien	2005.06.16
P-474 (u)	Submissions of the Office of the Auditor General / Argumentation du Bureau du Vérificateur général du Canada	2005.06.16
P-474 (v)	Written submissions by Mr. Stewart Bacon	2005.06.17
P-474 (w)	Représentations révisées de M. Jean-Marc Bard	2005.06.17
P-474 (x)	Représentations de Mme Christiane Beaulieu	2005.06.17
P-474 (y)	Représentation écrite de M. Michel Béliveau	2005.06.17
P-474 (z)	Written submissions of Wendy Cumming	2005.06.17
P-474 (aa)	Représentations écrites de M. Roger Desjeans	2005.06.17
P-474 (bb)	Written submissions of M. Alain Guilbert / Présentation écrite de M. Alain Guilbert	2005.06.17
P-474 (cc)	Représentations écrites de M. Martin Spalding et M. Jean Laflamme	2005.06.17
P-474 (dd)	Représentation écrites de M. Bernard Michaud	2005.06.17
P-474 (ee)	Written submission of Micheline Montreuil	2005.06.17
P-474 (ff)	Représentations écrites de M. Alain Renaud	2005.06.17
P-474 (gg)	Représentations du Procureur général du Canada – Final submissions of the Attorney General of Canada	2005.06.17
P-474 (hh)	Final submissions of Norman Steinberg and Steven Turner	2005.06.17
P-474 (ii)	Submissions of Mario Parent	2005.06.17
P-475	Agreed Statement of Facts – Paul Coffin	2005.06.14

Appendix G

RULINGS

Ruling on Standing (July 5, 2004)

Introduction

I have been appointed by Order in Council P.C. 2004-110, sometimes referred to in this Ruling as the "Terms of Reference" or "mandate", to conduct a factual inquiry and then to make recommendations. In the first part of my mandate, I am to investigate and report on the questions raised by Chapters 3 and 4 of the November 2003 Report of the Auditor General of Canada to the House of Commons with regard to the sponsorship program and advertising activities of the Government of Canada, including

i. the creation of the sponsorship program,

ii. the selection of communications and advertising agencies,

iii. the management of the sponsorship program and advertising activities by government officials at all levels,

iv. the receipt and use of any funds or commissions disbursed in connection with the sponsorship program and advertising activities by any person or organization, and

v.   any other circumstance directly related to the sponsorship program and advertising activities that the Commissioner considers relevant to fulfilling his mandate.

The first part of the mandate is referred to in this Ruling as the "Factual Inquiry".

The second part of my mandate is to make any recommendations that I consider advisable based upon the findings in the Factual Inquiry to prevent mismanagement of sponsorship programs or advertising activities in the future, taking into account certain initiatives announced by the Government of Canada on February 10, 2004 which are detailed in the Order in Council.

This latter aspect of my mandate is referred to as the "Recommendations".

The following paragraphs in the Terms of Reference are relevant to this Ruling:

e.   the Commissioner be authorized to adopt any procedures and methods that he may consider expedient for the proper conduct of the inquiry, and to sit at any times and in any places in Canada that he may decide;

f.   the Commissioner be authorized to grant to any person who satisfies him that he or she has a substantial and direct interest in the subject-matter of the inquiry an opportunity during the inquiry to give evidence and to examine or cross-examine witnesses personally or by counsel on evidence relevant to the person's interest;

A. Factual Inquiry

As already announced on May 7, 2004, I will conduct the Factual Inquiry by way of evidentiary hearings at which witnesses who give evidence under oath or affirmation will be examined and cross-examined. Documents will be produced, by these witnesses or by other means. I will receive closing submissions at the end of the Factual Inquiry.

The Draft Rules of Practice and Procedure proposed for use in the Factual Inquiry were announced in my Opening Statement made on May 7, 2004 and were published on the Commission's web site, www.gomery.ca. I invited interested parties to suggest modifications to these Rules not later than May 31, 2004. Following receipt of one submission from counsel representing the Government of Canada, articles 17, 39 and 40 of the Draft Rules have been amended. I draw the attention of interested parties to other changes in the Draft Rules to the definitions of the terms "full standing participant" and "partial standing participant". From now on a full standing participant will be known as a Party and a partial standing participant as an Intervenor. The Rules in final form have been published on the Commission's web site. Persons or groups participating in the Inquiry should visit our web site regularly for information on practical details and scheduling.

B. Recommendations

The formulation of the Commission's recommendations will follow the completion of the Factual Inquiry and will not be preceded by further formal evidentiary hearings. In due course the Commission will announce the procedure it intends to follow preparatory to the formulation of its recommendations.

Guiding Principles on Standing

In its Opening Statement the Commission invited persons interested in the Factual Inquiry to apply for standing not later than May 31, 2004. Prior to that date, I received thirteen applications from parties seeking standing as Parties or as Intervenors. Since that date, I have received requests to extend the delays from two applicants who wish to apply for standing. All fifteen applications were the subject of oral presentations in Ottawa on June 21 and 22, 2004. At that time I exercised my discretion to grant the requests of the two late applicants to be heard on the merits of their applications. I also received a late request from a private citizen which I dismissed prior to the hearings both as being outside the delay and for not disclosing a sufficient interest.

Before I address the merits of each of the fifteen applications, it is useful to summarize the general principles that have guided my decision on standing.

I am committed to ensuring that the Inquiry is both fair and thorough, and that in the course of the Inquiry I obtain and consider all relevant information relating to the issues identified in the Terms of Reference.

The Inquiry will examine not only what happened with respect to the sponsorship program and the advertising activities of the government as described in the Report of the Auditor General, but will also examine the circumstances surrounding the creation of the sponsorship program, its origins in preceding government initiatives, and the motivations, whether valid or not, for the manner in which it was organized. Similarly, the Inquiry will investigate the reasons why and how the government's sponsorship program and advertising activities were administered as they were. I intend to interpret the scope of my mandate broadly, with a view to understanding the extent to which these government activities were mismanaged, if indeed they were, and any improper use of the funds disbursed, if that occurred. Only in this way will it be possible to formulate intelligent recommendations to prevent mismanagement of similar activities in the future.

At the same time, I must continually bear in mind the importance of completing this Inquiry as expeditiously as is reasonably possible, particularly in light of paragraph (l) of the Terms of Reference which directs me to submit my Report on an urgent basis. In the past, some public inquiries have suffered from diminished credibility because of undue delay. I intend to act so as to avoid delay, repetition and the presentation of irrelevant or unhelpful evidence which will not assist me in making the findings called for by the mandate.

One of the principles which will guide the conduct of this Inquiry is that of transparency and openness. However, some prospective witnesses are facing criminal charges relating to the subject matter of the Inquiry and it may be necessary to hear all or parts of their evidence *in camera* or subject to an order of non-publication, in order to assure their right to a fair trial. The Commission may be requested to hear other witnesses *in camera* or confidentially for other reasons. These matters will be dealt with by the Commission as they arise but to the greatest extent possible I will strive to ensure that the work of the Inquiry is accessible to the public and as open as possible.

I will rely upon Commission counsel to assist me throughout the Inquiry. They will ensure the orderly conduct of the Inquiry and have standing throughout. Commission counsel have the primary responsibility for representing the public interest, including the responsibility to ensure that all facts and circumstances that bear upon the public interest are brought to my attention. Commission counsel do not represent any particular interest or point of view, and their role is not adversarial or partisan.

As provided under the Rules of Procedure and Practice, there are two categories of participation in the Factual Inquiry. It is foreseen that parties may be either:

i.   **Parties**, because their rights are directly and substantially affected by the Factual Inquiry; or

ii. **Intervenors**, where they are found to have clearly ascertainable interests and perspectives useful to the Commission's mandate. In such cases I am entitled to determine special conditions under which a party may participate.

In addition, any witness called to testify may be represented by counsel while testifying, and may be questioned by his own counsel. In other words, counsel for a witness will have standing for the purpose of his or her client's testimony at the Inquiry.

As will be seen from what follows, I have not granted to some applicants the right to participate that they sought. However, should circumstances change during the course of the hearing, I will be prepared to reconsider the matter and vary my earlier Ruling. For example, applicants having intervenor standing may apply for party standing if circumstances warrant.

What constitutes "a substantial and direct interest in the subject matter of the Inquiry"? Based upon what has been decided in comparable cases, the interest of the applicant may be the protection of a legal interest in the sense that the outcome of the Inquiry may affect the legal status or property interests of the applicant, or it may be as insubstantial as the applicant's sense of well-being or fear of an adverse effect upon his or her reputation. Even if such a fear proves to be unfounded, it may be serious and objectively reasonable enough to warrant party or intervenor standing in the Inquiry. What does not constitute a valid reason for a participant's standing is mere concern about the issues to be examined, if the concern is not based upon the possible consequences to the personal interests of the person expressing the concern. As was stated by Campbell J. in *Range Representative on Administrative Segregation Kingston Penitentiary* v. Ontario (1989), 39 Admin. L.R. at p. 13, dealing with a coroner's inquest:

> Mere concern about the issues to be canvassed at the inquest, however deep and genuine, is not enough to constitute direct and substantial interest. Neither is expertise in the subject matter of the inquest or the particular issues of fact that will arise. It is not enough that an individual has a useful perspective that might assist the coroner.

This extract was cited with approval by Mr. Justice O'Connor in his Ruling dated May 4, 2004 in the context of the Arar Commission of Inquiry.

This having been said, it is not possible to enumerate an exhaustive list of the factors to be taken into consideration when determining whether an applicant's interest is sufficiently substantial and direct to the subject matter of the Inquiry. The Terms of Reference, in stating that the Commissioner must be satisfied that an applicant has such an interest, leave me with a certain degree of discretion, which must be exercised judiciously, to decide which persons or groups shall be authorized to participate, and to what degree.

Disposition

A. Party Standing

I come to the conclusion, for the reasons given in each case, that the following persons or organizations have rights, privileges or interests that may be affected by the outcome of the Factual Inquiry. They therefore have a substantial and direct interest in the subject matter of the Inquiry sufficient to warrant being granted party standing, and will be entitled in each case to participate fully in the Inquiry with respect to the matters relevant to their interests.

1. **Attorney General of Canada, representing the Government of Canada.** The Government of Canada administered the sponsorship program. It authorized and paid for sponsorship grants and commissions, and authorized as well certain advertising activities, all at the heart of the November 2003 Auditor General's Report and concerns. It risks being reproached to the extent that there was any mismanagement or impropriety. The Attorney General represents not only the Government of Canada but also its employees and representatives, many of whom will be called to testify. His concerns are substantial and he has the required interest to participate fully in all phases of the Inquiry.

2. **Canada Post Corporation**
   Two transactions involving this Crown Corporation are directly referred to in the Auditor General's Report as giving cause for concern in the context of the sponsorship program. It is probable that Canada Post's methods and procedures in selecting advertising agencies will also be examined in the course of the Inquiry. It should therefore be granted party standing for Phases IA and IB of the Inquiry.

3. **VIA Rail Corporation**
   Like Canada Post, VIA Rail is a Crown corporation specifically mentioned in the Report of the Auditor General, and will be the subject of evidence to be presented in Phases IA and IB of the Inquiry. Some of its present and former employees will be heard as witnesses. It is entitled to be represented throughout the Factual Inquiry and to participate fully.

4.   **The Right Honourable Jean Chrétien**
     Mr. Chrétien was the Prime Minister of Canada during the relevant
     period when the sponsorship program was administered. He alleges
     that he had a unique role in the creation of the program. It is not
     unreasonable to consider, as pleaded by his counsel, that he may be
     directly and substantially affected by the findings of fact or
     recommendations resulting from the Inquiry. He seeks standing as
     a Party for Phases IA and IB. It appears that his interest is direct
     and substantial and, accordingly, he will be entitled to be represented
     throughout the Factual Inquiry and to participate fully.

5.   **The Honourable Alfonso Gagliano**
     Mr. Gagliano was Minister of Public Works and General Services
     from June 11, 1997 until January 14, 2002, and his ministry oversaw
     the administration of the sponsorship program during that period.
     At that time, he also had other ministerial responsibilities which may
     be relevant. He alleges that his reputation has been adversely affected
     by the findings of the Auditor General in her Report. He has
     therefore a direct and substantial interest in many aspects of the Factual
     Inquiry and will have the right as a Party to fully participate in it.

6.   **Joseph Charles Guité**
     Mr. Guité describes himself in his application as a senior public servant
     and the central figure involved in the management of the sponsorship
     program and advertising activities. He is now the subject of a
     criminal prosecution directly related to the matters dealt with in the
     Auditor General's Report. He will surely have to testify at the
     Inquiry. His reputation is at risk and his direct interest in the issues
     to be dealt with by the Commission is apparent and substantial.

7.   **Jean Lafleur**
     Until the business was sold as of January 1, 2001 to Communications
     Groupdirect Inc., Mr. Lafleur, as president of Jean Lafleur
     Communication Marketing Inc., was actively involved in the
     transaction and execution of numerous sponsorship contracts and
     related advertising. He or his firm received substantial revenues in
     the form of commissions and other remuneration as a result of the

sponsorship program, and are the subject of unfavourable comments in the Report of the Auditor General. His direct and substantial interest is evident.

8. Jean Pelletier

Mr. Pelletier acted as Director of the Office of the Prime Minister of Canada from November 4, 1993 until his retirement on June 30, 2001. He alleges that in that capacity he had a direct knowledge of the circumstances surrounding the creation of the sponsorship program and its objectives, although he denies any direct involvement or knowledge of its administration. Nevertheless, there have been public suggestions that he had some degree of implication in the management of the program, or knowledge of at least some of the matters referred to in the Report of the Auditor General. These suggestions have, according to Mr. Pelletier's application, put at risk his reputation as a competent and honest public servant. The protection of his reputation is the primary reason for Mr. Pelletier's application for standing as a Party. His concern is legitimate.

9. Ranald Quail

Mr. Quail served as Deputy Minister of Public Works and Government Services Canada from July 1993 until April 1, 2001. He was the most senior official in that government department during the time period which will be the focus of the Inquiry. As such, he was at least nominally responsible for the proper administration of the sponsorship program and advertising activities which are the subject of the Auditor General's Report. He has an interest in defending his record as a public servant and, specifically, his conduct and actions during the period relevant to the Inquiry. As his counsel points out, Mr. Quail's reputation may well be affected by the observations and findings of the Commission. For these reasons, he is entitled to standing as a Party.

10. Business Development Bank of Canada

The Business Development Bank of Canada is a Crown corporation which is the subject of unfavourable comments in the Auditor General's Report. For the reasons already given with respect to

Canada Post and VIA Rail, it should have the right to participate in the Inquiry, as a Party.

B. Intervenor Standing

I am persuaded, for the reasons given in each case, that the following applicants should have standing before the Inquiry as Intervenors, since, although they do not appear to have a direct and substantial interest in the subject matter of the Inquiry, they have clearly ascertainable interests and perspectives essential to the Commission's mandate.

1. B.C.P. Ltd.

B.C.P. Ltd. is a public relations firm which is mentioned in the Report of the Auditor General in relation to a sponsorship contract awarded to Tourism Canada. It seeks intervenor status only to enable it to correct any inaccuracies in the Report or misperceptions created by it. It should be granted the status it has requested.

2. Office of the Auditor General of Canada

Since the mandate of the Commission is directly related to the Report of the Auditor General, the latter's participation in the Factual Inquiry is essential. She has a useful perspective on the issues relevant to the Commission's mandate. At the time she and other representatives of her office are called upon to testify, they will be entitled to representation by their counsel, including the right to re-examine, and the Office should be in a position to make submissions to the Inquiry at its conclusion.

3. The Public Service Integrity Officer

On November 6, 2001, by Order in Council, Dr. Edward Keyserlingk was appointed as the Government's first Public Service Integrity Officer, to act in that capacity in accordance with the *Policy on the Internal Disclosure of Information concerning Wrongdoing in the Workplace* adopted by the Treasury Board of Canada pursuant to Section 11(2) of the *Financial Administration Act*. Dr. Keyserlingk's mandate is to deal with internal disclosures by public servants, to investigate allegations of wrongdoing in the public service, and to protect from reprisal public servants who make good faith disclosures. He seeks party standing so as to effectively offer protection against reprisal to public servants who will appear before the Commission.

Public servants are automatically entitled to be represented by counsel for the Government of Canada, unless they opt to be represented by counsel of their own choosing for the purposes of their testimony before the Commission. If they choose to be represented by counsel for Dr. Keyserlingk, the latter will automatically have standing to put questions to the witness and generally to act on his or her behalf. If the witness chooses to be represented by the Attorney General of Canada or by another attorney, Dr. Keyserlingk's counsel would have no right to intervene.

Nevertheless, the mandate of the applicant entitles him to be present throughout as an Intervenor, since he may have valuable perspectives and representations to offer, especially at the close of the Factual Inquiry.

4. **Conservative Party of Canada**

The Conservative Party of Canada, like the Bloc Québécois, seeks full standing as a Party. It alleges that it has a direct and substantial interest in the issues to be considered in Phase IB of the Inquiry, in the following respects:

i. it is interested to identify those persons or organizations who received the funds disbursed by the government, to know the purpose for which the funds were disbursed, and the extent of the value for money received by the Government of Canada.

ii. it is interested to determine whether there was political influence on the distribution of the funds; and

iii. it is interested to inquire into the sufficiency of external monitoring and financial controls used by the recipients of the funds.

These would clearly be questions relevant to the Commission's mandate, and central to its Inquiry, especially in Phase IB, but it is not at all apparent that a political party, in this case one opposed to the party in power, has a direct and substantial interest of its own in these questions, other than its partisan interests. These play an essential role within the political system but should not form part of the Commission's proceedings. Any misconduct which the Commission might find could result in political consequences, whether in Parliament or in an election, and therefore could be of great importance politically to the applicant. However, such political consequences should not be within the Commission's contemplation when drafting its Report and recommendations.

On the other hand, to the extent that the applicant's interests are not purely partisan and are those of the public interest, they are not distinct from those of every citizen concerned to understand the matters which are the object of the Inquiry.

I come to the conclusion that the applicant does not have a direct and substantial interest, as that expression has been defined in the jurisprudence cited to me, in the issues before the Commission.

There is an additional reason why political parties should not be given party standing. The Commission's jurisdiction is limited to an examination of the administration of the sponsorship program and advertising activities of the government, and to uncover all relevant facts resulting from any mismanagement or impropriety in the course of that administration or inappropriate use of the funds disbursed. The mandate of the Commission does not extend to an assessment of the political wisdom of the sponsorship program; that is a matter of government policy which the Commission has no mandate to examine, although it will inevitably learn, in the course of the hearings, what motivated the government to create the program and to disburse funds in accordance with the policy objectives it sought to promote. If the Commission were to permit a debate to occur in the course of the Inquiry as to the legitimacy of those objectives, or as to the desirability, from the public's point of view, of the sponsorship program and advertising activities of the government, the Commission would be distracted from its real objectives, and would waste valuable time in examining questions better left to the political arena. As was stated by Mr. Justice Dennis O'Connor in his Ruling on Standing and Funding at the Walkerton Inquiry, it is generally not desirable that a public inquiry be allowed to become a partisan debate between opposing political factions; such debates are better left to another forum.

I adopt his reasoning entirely; he says, with reference to a request by the Ontario New Democratic Party for standing, the following at page 81 of his Report.

> The second ground upon which the ONDP Group claims an interest for which it ought to be granted standing is that the ONDP was vocal in calling for the government to establish this Inquiry. In my view, the fact that a political party or its members call for the government to establish a public inquiry, without more, does not create an interest within the meaning of s.5(1) of the Act.

> Finally, I do not think that this is a case in which I should exercise my discretion to grant standing. I say this for two reasons. First, parties who have been granted standing will bring a sufficiently broad range of perspectives to enable me to fulfil my mandate. In granting standing, I have attempted to ensure that all perspectives, and in particular those such as the ones held by this applicant, which question the effect of government policies, practices and procedures, are fully represented. It is essential that there be a thorough examination of these factors in relation to the events in Walkerton. I am satisfied that this will occur.

> The second reason why I am not inclined to grant this group standing is that it is, in my view, generally undesirable to use public inquiries to have political parties advance their positions or policies. There are other more appropriate arenas for them to do so. Mr. Jacobs, counsel for the ONDP Group, recognized this concern and assured me that this was not the motivation underlying the application. I accept Mr. Jacobs' assurance without reservation. Nevertheless, I think there is a danger that this applicant's participation could be viewed by the public as politicizing the Inquiry in a partisan way. To the extent possible, that result should be avoided.

> Finally, I note that the considerations in granting standing to a political party differ from those which apply to a

government. Governments play a different role and have different responsibilities than do political parties. Moreover, the ONDP, unlike any other applicant, will have an opportunity to participate in the subject matter of the Inquiry by responding to my Report in the Legislature.

Although it is true that in the past some public inquiries have granted standing to political parties, others have refused such standing. It may be concluded that each case has to be decided on its individual merits.

In the circumstances of the present Commission, I find that it would be undesirable to give party standing to political parties which were, at the time of the events with which the Commission is concerned, in opposition to the government.

Nevertheless, I am satisfied that the applicant has clearly ascertainable interests and perspectives essential to the Commission's mandate, and that its participation as an Intervenor would enhance the work of the Commission in both Phases IA and IB. The Conservative Party of Canada represents a substantial body of opinion in Canada. It has a valuable perspective on public administration, the roles of office-holders and parliamentarians, and the process through which public funds are disbursed. The Commission would accordingly benefit from its participation, assistance and representations as an Intervenor.

5. Bloc Québécois
The application of the Bloc Québécois will be dealt with in the same manner as that of the Conservative Party of Canada, for the same reasons. One additional comment is necessary, because of allegations made on its behalf in its written application, and repeated at the hearing on June 22nd.

The Bloc Québécois alleges that it has a particular role to play in the Inquiry because of its unique position as a political party which advocates the sovereignty of the Province of Quebec and its eventual independence from the Canadian federation. Firstly, it alleges that the stated objective of the sponsorship program was the promotion of federalism in Quebec, and that this promotion sought to distort the political debate and to influence unfairly Quebec voters away from the political option which the Bloc Québécois seeks to encourage. Secondly, it alleges that funds originating from the sponsorship program and advertising activities of the government were diverted into the electoral funds of the Liberal Party of Canada, to the detriment of the Bloc Québécois; this allegation, however, is not to be found in the Report of the Auditor General.

The applicant seeks to be allowed to introduce evidence in relation to these allegations into the hearings before the Commission.

These are two conceptually distinct grounds. The issue of whether public funds should have been used to promote federalism in Quebec is a matter of political debate. It should be dealt with in the political forum. As earlier stated, it does not form part of the Commission's mandate. This is not, therefore, a basis for the Bloc Québécois to be granted party standing.

In contrast, the allegations with respect to the diversion of public funds to a particular political party fall squarely within the Commission's mandate. It is not necessary to grant party status to the Bloc Québécois in order for the Commission to deal with possible evidence on this matter.

Accordingly, the Bloc Québécois' application for party standing is denied. However, for the reasons set out in relation to the Conservative Party application, it is granted status as Intervenor.

John H. Gomery, Commissioner

July 5, 2004

Ruling on Funding (July 19, 2004)

By the Order in Council dated February 19, 2004, I am authorized to recommend funding to a party who has been granted standing at the Inquiry.

The relevant paragraph reads as follows:

> (h) for purposes of the investigation referred to in paragraph (a), the Commissioner be authorized to recommend funding, in accordance with approved guidelines respecting rates of remuneration and reimbursement and the assessment of accounts, to a party who has been granted standing at the inquiry, to the extent of the party's interest, where in the Commissioner's view the party would not otherwise be able to participate in the inquiry;

Subsequently the Treasury Board approved funding guidelines which may be found on the Commission's website.

In the *Rules of Practice and Procedure* which have been adopted by the Commission, the criteria for an application for funding are set out in Rule 11, which reads:

In order to qualify for a funding recommendation, a party must:

a. establish the party's inability to participate in the Inquiry without funding and the absence of an alternative means of funding:

b. provide a satisfactory plan as to how it intends to use the funds and account for them;

c. demonstrate sufficient interest and proposed involvement in the Inquiry; and

d. establish a special expertise or experience with respect to the Commission's mandate.

Of the fifteen persons and organizations that have been granted either party or intervenor standing at Phases IA and IB of the Inquiry, three have submitted applications for funding, or, should I say more accurately, applications for a recommendation for funding, since the Order in Council makes it clear that my authority is limited to making a recommendation.

The three applicants are Mr. Joseph Charles Guité, the Conservative Party of Canada, and the Bloc Québécois.

Joseph Charles Guité

Mr. Guité alleges in his application that he has already been exposed to substantial expense for legal representation before the House of Commons Public Accounts Committee as well as before the criminal courts, where he is facing accusations directly related to the role he played in the administration of the sponsorship program. His participation in the Inquiry as a Party will involve him in further legal costs and disbursements. He acknowledges that in virtue of his status as a former public servant, some of the fees of his personal attorney who appeared with him before the Public Accounts Committee have been supported by the government in accordance with the *Treasury Board Policy on the Indemnification of and Legal Assistance for Crown Servants* ("Treasury Board Policy"), but in his application he says that he has not yet received confirmation from the Department of Public Works and Government Services Canada that this same policy will apply to the services of his attorneys before the present Inquiry.

Mr. Guité refers in his application to considerable legal expense involved in defending the criminal charges of which he has been accused, but this is not a relevant consideration in the present context.

With reference to his financial circumstances and his ability to participate in the Inquiry without government funding, Mr. Guité alleges, somewhat laconically, that "a significant portion, if not all of my liquid assets, are being expended on the retaining of legal counsel to represent me, on the criminal charges before the Quebec Superior Court of Justice," and that "my personal and financial circumstances are such that I do not have the financial resources available to retain legal counsel to represent my interests" before the Inquiry. A more detailed description of his "personal and financial circumstances" would have been advisable, to enable me to assess Mr. Guité's ability or inability, as the case may be, to pay his lawyer.

Be that as it may, it is almost certain that his legal expenses before the Inquiry will be met, as they have been previously with respect to his representation before the Public Accounts Committee, in accordance with Treasury Board Policy. If for some reason they are not, I recommend that they be funded in accordance with the Treasury Board guidelines.

The Conservative Party of Canada

The Conservative Party of Canada has been granted the standing of an Intervenor before the Inquiry. Its application for a funding recommendation states that it has limited revenues consisting of an allowance allocated to it pursuant to sections 435.01 and 435.02 of the *Elections Act*, and the donations it receives from its supporters. The latter are, by the effect of recent amendments to the *Elections Act* and the *Income Tax Act*, now restricted to a maximum of $5,000.00 per year from any one person; donations or contributions from corporations and trade unions are prohibited. According to its application, the budget of the Conservative Party of Canada is entirely used to cover its expenses to run its national operations and to support the election campaign expenses of its candidates. It did not, in its 2004 budget, make any provision for the expense of participating in the Inquiry, which arose after the beginning of the year. It will receive no further allocation in accordance with the *Elections Act* until January 2005. It says that contributions from its supporters tend to diminish after an election.

The application does not identify the amount allocated from government funds to the Conservative Party of Canada in 2004, but as appears from a press release dated December 11, 2003 issued by the Chief Electoral Officer of Canada, attached as Appendix A, the Conservative Party of Canada received at the beginning of 2004 the sum of $8,476,872.25. This amount is subject to revision based upon the number of valid votes cast in its favour in the 38th general election held on June 28, 2004, but should not be significantly different in the future. Accordingly, starting in January 2005, the Conservative Party will be entitled to receive quarterly instalments of more than $2 million each.

Notwithstanding these very considerable resources, the applicant asserts that it is unable to participate in the Inquiry without funding, because its budget is entirely committed to its regular political activities. It seeks funding only to the extent necessary to a limited participation in the Inquiry, which it describes in detail in its application. It alleges that without such funding, it will be unable to participate in the Inquiry as an Intervenor.

The foregoing has led me to reflect upon whether it is reasonable and appropriate to require a political party to rely upon the funds allocated to it by reason of ss. 435.01 and 435.02 of the *Elections Act* for the purposes of its legal representation before a commission of inquiry. After careful consideration I have come to the conclusion that I should not impose such a requirement upon the applicant.

As its title indicates, the main purpose of the *Elections Act* is to regulate elections. It may therefore be assumed that the recent amendments to the *Elections Act* that provide for public financing of political parties anticipate that the funds so provided from public sources will be primarily used by political parties so as to promote the possibility that some of their candidates will be elected to Parliament in a general election. It may also be assumed that they do not foresee that those funds will be used for non electoral and non political purposes such as the participation of a political party in the work of a commission of inquiry.

The Commission intends to ask the Conservative Party of Canada to refrain from promoting its political objectives in its submissions to the Inquiry; this should be apparent from its Ruling on standing. It would therefore be contradictory and unfair to require it to use its financial resources, provided under the *Elections Act*, normally dedicated to political purposes, to pay its lawyers for their services related to the work of the Inquiry.

It is this contradiction that has persuaded me to exercise my discretion to recommend limited funding to the applicant, generally but not entirely in accordance with its Plan for Use and Accounting which forms part of its Submissions, and which is attached as Appendix B. Accordingly:

a. funding is recommended for one junior and one senior lawyer, to work separately, the bulk of the work to be performed by the junior lawyer, under supervision by the senior lawyer who will make decisions and present closing submissions to the Inquiry;

b. funding is recommended for pre-hearing preparation limited to 40 hours of work for each lawyer, and for suggestions from time to time to Commission counsel and related representatives limited to 40 hours of work by the senior lawyer;

c. funding is recommended for review of daily transcripts and documents limited to three hours per day by the junior lawyer and one hour per day by the senior lawyer;

d. funding is recommended for necessary expenses and travel, it being taken for granted that in most instances the applicant's lawyers will not have to incur costs for copies of documents or transcripts, and will not need to travel to Ottawa or Montreal to take cognizance of exhibits;

e. funding is recommended for the preparation and presentation of closing submissions limited to 30 hours for each lawyer.

I will remain open to the possibility of amending these recommendations as circumstances dictate, on application.

Bloc Québécois

With respect to the application of the Bloc Québécois, it alleges that it intends to participate actively in the Inquiry. For example, it proposes to have an attorney present at the hearing at all times, whereas the Conservative Party would be satisfied to take cognizance of the daily transcripts, and does not propose to have a legal representative present throughout the hearing. The need for the Bloc Québécois to be present at all times at the hearing of witnesses is not established to my satisfaction.

With respect to its financial resources, the Bloc Québécois makes little attempt in its application to describe in detail its situation. It says only that its financial resources are used in connection with its regular political activities, and that no provision has been made for extraordinary costs such as those related to the Inquiry.

Its application for funding makes no mention of the amounts allocated and to be allocated to the Bloc Québécois as a result of the recent amendments to the *Elections Act*. According to Appendix A, it received in 2004 the sum of $2,411,022.25, and it may be assumed that it received additional donations from its own supporters. As a result of its success in the recent election, it will be receiving a greater allocation in the future than it received in 2004.

Nonetheless, the application alleges in paragraphs 7 and 8:

> 7. Les ressources financières dont dispose le Bloc Québécois ne permettent donc pas de couvrir des dépenses liées à de quelconques activités extraordinaires telle qu'une participation à une commission d'enquête. Aucune somme n'a donc été prévue et n'est disponible pour ce faire.

> 8. Dans les circonstances, il est clair que le Bloc Québécois est et sera incapable d'acquitter les sommes nécessaires à sa participation à la Commission d'enquête. Il n'est d'ailleurs pas en mesure d'obtenir de tels fonds, dont la somme est considérable, par d'autres sources de financement. L'assistance financière fournie par le gouvernement est donc essentielle à sa présence dans le cadre de l'enquête factuelle et des représentations finales qui suivent celle-ci.

These submissions and the considerations that have led me to conclude that the Conservative Party of Canada is entitled to public funding for the services of its attorneys in relation to the work of the Commission persuade me that the Bloc Québécois is equally entitled to a recommendation for funding. However, I am not persuaded that it deserves more generous funding than what I recommend for the Conservative Party. Accordingly, I exercise my discretion to recommend funding to the Bloc Québécois, but only to the same extent that it is recommended for the Conservative Party of Canada. If the Bloc Québécois chooses to instruct its attorneys to participate in the Inquiry to a greater extent, it will have to finance any additional legal costs so incurred from its own resources.

John H. Gomery, Commissioner

July 19, 2004

Supplementary Ruling on Funding (October 26, 2004)

Introduction

By my Ruling dated July 19, 2004, I recommended public funding to the Conservative Party of Canada and the Bloc Québécois, which have intervenor status before the Inquiry. They are entitled, as detailed in the Ruling, to payment of the fees of their lawyers limited to three hours a day for a junior lawyer and one hour per day for a senior lawyer, with additional amounts for pre-hearing preparation, for the representations during the hearings, and for closing submissions. At that time I stated that I would remain open to the possibility of amending these recommendations as circumstances might dictate, on application.

Both the Conservative Party and the Bloc Québécois are now applying for a recommendation for increased funding. At the same time the Liberal Party of Canada, which was granted intervenor status on September 13, 2004, asks for funding for the first time. All three applications were presented on October 20, 2004 and were taken under advisement. The present Ruling will deal with them together.

Analysis

The application of the Liberal Party of Canada takes it for granted that it would at least be entitled to the same funding recommendation as has been already granted to the two other political parties. At first glance this is a reasonable assumption, except that the belated arrival upon the scene of the Liberal Party of Canada, after the hearing of witnesses had commenced, reduces its need of the same allocation for pre-hearing preparation. In addition, it is not my intention to recommend funding on a retroactive basis, which means that the Liberal Party will be entitled to receive funding for the services of its attorneys only from the date of its application; whatever legal costs may have incurred prior to that date will have to be financed from its other resources.

All three applicants argue that the amounts allowed by my earlier Ruling are inadequate to enable them to participate in the Inquiry as fully as they would wish, and as needed to fulfill their responsibilities, as they define them. They refer to the voluminous documentation which has been and is being communicated to them as the hearings advance, and the time required to peruse it carefully. They also invoke the difficulty of reading and comprehending daily transcripts when the exhibits referred to by witnesses may not be readily at hand, and the impossibility of suggesting questions in a timely way to Commission counsel, for submission to witnesses.

On this latter question, there is clearly a misunderstanding as to the intended role of these Intervenors. Although section 8 of the Rules of Procedure and Practice indicates that an Intervenor's participation includes "the opportunity to suggest areas for examination of a certain witness by Commission counsel, failing which, the opportunity to request leave to examine the witness on such areas", this right is at the Commission's discretion. It should have been obvious to the parties concerned that since it was not contemplated that they would be present at the Inquiry's hearings but would limit their participation to an examination of the daily transcripts, they would be, for all practical purposes, unable to suggest particular questions to witnesses, who would usually have completed their testimony before any such suggestions could be submitted, on details of their testimony. In other words, time spent formulating such questions would be wasted time and unnecessary. The Intervenors should instead be giving their attention to suggesting areas of inquiry relevant to their perspectives as office-holders or parliamentarians.

In general, it appears to me, from the written applications and the oral representations made by counsel for the three applicants, that they have generally misapprehended the scope of their participation in this Inquiry, and what the Commission expects of them.

On July 5, 2004, when the Conservative Party of Canada and the Bloc Québécois were granted the status of Intervenors at the Inquiry, I took care to explain that they were not being granted full participation because of the danger that that would introduce an element of partisan debate to the Inquiry which would be better left to another forum. With the subsequent arrival upon the scene of the Liberal Party of Canada, this consideration is reinforced. The only reasons these political parties have been granted intervenor status are those expressed in the following extract from the decision, referring to the Conservative Party:

> *The Conservative Party of Canada represents a substantial body of opinion in Canada. It has a valuable perspective on public administration, the roles of office-holders and parliamentarians, and the process through which public funds are disbursed. The Commission would accordingly benefit from its participation, assistance and representations as an Intervenor.*

The same reasoning applies to the Bloc Québécois and the Liberal Party of Canada.

In my opinion, in order to assist the Commission's work, it is not necessary for the Intervenors to analyze the daily transcripts with the attention which would be required of a lawyer mandated to defend the interests of a client. The three applicants have no interests to defend in the Inquiry. To the extent that they have interests, these should not be the concern of their counsel, but rather the public interest. The transcripts need only be examined by them with a view to the submissions which they will be making from time to time, but mainly at the end of the Inquiry.

With respect to documentation, counsel for the Intervenors should take cognizance only of the documents which form part of the record, since it is only that evidence which I will take into consideration in making my findings and recommendations. The remaining documentation communicated to the other participants may be of interest to the latter, who have the interests of their respective clients to defend, but the Intervenors, who do not represent clients having direct and substantial interests effected by the Inquiry, may safely ignore it.

I am not persuaded that counsel for the Intervenors require more funding than what has already been recommended. Probably the task of summarizing the daily transcripts will take longer on some days than the three hours allowed, but almost certainly on other days less time will be required. Counsel should seek alternative methods of facilitating their work, with a view to economizing public funds as much as possible. The drain upon the public purse caused by the work of the Commission should be minimized.

I am conscious of the possibility that at some point in the future, it may be necessary for one or other of the present applicants to seek the standing of a full participant. Should such an application be justified, the party concerned will then be entitled to ask for a revision of my recommendation with respect to funding.

Disposition

The applications of the Conservative Party of Canada and Bloc Québécois for a modification of my Ruling dated July 19, 2004 on recommended funding are dismissed.

The application of the Liberal Party of Canada for funding is granted as follows:

I recommend that limited funding be granted to counsel for the Liberal Party of Canada to the same extent that was recommended to the Conservative Party of Canada in the Ruling dated July 19, 2004, except that pre-hearing preparation should be limited to 20 hours of work for each lawyer, and funding should not otherwise be granted for services performed prior to October 20, 2004.

John H. Gomery, Commissioner

October 26, 2004

Supplementary Ruling on Funding-Liberal Party of Canada (Quebec) (April 4, 2005)

The Liberal Party of Canada and the Liberal Party of Canada (Quebec)— (collectively the Liberal Party), filed a written application on April 4, 2005, supplemented by oral submissions on the same date, to change the Party's status in the current proceedings from that of an intervenor to that of a full party. As well, the application included a request for funding according to Treasury Board guidelines on the same basis as that accorded to other parties with full party status.

The Commissioner has ruled in favour of the Liberal Party of Canada and the Liberal Party of Canada(Quebec) application and makes a recommendation to the Treasury Board to amend the previous ruling of October 20, 2004 as follows:

Change a) to read:

   a.   funding is recommended for one junior and one senior lawyer. The junior lawyer will work under the supervision of the senior lawyer who will make decisions and present closing submissions to the Inquiry;

Item b) remains unchanged:

   b.   funding is recommended for pre-hearing preparation limited to 20 hours of work for each lawyer, and for suggestions from time to time to Commission counsel and related representatives limited to 40 hours of work by the senior lawyer;

Change c) to read:

   c.   counsel will be funded to a limit of 10 hours per diem, to include both preparation for and attendance at the hearings; the Applicant will only be reimbursed for one legal counsel to attend for any one hearing day;

Change d) to read:

   d.   funding is recommended for necessary expenses and travel;

Item e) remains unchanged:

e. funding is recommended for the preparation and presentation of closing submissions limited to 30 hours for each lawyer.

[signature: John H. Gomery]

John H. Gomery, Commissioner

April 4, 2005

Supplementary Ruling on Funding-Bloc Québécois (April 6, 2005)

The Bloc Québécois made a written application on April 5, 2005 for:

I.   A change from Intervenor status to full Party status; and

II. additional funding as a result

The Commissioner rejected the applicant's motion for a change from Intervenor to Party status. However he makes a recommendation to the Treasury Board to amend the previous ruling of July 19, 2004, to take effect as and from April 6, 2005, as follows:

Change a) to read:

a.   funding is recommended for one junior and one senior lawyer. The junior lawyer will work under the supervision of the senior lawyer who will perform the bulk of the work, make decisions and present closing submissions to the Inquiry;

Item b) remains unchanged:

b.   funding is recommended for pre-hearing preparation limited to 40 hours of work for each lawyer, and for suggestions from time to time to Commission counsel and related representatives limited to 40 hours of work by the senior lawyer;

Change c) to read:

c.   funding is recommended for the review of daily transcripts and documents limited to three hours per day for the junior lawyer or one hour per day for the senior lawyer; in the alternative funding is recommended for one legal counsel to prepare and attend the hearings to a limit of 8 hours per day;

Change d) to read:

d.   funding is recommended for necessary expenses and travel;

Item e) remains unchanged:

e.   funding is recommended for the preparation and presentation of closing submissions limited to 30 hours for each lawyer.

_____

John H. Gomery, Commissioner

April 6, 2005

Supplementary Ruling on Funding-Conservative Party of Canada (April 6, 2005)

The Conservative Party of Canada made a written application on April 6, 2005, supplemented by an oral submission on April 7, 2005 and, a further request on April 12, 2005 for:

I. Additional funding to enable its Counsel to attend the proceedings before the Commission; and

II. Permitting its Counsel on occasion to attend the hearings at Place Guy Favreau in Montreal through teleconferencing, videoconferencing or other similar technology.

The Commissioner has ruled in favour of the Conservative Party's application and makes recommendation to the Treasury Board to amend the previous ruling of July 19, 2004, to take effect as and from April 6, 2005, as follows:
Change a) to read:

a. funding is recommended for one junior and one senior lawyer. The junior lawyer will work under the supervision of the senior lawyer who will make decisions and present closing submissions to the Inquiry;

Item b) to remain unchanged:

b. funding is recommended for pre-hearing preparation limited to 40 hours of work for each lawyer, and for suggestions from time to time to Commission counsel and related representatives limited to 40 hours of work by the senior lawyer;

Change c) to read:

c. funding is recommended for the review of daily transcripts and documents limited to three hours per day for the junior lawyer or one hour per day for the senior lawyer; in the alternative funding is recommended for one legal counsel to prepare and attend the hearings either in person or through teleconferencing, videoconferencing or other similar technology, to a limit of 8 hours per day;

Change d) to read:

    d. funding is recommended for necessary expenses and travel;

Item e) remains unchanged:

    e. funding is recommended for the preparation and presentation of closing submissions limited to 30 hours for each lawyer.

_____

John H. Gomery, Commissioner

April 6, 2005

Ruling on *In Camera* Hearing (Mr. Joseph Guité) (October 28, 2004)

This ruling deals with an application made by Joseph Charles Guité for an *in camera* hearing of his testimony, or, subsidiarily, for a publication ban of his evidence, or, again subsidiarily, for a postponement of his testimony until after his criminal trial. Mr. Guité fears that the publicity which will result from his appearance before the Commission, which is scheduled to take place within the next two weeks, will make it impossible for him to have a fair trial on the criminal charges which are pending against him. He alleges that he expects that his criminal trial before a court composed of a judge and jury, will take place in Montreal at the January assizes, that is to say within the next two or three months.

There are three circumstances that are to be taken into consideration in deciding this application; these circumstances do not usually exist in other cases where publication bans and similar remedies are sought.

First, this is a public inquiry on questions of national importance. It is particularly important that the Canadian public be enabled to follow what occurs at the Commission and to read media reports of the evidence presented, unless there are compelling reasons not to allow free access to such reports. Since the inquiry is public, it is more important that there be no limitation on media access than if the inquiry were one conducted, for example, by a coroner.

Secondly, counsel for the Commission have undertaken not to adduce evidence before the Commission of the contracts that are the subject of the criminal charges upon which Mr. Guité is to be tried. Accordingly, Mr. Guité, in his testimony before the Commission, will not be compelled to say anything of an incriminating nature which might predispose a jury candidate to consider him guilty of the counts in the indictment.

Thirdly, Mr. Guité has already testified at some length before the Public Accounts Committee of the House of Commons. One may assume therefore that impact or shock value of his testimony before the Commission will be lessened. Publicity concerning his statements has already occurred, and to the extent that that publicity might affect the possibility of empanelling an impartial jury to try him, the damage has already occurred and would not be substantially aggravated by a repetition of that testimony

Nevertheless, it is to be expected that Mr. Guité's appearance before the Commission will be the occasion of extensive reporting and comment in the media. Many potential jurors will have heard about Mr. Guité and his involvement in the administration of the sponsorship program and advertising activities of the Government as a result of his appearance before the Commission. The question which his application raises is as follows: has he shown that that publicity will so jeopardize his chances of having a fair trial that steps should be taken to avoid such publicity by an *in camera* order, or a publication ban, or by postponing his appearance to a later date.

From the submissions made to me by counsel for the applicant, by Commission counsel, and by the other parties who have made submissions on this question, I retain that the decision of the Supreme Court of Canada in Dagenais, and the opinion of Mr. Justice Cory in the Westray case, are the leading authorities on the subject. I do not propose to make a detailed analysis of this jurisprudence; it would be presumptuous for me to comment on it in any case, since the rules have been very clearly established.

First of all, the rule as enunciated by Chief Justice Lamer in Dagenais is stated as follows[1]:

A publication ban should only be ordered when:

(a) *Such a ban is necessary in order to prevent a real and substantial risk to the fairness of the trial, because reasonably available alternative measures will not prevent the risk; and*

b) *The salutary effects of the publication ban outweigh the deleterious effects to the free expression of those affected by the ban.*

I take it that the same rule would apply to an application for an *in camera* hearing.

With respect to the criterion of necessity, it is well established by the jurisprudence that a publication ban is not necessary if there are reasonable alternatives to assure a fair trial to the accused person. In this case, the only threat to a fair trial is the possibility that the impartiality of prospective jurors will be affected by the publicity surrounding Mr. Guité's testimony before the Commission. Surely I am entitled to assume, in the absence of evidence to the contrary, that the Judge of the Superior Court of Quebec who will have the responsibility of supervising the selection of a jury for Mr. Guité's trial, will take the usual precautions to ensure that prospective jurors are untainted by pre-trial publicity. Any prospective jurors who may have heard about Mr. Guité's involvement in the sponsorship program and advertising activities of the Government, (and let me say that it is probable that some prospective jurors will not have heard any such reports, in spite of widespread publicity), will be carefully screened to determine if they have formed opinions unfavorable to the accused; if they have formed such opinions, it may be assumed that questions will be put to the candidate to find out whether or not those opinions are so firmly held that they cannot be changed in the light of the evidence to be presented by the Crown.

In this fashion, biased jury candidates are weeded out. I am also entitled to assume that the presiding judge will give the usual instructions to the jury, once it has been formed, that they should judge the case on the evidence presented at the trial and not on the basis of what they might have heard elsewhere. And finally, I believe that I am entitled to assume that the jurors will listen attentively to the judge's instructions and will comply with them. In other words, I am of the opinion that the usual procedures involved in the choosing of an impartial jury and the instructions to be given to it in the course of Mr. Guité's trial provide a reasonable alternative to what is requested here by Mr. Guité, and they therefore avoid the infringement to freedom of expression which is the inevitable consequence of an *in camera* hearing or a publication ban.

What I have already said is sufficient, in my opinion, to dispose of the matter, but I would like to add an additional comment on one issue, which was strongly urged by several counsel, concerning the evidentiary burden upon the person requesting a publication ban, and, to an even greater extent, on the person urging the more draconian remedy of an *in camera* hearing. This issue is dealt with as follows by Mr. Justice Cory in the Westray decision[2]:

6. *Those seeking to have the court ban the publication of evidence have the burden of establishing the necessity of the ban. That is to say they must demonstrate that the effect of publicizing the evidence will be to leave potential jurors irreparably prejudiced or so impair the presumption of innocence that a fair trial is impossible. Before relief is granted in order to preserve the right to a fair trial, satisfactory proof of the link between the publicity and its adverse effect must be given.*

7. *Assessment of the effect of the publicity on the right to a fair trial must take place in the context of the existing procedures to safeguard the selection of jurors. Further, the nature and extent of the publicity must be considered.*

8. *The applicant seeking the ban must establish that there are no alternative means available to prevent the harm the ban seeks to prevent.*

In the present case the applicant's only evidence goes to establishing that there has been, and presumably will be, extensive media coverage of the issues giving rise to the present inquiry and Mr. Guité's involvement in it. There is no evidence at all of the effect this publicity has had or will potentially have on the minds and opinions of jury candidates, and there is nothing to indicate that they will or might become irreparably prejudiced as a result. Mr. Auger argues that this absence of evidence may be overcome by the use of common sense. However, I cannot say that my own common sense, which has been to some extent sharpened by my experiences as judge who has presided over a number of jury trials, leads me to conclude that the minds and opinions of jurors are so readily influenced by the media that they lose irretrievably their ability to decide upon the guilt or innocence of an accused upon the basis of the evidence presented at a criminal trial, rather than upon the basis of what they see and hear on the television and in newspapers. In any event, regardless of my own personal beliefs and experiences, and what I like to think of as my common sense, Mr. Guité has quite simply failed to discharge his evidentiary burden of showing the possibility, much less the probability, of bias resulting from publicity, no matter how extensive.

With respect to the lesser remedy of postponing the testimony of Mr. Guité until after his criminal trial, present indications are that the trial will not take place before January 2005 and that it will last for from four to six weeks. In practical terms this means that if I were to accept his request to postpone his testimony, the postponement would have to be until about the end of February 2005, by which time all or most of Phase IA of the Inquiry would have been completed. This would completely distort the presentation of the evidence as it has been envisaged by counsel for the Commission and would make it difficult if not impossible to lead evidence in a logical way by other witnesses who had dealings with Mr. Guité. Just as Mr. Guité has rights to defend, other parties have rights and interests, the defense of which requires them and Commission counsel to know in advance what Mr. Guité has to say about his dealings with others. In all of the circumstances, I agree with the submission of Mr. Finkelstein that any postponement of Mr. Guité's testimony is an unacceptable interference with the orderly presentation of evidence before the Commission, an interference unjustified when weighed against the prejudice which he alleges pre-trial publicity might cause to him. As already indicated, I am not persuaded that any such prejudice is irreparable and cannot be avoided by other alternatives such as careful jury selection.

For these reasons, Mr. Guité's application is dismissed.

John H. Gomery, Commissioner

October 28, 2004

1   Dagenais v. Canadian Broadcasting Corp. , [1994] 3 S.C.R. 835 at 878.
2   Phillips v. N.S. (Westray Mine Inquiry), [1995] 2 S.C.R. 98 at 173-174.

Ruling on Parliamentary Immunity (November 22, 2004)

Counsel for the House of Commons has advised me that her client has decided by motion to reaffirm the immunity and privilege which, according to her submission, attach to the testimony of Mr. Guité before the Public Accounts Committee, and not to waive that privilege. I am grateful to the House of Commons for the dispatch with which it considered and dealt with this issue.

This morning counsel for Mr. Guité presents a motion by which he reasserts his pretension that the transcription of his client's testimony before the Public Accounts Committee should not be used or referred to in any way during his cross-examination. In addition to the argument based upon parliamentary privilege, he invokes certain promises made to him prior to testifying to the effect that his testimony would not be used in other proceedings. These promises appear to have been an important consideration in the deliberations of the Committee of the House of Commons which recommended that no waiver be given. Mr. Guité asks that I issue an order accordingly, and maintain his objection to the use of any evidence previously given by him before the Public Accounts Committee.

Counsel for Mr. Pelletier who is cross-examining Mr. Guité, as well as counsel for certain other parties who will wish to cross-examine, wish to use the transcriptions as evidence of prior statements made by the witness which are, according to their pretensions, inconsistent with the testimony given before this Commission; in this way they propose to attack the credibility of the witness and the probative value of his testimony. Counsel for the House of Commons appeared before the Commission on October 18, 2004 and again on October 25, 2004, to argue that the use of transcripts or evidence given before any House of Commons Committee is constitutionally impermissible.

The objection to any admission of the PAC transcripts is based on the parliamentary privilege of "free speech" which is part of the Constitution of Canada by virtue of the preamble and s. 18 of the *Constitution Act, 1867* and s. 4 of the *Parliament of Canada Act*, R.S.C. 1985, c. P-1. Section 4 confirms the privileges of our Parliament and its members with reference to the privileges of the United Kingdom House of Commons as at

Confederation, which then included the parliamentary freedom of speech guaranteed by Article 9 of the United Kingdom's 1689 *Bill of Rights*. Article 9 provides "That the Freedom of Speech, and Debates or Proceedings in Parliament, ought not to be impeached or questioned in any Court or Place out of Parliament".

It is not suggested by any of the parties contesting the objection that Article 9 does not apply to the proceedings of committees of the House of Commons, but they argue that it applies only to what is said by members of Parliament, and does not extend to what is said by persons appearing as witnesses before Parliament or its committees. Counsel for these parties argue that Article 9 was not intended to apply to such witnesses but to the statements made in debate by parliamentarians themselves and that the purpose of the enactment was to protect the latter from civil or criminal proceedings based upon such statements. Its objective was not, according to their submission, to protect from scrutiny in the Courts the declarations made by witnesses before parliamentary committees which they later contradicted in court proceedings, or which are inconsistent with their testimony. They note the historical context in which the *Bill of Rights* was enacted, as part of legislation which brought William of Orange and his wife Mary to the throne of England, after the reigns of the Stuarts which had been marked by conflict between the Monarchy and Parliament. In 1689 parliamentarians clearly wished to ensure their immunity from prosecution for what was said in parliamentary debate, but it may be doubted that they were thinking of the testimony of witnesses before parliamentary committees. It may even be doubted that parliamentary committees existed in 1689, at least as we know them today.

One of the difficulties I have in deciding whether to maintain or dismiss the objection is that there is no Canadian case directly dealing with the issue. I am referred, however, to jurisprudence in cases alleged to be persuasive originating in other countries which have, like Canada, inherited the Westminster form of parliamentary government and the protections afforded by the *Bill of Rights* of 1689. Of this jurisprudence two cases stand out, the decision of Mr. Justice Hunt in the Australian case of *R. v. Murphy* (1986) 64 A.L.R. 498 and the decision of the Judicial Committee of the Privy Council, in an appeal from a decision of the Courts of New Zealand, in *Prebble v. Television New Zealand Ltd.* (1995) I A.C. 321. Sadly, these two decisions are at the same time well-reasoned, persuasive and completely contradictory. The parties contesting the objection, who argue that parliamentary immunity does not attach to the transcripts of Mr. Guité's testimony before the Public Accounts Committee, rely upon the reasons for judgment of Mr. Justice Hunt, which include the following extract from page 8 of his Judgment:

> *What is meant by the declaration that "freedom of speech. . . in Parliament ought not to be impeached or questioned in any court or place out of Parliament" is, in my view, that no court proceedings (or proceedings of a similar nature) having legal consequences against a member of Parliament (or a witness before a parliamentary committee) are permitted which by those legal consequences have the effect of preventing that member (or committee witness) exercising his freedom of speech in Parliament (or before a committee) or of punishing him for having done so. In other words, the phrase "impeached or questioned in any court or place out of Parliament" in Art. 9 should be interpreted in the sense that the exercise of the freedom of speech given to members of Parliament (and committee witnesses) may not be challenged by way of court (or similar) process having legal consequences for such persons because they had exercised that freedom.*

He continues at page 11 as follows:

> *Freedom of speech in Parliament is not now, nor was it in 1901 or even in 1688, so sensitive a flower that, although the accuracy and the honesty of what is said by members of Parliament (or witnesses before parliamentary committees) can be severely challenged in the media or in public, it cannot be challenged in the same way in the courts of law. It is only where legal consequences are to be visited upon such members or witnesses for what was said or done by them in Parliament that they can be prevented by challenges in the courts of law from exercising their freedom of speech in Parliament. It is only when that is the consequence of the challenge that freedom of speech in Parliament needs any greater protection from what is said or done in the courts of law than it does from what is said or done in the media or in public.*

This decision so alarmed the Parliament of Australia that it promptly enacted legislation to explicitly affirm the parliamentary privilege argument rejected by Mr. Justice Hunt, by the *Parliamentary Privileges Act* of 1987.

The opposing view, upon which counsel for the House of Commons and Mr. Guité rely, is enunciated in the Privy Council decision in *Prebble v. Television New Zealand Ltd.*, which takes a much broader view of the immunity created by Article 9 of the *Bill of Rights*. Lord Browne-Wilkinson expressly disagrees with the conclusions reached by Mr. Justice Hunt, and says in his opinion that Article 9 of the *Bill of Rights* is a manifestation of the principle that the courts and Parliament should recognize their respective constitutional roles and that one should not be allowed to challenge in any way what is said or done in the other. He continues as follows at p. 332 of the reported decision:

> *According to conventional wisdom, the combined operation of article 9 and that wider principle would undoubtedly prohibit any suggestion in the present action (whether by way of direct evidence, cross-examination or submission) that statements were made in the House which were lies or motivated by a desire to mislead.*

After expressing, politely but firmly, his profound disagreement with the conclusions of Mr. Justice Hunt in *R. vs. Murphy*, his Lordship concludes as follows (p. 334):

> *Moreover to allow it to be suggested in cross-examination or submission that a member or witness was lying to the House could lead to exactly that conflict between the courts and Parliament which the wider principle of non-intervention is designed to avoid. Misleading the House is a contempt of the House punishable by the House: if a court were also to be permitted to decide whether or not a member or witness had misled the House there would be a serious risk of conflicting decisions on the issue.*

It should be noted that decisions of the Privy Council rendered in 1995 are not binding on Canadian courts, although of course its views as to the proper interpretation to be given to an English statute such as the *Bill of Rights* of 1689 should be given great weight.

Before I undertake to choose between contradictory precedents, I must first consider the particular context in which the present dispute arises. Certain important distinctions from the cases mentioned are apparent. First of all, I am not here sitting as a court of law, but am presiding over a Commission of Inquiry, which has the mandate to make factual findings in order to make, subsequently, recommendations to prevent mismanagement of sponsorship programs or advertising activities of the Government of Canada in the future. The Terms of Reference by which the Commission was created require me to submit, on an urgent basis, reports to the Governor in Council, and I interpret this requirement to mean that as Commissioner I should avoid, to the greatest degree possible, legal entanglements that would have the effect of delaying the Commission's hearings and the submission of its reports. Since the Terms of Reference forbid me to make findings of civil or criminal responsibility, the present Commission is not at all similar to a court, although some of its procedures are comparable to what occurs during a trial. I also note that the Terms of Reference authorize the Commissioner "to adopt any procedures and methods that he may consider expedient for the proper conduct of the inquiry", meaning that the usual rules with respect to procedure and the admissibility of evidence do not apply, the only limitation to my liberty to proceed as I deem expedient and appropriate being my obligation to act fairly and in accordance with the requirements of natural justice.

Another distinguishing factor should be noted. This is a public inquiry into matters of great interest to the public, which relies upon the media for information concerning the evidence. The hearings are televised, as were the hearings before the Public Accounts Committee. Should I decide to maintain the objection, I would be in the seemingly paradoxical situation of deciding to exclude from consideration by the Commission testimony which has been available to the population in general and which has been widely commented upon in the media. However, this is not so paradoxical as it may at first appear. Facts having their source in privileged communications are often denied to judges and juries, as triers of questions of fact, yet no one contests the legal validity of their eventual findings and verdict.

The final distinction is the explicit promise made to Mr. Guité by the Public Accounts Committee that he would benefit from parliamentary immunity. From the case reports it does not appear that a similar promise was made to the witness concerned in the cases of *Murphy and Prebble*.

Should I decide the objection by authorizing the use of the transcripts for the purposes of cross-examination, I would undoubtedly have the advantage of knowing to what extent Mr. Guité may have made declarations to the Public Accounts Committee which may be inconsistent with his testimony before the Commission, but this would be at the cost of the risk of provoking an application for judicial review of my decision and the possibility of a stay of the hearings of the Commission. This is, in my opinion, a much greater danger and disadvantage to the completion of my mandate than being deprived of the use of the transcripts.

It should be remembered that questions to a witness concerning prior inconsistent statements have for their sole objective the undermining of the witness's credibility. They do not serve to put into evidence the earlier testimony of the witness; only what the witness says in his or her deposition before this Commission has what we call probative value. It should also be recalled that such questions are only one method of attacking a witness's credibility. All of the other means of assessing and testing credibility remain. In my view, even without the use of his prior testimony, I should be able to come to satisfactory conclusions concerning the credibility of Mr. Guité, based upon my experience as a judge, the documentation in the record, prior inconsistent statements he may have made elsewhere than before that particular Committee, and the usual indicia upon which triers of fact rely, such as the manner in which witnesses testify, contradictions, if any, in their testimony and the evidence of other witnesses.

In my view it is important that this Commission should not be seen to encroach in any way upon the privileges and immunities of the Parliament of Canada, and should respect the promises and undertakings it made to Mr. Guité. For this reason and for the practical reason that it is desirable and necessary to proceed with the work of this Commission of Inquiry without interruption, I propose to maintain the objection. Should this Ruling give rise to an application for judicial review by the parties contesting the objection or by one of them, in the event that my Ruling on the objection is eventually overturned before the Report of the Commission has been produced, Mr. Guité could, if necessary, be recalled to be questioned concerning the allegedly contradictory statements made previously. In other words, nothing will have been done that cannot be subsequently corrected.

For the time being, the objection is maintained and counsel are prohibited from asking Mr. Guité any question based upon an allegedly contradictory declaration made by him before the Public Accounts Committee of the House of Commons.

John H. Gomery, Commissioner

November 22, 2004

Ruling on Motion for Recusal (February 1, 2005)

A Motion presented on behalf of the Right Honourable Jean Chrétien asks me to recuse myself as Commissioner of this Inquiry.

Before dealing with some of the specific allegations made in support of the Motion, I would like to make a few remarks of a general nature.

I realize now, with the benefit of hindsight, that it was an error for me to agree to be interviewed by the media before Christmas. I also recognize that some of the statements made by me during those interviews were ill-advised and inappropriate. My inexperience in handling the media is obvious to everyone, and has served to detract attention from the real objective of the Inquiry, which is to get at the truth of the matters which were the subject of Chapters 3 and 4 of the Report of the Auditor General. I very much regret this distraction.

However, the question raised by Mr. Chrétien's Motion is not whether the interviews and the statements were ill-advised and inappropriate, but whether they demonstrate a reasonable apprehension of bias on my part, as that expression has been explained by the Courts, most recently in the *Beno* and *Krever* decisions.

In the representations made before me on January 11th, Mr. Scott declared and I quote: "You have closed your mind". That statement was factually incorrect; I am the only person in the world who could know if I had closed my mind, and I said then, to reassure Mr. Scott and others, that my mind remained open. It is still open today and I repeat that I have not yet reached any final conclusion on any of the questions which this Inquiry calls upon me to decide.

The arguments made in support of the Motion no longer appear to be that I am actually biased but rather that a reasonably well-informed person would conclude from the remarks that I made to journalists that I am biased, in spite of my reassurances to the contrary, and that I cannot be counted upon to decide fairly the matters which are to be decided. In paragraph 31 of the Motion, certain facts are cited in support of this proposition, which I would like to deal with briefly.

When I referred to the report of the Auditor General, I am quoted as saying that I "was coming" to the same conclusions as she did, not that I had so concluded. In other words, I indicated that my mental processes were ongoing; I have not closed my mind to contrary evidence, should such evidence be adduced.

When I made reference to autographed golf balls, I said that it was disappointing to have heard evidence that a Prime Minister *would* allow (note the use of the conditional tense) his name to be used in this way. My mind remains open to any reasonable explanation, and it is a small point in any event. I am looking forward to hearing Mr. Chrétien's testimony.

I have heard contradictory evidence, from various witnesses. I must conclude that some witnesses have not been truthful, but I did not say which witness or witnesses I was talking about, or indicate which of the conflicting versions I may be inclined to prefer. As to the relative truthfulness of various witnesses, these are conclusions I will draw only in light of all the evidence thus far and yet to come.

Finally, my description of Mr. Guité and the characterization of him as a "charming scamp", which is admittedly the kind of colourful language that judges should avoid using, does not in any way betray how I feel about his credibility. Sometimes charming people are credible and sometimes not. It is too soon to decide what weight I will give to Mr. Guité's testimony. That remains to be decided when the hearings are completed. The other matters referred to in subparagraph (c) of paragraph 31, namely the admissibility of testimony before the Public Accounts Committee and the decision to exclude evidence relating to outstanding criminal charges are raised in an application for judicial review which is pending before the Federal Court, upon which I should not comment.

The Motion refers to the political past of the Commission's lead counsel, Me. Bernard Roy. It acknowledges that those political activities ended more than fifteen years ago. His past was known to all parties concerned from the time I made the appointment, and is totally irrelevant to the subject-matter of the Inquiry. Me. Roy should be judged solely on the basis of his work for the Inquiry, which has been professional, impartial and objective. He has my full confidence. My conduct of the Inquiry has not been in any way influenced or affected by what Me. Roy might have done in the 1980's, or by any political views that he has now or may have had in the past.

I do not concede that anything that I said, or the language that I used, would persuade a reasonably well-informed and fair-minded person, viewing the matter realistically and practically, that I am biased or partial, or that I have closed my mind and come to conclusions prematurely about the issues with which this Commission is concerned, or that the proceedings are being conducted unfairly. After giving the matter careful consideration, I am firmly of the opinion that a reasonable, well-informed and fair-minded person understands the difference between committing an error and being biased.

I note that the Applicant's complaint about the phrasing of my question to Mr. Beaudoin has taken a small number of lines out of the much larger context in which the exchange took place. As to the comments made to certain journalists by Mr. Perreault, the Commission media spokesman, I wish to state that those comments were made without my knowledge. In any event, Mr. Perreault simply stated the content of e-mails received—a matter of fact.

I consider that it is my duty to take into account the work that has already been accomplished by the Commission, including extensive preparations and more than 60 days of hearings extending over a period of nearly five months. The recusal of its sole Commissioner would place all parties, including the witnesses who have already been heard and those who have not yet testified, in a position of stressful uncertainty, and would necessitate lengthy delays and huge costs in addition to those already incurred. The public interest would be badly served by a suspension of the hearings for any reason.

For these reasons I dismiss the Application for my recusal as Commissioner of this Inquiry.

John H. Gomery, Commissioner

February 1, 2005

Ruling on Applications for Publication Ban (March 29, 2005)

This Ruling deals with three applications, filed respectively on behalf of Jean S. Brault, Paul Coffin and Joseph Charles Guité, each having been charged by the Attorney General of Quebec in preferred indictments with multiple counts of fraud and conspiracy under the *Criminal Code*. Their trials, before courts composed of a Quebec Superior Court judge and jury, are scheduled to begin on May 2, 2005 and are expected to last from four to six weeks. In the meantime they have been subpoenaed to appear before this Commission to testify concerning matters relevant to its mandate. The applications ask that their testimony be made subject to a publication ban to have effect until the completion of their criminal trials.

The expression "publication ban" as it is used in this decision, should be taken to have the meaning those words have been given in subsection 486(4.9) of the *Criminal Code*, which states that "no person shall publish in any way (…) any evidence taken, information given or submissions made at a hearing", in this case, a hearing of the Commission. In my interpretation of this disposition, "broadcast" includes a posting on the Internet.

The word "broadcast" means "broadcast to the public", so that a publication ban would not prohibit a television broadcaster such as CPAC from continuing to capture the television images and sound of the Commission's proceedings, and from transmitting them to the media room and other in-house outlets, as it does at present. Rule 50 of the Commission's *Rules of Procedure and Practice* should not be construed so as to prevent this practice.

All three applicants request that the publication ban should be made to apply not only to their own testimony, but also to the testimony of others which relates to the criminal charges they are facing. It should be remembered, however, that at the very beginning of the hearings counsel for the Commission agreed and undertook not to adduce evidence before the Commission relating to the matters that are the subject of the criminal charges which the applicants are facing. This undertaking will continue to be respected. The testimony of the applicants themselves may give rise to other problems, such as impressions that potential jurors might receive with respect to their character or conduct; this difficulty will be dealt with later, but for now, I will say, for reasons that will be explained later, that I am not convinced that there is any justification for a publication ban with respect to the evidence introduced by persons other than the applicants themselves.

The applications in written form presented by Messrs. Coffin and Guité also ask that their testimony be heard *in camera*, but in their oral representations before me no arguments in favor of an *in camera* hearing were formulated, and I have concluded that this aspect of the applications has either been withdrawn, or is not their true objective.

In the application presented on behalf of Mr. Guité he requests, as an alternative conclusion, that his appearance before the Commission to testify be postponed until after his criminal trial. This request will not be granted since a publication ban, if it is granted, gives him equivalent relief. In addition, the postponement of his testimony would disrupt the orderly presentation of evidence and unduly delay the completion of the Commission's hearings, and the production of its first Report, a matter of considerable urgency.

Accordingly, the sole issue which remains to be decided is whether or not there should be a publication ban with respect to the testimony of the applicants, and if so, its scope and duration.

All of the applicants allege that the media attention which will be given to their appearances before the Commission will make it impossible for them to have a fair trial, since the jury selected to try them will inevitably be influenced by that publicity. They point to paragraph (k) of the Commission's Terms of Reference which directs me "to ensure that the conduct of the inquiry does not jeopardize any ongoing criminal investigation or criminal proceedings"; they argue that if the effect of their testimony before the Commission is to make it impossible for them to have a fair trial, I will have failed to fulfill this obligation.

The applications are contested by Mr. Bantey representing a consortium of newspapers and broadcast media. He submits that all of the reasons given in my Ruling of October 28, 2004 for refusing a publication ban which was then requested by Mr. Guité still apply, and that there is no reason alleged or evidence offered to support a modification of that Ruling. Counsel for the Auditor General of Canada, the Attorney General of Quebec, the

Attorney General of Canada and counsel for the Commission itself, all indicate in their representations that if a publication ban is contemplated, it should be limited as to its duration and scope, so as to conform to the principles enunciated by Chief Justice Lamer for the majority of the Supreme Court of Canada in the *Dagenais case*[1], by Mr. Justice Cory in the *Westray case*[2], and by the Supreme Court, unanimously, in *Mentuck*[3].

This matter is a classic case where a balance must be found between two constitutionally protected rights, the right of the public to be informed of matters affecting them, guaranteed by section 2 of the *Canadian Charter of Rights and Freedoms*[4], and the right of every person accused of a crime to have a fair trial, guaranteed by section 11(d) of the *Charter*. It should be noted that Canadian citizens have an interest in the protection of both of these rights, since the freedom of the press is an essential value in a democracy, and the guarantee that every person is presumed innocent and cannot be found guilty of a criminal offence without undergoing a fair trial is for the protection of us all.

I do not propose to repeat in detail what I said in my decision of October 28, 2004; the reasons that were given then continue to be valid, but it must be again recalled that in their testimony before the Commission, the applicants will not be questioned with respect to the matters underlying any of the criminal charges upon which they are to be tried in May. Accordingly, they have no reason to fear self-incrimination on those charges. I also wish to emphasize that the fundamental responsibility for assuming that accused persons have a fair trial rests primarily upon the court that tries them, which has many means at its disposal to ensure that the citizens chosen as jurors are impartial and able to decide upon the guilt or innocence of the accused based only upon the evidence presented at their trial, and not upon what they may have heard elsewhere.

Nevertheless, I am obliged to take into account the great interest with which the proceedings of the Commission have been followed by the public, as evidenced by extensive media and broadcast coverage and commentary. As the Supreme Court of Canada commented recently in *Krymowski*[5], a court may accept without the requirement of proof facts that are either

"(1) so notorious or generally accepted as not to be the subject of debate amongst reasonable persons; or (2) capable of immediate and accurate demonstration by resort to readily accessible sources of indisputable accuracy."

Judging by the number of journalists and cameramen who are present at the hearings, the intensity of this media coverage has increased since Mr. Guité first testified before me in Ottawa in November. Media reports of which I am aware refer to a high degree of public indignation at certain recent revelations in the evidence presented before the Commission. Applying judicial experience and common sense, these factors probably make it more difficult than previously to empanel an impartial and dispassionate jury.

The problem is aggravated by the circumstance that the testimony of the applicants will be presented before the Commission only a few weeks or days before the commencement of their trials. It may not be easy for potential jurors to distinguish between the facts admitted into evidence in the criminal trials and the facts, possibly of a prejudicial nature, which will be disclosed in the evidence presented during their appearances before the Commission.

Mr. Bantey takes the position that in spite of these factors, it should be possible to select, by a careful screening process, jurors who either have not followed the media coverage of the proceedings of the Commission, or who have not formed opinions favorable or unfavorable to the applicants. Furthermore, he argues that no evidence has been presented by the applicants to demonstrate that the depositions of the applicants will leave potential jurors irreparably prejudiced or impair the presumption of innocence.

These arguments have two inherent weaknesses.

First of all, in spite of the efficiency and effectiveness of the screening process, Mr. Justice Cory, in his opinion in *Westray*, does not entirely exclude the necessity, in some cases, of a publication ban. In other words, it must be foreseen that in some cases, admittedly cases of an exceptional nature, the pool of potential jurors may be irreparably tainted by information that has been disseminated prior to the criminal trial.

Secondly, the difficulty for an accused person to demonstrate, by an evidentiary process, that future publicity will cause him an irreparable prejudice, should not be underestimated. I cannot imagine how one is to assess the effect that revelations will have upon the public consciousness, particularly when one does not know what the revelations will be, the extent to which they will be reported by the media, and in what terms. The burden of proof imposed upon an applicant for a publication ban[6], presupposes that the extent and nature of the publicity is already known and measurable, whereas in the present matter, where the applicants have not yet testified, the possibly prejudicial effect of their depositions and how they may be reported and commented upon can only be guessed.

Mr. Justice Cory expresses the opinion that the hearings of a public inquiry do not in general present an unacceptable risk to the *Charter* right of an accused to have a fair trial, expressing himself on this subject in the following terms:

> *Often the publicity pertaining to the evidence given at the Inquiry will have little effect on potential jurors. The impact may be fleeting and quickly fade away. How very quickly the details of a news story can be forgotten. The passage of a very few days may suffice to dim if not obliterate the memory of the reporting of Inquiry evidence. The likelihood of a prejudicial effect upon fair trial rights may be small indeed, a minor item washed away in the flood of information generated daily by the media.[7]*

It is on the basis of this passage that I have concluded that there is no justification for a publication ban with respect to the evidence produced by persons other than the applicants themselves.

Mr. Justice Cory sees the matter differently however when the evidence before the public inquiry is the testimony of the persons accused of criminal offences. He is of the view that in those cases a publication ban may be necessary, as appears from the following passage:

> *However, the publication of the testimony of the two accused managers presents a very different situation. Obviously anything said by the accused will have a far greater impact than the evidence of many other witnesses. There is a real possibility that it will be stressed in media reports and well remembered by potential jurors. Yet, as accused, the managers can never be required to testify at their trial. The publication of their evidence at the Inquiry might mean that potential jurors would have been exposed to testimony that they might never hear at the trial. This coupled with the fact that it*

came from the accused themselves would make it difficult for jurors, despite their good intentions and the best of instructions from the trial judge to set it aside and leave it out of their considerations. In respect of this evidence, then, there is a clearly identifiable and serious risk that the fair trial rights of the two accused will be jeopardized.[8]

I am of the opinion, notwithstanding the undertaking made by Commission counsel, that the foregoing citation is applicable to the present hearings. A publication ban is needed, as a precaution, with respect to the testimony of the applicants and evidence presented during their depositions, in order to prevent a serious risk to the proper administration of justice, because reasonable alternative measures cannot be sure to prevent that risk.

Since publication bans should be limited as to their duration, scope and content, in order to minimally restrict the freedom of the press and the right of free expression that it represents, I will impose a publication ban only until the moment at the end of the criminal trial of the applicant concerned when jurors are sequestered to deliberate. In the meantime, at the end of the deposition of each of the applicants, I will be prepared to hear representations from interested parties, including counsel for the media, on the question of whether some or all of the deposition should be immediately released from the publication ban, taking into consideration the effect that such a release might have upon forthcoming jury selection.

For these reasons, the three motions are granted in part, and I order

(1) That the testimony of Jean S. Brault, Paul Coffin and Joseph Charles Guité before this Commission of Inquiry during Phase IB of its hearings, and any written evidence presented or referred to during their depositions, or any representations by counsel with respect thereto, shall be the subject of a publication ban as that term is used in subsection 486(4.9) of the *Criminal Code*, to remain in effect until the completion of the trial of the witness concerned before the Superior Court of Quebec, when the jury is sequestered to deliberate, unless ordered otherwise in the meantime;

(2) That upon the completion of the deposition of each of these witnesses, I will hear representations by counsel for interested parties who may request the immediate release from the effect of the

publication ban of the deposition of the witness concerned, or a part or parts thereof.

(3) That notwithstanding Rule 50 of the Commission's *Rules of Procedure and Practice*, CPAC may continue to capture the television images and sound of the Commission's proceedings, and to transmit them to the media room and other in-house outlets, as it does at present.

John H. Gomery, Commissioner

March 29, 2005

[1] Dagenais v. CBC, [1994] 3 SCR 835

[2] Phillips v. Nova Scotia, [1995] 2 SCR 97 (Westray)

[3] R. v. Mentuck, [2001] SCR 442

[4] Schedule B to the Constitution Act, 1982, enacted as the Canada Act, 1982 (U.K.), c. 11

[5] R. v. Krymowski, 2005 SCC 7 at para. 22

[6] Westray at pages 173-4

[7] Westray at page 177

[8] Westray at pages 177-8

Ruling Modifying Publication Ban (Jean S. Brault) (April 7, 2005)

On March 29, 2005 a publication ban was ordered with respect to the testimony of Jean S. Brault, which was then about to begin, and I undertook to hear representations by counsel for interested parties at the end of his deposition to determine if the ban should be released in whole or in part. His testimony ended yesterday afternoon. Counsel for Mr. Brault, supported by counsel for Mr. Guité, asks that the publication ban remain in effect until the completion of the trial of their clients, now fixed to begin on June 6th. All of the other parties that have made representations submit that it should be lifted, in whole or in part, except for counsel for Mr. Welch, who does not have standing, and who wants a delay to consider his position. This application cannot be granted; the interests of the other parties are of greater importance.

I am of the opinion that almost all of Mr. Brault's testimony and the documentation filed as part of his evidence have little to do with the accusations of fraud and conspiracy that he is facing. It is in the public interest that this evidence, with only a few exceptions, be made available to the public, remembering that publication bans constitute a violation of constitutional rights and are to be imposed rarely, particularly in the context of a public inquiry. At the time the ban was imposed, I did not know what Mr. Brault would say, and imposed the ban as a precaution, to prevent a possible prejudice to his right to a fair trial before an impartial jury. I will make a few exceptions to this general release, recalling the remarks of Mr. Justice Lamer in Dagenais c. C.B.C., [1994] 3 R.C.S. 835 at page 886 where he states:

> *Lorsque le procès est précédé d'une période intense de publicité relativement à des questions qui feront l'objet du procès, la situation est plus problématique. L'impact des directives est alors considérablement atténué. La publicité peut créer, dans l'esprit du jury, des impressions qui ne peuvent être consciemment dissipées. Le jury risque en fin de compte d'être incapable de distinguer la preuve entendue au procès de l'information implantée par un déversement continu de publicité.*

The evidence of the frequency of the contacts between Mr. Brault and Mr. Guité, and of the dealings they had, as described in Mr. Brault's testimony, could leave impressions in the minds of potential jurors, impressions that they might have difficulty to set aside, that they conspired together or were motivated by a common desire to derive improper benefits from their relationship. To reduce the possibility of such impressions being created, a few portions of Mr. Brault's testimony as identified below, and a few exhibits, will remain subject to the publication ban until after their trial.

Accordingly, the publication ban ordered on March 29, 2005, is lifted with respect to the deposition of Jean S. Brault and all representations by counsel made with respect to it, except for

1) The following portions of the transcription of Mr. Brault's testimony and the related portions of the broadcast tapes, namely:

   a. Volume 88, for March 30, 2005, page 15688, line 3 to page 15690, line 13;

   b. Volume 89, for March 31, 2005, page 15806, line 9 to page 15807, line 8;

   c. Volume 90, for April 1, 2005, page 15926, line 10 to page 15932, line 10;

   d. Volume 91, for April 4, 2005, page 16027, line 9 to page 16028, line 20, and page 16032, line 17 to page 16058, line 3;

   e. Volume 92, for April 5, 2005, page 16284, line 21 to page 16297, line 17, and page 16303, line 4 to page 16312, line 11;

   f. Volume 93, for April 6, 2005, page 16557, line 7 to line 18;

2)

   a. Exhibit C313, page 78

   b. Exhibit C299, pages 9 to 27 inclusive including the addenda following page 9, and pages 33 to 59.

John H. Gomery

John H. Gomery, Commissioner

April 7, 2005

Ruling Modifying Publication Ban (Paul Coffin) (April 27, 2005)

On March 29, 2005 a publication ban was ordered with respect to the testimony of Paul Coffin, and I undertook to hear representations by counsel for interested parties at the end of his deposition to determine if the ban should be released in whole or in part. His testimony ended this morning.

Counsel for Mr. Coffin asks that all or most of their client's testimony should remain subject to the publication ban until after his criminal trial, which will begin in mid June. Counsel for the Commission takes the position that only selected portions of the testimony should remain subject to the ban, those portions containing references to billing practices used by Mr. Coffin which were in some respects similar to those which are the subject of the criminal charges. The Crown prosecutor concerned supports this submission. All of the other parties who have made representations on this issue are in favor of a complete lifting of the ban.

None of the questions put to Mr. Coffin refer specifically to the criminal charges, but in two of his answers he made statements that might, correctly or incorrectly, be considered by potential jurors to be admissions of the fraudulent acts which will be the subject of his trial. Since the purpose of the publication ban was to protect Mr. Coffin from a breach of his right not to incriminate himself, those statements should not be published. All of the remainder of his testimony should be made available to the public; there is no serious danger that his actions and conduct which he describes could be confused with the actions and conduct which are the subject of the indictment.

Accordingly the publication ban ordered on March 29, 2005 is lifted with respect to the deposition of Paul Coffin and all representations by counsel made with respect to it, except for the following portions of the transcription of Mr. Coffin's testimony for April 26, 2005 and the related portions of the broadcast tapes, namely:

a. Page 19459, line 16 to page 19460, line 13;

b. Page 19496, lines 1 to 19.

John H. Gomery

John H. Gomery, Commissioner

April 27, 2005

Ruling Modifying Publication Ban (Joseph Charles Guité)
(May 4, 2005)

On March 29, 2005 a publication ban was ordered with respect to the testimony of Joseph Charles Guité, and I undertook to hear representations by counsel for interested parties at the end of his deposition to determine if the ban should be released in whole or in part. His cross-examination ended this morning and I have heard representations from all interested parties.

The importance of a publication ban in the case of Mr. Guité is lessened by the fact that his trial has been postponed to June 6, 2005 and may well be postponed again to a date in September.

However, to be consistent, there should remain in effect a publication ban with respect only to certain dealings that Mr. Guité had with Mr. Brault, considering that they are accused of criminal conspiracies. The lifting of the ban will be postponed until 3:30 this afternoon, so that Mr. Justice Brunton, who is seized with the record in the Quebec Superior Court, will have an opportunity to take such measures as he deems necessary to protect the rights of the accused to a fair trial. I apologize to my colleague for the short delay within which he will be obliged to act, but the right of the public to be informed of the testimony of Mr. Guité should not be compromised for longer than has already occurred.

Accordingly, the publication ban is to be lifted, as of 3:30 p.m. with respect to the testimony of Joseph Charles Guité, except for:

1) The transcript and broadcast tapes with respect to the representations made by Me. Bernard Roy today between 12:15 and 12:30;

2) Exhibit 376A, pages 293, 294 and 295;

3) The following portions of the transcription of Mr. Guité's testimony and the related portions of the broadcast tapes:

a.   Volume 108, page 19710, line 13 to page 19716, line 7;
b.   Volume 110, page 20106, line 22 to page 20109, line 8.

John H. Gomery

John H. Gomery, Commissioner

May 4, 2005

Ruling on Confidentiality Order (April 13, 2005)

The applicants, Malcom Media Inc. and Luc Lemay, have requested that I order that some of the documents that Commission Counsel intend to file as evidence be kept confidential and not disclosed to anyone unless a confidentiality agreement is signed.

In effect, the request amounts to a kind of no-publication order for these documents, which are the financial statements for a trust and corporations for which Mr. Lemay was the guiding spirit and principal stockholder. Mr. Lemay alleges that disclosure of these financial statements would be prejudicial to him vis-à-vis his competitors, his clients, his suppliers and potential purchasers of his companies.

I have no doubt that the disclosure of this financial information would have a negative impact on the intentions and business interests of the applicants, and constitute an invasion of their privacy. However, this is a public investigation of considerable interest to the people of Canada. Non-disclosure of the financial position of the applicants in all its details would deprive Canadians of a source of information that could help them, and the Commission itself, acquire a better understanding of where the sponsorship money paid by the Government of Canada went.

In *Sierra Club of Canada v. Canada (Minister of Finance)* [2002] 2 S.C.R. 522, Iacobucci J. in paragraph 53 of his reasons, summarized the rules to be followed when a litigant requests a confidentiality order, as follows:

> *A confidentiality order under Rule 151 should only be granted when:*
>
> a. *such an order is necessary in order to prevent a serious risk to an important interest, including a commercial interest, in the context of litigation because reasonably alternative measures will not prevent the risk; and*
>
> b. *the salutary effects of the confidentiality order, including the effects on the right of civil litigants to a fair trial, outweigh its deleterious effects, including the effects on the right to free expression, which in this context includes the public interest in open and accessible court proceedings.*

In the following paragraphs he added that to constitute a serious risk to an important interest, the risk must be real and important, insofar as it is solidly substantiated by the evidence and poses a serious threat to the commercial interest in question.

According to Mr. Justice Iacobucci, the interest in question cannot merely be specific to the party requesting the order but also one which can be expressed in terms of a public interest in confidentiality.

This requirement is not met in this case. The public interest requires complete disclosure of the financial statements in question. Moreover, within the context of this Commission of Inquiry, freedom of expression, a fundamental right, must be respected and protected, even at the expense of private interests, particularly strictly commercial interests.

For these reasons I dismiss the request.

John H. Gomery

_____

John H. Gomery, Commissioner

April 13, 2005

Ruling on Public Accounts Committee Evidence (May 20, 2005)

On October 18 and 25, 2004 I heard argument on Mr. Guité's objection to the attempt by Mr. Gagliano's counsel to cross-examine Mr. Guité on the basis of his prior testimony before the House of Commons' Standing Committee on Public Accounts ("PAC") in April of the same year. Mr. Gagliano was supported in his attempt by counsel for two other parties, Messrs. Chrétien and Pelletier, and was opposed by counsel for Mr. Guité. Mr. Guité's counsel, as well as counsel for the House of Commons, took the position that parliamentary privilege precluded the use of Mr. Guité's testimony for the purpose of impugning his credibility.

My decision dated November 22, 2004 was to exclude the use of the PAC testimony. I expressed the view that even without the testimony I had sufficient means to assess Mr. Guité's credibility; it was therefore unnecessary for me to make a final determination whether or not parliamentary privilege forbade the use of the PAC testimony to impugn Mr. Guité's credibility.

My decision not to allow the PAC testimony into evidence was upheld by the Federal Court on judicial review by a decision dated April 27, 2005. However, Madam Justice Tremblay-Lamer's conclusion was based on an assessment of the law of parliamentary privilege as it applied to the PAC testimony. She concluded that the essential test was whether, in order to ensure the effective operation of parliamentary committees, it was necessary to forbid the cross-examination of committee witnesses in any other forum, using transcripts of their committee testimony, and found that it was necessary to preclude cross-examination based on committee testimony, so as to encourage witnesses to testify openly before parliamentary committees, to allow the committee to exercise its investigatory function and to avoid contradictory findings of fact.

Mr. Gagliano's present application asks that I order deposit of the PAC transcripts and the corresponding audio-visual recordings into the record. Furthermore, basing himself on the last factor mentioned by Justice Tremblay-Lamer, namely the necessity of avoiding contradictory findings of fact, Mr. Gagliano asks for an additional order substituting the PAC evidence for this Commission's examination and cross-examination of Mr. Guité in November last year and in April and May this year. The application was argued before me on May 13, 2005 by counsel for Mr. Gagliano, for the House of Commons (accorded standing for the purposes of this application), for the Government of Canada and for this Commission. I was advised in writing by Mr. Guité's counsel that he opposed the application.

The first proposition of Mr. Gagliano's argument is that the filing of the PAC testimony as evidence of historical fact would not of itself violate parliamentary privilege. His second proposition is that Mr. Guité's PAC testimony should be admitted into evidence because its content is relevant to the Commission's inquiry, and essential to Mr. Gagliano's natural justice right to present evidence that contradicts Commission testimony that is adverse to his interests. His third proposition is that, according to the recent Federal Court decision, I am obliged to disregard Mr. Guité's allegedly inconsistent Commission testimony because the law concerning parliamentary privilege determines that the PAC testimony cannot be questioned. Finally, it is argued that Mr. Guité's PAC testimony meets the admissibility criteria specified by the Supreme Court of Canada in the *K.G.B.* decision.[1]

Mr. Gagliano's written submission adds that Mr. Guité's PAC testimony is likely to have been more frank and open than his "unprotected" testimony before this Commission because he was advised that his PAC testimony would be protected by parliamentary privilege; it follows that excluding the PAC testimony from the record would mean depriving this Commission of the best evidence available.

The principal argument opposing Mr. Gagliano's application was presented by counsel for the House of Commons, who argued that the mere admission of the PAC testimony into evidence, remembering that parliamentary privilege precludes an evaluation of the content of that testimony for credibility and weight, would frustrate the Commission's obligation to draw conclusions based upon its own evaluation of the evidence. It is obvious that Mr. Gagliano's real purpose is to admit the prior testimony for the truth of its contents rather than as a simple fact. It was also argued that admitting the testimony would frustrate this Commission's procedural fairness obligations, in particular its obligation to allow Mr. Guité an opportunity to try to explain any contradictions between his prior and current testimony. I was reminded that I had already come to the conclusion that I am able to assess Mr. Guité's credibility without resorting to the PAC testimony. Since the Committee has not itself evaluated the testimony or Mr. Guité's credibility, the potential for contradictory findings would remain. Finally, it was argued that the common law "best evidence" rule cannot prevail over a rule of privilege.

Counsel for the Government of Canada supported the House of Commons in its submissions, and added that, to the extent that Mr. Gagliano's argument relied on the principles of natural justice, the Supreme Court of Canada decisions in *Ocean Port*[2] and *Donahoe (New Brunswick Broadcasting)*[3] stand for the proposition that those principles may give way to conflicting statutory provisions (absent an overriding constitutional provision) and must give way to conflicting rules of constitutional law.

Commission counsel argued by analogy for the exclusion of the evidence on the basis of the common law rule that one cannot resort to the principles of natural justice to override professional privilege. He also noted that the *KGB* rules for the admission of prior contradictory statements only operate where the evidence sought to be introduced is otherwise admissible.

There is superficial merit to Mr. Gagliano's argument that the mere admission of the PAC testimony into evidence would not violate parliamentary privilege. Certainly, as noted in Mr. Gagliano's written submissions, the Judicial Committee of the Privy Council said in the *Prebble*[4] decision that courts may admit Hansard into evidence "to prove what was done and said in Parliament as a matter of history"[5]. However, on closer examination, the case law cited by the Applicant provides him little support in the particular circumstances of this case.

In *Comalco*[6], a decision of the Supreme Court of the Australian Capital Territory, the plaintiff corporation sued the media for defamation in a television program, in which were cited statements reportedly made by a government minister in the territorial legislature. In its defence, the media sought to adduce those statements in evidence and parliamentary privilege was invoked to preclude admission. The Australian Court reviewed a number of authorities, including the English defamation case of *Church of Scientology v. Johnson-Smith*[7] in which the plaintiff had alleged that the defendant member of Parliament had consistently attacked the Church of Scientology in the House of Commons. The English Court excluded the particulars that relied on Hansard to establish what was said in the House. Subsequently, in *Comalco*, the Australian Court clarified that the Church of Scientology ruling was that the defendant's statements in the House could not be used against him on the issue of malice, but not that Hansard was itself inadmissible. The Australian Court concluded[8] :

> ... I think that the way in which the court complies with Art 9 of the Bill of Rights 1689, and with the law of the privileges of Parliament, is not by refusing to admit evidence of what was said in Parliament, but by refusing to allow the substance of what was said in Parliament to be the subject of any submission or inference. The court upholds the privileges of Parliament, not by a rule as to the admissibility of evidence, but by its control over the pleadings and the proceedings in court.

Accordingly, passages from Hansard were held to be admissible solely to establish the fact that certain statements were made by the Minister, given their possible relevance to the defence of fair comment.

The House of Lords decision in *Pepper v. Hart*[9] was principally about the rule that prevented British courts from relying on Hansard as a statutory interpretation tool, a rule already rejected by Canadian courts. There was some discussion whether the simple act of admitting Hansard into evidence breached parliamentary privilege. In answering that question, the Law Lords focused on whether the admission of Hansard as a tool to resolve an ambiguity in statutory language would involve "any impeachment, or questioning of the freedom of speech or debates or proceedings in Parliament." The Attorney-General had argued that such use would entail a "questioning" of the freedom of speech or debate. Lord Browne-Wilkinson, with whom the other Law Lords expressed their agreement, held that "...the use of clear ministerial statements by the court as a guide to the construction of ambiguous legislation would not contravene article 9." He continued: "No doubt all judges will be astute to ensure that counsel does not in any way impugn or criticise the Minister's statements or his reasoning."[10]

In *Clarke*[11] , the defendant was charged with inciting a riot on the steps of the Ontario legislature. The Court allowed him to enter correspondence between himself and the Speaker's Office for the purpose of establishing his state of mind, but prohibited the use of the same documents to criticise or review the actions of the Speaker's Office or the Speaker's decisions.

Finally, although the *Prebble* case clearly supports the admission of Hansard as proof of the historical fact of certain things having been said in Parliament, the Law Lords very clearly limited the uses to which such evidence could be put, and placed certain oversight obligations on the court admitting the evidence[12]:

> ... Thus, in the present action, there cannot be any objection to it being proved what the plaintiff or the Prime Minister said in the House ... or that the State-Owned Enterprises Act 1986 was passed.... It will be for the trial judge to ensure that the proof of these historical facts is not used to suggest that the words were improperly spoken or the statute passed to achieve an improper purpose.

They continued[13]:

> It is clear that, on the pleadings as they presently stand, the defendant intends to rely on these matters not purely as a matter of history, but as part of the alleged conspiracy or its implementation. Therefore, in their Lordships' view, Smellie J. was right to strike them out. But their Lordships wish to make it clear that if the defendant wishes at the trial to allege the occurrence of events or the saying of certain words in Parliament without any accompanying allegation of impropriety or any other questioning there is no objection to that course.

In my view, the superficial attractiveness of Mr. Gagliano's argument that parliamentary privilege allows the admission of Mr. Guité's PAC testimony into evidence before this Commission disappears when one realises that the real purpose in admitting the testimony would be to establish what he affirmed. The fact that Mr. Guité testified is not contested; what Mr. Gagliano really wants to prove is that Mr. Guité may have made statements before the PAC which cannot be reconciled with his testimony before the Commission. This is directly contrary to the Federal Court decision on Mr. Gagliano's prior application; the record of Mr. Guité's PAC testimony cannot be used to test his credibility. In order to establish its allegedly contradictory nature, I would have to examine the PAC testimony and compare it to the testimony given before me. In my view, such an exercise is far too closely-related to the cross-examination that, according to Justice Tremblay-Lamer, is forbidden by parliamentary privilege.

For the purpose of the exercise of my discretion to control the proceedings before me, I find that the principal value of the jurisprudence cited above lies in their reminder of the care that must be taken by a tribunal if it is suggested that a record of parliamentary proceedings should be made part of the record. The tribunal must "refuse to allow the substance of what was said... to be the subject of any submission or inference,"[14] and must also "ensure that counsel does not in any way impugn or criticise the speaker's statements or reasoning"[15] and ensure that the admission of the transcripts or audio-visual recording "is not accompanied by any allegation of impropriety or any other questioning."[16].

With reference to the second conclusion of Mr. Gagliano's application, he argues that in the event I admit the transcript of the PAC testimony into evidence, I should then substitute it for the testimony given before this Commission. However, since Mr. Guité's PAC testimony is not evidence made in accordance with the Rules of the Commission, I cannot accept it without prior cross-examination, among other reasons. If I were inclined to defer to the Committee's assessment of Mr. Guité's testimony, I could not use the PAC testimony as evidence since the Committee has not yet reported. Indeed, reliance on the PAC testimony might ultimately lead to contradictory findings as between this Commission and PAC since PAC might eventually reject some or all of the testimony I had accepted.

In conclusion, since the Federal Court has decided that Mr. Guité's PAC testimony cannot be questioned, weighed or assessed for credibility by any body other than Parliament itself, and cannot be used against Mr. Guité in the Commission's proceedings, I find that the admission of Mr. Guité's PAC testimony would serve no useful purpose. I therefore exercise my discretion to continue to exclude that testimony from the record before me.

Mr. Gagliano's application is dismissed.

John H. Gomery

John H. Gomery, Commissioner

May 20, 2005

1   Her Majesty the Queen v. K.G.B., [1993] I S.C.R. 740

2   Ocean Port Hotel Ltd. v. British Columbia (General Manager, Liquor Control and Licensing Branch), [2001] 2 S.C.R. 781

3   New Brunswick Broadcasting Co. v. Nova Scotia (Speaker of the House of Assembly), [1993] I S.C.R. 319

4   Prebble v. Television New Zealand Ltd., [1995] I A.C. 321 (P.C.)

5   Ibid., at p. 337

6   Comalco Ltd. v. Australian Broadcasting Corporation, (1983) 50 A.C.T.R. I (S.C.)

7   Church of Scientology of California v. Johnson-Smith, [1972] I QB 522

8   Comalco, at p. 5

9   Pepper (Inspector of Taxes) v. Hart, [1993] A.C. 593 (H.L.(E.))

10 Ibid., at p. 639

11 Her Majesty the Queen v. John Clarke et al., unreported, Superior Court of Justice (Ontario), court file no. 0075/02, April 2, 2003

12 Prebble, at p. 337

13 Ibid., at p. 337

14 Comalco

15 Pepper v. Hart

16 Prebble

Ruling on Motion Pertaining to the Role of Commission Counsel

Volume 131, June 2, 2005

Page: 24877 Line 4 to 10

THE COMMISSIONER: Thank you very much.

I am going to dismiss the motion. I think that it has been apparent to everybody, as I have heard it, that I am unsympathetic to the proposition that I would be influenced improperly by facts that I might hear about, other than the facts that I have heard about in this room or in the room that we occupied when the hearings were going in Ottawa.

H

APPENDIX H

DEMERS ADMINISTRATIVE REVIEW

H. PIERRE TREMBLAY

P. Tremblay now occupies a position of vice-president at the EX-04 level at the Canadian Food Inspection Agency. During the period under review, he occupied a position of director at the EX-02 level, and then (interim) executive director at the EX-04 level.

The Committee met Pierre Tremblay on two occasions, on October 20 and 27, 2003. At the first meeting, P. Tremblay asked the Committee for a version of the Kroll Report in both official languages. The Committee said there was no French version. P. Tremblay asked that the Kroll Report and the Committee Report be made available in the two official languages, as the law provides for. He specifically required that it be mentioned in this report. At the beginning of the October 20 meeting, P. Tremblay said his lawyer could not attend the meeting, that he had not had time to read the excerpt from the Kroll Report and had advised him to note the questions likely to overlap the RCMP investigation so they can be analysed and answered in written form. P. Tremblay said he was ready to cooperate with the Committee to allow the administrative review to go forward. At the October 27 meeting, P. Tremblay said his doctors recommended against his taking part, but that he wanted to attend to show his cooperation and honesty.

P. Tremblay began the interview by tracing the history of his career and his arrival at Communication Coordination Services Branch (CCSB). About 1980, P. Tremblay was working for MP Jean-Robert Gauthier while completing a PhD. About 1985, after completing his thesis, P. Tremblay received an offer from MP Gauthier, then Chief Government Whip, who asked him to help him computerise the recording of House debates. During his work in Parliament from 1985 to 1994, P. Tremblay got to know Alphonso Gagliano. About 1994, Mr. Gagliano, then Chief Whip, was appointed Labour Minister. Minister Gagliano then hired P. Tremblay as executive assistant. When Minister Gagliano changed portfolio to head Public Works and Government Services Canada (PWGSC) in 1997, P. Tremblay followed him as executive assistant. When he arrived at PWGSC, according to P. Tremblay, Minister Gagliano asked Deputy Minister Ranald Quail to review the delegation of authority. Assistant Deputy Ministers Allan Williams and Jim Stobbe were in charge of the project. P. Tremblay said that in the spring of 1998, he himself did the monitoring with them to ensure the delegation was reviewed. Therefore, P. Tremblay said, he was reasonably familiar with the matter of delegation of authority at PWGSC.

P. Tremblay specified that Minister Gagliano asked Deputy Minister R. Quail to set up CCSB. In 1998, J.C. Guité asked P. Tremblay for the names of persons who could be good candidates to replace him as he was preparing for his retirement. He was looking for someone likely to get along well with the Minister. P. Tremblay himself was then considering a transfer into the civil service, so he informed Messrs. Gagliano and Quail of his interest in moving to CCSB. P. Tremblay said Messrs. Gagliano and Quail made sure he passed all the necessary tests (language, in-basket test, interview with CSC) to abide by the standards of eligibility for a CCSB position. In February 1999, P. Tremblay was appointed director of strategic communications, an

EX-02 level position, at CCSB. His work was to assist the Cabinet Committee on Communication on behalf of CCSB for the PWGSC Minister. This committee was made up of representatives from CCSB, the Privy Council Office and the Canada Information Office and met once a week.

P. Tremblay emphasizes that most of the events involving him in the Kroll Report occurred about April 1999, a few weeks after his arrival at CCSB, when J.C. Guité was still executive director. P. Tremblay says he signed for J.C. Guité when the latter was absent, but also sometimes when he was present because J.C. Guité was grooming him to take over the Sponsorship Program. P. Tremblay explains that, up until the time he arrived, there was no set budget for sponsorships. The person responsible for national unity in the Prime Minister's Office decided at year's end what sums were to be allocated to the Sponsorship Program. P. Tremblay claims the budget allocated to sponsorships since 1993 was hidden and that even the Auditor General had not been able to identify it. J.C. Guité, therefore, could not promise sponsorships for the next fiscal year, but would still negotiate them, confident he would later get the necessary budget. This is, he believes, why so many sponsorships were signed at the beginning of the fiscal year, in April. P. Tremblay says that, when he was appointed interim executive director in September 1999, he asked Deputy Minister R. Quail to change this method of accounting. With the help of Ralph Sprague (DG, Finance), P. Tremblay prepared a submission for the Treasury Board (TB). This submission was signed by Minister Gagliano and Prime Minister Jean Chrétien because the money came from the Unity Reserve. For the following years starting in 2000/2001, CCSB received an annual budget of $40 million for three years, which made it possible to improve the management of sponsorships.

P. Tremblay explains that traditionally, in this type of industry, communication agencies (CAs) contact event organizers and get a commission (approximately 25%) for finding them sponsorships. P. Tremblay says that in October 1999, soon after his appointment as interim executive director, he sent a letter to all event organizers who had received sponsorships in the past, saying all sponsorship applications from then on should be sent to him directly instead of through CAs. CAs were also informed of this new rule, and afterwards the call for tenders was changed accordingly. The Committee pointed out to Mr. Tremblay that documents on file showed these letters were in fact sent in the fall of 2000, that is, after the internal audit report. P. Tremblay replies that he thought he had sent the letters in the fall of 1999, but his memory may be failing him.

P. Tremblay explains that, for a number of years, every department had sponsorship budgets and that all was not perfectly coordinated. Indeed, he says that, in some cases, CCSB talked with Sport Canada and Heritage Canada to ensure that all three did not sponsor the same event.

P. Tremblay says that as soon as he was appointed interim executive director, he kept Deputy Minister R. Quail informed of his activities in regular personal meetings. In the matter of sponsorships, he also met Minister Gagliano just as regularly. The Committee asks Mr. Tremblay to specify the reason for these meetings and what information was shared. P. Tremblay says he met the Deputy Minister and the Minister, not necessarily in that order, on a weekly basis and presented them with the list of events proposed, rejected or accepted, with the dates, the location, the amount of sponsorship and commissions to be paid to the distribution agency (DA) and the CA, for the Minister's approval.

P. Tremblay says that, since Minister Gagliano was responsible for the Program, it was normal to share with him the list of events to make sure the sponsorships were congruent with the situation of the moment and would not cause any political problems. As an example, P. Tremblay says that if the cause of women in the regions was the topic of the day, an event targeting women in a region would be encouraged. Other types of events for which a federal government sponsorship might cause a controversy were also discussed with the Minister to see if he had any objection. He adds that there were at times mixed sponsorships, for instance Via Rail and the Government of Canada, which sponsored the National Hockey League. P. Tremblay stresses that R. Quail never commented on his delegation of authority with regard to the points raised in the Kroll Report. P. Tremblay says R. Quail concerned himself mainly with the amounts of the sponsorships, not the choice of events, to make sure everything stayed within the limits of the budget.

The Committee asks P. Tremblay to explain his understanding of the delegation of authority. P. Tremblay says the process he put into place after the CCSB 2000 audit gave him the delegation necessary for the competitive markets granted through the electronic media. He adds that the action plan of this 2000 audit included the training of employees and the increase in resources.

The Committee asks P. Tremblay to explain why so many sponsorships were directed to Quebec. P. Tremblay replies that Prime Minister Chrétien himself said in the House that it was to ensure greater visibility for the federal government in Quebec following the referendum. On the other hand, P. Tremblay says Minister Gagliano did not prevent him from accepting sponsorships outside Quebec. P. Tremblay says he tried to be fair in considering similar applications from other provinces. P. Tremblay says there were no guidelines for selecting the sponsorships until Evelyn Marcoux in 1999 proposed some that were approved by the Minister and the Deputy Minister a little later. These guidelines did not include any national unity criteria, but referred rather to what the Government of Canada had to offer Canadians.

P. Tremblay continues, saying that when he became interim executive director, he also did some housecleaning of promotional items (T-shirts, flags, lapel pins, etc.). He gave the entire CCSB stock to embassies and other organizations. To replace these assorted items, he had T-shirts made to distribute to CAs.

The Committee asks P. Tremblay to explain Huguette Tremblay's role in the Sponsorship Program. P. Tremblay replies that she handled contract documents, finances and was in contact with the DAs and CAs. He says that, when she initialled a document, it was to confirm that everything was according to standards. The Committee asks how the invoices were presented to him. P. Tremblay says he would receive the request for goods and services and the invoice, but does not remember whether the contract was attached. In any case, he says the contracts were standard. P. Tremblay says he could not check the detail of every invoice and he had to trust someone. The Committee asks if he checked the invoices before signing them as required by Section 34 of the *Financial Administration Act* (FAA). P. Tremblay says that before he was appointed executive director, that is, from February to August

1999, he did not really check them because he trusted the system put into place by J.C. Guité and he trusted Huguette Tremblay in general. P. Tremblay says that after his appointment as interim executive director in the fall of 1999, he required post-mortems for every contract. Records show that this requirement was set rather in the fall of 2000, after the controlled audit.

1. General: Elements of non-compliance with market policies/rules relating to calls for tenders and selection of bid:

The Committee asks P. Tremblay what his involvement was in the development of the CA list established in 1999. P. Tremblay says he received the list J.C. Guité had drawn up and continued to use it until a new process was set up to improve the selection system. He says that, as far as he knows, seven of the list of ten CAs mentioned in the Kroll Report were used. He explains that sponsorship applications were submitted to J.C. Guité by CAs and it was generally those agencies that got the contract. He adds that sometimes J.C. Guité would ask a CA to sound out an event organizer, and he sometimes did the same thing.

Specific analysis/conclusion: Although P. Tremblay could have changed the system in place upon his appointment as executive director, well before it was recommended by the 2000 internal audit, the Committee finds that P. Tremblay had been led to believe sincerely the system was adequate. Consequently, the Committee feels he could not be held responsible for this.

2. General: Elements of non-compliance with delegation of authority and splitting of contracts:

In short, P. Tremblay says he used the delegation grid applicable to competitive markets granted by the electronic media. He consulted the Deputy Minister and the Minister every week and submitted for their approval a detailed report on sponsorship applications. Because of this, he feels, policy requirements and rules applicable to the approval of markets were respected.

3. Specific events in the Kroll Report:

P. Tremblay reminds us that his superiors never indicated to him that he went beyond his delegation of authority as he reported to them in detail every week on the sponsorship applications. That is why he rejects the findings of the Kroll Report in this matter. He adds that, given his consultations with the Minister, he rejects any element of non-compliance indicating that the Minister had apparently not been informed as prescribed by the conditions of the delegation of authority.

Events 37, 41, 40, 43, 35, 32, 29, 26, 48, 47, 45, 44, 38, 39 (re-numbering applied in the Kroll Report of June 2003)
(Contracts #EPO43-9-0005, 0013, 0010, 0006, 0016, 0011, 0012, 0015, 0002, 0003, 0008, 0004, 0001, 0007)
Salons/Soirées/Magazines/Almanach

These files concern Section 34 of the Financial Administration Act (FAA). The Kroll Report revealed full payment was made on April 20, 1999, while the contract was dated April 1, 1999. Nothing in the file indicates the event was held prior to April 20. According to the contract, only 80% of the amount was to be paid before the event.

P. Tremblay explains that he had been in his position only a few weeks when he signed these invoices while he was DG of strategic communications under J.C. Guité. The invoices had been initialled by Huguette Tremblay. J.C. Guité then instructed him on what he had to do and he confirmed that everything was in accordance with rules and policies. Since these contracts had been negotiated and signed by J.C. Guité himself, P. Tremblay says he did not question the invoices submitted. He now realizes he should have. P. Tremblay cannot offer any evidence confirming the dates and the actual staging of those salons/soirées because he verified none of these files that were initiated by J.C. Guité. The Committee asks whether it was possible those invoices dated April 20, 1999, were for events held the previous year. P. Tremblay says it is not impossible, but he believes they were for the current year. He adds that J.C. Guité often exceeded the budget of the Sponsorship Program, but did not worry because he was confident he would obtain the necessary funds. The Committee asks P. Tremblay to comment on the value of these sponsorships compared with other similar events in Canada. P. Tremblay replies that the value depends on many criteria, such as the targeted public and the kind of vehicle used.

Specific analysis/conclusion: Taking into account the findings described in C-3 (Section C), added to the following attenuating factors:

- The invoices were submitted to him shortly after P. Tremblay arrived at CCSB while he was still in a period of apprenticeship under J.C. Guité;

- the fact that J.C. Guité, according to Huguette Tremblay, authorized single, full payments only exceptionally.

The Committee is of the opinion that P. Tremblay did not comply with the provisions of Section 34 of the FAA and, thus, was negligent but the seriousness of that negligence is attenuated by the above-mentioned circumstances.

Event #30 (contract # EPO43-9-0014) National Magazines:

Section 34 of the FAA: The element of non-compliance is the same as in the previous case, except for a third-party invoice dated after April 20, 1999. P. Tremblay does not remember the details of this case, but remembers discussing it with J.C. Guité.

Specific analysis/conclusion: The Committee's conclusions are the same as for the previous event.

Event #33 (contract # EPO43-9-0009) Production and Planning Cost:

Section 34 of the FAA: This concerns production/planning for all previous events.

P. Tremblay notes Huguette Tremblay did not initial this invoice of May 3, 1999, but adds that, in this case, J.C. Guité would have indicated to him that he could sign. P. Tremblay says that, in the case of production/planning, it is possible the work was carried out by the CA before the May 3, 1999, signature. In contrast, P. Tremblay confirms that, according to him, all the salons/soirées in question were not held in April, but rather in the course of the year.

Specific analysis/conclusion: The Committee notes that Huguette Tremblay did not initial this item. In addition, contrary to the payment of the sponsorship itself, it seems the CA work could not be adequately assessed. The Committee must take into account the fact that these invoices were submitted to P. Tremblay shortly after he arrived at CCSB while he was still in a period of apprenticeship under J.C. Guité. The Committee is of the opinion that P. Tremblay did not comply with the provisions of Section 34 of the FAA and, thus, was negligent but the seriousness of that negligence is attenuated by the preceding.

Event #160 (contract # EN771-8-0077) 125th Notre-Dame du Laus:

Section 34 of the FAA—Contract of $21,000 value; some items in one invoice are for work carried out after the period covered by the contract.

P. Tremblay does not remember this small event. Here again, the invoice of August 30, 1999, bore the initials of Huguette Tremblay. However, he did not check the details.

Specific analysis/conclusion: Taking into account the findings described in C-3 (Section C), added to the following attenuating factors:

- These invoices were submitted to him while he was still in a period of apprenticeship under J.C. Guité;
- the relatively low value of these invoices.

The Committee is of the opinion that P. Tremblay did not comply with the provisions of Section 34 of the FAA and, thus, was negligent but the seriousness of that negligence is attenuated by the above-mentioned circumstances.

Event #75 (contract # EPO43-9-0133) Jeux de la Francophonie:

Section 34 of the FAA: Indication of double payment.

P. Tremblay never realized anything was wrong with this $4,950 invoice of June 4, 1999. He believes it may have been an administrative error.

Specific analysis/conclusion: The other invoice was paid by David Myer on June 14, 1999. The Committee is of the opinion that it is indeed an administrative error and the signatory here was not negligent.

- Non-compliance with conditions of delegation of authority:

P. Tremblay notes that, while J.C. Guité was executive director and he was in the Minister's office, J.C. Guité met the Minister every three or four weeks, almost always in his presence. Exceptionally, in the minister's absence, J.C. Guité would meet with P. Tremblay or his successor, Jean-Marc Bard. P. Tremblay says that he discovered only later, after his transfer to CCSB, that J.C. Guité did not inform the Minister of all the events.

Specific analysis/conclusion: The Committee applies the findings described in C-1 to this element of non-compliance. The Committee does not conclude there was any negligence.

- Elements of non-compliance concerning competitive markets:

P. Tremblay says that in the minds of CCSB employees, the system in place complied with rules applicable to the state's competitive markets. He adds the short time limits in which the contracts were granted would not have allowed competitive bids; besides, the 12% rate provided in the contract was fixed. He says the distribution of markets among CAs improved with time.

The Committee wonders whether the decisions to grant a contract to one CA or another were motivated by political considerations. To this, P. Tremblay replies that CAs were paid for their work and that, if any of them contributed to political parties, they had to declare it to Canada's Chief Electoral Officer, as the applicable legislation requires. P. Tremblay goes on to say some agencies were known to have ties with different political parties. P. Tremblay adds that he never took into account the CA's political affiliations in his choices and that the minister never told him to which CA a contract should be given. The minister, he believes, was only interested in the visibility of the sponsorship and its importance. He further says that it was the same when J.C. Guité met the minister while he was his executive assistant.

Specific analysis/conclusion: The Committee applies the findings described in C-1 to this element of non-compliance. The Committee does not conclude there was negligence here.

Event #9 (contract # EP043-9-0037) Pan American Games:

Contract exceeding the level of delegated authority and non-compliance with conditions of the delegation of authority.

About this September 10, 1999, change in the contract, P. Tremblay says he believes he had the Minister's verbal approval, given at the weekly meetings. The latter was also informed of the changes later brought to the contracts.

Specific analysis/conclusion: Further to the explanations given by P. Tremblay, the Committee finds he had the necessary authority for the changes granted through the electronic media. The Committee applies the findings described in C-1 to the elements of non-compliance. The Committee does not conclude there was any negligence.

Event #16 (contract # EN771-7-0027) Hot Air Balloon Leases:

Payment possibly made twice.

P. Tremblay does not remember this invoice which apparently was paid twice; the other signed by Mario Parent. P. Tremblay explains that Christiane Bouvier, under Ralph Sprague, was the person in Finance paying these invoices.

Specific analysis/conclusion: The Committee checked this case with Finance. They said upon verification that only one payment was made for this transaction. The Committee, therefore, withdraws this element from the list included in the Kroll Report.

Event #31 (contract # EP043-9-0166) Atlantic Salmon:

Section 34 of the FAA—Lump-sum payment lacking a basis for confirming whether the rate of payment authorized in the contract is respected.

P. Tremblay signed this invoice on May 31, 1999. It does not bear Huguette Tremblay's initials. P. Tremblay claims he had instructions from J.C. Guité before signing it. He adds that this event (Atlantic salmon) is one of the first he eliminated when he became interim executive director. Having attended one of these events with J.C. Guité, he could see the visibility offered by the sponsorship was too limited.

Specific analysis/conclusion: The Committee notes Huguette Tremblay did not put her initials here. The Committee must take into account the following attenuating factors:

- The fact that these invoices were submitted to P. Tremblay shortly after his arrival at CCSB while he was still in a period of apprenticeship under J.C. Guité;

- the relatively low value of this invoice.

The Committee is of the opinion that P. Tremblay did not comply with the provisions of Section 34 of the FAA and, thus, was negligent but the seriousness of that negligence is attenuated by the above-mentioned circumstances.

Event #94 (contract # EP043-9-0040) CFL:

Section 34 of the FAA—Lump-sum payment lacking a basis for confirming whether the rate of payment authorized in the contract is respected.

P. Tremblay signed this invoice on December 31, 1999. P. Tremblay trusted Huguette Tremblay's initials. He claims he discussed it with her and told her to make sure everything was in order. She had done the same work for J.C. Guité, and P. Tremblay asked her to continue. Sometimes, Huguette Tremblay would question an invoice and P. Tremblay asked her to check with the CA.

P. Tremblay says he believes she did her best in the circumstances, but resources were insufficient given the workload.

Specific analysis/conclusion: The Committee considers that from September 1999, when P. Tremblay became interim executive director, he was responsible for making sure he assigned very clear tasks to his staff concerning their financial and contract responsibilities. He also had to make sure they carried out their tasks appropriately. As a consequence, the Committee does not accept P. Tremblay's defence that he believed Huguette Tremblay's initials meant the invoices complied on every point, including financially, with the contract. The Committee is of the opinion that P. Tremblay did not comply with the provisions of Section 34 of the FAA and, thus, was negligent.

Event #97 (contract # EP043-9-0046) Attractions Canada:

Four items under Section 34 of the FAA:

1. A sum totalling $62,000 in profit margin (spread over 28 invoices) was paid for services rendered by an agency strategically allied to the CA under contract, contrary to the terms and conditions of the contract.

2. A sum totalling $10,000 in profit margin was paid to an agency for 6 invoices covering work carried out by an agency strategically allied to the CA under contract, contrary to the terms and conditions of the contract.

3. Lump-sum payment lacking a basis for confirming whether the rate of payment authorized in the contract is respected.

4. Certain items in one invoice are for work carried out before or after the period covered by the contract.

P. Tremblay asks that a copy of his statement on Bill C-5 to the June 6, 2000, meeting of the Industry Committee, in which he commented on the *Attractions Canada* file, be appended to the report. He adds that the *Attractions Canada* file had been specifically assigned to Huguette Tremblay. He repeats that he did not check the invoices in detail. The invoices are dated from June 1999 to June 2000 and bear Huguette Tremblay's initials. Huguette Tremblay has confirmed that she checked the invoices and the calculations, and that she knew also that the agencies that received such a profit margin had a strategic alliance with the CA.

Specific analysis/conclusion: The Committee considers that from September 1999, when P. Tremblay became interim executive director, he was responsible for making sure he assigned very clear tasks to his staff concerning their financial and contract responsibilities. He also had to make sure they carried out their tasks appropriately. As a consequence, the Committee does not accept P. Tremblay's defence that he believed Huguette Tremblay's initials meant the invoices complied on every point, including financially, with the contract. Therefore, the Committee is of the opinion that P. Tremblay did not comply with the provisions of Section 34 of the FAA and, thus, was negligent with regard to invoices signed after September 1, 1999.

As to invoices prior to September 1, 1999, the Committee accepts as an attenuating factor the findings described in C-3, added to the fact that P. Tremblay was still in a period of apprenticeship under J.C. Guité. With regard to these invoices, the Committee is of the opinion that P. Tremblay did not comply with the provisions of Section 34 of the FAA and, thus, was negligent but the seriousness of that negligence is attenuated by these circumstances.

Event #112 (contract # EP043-9-0057) Canadian Grand Prix:

Section 34 of the FAA. The Kroll Report indicates full payment was made on June 1, 1999, when the event had not yet been held. According to the contract, only 80% of the amount should have been paid before the event took place.

P. Tremblay says that, when he signed this invoice on June 1, 1999, the Canadian Grand Prix event was to take place soon after, early in June, and all the advertising was already on the site. There again, he says he trusted J.C. Guité and Huguette Tremblay, who put her initials on the invoice.

Specific analysis/conclusion: Taking into account the findings described in C-3 (Section C), added to the following attenuating factors:

- These invoices were submitted to P. Tremblay shortly after he arrived at CCSB and while he was still in a period of apprenticeship under J.C. Guité;

- the fact that J.C. Guité, according to Huguette Tremblay, on an exceptional basis authorised single, full payments.

The Committee is of the opinion that P. Tremblay did not comply with the provisions of Section 34 of the FAA and, thus, was negligent but the seriousness of that negligence is attenuated by the above-mentioned circumstances.

Event #113 (contract # EP043-9-0066) VIA Magazine:

Section 34 of the FAA—Payment of 9 invoices at a rate not provided in the contract; no information indicating what portion of the payment went to the CA and to VIA; no copies of the magazine in the file to confirm that the advertising was indeed placed in it.

P. Tremblay says that, in the case of VIA Magazine, he saw the finished product because VIA regularly sent them copies. In contrast, he says he did not look at each magazine specifically when he signed the invoices. The invoices, dated July 1999 to March 2000, all bore Huguette Tremblay's initials.

Specific analysis/conclusion: P. Tremblay did not make any detailed check when he signed the magazine's invoices. The Committee got a note from a VIA representative indicating all the magazines were published as expected during the fiscal year in question and he gave us two copies (June and November 1999). The Committee considers that from September 1999, when P. Tremblay became interim executive director, he was responsible for making sure he assigned very clear tasks to his staff concerning their financial and contract responsibilities. He also had to make sure they carried out their tasks appropriately. As a consequence, the Committee does not accept P. Tremblay's defence that he believed Huguette Tremblay's initials meant the invoices complied on every point, including financially, with the contract. Therefore, the Committee is of the opinion that P. Tremblay did not comply with the provisions of Section 34 of the FAA and, thus, was negligent with regard to non-compliance, except for the reservation expressed above concerning the proof of publication of the magazine.

Event #126 (contract # EP043-9-0048) China Project:

Section 34 of the FAA—Payment made without documents to determine whether the invoice was in accordance with the terms of the contract.

P. Tremblay signed this invoice on August 1, 1999, and Huguette Tremblay put her initials on it. He says that Andrée LaRose was almost exclusively in charge of this file. He adds that this project did not really constitute a sponsorship because, in his view, it was more a TV production. It refers to a Canadian living in China who gave English courses on Chinese television and had a considerable audience. P. Tremblay does not remember the details of this payment, but he says it would have been made in three stages. The Committee asks P. Tremblay how he could check the payment since there is no written proof in the file. P. Tremblay says he does not know why there is no written proof in the file, but adds that Huguette Tremblay checked before he signed. P. Tremblay repeats that this was specifically a TV production in spite of the fact that the budget came from the Sponsorship Program.

Specific analysis/conclusion: The Committee takes into account the findings described in C-3 as well as the attenuating factor that these invoices were submitted to him while he was still in a period of apprenticeship under J.C. Guité. The Committee notes, however, that the amount in question was very high and that it was also the last payment under this contract. The Committee is of the opinion that P. Tremblay did not comply with the provisions of Section 34 of the FAA and, thus, was negligent.

Event #28 (contract # EP043-9-0145) Opportunity analysis:

Section 34 of the FAA—Kroll reports that it is impossible to determine whether the agency fulfilled its obligations under the contract at the end of which an analysis report was to be produced (value of $575,000). Such a report was indeed produced, but it is not clear whether it respects the contract since, for instance, most of the events listed in the report had already been held before the contract came into effect.

P. Tremblay says the RCMP is investigating this file and, therefore, he does not want to talk about it in detail. He says this is the third Groupaction contract checked by the Auditor General in 2002 and the only one that produced a report on file. He also says this project was initiated by J.C. Guité, and that he himself only signed a few invoices. He says J.C. Guité commented afterwards that verbal advice had been given beyond the reports commissioned under these contracts. The Committee questions him about the assessment of this report that the Auditor General described as scandalous and of dubious value. P. Tremblay replies that it seems to him it was was dearly paid for and that he perhaps should not have signed. He trusted J.-C. Guité, who said verbal advice had been part of the product/service received.

Specific analysis/conclusion: The contract itself was signed by J.C. Guité on May 1, 1999, while P. Tremblay occupied the position of DG. P. Tremblay signed the 4 invoices relating to the product in June ($214,000), August ($223,000), September ($164,000) 1999, and in February 2000 ($12,000). They were all initialled by Huguette Tremblay. The report was sent by Groupaction on October 10, 1999. It is difficult to draw a clear conclusion since P. Tremblay refused to discuss the matter in detail. The Committee is of the opinion that the fact the contract was initiated by J.C. Guité does not discharge P. Tremblay of his responsibility in signing the invoices. J.C. Guité's claim that verbal advice was provided in addition to the report is not a convincing defence since P. Tremblay signed the last two invoices and received the report while he was interim executive director. Consequently, if verbal advice had been provided, P. Tremblay should have been aware of it, which he did not mention. On the basis of the available information, the Committee concludes that P. Tremblay has, at the very least, been seriously negligent in signing the invoices relating to this product, which he himself finds was dearly paid for.

Event #100 (contract # EP043-9-0234) Canadian Encyclopaedia:

- File about which Kroll says it is not clear whether Section 34 of the FAA was respected. The Office of the Millennium circumvented the restrictions within its mandate by using CCSB to achieve its goal:

The Committee requests an explanation of why a contract of zero value ($0) was concluded. P. Tremblay explains the context of this file: J.C. Guité, along with P. Tremblay, met Janice Oliver who worked for Minister Herb Gray. She wanted CCSB to take care of the translation and distribution of an encyclopaedia since this was not within the mandate of the Office of the Millennium. P. Tremblay met with Mr. Gray's Deputy Minister and his Assistant Deputy Minister responsible for finances. The latter made an account transfer to CCSB. P. Tremblay does not remember why the contract was of zero value ($0). P. Tremblay adds that only a small part of the sponsorship budget was used to ensure delivery and storage through a CA. The Committee asks whether this type of arrangement was frequent and why the DA received 3%. P. Tremblay says he does not remember the administrative details, but that the Office of the Millennium could not do it directly within its mandate. The Committee points out the file shows the CA charged $100,000 for printing, and that this invoice was rejected. Was it because of the zero-value contract? P. Tremblay says he does not remember the details of this contract which was initiated by J.C. Guité.

Specific analysis/conclusion: P. Tremblay signed this contract on September 1, 1999, the day he became interim executive director. Considering the ambiguity surrounding this case, which Kroll could not resolve either, the Committee cannot conclude there was any form of misconduct respecting Section 34 of the FAA.

- Elements of non-compliance regarding competitive markets given the zero-value contract:

Specific analysis/conclusion: The Committee obtained a legal opinion stating that a zero-value request for goods and services did not relieve CCSB from its obligations with respect to the competitive process on the state's markets. The Committee applies the findings described in C-1 to the elements mentioned for this event. The Committee does not conclude there was negligence.

Event #74 (contract # EP043-9-0105) Laszlo 50 Canadians 2000:

Section 34 of the FAA—Payment of 7 invoices between April and November 1999 showing an hourly rate not authorized in the contract.

The Committee asks why the invoices were paid when the rates were not in accordance with those in the contract. P. Tremblay says he received piles of invoices and trusted Huguette Tremblay to check them. He claims the work was done. He adds that J.C. Guité's custom was to give verbal approval and the relevant papers followed. It is to be noted that 3 of the 7 invoices during the period of April and May 1999 do not bear Huguette Tremblay's initials.

Specific analysis/conclusion: The Committee considers that from September 1999, when P. Tremblay became interim executive director, he was responsible for making sure he assigned very clear tasks to his staff concerning their financial and contract responsibilities. He also had to make sure they carried out their tasks appropriately. As a consequence, the Committee does not accept P. Tremblay's defence that he believed Huguette Tremblay's initials meant the invoices complied on every point, including financially, with the contract. Therefore, the Committee is of the opinion that P. Tremblay did not comply with the provisions of Section 34 of the FAA and, thus, was negligent with regard to invoices signed after September 1, 1999.

As to invoices prior to September 1, 1999, on which Huguette Tremblay's initials appear, the Committee accepts as an attenuating factor the findings described in C-3, added to the fact that P. Tremblay was still in a period of apprenticeship under J.C. Guité. The Committee is of the opinion that P. Tremblay did not comply with the provisions of Section 34 of the FAA and, thus, was negligent but this negligence was attenuated by the preceding.

As to invoices prior to September 1, 1999, on which Huguette Tremblay's initials do not appear, the Committee continues to note the attenuating factor that P. Tremblay was working under the direction of J.C. Guité. The Committee is of the opinion that P. Tremblay did not comply with the provisions of Section 34 of the FAA and, thus, was negligent but the seriousness of that negligence is attenuated by the above circumstance.

Event #98 (contract # EP043-9-0261) Maurice Richard Production series:

- Elements of non-compliance regarding competitive markets:

Specific analysis/conclusion: The Committee applies the findings described in C-I to the elements mentioned for this event.

- Additional element noticed by the Committee: Demand for goods and services and $750,000 contract signed by P. Tremblay in December 1999, including an additional commission of $112,000 to a CA for which there is no documentation proving the product/service was delivered.

The Committee submits to P. Tremblay the QRT (Quick Response Team) note contained in the Kroll Report concerning the invoice signed by David Myer. The note says Huguette Tremblay indicated the amount of $750,000 was intended to reimburse VIA for its previous year's contribution to the Maurice Richard Series presented by Radio-Canada. P. Tremblay says the *Maurice Richard* file began with J.C. Guité and, as he recalls, the Canada Information Office was involved, having paid for part of the production. The Committee asks P. Tremblay to comment on the QRT note. P. Tremblay replies that, if such were the case, it was for something negotiated by J.C. Guité, but he does not remember. The Committee wonders about the types of financial arrangements between such organizations. P. Tremblay explains that, for instance, to be the main sponsor of an event and thus derive maximum visibility, CCSB and VIA or Canada Post would sometimes pool their contributions to a sponsorship. Afterwards, one of the organizations would take responsibility for the coordination and the others would transfer their contributions to it. The Committee points out a payment for the previous year might indicate the CA had been paid only to transfer a cheque. The Committee wonders about the indication in the contract that it is a production service. P. Tremblay specifies that Robert Guy Scully's agency produced the series, but that the CA perhaps also contributed to it. The Committee points out that, according to the QRT note, this payment was for an event already past and asks whether CAs were ever paid merely to transfer a cheque. P. Tremblay says he does not believe so. The Committee stresses that account transfers cannot be effected with a Crown Corporation and asks how money is transferred in such cases. P. Tremblay replies that he does not remember because there were about 350 to 400 sponsorships per year and he cannot remember the details of each file. The Committee suggests to P. Tremblay that, given the peculiarity of the transaction relating to this file as described by Huguette Tremblay, he should remember. The Committee finally asks whether this file appeared on the list given to the Deputy Minister and the Minister. P. Tremblay says it did, and he adds that he was not saying Huguette Tremblay was wrong, but he does not remember the details, that's all.

Specific analysis/conclusion: During her interview, Huguette Tremblay recalled having approached P. Tremblay about the request for goods and services because there were no documents to support it. She said P. Tremblay told her to proceed without asking questions. Afterwards, Huguette Tremblay said that when the time came to finalize the file, she had to phone the CA to begin the invoicing. At that point, it became obvious to her that her CA interlocutor did not know how to present this invoice for an event already past. Huguette Tremblay said she believed the CA did not do the work billed in this invoice. The Committee finds this transaction highly questionable. The defence that a special arrangement had been negotiated by J.C. Guité does not stand up to analysis, according to the Committee, since P. Tremblay had well and truly been interim executive director for several months when the request for goods and services and the contract were signed. The lack of documents makes it impossible to draw firm conclusions, but, on the basis of the available information, the Committee concludes that P. Tremblay, at the very least, showed serious neglect by signing the request for goods and services and the contract relating to this event.

Event #25 (contract # EN771-8-0002) Parc des champs de bataille, Quebec City:

Section 34 of the FAA—Some elements of non-compliance appearing in 5 invoices, signed between May and July 1999, concerning work carried out after the period specified in the contract.

The Committee questions the expenses incurred after the period specified in the contract. P. Tremblay says he trusted Huguette Tremblay, who initialled the invoices, and that he did not check every single one. The Committee asks what instructions were given to Huguette Tremblay and Isabelle Roy when he became executive director. P. Tremblay says he asked Isabelle Roy to handle negotiations with the CAs while Huguette Tremblay would continue to take care of the administrative part of the invoices and other related matters. The Committee asks if Huguette Tremblay's role included verifying the delivery of the product/service provided for in the contract. P. Tremblay says it did, adding that, after September 1999, she would confirm it by checking if the post-mortem received by Isabelle Roy, who worked next to her, was in the file.

Specific analysis/conclusion: The records indicate that it was rather in the fall of 2000, following the internal audit, that the systematic verification of post-mortems was introduced. Taking into account the findings described in C-3, added to the following attenuating factors:

- These invoices were submitted to him while he was still in a period of apprenticeship under J.C. Guité;

- the relatively low value of these invoices.

The Committee is of the opinion that P. Tremblay did not comply with the provisions of Section 34 of the FAA and, thus, was negligent but the seriousness of that negligence is attenuated by the above-mentioned circumstances.

Event #72 (contract # EP043-9-0050) Promotional items:

Contract exceeding the delegated authority:

P. Tremblay says the Minister's office was aware of this situation. J.C. Guité purchased all kinds of promotional items. P. Tremblay's approach differed from his predecessor's by concentrating on one item per event to simplify and eliminate stocks.

Specific analysis/conclusion: The Committee applies the findings described in C-1 to the elements mentioned for this event. The Committee does not conclude there was any negligence.

4   General:

The Committee questioned P. Tremblay on the training he received when he joined the civil service. He said that, before joining CCSB, he took a two-day course on in-house procedure in the federal government, but did not have any training in the management of public finances. In the Minister's office, he had occasional briefings on various topics, such as employment equity, the role of the Auditor General, etc. Finally, he said that at the Canadian Food Inspection Agency, he took part in a one-and-a-half-day course on the *Financial Administration Act* for the first time in his career. The Committee asks whether CCSB employees had the benefit of training programs following the 2000 internal audit. P. Tremblay said he would need to consult the action plan to make sure.

The Committee asks whether VIP passes and other such items were well used and controlled. P. Tremblay replies that some employees attended the events as part of their work to network with the CAs and took this opportunity to check the visibility offered by the sponsorship. When he assumed the post of interim executive director, he made sure those passes would transit by him to control their distribution.

The Committee then sought P. Tremblay's comments on the news story published a few days before the second interview, saying the Auditor General's next report would charge that Crown Corporations had been used to divert money. The same story suggested there were also serious problems with advertising contracts. P. Tremblay replies that he has no idea about it; that he concluded partnerships with Crown Corporations and transferred money in both directions, but always for a legitimate purpose. The Committee asks again whether CAs could receive commissions merely for transferring funds. P. Tremblay answers negatively.

The Committee asks P. Tremblay to explain the fact that in a file initiated under his rule on April 1, 2000, concerning the Old Port of Montreal (EP043-0-0113), we see that sponsorship funds were allotted to the purchase of a giant screen, and therefore, were for a capital expenditure. P. Tremblay replies the screen was used to promote Canada and, as the record shows, it was considered as a promotional tool for the lifespan of the screen. The Committee then asks why the CA got a commission. P. Tremblay replies that the firm was our intermediary, did design, had negotiated with the Old Port where to locate the screen, in addition to producing elements of visibility that would appear on this screen.

As a general conclusion, P. Tremblay says there may have been some administrative errors and other imperfect transactions, but at any given time he was not the only manager involved. The Treasury Board, the Deputy Minister, the Minister, other agencies like the CIO or the Office of the Millennium were also involved. He says he has a clear conscience because he did not do anything to embezzle Crown money or steal anything. He says he cooperated as best he could with this administrative review.

General analysis/conclusion:

The Committee is of the opinion that P. Tremblay showed unacceptable laxity and lack of rigour for a civil servant of his level.

As director general of strategic communications through the period of February to August 1999, he should have at least questioned established practices. It should be noted that a great number of the offences blamed on him were committed during that period.

Through the period of September 1999 to March 2000, while he was interim executive director, P. Tremblay knew or should have known, having worked for several months with J.C. Guité, that the management of sponsorships was grossly deficient. Nevertheless, he made no substantial changes. He continued to approve poorly documented transactions, thus contrary to the Treasury Board's policy requirements regarding the state's markets and the audit of accounts. He should have understood and clarified the responsibilities of employees under his authority and this, upon his appointment as interim executive director, in addition to making sure there was no misunderstanding in this respect with his other managers.

P. Tremblay has attempted to explain the elements of non-compliance mentioned in the Kroll Report. However, the elements for which his explanations are non-existent or are not convincing are such that they assume great importance and surely constitute very serious negligence deserving a proportionate disciplinary measure.

I

———

STAFF OF THE COMMISSION

Executive

Commissionner John H. Gomery
- Snowball, Laura—Legal Counsel
- Hoffer, Maxine—Executive Assistant (Montréal)

Cook, Sheila-Marie
Executive Director and Commission Secretary (Administration, Finance, Communication / Publications)

Roy, Bernard (Montréal)
Lead Counsel (Legal)

Savoie, Donald
Special Advisor (Research)

Office of the Executive Director

Cook, Sheila-Marie
- Robitaille, Caroline—Executive Assistant

Administration/Finance:

Ariano, Wanda
Manager, Administrative Services

Bouchard, Jocelyne (Ottawa)
Administrative Assistant

Brook, Dennis (Ottawa)
Information Technician

Châteauvert, Marie
Receptionist

Cérant, Marie Paule (Montréal)
Administrative Assistant

Cooke, Lynne
Finance Officer

Doherty, Mike
Manager, Financial Services

Duquette, Julie (Montréal)
Manager, Administrative Services

Gauthier, Michel
Information Technician

Godbout, Gail
Manager, Human Resources

Godin, Denis
Clerk/Messenger

Hooper, Anne (Ottawa)
Librarian

Hughes, Alice
Secretary

Karmali, Nadira
Coordinator, Administrative Services

Napoletano, Louis/Ronald Tremblay (Mtl)
Information Technician

Ostojic, Milos (Montréal)
    Clerk/Messenger

Plante, Julien (Montréal)
    Librarian

Smith, Éric
    Finance Clerk

Skwiercz, Marc
    Receptionist

Thériault, France (Montréal)
    Receptionist

Thomas, Roger
    Manager, Printing and Offices Services

Communication:

Perreault, François
    Commission Spokesperson

Publications: (Editorial Staff and Researchers)

Enman, Charles
    Researcher

Gussman, Tom
    Strategic Editor

Léger, Sylvie
    Researcher

Liebman, Dan
    Copy Editor

Lutes, Kim
    Editorial Assistant

Maude-McDougall, Mary
    Researcher

Moschopoulos, Ourania
    Researcher

Oscapella, Eugene
    Researcher

Sadinsky, Ian
Strategic Editor

Shipton, Rosemary
Researcher

Research Office

Savoie, Donald
- Benoît, Ginette—Executive Assistant

Dickerson, Ken
Research Analyst

Guérette, Hélène
Research Analyst

Office of the Lead Counsel

Roy, Bernard
- Lepage, Josée—Manager, Legal Services

Bordan, Gregory
Legal Counsel

Corbeil, Myriam
Legal Counsel

Cossette, Marie
Senior Counsel

Cournoyer, Guy
Associate Counsel

Finkelstein, Neil
Co-Counsel

Gervais, Marie-Christine
Legal Counsel

Kanya-Forstner, Charlotte
Legal Counsel

Lachance, Steve
Associate Registrar

Landry-Schönbeck, Rosalie
    Legal Counsel

Lortie, Renault-François
    Legal Counsel

Martel, Reine
    Legal Secretary

Nunnelley Sophie
    Legal Counsel

Richard, Simon
    Legal Counsel

Robert-Blanchard, Véronique
    Legal Counsel

Roy, Serge
    Registrar

Thouin, Isabelle
    Legal Secretary